KABUKI

FIVE CLASSIC PLAYS

Frontispiece :

Sukeroku on his first entrance, hair tied in a fashionable purple headband, umbrella held jauntily over the shoulder, a peony crest marking his black kimono. (*Sukeroku:* Ichikawa Ebizō)

Kabuki

FIVE CLASSIC PLAYS

Translated by
James R. Brandon

Harvard University Press

Cambridge, Massachusetts
and
London, England
1975

Library of Congress Catalog Card Number 74–82192
ISBN 0–674–30485–3

Printed in the United States of America

UNESCO Collection of Representative Works
Japanese Series
This book has been accepted in the series of translations from Japanese literature
sponsored by the United Nations Educational, Scientific and Cultural Organization (UNESCO).

For Ken

Preface

Kabuki is one of the world's great stage arts. The Western spectator fortunate enough to sit in a kabuki audience during even a single performance is almost certain to be swept away by the dynamic theatricality of the experience. The translations in this volume are an attempt to recreate, as best as can be done with words and photographs, five plays from the standard repertory as they might be seen and heard in performance. Of the three hundred or so plays in the current repertory, scarcely half a dozen are available in English translations (see Bibliography). Some scholars have shied away from translating kabuki because it is not a "literary" form, and others have been deterred from translating text alone because of the very importance of contributory theatrical elements—music, song, dance, spectacle, acting.

The problems of translating kabuki plays are considerable. Some are discouragingly long (twenty, even thirty, times the length of a nō play). The original texts of many early plays are no longer extant, and we are forced to choose among later versions. Since it was the rule to revise the script each time a play was revived, precisely those favorites of the repertory which have stood the test of time and which merit translation are the ones which exist in the most variant versions. Kabuki dialogue is liberally sprinkled with puns and word play, and many passages are composed in meter, posing difficulties to the translator. Published scripts contain scant stage directions, so the translator must go to current productions, to prints, and to commentaries and must speak with performers to search out production details. Some plays, interesting when performed, lose too much in transition to the printed word to warrant translation. Still, there are several score of plays which are superior drama and which exemplify the remarkable nature of kabuki theatrical art. I have tried to choose from among these for this volume.

Four of the five plays are regularly staged and might be seen at any time; the fifth, less often staged, is a recognized masterpiece of one of kabuki's most highly regarded playwrights, Tsuruya Namboku IV. They represent basic dramatic types (history, domestic, "true" domestic, and dance plays) and performance styles (the bravura style of Edo [Tokyo], the soft style of Kyoto, and the puppet-derived style of Osaka). The plays are from the years 1712–1817, the first hundred years during which complete kabuki scripts have been preserved. Within this time span, I have chosen more plays from the earliest period (Genroku: 1688–1730), because this was when characteristics basic to kabuki were being formed. Space limitations make it impossible to include more plays; translations of some of the extremely interesting plays of the following century (1830–1930) could well make up another volume. On the basis of current popularity, it might be argued that more than one puppet adaptation deserves inclusion, for puppet plays account for perhaps a third of the twentieth-century repertory. It seems appropriate in a collection of kabuki drama, however, to concentrate on those plays which were created by kabuki artists.

Performance of texts, rather than texts themselves, have been translated. I made a preliminary list of about fifty plays in the repertory that might, I felt, be profitably translated. Among these some thirty were staged while I was in Japan (1958–1961 and 1966–1968). Performance tapes were made of those productions and included simultaneous commentary and stage directions. When translating, the published text was compared with the performance tape so that details of the production could be taken from the tape. There are difficulties with this approach of course. It is often hard to distinguish between staging practices which are contemporary and those of the original production, or at least of earlier periods. When a distinction could be made, in general I have chosen the earlier of the possibilities. Many kabuki plays are performed in abridged versions, presenting a perplexing problem of selection. The principle I have followed has been to translate either long plays in their entirety (or near to it), or abridgments which have become recognized classics in that form over the years. In other words, abridgments made for reasons of passing convenience have not been used.

Translating the text of a play differs from translating a poem or a novel. The words of dialogue spoken by a character in a play cannot be the focus of translation; they are only the surface manifestation of underlying thoughts, motives, and emotions that should be the major concern of the translator. Authenticity of translation lies in faithfulness to the broad intent of an act, a scene, or a passage of dialogue, and only secondarily in faithfulness to the surface words. The translations here have been written with the aim of faithfully recreating the "subtext" of human relationships the kabuki texts imply. This does not mean the plays have been freely translated; no deliberate attempt has been made to depart from either the spirit or the basic content of the texts. It is hoped the English text will suggest the differences in emotional makeup and social status of characters which are clear in the Japanese texts. When a playwright consciously uses metrical lines (usually in alternating phrases of seven and five syllables), abrupt or incomplete sentences, or long and intricately composed lines, these stylistic features are maintained as much as possible in English. I have sought English equivalents for the puns and word play, so important to the spirit of kabuki. Technical terms for acts, scenes, and performance and language techniques that are discussed in the introduction are identified by marginal note where they occur in the text. (Verbal play occurs so extensively that only some examples are indicated by marginal notes.) Descriptions of stage settings, costuming, makeup, stage movement, dance, names of musical selections, and sound effects in the texts are taken from Japanese texts and from performance tapes.

My aim has been to write translations that are performable. At the University of Hawaii three of the translations have been staged in recent years: *Sukeroku: Flower of Edo* (1970), *Narukami the Thunder God* (taken from *Saint Narukami and the God Fudō*) (1973), and *The Scarlet Princess of Edo* (1974).

I am indebted to a number of scholars and artists for their advice and generous assistance: Onoe Kurōemon, the actor who first guided my tentative footsteps along kabuki's labyrinths; Professor Gunji Masakatsu, scholar and director of *The Scarlet Princess of Edo;* Tobe Ginsaku, who directed *Saint Narukami and the God Fudō;* Professor Kawatake Toshio, colleague and mentor at Waseda University; Ariyoshi Sawako, for sharing her detailed notes on Namboku; the management and staff of the National Theater of Japan and of the Kabuki-za in Tokyo, for allowing me complete access to their facilities; the actors Nakamura Matagorō II and Onoe Baikō VII; the musicians Kineya Rokurirō, Mochizuki Tasaku, Nozawa Matsunosuke, and Tanaka Denzaemon; Nakamura Tōkichi, who instructed me in sound effects; Bandō Yaenosuke, my *tate* instructor; my dance teacher Fujima Kanshino; Sekiguchi Masao for translation assistance; Professor Kishibe Shigeo; Sasaki Einosuke; Ōki Yasushi; Mrs. Maki Yukiko; and Professors William Ross, Hideya Kumata, and Earle Ernst for their encouragement of this study. The translations were begun while holding a Fulbright-Hays research grant, 1966–1968, at Waseda University in Tokyo. I wish to express my appreciation for this financial support and for supplementary grants from Michigan State University International Programs and from the University Research Council and the Asian Studies Program of the University of Hawaii that made possible the completion of the study.

Honolulu

J.R.B.

Contents

Illustration Credits

Frontispiece: Umemura Yutaka

Following page 70: Shiratama, surrounded; Sukeroku enters; He holds; Stamping loudly; He strides; "If you . . ."; Challenged by; Sembei demands; The effeminate; Dandy places; Sukeroku hides—Umemura Yutaka. Sembei and—Howard Hamilton. Discovered by—Shōchiku Company. For their—J. R. Brandon.

Following page 124: Promised restoration; Danjō is; Mimbu crosses; The actor; Danjō forces—National Theater of Japan, Research Department. The revolving; The high; Kazuma is; The garden; Danjō slaps; Iron dagger—Gotō Katsuichi. At the signal; Suddenly he—National Theater of Japan, Stage Department. When Danjō—Umemura Yutaka.

Following page 156: Lady Taema; Hayakumo wears; Hayakumo's disguise; Narukami begins; Basting threads—Gotō Katsuichi. To signify; The Guardian; The final—National Theater of Japan, Stage Department. Narukami innocently; "What silliness . . ."; The imperial—National Theater of Japan, Research Department.

Following page 182: Prince Atsumori; Far out; Kumagai has; Kumagai draws; "His head . . ."; Kumagai thrusts; The act ends—Umemura Yutaka. The formal; "Ahh! Isn't . . ."; "My son's . . ."—J. R. Brandon.

Following page 208: Kumagai concludes; Then Kumagai; Yoshitsune views—Umemura Yutaka. Lady Fuji; "When the . . ."; Sagami shows; "When he . . ."; Lady Fuji; Kumagi exits—J. R. Brandon. Kumagai prevents; Kumagai abandons—Shōchiku Company.

Following page 226: Izaemon stops; Waiting for; Yugiri enters; Yugiri kneels; "Stop it . . ."; "There's no harm . . ."; "From the day . . ."; A Clerk—Umemura Yutaka. In front; "This Izaemon . . ."—Shōchiku Company.

Following page 262: Seigen comforts; "Princess Sakura . . ."—National Theater of Japan, Stage Department. All others from National Theater of Japan, Research Department.

Following page 308: All from National Theater of Japan, Research Department.

Following page 324: All from National Theater of Japan, Research Department.

Following page 346: All from National Theater of Japan, Research Department.

KABUKI

FIVE CLASSIC PLAYS

Introduction

The earliest complete kabuki play scripts that survive date from the Genroku period (1688–ca. 1730). They represent a mature drama, for kabuki had already been in existence a century. Reading them, or seeing productions based on them, certain characteristics immediately strike us. Plots are strong and muscular, complexly developed over four, five, or six acts. Their stories concern intrigue, love, and struggles for power. Characterization is vivid and compelling. Events from history or legend mix with scenes of everyday life. The plays share with *ukiyoe* wood-block prints, like kabuki a popular art and of the same time, boldness of artistic form and a love of sensuous, colorful display. Some elements can be traced back to *nō* and to *kyōgen*, the aristocratic dance-drama and the comic theater of Japan's medieval period. And borrowings from contemporary *jōruri* puppet drama can be found. Yet the plays of early kabuki differ notably from their predecessors in spirit and in form. Above all, they introduce into Japanese drama a new spirit of vitality, even brashness, and a tremendous sense of theatrical élan. These are qualities of popular theater, which kabuki has been since its inception.

The first kabuki performances took place around 1600. In 1603 it is recorded that a young woman named Okuni, calling herself a priestess of the Izumo Shrine, danced the *kabuki odori*, or "kabuki dance," on a temporary stage set up in the dry bed of the Kamo River in Kyoto. She and her troupe sold tickets for stage performances during the day and, it is presumed, sold their favors to customers at night as prostitutes. Okuni's new dance was lively and sensuously appealing. Though perhaps not explicitly licentious it was so unusual that it attracted great attention. (Kabuki means "strange," "inclined," "far out.")

The early seventeenth century saw the rapid growth of major cities in Japan; a distinctive middle-class, urban, moneyed culture was emerging. The rising wealthy merchant, the town wit, and the dandy alike were seeking new entertainment. Kabuki very quickly developed into an urban fad as scores of professional troupes adopted Okuni's style of performance, calling themselves "kabuki people" (*kabukimono*). Before long, kabuki was to become the pivotal art form of Japanese urban culture.

Many of the first troupes to perform in kabuki style were composed mostly of professional prostitutes. As a result, the earliest kabuki is termed "women's kabuki" (*onna kabuki*) or "prostitutes' kabuki" (*yūjo kabuki*). Actually, comic roles (*saruwaka*) were always played by men, as were other roles at times. Some troupes were made up of boys between the ages of about ten and thirteen, chosen for their attractiveness. Though young, they too were professionals who, like the women, performed during the day and sold sexual favors at night. When the Tokugawa Shōgunate, the military government of Japan, banned women from the public stage in 1629, the only troupes remaining to perform kabuki were these. "Boys' kabuki" (*wakashū kabuki*), as it was called, continued for another twenty-three years, until in 1652 young boys as well as women were forbidden by the Shōgunate to act in kabuki.

According to traditional accounts, after a year had passed in which no kabuki was allowed, theaters were given permission to reopen on condition that all performers would be adult males and that productions would be "fully acted plays" (*monomane kyōgen zukushi*), instead of the previous variety shows of independent songs, dances, and sketches. Theater managers accepted these conditions and the period of "adult male kabuki" (*yarō kabuki*) began. Naturally we need not believe that thereafter sodomy ceased to be part of the actor's profession, that full-blown drama instantly appeared, or that artistic standards magically improved, as is sometimes suggested. But favorable conditions now existed for the creation of a serious dramatic art. The yarō period (1653–1688) is often overlooked, but it was during this time that many of the significant features of mature kabuki evolved. Already during the wakashū period standard scenes were the assignation at a brothel (*keiseigai*), swaggering through the streets by the dapper hero (*tanzen roppō*), and the flight of lovers (*michiyuki*). In 1655 a commentator noted that fighting scenes (*tachimawari*) were being so skillfully done at the Yamamura Theater in Edo that people were talking about nothing else.[1] Performers of female roles, *onnagata*, were distinguished from

1. Ihara Toshirō, *Kabuki Nempyō* (Chronology of Kabuki; Tokyo: Iwanami Shoten, 1956), I, 69.

performers of male roles (*otokogata*) on playbills as early as 1644; during the 1660s and 1670s female impersonation became an art. Prior to 1664 kabuki programs consisted of unrelated, short items: in 1662 the program at the Kodennai Theater in Edo contained seventeen separate pieces in the fifth month, and at the Inishie Theater fifteen in the eighth month.[2] But in 1664 dramas of two, three, and four linked acts were performed in Osaka and Edo. About the same time stage settings came into use and the act curtain made its appearance, probably to facilitate changing the various sets being called for in the new multiact plays. Playwriting became a specialized profession, as the inclusion of the author's name on kabuki playbills after 1680 indicates, and the first illustrated play-books (*eiri kyōgenbon*) containing excerpts of dialogue and summaries of action began to be published in Kyoto in 1688, the first year of Genroku (and about ten years later in Edo). Thus, by the beginning of the Genroku era basic characteristics of kabuki playwriting had been established that would persist for two hundred years—until Japan was opened to contact with the West in 1868.

A townsman's art, kabuki was viewed with grave suspicion by Japan's ruling samurai warrior class. In the first place, its performers were social pariahs, "beggars of the riverbed," scarcely higher than outcasts in the social system. The authorities accepted the fact that the townsman (artisan or merchant, collectively called *chōnin*) required entertainment, but they feared social disruption and possible contamination of their own class if such entertainments were not carefully regulated. So the two chief entertainments of the great cities, kabuki and prostitution, were licensed and placed in segregated areas where they could be closely watched. The immediate reason for the ban on women in kabuki was a violent brawl that erupted between rival samurai at a performance by the prostitute Yoshino of a nō play in Kyoto in 1629. Spectators were injured and the stage demolished. The resulting government regulation prohibited women from performing nō, jōruri puppet plays, and kabuki.[3] The ban on women in kabuki, therefore, can be seen as part of the government's larger policy of separating prostitution from performing and confining each profession in its own area. (Yoshiwara, the main quarter set up for prostitution in Edo, was completed in 1626, or just three years before public stages were closed to prostitutes.) In the second place, kabuki was hardly an art at all in the eyes of the samurai. It is true that individual government officials, including some of the highest rank, became enamoured of

2. Ibid., pp. 87–89.
3. Ihara quotes from the edicts issued in November 1629 in both Kyoto and in Edo; ibid., p. 49.

kabuki, but as a class the samurai patronized austere and restrained nō drama and could see in kabuki's direct action and high-spirited acting little more than frivolous vulgarity.

It must have been profoundly disturbing for Shōgunate officials to realize that every day tens of thousands of spectators at theaters in Kyoto, Osaka, and Edo were being exposed to plays that glorified the commoner. The mere existence of plays about the daily lives of the lower classes conferred on these lives a value which the authorities wished to deny. Plays about contemporary urban life go back to the earliest days of kabuki. Okuni acted the role of a young samurai, foppishly dressed in the latest fashion, who goes to a public house of assignation, meets a prostitute, dallies with her, and joins in singing and dancing to popular tunes of the day. An account from the Genroku period says, "Lately it has become the rage to stage, the following day, adulterous affairs and scandal which occur in the city the preceding day. Not even the names of the people are changed and the audience finds this very interesting."[4] Plays of current events were called "living newspapers" (*kiwamono*) or, in the slang of the day, "overnight pickles" (*ichiyazuke*). The many accounts of plays appearing on the stage a single day after a murder or suicide probably cannot be taken literally, but it is said that Chikamatsu Tokusan dashed off his famous overnight pickles play of multiple and gory murders, *Sounds at Ise and the Sleeping Sword of Love*, in just three days.[5] Kabuki playwrights continued to dramatize current events through two and a half centuries, which helps explain why there is no "typical" kabuki play. Rather, half a dozen general types of plays evolved at different times in response to different dramatic materials and social conditions.

The Shōgunate rulers looked askance at plays that dramatized current events for the obvious reason that the dramatists' views of these events were bound to differ from the official view. Eventually plays about two types of contemporary events were banned as being particularly disruptive to society: lovers' suicides and scandals in important samurai families. Both were extremely popular in early Genroku. In 1722, plays dramatizing recent love suicides (*shinjū*), or that had the word shinjū in their title, were banned on the grounds that seeing them would incite spectators to commit suicide themselves. There was no way to evade this regulation. The fact that this prohibition was enforced for many years undoubtedly

4. Quoted in Gunji Masakatsu, *Kabuki no Hassō* (Formation of Kabuki; Tokyo: Kōbundō, 1959), p. 193.
5. *Engeki Hyakka Daijiten* (Encyclopedia of Theater; Tokyo: Heibonsha, 1960), I, 145.

hastened the decline of kabuki in Osaka and Kyoto, where love suicide plays formed an important part of the repertory. Current happenings within samurai feudal houses were of intense interest to kabuki's plebian audiences, but their dramatization, too, was forbidden, probably as early as 1703. This ban proved uninforceable, however, for playwrights simply altered characters' names and placed events in an earlier period, usually Kamakura (1185–1333) or Ashikaga (1336–1568). In time a whole system of conventional parallels between places, situations, people, and events from past and present developed. This "matching" of present and past, which became an important part of kabuki dramatic practice, is called *mitate*. Often a major figure first appears "in disguise" (*yatsushi*), only to reveal himself in a crucial moment to be "in reality" (*jitsu wa*) a person from a different historical period (Sukeroku, for example, in *Sukeroku: Flower of Edo*). Mitate was a transparent device, and the audience easily identified the actual contemporary event from its historical parallel, but the letter of the law was not broken.

Because of the restricted social environment in which kabuki artists worked, Japan's isolation from outside contacts, and oppressive government restrictions, kabuki plays developed many characteristics of a game played by audience and performers. Like a game it had certain rules, such as mitate, yatsushi, and jitsu wa, and playing according to the rules became in itself an important source of enjoyment and pleasure for an audience. Undoubtedly the game approach stimulated writers and actors to perfect kabuki's artistic qualities and helped sustain the form's delightful spirit of playfulness.

THE PLAYS

THE GENROKU PERIOD

By the beginning of the Genroku period, in the late seventeenth century, three major divisions of kabuki drama were recognized: *sewamono*, or plays about the lives of contemporary commoners; history plays, known as *jidaimono*; and dance pieces, called *shosagoto* (*keigoto* in Kyoto and Osaka). Dances (which will be discussed later) and sketches of contemporary life were among the earliest kabuki pieces. The most important topical situation was that of the young town dandy visiting a courtesan in the licensed quarter. Three generations continued the situation, first performed by Okuni, in hundreds upon hundreds of plays, until it evolved in

Genroku into the so-called "prostitute" or "prostitute-buying" (*keisei* or *keiseigai*) play.

The prostitute play is particularly characteristic of Kyoto (and Osaka) kabuki, and it was Kyoto actor, Sakata Tōjūrō (1644–1709), who brought the genre to perfection. Tōjūrō was admired as an actor of impeccable taste. The story is told of how he received a farewell gift from Nakamura Shichisaburō (1662–1708), a fellow actor and warm friend, who was leaving Kyoto. Thinking it would be too mechanical to return the gift immediately, Tōjūrō did nothing. After several months porters sent by Tōjūrō arrived at Shichisaburō's door in Edo, carrying a great jar in a crate and a letter which read, "I hereby present you with a jar of water from the River Kamo. Please use it for your New Year's tea."[6]

In 1678 Tōjūrō created the role of Fujiya Izaemon in the play *New Year's Remembrance of Yūgiri*. He played Izaemon as a wealthy and pampered young man-about-town, drawing gentle laughter with his portrait of the elegantly handsome hero who pouts childlishly as he awaits Yūgiri, the courtesan he loves. Tōjūrō's unique blend of sensuousness and comic helplessness was called *wagoto*, literally "soft style," acting. A current saying described the wagoto part as "a lover's role played with the heart of a comedian."[7] A sociologist or psychiatrist might wish to explore why, at least in art, the foolish, ineffectual hero was the favorite of courtesans. Tōjūrō's performance was extremely well received; in order to satisfy public demand he played Izaemon four times that year and, in all, eighteen times during his acting career. No other kabuki actor before or since has been so intimately connected with a single role. Thereafter he played similar wagoto leading roles in scores of plays in Kyoto and Osaka; "all things considered, he spent practically his whole life doing keisei pieces."[8]

Just as the role of Izaemon is taken, even today, as the model for wagoto acting, the Yūgiri-Izaemon story, dramatized in *Love Letter from the Licensed Quarter* (1712), is typical of the mature prostitute play. The basic situation is as follows. Izaemon has squandered a small fortune on the courtesan Yūgiri of the Shinmachi licensed quarter in Osaka. As a result, his wealthy family has disowned him. After wandering pathetically for two years Izaemon returns to the quarter, yearning to meet Yūgiri. He is so put out at having to appear as a virtual outcast in the quarter where his money used to

6. Charles J. Dunn and Bunzō Torigoe, *The Actors' Analects: Yakusha Rongo* (New York: Columbia University Press, 1969), p. 135.

7. *Daijten*, VI, 65.

8. Dunn, *Analects*, p. 102.

buy him every attention and favor, that when Yūgiri finally comes to meet him he pouts and pretends he is interested in her no longer. He accuses her of being unfaithful. They quarrel. She tells him she had become so ill worrying about his safety, she only this day has consented to meet guests. As they tenderly make up, family servants fortuitously rush on carrying chests of money to pay Izaemon's debts and buy off Yūgiri's contract with the brothel. Typical elements of the prostitute-buying genre are found here: the disinherited hero's return to the licensed quarter in disguise (*yatsushi*), the lovers' quarrel (*kuzetsu*), and the love scene (*nuregoto*). It is difficult now to judge how explicitly erotic the love scenes were in Genroku kabuki. Stage directions are few, but Tōjūrō criticized scenes staged at other theaters that showed lovers together in bed.[9] In all likelihood Genroku prostitute plays were more sensual than we might imagine reading present scripts. They were also elegantly stylish, reflecting the urbane sophistication cultivated by habitués of licensed quarters. It has been suggested one reason people flocked to see prostitute plays was that they instructed the spectator on how to carry off with the proper finesse a visit to the quarter. There is no villain or antagonist role in the typical prostitute play, and conflict, largely limited to the bickering of the lovers, remains on a low level. As we will see, this contrasts markedly with history plays as well as other types of contemporary sewamono. The typical prostitute play is casual and lighthearted.

The role of Yūgiri was based on a widely known courtesan of that name from the Osaka Shinmachi prostitute quarter, who died suddenly in 1678. Within a month Tōjūrō had opened in *New Year's Remembrance of Yūgiri* (whether in Kyoto or Osaka is unclear). This can be considered the first important "overnight pickles" play. Its great success encouraged managers to base other plays on the latest town scandal. In the spring of 1683 the Osaka courtesan Yamato Ichinojō and her patron, Goze Choemon, for unknown reasons took their lives together. Plays about this sensational event immediately opened at three major kabuki theaters in Osaka. Very probably these were the first love suicide, or shinjū, plays to be staged in Japan (the word "shinjū" appears in a kabuki play title in 1662, but the plot of the play is unknown).[10] The popular actor-manager Iwai Hanshirō I played at his theater in Osaka *The Love Suicides at Toribeyama* in 1685, and in 1686 *The Love Suicides at Mikatsu*. The latter was such a success it ran one-

9. Ibid., p. 136.
10. See Ihara, *Nempyō*, I, 87–89, 147.

hundred fifty performances. By the end of the century a dozen similar plays had been staged in kabuki. The love suicide play can be seen as a development of the prostitute play in which the relationship of the courtesan and her patron is carried past the stage of courtship and casual dalliance to its tragic denouement in death. A third type of contemporary sewamono play dramatized recent scandalous murders (*satsujinmono*). Again, a courtesan and her patron were usually major characters. The murder scenes in *The Scarlet Princess of Edo*, written more than a century later, are descendents of the Genroku period murder play.

Following the immense popularity which kabuki's domestic plays gained in the two and a half decades since Tōjūrō captivated audiences in *New Year's Remembrance of Yūgiri*, the form was transplanted into jōruri puppet drama by Chikamatsu Monzaemon (1653–1724), a brilliant playwright of both kabuki and jōruri texts. In 1703 a young merchant and a prostitute, who were in love, killed themselves at Sonezaki Shrine in Osaka. Within days kabuki dramatizations of the event were playing at three theaters, and a few weeks later Chikamatsu's puppet play *The Love Suicides at Sonezaki*[11] opened in Osaka. It was the first jōruri domestic play. (Before this the puppet repertory had been made up of religious and history pieces.) It was well received and Chikamatsu went on to write many more. By the time he composed *The Love Suicides at Sonezaki*, Chikamatsu was an old hand at writing sewamono plays. For twenty years he had been a staff playwright for Sakata Tōjūrō in Kyoto, writing an estimated twenty to thirty kabuki plays, most of which included prostitute-buying scenes. In *The Love Suicides at Sonezaki*, Chikamatsu recreated in jōruri the familiar kabuki prostitute-buying situation and kabuki's wagoto comic-lover hero. In later works he was to move away from the kabuki model and write suicide plays, more somber in mood, emphasizing the family obligations of the hero that would make his love for a prostitute untenable.

History plays, or jidaimono, developed in kabuki some decades after contemporary plays. During the 1660s scenes were staged of warriors fighting (*budōgoto*) with spears and swords. These may have been stimulated by warrior or demon plays from the nō repertory or by the violent battle scenes typical of "old jōruri" (*kojōruri*), as puppet drama before Chikamatsu's time was called. By Genroku, two kinds of kabuki history plays were identifiable. Contemporary assassinations, vendettas, and power struggles

---

11. Translated in Donald Keene, *Major Plays of Chikamatsu* (New York: Columbia University Press, 1961).

within the ruling samurai class were put on stage as *oiemono*, or "feudal house" plays. For example, a number of oiemono history plays were based on a famous incident which occurred during the Genroku period. In 1703 forty-seven retainers of Lord Asano of Akō, having illegally slain a high official of the Shōgun's court who was responsible for their master's disgrace and death, committed mass suicide by disembowelment (*seppuku*). No event had so shocked and aroused the nation for a hundred years. The death of the forty-seven occurred on February 4; twelve days later, on February 16, a kabuki play alluding to the incident opened in Edo. Keenly aware that public sympathy lay with the executed men, three days after the play opened the government simultaneously closed it and banned dramatization of contemporary events concerning samurai. After this mitate came into general use, whereby contemporary events were safely placed in the past. Accordingly, when the next play on the Akō incident was written—by Chikamatsu Monzaemon—and staged in 1706, the event was placed in the Taiheiki World of the fourteenth century and Lord Asano was identified as Enya Hangan, a historical figure of that far-off period. Later plays based on the incident, including the famous *Chūshin-gura: The Treasury of Loyal Retainers*, followed this example. (Strictly speaking, the first oiemono plays about the Akō incident were not "history" plays at all: they were contemporary plays disguised as historical drama.)

In January 1664 kabuki theaters were prohibited from performing "Shimabara plays," as plays about prostitutes were often called. (Shimabara was the major licensed quarter in Kyoto.) Also, "the acting of courtesans' roles was resolutely forbidden."[12] Henceforth writers in Kyoto and Osaka disguised the prostitute-buying situation by working it into a three-, four-, or five-act oiemono history play. In a typical oiemono play the young heir to a feudal house would be deposed by a scheming clan retainer or relative and forced to escape in the disguise of a commoner. Often wearing a "paper kimono" symbolic of his poverty, he visits the licensed quarter for the usual wagoto love scene with a courtesan. At the end of the play, the evil retainer is defeated by retainers loyal to the house and the young heir is reinstated. Tōjūrō played scores of wagoto roles of this type. It seems that Kyoto audiences especially appreciated the contrast in oiemono plays between delicate wagoto acting and active samurai scenes.

A second type of history play, the *ōchōmono* or "imperial court"

12. Ihara, *Nempyō*, I, 93. Similar prohibitions decreed in 1655 and in 1658 seem not to have been observed.

play, was extremely popular with audiences in Edo. Also called "court history" plays (*ōdaimono*), they were set in the days of the ancient Heian court (794–1160) and were acted in a highly exaggerated, bravura style known as *aragoto* (literally, "rough style"). Aragoto acting is said to have originated with the first stage appearance, in 1673, of Ichikawa Danjūrō I (1660–1704). Playing the role of Kimpira, superhuman son of one of the Four Guardian Generals, he created a sensation when he entered the stage wearing bold "black and red makeup,"[13] rampaged up the side of a mountain, and single-handedly demolished a number of opponents. The impress of Danjūrō's bravura acting style carried over to some fifty plays which he composed under the pen name Mimasu Yahyōgo. Of these, *Indestructible* (1680), *Saint Narukami* (1684), *Wait a Moment!* (1697), *The God Fudō* (1697), and *Pulling the Elephant* (1701) are performed today. Originally, each was conceived as a single scene or act in an all-day play. Subsequently they were rewritten and incorporated in other long plays on many occasions. In time they began to be staged as independent one-act plays, the way they are now performed. *Wait a Moment!* has been produced in several hundred versions, and since early Genroku until the end of the nineteenth century theaters in Edo have traditionally incorporated into each season's opening play its simple situation of the hero saving the lives of the good faction by simultaneously lopping off eight enemy heads. Records substantiate at least ninety-six major productions of *Saint Narukami* and thirteen of *The God Fudō* since their premieres.

The last two give their names to the all-day imperial court play *Saint Narukami and the God Fudō*, staged in Osaka in 1742. Ichikawa Danjūrō II (1688–1758), son of the first Danjūrō, had been paid 2000 gold *ryō* (between $60,000 and $90,000) to come from Edo to play at the Sadoshima Theater in Osaka that season. Naturally he hoped to attract large audiences by playing aragoto style plays, his family's specialty, in order to justify this unprecedented salary. The opening production was moderately successful; the second, a revenge play concerning the Soga brothers, was poorly received and withdrawn after ten days. The theater manager, Sadoshima Chōgoro, describes what happened next: "Then when the dressing-room and the front got around to discussing the third program, and what should be in it, all sorts of things were suggested, but we came to no conclusion. At this point Hakuen (Danjūrō) suggested that we put on *Narukami* next. I said that if we did this

13. Most Japanese writers believe this marked the beginning of the distinctively bold makeup known as *kumadori* (e.g., *Daijiten*, I, 170).

play, there would be no need for a plot to be thought up. I joined the old play on to an introduction . . . Reverberations of the 'thunder god' (Narukami) not only reached the neighboring provinces, as was to be expected, but also there came to Osaka a great number of people even from distant parts especially to see . . . *Narukami*. It was universally well received, and the crowds were packed so tight that one could not force one's way through them. Many connoisseurs of the art from Kyoto came to Osaka to see his performance . . . What a fantastic genius he had, thus to excel even when not in view of the audience!"[14] The plot suggested by Chōgorō included Saint Narukami's death. Danjūrō objected to playing the role of a hero who was defeated, for supernatural strength and invincibility were the essence of aragoto style. But Chōgorō prevailed, *Saint Narukami and the God Fudō* opened as he suggested, and played 170 days, an exceptionally long run at that time. The clamor to see Danjūrō was so great that he was able to take off but a single day during the seven months the play ran and within a few days of Danjūrō's closing, the Mandayū Theater in Kyoto was ready with its own version of the play under the very same title.[15]

As the incident about the play's composition indicates, several casts of characters, originally unrelated, were woven together in a long play intended to last from early morning until dusk. These characters belong to well-defined "worlds", called *sekai* in kabuki. First in importance in this play is the Disputed Throne World of the Heian imperial court, set during the time of regent Fujiwara Mototsune and Emperor Yōzei in the ninth century. The story concerns Prince Hayakumo's scheme to depose the infant emperor, on the pretext that a mere child is incapable of interceding with the gods to end a terrible drought which is ravaging the land. The powerful Ono clan is a firm supporter of the emperor and is the Prince's major opponent. Hayakumo steals the clan's precious poem card, thereby humiliating the clan and at the same time preventing the card's use to bring rain (immersed in water, it possesses the power to cause rain to fall). And, because Princess Nishiki of the Ono clan is engaged to Bun'ya Toyohide, another supporter of the emperor, Hayakumo has an accomplice cause her hair to mysteriously stand on end in order to force an end to their relationship. Both of these intrigues are exposed by Kumadera Danjō, a retainer

14. Dunn, *Analects*, p. 155.
15. A successful play could always be counted on to have its imitators and rivals at other theaters. The poster at the Mandayū Theater in Kyoto specifically referred to Danjurō's seven-month run, adding that "since so many people wanted to see the play, fortunately the actor Iseburō was able to play it" in Kyoto (see Ihara, *Nempyō*, II, 285).

of Toyohide, in the "Whisker Tweezers" scene. In amusingly exaggerated aragoto fashion, Danjō threatens to send the poem card thief "to hell," and he discovers that a magnet in the ceiling is drawing into the air iron ornaments in the princess's hair. A second world is that of Saint Narukami and Lady Taema, a legendary world set in India. Narukami holds the Dragon Gods of rain captive with a magic spell and so causes the drought. Taema undertakes to seduce him in order to break the spell and release the rain-making Dragon Gods, on the condition that she will be allowed to marry Toyohide, whom she loves. A third world is that of the God Fudō. In the play's final scenes Fudō defeats Prince Hayakumo, the Ono clan's position is secured, Taema marries Toyohide, and Danjō kills Narukami, thus assuring Taema's safety and the freedom of the Dragon Gods on whom the prosperity of the realm depends.

Saint Narukami and the God Fudō is an appealingly innocent play. Worlds are joined together loosely, with important scenes and acts virtually independent plays. It evokes a simple and distant age from the past. Evil and good engage in epochal struggle for mastery of the nation, with the imperial throne itself the prize. It seems natural for the emperor to assume that his authority derives directly from the Sun Goddess. Many scenes are theatrically powerful. Pious Narukami transforms himself into a raging thunder god. Fudō makes an awesome descent from the heavens to resolve the play—a literal *deus ex machina.* It is easy to see how broadly stylized aragoto elocution and movement techniques were created for plays conceived on such a grand scale. *Saint Narukami and the God Fudō* could be pompous and boring were its grandiloquent scenes not tempered with delightful, straightforward humor. Danjō attempts to seduce the boy Hidetarō and Makiginu, a lady-in-waiting, with such zest and good humor that we are totally disarmed. While Lady Taema's seduction of Narukami is one of kabuki's most explicitly sexual scenes, it is also exceptionally witty and entertaining. We find the business of the magnet lifting Princess Nishiki's hair and then the tweezers and the knife, in the "Whisker Tweezers" scene, good fun and little more. Danjō's lines are enlivened by word play, and even Prince Hayakumo, the villain of the piece, puns that his henchmen's plot to take control of the Ono clan is "a play" that is "too small, too small," while his scheme to depose the emperor is "a grand masquerade." Kiyoyuki, the white-haired sage buried alive by Prince Hayakumo, laughingly attributes his survival to gluttony: after a hundred days in the ground "the delicious smell of rice cakes roused me and I followed my nose to the surface."

A number of qualities are shared by Genroku plays regardless of their place of origin, yet Japanese commentators have always remarked on the differences between plays written for Kyoto and for Edo audiences. The playwright Namiki Shōzō II (d. 1807) wrote in the early nineteenth century: "The spirit of Kyoto is gentle and from ancient times six-tenths of the plays that please are love stories, lacking in vigor and too softly composed. They have the heart of a woman. They are like a person's 'skin.' The spirit of Edo is violent and seven-tenths of the plays that please are prodigious imperial court plays, packed with action, strong in plot, unsuited to a woman's taste. They have the heart of a samurai. They are like a person's 'bones.' "[16]

In practice, the styles of the two cities often mingled. Perhaps the most successful blend of Edo bravura and Kyoto comic-eroticism is found in the Genroku period play *Sukeroku: Flower of Edo* (1713). It was written for Danjūrō II, who in addition to carrying on the bravura acting tradition of his father was also well acquainted with the soft acting tradition of Kyoto-Osaka. When young, Danjūrō certainly had seen Nakamura Shichisaburo play wagoto roles in Edo with a skill rivaling that of Tōjūrō. Three years after *Sukeroku: Flower of Edo* was written, Danjūrō himself played the wagoto role of Hanshichi in *The Love Suicides of Hanshichi and Sankatsu* at the Nakamura Theater in Edo to great acclaim.[17] In some ways Sukeroku, the play's hero, is a strutting, quarreling *otokodate*, or "chivalrous commoner," of the type that Edo audiences loved. The otokodate was a manifestation of contemporary life in vigorous Edo. Young townsmen would parade by the bathhouses where cheap prostitutes worked, swaggering, bragging, and showing off. The bravest might challenge samurai to a fight. But Sukeroku is also part wagoto lover. Instead of wearing the vast, padded garments of an aragoto hero, Danjūrō played Sukeroku wearing first a chic black kimono and later a "paper kimono" such as Izaemon wears in *Love Letter from the Licensed Quarter*. As accouterments of a dashing lover, he tied a luxurious purple headband of silk around his hairdo and tucked a flute into his sash. His makeup of narrow black and red lines over a delicate white base was the softest aragoto type. In the character of Shimbei, Sukeroku's gentle and humorously self-effacing brother, we have a pure wagoto role. The play begins as

16. From *Kezairoku* (ca. 1801–1804), quoted in Urayama Masao and Matsuzaki Hitoshi, ed., *Kabuki Kyakuhonshū* (Collection of Kabuki Plays; Tokyo: Iwanami Shoten, 1960), I, 8.

17. Ihara, *Nempyō*, I, 464.

a prostitute-buying sewamono, set in Edo's Yoshiwara licensed quarter. Sukeroku and the courtesan Agemaki quarrel during their love scene, as in every prostitute-buying play. But with Sukeroku's revelation that he is "in reality" Soga Gorō, a famous warrior from the twelfth century, only pretending to be a commoner in order to find a stolen sword and to avenge his father's murder, historical and contemporary worlds come to exist simultaneously. Shinbei is then shown to be Soga Jūrō, Gorō's elder brother, and the enemy samurai Ikyū suddenly reveals himself in a spectacular costume change (*miarawashi*) to be none other than the Heike general Heinai Zaemon. Edo audiences loved to play the mitate game of matching worlds from the present with those of the past.

Sukeroku: Flower of Edo is one of kabuki's most scintillating plays. Its costuming and staging are colorful. It contains magnificent procession scenes, active sword fights, and a scene in which Sukeroku plunges into a brimming vat, sending water cascading onto the floor. Its long speeches are famous, among them Agemaki's scathing put-down (*akutai*) of Ikyū and Sukeroku's nonstop "name-saying" speech (*nanori*). Sukeroku and Shinbei provide twenty mintues of outrageous slapstick when they force passersby to crawl between their legs. Because this scene is ad-libbed (*sutezerifu*), it varies from production to production, even from performance to performance. *Sukeroku: Flower of Edo* is unique; there is no other play like it, yet it sums up the characteristics of Genroku kabuki—sensuality, vitality, optimism, and good-natured fun.

PUPPET ADAPTATIONS

Plays written through the Genroku period are called "pure" (*junsui*) kabuki. Written for kabuki by kabuki playwrights they are different in many ways from the puppet play adaptations (*maruhonmono*, *dendenmono*, or *gidayū kyōgen*) that came to occupy an important place in the kabuki repertory from the Horeki period (1751–1764) on. Puppet and kabuki theaters had existed side-by-side in the entertainment quarters of the three cities since the early 1600s. In the hundred years following, neither jōruri nor kabuki borrowed extensively from the other. Occasional instances can be noted, as when Danjūrō I based some of his portrayal of the aragoto hero on Kimpira jōruri, a knockabout puppet play popular in Edo in the mid-1600s. Considering the physical proximity of kabuki and jōruri theaters in the entertainment quarters and the fact that their audiences were almost the same, it is surprising that so little interchange between them took place. One probable reason is that kabuki and "old jōruri" were quite different art forms. Kabuki was a dialogue and dance drama; jōruri was not so much a first-person play as a narrative epic, incidentally illustrated by actions of hand puppets. But gradually during the Genroku period, jōruri became "kabuki-ized." Although it never completely abandoned its distinctive narrative style, the amount of narrative decreased significantly from Chikamatsu's time onward, while the amount of first-person dialogue increased proportionally. Between 1720 and 1735 revolutionary changes occurred in the type of puppet used and in manipulation technique. The simple one-man hand puppet was replaced by a complex doll, three-quarters life-size, that had movable eyes, eyebrows, mouth, hands, and fingers and required three men to operate. In the past a single chanter (singer) had performed a scene; now a scene was divided into sections and a different chanter took each. By the mid-1700s half a dozen chanters appeared simultaneously in some scenes, each, like an actor, taking a single role. Audiences were entranced by this new type of puppet performance. They jammed the puppet houses, marveling at the realism with which the dolls of wood, paint, and cloth were able to recreate scenes of daily life, dusting, pouring tea, eating, playing a musical instrument, or sobbing piteously in a moment of high emotion, as chanters placed in the characters' mouths moving dialogue and fused the whole together with soaring passages of sung narration. Earlier plays, including Chikamatsu's, no longer suited the new performing style, and scores of new ones were composed for the versatile, lifelike puppets. Over a span of just six years, four highly acclaimed jōruri plays were written: *The House of Sugawara* (1746),[18] *Yoshitsune and the Thousand Cherry Trees* (1747), *Chūshingura: The Treasury of Loyal Retainers* (1748)[19] — the "Three Great Masterpieces" of jōruri—and *Chronicle of the Battle of Ichinotani* (1751). Their popularity was so instantaneous that within months they were being staged by kabuki actors also. Not only were new themes and dramatic materials thereby introduced to kabuki, but the singing style, the Takemoto (or Gidayū) *shamisen* music, and the puppet movement techniques of jōruri theater were deliberately taken over as well. The transposition of complete puppet plays into the kabuki repertory is said to have

18. Translated in Earle Ernst, ed., *Three Japanese Plays* (New York: Oxford University Press, 1959).
19. Donald Keene, trans., *Chūshingura: The Treasury of Loyal Retainers* (New York: Columbia University Press, 1970).

begun with *Yoshitsune and the Thousand Cherry Trees* at the Nakamura Theater in Edo in May 1748, when a chanter, three shamisen players, and six puppeteers were invited from the Takemoto Puppet Theater in Osaka to direct rehearsals.[20] The kabuki version played to full houses for seventy days, establishing a pattern of direct borrowing that continued for several decades. The period 1750–1770 therefore marks a radical departure from kabuki's previous history.

Chronicle of the Battle of Ichinotani takes place in the second month of 1184, when Genji armies, under the command of Minamoto Yoshitsune, are defeating the Heike and wresting from them control of the nation. Of the play's original five acts, two are still performed. On the beach of Suma Bay, Kumagai, a Genji general, unhorses and beheads a young enemy warrior, described as the ex-emperor's son and Heike heir, Prince Atsumori. The next scene is at Kumagai's battle camp. He is attacked by Atsumori's mother, Lady Fuji, who has been driven wild with grief by the death of her son. Kumagai is able to calm her by recounting each step of the boy's noble death, in a moving narrative (*monogatari*). Yoshitsune appears and demands to see Atsumori's head. When Kumagai presents it for verification (*kubijikken*), his wife, Sagami, gasps with astonishment. The head is not that of Atsumori, but of their own son, Kojirō. Knowing it was Yoshitsune's wish that the child of the emperor be spared, Kojirō willingly substituted himself for Atsumori during battle so that Kumagai would behead him in place of Atsumori. Husband and wife struggle to maintain their composure and protect the secret of the head's identity, as Sagami lovingly cradles Kojirō's head to her breast in a bitter, suppressed scene of lamentation (*kudoki*). Lady Fuji also sees the head and joins their weeping. The act (and the play in its present form) ends as Kumagai strips off his armor to reveal beneath it a monk's garb. He renounces his rank and begins a wandering life dedicated to praying for the repose of Kojirō's soul.

Not all history puppet plays written at this time are set during the bloody Heike-Genji conflict, but a similar quality of emotional torment and anguish runs through them, setting them apart from the majority of kabuki plays. Perhaps the most descriptive term would be "feudal war" plays (usually they are called simply *jidai*,

---

20. Ihara, *Nempyō*, III, 10; the names of the artists invited to Edo do not appear on the original jōruri playbill (see Tōkyō Ongaku Gakkō, *Kinsei Hōgaku Nempyō: Gidayū Bushi no Bu* [Tokyo: Rokugōkan, 1927], p. 104), indicating either that they had not performed in Osaka or that their parts there had been minor, which opens up the possibility that the kabuki version was less authentic than is usually thought.

or "period," plays). Typically there is a prolonged scene of physical suffering followed by death. In *Chronicle of the Battle of Ichinotani*, after Princess Tamaori is wounded, she clings to life for many minutes, blinded and in great pain, before she finally succumbs. Such scenes are almost certainly related to "wounded" (*teoigoto*) scenes in *budō* fighting plays of pre-Genroku kabuki. More important, a "sincere" hero (*jitsugoto*) is featured in a moving scene of sacrifice. The hero commits suicide or, as in *Chronicle of the Battle of Ichinotani*, he causes or is forced to endure the death of a beloved family member. This climactic scene usually occurs at the midpoint of the five-act play: in the final section (*kiri*) of the third act (*sandan*). Although it is part of a "history" play, Japanese consider the *sandan no kiri* suicide or family sacrifice a *sewa*, or "domestic," scene. In it the pomp of history is laid aside, and characters bare their hearts as husband and wife, parent and child. In *Chronicle of the Battle of Ichinotani*, duty (*giri*) impells Kumagai to kill his son, although his human feelings (*ninjō*) rebel against the act. The conflict is intensely dramatic and might be handled in a number of ways. Kumagai might unblinkingly follow the dictates of giri, in which case he would kill his son without hesitation and in the aftermath would show no outward sign of remorse or grief (although he might feel both). Ideally, this is what the samurai code calls for. In fact, both Kumagai and Sagami fail to control their emotions. They act like middle-class parents. He vacillates for ten minutes before Hirayama's taunts compel him to behead Kojirō. (Kojirō on the contrary dies with perfect composure, in accordance with the code.) Sagami weeps openly and at length. It is human and understandable that they would give way to their deep grief over the loss of their son; but these are not the actions of noble, historical figures, solely motivated by samurai codes of conduct. In general, the feudal war play, especially its sandan no kiri climax, represents a kind of bourgeois domestication of samurai ethics.

The typical scene of lamentation in jōruri reaches its culmination in a flood of anguished tears and is called a "great conclusion" (*ōotoshi*), thus distinguishing it from other standard endings of scenes. Significantly, no term in kabuki drama identifies a crying scene. Several explanations have been advanced for the prevalence and the importance of tearful scenes in puppet drama. It may be that a narrative art, with its commentary and description, is especially effective in creating moods of melancholy and of pathos. Or, perhaps puppets that are nearly, but not quite, human can only be brought fully to life by projecting into them the most intense emotions. We can imagine that the jōruri audience of merchants and townsmen found comfort in seeing their samurai betters dissolve into tears of grief, as they themselves would do. Osaka is the home of jōruri puppet theater. *Chronicle of the Battle of Ichinotani* and the other great puppet dramas were written and performed for Osaka audiences. It is often suggested that, for unexplained reasons, these audiences have been particularly susceptible to tearful stories. Namiki Shōzō, who was born in Osaka, concluded his comparison of plays in the three cities with the sardonic observation that, "the spirit of Osaka is logical to a fault, and eight-tenths of the plays that please are concerned with duty (giri), filled with boring explanation, and designed for the heart of the chivalrous townsman. They are like a person's 'flesh.'"[21]

The relationship between kabuki and jōruri drama was considerably more complex than this brief outline may suggest. When Danjūrō I appeared on stage for the first time, in 1673 at the age of thirteen, his role of Kintoki (Kimpira's son) already had been popular with puppet audiences for at least two decades. In the Kyoto Mandayū Theater's 1694 production of *Five Roads and the Official of Death* scenes of miraculous resurrections and roles for three villains reflect borrowings from old jōruri.[22] Chikamatsu's highly successful puppet play *The Battles of Coxinga* (1715)[23] inspired kabuki playwrights to write similar plays. At about this time, the actor Otowa Jirosaburō refused to play in pieces "which used the chanting that goes with the puppets,"[24] indicating that puppet performing techniques were being borrowed at least occasionally by kabuki. As often as not a play was staged first as kabuki and later adapted to the puppet stage. (A kabuki play about the battle of Ichinotani was performed in Kyoto as early as 1691, sixty years before *Chronicle of the Battle of Ichinotani* was written.) But sometimes it was the other way around. Other plays, like the famous *Incense of Loyalty for a Late Master*, passed back and forth between kabuki and jōruri so often that it is impossible to attribute them to one form or the other. With the adaptation of *Yoshitsune and the Thousand Cherry Trees* to kabuki, jōruri chanter and shamisen teams (chobo) became a part of every kabuki troupe. While actors took over the lines of dialogue, the jōruri chanter sat to the left of the stage, as in the puppet theater, and delivered the narrative sections. Numerous changes occurred, such as the reduction of the

21. Urayama, *Kyakuhonshū*, I, 8.
22. Kawatake Shigetoshi, *Nihon Gikyokushi* (History of Japanese Drama; Tokyo: Nan'undō, 1964), pp. 344–346.
23. Translated in Keene, *Chikamatsu*.
24. Dunn, *Analects*, p. 112.

amount of Takemoto music to meet the requirements of kabuki acting, but the basic jōruri style of performance was carried over onto the live stage.

Maruhon plays, as puppet adaptations in kabuki are usually called, are excellent theater pieces and their incorporation into the repertory enriched the drama. But jōruri has a "thickness" of style; it emphasizes emotionalism and contains little humor, and the puppets depend upon small, realistic movements (*furi*) for effect. Such qualities are fundamentally antithetical to kabuki artistic style. Because text, chanting (or singing), music, and movement in jōruri fuse into a single pattern, the kabuki actor lost some of his freedom to improvise. But audiences enjoyed seeing actors perform drama written for puppets, and the best plays soon became part of both repertories. It is often said that kabuki acting style changed under jōruri influence, and it would be interesting to have this subject studied in detail. We can note, however, that kabuki writers demonstrated no interest in following jōruri dramatic form. With but one exception during the next hundred years, no kabuki playwright composed new works using jōruri narrative technique. (The exception was Namiki Shōzō whose father was one of the authors of *Chronicle of the Battle of Ichinotani*.)

DANCE PLAYS

This remarkable period of creativity in jōruri writing ended almost as suddenly as it had begun and by the end of the Hōreki period kabuki had returned to its own resources for new drama. The center of kabuki activity shifted from Kyoto and Osaka, and thereafter almost all important new plays came from Edo playwrights. Two new directions in Edo kabuki are noteworthy. During the Tenmei period (1781–1788) playwrights such as Horikoshi Nisōji (1721–1781?) and Sakurada Jisuke I (1734–1806) created a new style of dramatic dance play (*buyō geki*). Prior to this time a michiyuki "travel dance" was an integrated scene within the main play (*hon kyōgen*); otherwise kabuki dance tended to be nondramatic. The very important solo dance piece (shosagoto or buyō) by the onnagata actor was designed to exhibit the physical attractiveness of the actor and to display his skill in portraying feminine elegance. If performed at the end of the program it was called "final piece," *kiri kyōgen*, and might be given a title separate from the main play. The other main type of dance, *ōdori*, was a lively group dance performed by the entire company. As a rule ōdori were not given titles but were simply announced to the audience at the conclusion of the main play. An interesting account of one such informal dance is found in the illustrated play book for the four-act history play *The Biography of the Genji-Heike Thunder God*, written and performed in 1698 by Danjūrō I. This play marked the retirement at the age of forty-two of the troupe's lead onnagata, Ogino Sawanojō. At the end of the last act the text continues: "And now Danjūrō announced to the audience, 'At this time Sawanojō resumes his manhood. This, then, is his farewell appearance.' With the entire cast urging him on, Sawanojō made a swaggering entrance (*roppō*) dressed like a man with his hair done in masculine fashion. At this point Sawanojō performed an active entrance dance, looking the height of male handsomeness in his final appearance. Crying 'How difficult,' the entire cast without exception began a group dance (*ōodori*) as encouragement for him to continue. It was a never-to-be-forgotten sight, child actors decorating themselves with flowers, male leads doing the Ten Thousand Bushels Dance, others saying 'Me too, me too,' as they danced Edo's famous Straw Bag Dance. The actor Yanaginosuke, too, did the Straw Bag Dance and to 'Congratulations, congratulations,' all joined the auspicious group dance."[25]

Almost a century would pass before casual nondramatic dances yielded gradually to danced plays in which the leading man as well as the onnagata would take major dance roles. When this occurred dance-dramas with plots and conflicts became possible. Horikoshi established the custom of each full-length play's containing a dance scene or act. New types of music created especially for dance plays combined the narrative qualities of Takemoto music (the music of jōruri puppet drama) and the lyric qualities of kabuki's usual Nagauta music. Tokiwazu, Kiyomoto, and Tomimoto were the most important of these new musical styles.

A craze for dance plays swept kabuki that continued through the nineteenth century. While some wholly new ones were created, many favorite plays were adapted to dance. To mention just one example, dance sequences were added to *Narukami* when it was performed as an independent play by Danjūrō VII and VIII in the mid-nineteenth century. Taema's scenes especially were accompanied by various styles of music: Kiyomoto music for Danjūrō VII's production in 1836, Tokiwazu and Takemoto music for Danjūrō VIII's production in 1843, and Kiyomoto and Takemoto music eight years later in 1851. The dance play translated here is *Love Letter from the Licensed Quarter*, staged for the first time under that title in

25. Takano Tasuyuki and Kuroki Kanzō, eds., *Genroku Kabuki Kessakushū* (Masterpieces of Genroku Kabuki; Tokyo: Waseda Daigaku Shuppanbu, 1939), I, 150.

1780. It is a dance adaptation of the well-known Yūgiri-Izaemon story from the Genroku period. It is an unusual dance play in that the first scene is dialogue drama while the last half of the play is dance; it is sometimes called a *han-buyō*, "half-dance," for this reason. In other respects it contains typical elements of mature kabuki dance-drama. The story is well developed and is enacted by several characters; dialogue sections alternate with sections of dance; and variety of musical effect is achieved by the use of more than a single type of music (Takemoto and Kiyomoto or Tokiwazu). Although the dramatic content of the piece is of considerable interest, it is not the sole focus of attention. An important aim of the piece is to produce aesthetic delight through the beautiful sounds of music and singing, elegant costuming, and pleasing patterns of dance movement. Two groups of musicians are seated in full view of the audience in order to add color and weight to the visual composition. The play lasts about an hour in performance. Staged as the last piece (kiri kyōgen) of a long day's program, it restores the spectator to a pleasant and relaxed frame of mind before he leaves the theater.

TRUE DOMESTIC PLAYS

A second new type of play evolved in the city of Edo beginning in the Kasei period (1804–1830).[26] Called *kizewamono*, "true sewamono," plays dramatizing a dark substrata of violence and immorality that lay beneath the outward opulence of the period began to be written. In the early nineteenth century the fabric of Tokugawa feudal society was beginning to unravel: powerful samurai were deeply in debt to the very merchants they despised; natural disasters and oppressive taxation caused futile peasant uprisings; the number of masterless, wandering samurai (*rōnin*) grew dangerously large. Sakurada Jisuke I and Namiki Gohei I (1747–1808) had put peasants and low-ranking commoners on stage, but it remained for Tsuruya Namboku IV (1755–1829) to create a new form of drama in which thieves, murderers, pimps, swindlers, renegade monks, and street whores played central roles.

Namboku was typical of kabuki playwrights in that he spent his whole life in the theater. At the age of twenty-two he was accepted as a "see and learn" (*minarai*) apprentice on Sakurada Jisuke's writing staff at the Nakamura Theater. During the next thirty years he worked his way up from Third Assistant Playwright to Second

26. The two eras, Bunka (1804–1817) and Bunsei (1818–1830), taken together are called Kasei.

Assistant Playwright at Edo's major kabuki houses, the Ichimura Theater, the Morita Theater, and the Kawarazaki Theater. By the time he achieved the rank of Chief Playwright at the age of fifty-three, he knew the art of kabuki intimately. He wrote every type of play prolifically. In the last two decades of his life he was chief author of 125 scripts. Like most playwrights of his time, Namboku seems to have had little formal education, yet he reveals intuitive understanding of the society of his time. A major Japanese criticism of Namboku's writing has been that it lacks delicacy and at times is almost brutal. Critics call his plays "overripe," because he mirrored the reality of late feudal times when corruption and venality were seen everywhere and traditional loyalty seemed a rare virtue indeed. Whatever qualms one may have regarding Namboku's unsavory materials, as a dramatist and a humorist he has no equal in kabuki.

Namboku wrote *The Scarlet Princess of Edo* in 1817. It is an all-day, *jidai-sewamono*, or "mixed history-domestic play" (actually *jidai-kizewamono* would be more exact). In the history part of the play, plots from two worlds intertwine. From the Sumida River World he has taken the story of Akugorō's scheme to usurp control of the House of Yoshida. And from the Sakura-Seigen World, he has taken the story of Priest Seigen's unrequited love for Sakura. Namboku makes Sakura both the object of Seigen's love and a princess of the House of Yoshida, thus joining together the two worlds. The second part of the play moves into the kizewamono world of Tsurigane Gonsuke, a callous scoundrel who seduces Princess Sakura, sells her into prostitution, and fathers her illegitimate child.

Namboku's inventiveness and virtuosity are apparent at every turn in the way he infuses new life into standard situations. An important concern of kabuki writers of every period was how to interweave historical and contemporary materials. We have seen—in *Sukeroku: Flower of Edo*, for example—how a contemporary figure may reveal himself to be a famous historical personage, following the fanciful game of mitate. In *The Scarlet Princess of Edo*, Namboku turns the game into shocking reality: he dramatizes the descent of his main characters, Princess Sakura and the priest Seigen, from exalted aristocrats to outcasts. No theatrical trick or convention is involved. In Namboku's society thieves and samurai do not live in isolated worlds; they rub shoulders. He gives the usually insipid "scarlet princess' (*aka hime*) role unusual range and interest. It is wonderfully inventive to have Gonsuke send Princess Sakura out to be vulgarized (the opposite of Shaw's *Pygmalion*). When she returns, she has been, as Gonsuke laughingly remarks, "chopped down the middle, half princess, half bitch." Such a character had never been seen in kabuki before. The usual place for a lovers' suicide journey is well into a play, but Namboku dared open *The Scarlet Princess of Edo* with Seigen and his boy lover traveling to the cliffs at Enoshima to die together. And instead of the usual romantic ending, with the lovers tearfully dying in each others' arms, Namboku mordantly sends the boy to his death alone. Seigen decides to live. He is afraid to die! The scene in which Naga-ura and Zangetsu are kicked out of the temple by Gonsuke and prepare to depart is a very funny spoof of the standard, pathetic michiyuki journey. "Gunjibei's Village School" scene is a deliberate takeoff (*modoki*) of two famous jōruri plays: the opening is like the "Village School" scene ("Terakoya") in *The House of Sugawara*, and it concludes with a double child-sacrifice modeled on *A Woman's Sacrifice on Mount Imose* (1771).

Namboku does not make the moral disarray of his times a topic of discussion, but we see clear evidence of it in *The Scarlet Princess of Edo*. Characters pray and observe traditional Buddhist pieties, but the appearance of Seigen's ghost is made a joke, presumably because many in the audience did not take this Buddhist idea seriously. The humor, black and bitter and rising from a mood of pessimism, is totally unlike the sunny humor of Genroku drama. In earlier times thefts or murders in sewamono plays were presented as aberrations in the conduct of otherwise normal townsmen. In contrast, Gonsuke is a cold-blooded professional criminal, who murders and steals as a way of life. The scenes of brutal murder (*koroshiba*) and of blackmail or extortion (*yusuriba*) in the play are typical of kizewamono. Gonsuke strangling a maid, kicking her body into the moat, and then humming a snatch of a nō song as he saunters away, is a chilling portrait of human behavior.

It would be wrong to think that Namboku was writing here a "realistic" drama. Namboku was a master of kabuki art. His aim, even in seemingly "real" scenes, was to create a sense of beauty irrespective of subject matter. The extended murder scenes in which Seigen tries to kill Sakura and when Sakura kills Gonsuke illustrate this. At first they may seem sordidly real, but in performance they are eerily beautiful. Delicately lyric music accompanies actions that are executed in artfully choreographed dance patterns. Namboku pioneered using the Japanese poetic form of alternating phrases of seven and of five syllables (*shichigochō*) for long passages of kabuki dialogue. It is impossible to take realistically a scene like Gonsuke's audacious blackmailing of Ojū and Sentarō when we hear their three voices rising and falling in cadence as they argue and challenge each other in regular seven-five phrases. The long section of shichigochō which opens the scene in which Seigen and Sakura pass in the night, contributes much to that scene's beauty.

Unfortunately for Namboku's reputation as a playwright, shortly after his death Japan's feudal system collapsed and the nation was opened to the West. His plays concerned a disreputable period which most Japanese earnestly wished to forget. And, with the importation from the West of Victorian standards of art and taste their eroticism and irreverent humor came to be considered offensive. Namboku has been out of fashion for many years. However, it appears that his works are being rediscovered and that a reevaluation of his reputation is under way. What once struck observers as Namboku's "realism" is now seen as a return to kabuki's original concern for contemporary events. Perhaps Namboku's greatest contribution to kabuki drama is that he applies the stylized vision of the history play (influenced by Edo aragoto) to current events, events which often concerned people from the depths of society, thereby creating a new and beautifully stylized yet contemporary play, the kizewamono.

THE PLAYWRITING SYSTEM

The typical kabuki performance began around three in the morning and continued until dusk. Consequently, playwrights had to create fourteen- to fifteen-hour programs. It was possible to do this because writers worked within well established frames of reference. To begin with, the day's program was divided into parts. A ceremonial dance play, *Sanbasō*, opened the bill, followed by one of a theater's two or three standard "house plays" (*waki kyōgen*), usually a comic dance or sketch adapted from the kyōgen comedies that are associated with nō. Because everyone in the company knew these plays, they required no preparation. Then followed one or two short practice plays (*jobiraki* or *futateme*), written by apprentice playwrights and performed by young actors as part of their training. These preliminary plays were of little importance and few spectators came to the theater at such an early hour. The main play was the hon kyōgen, written by the chief playwright and his top assistants and performed by the stars of the troupe. Hon kyōgen began around seven in the morning and continued through the day until the theater closed. Depending upon the circumstances, there could be several main plays, but for the most important programs of the year it was usual to write a single multiact play that would run ten to twelve hours in playing, called *tōshi kyōgen* (literally, "straight-through play"). *Saint Narukami and the God Fudō* and *The Scarlet Princess of Edo* were written, and are translated, as tōshi kyōgen.

At the beginning of each theater season, worlds (sekai) to be used for main plays throughout the year were decided on by the chief playwright of a troupe in consultation with the actor-manager (*zagashira*), the theater owner, and sometimes other actors. A world was a well-known situation with an established set of characters; it was rarely invented by a playwright. Precisely because a world was already significant in legend or history, or in the case of sewamono through public scandal, it was considered appropriate for the stage. Many historical worlds encompass the great events and figures of Japanese history from the time of the Heian emperors in the ninth century down to the years immediately preceding kabuki's founding.[27] An imperial court play could be set in the Disputed Throne World, with the famous poets Ono Komachi or Ariwara Narihira or the regent Fujiwara Mototsune as major characters; in the Ise World of Narihira's brother the courtier Yukihira and the sisters Matsukaze and Murasame who love him; or in the Pre-Great Peace World, which included such important figures as the Four Guardian Generals and Yorimitsu (Raiko), who were instrumental in suppressing the revolts of Taira Masakado. All are set in the ninth and tenth centuries. The Heike World, largely based on the epic, *The Tale of the Heike* (*Heike Monogatari*), is one of the most wideranging. The period covered is barely thirty years, 1156–1185, but during that time the total destruction of the Heike clan by the Genji occurs, giving ample material for several cycles of plays featuring the Heike Prince Atsumori; Heike generals Kagekiyo, Shunkan, Shigemori, Sanemori, and Kiyomori; and the Genji general Kumagai. The melancholy nature of the Heike World derives chiefly from the fact that the defeated Heike more than the victorious Genji are made central dramatic figures. Minamoto Yoshitsune, the Genji general most responsible for defeating the Heike, naturally appears in many plays of the Heike World as a fearless and brilliant warrior. But there is also a separate Yoshitsune World devoted to incidents in his personal life, involving especially his retainer Benkei and his mistress Shizuka, in such plays as *The Subscription List*, *Yoshitsune and the Thousand Cherry Trees*, *Benkei at the Bridge*, and *Benkei in the Boat*. The most popular of all worlds in Edo was the Soga World, whose perennial heroes are the powerful Soga Gorō and his gentle elder brother Soga Jūrō.

27. See Izuka Tomoichirō, *Kabuki Saiken* (Survey of Kabuki Drama; Tokyo: Daiichi Shobō, 1926). Some six thousand kabuki plays are classified according to worlds and sub-worlds.

In 1193, in the first decade of the Kamakura era, the brothers avenged the murder of their father which had occurred eighteen years earlier; this incident inspired uncounted hundreds of revenge plays with Gorō and Jūrō as their heroes. The World of the Hōjō Regents is set in the Kamakura period, ca. 1185–1333, while the World of Great Peace is set in the period of the Northern and Southern Courts immediately following (ca. 1336–1392), when ironically the Shōgunate rulers in Kamakura were engaged in constant battle with supporters of the emperor in Kyoto. These two worlds are of particular interest. When contemporary events concerning samurai had to be hidden through mitate they were usually placed in these periods, which were safely "historical" yet not too remote. Less numerous but still important were worlds based on early myths and legends: the World of Narukami the Thunder God, the World of the God Fudō, the World of the Angel's Robe, the Dojō Temple Maid World, and others. When a once current event became staple dramatic material over a period of years, it, too, was called a world. There are scores of sewamono worlds, including the World of Yūgiri-Izaemon.

Each world had a special emotional quality and tone which was carefully matched to suit the season of the year in which a play was produced. A theater staged five or six productions annually: the November *kaomise*, "face-showing," production which opened the new theatrical season; January, the New Year's production; March, the spring production; May; the late summer production in July or August; and sometimes a special fall production in September. The first production of the new season was in the eleventh lunar month. An imperial court world was appropriate, for it gave members of the newly formed troupe an opportunity to introduce themselves (kaomise) to their audience in impressive scenes. In Edo, the New Year was a gala season that called invariably for a play set in the Soga World, while in Kyoto and Osaka a prostitute-buying world was traditional. The spring production, during the Girls' Festival, required a play centering on love (*The Scarlet Princess of Edo* is a spring play). Revenge plays were suitable during the Boys' Festival in the fifth month, considered one of the less important productions of the year. The late summer production was second in importance only to New Year's, and was scheduled during the Bon Festival, honoring souls of the dead; worlds concerned with love suicides, murders, the return of a vengeful spirit, or child sacrifice were appropriate to this season (Bon was a favorite season for puppet play revivals). Before disbanding in early autumn, a troupe might stage a special "farewell" (*nagori*) performance in honor of an actor who would be gone next season.

In the earliest days of kabuki the actor created his own plays, first through improvising dialogue during performance (*kuchidate*), and then by writing out his dialogue in advance of performance. During the Genroku period the playwright emerged as a specialized artist in the theater troupe. His function was to provide scenes suitable to the talents of a known group of actors who were under contract for the year. The actors numbered from forty to sixty; each was a specialist in a certain type of role: leading man (*tachi-yaku*), leading female (*tateoyama*), mature or elderly woman (*kashagata*), villain (*katakiyaku*), comic (*dōkeyaku*), adolescent boy (*wakashūgata*), fighters and acrobats (*yoten*), and others. The writer's script was not an end in itself; it was considered just one part of the process of achieving a satisfactory performance. The following remarks by the playwright Kaneko Kichizaemon, who collaborated with Chikamatsu Momzaemon in the writing of *Second Sequel to Buddha in the Field* (1699), suggest how much a writer depended upon the actor to adapt a text in performance. "The various ways in which he (Tōjūrō) tried unobtrusively to waste time were very comic and done with many actions. On the opening day, the fifteenth day of the seventh month, the audience were bored with this by-play, and there were various shouts of 'Get on with it,' 'Pack it in,' and this act finished in confusion. However, when the performance came to an end I went to express my thanks to Tōjūrō and said, 'In that comic bit you do, Chikamatsu and I wrote the words between us, but the audience does not understand it. There's nothing else for it but for you to cut out half the lines.' On the sixteenth I went to see him play again. There were more people in the audience than I had expected, and they were greatly amused by the comic passage. There were many shouts of 'Tōjūrō, keep it going, don't stop yet!' That evening Tōjūrō came up to me and . . . I said, 'What a difference from yesterday! After all, you added more words and spun it out even more, and yet they wanted more. Audiences in the seventh month are different from what they are in the rest of the year, and it is very difficult to find out what they want.' "[28] Kabuki is often criticized for placing such great emphasis upon the actor, but in fact this is a characteristic common in Japanese performing arts. (Zeami admonished the nō actor always to suit his performance to the occasion and to the nature of the

28. Dunn, *Analects*, pp. 82–83.

audience, and he, to a greater degree than any other well-known actor in the long history of Japanese theater, both composed and performed in his own plays.)

As a rule several writers collaborated in composing an all-day play. The chief playwright of the troupe was responsible for the entire work; he would develop an outline of the action in conjunction with the theater manager and the leading actor and would write the most important acts (sewamono and dance) himself. The second and third ranking playwrights on the troupe staff would rough out dialogue for the rest of the play under his supervision. Because a single writer held ultimate responsibility over the whole play we find somewhat greater unity in even the longest kabuki texts than in comparative jōruri texts, where each act is the work of a different author. As a consequence, it is easier to pull a single act out of a jōruri play and perform it as an independent piece than in kabuki.

An all-day play consisted of a long (four- to six-act) jidai or history section and a shorter (one- to three-act) sewa or contemporary section. On the face of it this division appears to be concerned with content or subject matter. It is also closely related to the artistic principle of great antiquity in Japanese performing arts that mood, emotional quality, and tempo must be varied constantly in the course of performance in order to maintain audience interest. The concept finds formal expression in the *jo-ha-kyū* (introduction, development, climax) organization of *gagaku* music and nō drama. Consequently, the kabuki writer did not have to rely solely on plot or thematic connections to knit his play together. He also linked acts and scenes in terms of color, atmosphere, tempo, and even variation in style of acting. The audience perceived the succession of scenes and acts through the full day's performance as components of an overall artistic progression.

The playwright could establish a basic mood for a section of the play through his selection of type of history or domestic play. An imperial court play would be austere and impressive, normally containing an audience scene in the imperial palace (*goten*). A feudal war play engendered a melancholy atmosphere through scenes of warfare (*shuraba*), suicide by disembowelment (*seppuku*), child sacrifice (*migawari*), head verification (*kubijikken*), or lamentation (*kudoki*). A feudal house play, concerned with a struggle for clan succession or revenge, seemed closer to the audience's lives and would have a revelation scene (*jitsu wa*) and possibly the wounding of a hero (*teoigoto*). Variety was possible in the contemporary section as well. The prostitute-buying play was erotic and humorous, with a love scene (*nureba*) and lovers' quarrel (*kuzetsu*). The mood of a love suicide play was set by the romantically sad journey (*michiyuki*) and double death (*shinjū*) scenes. Murder (*koroshiba*) and extortion (*yusuriba*) scenes made the "true" domestic play a corrosive experience.

Other types of scenes might appear in a play, regardless of whether it was a history or domestic piece. Since the audience was at the theater all day and often straggled back to their seats many minutes after an intermission was over (an intermission could last an hour), acts began with unimportant "filler" scenes featuring characters with only small parts in the main story. A good deal of recapitulation was considered necessary in all-day plays because of the long intermissions and because a spectator might come in to watch only an act or two. Both introductory filler scenes and recapitulated exposition are noticeable in *The Scarlet Princess of Edo*, the longest play in this book. Each time Seigen reappears he recalls the reasons for his downfall and stresses anew how sad it is that he and Princess Sakura had passed in the night at Mimeguri Shrine. Repetition tends to make these scenes more lyrical in quality than they ordinarily would be. As the characters reminisce about their past, they become increasingly vulnerable and sympathetic. To heighten the poetic quality of such scenes, dialogue may be written in metric lines that call for elegant delivery. Humorous stories taken from professional storytellers (*rakugo*) were often inserted. Told with lively gestures and mime, these stories, called *shikatabanashi* in kabuki, were especially popular in the Kasei period. Major entrances (*deha* or *de*) and exits (*hikkomi*) were developed into important scenes for stars of a troupe; Sukeroku's entrance and Saint Narukami's exit are famous examples. Other familiar scenes include those in which the hero is forced to endure a beating (*chōchaku*) or accept harsh criticism (*iken*).

In Kyoto and Osaka the history and the contemporary sections of a program might be written as independent main plays. The contemporary section, or sewamono, was then called kiri kyōgen, "final play." Apparently the first time a play was so styled was in 1684, when Chikamatsu wrote *Seventh Anniversary of Yūgiri's Death* as a two-scene kiri kyōgen to follow the three-act *Komachi and the Hundred Nights*, an imperial court play set in the Disputed Throne World.[29] Plot and characters of the two plays were not related to each other. *Seventh Anniversary of Yūgiri's Death* is purely sewamono, a play having no connection with a historical

29. See Kawatake, *Gikyokushi*, pp. 354–355, and Takano, *Kessakushū*, II, 1–3.

world. Tōjūrō's six earlier Yūgiri-Izaemon plays may have been of the same type but, lacking scripts for them, we cannot be sure.

In Edo it was usual to write one all-day play which contained related history and domestic sections for the important productions of the year: the season opening, New Year's, and spring. In 1796 the playwright Namiki Gohei I introduced Edo to the Kyoto-Osaka system of writing separate history and contemporary main plays. It was not generally adopted there, however, and until the Meiji era Edo playwrights continued to link the two sections under a single title. For example, Namboku's *The Scarlet Princess of Edo*, an all-day play containing history and contemporary sections, was written in Edo two decades after Gohei's introduction of the Kyoto-Osaka system.

Traditionally, the main play, although important, was thought of in relation to the entire program. All the acts written especially for a program were numbered consecutively. *Sanbasō* and the house play (waki kyōgen) were fixed pieces, not newly composed and therefore not numbered, but the new jobiraki and futateme which followed were identified as the first and second pieces ("futateme" means literally "second piece"). Since the main play came next, the "third piece" (*mitateme*) on the program was the first act of the main play, the "fourth piece" (*yontateme*) of the main play was the second act, the "fifth piece" (*gotateme*) was the third act, and the "sixth piece" (*rokutateme*) was the fourth and usually final act. The acts of *Saint Narukami and the God Fudō* are numbered this way. In the early nineteenth century the system began to change. The preliminary pieces became less important and numbering began only with the acts of the main play: *jomaku* ("introductory act"), *nimakume* ("second act"), *sanmakume* ("third act"), *yonmakume* ("fourth act"), and so on. Acts of *The Scarlet Princess of Edo* are numbered this way. The first act of the main play was given special names: in Edo *jomaku*, in Kyoto and Osaka *kuchiake* ("opening"), and for jōruri puppet plays *daijo* ("great opening").

The writer who could work with freshness and originality within these several frames of reference was eagerly sought after. No playwright became famous by repeating clichés of past generations. It is true that the worlds did have fixed casts of characters, but within worlds a writer had wide latitude to invent whatever plot (*shukō*) he wished. Writers have written plots portraying Sukeroku, for example, as Tahatanosuke from the Temple of the Highway, as a commoner, as an outcast, as Soga Gorō, and as a lover who commits suicide. The historical facts of the Heike-Genji conflict tell us that Atsumori was slain on Suma Beach; this did not prevent the authors

of *Chronicle of the Battle of Ichinotani* from allowing him to live.
In fact, sacrificing one's child for one's lord is dramatic fiction; there
is no historical instance of it in Japan. Nor was it a restriction on a
writer's imagination for worlds to be clearly demarked and understood. The number of possibilities, after all, was enormous: two-
hundred and seventy-five worlds and sub-worlds have been described
by the kabuki scholar Izuka Tomoichirō.[30] If a writer wished, he
could compose plays all his life without repeating worlds. (The fact
that certain worlds were repeatedly dramatized suggests that they
were rich in dramatic possibilities, not that a writer was restricted
to them.)

Similarly, the elaborate system of classifying role types was scarcely a factor limiting creativity (at least during the time under consideration in this book). The choice within categories was a large one,
Forty-two distinct role types are identified by one scholar.[31]
Among villain roles Ikyū is a villain striving for power (*jitsuaku*),
Prince Hayakumo a court villain (*kugeaku*), and Gengo a comic
villain (*handō*). The courtesan is one of the half-dozen types of
leading woman's role, and the nature of the courtesan is different
in Kyoto-Osaka and in Edo: Yūgiri is gentle, loving, and comic in
the style of Kyoto and Osaka; Agemaki is strong-willed, fiercely
protective, independent, clever, and adept in public display. Sembei
is a comic role, as are Black Cloud and White Cloud, yet they bear
no particular resemblance. Among the seven or eight kinds of
tachiyaku, or leading male role are wagoto, aragoto, and jitsugoto
roles. It would be hard to imagine two more dissimilar characters
than Izaemon, a wagoto role, and Kumagai, a jitsugoto role. Kumadera Danjō, Saint Narukami, and Fudō all are classified as aragoto
leading roles. Yet how different they are! Danjō is clever, brash, and
devil-may-care; Narukami is naive and emotional (we cannot imagine
Lady Taema tricking Danjō as she does him); Fudō is an implacable,
powerful god. These few examples could be multiplied many times.
Furthermore, nothing prevented a playwright from creating a character quite unlike any before, though in fact it would have to be
classified within one of the standard categories of roles. Sukeroku,
Gonsuke, and Princess Sakura are such *sui generis* roles; they were
intended to be unique and their uniqueness undoubtedly accounts
for much of our interest in the plays in which they appear. Like
Shakespeare and Molière, who also wrote for specific actors, the
kabuki author tried to capitalize on each performer's special abili-

30. Izuka, *Saiken.*
31. Gunji Masakatsu in *Kabuki* (Palo Alto, Calif.: Kōdansha International, 1969),
pp. 179–191.

ties. Knowing that Iwai Hanshirō V would play Princess Sakura, it is said that Namboku purposely created an extremely complex role to take advantage of Hanshirō's unusual versatility.[32]

Finally, the fact that ad-libbing was normal in kabuki contributed to creativity of play composition. Even today group scenes and many lines spoken as a character enters or exits are ad-libbed. Major speeches as well might be contributed by the actor. This is especially true of plays in aragoto style, where some speeches were rewritten (by the actor or by a writer for the actor) for each new production. As an extreme case, one edition of *Wait a Moment!* includes forty-two versions of the hero's name-saying speech delivered on different occasions.[33]

RELIGIOUS BACKGROUND

Because kabuki has been a secular and commercial theater for so long, its roots in religious beliefs and practices are easy to overlook. Kabuki's bimonthly productions were timed to open in celebration of native Shintō seasonal festivals: New Year's; the Doll Festival for girls (third day of the third lunar month); the Boys' Festival (fifth day of the fifth month); the Star Festival (seventh day of the seventh month); and the Bon Festival for the Dead, a Buddhist festival falling between the thirteenth and sixteenth days of the seventh month. In the *Sanbasō* ritual performance we can see a survival of Shintō shrine dances dating back a thousand years prior to kabuki. Many of the dances Okuni performed were secularized versions of Buddhist and Shintō dances of worship and of prayer (*nembutsu* and *ennen*) as well as folk dances of a less religious cast.

A number of dramatic situations cannot properly be understood except in terms of popular religious beliefs. It was assumed that gods and spirits could manifest themselves to the living on earth. This manifestation could take a number of forms. A god, such as Fudō, appears of his own volition. Through powers derived from esoteric Buddhism, Saint Narukami transforms himself into a demonic thunder god. The soul of a person who has died in torment remains tied to the earthly object of his desire in Buddhist belief, hence Seigen's soul appears before Sakura, whom he loves. Lady Fuji hopes that through prayers she can meet the spirit of her dead son one last time. The soul of a powerful human who has died in

---

32. See Takeshiba Sōtarō et al., ed., *Tsuruya Namboku Zenshū* (Complete Plays of Tsuruya Namboku; Tokyo: San'ichi Shobō, 1971), VI, 497.

33. Kawatake Shigetoshi, ed., *Kabuki Meisakushū* (Famous Kabuki Plays; Tokyo: Kōdansha, 1936), II, 913–933.

torment remains bound to earth, out of hatred for an enemy who survives him. He is known as *arahitogami* ("violent man-god"), and can assist those who worship him. After Soga Gorō died, he came to be worshiped as an arahitogami, a fact that helps explain the Soga brothers' phenomenal popularity as dramatic heroes. Connected with this belief was the custom in medieval times of propitiating powerful and violent spirits through dance (*goryōe*).[34] From this evolved the practice of performing a play about a deceased person as a means of honoring and placating its spirit. Tōjūrō performed Yūgiri-Izaemon plays in honor of Yūgiri's death, on the first, third, seventh, thirteenth, and seventeenth anniversaries of her death. Chikamatsu wrote his jōruri, *Yūgiri and the Straits of Naruto*, in honor of the thirty-third anniversary of her death. It has even been speculated that the name Gorō is a contraction of *goryō*, the generic term for powerful spirits of the departed. It is probable that the kudoki lamentation scene of jōruri plays derives from the Buddhist confession (*sange*), in which one's carnal sins are recalled and thereby expiated.

Characters in the plays express belief in concepts of popular Buddhism: salvation after death through the invocation of Amida Buddha (*Namu Amida Butsu*) in the Pure Land sect or of the Lotus Sutra (*Namu Myō Hō Renge Kyō*) in the Nichiren sect, reincarnation, and the chain of causation (*karma* or *inga*) whereby a person's present condition in life is seen to be the result of his actions in previous lives. Shiragiku, the boy page in love with Seigen (in *The Scarlet Princess of Edo*), willingly kills himself believing they will be reunited in their next lives. Kumagai renounces the world saying, "From this moment let me take the monk's name Renshō and turn my steps toward Amida Buddha's Western Paradise, where Kojirō, embarked before me upon the Nine Stages of Bliss, and I shall one day sit together on the same lotus. Namu Amida Butsu, Namu Amida Butsu." Seigen pleads with Princess Sakura to recognize "our ties of love, ordained by karma," adding that, if she cannot, at least they should die together so "bliss will be ours together, sharing the same lotus leaf" in the next life. We can note that Princess Sakura does not accept either argument and refuses to do what Seigen wishes.

It might be thought that characters believing in karma would lose the will to act and, imbued with fatalism, would allow the present to be passively shaped by the past. Obviously this is not the case.

34. See Gunji, *Hassō*, pp. 41–46, and Ogasawara Kyōko, *Kabuki no Tanjō* (Birth of Kabuki; Tokyo: Meiji Shoin, 1972), pp. 13–23.

Perhaps because characters cannot know what their karma will be they have to act as if there were no karma. Certainly Sukeroku does not resign himself to misfortune, saying it is "destiny" that his father was killed; he searches for his father's murderer until he is successful. Prince Hayakumo does not take being passed over for accession to the throne as a sign of past misdeeds. Although he eventually fails, throughout the play he attempts to wrest the throne from the emperor. Gonsuke and Zangetsu in *The Scarlet Princess of Edo*, scramble tenaciously to change their lot, even in the face of continued adversity. Perhaps the most that can be said is that belief in karma is a consolation in final extremity, when every possibility of success is gone.

One further interesting dramatic concept derives from Buddhism. Often characters will meet unexpectedly, saying, "This is a fortunate meeting." The Western reader will be tempted to call this mere coincidence and conclude that the playwright lacks skill. These meetings occur in kabuki because it is believed that people are drawn together by their past associations in this or previous lives. Thus, it is not strange that twice Gonsuke unexpectedly meets Princess Sakura in *The Scarlet Princess of Edo*. They are lovers, drawn to each other. They are fated to meet.

THEMES

Obligation to fulfill one's duty (giri), the struggle for power, love, and the search for money are recurring themes in the plays. Minor characters leap to obey the call of giri, and just as quickly may lose their lives. Since we do not know them, we cannot grieve. They provide a moment of action and are gone. Heroes of the early history plays enthusiastically carry out the dictates of giri. Invariably they are successful: Danjō happily and easily ferrets out the enemies of the House of Ono; Sukeroku relishes the task of finding and avenging the murderer of his father. But Gunsuke the umbrella-maker in *The Scarlet Princess of Edo* dies protecting the honor of his clan, and his death is touching. It is heartbreaking to watch Kumagai, or Gunjibei and Hanbei (in *The Scarlet Princess of Edo*) kill a son, a daughter, or a younger brother, for although they do as duty demands the act conflicts with ninjō, or human feelings. As already noted, it is a special characteristic of puppet drama to place a hero in a giri-ninjō conflict and then resolve the conflict in favor of giri. This is not characteristic of kabuki drama, however. The famous giri-ninjō conflict in the kabuki play *The Subscription*

List[35] is resolved in favor of ninjō: Togashi, a samurai, deliberately disobeys his lord's orders to capture Yoshitsune and, out of human sympathy, allows him to escape. In a situation more typical of kabuki than of jōruri, Seigen follows human feelings when he accepts the blame for dispoiling Princess Sakura, although he is not at fault. His act contains a good bit of self-interest, but it also springs from ninjō, for it is natural, spontaneous, and in part generous, not the result of social rules or obligations.

In kabuki, duty conflicts with other motives more than with human feelings. Prince Hayakumo is obsessed by a will to power that overrides his obligations of loyalty to the emperor. It is said that audiences admired a strong figure with a will to power. Perhaps the common people, themselves subjected to oppressive demands of giri in daily life, found vicarious pleasure in seeing a powerful figure like Prince Hayakumo flaunt his contempt for duty. In any case, the conflict between a villain's egoistic will to power and a hero's dedication to fulfilling the demands of duty to one's lord provided kabuki writers with a strong dramatic situation. *Saint Narukami and the God Fudō* is the only play in which the morality of giri's demands is debated. Hayakumo and Narukami both present a well-reasoned defense for disloyalty to the emperor. (Despite the fact that it is monstrous to ask Kumagai to sacrifice his son out of loyalty, no one questions Yoshitsune's moral right to do so.) Izaemon has an obligation to his family and he disregards it. Yet obligations of giri are scarcely mentioned in *Love Letter from the Licensed Quarter*. The dramatic issue presented is "will he get the money he needs?"—not "should he get it?"

Sexual love motivates the actions of many characters. (Among the five plays in the book only in *Chronicle of the Battle of Ichinotani* is love not a motive of major importance.) Affairs and liaisons are passed off without moralizing. The fact that Lady Taema makes love to Narukami in order to marry Toyohide, with whom she is currently having an affair, arouses no comment. Danjō's peccadilloes are passed off as jokes. Surprisingly, only Namboku, supposedly a "decadent" playwright, suggests that dire consequences may result from illicit sexual adventures: *The Scarlet Princess of Edo* graphically attributes to lust the fall of five people—Shiragiku, Sakura, Seigen, Zangetsu, and Nagaura. Money is perhaps the overriding theme in domestic or contemporary plays. Izaemon's difficulties are resolved instantly when money is received from his family.

35. Translated in James R. Brandon, ed., *Traditional Asian Plays* (New York: Hill and Wang, 1972).

Gonsuke kills for money; he blackmails and swindles, adopts a child, and sells two women, including his wife, into prostitution for it. In contrast, money is not even mentioned in most history plays, for it was held in contempt by members of both the warrior class and the imperial aristocracy. That Akugorō, a high-ranking samurai, hires a common killer and promises to reward him with gold in *The Scarlet Princess of Edo* provides a telling insight into the confused morality of the time in which Namboku lived. And there is little honor left to the warrior class when Akugorō can be slain by this same wretched gangster. The daily concerns of the urban audience that attended kabuki centered on earning a living, seeking out pleasure and love, and being part of the exciting and ever-changing bustle of activity that was life in the great cities. At the same time, people were curious about the momentous events which occurred in worlds inhabited by their samurai rulers and a distant imperial aristocracy. It is this dual reality of the audience which the plays of kabuki reflect, a duality which in the plays consists on the one hand of a highly particular depiction of the actuality of daily life of the urban commoner and on the other of a fanciful, romantic approach to history and to the nobility.

LANGUAGE

Kabuki scripts are written in vigorous, conversational prose. A character's social status and relation to other characters is indicated by the "level of politeness" of the Japanese he speaks. Prince Hayakumo's language is elegant, Gonsuke's is vulgar. (The attempt has been made to mirror these levels in translation.) A great deal of attention is devoted to the effects of language in kabuki. One example of this is the scene in which Princess Sakura, returned from the prostitute's quarter, switches in mid-sentence from formal palace speech to the argot of a whore and back again. In an imperial court play complete, carefully balanced sentences create an impression of dignity. In the contemporary sections of a play like *The Scarlet Princess of Edo* broken phrases suggest incomplete thoughts, and a line will be left incomplete to engender suspense or create a feeling of informality. A stylistic device especially common in history plays is quoting from a classical poem. Members of the court were skilled in poetry composition so it was not strange for a character to recite a poem. Most are *waka* (*tanka*), in 31 syllables, divided into phrases of 5–7–5–7–7 syllables. Lady Taema draws out Narukami by pretending to have forgotten the last two phrases of a waka she quotes. As she hopes, he supplies the missing line. The poem Kohina writes on the umbrella is a waka.

The intricately composed major speech, consisting of numerous interconnected phrases that gradually build to a climax, is a special feature of kabuki drama. It is often called *tsurane*, a term that refers to the forceful style of elocution.[36] A speech for a hero, heroine, or villain can be extremely long. Such extended speeches do not exist in nō drama and seldom are found in jōruri (where even a major speech like Kumagai's monogatari will be broken up into short segments by narration). The final line of Sukeroku's name-saying speech in Japanese consists of ten interlocking phrases, of 125 syllables (in translation, nine phrases of 100 syllables). Agemaki, in the same play, reviles Ikyū in a famous speech, made up of twelve phrases of 143 syllables, all linked together in a single sentence. One of the longest speeches in kabuki is Narukami's condemnation of Taema (the longest sentence in it runs 249 syllables). Playwrights used numerous poetic devices to enhance the complexity and beauty of these set-piece speeches.

A major speech may be divided among several characters. When a group of people each take a portion of one speech in sequence, with all joining in on the final phrase, it is called *watarizerifu*, "passed-along dialogue." Essentially an arbitrary artistic device, for each character knowingly speaks part of a common thought, connected dialogue produces a pleasing formal effect when spoken. It has been part of the kabuki playwright's technique at least since the yarō period.[37] Similar to passed-along dialogue, and perhaps even more effective when heard in the theater, is "divided dialogue," *warizerifu* (also *kakeai*, "exchange"). A section of divided dialogue is written for two characters only. It might be described as a joint soliloquy in which two characters alternately speak their thoughts out loud. Neither is aware of the other's presence. Gradually, however, their thoughts converge until by the last line they are the same and they speak the final phrase in unison. Princess Sakura and Seigen speak divided dialogue when they pass in the night without meeting.

The poetic and rhythmic qualities of both passed-along and divided dialogue are enhanced when they are composed of lines of seven

36. Tsurane is most often applied to one person's long speech, but it can also refer to "divided" or "passed-along" dialogue of several persons (see *Daijiten*, IV, 44, and Yamamoto Jirō et al., *Kabuki Jiten* [Dictionary of Kabuki; Tokyo: Jitsugyō no Nihonsha, 1972], p. 250).

37. Watarizerifu is mentioned as being used in the play *The Rōnin and the Sake Cup*, probably staged around 1665 (Dunn, *Analects*, p. 38).

and five syllables. Songs and jōruri narrative passages normally are written in this "seven-five" poetic form, also. It is considered banal, however, to force lines to fit the meter exactly, so a line may consist of thirteen syllables (eight and five or seven and six), or fourteen (eight and six or seven and seven), or occasionally more. In the translations in this book shichigochō lines are given in English with the same syllable count as in the original (a semi-colon marks the end of a line). This is done so that in English-language performance rhythmic effects similar to those in Japanese can be achieved. In *The Scarlet Princess of Edo*, Act V, Scene 1, Seigen is given a long monologue mostly written in shichigochō which shows different line lengths. "Just a few moments ago / while I was sleeping; I saw in a dreaming state / you Princess Sakura; toward whom my deep bitterness welled / as if to cry out; when the crying of the infant / aroused consciousness; my eyes slowly opening / to look on this robe." (*Ima shibaraku mo / modoromishi; yume no kokoji ni / mamieshi hime; urami no take o to / omō uchi; kono ko no sewaru ni / kokorozuki; mezamete mireba / kono kosode.*) The five lines in the sentence contain: twelve syllables (seven-five), thirteen (seven-six), thirteen (eight-five), thirteen (eight-five), and twelve (seven-five). Some narrative passages in *Chronicle of the Battle of Ichinotani* are also in shichigochō. They are delivered in a chanting style that makes the seven-five syllable pattern almost indiscernible, and are translated in unmetered prose.

Another rhythmic pattern often used by kabuki writers is called *kuriage*, "raising up." When opponents challenge each other, they build a scene to a high pitch, often shouting alternately to each other, "Sa! Sa! Sa!" meaning, roughly, "Well? Well? Well?" The lines accelerate until the characters are speaking in unison. Or, at the end of a long speech a character will demand of his opponent, "Well? Well? Answer me! Answer me!" to raise the emotional level of the scene suddenly.

These writing techniques are either unknown or little used in other Japanese drama. Two other poetic devices—*engo*, "related words," and *kakekotoba*, "pivot words"—are common to traditional drama and other literature as well. It is not necessary to discuss them in detail, for they are described in works on Japanese litera-ture.[38] Briefly, related words are synonyms or words with sug-gestively similar meanings and a pivot word is a single word, a homonym, with one meaning when read with the phrase preceding it and another meaning when read with the phrase following it.

38. E.g., Keene, *Chikamatsu*, pp. 27–29.

When Lady Taema is describing her nighttime visit to her beloved, she purposely says "river," "splash," "damp," "moistness," and "dew," all engo or words related to wetness and hence connoting lovemaking. The word "bound" is a pivot word in the phrase "lustrous black hair was bound to be alluring," meaning either "tied" or "certain to be" depending on which phrase it is related to (*The Scarlet Princess of Edo*, Act V). A two-word phrase, *omoiiri Enoshima*, from the same play illustrates some of the allusive complexities that are possible. *Omoiiri* means "deep in thought" while *Enoshima* is the name of a famous ocean cliff near Kamakura. The literal meaning of the two words, then, is "deep in thought [at] Enoshima." But *iri* and *e* can also combine to make *irie*, becoming a kind of pivot word, which, since it means "cove" of a seacoast, is also a related word with Enoshima. (A new related word is created in English if the phrase is translated "sunk in thought at Enoshima.") The difficulty which some passages present suggests that audiences were not necessarily expected to grasp each allusion or play on words.

Verbal humor is a striking feature of kabuki scripts, taking the form of innumerable puns, rhyming games, and wordplay of other kinds. Since puns (*share*) are based on sound similarity, they seldom can be directly translated from Japanese into English. Similar puns in English, therefore, have been sought in order to preserve the playful spirit of kabuki in these translations. Nonsense rhymes (*goroawase*) such as Shinbei's exclamation "*Sukenari, kaminari!*" are in a play for the sheer fun of sound, much as we might say "Middletown, diddletown." Shinbei also uses front-and-end rhyme (*shiritori monku*, literally "end-taking phrase") in which the last word or syllable of a phrase is repeated as the first word or syllable of the next phrase ("anger the wielder of this stave, stave off my blows as you will, willingly will I slice you through"). A famous "running pun" (*nani-nani zukushi*) occurs in Sembei's challenge to Sukeroku. He repeats the word *sembei* six times with different meanings. In the same play Ikyū and Agemaki joust with puns in several scenes. In response to Agemaki's request that he count the stars in the sky, Ikyū retorts, "While I am counting your stars, will you be counting on your star-crossed lover?"

A few writing techniques of the puppet theater are found in kabuki adaptations of jōruri plays. A special section of narrative (*makura*, literally "pillow") describes the setting, time, and circumstances at the opening of each new act. The concluding speeches (*dangiri*) of a scene which draw the threads of the action together are composed of deliberately dense, forceful phrases. Pent-up emotions may burst forth in a single impassioned line (*tatekotoba*), as in the conclusion of *Chronicle of the Battle of Ichinotani*.

PERFORMANCE

The five plays translated here are intended to be performed within certain acting and stage conventions. They were written for a playhouse with a small stage (thirty feet or so in width) and with the audience close by. Even when relatively lavish scenery was used the actor was the undisputed center of attention. (Today's kabuki stages are so large the actor's presence is diminished considerably.) A main curtain was pushed to the side to open and to close an act. A scenery curtain, released from above and falling to the floor, could suddenly reveal a new scene (*Saint Narukami and the God Fudō*, Act II, Scene 2, for example). An important character could with stunning effect enter (de) or exit (hikkomi) directly through the audience on an extension of the stage running to the rear of the auditorium, called the *hanamichi*, "flower way." Sukeroku's entrance is the longest and most beautiful in kabuki; he dances on the hanamichi for fifteen minutes before continuing onto the main stage. Six times in *The Scarlet Princess of Edo* grand processions move down the main hanamichi stage right; three times processions appear simultaneously on the main hanamichi and a second, temporary hanamichi stage left. Entering or exiting, characters pause for effect at a point seven-tenths the distance from the back of the auditorium to the stage, the "seven-three" (*shichisan*) position. Here they can be seen by everyone in the house. Posed in the midst of the audience, their actions or words are particularly effective.[39]

The kabuki actor brings to a play three abilities, indicated by the old saying, "first, voice; second, movement; third, physical attractiveness."[40] It is not strange that the skill most prized in the actor is elocution. Many writing techniques make extraordinary demands upon the actor's voice. Unfortunately vocal techniques cannot be very satisfactorily described in words, but some important ones used by the actor are indicated in these translations. One is *ippon chōshi*, "continuous pattern." Primarily an aragoto technique, it is

39. Up until the Meiji period the "seven-three" position was seven-tenths the distance *from* the stage toward the rear of the house, placing the actor deep in the auditorium. After Western-style, projecting balconies came to be built, the actor was moved closer to the stage in order to remain visible to everyone in the theater.

40. The source of the saying is unclear but it is constantly quoted in slightly varying ways (see, e.g., *Daijiten*, III, 381, and Yamamoto, *Jiten*, p. 249).

used to build a major speech to a furious climax. Apparently it was part of the actor's technique from early in the Genroku period. Words are delivered at machine-gun speed, without a break and without major inflection. It is used by the actor playing Sukeroku, in the name-saying speech beginning "A headband of purple . . . ," and again "All Edo's eight-hundred-and-eight districts . . ." Ippon chōshi requires breath control beyond the ability of all but the finest actors. Another technique, borrowed from the puppet theater, is called *nori*, or "riding" the rhythm of the shamisen. It is used for brief passages—seldom more than a single line—in *Chronicle of the Battle of Ichinotani*. In sections where the original jōruri text is marked "riding dialogue" (*kotoba noru*), the actor imitates the jōruri chanter, speaking in regular, metronomelike rhythm, each syllable timed to a chord of shamisen music. Last is the vocal technique used by actors when delivering sections of shichigochō dialogue. The voice follows a cadenced pattern, gently rising and falling within each seven or five syllable phrase. The superior actor avoids making either rhythm or melody too obvious. He suffuses his lines with emotional warmth, purposely introducing small variations of rhythm and inflection. When a long section of seven-five dialogue is properly delivered, it is only after a time that the spectator gradually begins to notice the lines' subtly lilting cadences (see, for example, the entrance of Sakura and Seigen in *The Scarlet Princess of Edo*, Act IV, Scene 1). This style of delivery in a long seven-five speech by a major character is sometimes called *yakuharai*.

Perhaps because of difficulties posed by language, Western observers have been more conscious of movement techniques than of vocal techniques, and as a consequence much has been written about them. Three basic movement techniques are identified in the translations. The *mie* highlights a crucial moment in a scene. It is a pose that functions as a kind of visual exclamation point. The actor moves into a powerful stance, rotates his head with a snap at the end of the movement, and freezes, glaring strongly (often with one eye crossed over the other, *nirami*) to magnify the impression of strength which lies at the heart of the mie's meaning. A mie may punctuate the end of a line of dialogue. Sukeroku executes a powerful mie as he concludes his name-saying speech, saying, "Scum! Bow before this face! Worship . . . it!" Or it may punctuate the end of a movement phrase. No dialogue is spoken while Narukami fights the monks; mie punctuate the end of each movement sequence. All fighting scenes (tachimawari) follow this pattern. In reading the plays, one should imagine a scene rising to a climax in a mie, pausing as the mie is held, dropping in tension as the action once more resumes, then building again to another high point and another mie.

A second major movement technique, called *tate*, identifies the some two hundred specific movements used in fighting with sword, spear, or lance and in hand-to-hand combat. It is beyond the scope of this book to identify each movement by name but fighting scenes choreographed using sequences of these movements are identified as tate scenes. Other fighting scenes which do not use the conventionalized tate movements—such as Seigen's attempt to murder Princess Sakura—are identified in marginal notes by the general term tachimawari. Great attention is paid to visual effect in tachimawari scenes through formalized movements and mie poses.

Third is the entrance and exit technique known as roppō, meaning "six directions" and indicating a highly stylized, masculine, dance-like movement down the hanamichi. According to one, possibly apochryphal, account, the actor Nagoya Sanza did the first roppō dance during Okuni's time.[41] Certainly swaggering entrances and exits were important to male acting many decades before the Genroku period in Kyoto-Osaka and in Edo. Roppō were used for major danced entrances during Genroku, as can be seen in Dan-jūrō's 1698 production of *Narukami*, already described. In time the term came to apply almost exclusively to exits by an aragoto hero. The raging hatred Narukami feels for Lady Taema finds expression in a fierce and powerful "flying roppō" (*tobi roppō*) as he pursues her down the hanamichi at the end of the scene.

The personal attractiveness of the actor is a factor in any theater form, but the audience-actor relationship in kabuki has a special dimension. It is part of the "game" of kabuki for the spectator to see the actor-as-actor as well as a character in a drama. This attitude finds expression in several unusual conventions. A stage assistant (*kōken*) moves unobtrusively about the stage (dressed either in black or in formal costume). He is a pupil of a major actor. It is he who hands Danjō his tweezers, takes away Sukeroku's clogs and fixes the flute in his sash, or gives Princess Sakura the dropped incense box. A stage assistant helps Ikyū to remove his kimono to reveal himself "in reality" as Heinai Zaemon. Two assistants help Narukami change his costume as he transforms himself, before the eyes of the audience, into a thunder god. When the actor playing Danjō finishes his first big scene, a stage assistant will bring out a cup of tea to slake the actor's thirst.

41. Dunn, *Analects*, p. 138.

Recognition of the actor-as-actor is made explicit when Narukami says he will change his name to "the lecher, Ichikawa Danjūrō!" The heroine of a ghost story is described by Gonsuke as "a dead ringer for the kabuki actor Hanshirō," the actor just ten feet away on stage playing the role of Princess Sakura. Sukeroku says there is a snake running loose in Yoshiwara that "makes a fierce face, has white hair, a beard, and looks exactly like the actor Yamanaka Heikurō," describing the actor playing the role of Ikyū. Of course it is a joke for an actor to refer to himself or another actor by name, but the Japanese spectator considered it a perfectly reasonable joke. After all, an actor is an actor, even when playing a role. (The Western "realistic" convention of pretending that actors do not exist on stage but only characters do is much more fanciful.)

Formal announcements, kōjō, to the audience are part of most plays. The troupe's leading actor (called zagashira or zatō, literally "troupe head") often addressed the audience to introduce a child actor and ask for the audience's support through the years or to comment on special circumstance of a production. Or the kōjō could be made by the theater's Stage Manager, a not very important position (called tōdori). The main play would be introduced before the opening scene (Sukeroku: Flower of Edo) or within an early scene (Saint Narukami and the God Fudō). A shorter play might not be introduced at all (Love Letter from the Licensed Quarter). Each day's program ended with the conventional words, "With this we conclude today's performance." We note that the final kōjō in The Scarlet Princess of Edo warns that the day's program is not yet over and that a dance scene follows the main play. The kōjō, wherever it occurs, breaks out of the bounds of the drama proper by calling attention to the play as an event, to the audience as spectators, and to the actors as artists performing for the audience's enjoyment.

Regardless of the role they were playing, actors wore costumes decorated with their acting family crest, thereby reinforcing their dual identity. When a spectator was pleased he would call out encouragement to the actor: "Best in Japan!" or "We've waited for this!" or "Like your father!" It would be pleasant to believe that all the ringing shouts coming from the balcony were spontaneous, but this was not the case. To encourage the audience, actors sent their pupils and employees into the gallery as a professional claque (koeban), with precise instructions of where and what to cry out. We know that actors controlled the claque, for Namboku writes in a stage direction just before Hanjūrō is beheaded in The Scarlet Princess of Edo: "There should be no calls from the claque."

Three sources of musical accompaniment are identified in the translations: Nagauta style music of the *geza* ("offstage") ensemble, dance music, and Takemoto music taken from the puppet theater. The standard kabuki music is that of the geza ensemble of musicians and singers who perform offstage right. These musicians watch the action of the play and provide appropriate background music. Geza music plays quietly during dialogue, sets the mood for a scene as the curtain opens, accompanies actions, or "fills" time while a character makes a long entrance or exit (for example, Agemaki's first entrance in *Sukeroku: Flower of Edo*). Instruments include stringed instruments, of which the three-stringed shamisen is most important, several types of flutes, and drums, gongs, and bells in a score of kinds and sizes. Music is selected to match the emotional quality of play and scene. The Imperial Palace is introduced in *Saint Narukami and the God Fudō* by the austere strains of Goten, "Palace," played by drums and flute. Sugagaki, a sensuous shamisen melody heard in daily life in the prostitutes' quarters, accompanies the entrance of courtesans in *Sukeroku: Flower of Edo*. Battle scenes of *Chronicle of the Battle of Ichinotani* are heralded by crashing cymbals and beating drums of Tōyose, signaling the army's "Approach." The song *Jizōkyō*, "Saint Jizō's Prayer," is sung by four or five singers because a powerful effect is required during the fight between Princess Sakura and Seigen. A hauntingly beautiful mood is created when *Doku Gin*, "Solo Air," is sung by a single voice from behind the geza blinds to underscore Princess Sakura's melancholy entrance on the hanamichi in the Mimeguri Shrine Scene. (This type of delicate solo, which accompanies the many touching scenes of female mime in kabuki, is called *meriyasu*.) Of special interest are the various atmospheric patterns beat out on kabuki's unique large drum (*ōdaiko*). Ama Oto, "Rain Pattern," is a light tapping pattern. A crescendo of rapid beats suddenly falling off is Nami Oto, "Wave Pattern." Kaminari Oto, "Thunder," booms out in rolling beats. There are a dozen such patterns. In all, over four-hundred geza melodies and rhythms are used in kabuki. Names of compositions called for in performance are given in the text, and where possible they have been translated. The system of musical cuing for the geza is given in Appendix C. The second type, dance music, is found in the translations in *Love Letter from the Licensed Quarter*, where a Tokiwazu ensemble sings and plays instrumental interludes to accompany dance and mime portions of the play. The Tokiwazu shamisen players and the singers sit on stage in view of the audience.

The third type of music, Takemoto, accompanies all of *Chronicle of the Battle of Ichinotani* and parts of *Love Letter from the Licensed Quarter*. In terms of musical style, instrumentation, and singing technique the Takemoto music is the same in both plays, but its function and effect upon the audience are different: narrative and supplementary in the history play, lyric and continuous in the dance play. This difference is explained by the dissimilar patterns in which the two original jōruri texts were adapted for kabuki. To recapitulate, a jōruri text consists of narrative, almost entirely sung to shamisen accompaniment, and dialogue, which is accompanied only in part by shamisen music. *Chronicle of the Battle of Ichinotani* was brought into kabuki as a dialogue drama. Narrative passages were mostly retained as is, but dialogue sections were given to actors to be spoken and whatever shamisen music was originally called for usually was eliminated. That is, sung dialogue accompanied by shamisen was replaced by spoken and unaccompanied speech. This occurs throughout the play but a particularly striking example is the dangiri, or final section, of Act III. In jōruri this section is intended to build an act musically to a vigorous climax. Almost all words, dialogue and narrative, are sung at a furious rate to cascades of shamisen notes tumbling over each other. But when the play is given as kabuki the dangiri is performed largely as spoken dialogue without music. In short, compared to the jōruri performance, the performance of *Chronicle of the Battle of Ichinotani* in kabuki contains less Takemoto singing and less Takemoto shamisen playing. *Love Letter from the Licensed Quarter*, on the other hand, has been made into a kabuki dance play and contains more music than does Chikamatsu's original jōruri. Geza songs in Nagauta style and Tokiwazu singing have been added. If we look at Yūgiri's final long monologue we find that some of it was to be spoken, some sung in jōruri. The monologue could be spoken by the kabuki actor, and if the play were being adapted as a straight domestic dialogue drama it would be spoken. In *Love Letter from the Licensed Quarter*, however, the entire monologue is sung by the Takemoto singer to melodic shamisen accompaniment, and Yūgiri merely dances and mimes the action, thereby encouraging the audience to respond less to the story and more to musical and dance effects in the scene.[42]

42. The standard structure of a kabuki dance play—musical introduction (*oki*), entrance (*de*) and travel scene (*michiyuki*), female lamentation (*kudoki*), male narrative (*katari*), lively dance often by a group (*odoriji*), and closing dance which may be a fighting scene (*chirashi* or *dangiri*)—is not found in either play. *Love Letter from the Licensed Quarter*

Two types of sound effects are indicated in the translations. Sharp and penetrating clacks of hard wooden clappers (*ki* or *hyōshigi*) provide stage cues. A single loud clack signals actors to begin, the stage to revolve, or a curtain to fall; two loud clacks signal music to begin; and continuous clacking (*kizami*) accompanies opening and closing of the act curtain. Two, somewhat smaller, wooden clappers (*tsuke*) are beat on a flat board placed in view of the audience on the stage by the left proscenium arch. Tsuke beats emphasize movements of the actors: for falling, a double beat (*batan*); to "fill" a mie with sound, a triple beat (*battari*); to accompany a running figure, continuous rapid beats (*bata-bata*); and a furious crescendo of rapid beats (*uchiage*) leads up to a tableau preceding a final curtain. Ki patterns are analyzed and described in more detail in Appendix A and tsuke patterns in Appendix B.

CONCLUSION

How are we to evaluate the plays of kabuki? At the turn of the century and for several decades thereafter they were consistently underrated by such scholars as Tsubouchi Shōyō, who, while cherishing much that he found, judged kabuki by the criteria of realistic Western dramaturgy and found the native form wanting. Today we are more fortunate. We know the futility of applying to the art of one culture artistic standards derived from another. We can see that the best kabuki dramas are superb examples of the playwright's art. They are straightforward, gripping, very largely eschewing the sentimentality found so often in popular arts. Historical conditions, which included government control and often suppression, precluded the kind of direct discussion of issues found in Western drama. But the experience of the urban commoner is presented on the stage with understanding and honesty. Without moralizing, the kabuki author allows actions to speak for themselves.

The plays of kabuki are painted in rich hues. They lack the mystic allusiveness of nō drama and share little of the intense and searing emotional power of jōruri. But compared to nō the dramatic range is broader and there is greater flexibility and variety of form, mood, and character development than in puppet drama. It is a remarkable artistic achievement to have created, within the space

---

is not a full dance play and only the kudoki section can be clearly identified. In a multiact puppet play is it never possible to follow the musical structure intended for a relatively short dance piece. In puppet drama the terms kudoki and monogatari indicate the type of scene, not the type of music.

of a little more than a century and a half, the formal beauty and marvelous storytelling qualities of *Saint Narukami and the God Fudō*, the gentle eroticism of *Love Letter from the Licensed Quarter*, the irresistible vitality and brilliant humor of *Sukeroku: Flower of Edo*, and the frighteningly real castoffs of society found in *The Scarlet Princess of Edo*. For too long the dexterity with which the kabuki writer has handled his dialogue has been overlooked; the dialogue of most Western plays is palid, indeed, beside the richly suggestive wordplay found in kabuki. Minor characters tend to stereotype, but major characters are drawn with refreshing humanness. We sense immediately the truth of Sukeroku's vanity, Gonsuke's total self-interest, or Izaemon's weakness of character. When the dramatic elements of the texts are combined with dance, music, mime, and song and are performed within kabuki's richly stylized acting techniques, the plays represent one of the world's great examples of "total theater."

At its best kabuki drama is dazzling in its virtuosity; at its worst it can be pompous, hollow, a mere show of effects. Increasingly from the middle of the nineteenth century, plays became routine works, drawing on the ideas and techniques of earlier times. But during the period of these five plays kabuki was still boldly original and the spirit of creativity ran strong. In their various ways the plays translated here celebrate an overriding sensuous joy of existence that rises above restraints of society and imperfections of the human spirit.

Sukeroku: Flower of Edo

SUKEROKU YUKARI NO EDO ZAKURA

by Tsuuchi Jihei II and Tsuuchi Hanemon

First performed in March–April 1713 at the Yamamura Theater in Edo as the second or domestic part (sewamono) of an all-day play (tōshi kyōgen) with the fanciful title *Protection of the Cherries of Flower Mansion*, this play was written for Ichikawa Danjūrō II, who played Sukeroku. The exact circumstances of its authorship are unclear, but it is believed that Tsuuchi Jihei II, son of Danjūrō I's favorite playwright, was consulted about the script and that most of the writing is the work of Tsuuchi Hanemon, the Yamamura Theater's chief playwright. Jihei is credited with establishing the four-act form in kabuki and the two-part, history-domestic form of play. We do not know what the entire play was about, but the world of Agemaki and Sukeroku had been used for plays for thirty years. Conflicting accounts say a courtesan, Agemaki, and her lover, Sukeroku, killed themselves in Osaka in either 1673 or 1709. Regardless of the historical facts, several Agemaki-Sukeroku love suicide plays were played on Kyoto and Osaka kabuki stages in 1675 and others were to follow. The 1713 production in Edo abandoned the suicide plot popular in Kyoto and Osaka for a new one telling how Sukeroku, with the help of his brother Shinbei, kills Ikyū, a samurai rival. Jihei rewrote the play for Danjūrō three years later, keeping the basic story but setting it within the world of the Soga brothers. Danjūrō added the long danced entrance with the umbrella and played Sukeroku closer to soft wagoto style than in 1713. At the age of sixty-two, Danjūrō revived the play once more (1749). He further refined the acting (and presumably the dialogue as well), and changed the original Itchū Bushi music to Katō Bushi style music for his first entrance. Cherry trees, once associated with gardens of the aristocracy, were planted in Yoshiwara for the first time that spring, and Danjūrō lined the hanamichi with cherry trees in full bloom. Fujimoto Tobun, the chief playwright, placed the story within another all-day play (*Story of the Brothers Named Soga*). The Katō Bushi music heard in performances today was composed for the 1761 production in which Danjūrō III played Shinbei. Shortly after that *Sukeroku: Flower of Edo* began to be performed as an independent one-act play. For the 1832 production, Danjūrō VII called it one of the "Eighteen Favorite Plays" (*jūhachiban*) of the Ichikawa family, the first of this group of famous plays to be so designated. Onoe Kikugorō V, an extremely popular actor, replaced the Katō Bushi music with Tokiwazu music when he played Sukeroku in 1870, and his son, Kikugorō VI, performed the role to Kiyomoto music in 1915. Either Katō Bushi or Kiyomoto music can be heard in current productions.

Because the play has been performed by every generation since 1713, it maintains many elements of its original Genroku style. It seems likely that Sukeroku's long entrance dance was created to take advantage of the recently created hanamichi (probably for the play's second or third production). The play shows close connections with life in old Edo. The Katō Bushi musicians were well-to-do merchants who were avid patrons of kabuki and of Danjūrō. Amateurs, they vied for the chance to appear on the kabuki stage. (This was what prompted Kikugorō to switch to professional Kiyomoto musicians.) Houses of assignation in Yoshiwara sent Danjūrō gifts of sake and costumes, and decorated the theater with lanterns advertising their establishments. The Sugagaki melody heard throughout the play was familiar to the audience as the music which accompanied real courtesans when they promenaded through the streets of Yoshiwara. Sugagaki is used in a unique way. Instead of being played quietly in the background during speeches, a single chord is played in the pause between phrases. The effect is unusually formal and sophisticated. A cast of more than eighty actors is generally employed to create a sense of color and spectacle. The many long speeches call for accomplished elocution. Comic scenes can be improvised as much as today's actor dares; in the role of the Dandy especially, actors include contemporary references (a popular dance, exiting with a hula hoop, using the baseball term "double-header" to describe the experience of going between the legs of first Sukeroku and then Shinbei). The longest versions of the play today may last three hours, but it is usually reduced to two hours by cutting a superfluous opening scene of exposition between Agemaki, Shinbei, and Mankō (as in the translation). The love scene between Agemaki and Sukeroku, although no longer performed, is included in the translation.

The play has a simple sequential construction for the most part, and several situations are repeated. It is essential to the plot that Sukeroku and Ikyū be in disguise and that they reveal themselves later to be "in reality" (jitsu wa) other people. But when the disguise device is repeated by Mankō, Shinbei, and even the Samurai, it is obvious that it is being done for mere theatrical effect. Sukeroku and Shinbei have three encounters with passersby, but this could be reduced to two or to one or all could be eliminated without changing the plot (although the scenes are the funniest in the play). The play may end as it does in the translation—with Sukeroku emerging from a vat filled with water (the ending favored today by Nakamura Kanzaburō XVII)—or the vat scene may be cut and the play end immediately after Ikyū is killed (favored by the late Danjūrō XI).

The text for *Sukeroku: Flower of Edo* exists in many versions, but the variations among them are not significant. The oldest extant text is that attributed to Sakurada Jisuke used for the 1779 production. The translation is based primarily on the annotated text in Gunji Masakatsu, ed., *Kabuki Jūhachibanshū* (Collection of Eighteen Favorite Plays; Tokyo: Iwanami Shoten, 1965). Also consulted were texts in Toita Yasuji, ed., *Kabuki Meisakusen* (Selected Kabuki Classics; Tokyo: Sōgensha, 1956), vol. 15; Atsumi Seitarō, ed., *Nihon Gikyoku Zenshū* (Complete Japanese Drama; Tokyo: Shunyōdō, 1931), vol. 1; and Kawatake Shigetoshi, ed., *Kabuki Jūhachibanshū* (Collection of Eighteen Favorite Plays; Tokyo: Asahi Shimbunsha, 1952); and the text, as performed by the late Danjūrō XI in 1962, published as a brochure with Victor Record set SJ-3001–3. Stage directions are taken from performances of the play by Nakamura Kanzaburō XVII (Kabuki-za, Tokyo, May 1967) and by Ichikawa Ebizō X (Kabuki-za, Tokyo, November 1969).

Sukeroku: Flower of Edo

SCENE 1

[*Deep beats of the large drum and sharp notes of the flute playing* Tōri Kagura, *"Shrine Dance Procession," drift through the striped kabuki curtain. Two sharp ki clacks signal the curtain to open.*]

CHORUS [*offstage, sings* Dote no Chōchin, *"Lanterns on the Embankment," to shamisen accompaniment, as drum and flute continue* Tōri Kagura] :
Rows of paper lanterns glow,
>Yoshiwara's nighttime brillance, bright as the moonlight;
>The pleasure quarter beckons, angling, drawing men;
>Alluring, luring, luring, to Yoshiwara.

[*Accelerating clacks of the ki accompany the opening of the curtain. Music and ki fade to silence. The scene is the front of the Three Harbors, a fashionable house of prostitution in the licensed quarter of Yoshiwara, in Edo (Tokyo). Heavy grillwork covers most of the building exposed to the street, except stage left where a divided curtain covers the entrance. The building is painted bright red and is decorated with black and gold designs. Masses of lighted paper lanterns, alternately red and green, form a brilliant display on either side. A huge vat marked "For Fire," topped by a pyramid of wooden buckets, occupies a corner stage right. Sprigs of spring cherry blooms hang across the width of the stage. A number of simple benches, covered with crimson cloths, face the street. The* STAGE MANAGER *in dark kimono and formal outer garments, enters from the right and kneels center stage. He places his fan before him and bows ceremoniously.*]

kōjō   STAGE MANAGER: Hear ye to the east and to the west! May I respectfully introduce as our play "Sukeroku: Flower of Edo," first performed by Ichikawa Danjūrō II in 1713—the third year of Shōtoku—and now a classic of the Edo stage.[1] [*Bows deeply.*] May you all, east and west, find pleasure and enjoyment in this, our spring play! [*Glancing back.*] Katō Bushi musicians, will you please begin!

---

1. The stage announcement (kōjō) was changed for each production. This one dates from some time after the 1713 production, but which production is not clear.

[*He bows low, rises, and exits right. The blinds center roll up, and seen seated inside the house are a dozen Katō Bushi shamisen* PLAYERS *and a* CHORUS *of as many singers.*]

KATŌ BUSHI CHORUS [*singing to shamisen music*] :

In springtime hazes,
   Blooms pink as Mount Yoshino fill Yoshiwara.
Tender shoots and gentle buds flourish in our view;
   Of the Mountain Entrance House and the Three Harbors;
   Where the bursting cherries of Edo flower.

[*A distant temple bell tolls. As the* CHORUS *continues, a* WATCHMAN *enters from each direction, striking a metal staff on the ground to warn residents of the ever-present danger of fire at night. Each is nattily dressed in a dark blue happi coat and light blue, snug-fitting trousers, and carries a lighted lantern. They meet center, bow in greeting, and pass in opposite directions. The temple bell tolls in the distance.*]

KATŌ BUSHI CHORUS [*continuing*] :

Fragrance of the evening drifting on the winds.
   Is the tolling temple bell that of Ueno;
   Or Asakusa famous for the Flower of Edo?

[*The blinds drop. The bell tolls. Offstage, large drum and nō flute play stately* Tōri Kagura *and shamisen play* Sugagaki, *a special melody associated with the licensed district. Black-robed and hooded* STAGE ASSISTANTS *hold back the entrance curtain of the Three Harbors and five luxuriously dressed* COURTESANS *enter. The richly brocaded silk robe and hanging sash of each is of contrasting color and pattern. Their hair is piled high, in an elaborate style indicating they are courtesans of high rank. Each rests a hand on the shoulder of a young* ATTENDANT *to help maintain balance while sweeping forward regally on foot-high lacquered clogs. Two younger* PROSTITUTES *follow each courtesan. They stop center and pose. They speak with calculated elegance, in phrases of seven and five syllables, their voices first rising then trailing off insinuatingly. A quiet chord of* Sugagaki *punctuates the end of each phrase.*]

watarizerifu   FIRST COURTESAN: Ahh, ahh, everyone, gaze upon the view. Yoshiwara's cherry pink petals opening; is it not a wonderous thing, our springtime beauty?

shichigochō   SECOND COURTESAN: Another spring's fresh blossoms bursting wide with love; another season's dewy beautiful young buds . . .

THIRD COURTESAN: . . . the buds of Yoshiwara flower before man's eyes; softly bloom then fade away scattered in the wind.

FOURTH COURTESAN: Men's hearts steeped in spring's pleasures cherish your spring love . . .

FIFTH COURTESAN: . . . dwell well upon the beauties . . .

ALL [*in unison*] : . . . of Yoshiwara!

FIRST COURTESAN [*looking down the hanamichi*] : Ahh, ahh. The pride of Yoshiwara.

SECOND COURTESAN: I see a lantern . . .

THIRD COURTESAN . . . marked with the Three Harbors crest!

FOURTH COURTESAN: It is . . .

ALL [*greatly prolonging the word*] : . . . Agemaki!

CHORUS [*sings* Yami no Yo, *"The Dark of Night," from offstage to accompaniment of shamisen, as large drum and nō flute play* Tōri Kagura, *and stick drum and hand bell play slow* Watari Byōshi, *"Crossing Over"*] :
In a moonless night only Yoshiwara shines;
　　As bright as the moon . . . the moon, the moon.

[*During the song* AGEMAKI, *a courtesan of the highest rank, enters the hanamichi with her retinue, consisting of a* LANTERN BEARER, *a* MALE ATTENDANT *holding a large parasol over her head, another* ATTENDANT *upon whom she rests her hand as she walks, several younger* COURTESANS, *two* CHILD MAIDS *in bright red kimonos with trailing sleeves who carry trays with drinking and smoking implements, a* FEMALE ATTENDANT *in deep purple kimono, six adolescent* COURTESANS *in pastel kimonos of different colors, an elderly* CHAPERON *in black kimono, with two more* MALE ATTENDANTS *bringing up the rear.* AGEMAKI *walks with undulating, wide-sweeping "figure-eight" steps of a first-rank courtesan, a style both elegant and provocative. She has been drinking and her movements betray her condition. She stumbles slightly. At seven-three she faces the audience and poses elegantly. Offstage shamisen continue* Yami no Yo *quietly in the background.*]

watarizerifu　FIRST COURTESAN [*gently chiding*] : My, look at Agemaki, how can she manage . . .

shichigochō　SECOND COURTESAN: . . . listing like a sail boat in a gusty wind?

THIRD COURTESAN: For shame, a reeling courtesan, leading her parade.

FOURTH COURTESAN: Agemaki, where did you . . .

FIFTH COURTESAN: . . . when did you . . .

FIRST COURTESAN: . . . get so . . .

ALL: . . . intoxicated? [*Prolonged.*] Ehhhh?

AGEMAKI [*grandly*] : Indeed, such an elegant assemblage greets me on my return.

[*She catches her balance. Though inebriated, she still shows the wit and poise which make her the most sought-after courtesan in the quarter.*]
Where did I, when did I, become intoxicated did you say? From the youth at the Pines, from a foul-mouthed samurai, from every corner hands thrust upon me brimming cups of wine when I pass through the streets of Yoshiwara. [*Mimes receiving cup and drinking.*] My mere appearance puts to flight the greatest sots of Edo, with a "pardon me, I must go." [*Delicately covering her mouth.*] Ha, ha! For Agemaki, pride of the House of Three Harbors, drinks but does not . . . become intoxicated. [*She lurches.*]

MAID [*tiny, high voice*] : Mistress. Take care.

AGEMAKI [*kindly*] : I hear a small one's large opinion. Little one, do not fear. I am not incapacitated.

watarizerifu　FEMALE ATTENDANT [*respectfully bowing*] : You may say, that, Mistress, but the cherry's pink blossoms . . .

FIRST YOUNG COURTESAN: . . . are seen in your face . . .

SECOND YOUNG COURTESAN: . . . a blushing shadow of the . . .

THIRD YOUNG COURTESAN: . . . night-flowering cherry.

FOURTH YOUNG COURTESAN: We can clearly see you are . . .

ALL: . . . intoxicated.

CHAPERON [*sternly*] : Child, bring medicine for your mistress.

CHILD [*holding up tray*] : Mistress. May the Plum Blossom Sleeve brush your illness away.

AGEMAKI [*idly*] : Isn't there a poem . . . "Whose sleeve stirs the fragrance of plum blossoms?"[2]

CHILD: Medicine, Mistress, called . . .

AGEMAKI: Plum Blossom Sleeve. How amusing. Thank you, Child.

[*Music tapers off. The female* ATTENDANT *mimes pouring water, then powder from a packet into the cup held by the* CHILD. *She politely offers the cup and holds tissue to cover* AGEMAKI's *mouth as she drinks.*]

CHAPERON: And now, Agemaki . . .

ALL [*bowing*] : . . . let us go.

AGEMAKI [*with great dignity and formality*] : Children . . . we go!

CHILDREN [*high, prolonged*] : Aiiii!

CHORUS [*repeats* Yami no Yo *with different lyrics, to* Tōri Kagura *and* Watari Byōshi *accompaniment*] :

Where are they floating, delicate pink mists of spring?
  On Mount Miyoshino . . . the flowers, the flowers.

[AGEMAKI *crosses onto the stage. At the bench center she turns upstage and poses as her robe is lowered by a* STAGE ASSISTANT *and her attendants. The women follow* AGEMAKI's *lead, facing front and sitting as she does. The five* COURTESANS *sit in a row at the back and the lesser* PROSTITUTES *on benches to the side. Music ends.* WOMAN *comes out of the Three Harbors to fast* Sugagaki *shamisen music.*]

WOMAN: Mistress Agemaki, Sukeroku's mother sends this letter.

[*Surprised,* AGEMAKI *takes the letter, gives the envelope to a* STAGE ASSISTANT, *scans a few lines, and poses. The bell tolls.*]

AGEMAKI: Because of Sukeroku, a quarreling son, a mother's life is black.

[*She reads more.*] Because of Sukeroku, my quarreling lover, my life, too, is black. How pitiful is woman's fate.

[*She poses. The bell tolls. The curtain at the end of the hanamichi is flicked open. The blinds upstage center are raised revealing a dozen Katō Bushi shamisen* PLAYERS *and* CHORUS *of singers. They sing as the wealthy samurai* IKYŪ *and his retinue enter.*]

KATŌ BUSHI CHORUS [*to shamisen accompaniment*] :

Multitudes throng up and down in Yoshiwara;
  Floating, drifting with no aim but joy and pleasure.
Men of wealth and power, too, parade in splendor;

---

2. "Who stirs the plum blossoms with their sleeve?" in the *Shinkokin* (1205), and similar poems, probably inspired the name of this hangover medicine which was a big seller in Yoshiwara in the early 1700s.

It is a transient world of passing pleasure.

[*First to enter is IKYŪ, old, bearded, dressed in a magnificent robe of gold, cream, and white embroidered silk. By his side and with her hand resting on his shoulder, walks the high-ranking courtesan, SHIRATAMA. Her costume and elaborate wig are like AGEMAKI's except in color. With a MALE ATTENDANT holding an umbrella high over her head, she moves past seven-three and stops. IKYŪ stops at seven-three and turns. Six RETAINERS, dressed in blue and white summer kimonos, carry his long sword, sword rack, armrest, tobacco box, and incense stand. No one on stage is aware of their presence. The blinds fall. Offstage shamisen play quiet Sugagaki between phrases of dialogue.*]

watarizerifu   FIRST RETAINER: Master Ikyū, noble lord . . .

shichigochō   SECOND RETAINER: . . . have you chosen her . . .

THIRD RETAINER: . . . who will be the lucky whore . . .

FOURTH RETAINER: . . . to share your bed . . .

ALL [*prolonged*] : . . . tonight!

IKYŪ [*heavy, insinuating voice*] : The whore Agemaki is a treasure among a thousand pillows but unfortunately will not be swayed by the strength of China nor lured by gold. Each time she rebuffs me. [*Vilely.*] Tonight will my ardor be dampened by the rain or quickened by Yoshiwara's dewy petals? [*Sees the group onstage.*] Ha, ha! See the one in back. Is she the new one you were speaking of?

RETAINER [*leans forward, poses*] : Boss! They say she's like a virgin!

IKYŪ: Splendid! I have an urge to spend some time with her.

SHIRATAMA [*haughtily, not looking at him*] : Ikyū, Agemaki will despise you, if you are fickle. Or is your interest in her gone?

IKYŪ [*unctuously*] : Shiratama, renowned in the five districts of Yoshiwara, plead my suit with Agemaki.

SHIRATAMA: Are you sincere?

IKYŪ: Constantly she meets another patron who is never seen. [*Turns front, furious.*] I will not have it!

SHIRATAMA: Dear Ikyū, nothing I can say will help, but if you wish I shall.

IKYŪ: Yes. Speak with her. [*She nods coolly.*]

RETAINERS [*in unison*] : Then Master . . . ?

IKYŪ [*poses haughtily*] : We go!

[*The procession moves majestically on stage, as shaimsen play Sugagaki and the large drum and flute play Tōri Kagura. IKYŪ ponderously settles himself on a bench stage left, sitting on a white silk cushion brought out of the Three Harbors by a CHILD MAID. His sword rack, pipe, armrest, and incense stand are placed around him and his RETAINERS retire to a side bench left. He casually smokes a beautiful filigreed silver pipe as he waits for AGEMAKI to acknowledge him. When she does not, he glances furtively in her direction. The COURTESANS have been waiting for this and they gently taunt him.*]

FIRST COURTESAN: Great Ikyū . . .

ALL: . . . is in our presence.

[*The end of each phrase is punctuated by a chord of Sugagaki music.*]

IKYŪ [*with heavy sarcasm*]: Kind whores, my name is known . . . by some, I see.

SECOND COURTESAN [*gently baiting him*]: Not know Lord Ikyū, greatest samurai of Edo?

THIRD COURTESAN: Even I, insignificant sparrow of a courtesan, know wealthy master Ikyū.

IKYŪ [*leering, but facing front*]: You please me, whores. Later we shall meet.

FOURTH COURTESAN: Oh, Lord Ikyū . . .

FIFTH COURTESAN: . . . tonight is your favorite occupied?

IKYŪ: My favorite?

FIFTH COURTESAN: You know her name.

IKYŪ [*slaps pipe on bench*]: Agemaki, do you mean?

AGEMAKI [*coldly*]: Ehh?

ALL [*giggling*]: Ikyū is in your presence!

AGEMAKI [*looks obliquely at him*]: Indeed? An ostentatious customer. I have been waiting for you.

IKYŪ [*sneering*]: Ehh? Me! You wait, you mean, for Sukeroku! [*Poses.*]

SHIRATAMA: Truly, Ikyū, you are churlish. Spiteful ways do not persuade.

IKYŪ [*catches himself*]: You are right—"we carve Buddha's statue and give it no soul."[3] [*Nods slightly in her direction.*] I beseech you.

SHIRATAMA: Soft words reach my heart. [*To* AGEMAKI.] Dear Agemaki, let me as a friend gently ask—meet with Lord Ikyū. His generosity is legend in the quarter. How can his words offend? If you do not wish to sleep with him, deign at least to meet and drink in private.

AGEMAKI [*with haughty superiority*]: Indeed. Not that I deign not to meet privately, Lord Ikyū, but . . .

IKYŪ [*face ugly with rage*]: . . . but, in truth, you wait for Sukeroku!

AGEMAKI [*feigning disinterest*]: Sukeroku, you say?

IKYŪ: Do you think I do not know the one you see is Sukeroku?

AGEMAKI: I meet whom I please.

IKYŪ: Take care, whore. I have the money to meet you when I please. [*Strongly, drawing out his words.*] I hate this Sukeroku! [*Speaking front, contemptuously.*] You know, whores, don't you, this Sukeroku is a petty thief?

AGEMAKI [*poses in surprise*]: Ehhh?

IKYŪ: Watch him when he fights, if you can call it a fight the way his hand slides round the other fellow's hip searching out his wallet. A pickpocket is what he is. Tell me, Agemaki, how long will a great courtesan relish the company of a vagabond?

AGEMAKI [*sadly, to herself*]: Truly, he does not bring happiness. And yet for all that, Sukeroku . . .

IKYŪ [*sneering*]: . . . charms you?

AGEMAKI [*poses, serenely*]: He is my charmed fate.

IKYŪ [*bursting out angrily*]: You are bewitched by the devil you mean! Will

3. We forget what is most important. A maxim in *Kefukigusa* (1645), a collection of poems, by Matsue Shigeyori.

you keep him as your lover, Agemaki, until you've been stripped naked?[4]
It will be piteous to see!

AGEMAKI: You may say I jilt wealthy patrons to meet my lover. You may say
I am a fool. But to say my Sukeroku is a thief, Ikyū, is insupportable!
[*She glances haughtily at him and poses.*]

IKYŪ: What? [*Mocking.*] Insupportable? The whore that's fool enough to
love a gutter rat will end up in the gutter with him. Love a thief and you
will learn to love his light-fingered ways. Before you know it you'll be
lifting patrons' wallets while they sleep. And when you are thrown into
the street, the two of you beggars, do you think your heart will care for
Sukeroku then? [*Poses, sneering.*] Insupportable, indeed. Unsupportable,
you mean!

AGEMAKI [*regally*]: You are a tiresome old man, Ikyū. Do you think I fear
your anger because I give my love secretly to Sukeroku? Do you want to
strike me here, before everyone? Do you want to cut me down with your
sword? You may, but I will not take you as my lover. I am Agemaki, of the
House of Three Harbors. I love a man—Sukeroku! [*Slyly.*] Since I am
paramour to the devil, possessed by his spirit, as you say, I shall revile you
with a devil's tongue.[5]
[*Music stops. She stamps and poses, holding her robe grandly open. She
slips off the robe to reveal a brilliant red inner kimono. She gestures with
her long silver pipe held vertically in her right hand to indicate* SUKEROKU;
her left index finger disparagingly indicates IKYŪ. *Sugagaki* resumes.]

akutai

Compare Sukeroku and Ikyū, side by side. Here is the one, a young stag,
here is the other, an old crab. White and black, like snow and ink. One the
the broad ocean, one a mire of mud; one deep, one shallow, as the courtesan's beloved and the prostitute's customer. Black is the courtesan's life
bereft of her beloved, but in her blackest life, in the blackest night, she
could not mistake Sukeroku for Ikyū! Ha, ha! Ha, ha, ha!
[*Enraged,* IKYŪ *partially draws. Music stops. She faces him disdainfully,
speaking rapidly, caustically.*]
Ah, will you strike me? Kill me if you wish, but I will not give up my
Sukeroku. [*He hesitates.*] Come, come, great Ikyū. Strike me! Kill me, if
you dare!

IKYŪ [*furiously slams the sword back in the scabbard*]: Go!

AGEMAKI: Where?

share

IKYŪ: To . . . to the devil!

AGEMAKI: You do not mind, great Lord Ikyū, that I go to meet my Sukeroku?

IKYŪ [*roaring*]: Get out!
[*He poses, one hand inside his kimono sleeve, the other resting on the hilt
of the sword in his sash. She looks at him contemptuously a moment, then*

---

4. From the saying that a woman deeply in love cares nothing for herself, even to
giving the clothes off her back for her lover.

5. Quoted as a folk saying by Motoori Norinaga (1730–1801) in *Tamakatsuma*, a
collection of essays, though it may have been current earlier than this. Literally,
"they say the wife of the devil should be a devil herself."

turns upstage so her ATTENDANTS *can lift and secure her voluminous robe preparatory to walking. Offstage shamisen play* Sugagaki *and the large drum and nō flute* Tori Kagura. AGEMAKI *turns and moves regally, provocatively onto the hanamichi followed by her retinue. When she reaches seven-three,* SHIRATAMA *rises and steps forward.*]

SHIRATAMA: Please stop, Agemaki.

[*The procession stops. Shamisen continue playing* Sugagaki *quietly in the background.*]

You are leaving rashly. Can you tell what your misfortune may be, or that of the one you care for, if you go this way? Like a younger sister, I speak out of turn, but say it still—please return, Agemaki. For all our sakes.

AGEMAKI [*looking out at audience*]: Joyfully I go to my dear love, yet I will not disregard the words of a friend.

SHIRATAMA: You will return?

AGEMAKI; Aiii.

[*The procession music resumes,* AGEMAKI *turns and moves back to the stage followed by her retinue. She stops before* IKYŪ. *The music tapers off.*]

Ikyū, we shall not meet again. Shiratama.

SHIRATAMA: Agemaki.

AGEMAKI: Children.

BOTH [*flaunting their disdain for* IKYŪ]: We . . . go!

CHILDREN: Aiii!

CHORUS [*sings* Yami no Yo *offstage, to shamisen accompaniment as large drum, and noh flute play* Tōri Kagura *and stick drum and hand bell play* Watari Byōshi]:

In a moonless night only Yoshiwara shines;

  As bright as the moon . . . the moon, the moon.

[AGEMAKI *sweeps past* IKYŪ, *pauses, casts him a withering look over her shoulder, and enters the Three Harbors, followed by her retinue.* SHIRATAMA *and her retinue follow. The offstage music stops and the clear notes of a bamboo flute are heard at the end of the hanamichi.*]

watarizerifu   FIRST COURTESAN: The sound of a flute . . .

SECOND COURTESAN: . . . could it be a wandering monk . . .

THIRD COURTESAN: . . . or a passerby?

FOURTH COURTESAN: Ah, indeed . . .

[*Rising, they flick their left arms inside voluminous kimono sleeves, and pose expectantly.*]

ALL [*looking down the hanamichi*]: . . . he comes!

[*Single ki clack. The distant temple bell tolls. The blinds covering the interior of the Three Harbors roll up again to show the Katō Bushi ensemble. They begin a lively instrumental prelude to* SUKEROKU's *entrance. The* COURTESANS *sit. A* RETAINER *hands* IKYŪ *his silver pipe, which he smokes complacently.*]

KATŌ BUSHI CHORUS:

Hear the shamisen sounding bright Sugagaki;

Arousing our memories in the gay quarter;

When a bird returns homeward he is called lover;

Is it not so in the midst of flowering grasses?

deha

[The curtain at the end of the hanamichi flies open and SUKEROKU *swiftly enters. He strides to the seven-three position, wearing high clogs, half-crouching under a partially closed paper umbrella. He stops, stands boldly erect, flourishes the umbrella overhead, and poses. He is dressed in a solid black kimono piped in red and pale blue. An elaborate brocade sash is figured with the Ichikawa acting crest; from it dangles a lacquered tobacco pouch and a bamboo flute is tucked in it at the back. A purple headband holds his stylish hair in place. Thin but bold lines of red and black highlight the pure white makeup of his face. The audience applauds his entrance.]*

KATŌ BUSHI CHORUS [*continuing*]:

Impregnated kimono crest of Five Seasons;

Symbol of year's waiting, steeped deeply in love;[6]

*[*SUKEROKU *flicks his right arm in his sleeve, and looks at the crest dyed in the fabric. He plants his right foot forward, holds the umbrella overhead, and looks toward the audience, shifts position and poses looking in the opposite direction. He holds the umbrella in his other hand, and strides away from the stage, stops, looks back, and poses elegantly.]*

Waiting for their time to come, sleeping moist with love;

Dampened by the quarter's rain, the spring's bitter cold.

[He closes the umbrella and poses with it held under his chin as if sleeping. He flicks the umbrella open and poses with it overhead, gazing up at the rainy sky, first in one direction then another.]

FIRST COURTESAN: Dear Sukeroku . . .

ALL: . . . your headband . . . ?

SUKEROKU: Ah! Is it strange?

KATŌ BUSHI CHORUS [*continuing*]:

A headband such as this one in times long ago;

Spoke through its purple color of abiding ties;[7]

[He stands with the umbrella held overhead, and slowly points with pride to his headband. He pivots and looks intently toward the Three Harbors, indicating his tie is with AGEMAKI.]

This colored band if you permit, shall be seen by all;

[He folds the umbrella closed, holds it up reverently to his forehead, and bows slightly to the COURTESANS. *Then he straightens and poses with the umbrella open overhead.]*

In changed times like the unchanged needles of the pine;

[He rests the umbrella shaft on his left shoulder, leans back, and gazes upward as if looking at a tall pine; he shifts the umbrella to the right shoulder and poses in the other direction.]

6. The lyrics contain a number of kakekotoba and engo.

7. Alluding to a poem in the *Kokinshū* (905), that describes purple as the color which indicates ties of love.

Binding up a spray of hair dangling at the back;
  Blown by the breezes of the wind, on the dike of cherries;
  The eye falls on the willow, snowfalls of blossoms;
[*Stamping twice as if halted on the dike, he looks in the direction of the Three Harbors, points toward it with the open umbrella, strikes his chest with his fist, and poses in a powerful mie to battari tsuke beats.*]
Piling on the umbrella, in Yoshiwara;
[*He bows his head beneath a kimono sleeve, as if heavy-laden with snow.*]
Lying in the spot between Mount Fuji and Mount Tsukuba;
  The grass lies silently though parted by his clogs.
[*Closing the umbrella, he leaps with legs spread widely apart. Looking up to the left at Mount Fuji, he straightens up slightly; shifting the umbrella to the other hand, he looks up to the right at Mount Tsukuba and stands erect. He pivots, scuffing nonchalantly with his clog. A* STAGE ASSISTANT *takes the umbrella.*]
A stylish tobacco pouch, double kimono;
[*Turning his back to the audience, he places his hands on the tobacco pouch at the back of his sash. He faces front and adjusts the lapels of his kimono with a fastidious gesture.*]
Do not hurry, do not rush;
  The world is transient, a wheel that turns;
  Time passes by day by day as expected.
[*Assuming a soft wagoto pose, he places the umbrella on its edge, half-covers his face, and gently rocks the umbrella back and forth. Reverting to his usual swaggering self, he flicks the umbrella over his shoulder and poses strongly.*]
It is to be expected that lovers quarrel;
  That sweet words of endearment will follow harsh words.
[*Miffed, he turns and struts away from the stage. He stops, poses, then strides back to the seven-three, gazing at the stage.*]
You are charming! You are marvelous!

[*He poses elegantly, with the umbrella slanted overhead.*]
SUKEROKU: It is for you! For you!
KATŌ BUSHI CHORUS [*continuing*]:
  Agemaki of Three Harbors, passionate sincerity;
  Thus Sukeroku passes by lined-up courtesans;
    With a dashing air!

tanzen roppō [SUKEROKU *swaggers onto the main stage. One-handed he snaps open the umbrella and, with a flourish, flicks it over his head. He thrusts his left fist through his kimono breast, and poses in a vigorous mie. The audience applauds and shouts. The blind falls, concealing the Katō Bushi ensemble.* SUKEROKU *relaxes the mie, passing the umbrella to a* STAGE ASSISTANT. *He preens. The* COURTESANS *flutter about him. Though he does not look at* IKYŪ *he is acutely aware of his presence.*]

watarizerifu FIRST COURTESAN: Sukeroku . . .
SECOND COURTESAN: . . . rapturously, we . . .

ALL: . . . welcome you!

THIRD COURTESAN: Stay with us!

> [*They tug him by the sleeves first one way, then the other, as they ad-lib, "Stay with me," "With me," "No, with me."*]

SUKEROKU [*gallantly*] : What a lineup of beautiful faces. [*Women titter.*] I suppose I can squeeze in somewhere?

ALL: Please do.

SUKEROKU [*expansively*] : Move over, girls, make way for a man.

> [*Shamisen offstage play rapid Sugagaki as* SUKEROKU *strides to the bench right and sits with a flourish.* COURTESANS *sweep past him, piling both upturned hands full of pipes, ad-libbing "Here Sukeroku," "Take mine, Sukeroku," "No, take mine." He chuckles.* Sugagaki *chords continue between dialogue phrases.*]

share

This beats my wildest pipe dream. Be careful, girls, my heart may go up in smoke! Ha, ha!

> [*He slaps the pipes down on the bench, then nonchalantly takes up one to smoke.*]

ALL [*laughing in unison*] : Ah-ha! Ah-ha!

> [IKYŪ *frowns, for it is a sign of affection to pass a man a lighted pipe.*]

IKYŪ [*ominously*] : Whores, I'll have one of your pipes.

watarizerifu

FIRST COURTESAN [*sweetly*] : We should like to, noble Ikyū . . .

SECOND COURTESAN: . . . except our pipes . . .

ALL: . . . are gone.

IKYŪ [*reacts*] : Your pipes are gone?

THIRD COURTESAN: Indeed, they all have been taken.

IKYŪ [*ominously*] : All? Taken, by . . . ?

SUKEROKU [*brusquely, not looking*] : . . . by me. Why deny it, I attract the whores. Their hearts beat faster when I show up at Yoshiwara's Great Gate. Up and down the quarter they come running. Pipes shower down on me like the falling rain. [*Strongly.*] I am flooded with them! [*Lightly again.*] Why, last night in front of the Pines, I hardly sat down before the pipes piled up till they looked, so help me God, like a damned tobacco display. If you can't get a trivial sign of affection from the whores, what's the pleasure playing in the pleasure quarters? Ha, ha, ha! No titled noble, no fat moneybags can begin to buy what the whores of Edo give me for free every day. So, did someone say he wants a pipe? I'm the one to give it to him.

> [*He slaps his pipe down and picks up another. With studied nonchalance he crosses to the bench center. Kicking off one clog, he plops down on the bench, slaps the pipe between his toes, and thrusts his leg insultingly in* IKYŪ's *direction.*]

You say you want a pipe? Here! Smoke it!

> [SUKEROKU *brings his left fist out of the breast of his kimono, leans back on his right hand, and poses belligerently. Music stops. Without a word* IKYŪ *reaches out for the pipe, cannot find it and slowly turns until he sees* SUKEROKU's *foot. He reacts, then quickly catches himself; he so*

[*despises* SUKEROKU *he pretends to be unperturbed by this gross insult. He looks front without moving.*]

akutai IKYŪ [*low, grating laugh*] : Ha, ha! Ha, ha! Ha, ha, ha! How sad, has this splendid fellow no arms? Do his hands stink of fish paste that he hides them in shame? Has he educated feet like a wine-presser?[8] I see low trash masquerade as chivalrous youth. The spirit of chivalry protects justice, is moral, is respectful, and . . . is not quarrelsome. A man of fashion cultivates refinement as a matter of pride. He who cannot discern proper decorum from ill-bred behavior is a wretch beneath contempt. The quarter is filled with buzzing idlers. [*Derisively.*] When a mosquito irritates with its buzz, buzz, buzz, clap your hand . . .

[*He stamps forward with his right foot and gestures squashing a mosquito between his palms.*]

. . . and it is gone! Ha, ha, ha!

[*Poses in a strong mie to loud battari tsuke beats.* SUKEROKU *drops his pose and passes the pipe to a* STAGE ASSISTANT. *He sits center unperturbed.*]

SUKEROKU [*easily*] : It is written in the warrior's code, tactics should be flexible. Suit the method to the object, the style to the man: reason with a wise man, but kick a mule in the ass. I deflate the pompous braggart with a touch of my clog. Only when the brave resist do I draw my sword. Not birth, not training mark the courageous from the weak. The test of the chivalrous simply is—once drawn, does your sword cut through? [*Roaring.*] What do you think I am? Senile old fool!

[*He plants his right foot forward and poses in a mie, to battari tsuke beats.* IKYŪ *motions to his* RETAINERS. *They serve him a cup of rice wine which he drinks as* SUKEROKU *continues.*]

By the way, whores, have you heard? A great snake is running loose in Yoshiwara.

ALL [*drawing back in fright*] : Ehh?

SUKEROKU: Oh, he's a harmless enough snake girls. He makes a fierce face, has white hair, a beard, and looks exactly like the actor Yamanaka Heikurō.[9] A very queer snake, he never tires of being reviled. He crawls back nightly though every slut in the quarter despises him. And the creature has lice in his beard, did you know that? So bad he fumigates it. Otherwise people couldn't stand to be near him. God, the reptile stinks!

[SUKEROKU *rises, scuffs his clog derisively in* IKYŪ's *direction, and crosses right. He sits facing upstage, closed out of the ensuing scene.* IKYŪ *trembles with fury and indignation, but does not move. Offstage shamisen play rapid* Sugagaki *and drum and flute play* Tōri Kagura. MOMBEI, *a blustering bully, stamps out from the Three Harbors, to alternating batan and battari tsuke beats. He wears clogs and carries a small towel in one hand. With the other, he holds closed his flapping cotton bath kimono, for in his rush he has forgotten a sash. He is raging, and nothing the* WOMAN *of the house can do will calm him.*]

8. Literally "skilled feet of a *fu* (wheat-flour cake) maker."
9. The name of the actor playing Ikyū; Yamanaka Heikurō played the part in 1713.

MOMBEI: Where are they? Where are they? [*She tugs at his sleeve.*] No! Bring me those sluts!

WOMAN: There, there, Mombei, simmer down. What will people say, hearing all this noise?

IKYŪ [*annoyed*] : Mombei. What's the grumbling about?

MOMBEI [*surprised*] : Oh, it's you, Boss. Listen to this story.
[*Sugagaki continues between phrases.* MOMBEI *appeals to* IKYŪ.]
Do you see that old witch there? She thinks I'm going to pay for the same women twice. [*Glares at her.*] I won't, I won't! Hag!

WOMAN [*joshing him*] : Oh, Mombei, you get too excited. You make the girls shy. Witch, hag, or virgin, you grab us all. Ho, ho!
[*Hiding her laughter behind a sleeve, she retreats right.*]

MOMBEI: Ehhh? You'd better not fool with a samurai, whore.
[*Drawing himself up, he tells his tale, alternately bombastic and whining.*]
I, exalted Kanpera Mombei, drank too much, and so I went into this whorehouse for a bath. Send in the girls to scrub my back, I said. Of course, as you wish, at once, you said. So I went on ahead, got into the bath alone, and alone I waited and waited and waited, without a damned whore in sight. I half melted in the heat! [*Wipes face with towel. Thundering.*]
Has someone bought up all the women in the quarter? You! Throw those round-heels in my bath! Everyone! I'll feast on slut soup!

watarizerifu

FIRST COURTESAN [*with sweet disdain*] : My, my, dear angry Mombei, do you think you are the only customer in Yoshiwara?

SECOND COURTESAN: Control your passion . . .

THIRD COURTESAN: . . . let patience be your guide . . .

FOURTH COURTESAN: Why, Mombei dear, your face is purple . . .

FIFTH COURTESAN: . . . seeing it, makes us . . .

ALL [*in unison*] : Ah-ha! Ah-ha!

FIRST COURTESAN: . . . laugh! [*They break into peels of laughter.*]

MOMBEI [*whining*] : Noisy bowlegs, pay me some respect.

SECOND COURTESAN [*mocking*] : Your face . . .

ALL: . . . looks so dreadful!

MOMBEI [*insultingly*] : Masters, haul out your sluts! Tie a rope around their bellies and lead them into the center of Yoshiwara where I can tick them off as I recite a million "Namu Amida Butsus"!

FIRST COURTESAN: Do you think you'll so easily get through a rosary of courtesans?

MOMBEI: You dare laugh at me? We'll see how much you laugh when I'm through with you![10]
[*Offstage shamisen play fast* Sugagaki *and large drum and flute play* Tōri Kagura. MOMBEI *flicks the towel over his shoulder and with his free hand grabs the* WOMAN *and tries to drag her into the Three Harbors. All the women try to prevent this and in the melee which follows a* NOODLE VENDOR *trots down the hanamichi, finds no way through, and, to* batan

10. Instead of saying *harai kiyomeru* (ritual purification), he says the nonsensical *warai kiyomeru*, "laughing purification," as a pun.

tsuke beats, accidently bumps MOMBEI. *They stagger apart.* MOMBEI
holds his head.]

Owww! Owww!

VENDOR [*bows briskly*] : Sorry about that.

[*Music slows and shamisen continue to play quietly in the background.
The* NOODLE VENDOR *wears a dark blue happi coat. A red waistcloth—a
sign of affectation for a commoner—falls to his knees. A small towel is
wrapped around his head. A black lacquered box of noodles sways from
one end of a pole which he carries over the shoulder.*]

MOMBEI [*belligerently*] : What do you mean, "sorry"? You smashed into me
with a box of noodles. [*With each epithet he moves a step closer.*] Idiot!
Fool! Noodle-brain! Use your eyes!

VENDOR [*smartly puts box down*] : I said it once, I say it again. [*Takes off
towel, and bows briskly.*] I am sorry about that. Girls, tell him it was an
accident.

FIRST COURTESAN: Dearest Mombei, forgive him . . .

ALL: . . . please.

MOMBEI: Never.

VENDOR: Ehh? Never? [*Challenging.*] And so?

MOMBEI: So?

VENDOR: Do as you damn please!

[*He flicks up his happi coat and with a flourish sits cross-legged on the
floor.*[11] *Offstage* Sugagaki *accelerate.* MOMBEI *raises his hand to strike,
but* SUKEROKU *moves between them and effortlessly grasps* MOMBEI's
hand, bending it back to loud batan tsuke beats. Sugagaki *quiets. The*
VENDOR *moves stage right.*]

MOMBEI: Oww! Oww!

SUKEROKU [*casually forcing him left*] : Forgive him. Eh?

MOMBEI [*outraged but helpless*] : Forgive him? Eh?

SUKEROKU: Yes, yes, Do it, eh?

MOMBEI [*imitating*] : Do it, eh? [SUKEROKU *releases his hand.*] "Do it"
sticks in my craw. [*Looks* SUKEROKU *over.*] You look like you've been
around, friend, how is it you don't know me?

SUKEROKU [*lightly*] : Not know you? In Yoshiwara, in all Edo, is there
someone who does not know you?

MOMBEI [*happily*] : Ho, ho! You know me?

SUKEROKU [*turning casually away*] : I never heard of you.

MOMBEI: He picks a man up then he lets him down.

SUKEROKU [*back to* MOMBEI] : Who would know trash like you?

nanori MOMBEI [*makes a face of impotent rage*] : Villain! Blackguard! Hmm. Since
you don't know who I am, it's clear this is your baptismal trip to Yoshiwara. So, little baby, listen to what I have to say and it will be your
inoculation against . . . the pox!

11. In some versions of the play the Noodle Vendor here delivers a clever *uirouri*
speech (salesman's pitch). The punning and rapid-fire banter of the Edo barker were
once very popular with kabuki audiences.

[*Gestures broadly toward* IKYŪ: *lifts both open palms and bows in a gesture of respect.*]

First, this is my revered Master, the illustrious warrior Ikyū. Taking the Kan of my name from Kan'u, the Chinese general of the Three Kingdoms whose flowing Cloud Beard reminds us of Lord Ikyū, and the Mon of my name signifying a treasured temple gate, I am the samurai Kanpera Mombei, wealthy powerful Kanpera Mombei! [*He rubs his fat belly.*] Take off that insulting purple headband when you stand before me. [*Stamps forward with his right foot and makes a threatening gesture with his raised fist.*] On your knees! Bow down three times!

SUKEROKU [*blithely, not looking*]: Thanks for the history recitation, friend. You must be famished after such a speech. And, as luck would have it, here's a noodle vendor. I think you should eat. [MOMBEI *looks amazed.*] No, no, don't say no; I'm buying. [*Crossing.*] Make it one.

VENDOR [*with a professional flourish, heaps noodles onto a small wooden box*]: One noodles with fish, coming up.

SUKEROKU [*sniffs them as he crosses to* MOMBEI]: Fish or no, I won't guarantee, but here, Mombei I serve you. [*Strikes a pose and thrusts the noodles under* MOMBEI's *nose.*] Have some noodles.

MOMBEI [*plaintively*]: Who? Me?

SUKEROKU [*lightly mocking*]: Yes. You.

MOMBEI: I don't like the way you're . . . it's not p-p-proper . . .

SUKEROKU: He says he wants pepper. [*He flicks pepper from the lid of the box into* MOMBEI's *face.*]

MOMBEI [*sneezing*]: I don't want noodles, I tell you!

SUKEROKU [*pushing the box under* MOMBEI's *nose again*]: Should I help you?

MOMBEI: I hate noodles! I hate them!

SUKEROKU: Then I'll serve them to you!

[*Offstage shamisen play fast, loud* Sugagaki *as the large drum and flute play* Tōri Kagura. SUKEROKU *brings the noodles up behind* MOMBEI's *back, where he cannot see them, and dumps the box upside-down on his head.* MOMBEI *falls, shocked, to the ground to series of double tsuke beats that taper off into silence. A* STAGE ASSISTANT *removes the box.* SUKEROKU *motions the* VENDOR *to leave.*]

VENDOR [*passes* MOMBEI, *stops, and turns*]: Spectacular!

[VENDOR *trots briskly off left.* SUKEROKU *sits on the center bench as if nothing had happened.* MOMBEI's *lackey* SEMBEI *enters from inside the Three Harbors. He is dressed as a comic villain: yellow hose, green socks, tucked-up trousers, stiff outer garment over the shoulders, and makeup of red and white markings edged with black. He walks with a little hopping gait and when he stands he bends his knees and cocks his head forward, as if in a perpetual subservient bow.* SEMBEI *carries* MOMBEI's *long sword wrapped in his regular kimono. Music stops.*]

SEMBEI: Master, Master!

MOMBEI [*groaning*]: I'm dying! I'm dying!

SEMBEI: What is it? What happened?

MOMBEI: How badly am I wounded, Sembei? Look.

SEMBEI [*horrified*] : Wounded?

> [*Peers from one side then the other. From behind* MOMBEI, *he picks apart the noodles and inspects his head.*]

There's no wound here, Master.

MOMBEI [*lip quivering*] : The blood is dripping, dripping, dripping. [*Puts his hand up and feels the noodles. He almost weeps.*] My brains are . . . [*Brings down a handful and sees them for the first time.*] I thought I was mortally wounded, but . . . noodles!

SEMBEI [*front, covering a smile*] : It is killing.

> [MOMBEI *throws the noodles over his shoulder; they are removed instantly by a waiting* STAGE ASSISTANT. *A dozen* RUFFIANS, *part of* MOMBEI's *gang, force their way on from the right. Their clothes are dirty and disheveled. They carry long poles and some have one shoulder bared, ready to fight.*]

MOMBEI [*seizing his sword and kimono*] : Annihilate him!

RUFFIANS [*brandishing their poles*] : We will!

> [*Offstage shamisen play rapid* Sugagaki *and large drum and flute* Tōri Kagura. *Bata-bata tsuke beats accelerate as* SEMBEI *gestures the swaggering* MOMBEI *into the Three Harbors, then follows him off. The* RUFFIANS *advance in formation on* SUKEROKU. *Music softens.*]

SUKEROKU: Striplings! What are you doing with those poles? Touch me and they'll build a mountain in Yoshiwara with your corpses! [*Strikes a fierce pose.*]

RUFFIANS [*cowed*] : Ehhh?

> [*The* RUFFIANS *fall back, then one by one slip away. Casually* SUKEROKU *sits.* SEMBEI *reenters, expecting to see* SUKEROKU *beaten. He is amazed to see the men retreating. He collects himself, crosses center, and begins a challenging speech, emphasizing each phrase with exaggerated posturing and rhetorical tricks.*]

SEMBEI: Ahem, ahem. [*Stepping forward on each word.*] You are a rascal. Your father was a rascal. Your father's father was a rascal and obviously made the original mistake. Ahem. Ahem. [*Bends his knees and leans forward.*] I do not recall any rascal who has opposed my patrician master Mombei. [*Cocks his head at* SUKEROKU.] And now, sir, you, sir, heap insults upon his head, sir, in the form of noodles. Cheap noodles. [*Points to his head, then to* SUKEROKU's.] You are a rascal! Apologize!
[*He strikes a pose, fists doubled and left leg thrust forward. When* SUKEROKU *ignores him, the pose wilts.*]

Sembei zukushi Apologize? Ahem, ahem. [*Runs hand up and down kimono collar, straightening it.*] My name, sir, is Morning Glory Sembei. Some days some pay Sembei—for their insolence. Today, sir, you pay Sembei, sir, for yours. Pay today to Morning Glory Sembei. Prepare to be pummeled by a man![12]

12. This famous passage contains many plays on words, the most elaborate of which is a sixfold pun on Sembei's name, a homonym for rice crackers.

Shiratama, surrounded by her retinue, poses in front of the House of Three
Harbors before she sits. (*Shiratama:* Nakamura Shikan; *Attendant:* Nakamura
Shōsaburō) Page 59

Sukeroku enters on the hanamichi: Flicking his arm in the sleeve of his kimono to show the peony crest dyed in the fabric, he plants one foot forward and leans back, glancing up under the opened umbrella. The Chorus sings: "Impregnated kimono crest of Five Seasons, symbol of year's waiting, steeped deeply in love." (*Sukeroku:* Nakamura Kanzaburō) Page 63

He holds the closed umbrella before him. "Sleeping moist with love, dampened by the quarter's rain, the spring's bitter cold." (*Sukeroku:* Ichikawa Danjūrō) Page 63

Stamping loudly with his wooden clogs, he flicks the umbrella under his arm, strikes his chest with his fist, and poses in a powerful mie, glaring at Ikyū. "The eye falls on the willow, snowfalls of blossoms piling on the umbrella in Yoshiwara." (*Sukeroku:* Ichikawa Danjūrō) Page 64

He strides onto the main stage and poses proudly, umbrella overhead and left fist thrust out of the breast of his kimono. The actor's Stage Assistant watches, ready to take the umbrella. Kiyomoto Chorus behind the blinds sing, "Thus Sukeroku passes by lined-up courtesans with a dashing air!" (*Sukeroku:* Nakamura Kanzaburō) Page 64

"If you can't get a trivial sign of affection from the whores, what's the pleasure playing in the pleasure quarters? Ha, ha, ha! No titled noble, no fat moneybags can begin to buy what the whores of Edo give me for free every day. So, did someone say he wants a pipe? I'm the one to give it to him." (*Sukeroku:* Ichikawa Danjūrō) Page 65

Challenged by Mombei, the Noodle Vendor sits defiantly. "Do as you damn please!" (*Noodle Vendor:* Ichimura Takenojō; *Mombei:* Jitsukawa Enjaku)

Sembei demands an apology from Sukeroku. "I do not recall any rascal who
has opposed my patrician master Mombei. And now, sir, you, sir, heap insults
upon his head, sir, in the form of noodles. Cheap noodles." (*Sembei:* Ichikawa
Nedanji; *Sukeroku:* Nakamura Kanzaburō) Page 70

Sembei and Mombei fall to the ground in fright as Sukeroku strikes his chest
with his fist and poses in a ferocious mie. "Scum! Bow before this face!
Worship it!" (*Sukeroku:* Ichikawa Danjūrō) Page 72

The effeminate Samurai is shocked that Shinbei orders him to crawl through his legs. A Stage Assistant watches behind the bench. "Pass between your legs too?" (*Shinbei:* Nakamura Ganjirō; *Samurai:* Sawamura Gennosuke) Page 77

Dandy places a white handkerchief on his head as he prepares to crawl between Sukeroku's legs. (*Sukeroku:* Nakamura Kanzaburō; *Dandy:* Sawamura Tosshō) Page 79

Discovered by Ikyū, Sukeroku is about to draw his sword. Agemaki restrains him. (*Agemaki:* Nakamura Utaemon; *Sukeroku:* Ichikawa Danjūrō; *Ikyū:* Bandō Mitsugorō) Page 86

For their final battle Sukeroku and Ikyū strip down to white kimonos. Ikyū is tricked by Sukeroku into believing his opponent is wounded and so drops his guard. At that moment Sukeroku plunges his sword into Ikyū's side. He twists the blade cruelly in the wound. Ikyū gasps, his fingers claw the air. (*Sukeroku:* Nakamura Kanzaburō; *Ikyū:* Ichikawa Danzō) Page 90

Sukeroku hides from Constables by leaping into a huge vat of water. Water cascades onto the stage. He knocks the bottom out of a bucket that he will place over his head that he cannot be seen. A crouching Stage Assistant watches. (*Sukeroku:* Nakamura Kanzaburō) Page 90

[*After striking a ridiculous pose, he strides up to* SUKEROKU *and seizes his collar on both sides. He tugs but* SUKEROKU *does not budge. With a flick of the hand,* SUKEROKU *sends him sprawling. He lands on his buttocks to loud battari tsuke beats.* SEMBEI *holds his head and howls.* MOMBEI *reenters, having changed from his bathing kimono to a brown padded kimono. He runs over to* SEMBEI.]

SEMBEI [*rhythmically*] : Ohh! Ohh!

MOMBEI: Sembei, Sembei?

SEMBEI: Mombei, Mombei.

MOMBEI: Well? Well?

SEMBEI: I tripped, I tripped. Over a root. [*Points down.*]

MOMBEI [*kneeling to look*] : Tripped? Over a root? Truly, Sembei?

SEMBEI: Truly, Mombei.

[*They look at each other, nod in agreement, rise, and strut to either side of* SUKEROKU.]

MOMBEI [*fiercely*] : Who do you think you are? [*Stamps his right foot out and poses threateningly.*] Arrogant wretch!

SEMBEI [*same business*] : Yes, yes, who do you think . . .

BOTH [*stamp*] : . . . you are!

[*They strike identical poses, ludicrously leaning forward, fists raised threateningly.* SUKEROKU *does not look in their direction. He sits in a casual pose: right fist resting lightly on the hilt of his sword, left arm out of sight inside his kimono sleeve. When he begins speaking his voice is deceptively bouyant and casual. But inwardly,* SUKEROKU *rages at the effrontery of such fools.*]

nanori

SUKEROKU: No one but an ass sets foot in Yoshiwara not knowing my name. So hear it well.

[MOMBEI *and* SEMBEI, *enraged, strain forward.* SUKEROKU *moves his sword hand slightly; they tremble with fear.* SUKEROKU *smiles.*] Knowing my name should cure your malarial shakes. [MOMBEI *and* SEMBEI *subside.*] Write it three times on the palm of your hand as you pass through the quarter's Great Gate and no whore can refuse you. Do I appear to you small? My exploits are legend, talked about by everyone from the charcoal-selling hags of Hachiōji to toothless rustics in the fields. In the gay quarters I am the topic of gossip over pickled plums and tea. I spend without limit and the hell with the price.

ippon chōshi

[*Rapid, strong, rhythmic speech gradually builds to a climax.*] A headband of purple, the pride of Edo, dyed in Edo, binds my hair, the strands of which as you look through them frame a face which, if it graced an ukiyoe print, would make that picture famous in Japan! Who does not know this dragon in the water, growing stronger as his enemies increase? From the carousers at the pleasure houses of Golden Dragon Mountain[13] to the grim image of the ferocious god Fudō in Meguro, all Edo's eight-hundred-and-eight districts do not hide the man who does not know this

13. An allusion to Asakusa Temple, near Yoshiwara.

wearer of the crest of peonies, this dweller among the cherry blossoms of Yoshiwara, this youthful Sukeroku, Agemaki's Sukeroku! Scum! Bow before this face!

[*Still sitting, he stamps loudly with the right foot, to batan tsuke beats, and brings his right hand, spread wide, up past his face and over his head in a ferocious gesture.* MOMBEI *and* SEMBEI *collapse in fright.*]

Worship . . . it!

[*During the phrase, he executes a powerful mie to battari tsuke beats: left hand under the right elbow, right fist pressed against the chest, weight forward on the right foot.*]

MOMBEI and SEMBEI [*awed, each holding up a hand to ward him off*]: Ehhh!

SUKEROKU [*rising*]: Blockhead! Beanpaste brain! Outhouse ass! Get out of here. Get . . . out!

MOMBEI: Take him, Sembei!

SEMBEI [*drawing his sword*]: En garde!

tate

[*They draw their swords. Offstage shamisen play fast Oimawasu, "Chase Around," fighting music and the large drum and flute* Tōri Kagura. *A* STAGE ASSISTANT *pulls empty benches upstage. Batan and battari tsuke beats punctuate* SEMBEI's *and* MOMBEI's *attack. They strike alternately right and left.* SUKEROKU *seizes their wrists at the same instant. He looks at* SEMBEI's *blade, then throws him to the ground, stepping on* SEMBEI's *sword. He pulls* MOMBEI *forward to inspect his blade, kicks* SEMBEI *into a heap, and sends* MOMBEI *sprawling prostrate across* SEMBEI. *He strikes* MOMBEI's *back three times with the flat of* MOMBEI's *sword. Again* RUFFIANS *appear and advance on* SUKEROKU. *Music stops.*]

SUKEROKU [*poses in a mie,* MOMBEI's *sword over his head, as he speaks*]: Move and I will cut them through!

RUFFIANS: Ehh! [*They slip away rather than face* SUKEROKU.]

FIRST COURTESAN: Sukeroku . . .

ALL: . . . wonderful! Wonderful!

SUKEROKU [*throws the sword down disdainfully*]: Yattoko, totcha!!

[*Stamps out with his right foot, sweeping the right hand, palm open, up and out, then does the same to the left.*]

Untoko na!![14]

[*Sits with a flourish on the bench, crossing his arms in front of his chest. He poses. Then dropping the pose, he turns rudely to* IKYŪ.]

Old man, if you want me do it yourself. Look at your fools. Well? Well?

[*Taunting.*] Draw! Draw!

[IKYŪ *does not respond.* SUKEROKU *leaps up and throws his bench—helped by the* STAGE ASSISTANT—*toward* IKYŪ. MOMBEI *and* SEMBEI *crawl away right.* SUKEROKU *plants himself on the bench beside* IKYŪ, *and puts his left foot on* IKYŪ's *sword hilt, an incredibly insulting action.*]

What about it white beard? Hey, samurai, can't you speak? Are you deaf?

---

14. A powerful exclamation, without literal meaning, uttered by an aragoto hero to express great strength and anger.

Dumb? [*Pushes lightly, insolently with his foot.*] Hey, draw, draw. He's as quiet as a rat chased by a cat. [*Rises, briskly.*] It looks like the old fool's dead. Someone should perform the last rites for him then. I'll donate a candle for the corpse's head.

[*Removes a clog and puts it on IKYŪ's head, where it is held by a STAGE ASSISTANT. He carefully arranges his kimono, kneels facing IKYŪ, claps his hands three times, and with closed eyes intones a prayer.*]

"Namu Amida Butsu, Namu Amida Butsu." Oh, Great Beggar King of Hades receive your own.

[*In silence IKYŪ slowly reaches up, grasps the clog, and lowers it into view. He is enraged: he throws the clog over his shoulder, stamps, seizes his long sword, and begins to draw to batan tsuke beats.*]

Now things are getting interesting. Kill me, kill me, kill me!

[*SUKEROKU leaps up, slides the kimono from his right shoulder to free his arm for action, and pivots in toward IKYŪ with small sliding steps.*]

Draw, Ikyū! Draw!

[*SUKEROKU leans toward IKYŪ, exposing his neck as a target. The RUFFIANS sidle on from both sides of the stage.*]

IKYŪ [*hesitates a moment, then slams the sword back in its scabbard*] : I will not!

MOMBEI [*on his haunches piteously*] : Don't be a coward, Boss, it is discouraging!

SEMBEI: We are losing our samurai pride.

MOMBEI: What miserable warriors . . .

BOTH: . . . we . . . are.

IKYŪ [*grandly*] : You do not slit a rooster's throat with a sword. He is not worth my time. [*Rises.*] Mombei.

MOMBEI: Boss?

IKYŪ: Sembei.

SEMBEI: Boss?

IKYŪ [*archly*] : Watch for . . . pickpockets.

[*SUKEROKU strides over to IKYŪ's bench, takes his arm rest, and places it on the floor. With a flick of the sword he slices it through. To battari tsuke beats, the two halves fall apart. He strides back to his bench center.*]

SUKEROKU [*returning the sword to its scabbard*] : And that could be you.

tate

[*IKYŪ gestures to his RUFFIANS to attack, turns on his heel, and exits into the Three Harbors. MOMBEI, SEMBEI, and all the women follow. Offstage shamisen play very fast Oimawasu and the large drum and flute play Tōri Kagura. SUKEROKU kicks off his clogs, ready to fight. The RUFFIANS face him in two rows of ten each, poles ready. To single, regularly spaced tsuke beats they attack, moving from stage right to left, striking and passing in front of SUKEROKU alternately to right and left, as SUKEROKU moves through them. They turn, form two lines again, all pose in a mie. Again they attack, two by two, moving from stage left to right: SUKEROKU casually moves between them in the opposite direction. Using only the flute as a weapon, SUKEROKU glowers, forcing them*] *back. To loud bata-bata tsuke beats, the* RUFFIANS *rush onto the hanamichi and* SHINBEI, SUKEROKU's *meek elder brother, slips unnoticed among them. He is dressed in a wine-seller's light blue leggings, kimono, vest, and head cloth. He carries a thin staff. A white kerchief hides his face. He drops to his knees, head low. The* RUFFIANS *flee pellmell down the hanamichi.* SUKEROKU, *not seeing his brother, poses in a mie, flute brandished in the air.*]

SUKEROKU [*laughing*] : They can't speak and they cannot fight.

[*He turns upstage and a* STAGE ASSISTANT *helps him put on his clogs and slip his arm back into his kimono sleeve. He turns front and the* STAGE ASSISTANT *returns the flute to its place in his sash. He adjusts his kimono.*]

And now for a cup of wine in Agemaki's bed. [*Turns and struts away.*]

SHINBEI [*softly*] : Please don't go, Brother.

SUKEROKU [*stopping*] : Brother? Here's a joker if I ever heard one!

[*Over his shoulder.*] Don't "brother" me. I am Agemaki's Sukeroku and knight protector of Edo's Great Temple of Buddha. On your way, fellow!

[*Scuffs his clog at him and begins to go.*]

SHINBEI [*softly, rapidly*] : Agemaki's Sukeroku and knight protector of Edo's Great Temple of Buddha, wait a moment, Brother.

SUKEROKU: Again? [*Turns to see who it is.* SHINBEI *flattens himself even more.*] Fool with me, fellow, and you'll end up in a ditch with a houseboat up your nose. Hear me?

[*Scuffs his clog at* SHINBEI, *thrusts his fist derisively out his kimono breast, and struts away.*]

SHINBEI [*softly, as before*] : Please wait, Brother.

SUKEROKU [*annoyed*] : Again "brother." I warned you.

[*Strides onto the hanamichi. Seizes his collar, and hauls him, like a young puppy, center stage.*]

Now, who calls me "brother"?

SHINBEI [*kneels, takes off kerchief*] : It is I, Brother.

SUKEROKU [*amazed*] : Elder Brother. Jūrō! [*He is immediately respectful.*]

SHINBEI [*sadly*] : Gorō! I do not think you see me as your elder brother.[15]

SUKEROKU: I did not know you, dressed like a wine peddler. What are you doing in Yoshiwara?

SHINBEI [*pouting*] : You should know why I'm here. I'm here because someone was pushed in a ditch. I'm here because someone had a houseboat shoved up his nose. I'll tell you why I'm here dressed like Shinbei, a wine peddler.

[SUKEROKU *looks contrite. He quietly sits on a small stool brought forward by a* STAGE ASSISTANT. *Offstage shamisen play melancholy* Tada Aikata, *"Plain Melody," in the background.* SHINBEI *puts away his kerchief and composes himself.*]

iken

15. Soga Jūrō Sukenari and Soga Gorō Tokimune are the full names of the brothers. Within the family the final names would be used, but Jūrō and Gorō are used here for simplicity.

Every day mother and I heard stories of your fighting in Yoshiwara. Who pushed the man in the gravel pit? Sukeroku. Who laid to rest the man before the Temple of Eternal Peace? Sukeroku. Who cut down the cut-up of Takecho?[16] Sukeroku. The day the crows don't caw is the day Sukeroku doesn't fight in Yoshiwara, they say. She could not believe this wastrel called Sukeroku was her son, Gorō. So she sent me to the quarter to see and I saw—Gorō dumping noodles, Gorō placing a clog on a warrior's head. [*His lip trembles; he is close to tears.*] For eighteen years we have waited to avenge father's murder at Hakone Mountain, but now that the time has come, you disgrace yourself with quarreling and debauchery. Honor your parents is the first precept of morality, honor your elder brother is the second. You esteem neither. The bond between us is broken. You are no longer my brother Gorō. [*Covers his face with his hands.*] I cannot imagine the divine retribution your unfaithfulness will bring.

SUKEROKU [*quietly, respectfully*] : My quarreling is reprehensible, Brother, I know. Please believe I am doing it with a purpose, from deep filial obligation.

SHINBEI [*sniffing*] : You brawl in the quarter . . .

SUKEROKU [*head bowed*] : . . . out of filial obligation. I quarrel to find father's stolen sword, Tomokirimaru. I take the name of Sukeroku that I can roam disguised, bickering, insulting men that throng the quarter, forcing them to draw so I can see if they are wearing Tomokirimaru. Is this it, or this? [*He turns away.*] But since I am reproached by my mother and my elder brother for fighting, hereby I renounce it. I will shun all quarrels and become a monk. [*Closes his eyes and clasps his hands in prayer.*] Deign forgive my sins, oh holy Buddhas and Bodhisattvas. "Namu Amida Butsu, Namu Amida Butsu."

SHINBEI [*slaps his knee delightedly*] : I knew it was something like this. I take back what I said, Gorō. [*Shyly.*] Forgive me, Brother.
[SUKEROKU *turns away, mumbling prayers.* SHINBEI *is contrite. He faces front and slaps his mouth.*]
You're a bad mouth. Why did you say those things? You were wicked, wicked, wicked. [*He pinches his lip as punishment.*] Ouch!
[SHINBEI *rises and crosses behind* SUKEROKU *to face his brother from the left.*]
I was wrong, Brother. Forgive me?
[SUKEROKU, *pretending coldness, pivots right to turn away.* SHINBEI *scurries around to stage right to face him in this new position.*]
Gorō, please listen to me. I apologize. [SUKEROKU *turns left, and again* SHINBEI *follows.*] Don't be angry with me, please, Gorō.
[SUKEROKU *turns away,* SHINBEI *glances at* SUKEROKU's *back, looks front and poses.*]
Hmph! How inelegant. "In Yoshiwara, you have to worship Buddha's backside."[17] [*Crosses right and kneels facing* SUKEROKU.] Please forgive me, Brother.

16. A pun on *takechō* (Bamboo Ward) and *takewari* (cut in two down the middle).
17. The famous Asakusa Kannon statue faces away from Yoshiwara.

SUKEROKU [slyly looking up] : You won't be offended if I quarrel?

SHINBEI: Quarrel all you want. Wear a kimono with "I want to fight" written on it. [Mimes writing.]

SUKEROKU: I will fight, if you allow it.

SHINBEI: Make a meal of your quarrels. [Mimes eating.]

SUKEROKU: Ho, ho! [Drops his contrite pose and stands.] I will eat our enemies up!

SHINBEI: Take seconds if you want! [Laughs delightedly. Music stops.]

SUKEROKU: Ah, you set my heart at ease, Jūrō.

SHINBEI: And you mine, Gorō. [Rises. Pause, then looks shyly at SUKE-ROKU.] Brother, do you suppose I could help you find Tomokirimaru?

SUKEROKU [amused] : You, Jūrō?

SHINBEI: Do you know where it is?

SUKEROKU: Ikyū would not draw, even when I taunted him.

SHINBEI: He has a wicked face. [Hopefully.] I could fight by your side. I could back you up.

SUKEROKU [gently] : Dressed like that?

SHINBEI [realizing his peddler's dress is not suitable for a warrior's vendetta] : Oh . . . well . . .

[To look more masculine he ties a kerchief around his head, as fighters do, and thrusts the staff into his sash like a sword.]

There we are. Will . . . will this do?

SUKEROKU: Oh, yes, that is quite . . . excellent, Jūrō.

SHINBEI [nervous and excited] : All right, now teach me what to do.

SUKEROKU [seeing his brother is serious, he suppresses a smile and stands in a formal pose] : Very well, let me instruct you in the traditional art of fighting. Step one: fundamentals of the feet. Place your right foot firmly forward. [He does so.] Second, strike a pose with your arm so. [He flicks his right arm into his sleeve and brings the fist out the kimono breast.] Third, the challenge. [Bellicose.] Hey! Samurai! Don't shove me! I'll throw you in a ditch! I'll ram a houseboat up your nose! Hear me? [Stamps hard with his right foot, poses, and roars a challenge.] Well?! [He drops the pose and turns respectfully to SHINBEI.] That's what you do, Brother.

SHINBEI: That looks hard. [Sighs.] Well, let me try. Foot out. [He puts his foot out gingerly.] Arm in sleeve. [He has trouble doing it. He poses. Though he tries to be fierce, his voice remains meek and soft.] Hey, samurai, don't shove me, I'll throw you in a ditch, I'll ram a houseboat up your nose. Hear me? [He tries to stamp, the clog slips, and he almost falls.] Well . . . ?

SUKEROKU [gently] : You're doing this to provoke him, Jūrō. Anger him. Do it more strongly. [Demonstrating.] Hey! Samurai! Don't shove me! I'll throw you in a ditch! I'll ram a houseboat up your nose! Hear me? [Stamps and poses fiercely.] Well?! [He bows respectfully.] That's the way to do it, Jūrō.

SHINBEI: I think I have it. Here. [He does speak louder, but his gentle demeanor remains unchanged. SUKEROKU encourages him with empathic gestures.] Hey, Samurai. Don't shove me. I'll throw you in a ditch. I'll ram a houseboat up your nose. Hear me? [*Stamps and his clog slips again. The last line trails off helplessly.*] Well . . . ? [*Smiling happily.*] Was that good?

SUKEROKU [*bows to hide his smile*] : It was very good, Brother. [*Sees someone coming off left.*] Ah, here's luck, Jūrō. "A wandering crow is blown our way by the wind."

[SUKEROKU *and* SHINBEI *turn upstage to prepare for an encounter.* SHINBEI *continues practicing.*]

CHORUS [*sings* Kyō no Shiki, *"Four Seasons of Kyoto," to offstage accompaniment of shamisen and hand bell*] :

Soft symbol of spring;
>Come, come see the pink blossoms on Eastern Mountain;
>Color and fragrance combine, night-blooming cherry.

Man of mode or bumpkin;
>Both are intoxicated by spring's soft beauty.

[*During the song a* SAMURAI *enters. He wears the elegant long-sleeved kimono of a youth, with cloak and divided trousers over it. A wicker hat covers his face. A closed fan dangles from his fingertips.* SUKEROKU *confronts him, yanks his sword from its scabbard, inspects it, and contemptuously throws it to the ground. The terrified* SAMURAI *retrieves it and tries to pass.* SUKEROKU *spreads his legs, blocking his way. Music stops.*]

SUKEROKU: Hey, samurai! Pass between my legs! [*He lifts his kimono slightly.*]

sutezerifu

SAMURAI [*timid, cultivated voice*] : What's that? Pass between your legs? Not since I came from my mother's womb have I, at a gentlemen's insistence, passed between someone's legs. But if I must . . .

[*Offstage shamisen, stick drum, flute, and hand bell play spirited, humorous* Gion Bayashi, *"Gion Melody." He carefully prepares himself. He removes his hat, and we see he is not young as expected, but a heavily rouged and powdered middle-aged roué. He gets to his knees and pushes through first the hat, then his sandals, and finally his swords. Opening his fan and fanning himself, he crawls through on hands and knees. He picks up his things and turns to go, but* SHINBEI *blocks his path standing on tiptoe, knees quaking. Music stops.*]

SHINBEI [*quavering voice*] : Hey, samurai. Pass between my legs.

SAMURAI: Pass between your legs too?

[*He is about to protest, but sees* SUKEROKU's *glare, and subsides.* Gion Bayashi *melody resumes. The* SAMURAI *looks suspiciously at* SHINBEI *and decides to back through clutching everything in his hands. He escapes onto the hanamichi. At seven-three he carefully arranges his clothes, fans himself, and poses.*]

"I hear lovers quarreling; how embarrassing to pass between your legs; how embarrassing to pass between your legs."

[*He looks archly at* SHINBEI *and exits fanning himself.*]

CHORUS [*sings* Kyō no Shiki *to offstage shamisen and hand bell accompaniment*] :

Soft symbol of spring,

Come, come see the pink blossoms on Eastern Mountain.

SUKEROKU [*laughing*] : There's a strange one, Jūrō.

CHORUS [*sings Ryūkyū Bushi, "Song of Okinawa," in country accent, to shamisen accompaniment and rollicking folk rhythm, Fushi Mawashi, "Playing Music," played on the large drum and hand bell*] :

Rikyū[18] and Kagoshima. Ah!

Where's the land connecting you?

[*A loutish, gawking* COUNTRY SAMURAI *enters with his* SERVANT. *They wear thick kimonos of country design. The* SAMURAI's *hair is done up in a high, awkward style. A ruddy complexion is visible beneath black stubble of an unshaven face. It is obvious he and his* SERVANT *have never been to the big city before, let alone a licensed quarter.*]

sutezerifu SERVANT: Master, look. I never seen so many cherry blossoms. [*Eagerly.*] Should we go inside Yoshiwara? [*The* SAMURAI *nods happily.*]

[SUKEROKU *suddenly blocks their way, yanks out their swords, inspects the blades, then throws them down. The two look at each other in blank amazement. They pick up the swords.*]

SUKEROKU: Hey, samurai! Through my legs! [*He stamps and hikes his kimono.*]

SERVANT: It may be the custom here, Master. [*In dumb rage the* COUNTRY SAMURAI *begins to draw.*] No, Master, no!

[*Offstage shamisen, flute, and stick drum resume* Gion Bayashi. *The* COUNTRY SAMURAI *allows himself to be led by his* SERVANT *up to* SUKEROKU, *and with his assistance passes between* SUKEROKU's *legs after mumbling a short prayer. The* SERVANT *slides along on his belly, but even so* SUKEROKU *kicks him as he goes through.*]

SHINBEI [*legs quaking*] : Through my legs, samurai.

[*Again the* COUNTRY SAMURAI *reaches for his sword. The* SERVANT *sees* SUKEROKU *glaring at them, he tugs his master's sleeve, and gestures for him to look at* SUKEROKU. *Shaking his head in bewilderment, the uncomprehending* COUNTRY SAMURAI *falls to his knees and goes through, accidentally tickling* SHINBEI *as he passes. The* SERVANT *follows. They rush onto the hanamichi and stop at seven-three. Music ends. The* SERVANT *thinks.*]

SERVANT: Master, we've been had.

[*He reaches for his sword, but this time the* SAMURAI *stops him. As the offstage* CHORUS *sings, they look at each other, sigh with resignation, turn and strut off down the hanamichi.*]

CHORUS [*repeating* Ryūkyū Bushi] :

Rikyū and Kagoshima. Ah!

Where's the land connecting you?

SUKEROKU [*chuckling*] : He's a brave samurai, Brother.

CHORUS [*sings Yo Zakura, "Night Cherry," to brisk shamisen accompaniment as stick drum plays* Sawagi] :

18. Dialect for Ryūkyū (Okinawa).

Night-blooming cherry,
> The light-hearted wanderer, while dancing, dancing;
> In the shade of the blossoms, see there is someone;
> There is someone there.

[*A rich young* DANDY *enters. He wears no swords, and is modishly dressed in pastel green kimono with matching cloak. His makeup is handsomely white. He carries a half-open fan. Shamisen continues in the background.*]

sutezerifuDANDY: How smashing to float about this wild place, taking it all in. I'll never tire seeing the tender beauties of the quarter go by. They're so with it. They swing.

CHORUS [*repeats* Yo Zakura *to same accompaniment, as the* DANDY *flicks open his fan and ambles on*] :
Night-blooming cherry,
> The light-hearted wanderer, while dancing, dancing . . .

SUKEROKU [*blocking his way*] : Pass through here!

DANDY: What is that? What did you say? I am to pass through there? You must be putting me on, vulgar man. Even here in this paradise of the senses, you ask too much. [*He sees* SUKEROKU's *relentless attitude and sighs.*] Well, if I must, at least I shall travel in style. [*Looks archly at the audience.*] Hereafter this voyage shall be known as "Twenty Thousand Leagues Under the Seat." Let us begin. [Gion Bayashi *resumes. He prepares himself as if for a night out. He puts his fan away, then takes off his sandals and carefully pushes them through. He unfolds a white handkerchief which he places on his head to protect his hair. He removes a sachet from his kimono breast and scents himself here and there. After carefully arranging his clothes, he fastidiously crawls through on hands and knees. Rising, he sighs.*]

I thought I'd seen everything, but this is the end.

SHINBEI [*full of courage*] : Pass through here.

DANDY [*shocked*] : Again? Not again, not again through there? You can't mean it, you terrifying people, you're too much. I mean really, see Japan first, but you're out of your minds! [*He turns and sees* SUKEROKU *looking steadily at him.*]

Ohh. This is out of sight.

[*He looks at* SHINBEI *and sighs wearily. Again he fastidiously prepares. He pushes sandals through, places the cloth on his head, and adjusts his clothes. Approaching* SHINBEI *on his knees, he sniffs and makes a wry face. He holds a sleeve to his nose to filter the air but that doesn't work. With elegant nonchalance he dangles the sachet before* SHINBEI *and fans the scent between* SHINBEI's *legs. Then, holding the sachet between his teeth, he crawls through, bumping* SHINBEI *in the process and sending him flying upstage. He crosses to seven-three on the hanamichi. Music stops.*]

Really, look at me. My clothes are filthy, my hair ruined. How can I ever face the girls this way? Well I must, even if they spurn me. [*Brightens.*]

Who knows, I might just start a new fashion!

[*He flicks his fan open as a signal to the musicians. They play a lively popular song, chosen from among current hits, and the* DANDY *abandons himself to a brief dance in contemporary style. Another flick of the fan and the musicians return to* Yo Zakura. *Instantly reverting to character, he dances gracefully down the hanamichi and off.*]

CHORUS [*repeating original lyrics*]:

Night-blooming cherry,

The light-hearted wanderer, while dancing, dancing . . .

SUKEROKU [*laughing*]: He's a funny one, Jūro.

AGEMAKI [*off*]: Take care, traveling in the night.

SUKEROKU [*bristling*]: Agemaki? Seeing out a customer? "I wait for you," she said. I knew that whore was unfaithful.

SHINBEI: You tell her, Brother!

CHORUS [*sings* Fumi no Tayori, "*A Letter's Message*," *to shamisen and hand bell accompaniment*]:

Let us meet this evening,

She entreats in her letter.

[AGEMAKI, *no longer wearing her outer robe, politely ushers out of the Three Harbors, her "customer" who is dressed in the severe black kimono and wears the two swords of a samurai. A deep wicker hat completely covers the customer's face. There is no way to know this is* MANKŌ, *mother of* SUKEROKU *and* SHINBEI. SUKEROKU *blocks their way with outstretched arms. Offstage shamisen continues* Fumi no Tayori *in the background.*]

SUKEROKU [*viciously*]: Stop where you are, samurai!

AGEMAKI [*protecting* MANKŌ]: Sukeroku, don't be rash!

SUKEROKU: Don't meddle, slut!

AGEMAKI: You abuse me, Sukeroku.

SUKEROKU: What if I do?

SHINBEI: Yes, yes, what if he does?

[*Hurt,* AGEMAKI, *moves away.* SUKEROKU *stands belligerently blocking* MANKŌ's *way. She hesitates a moment, then deliberately stamps on his foot.* SUKEROKU *grabs her swords, but she holds them fast.*]

SUKEROKU [*roaring*]: Samurai! The street is wide but you step on my toes! [*Stamps foot out.*] Lick them clean!

AGEMAKI: You will regret this, Sukeroku.

SUKEROKU: Out of my business, whore.

SHINBEI: Yes.

AGEMAKI: I can see from your face you hate me.

SUKEROKU [*bitterly*]: With good reason. [*Turns to* MANKŌ.] Speak, samurai! Are you deaf, are you dumb?

SHINBEI: Deafy. Dummy. Speak . . .

SUKEROKU [*strongly*]: Show your face! Show it or I'll . . .

[*He poses before* MANKŌ. *Music stops. He seizes the brim of her hat, lifts it, and sees his mother's face.*]

AGEMAKI: Yes, lift the hat, Sukeroku. Then will you scar the face you see?
[*He falls back, speechless.*]

SHINBEI: My, my, what's this? Is the carnival over? Let me take my turn then.
[SUKEROKU *tugs his sleeve to dissuade him, but* SHINBEI *blithely brushes him off.*]

Release me. I will do it. [*Struts over to* MANKŌ.] Hey, samurai! See this foot and this foot? [*Hikes his kimono.*] This foot is for booting bottoms of boys who don't obey. This foot is for stuffing in your eye, an idea I

share

think I like very much. So, samurai, don't play footsie with me. [*He stamps, trying to strike a powerful pose, and falls to the ground, clutching his foot.*] Ouch. A gallant must not say ouch, so in silence I bear my pain. [*Rises, and poses with his hand on the little staff.*] I am the master of

shiritori

Agemaki's Sukeroku. Should you anger the wielder of this stave, stave off my blows as you will, willingly will I slice you through to the soles of your feet. So hats off. Pay me some respect . . .[19] [*He lifts the hat, sees his mother.*] Ah, ah, ah! I die!
[SHINBEI *falls weakly to his knees.* SUKEROKU *has removed his clogs and kneels facing his mother, his gaze downcast.*]

MANKŌ [*removes hat and speaks sadly to* SUKEROKU] : How heroic is Agemaki's Sukeroku. Gorō, my son, will you strike me, kick me?
[*She turns to* SHINBEI, *who is crawling away on his hands and knees, hidden under a red cloth from one of the benches thrown over him by a* STAGE ASSISTANT. MANKŌ *passes her hat to another* STAGE ASSISTANT *and seizes* SHINBEI *under the cloth.*]
Who is this contemptible one who helps you? Show your face.
[*She takes the cloth off and falls back amazed.*]
Jūrō, my eldest son!

share

SHINBEI [*a tiny voice*] : Sun or moon, I'll never shine again.[20]

MANKŌ: You too. How pitiful.
[*She removes her cloak and hands it to a* STAGE ASSISTANT *and poses.*]

SHINBEI: Where is there a hole I can crawl in?

MANKŌ [*sits bench center as offstage shamisen plays melancholy* Tada

iken

Aikata *in the background*] : Virtuous sons would be taking vengeance on their father's slayer. My sons take aliases and brawl in public places. So unutterably ashamed am I, a woman, unable to strike my husband's enemy, remiss in the upbringing of his sons. It is punishment for the sins committed in a previous life. I shall beg your father's forgiveness by giving my life in apology.
[SUKEROKU *and* SHINBEI *half rise to stop her, then* SUKEROKU *hangs his head in shame.*]

SHINBEI: Wait, Mother. Please let me explain for Gorō. Without father's

19. Shinbei's speech is filled with wordplay. He says, for example, *sori ashi* (bent toes) when he means Osaka's *sori hashi* (arched bridge). The word *ashi* means three things in the phrase *Awaji no ashi ka omoi*: "reeds of Awaji" (Awaji no *ashi*), a contraction for "I" (*washi*) in "I think" (*ashi ka omoi*), and "foot."

20. The pun in the text is on Sukenari, his name, and *kaminari* (thunder).

sword, Tomokirimaru, even Gorō cannot defeat father's enemy. All the power of the great noble Yoshitsune resides in it, for it was a gift from him. Purposely Gorō hides his true identity. Purposely he fights in the hope of finding Tomokirimaru.

MANKŌ: Gorō, is it true?

SUKEROKU [*still bowing low*] : It is, Mother. Tomokirimaru will lead us to our enemy. I swear father's spirit will be avenged.

SHINBEI: Forgive us, Mother. [*Both bow.*]

MANKŌ: It lightens my heart to know you remain faithful to your obligations. [*Gets kimono from STAGE ASSISTANT.*] Gorō, as you search for Tomokirimaru, you must not quarrel. Wear this robe of paper. Its fragility will counsel you in patience. For my sake, bear humiliations. For your father's sake, endure even blows.
[*She and SHINBEI move downstage, hiding SUKEROKU from view as the STAGE ASSISTANT removes his outer kimono, revealing beneath it one identical to that brought out by MANKŌ. They separate and the audience sees SUKEROKU dressed in a soft, silk kimono of dark purple and lavender sections, the latter with writing on them. This is the conventional representation of a kimono patched together from love letters.*]

SHINBEI: This is a marvelous precept of forbearance.

MANKŌ: It is time to go. Agemaki. [*Looks at her significantly.*] I am indebted for your help. [*Bows.*]

AGEMAKI [*returning the bow*] : The night wind grows strong. Take care.

MANKŌ: Jūrō, let us go.
[*SHINBEI gets MANKŌ's hat, his hat and cane from a STAGE ASSISTANT. MANKŌ moves past SUKEROKU, then turns back.*] Gorō.

SUKEROKU [*head low still*] : One thing remains before I join you, Mother.

MANKŌ: I shall be waiting.
[*Music stops. Silence. MANKŌ and SHINBEI move to the seven-three position on the hanamichi. MANKŌ looks appealingly at AGEMAKI, who rises and nods reassuringly. MANKŌ turns away and poses.*]

SHINBEI: Don't delay, Brother.

CHORUS [*sings Tada Uta, "Plain Song," to shamisen accompaniment*] :
Ahh!
Breezes blowing toward the pine.
[*MANKŌ slowly and with great dignity moves down the hanamichi to the melancholy music. SHINBEI follows. SUKEROKU does not move. AGEMAKI crosses to his side and gently touches his shoulder.*]

AGEMAKI: Put your worries aside, Sukeroku. Since you've promised to no longer quarrel, tonight we shall be together for as long as you wish.
[*He does not respond. She becomes coquettish.*] I must tease you though, at least a tiny bit. Imagine, not knowing who your mother was! Ho, ho!
[*She leans against him provocatively.*]

kuzetsu SUKEROKU [*coldly*] : Fool. Two swords and a hat don't make a samurai. I know my own mother.
[*Rises, she falls slightly off-balance. He crosses and sits on the bench center.*]

You're a two-faced whore, Agemaki.

AGEMAKI [*turns away in surprise*] : In spite of your mother's words, you are determined to quarrel, I see.

[*Offstage shamisen play* Asazuma, *"Asazuma Pleasure Boat," in the background.*]

It doesn't matter what I say, you don't listen to me, but really, Sukeroku, taunting every samurai that passes by is childishly absurd.

SUKEROKU [*reacts*] : You deliberately brought my mother here to get me out of the quarter. Lying whore.

AGEMAKI : I? What lie have I told you?

SUKEROKU : Do you think I don't know? Old white beard has been inside your kimono. [*Acting hurt.*] Now you want me out of the way. Damned faithless slut. [*He poses.*]

AGEMAKI [*her lower lip trembles, but she puts up a brave front*] : It makes me laugh—I, in bed, with Ikyū? Ha, ha!

SUKEROKU : Laugh, but I know he came to you and you slept with him.

AGEMAKI [*pouting*] : No, I won't have you say that. [*Slaps the floor with her hand for emphasis.*] Where did you hear this? Where?

SUKEROKU [*uncomfortable*] : Never mind where I heard it.

AGEMAKI [*crosses and sits beside him, wheedling*] : No, tell me. Where did you hear it?

SUKEROKU : I, uh, heard it in my ear.

AGEMAKI [*flounces*] : Oh! Who told you?

SUKEROKU : The one who told me . . .

AGEMAKI : . . . who told you is . . . ?

SUKEROKU : Well . . .

AGEMAKI : Well?

SUKEROKU : No one.

AGEMAKI [*pouting*] : Sukeroku. Without proof you believe this. Did you not say, in bed that time, "As long as I live I shall be grateful to Agemaki, the truest person I have ever known?"

SUKEROKU : I did.

AGEMAKI : You lied. Now you say Agemaki is a faithless slut. [*Looks at him gently.*] I swear I despise Ikyū. [SUKEROKU *does not react. She looks away and speaks with pride.*] I see you have grown tired of me. You want to say goodby without saying it, so you bring up this wild story about Ikyū. Or do you hope I will lose interest in you, and so save you the trouble of leaving me? Is that what you want? Is it? It is cruel of you, Sukeroku.

SUKEROKU [*covering his discomfiture*] : I will not press the point, if what you say is true. Look at me, Agemaki.

AGEMAKI [*rises coldly and sweeps right*] : It was said I have the appearance of a slut.

SUKEROKU : You heard me. If there's nothing to this Ikyū business, don't fuss so.

AGEMAKI [*taking a pipe from a* STAGE ASSISTANT *and pointedly not offering it to him*] : I am a lying whore.

SUKEROKU: I'll say nothing more about Ikyū. Come over here. [*She continues smoking.*] From the beginning I have treated you well, but it's clear you're just too conceited to appreciate me. Come, or I leave. And I will not be back. [*He rises, and poses.*] I am leaving the quarter for good. [*He expects her to stop him. When she doesn't, he glances at her.*] You're a fool, Agemaki. This is the end. [*He draws himself up and crosses grandly to the hanamichi.*]

AGEMAKI [*sadly, to herself*] : To cry in regret is useless, yet the things you have said . . . [*Lightly.*] Sit down.

SUKEROKU: Sit down? Aha!

[*He struts back and sits, thinking he has won.*]

AGEMAKI [*sweetly*] : From what young courtesan did you receive the umbrella with the peony crest?

SUKEROKU [*startled*] : Eh? I bought it. At Nihon Bridge.

AGEMAKI: Oh, do be silent.

SUKEROKU [*huffing*] : Don't speak like a boor to Sukeroku.

AGEMAKI: You are the boor, Sukeroku, and I am bored with you. Leave me [*She turns her back on him.*]

SUKEROKU: You twist everything I say! [*Sighs.*] I was wrong in everything. It was my fault.

AGEMAKI: All you said before?

SUKEROKU: A mistake.

AGEMAKI: Truly?

SUKEROKU: I swear it.

[*Music stops.*]

AGEMAKI [*savoring her victory*] : You were hateful.

SUKEROKU [*meekly*] : I was hateful.

AGEMAKI [*suddenly feminine again, she tenderly sits beside him*] : You were, dear Sukeroku.

SUKEROKU [*amorously embracing her*] : Dear, dear Agemaki!

[*He slides his hand into the breast of her kimono.*]

IKYŪ [*off*] : Agemaki? Agemaki?

SUKEROKU: Ikyū!

[SUKEROKU *leaps up, hand on sword hilt. Offstage shamisen play* Sugagaki *in the background.* AGEMAKI *restrains* SUKEROKU *and gestures for him to hide behind the bench. He does. She sits on the bench, whirling the trailing end of her robe over him. A* STAGE ASSISTANT *holds the robe over* SUKEROKU's *head.* IKYŪ *enters followed by two* CHILD MAIDS. *One places a white cushion on the bench, the other places an incense stand in front of it.* IKYŪ *sits.*]

IKYŪ: Ah, here you are, Agemaki.

AGEMAKI [*coolly*] : Ah, Ikyū.

IKYŪ: I said before inside, what happened earlier is water under the bridge. Now, it is rumored you will sleep with me tonight. Is it true?

AGEMAKI: Sleep with Ikyū?

IKYŪ: You will not?

AGEMAKI [*carefully*] : The lie that Agemaki will sleep with Ikyū . . . [IKYŪ *reacts angrily.*] . . . is no lie.

IKYŪ [*grandly takes her hand*] : Then to bed, whore.

AGEMAKI: No.

IKYŪ: No?

AGEMAKI: I have drunk too much and need fresh air. You go on to bed before me. Night air stiffens old bones.

IKYŪ: Then I shall wait in the night air with you! [*He laughs evilly.*] How it would infuriate your ruffian friend Sukeroku to see us here. Eh, Agemaki? [*He laughs and starts to slide close to* AGEMAKI. *The cloth shakes.* SUKEROKU *pinches* IKYŪ's *leg.*]

Ouch! Somebody pinched my leg.

AGEMAKI: Children, you are being naughty.

CHILD: Mistress, under your robe . . .

AGEMAKI [*silencing them*] : I will hear no excuses.

CHILD: But . . .

AGEMAKI: Silence.

CHILDREN: Aiii!

[SUKEROKU *stirs under her robe.*]

AGEMAKI [*under her breath*] : Don't come out.

IKYŪ: Don't come out?

AGEMAKI [*meaningfully*] : I was saying to the moon, do not come out . . .

IKYŪ [*mocking*] : The pure light of the moon? Shining in Yoshiwara?[21]

AGEMAKI: . . . from behind the clouds.

IKYŪ: Ah. The clouds . . .

AGEMAKI: . . . are hiding . . .

IKYŪ: . . . the moon? [*He shrugs.*] The moon is easily clouded, the flower easily scattered, they say. Eh, Agemaki? Ha, ha, ha! [*He reaches for his pipe.* SUKEROKU *slides the tobacco box out of his reach, filches the pipe, and casually smokes it himself.* IKYŪ *looks about suspiciously.*]

Who moved my tobacco box? Where's my pipe?

AGEMAKI: The children are naughty again. Go inside at once.

CHILDREN: Aiii!

[Sugagaki *music speeds up as they exit, then continues quietly between dialogue phrases.*]

IKYŪ: No, Agemaki, this time it was not the children. It was . . . [*He begins to slide close to her. She stops him, pointing to the sky.*]

AGEMAKI [*quickly*] : Ah, my, my, Ikyū, look. Look . . . the stars are out tonight.

IKYŪ: And what is so interesting about the stars that come out every night?

AGEMAKI [*pretending to pout*] : But tonight there are so many. Ikyū, count them for me.

IKYŪ: What? Count the stars for you?

21. A sarcastic reference to the well-known saying, "The moon will shine in its ebb quarter as soon as prostitutes are truthful and eggs have square corners."

AGEMAKI [*coquettishly*] : Yes.

share

IKYŪ [*with a wicked smile*] : And while I am counting your stars, will you be counting on your star-crossed lover? Count on then, count on. Ha, ha! [*Pointing.*] The bright one there is the Morning Star. Above that is the Big Dipper. Ah, and there is a falling star, but you know about them. Don't you, Agemaki?

AGEMAKI: No.

IKYŪ [*darkly insinuating*] : A star that flashes brightly through the quarter, streaking in at night to rob a patron of the woman he has purchased, is a falling star.[22] [*Enjoying the game, he points again.*] And there is the Weaving Maid, longing for her Cowherd lover to join her in the sky.[23] But the great Milky Way, called Ikyū, sits immovable between them so they cannot meet! Eh, Agemaki? Ha, ha, ha!
[SUKEROKU *pinches his leg again.*]
Ouch! Someone pinched my leg.

AGEMAKI: The children, Ikyū . . .

IKYŪ [*ominously*] : . . . are gone, Agemaki.

AGEMAKI: If not the children, then a mouse.

IKYŪ: A mouse?

AGEMAKI: Yes.

IKYŪ: A rat, you mean. A sewer rat, Agemaki. There he is.

AGEMAKI: Where?
[*Music stops.* IKYŪ *rises, pushes* AGEMAKI *behind him, and points with his sword.*]

IKYŪ: There!

SUKEROKU [*leaping out*] : Ikyū!

IKYŪ: Sukeroku!
[*To loud* batan tsuke *beats,* SUKEROKU *and* IKYŪ *face each other, ready to draw.* AGEMAKI *restrains* SUKEROKU.]

AGEMAKI: Wait!
[*She gestures commandingly for* IKYŪ *not to draw and sweeps her trailing robe protectively around* SUKEROKU, *stamps, and poses.* IKYŪ *seizes his sword with both hands, but does not draw.* SUKEROKU, *remembering his promise, falls to his knees, struggling to suppress his anger. All pose in a tense group* mie *to* battari tsuke *beats. Offstage shamisen and flute begin melancholy* Rokudan, *"Six Part Melody."*]

IKYŪ [*scathingly*] : Behind the skirts of the street slut Agemaki, hides the gutter rat Sukeroku, while the wise-beard old cat Ikyū sees it all! Sukeroku, you slink about like a thief. Is this the spirit in which you plan your great deed? [*Sneering.*] Soga Gorō the coward!

22. A pun on *yobai* (secretly slipping in to see a girl at night) and *yobai boshi* (falling star).

23. In Japanese mythology the brightness of Vega and Altair on either side of the Milky Way in midsummer is explained by the story of the Cowherd who is able to cross the river of the Milky Way to meet his beloved Weaving Maid each year on the seventh day of the seventh month.

SUKEROKU [*surprised, turns to face* IKYŪ] : If you know my name, you know I am no coward.

IKYŪ [*disdainfully faces front*] : Your father perished ignominiously. While you without the spirit to avenge him debauch with drink and whores, your father's murderer, Suketsune, lives in pomp at court. Do you think he is untouchable? Bah! Coward, must I beat some warrior's courage into you?

chōchaku

[*Music stops.* IKYŪ *strikes* SUKEROKU *on the head and shoulders five times with his heavy closed fan, each blow accented by batan tsuke beats.* SUKEROKU *grasps* IKYŪ's *wrist and they pose in a mie to battari tsuke beats.*)

SUKEROKU [*bitterly*] : Ikyū—fortunate man! How I envy you! For eighteen years I have searched out our family's enemy to strike him down. And now it is you who strike me! How bitter fate is. Revile me, beat me. I wear my mother's robe and will not draw! [*He releases* IKYŪ's *wrist, turns front, and clasps his hands together in agonized prayer.*] Strike, Ikyū! Strike me down!

IKYŪ: Hmm. To honor a parent's words shows you are not wholly lacking in resolution. Soga Gorō, listen.

[*Music resumes. He looks at* SUKEROKU *craftily, then places the incense stand center stage.*]

In achieving one's great ambition, you cannot be swayed by people's hatred or their love. Trifling with whores, petty squabbles erode your will. But join three wills together, Soga Gorō—you, your brother, and . . . one another—these three wills united beyond hate or love could achieve a father's murderer's death, the Shōgun's fall, even the rule of the nation itself! Together, nothing could stand against such strength. [*Indicates the stand. Meaningfully.*] No weight could crush the two Soga brothers if, like this incense stand, there were three pillars of support. But, lacking one you will fall like this.

[*Music stops.* IKYŪ *suddenly draws his sword and, to batan tsuke beats, slashes one leg from the stand, which falls to the floor.* SUKEROKU *seizes* IKYŪ's *hand and looks at the blade. Quickly realizing he has erred,* IKYŪ *replaces the sword in the scabbard to batan tsuke beats.* SUKEROKU *is about to draw.* AGEMAKI *comes between them. She restrains each with a hand gesture. The men glare fiercely at each other, hands on their swords. They pose in a group mie to battari tsuke beats.*]

CHORUS [*offstage repeats* Tada Uta *to shamisen accompaniment*] :
Ahh!
Breezes blowing toward the pine.

[IKYŪ *turns and walks ponderously toward the Three Harbors. He stops, slowly pivots, and looks at* SUKEROKU *with contempt and hatred. The music speeds up as he quickly exits.*]

AGEMAKI [*noticing*] : Your robe, Sukeroku, is torn.

SUKEROKU [*rising, with a laugh*] : Ha, ha. Then his fate is decided.

AGEMAKI: Is it . . . ?

SUKEROKU [*triumphantly*] : It is Tomokirimaru!

[*She reacts, then moves close and whispers a question into his ear. He nods emphatically.*]

Tonight I wait for . . .

[*He rushes onto the hanamichi to fast bata-bata tsuke beats. At seven-three he stops, steps out with his right foot to a sharp ki clack. He leans forward in an aggressive mie, both hands on the hilt of the sword, as he speaks.*]

. . . Ikyū!!

[*To fast tempo Kyokubachi, "Drum Stick Rhythm,"—played by the large drum, stick drum, and flute—and bata-bata tsuke beats, SUKEROKU runs down the hanamichi and off. AGEMAKI poses center stage, watching him. The curtain is run closed to gradually accelerating ki clacks. The large drum immediately begins beating Kaza Oto wind pattern. House lights remain low as the dance floor is removed. The interval is short. Kaza Oto becomes louder and with a single ki clack signal, offstage shamisen play fast Sugagaki. The curtain is run open to accelerating ki clacks. There is a moment of silence.*]

SCENE 2

[*The scene is the same, except that the huge water vat stage right has been moved downstage, the benches have been removed, and a slatted night gate now covers the entrance to the Three Harbors. It is night. Pale blue light comes up on the hanamichi. The large drum booms out Kaza Oto and to fast bata-bata tsuke beats, SUKEROKU rushes on. He wears a simple white kimono, tied with a pale blue sash, and white leggings. Hair falls about his shoulders wildly. At seven-three he stops, peers into the darkness, and poses in a mie, naked sword held behind him, to battari tsuke beats. To softly ominous Kaza Oto drum beats, SUKEROKU moves stealthily on stage. A time bell tolls in the distance. He slips behind the water vat.*]

CHORUS [*softly sings Fukete, "Nightfall," to quiet, offstage shamisen accompaniment*] :

Our slumbers in the evening are quickly broken;

By regrets of past summers knocking at the door.

[*During the song, SEMBEI, a MALE SERVANT of the Three Harbors, IKYŪ, and two young COURTESANS enter through a small door set into the front gate. SEMBEI hands a lighted lantern to the SERVANT. Offstage shamisen play Fukete Aikata in the background.*]

FIRST COURTESAN [*bowing politely*] : Tonight you're leaving so early.

SECOND COURTESAN: Every night it's someone different, Ikyū.

FIRST COURTESAN: Come again, noble Ikyū.

[*They bow politely. He takes his sword from the FIRST COURTESAN.*]

IKYŪ: It will be light soon. [*To SEMBEI.*] Come. Come.

SERVANT: I will go with you as far as the river bank.

SEMBEI [*snatching the lantern back*] : What good is that? Never fear. Sembei, a warrior, will lead the way. Come.

COURTESANS [*bowing*] : Good night, then.

[*The time bell tolls. The* COURTESANS *go inside. The men move right.*]

CHORUS [*repeats* Fukete] :

Deep slumbers in the evening are quickly broken;
  By regrets of past seasons knocking at the door.

[*The time bell tolls.*]

IKYŪ [*stopping*] : What time is it, Sembei?

SEMBEI: Three o'clock, Master.

IKYŪ [*glances about*] : Hurry, hurry.

[Kaza Oto *swells.* SUKEROKU *creeps forward in the dark. As the men move past him,* SUKEROKU *knocks the lantern to the ground to batan tsuke beats. The lights do not dim, but the scene is played as if in complete darkness.*]

What thief attacks without a word?

SUKEROKU: No thief, Ikyū!

IKYŪ: Sukeroku! Coward, sneak-thieving in the dark!

SUKEROKU: To avenge the honor of the Sogas I lie in wait for you, Ikyū.

[*Straining forward in the dark.*] Give me Tomokirimaru!

[*Offstage shamisen play* Yachio Jishi, *"Ageless Lion."*]

miarawashi IKYŪ [*strongly*] : I shall never part with this sword which belonged to Minamoto Yoshitsune, for the Minamoto clan are my hated enemies. I take the name of Ikyū, but now know who I really am: Ika Heinai Zaemon, general of the Taira!

[*A* STAGE ASSISTANT *helps him remove his robe and sash, revealing beneath a kimono of white tied with a soft purple sash. He stands, heels together, in a powerful mie, to battari tsuke beats.*]

SUKEROKU [*snarling*] : Tomokirimaru!

IKYŪ: With its strength I shall depose the usurping Minamoto from power and restore to rule once more the Taira clan! No power on earth will make me part with Tomokirimaru!

[*A* STAGE ASSISTANT *helps him tie a blue cloth around his head, as a sign he is prepared to fight.*]

SUKEROKU: I shall. Give it here!

IKYŪ: Draw, Sembei!

SEMBEI: Yes, Master!

tate [Yachio Jishi *music becomes faster,* Kaza Oto *rises and falls, and alternating tsuke patterns of batan and battari accompany the fighting scene which follows.* SEMBEI *takes his right arm out of his sleeve, and rushes at* SUKEROKU. *He strikes awkwardly right and left.* SUKEROKU *easily pushes him away with the flat of his sword.* SUKEROKU *and* IKYŪ *move center, where they strike and parry. They pose facing each other in a mie. The tempo becomes more deliberate. The flute adds its haunting sound to the shamisen.* SUKEROKU *holds off* IKYŪ's *determined thrusts, until* SUKEROKU *steps aside and* IKYŪ *is pushed stage right.* SEMBEI *attacks and is forced to the ground. He holds his sword horizontally over his head:* IKYŪ *and* SUKEROKU *rest their sword tips on it and the three pose in a*

89 Sukeroku: Flower of Edo

group *mie, to battari tsuke beats.* SEMBEI *rises, is slashed across the neck by* SUKEROKU, *staggers, and falls dead behind a lantern stand left. A head appears on the stand, as if the force of* SUKEROKU's *blow had sent it flying through the air.* SUKEROKU *and* IKYŪ *stand back to back, fall apart, and glare at each other. With sword tips touching, they pose in a mie, to battari tsuke beats. A* STAGE ASSISTANT *holds a black cloth in front of* SEMBEI, *and he goes off unseen. The two simultaneously slash at each other,* IKYŪ *screams, both clutch the base of their necks and fall. Loud* Kaza Oto. *They struggle to their feet and we see gashes of red on each, running from the top of the shoulder to the breast.* IKYŪ, *sensing where his opponent is, desperately jabs his elbow into* SUKEROKU's *stomach.* SUKEROKU *absorbs the blow with his hand, but pretends to have the wind knocked out of him and staggers, whirling stage left where he falls prostrate on his back.* IKYŪ, *at the hanamichi looks back, sees* SUKEROKU *fallen, and poses in a mie. Face contorted with pain,* IKYŪ *forces himself across the stage to where* SUKEROKU *has fallen. Thinking* SUKEROKU *is safely unconscious, he takes his time straddling his opponent and raising his sword in both hands for the final blow.* Bata-bata *and* Kaza Oto *crescendo. Suddenly* SUKEROKU *thrusts his sword up into* IKYŪ's *unprotected side. His ruse has worked. Holding his sword in place,* SUKEROKU *rises and forces* IKYŪ *center, turning him around and around. He twists the blade cruelly in the wound.* IKYŪ *gasps, his fingers claw the air. Staggering helplessly, he is slashed down the length of his back.* IKYŪ *groans, and falls. Music stops. In silence,* SUKEROKU *straddles his foe, and plunges his sword into* IKYŪ's *throat. Several* TOWNSPEOPLE *slip on and, in the dim light of lanterns they are carrying, witness the killing. They silently slip away to sound the alarm.* IKYŪ's *hand, still clutching Tomokirimaru, trembles violently.* SUKEROKU *twists the blade in* IKYŪ's *throat. His arm falls, the sword clatters to the ground.* IKYŪ *is dead.* SUKEROKU *holds Tomokirimaru high.*]

SUKEROKU: Tomokirimaru!

[IKYŪ *goes off unseen behind a black curtain held in front of him by a* STAGE ASSISTANT. *Booming drum beats of* Mitsu Daiko, *"Triple Beat," sound the alarm. From far off come cries of "Murder!" Startled,* SUKE-ROKU *holds the sword reverently to his forehead. Then he rushes to escape down the hanamichi. Cries of "Murder" from that direction force him back onto the stage. He moves left, then right; each time new shouts of "Murder" force him back. He falls weakly to one knee. Renewed shouts and ever louder and faster drum beats rouse him. Desperately, he looks for a way of escape. He sees the water vat and strikes at its pyramid of buckets with his sword. The buckets fall with a crash. He picks up one, knocks out the bottom with the hilt of his sword, and heaves it up into the vat. He climbs a ladder on the outside of the vat, poses for a moment on the edge, then plunges in causing a great wave of water to cascade onto the stage. He places the bucket over his head and disappears from sight.* Mitsu Daiko *drum beats pound unrelentingly. Several* CONSTABLES, *in*

dark blue jackets and trousers and carrying short metal rods of office,
rush down the hanamichi carrying a ladder. Shouting instructions and
encouragement to each other, they raise it and one runs nimbly up to
look about. He points to the Three Harbors. They rush onto the stage and
raise the ladder against the side of the Three Harbors. The same CON-
STABLE *runs up and looks again. This time he points off right. Shouting*
loudly, they run off, leaving the ladder in place. Drum beats become soft
and ominous; the shouting fades. The bucket moves, water splashes down.
SUKEROKU *rises slowly out of the water holding the bucket over his*
head. He poses in a mie, as the time bell tolls. The audience applauds and
shouts in appreciation. Offstage shamisen and flute play quiet Kono Ha,
"This Leaf." Three times SUKEROKU *tries to pull himself out of the vat,*
each time he falls back, causing a wave of water to cascade onto the floor.
Finally he heaves himself over the edge, staggers to the center of the stage,
and there falls unconscious, still clasping Tomokirimaru. Music stops. The
alarm drum begins booming again and shouts are heard offstage from all
directions. Rushing from the Three Harbors in her sleeping kimono,
AGEMAKI *takes in the situation at a glance. As* TOWNSPEOPLE *swarm*
on, she covers SUKEROKU *with the long train of her kimono.*]

YOUNG MAN: What's this, a woman?

SECOND YOUNG MAN: Whore, out of the way!

ALL: Stand aside! [*They brandish sticks and poles.*]

AGEMAKI: I shall not move.

YOUNG MAN: Is he inside?

SECOND YOUNG MAN: Where is he?

THIRD YOUNG MAN: He's here somewhere!

ALL: Bring him out!

AGEMAKI: Agemaki, pride of the House of Three Harbors, does not lie.

YOUNG MAN [*frustrated*] : I know she's hiding him.

SECOND YOUNG MAN: Tell us where he is.

ALL: Tell us! Quick!

 [*They raise their poles and sticks threateningly.*]

AGEMAKI [*haughtily*] : Stop. Let one of your poles mar the beauty of
 Agemaki, beware—darkness will descend on Yoshiwara. [*Men mutter.*]
 If you oppose Agemaki, Agemaki will oppose you. [*She strikes a regal
 pose and looks away disdainfully.*]

CONSTABLE [*coming on*] : In the dark, he could be anywhere. Spread out and
 look.

 [*To booming Mitsu Daiko, they run off in different directions. When they
 are gone, the drum shifts to faint, ominous Kaza Oto.* AGEMAKI *kneels
 beside* SUKEROKU, *sees his wound, takes off her robe and covers him.
 Then she climbs the side of the vat, wets her sash, returns, and squeezes a
 few drops of water into his mouth. He revives and clutches her.*]

SUKEROKU [*painfully sitting up*] : Ah, Agemaki. The water was turned red
 with my blood. My strength drained away until for a moment I fell
 unconscious. [*He stands, holding himself up with his sword.*]

AGEMAKI: Then you have found . . . ?

SUKEROKU [*holds sword high*] : Tomokirimaru!

AGEMAKI [*hands clasped*] : How grateful we all are.

SUKEROKU: And now to find Suketsune.

AGEMAKI: The quarter is filled with men searching for you. There is no
way out.

SUKEROKU [*sees ladder*] : I'm in luck! I'll go across the roofs.

AGEMAKI: And I will wait by the great gate, near the river bank. Be careful,
Sukeroku.

[*He climbs painfully to the top of the ladder. He looks back at her as she
kneels right and faces him.*]

SUKEROKU: Agemaki!

AGEMAKI: Sukeroku!

BOTH [*prolonged*] : Until . . . we . . . meet!

[*A sharp ki clack signals lights to come up full. Uchiage tsuke beats rise to
a furious crescendo, fade, then swell again: he raises Tomokirimaru over
head and clasps his wounded shoulder; she rises on her knees and looks
intently at him. They pose in a final mie.*]

kōjō   STAGE MANAGER [*enters quickly and kneels stage right*] : With this, we
conclude today's performance!

[*The STAGE MANAGER bows low. SUKEROKU and AGEMAKI pose.
The curtain is slowly walked closed to accelerating ki clacks as offstage
shamisen play Shinnai Maebiki, "Shinnai Prelude," and the large drum
Mitsu Daiko. A single ki clack signals the large drum to beat out Uchidashi,
indicating the day's performance is over.*]

Saint Narukami and the God Fudō

NARUKAMI FUDŌ KITAYAMA ZAKURA

by Tsuuchi Hanjurō, Yasuda Abun,
and Nakada Mansuke

This all-day (tōshi kyōgen) imperial court play (ōchōmono or ōdaimono) was performed January through July 1742 by the Sadoshima Chōgorō troupe at the Ōnishi Theater in Osaka. The play's great success is attributed to the skill with which favorite scenes of the visiting guest star from Edo, Ichikawa Danjūrō II, were melded with new materials. The first kabuki play about the seduction of a powerful ascetic by a court lady, the basic plot of *Saint Narukami*, was written and acted in by Danjūrō I in 1684. But the legend is ancient. It is found in the *Nalinika Jataka* stories in India and these were translated into Chinese around the fourth century. Erotic accounts of the story are included in the Japanese *Konjaku Monogatari* (eleventh century) and the *Taiheiki* (fourteenth century). A nō play on the subject (*Ikkaku Senin*, translated by Frank Hoff and William Packard, in *Traditional Asian Plays*) is austere and elliptical. Danjūrō returned to the graphic approach of the earlier chronicles in which the seduction was made central. To this he added the low comedy of the monks White Cloud and Black Cloud. In 1697 Danjūrō I also wrote and played the lead in *The God Fudō*, astonishing the audience with his portrayal of this fearsome deity. He and his son, Danjūrō II, revived *Saint Narukami* seven times and *The God Fudō* three times during the following half-century. For the 1742 production these two well-known plays were worked into the Disputed Throne World of the Heian court. Another act of the long play was *The Whisker Tweezers*, which capitalized on the discovery of lodestones in Japan in 1717. The three were revived frequently, usually as acts within long plays. Danjūrō VII included all three as independent, one-act plays in his selection of "Eighteen Favorite Plays." After the time of Danjūrō VIII (1823–1854) the plays fell into disfavor: *Saint Narukami* was not performed for a period of 49 years (1851–1900), *The Whisker Tweezers* for 59 years (1850–1909), and *The God Fudō* for 131 years (1780–1911). During his long career, Danjūrō IX (1838–1903) refused to perform any of them. It is said that the suicide of Danjūrō VIII in 1851 while performing the title role in *Saint Narukami* made him shun the play as unlucky. It also seems probable that he hesitated to perform *Saint Narukami* or *The Whisker Tweezers* because in the prudish atmosphere of turn-of-the-century Japan the eroticism of the plays was unacceptable. Morally offensive lines were expurgated in an important edition of *Saint Narukami* published in 1936. We know the plays today through revivals (based on the 1742 text) staged by Ichikawa Sadanji II between 1909 and 1911. *Saint Narukami* is particularly popular with modern audiences and has been produced more than fifty times in the past four decades.

It is probable that the authors chose the world of Fujiwara Mototsune (836–891) because he was a famous historical figure, the first of the powerful Fujiwara regents who controlled the government during the Heian era. This was a period of unprecedented natural disasters, and Mototsune was well known historically for his support of incantations and rituals to placate the vengeful spirits believed to have caused the famines and floods that plagued the country. The period thus provided a natural setting for the story of the drought in *Saint Narukami and the God Fudō*. At the same time audiences would have been familiar with many settings in the play: images of the God Fudō were venerated at a grotto in the mountains near the Arashiyama River, north of Kyoto, where Saint Narukami was said to have trapped the rain gods; the Shinsen Temple and its adjoining lake into which the Ono family poem card was to be immersed can still be seen on the imperial palace grounds in Kyoto; Tree Island Shrine stood outside the capital on the road to Osaka; and the remains of the ancient inner palace could probably still be identified.

The bravura style of the Ichikawa family is exemplified in the heroic roles of Danjō, Narukami, and Fudō (all played by Danjūrō II in 1742) and by the court villain (kugeaku) Hayakumo. Typical of the exaggerated style of aragoto, Danjō roars as he prepares to expose the spy in the ceiling, *"Yattoko totcha, untoko na!"* It is a made-up phrase that is intended to sound imposingly fierce (the same phrase is used in *Sukeroku: Flower of Edo*, and other aragoto plays). The play is sometimes described as the last important "conversation" play of "pure" kabuki, before the influence of the puppet theater. Except for short sections of Ōzatsuma narrative music when Saint Narukami enters and when he transforms himself into a Thunder God, music is entirely offstage atmospheric geza music. (The dance-mime sections accompanied by narrative music of onstage Takemoto, Tokiwazu, Nagauta, or Tomimoto ensembles seen in current productions of *Saint Narukami* as a one-act play were added between 1773 and 1843, and are not part of the 1742 text.)

The present translation is based on an abridged version of the 1742 text of *Saint Narukami and the God Fudō*, prepared for production at the National Theater of Japan in 1967. Tobe Ginsaku was adapter and director. Narukami's death at the hands of Danjō was not included in the production, and other smaller cuts were made. Many independent versions of *Saint Narukami, The God Fudō*, and *The Whisker Tweezers* have been published. Annotated texts in Gunji Masakatsu, ed., *Kabuki Jūhachibanshū*, were consulted as well as in Toita Yasuji, ed., *Kabuki Meisakusen* (vol. 15, 1956), and Kawatake Shigetoshi, ed., *Kabuki Jūhachibanshū*. Most stage directions are from the production of *Saint Narukami and The God Fudō*, National Theater of Japan, Tokyo, January 1967.

Saint Narukami
and the God Fudō

ACT I

SCENE 1   THE IMPERIAL PALACE

[*Two sharp clacks of the ki signal the* MUSICIANS *offstage right to begin*
Goten, *"Palace," drum and flute music associated with the court. Regular
beats of the stick drum alternate with clacks of ki as the curtain is slowly
pushed open; drum and ki accelerate, ending in two loud beats. The scene
is an audience hall of the Imperial Palace in Kyoto, a simple raised room
with connecting passages on either side. The restrained elegance of court
taste is apparent in the stark black, pale green, and gold color scheme of
pillars, beams, and bamboo blinds, now lowered, covering the room and
passageways from view. A sign reading "Saint Narukami and the God
Fudō" is hung on a pillar stage left, and on a similar pillar, stage left, a
sign indicates that the scene is The Imperial Palace. A dark blue curtain
decorated with the theater's crest, covers an exit into the garden, downstage left. Through vertical slits in the scenery, stage right, the offstage*
MUSICIANS *follow the play. No one is onstage. Two sharp clacks of the
ki signal the* MUSICIANS *to begin* Ōdaiko Sōban, *"Drum and Gong," music
played on the large drum, bells, and shamisen to accompany rain prayers.
From behind the curtain at the end of the hanamichi come wailing cries,
"Rain, rain, let it rain!" "Great Dragon Gods of Rain, hear us!" "Bring
rain, Dragon Gods!" A group of* FARMERS *and their* WIVES *enter from
the rear of the hanamichi and dance along the hanamichi through the
audience. They wear plain blue and brown cotton kimonos, the hems of
which are tucked up out of the way. Some wear straw rain cloaks or hats,
others wear towels over their heads. The women strike Buddhist prayer
bells, the men beat small tambourines. They perform an animated rain
dance, crouching, rising, turning, as if in a frenzy.*]

CHORUS [*offstage, sings a prayer for rain, accompanied by shamisen, large
drum, stick drum, flute, and bells playing* Amagoi Daiko, *"Rainmaking
Drum"*] :

Pray for springs of pure water, pray for falling rain;
　Go to the Emperor's palace, the palace of rain;
　Pray for rain at the palace of the Emperor.
Rains deluge! Rains fall! Rains pour!
　Oh, Great Dragon Gods of rain!
[*They are whirling wildly through the palace garden when an imperative voice calls out from the blinds, "Silence! Silence! Cease your clamor!" Shocked by the realization they have trespassed on imperial grounds, the* FARMERS *gasp and fall to their knees in terror. They whip off their headgear and press their faces to the ground.*]

FIRST FARMER [*voice quaking*] : My Lord, allow us to present . . .

ALL [*bowing in unison*] : . . . our petition.

MOTOTSUNE [*behind the blind*] : Raise the blinds that a petition may be received.

RETAINERS [*behind the blind*] : We shall.

[*Large drum and flute play impressive Sōgaku, "Court Music," as the blinds, running the full length of the stage, are rolled up to reveal the audience room. A huge spreading pine tree is painted on the gold background of sliding doors, at the rear center. A silk curtain, striped in white, purple, black, and red, covers the entrance to the inner chambers. Four court ministers, identified as imperial nobles by their voluminous robes with Chinese-style round collars, sit regally on the soft straw matting which covers the floor.* MOTOTSUNE, *regent and eldest adviser of the infant Emperor, wears an elegant robe of peach-colored silk and holds in his right hand the small cyprus wood symbol of his office. He wears a high curving black hat.* ONO HARUMICHI, *the Emperor's chief minister, sits immediately to his right, wearing a chaste black and gold robe. Two younger nobles,* TOYOHIDE *and* HARUMICHI's *son* HARUKAZE, *sit some distance to the right of their elders. Their robes are bright and youthful:* TOYOHIDE's *is apple green,* HARUKAZE's *is powder blue. They, like* HARUMICHI, *wear low, rounded hats of gold cloth, tied under the chin with a purple cord. Faces and hands are made up white, indicating their refined natures. They do not wear swords. Two samurai* RETAINERS, *wearing conservative-colored kimonos and stiff outer garments, kneel on either side of the nobles, a short sword in each sash.* TOYOHIDE *raises his fan slightly and glances over it at the* FARMERS. *He speaks delicately but imperiously.*]

TOYOHIDE: You are in the presence of Regent Mototsune. State your business instantly.

FARMERS: [*bowing, terrified*] : Ahh!

FIRST FARMER [*stammering*] : I-I-I will speak. I . . .

FIRST WIFE [*edging forward*] : Don't shilly-shally. Then I'll tell them.

[*Others ad-lib support. Offstage shamisen play* Seki Dera, *"Barrier Temple," in the background. Though frightened, she speaks strongly.*]

As your Lordships know, the rain doesn't fall and doesn't fall. We don't know the reason, but we farmers are at our wits' end.

SECOND FARMER [*gaining courage*] : It's the truth, Sir. Our rice fields are cracked and dry. There's no use thinking about watering them. The rivers are dry, the lakes are empty. It must be heaven's punishment.

SECOND WIFE [*glaring at* SECOND FARMER] : That's a dreadful thing to say. [*To the nobles.*] My Lords, we have beat drums and bells praying to the Dragon Gods for rain, but no matter what we do, not a single drop falls. [*Overcome, she weeps.*]

OLD WOMAN [*pitifully*] : Farmers weep, my Lords. Please, help turn our tears into rain.

[*They weep loudly and prostrate themselves.*]

THIRD WIFE [*desperately*] : Our Majesty the Mikado is called the Son of Heaven. We beg you, ask His Majesty to have the great Sun Goddess bring us rain!

THIRD FARMER [*bowing*] : Grant this favor . . .

ALL [*bowing low*] : . . . we humbly pray!

TOYOHIDE [*gently*] : Indeed, your Lordship, this time of drought is just cause for their petition.

[*Music ends.* MOTOTSUNE *speaks grandly, easily, as one who is above mundane problems.*]

MOTOTSUNE: Do not trouble yourselves, for, knowing that drought has fallen upon the land, though Mars has not entered that conjugation of the heavens usual for this condition, the Mikado himself and all members of his court, stricken to the heart with concern, offer prayers to Shintō and Buddhist deities of every shrine and temple in this Land of the Sun. Rest content. In time the Gods and Buddhas will bestow their protection once again.

[*The* FARMERS *are dismayed by his casual attitude.* HARUKAZE *tries to reassure them.*]

HARUKAZE [*strongly*] : Farmers! Think of the favor Regent Mototsune has bestowed, ordering the Imperial Council to concern itself with no other matter than this. As it deliberates, raise unceasing Shintō and Buddhist prayers.

FIRST WOMAN [*protesting*] : You say our Mikado, who is higher than the Gods, can't move the heavens? Surely then no one's going to listen to our prayers!

[*The nobles frown with displeasure.*]

HARUMICHI [*not deigning to look*] : Do not speak nonsense. Go home. Go!

HAYAKUMO [*offstage left*] : The farmers' words are reasonable! Listen to them!

[*All react with astonishment.*]

HARUKAZE: It is His Imperial Highness . . .

HARUKAZE and HARUMICHI: . . . the Prince!

[*With a crash of cymbals the curtain left is flicked open and* PRINCE HAYAKUMO *strides on to the portentous music,* Midare Taiko, *"Agitated Beat," played by large drum, stick drum, and flute. High black clogs emphasize the prince's imposing size. Heavy black and blue lines on white makeup accent menacing features. A huge mane of black hair sweeps over* his shoulders to below his waist. He wears a straw rain cape and carries a farmer's straw hat in one hand and a sickle in the other. Music stops.]

HARUMICHI [shocked almost speechless]: Your Imperial Highness, after two years' absence, what explains your presence here . . . dressed in peasant's clothes?

HAYAKUMO [grandly, facing front]: I address Regent Mototsune only! Receive me!

[With crashing cymbals, Midare Taiko resumes. HAYAKUMO removes his cape, which a RETAINER hangs over the veranda railing, revealing a magnificent gold, blue, and cream-colored silk outer robe, which covers a white inner kimono and gold and black trousers. Passing clogs and hat to a RETAINER, he deliberately mounts the stairs and moves to a tall stool a black-robed STAGE ASSISTANT places in the center of the room. Music stops with a loud crash as HAYAKUMO sits. His voice, when he speaks, shows his regal disdain of even those high nobles of the court.]

I, born the son of the late Mikado, rightful heir of the Seat of Ten Virtues,[1] was passed over by the Council of Nobles, who placed instead an infant, Yōzei,[2] on the Imperial Throne! And so I left the capital, to mix with townsmen and peasants, with whom I shared in recent days the misery of their lives, suffering through this drought. [With flattering politeness.] Worthy farmers, I hereby consecrate myself through prayer and meditation to bring, for the benefit of the whole world, the rains you seek. Place your trust in Imperial Prince Hayakumo and return to your homes.

[The FARMERS are overjoyed.]

FIRST FARMER: We are grateful, Your Highness! Thank you for your kind words!

SECOND FARMER [pleading]: Please, Your Highness . . .

ALL [bowing]: . . . answer our plea!

FIRST FARMER: Come, we can go now. Come.

CHORUS [sings offstage to Amagoi Daiko music]:
Rains deluge! Rains fall! Rains pour!
    Oh, Great Dragon Gods of rain!
[Bowing repeatedly, the FARMERS rise and go off happily during the song. The music ends with a crash of cymbals and drums. HAYAKUMO glares at MOTOTSUNE.]

HAYAKUMO: Mototsune! Listen!

[The prince's entrance music, Midare Taiko, plays ominously in the background.]

Incapacity of the infant Emperor causes this disaster! If he cannot address the heavens to bring the blessings of rain, there will be famine throughout the country. Soon the fields will grow wild and corpses of the dead will

1. One of the Emperor's duties was to offer protection against the Ten Evils described in Buddhism, hence the throne was called the Seat of Ten Virtues.

2. Ascended the throne in 876 at the age of eight and deposed by Mototsune eight years later as being criminally insane. In the play Mototsune is a loyal supporter of the Emperor.

make a mountain! Wearing wooden clogs to protect my feet from frost and a peasant's straw hat to ward off the heat of the sun, I myself cut the parched grass with this sickle, to discover the truth of our land's disaster. [*Gestures with the sickle.*] Is the Son of Heaven unconcerned with his subjects' misery? Mototsune, shouldn't you inform him?

MOTOTSUNE [*coldly*] : Your Highness speaks absurdities. To suggest that the Son of Heaven is incompetent shows incompetence itself. The Son of Heaven commands total respect which is beyond most peoples' understanding.

HAYAKUMO [*slyly*] : Who said otherwise? Who? But I ask: Is the world not suffering miseries because the rains no longer fall?

HARUMICHI [*temporizing*] : It is as Your Highness says, yet droughts of several years duration have been recorded numerous times in the past, without casting doubt on an Emperor's capacity to rule.

HARUKAZE: When snow fell during the sixth month of the year, during the reign of Emperor Temmu,[3] none dared say this act of heaven was the fault of the Emperor.

TOYOHIDE: In the past when inexplicable events occurred, the Great Council of State bore responsibility. Your view is unnecessary.

HAYAKUMO [*haughtily*] : Then tell me, illustrious members of the Great Council of State: How will you appeal to the Gods to bring rain? How will you end your subjects' misery? How? How!

TOYOHIDE [*turns to the prince, unable to suppress his anger*] : Saint Narukami and the scholar Abe Kiyoyuki have been summoned to the palace. No one is more skilled in nature's secrets than Kiyoyuki. When Narukami directs his incantations to the heavens rain will fall, the land will prosper!

HAYAKUMO [*pretending to be overjoyed*] : Ah! Then both seers are in the palace?

TOYOHIDE [*hesitates*] : They are summoned . . . though not yet arrived. [*Knowing they will not come,* HAYAKUMO *smiles. A* MESSENGER *runs onto the hanamichi and respectfully drops to one knee. His dark kimono is tucked up at the thighs for easy movement.*]

MESSENGER [*bowing briskly*] : I beg to report the monk White Cloud, acting as messenger for Saint Narukami, arrived, stated that his master would not come and would not meet your Lordship, rose, and departed, my Lords.

TOYOHIDE [*rising on one knee, surprised*] : What? Saint Narukami . . .

TOYOHIDE, HARUKAZE, and HARUMICHI [*prolonged*] : . . . will not . . . come?

MOTOTSUNE: Dispatch another messenger. At once.

MESSENGER [*bowing*] : Yes, my Lord. [*He hurries off right.*]

HAYAKUMO: Of course, of course. Narukami is no fool. Nothing will persuade him to enter the palace.

TOYOHIDE [*furious*] : How dare you say that?

HAYAKUMO: Do your memories fail you, courtiers? Then listen.

3. Reigned 673–686.

[*Offstage shamisen continues quietly in the background. Eyes flashing,* HAYAKUMO *speaks eloquently.*]

When, at the time Emperor Anjin was conceived as a girl child in his mother's womb, Saint Narukami, through his great Buddhist merit, offered prayers which altered the child's sex to that of a boy, requesting as reward for his miraculous deed that a temple be ordained for him. And in response, what was the Emperor's command?

MOTOTSUNE [*somberly*] : Indeed, the blessing of imperial favor was removed.

TOYOHIDE: Regardless of the merits of Narukami's act, the three thousand priests of Heizan would have pillaged the city in outrage if a temple had been ordained to him. For the country's safety, Narukami's request was denied.

HARUKAZE: Therefore, shortly after, Narukami was informed that any other request at all would be granted.

HAYAKUMO [*contemptuously*] : Promised any desire if he could assure the birth of an imperial prince, he fasted and endured the severest austerities in winter's bitter cold to gain the temple he desired. At last a prince was auspiciously born, but the temple was not built for him. No wonder Narukami raged when you begged him make "any other request at all!" He is stubborn. Nothing will change his hatred. And if he bent his prayers for rain it would not matter, for this drought is an act of heaven, and even the wizardry of Narukami cannot bring Heaven's intercession during the present Emperor's rule! [*Meaningfully.*] Mototsune, there will have to be some way other than offering prayers to eliminate the suffering of the people and their distress!

[*Music ends.*]

MOTOTSUNE: There is Abe Kiyoyuki. He has power to divine the secrets of the earth.

[*They glare at each other. Just then a voice calls out from the end of the hanamichi.*]

RETAINER [*offstage*] : Announcing Abe Kiyoyuki!

TOYOHIDE: Ahh! After long waiting . . .

HARUMICHI and HARUKAZE: . . . Kiyoyuki is here!

[*They look down the hanamichi as stick drum, flute, and bells play* Jo no Mai, *"Slow Dance," and Shamisen play* Tama no Gozen, *"Jewel Princess," announcing the entrance of a princess.* PRINCESS TAEMA *moves slowly to the seven-three position and stops. Over a kimono of pink silk held at the waist by a brilliant red sash, she wears a magnificent court robe of cream and pink silk, embroidered in flower and bird patterns of gold, silver, blue, and red. Her long sleeves almost trail on the floor. Her hair hangs down her back in a thick black strand, and on her head is a three-tiered tiara of silver flowers.* TAKINO, *her chief lady-in-waiting, stands behind her. Her robe is sober blue and black and her hair is done up in matronly fashion. A* MAID *stands respectfully to her rear. She is dressed in a simple kimono of peach-colored silk, fastened with a large slanted bow at the waist. Their makeup is pure white, with eyes lightly marked in black and lips in red. Shamisen continues* Tama no Gozen *in the background.*]

MAID [*looking about disappointed*] : It's not true. Though they call it the Great Inner Mountain, the only scenery around is rooftops.

TAKINO [*severely*] : Don't be silly, child. The palace is the Great Inner Mountain because it lies at the heart of the capital and stands as the pinnacle of all wisdom. Look to the hills west of Kyoto if it's mounds of earth you want to see!

TAEMA [*demurely*] : Although I was not told the reason my master Kiyoyuki is summoned to the palace, I have come willingly.

MAID [*slyly*] : All you can talk about is wanting to meet Lord Toyohide.

TAEMA [*blushing*] : Ahh! Here, here, do not speak rashly.

[*The* MAID *giggles and covers her face.* Jo no Mai *and* Tama no Gozen *music resume.* TAEMA *turns and crosses to the stage followed by her attendants. A* STAGE ASSISTANT *takes their sandals. Carefully arranging the folds of her dress,* TAEMA *kneels at the foot of the stairs.* TAKINO *and the* MAID *kneel behind her, taking care they do not look at the august nobles seated above them. They place their fingertips to the floor and bow respectfully.*]

HARUMICHI [*startled*] : What? It is not Abe Kiyoyuki . . .

HARUKAZE: . . . but Lady Taema?

TAEMA: Yes, Taema of the Clouds, granddaughter of Ōe Koretoki and disciple of Kiyoyuki. I attend you most respectfully in Kiyoyuki's place.

TOYOHIDE: But why?

TAEMA [*feigning surprise*] : Ah, my Lord Toyohide. [*She gives him a lingering glance, then bows coquettishly.*] We have not met for a long time. Some days ago, Master Kiyoyuki vanished from his house. When the imperial summons was received people were dispatched in every direction to find him, but his whereabouts remain unknown. On his behalf I have hurried to the palace.

TOYOHIDE [*frowning*] : Perhaps Kiyoyuki's disappearance portends some heavenly disaster. It is a foreboding sign.

HAYAKUMO: Your Prince understands the sage Kiyoyuki perfectly! Disturbed by the turmoil in the realm, he has retired from the world! [*Fixing her with a fierce gaze.*] So, Taema! Your arrival is most gratifying. I have spoken of my fondness for you and urged you to join my service many times. You always refused. Ha, ha! Do you come to accept my proposal today?

TAEMA [*protesting*] : No, no. I have come to meet Lord Toyo- . . . I mean, I come as Kiyoyuki's disciple.

HARUMICHI [*facing her*] : Lady Taema, he must discover, by power of divination, the reason drought grips the world.

TAEMA [*surprised*] : Eh? My Master? You have summoned him here . . .

TOYOHIDE: . . . yes, to bring rain through his great spiritual powers, Lady Taema.

MOTOTSUNE: From the Emperor down to the lowest subject, all suffer hardship. Lady Taema, you say the seer is gone. Find him, let him cause rain to fall, and you and your descendants shall occupy the highest place of honor at court.

TAEMA [*she gasps, and places a hand to her breast*] : You say the House of Ōe will be restored to honor, if I find Kiyoyuki and he ends this drought? [*She looks about agitated, gazes at* TOYOHIDE, *then bows to* MOTO-TSUNE.] Rather than restoration of our house, grant . . . another heartfelt desire.

MOTOTSUNE [*grandly*] : Speak. Any desire whatsoever shall be granted.

TAEMA [*realizing her temerity, she hesitates*] : Should I then, perhaps, tell you?

MAID [*saucily*] : Tell them, my Lady, what it is you want.

TAKINO: If it shames you, I can speak, my Lady.

TAEMA: No, I will. I will speak.

> [*She gestures for* TAKINO *to remain seated. Shamisen play* Chigusa, *"Blooming Flowers," quietly in the background.*]
> I would be most grateful to receive as my husband, Lord Toyohide, who sits before me.
> [*The three women bow. The nobles react with amazement to* TAEMA's *audacious request.* HARUMICHI *turns coldly to her.*]

HARUMICHI: No! Your love is forbidden! Toyohide is betrothed to Nishiki, my daughter. You cannot be Toyohide's wife, nor he your husband.

TAEMA [*softly, yet undaunted*] : An imperial edict could sanction our marriage, since they are merely engaged.

> [HARUMICHI *is scandalized.* TOYOHIDE *looks away, too embarrassed to speak.*]

MOTOTSUNE: And yet, to bring rain would be an act of rare merit, perhaps justifying . . .

> [TAEMA *looks up expectantly.* HARUMICHI *sees a way to recover the situation and he quickly turns to his son.*]

HARUMICHI: Harukaze, our House possesses the precious poem card of our ancestor, Ono Komachi.[4] If it is immersed in the waters of Shinsen Garden while earnestly praying for rain, whether Kiyoyuki or Saint Narukami are found or not, rain must fall.

> [HARUKAZE *blushes; the poem was entrusted to him, but he no longer has it.*]

HARUKAZE: But, surely, we cannot depend . . .

MOTOTSUNE [*pleased*] : What an excellent idea: Taema will enlist Kiyoyuki's aid and Ono Komachi's poem shall be immersed in the Shinzen Garden pool. Done together, surely rain will fall. All shall be reported to his Majesty the Emperor!

HAYAKUMO [*scathingly*] : Do you think your puny efforts will draw down rain from heaven? Ha! Pray as much as you want, you cannot bring rain!

> [*He looks commandingly at* TAEMA. *She places her fingertips to the ground and bows.*]

---

4. Ono Komachi, a legendary beauty of the Heian court and the subject of several nō plays. She was famous for her cleverness at poetic composition, a good example of which is this prayer for rain, in which the pivotal word *ama*, "heaven," is also a homonym for "rain." The poem on the card goes, "In the Land of the Sun, it is reasonable that the sun shines, yet being under the ama . . . "

Taema, you are not like most women. You would do well to submit to my heart's demands.

TAKINO [*quickly interrupting*] : No, my Prince. Lady Taema will cause magnificent rain. She and Lord Toyohide . . .

HARUMICHI [*interrupting her*] : Toyohide is promised in marriage to the House of Ono. You shall not break your oath, Toyohide!

TOYOHIDE [*glancing covertly at TAEMA*] : That is a private matter. If state duties require it . . .

TAEMA [*looks longingly at TOYOHIDE, then bows*] : Please grant my request.

MOTOTSUNE [*temporizing*] : Hmm. We cannot decide until the rain falls. [*Rapid bata-bata tsuke beats. The curtain left flies open and KANZŌ, an underling of the prince rushes on. He wears a dark padded kimono which reaches to the knee. His face is deep, reddish-brown, indicating his base nature. Kneeling stage left, he bows to HAYAKUMO.*]

KANZŌ [*roughly*] : Prince, I must speak.

HAYAKUMO: Yes?

KANZŌ: The heat has become so fierce farmers are now collapsing with fever. [*The nobles look at one another helplessly. HAYAKUMO smiles contemptuously.*]

HAYAKUMO: Ah, then you see it is as he says. The regime is incompetent. [*Rises and poses. He speaks in a lightly mocking tone.*] Mototsune. Great Lords. Consider this well.

[*A sharp clack of the ki. Large drum, stick drum, flute, bells, and shamisen play* Goten, *"Palace." All move into a tableau: TAEMA rises on her knees and looks at HAYAKUMO; HAYAKUMO glares at TOYOHIDE; TOYO-HIDE edges forward to gaze at TAEMA; the others face front. All pose. Another sharp ki clack signals the stage to revolve. TAEMA and HAYA-KUMO look at each other, then turn sharply away and face front. HAYA-KUMO steps forward and poses with the sickle held over his head. The tableau moves out of sight and the next scene comes into view.*]

SCENE 2   TREE ISLAND SHRINE

[*Kaza Oto drum pattern rises and falls, indicating wind blowing over a desolate scene. The entrance to Tree Island Shrine. All that can be seen in the dim light are heavy stone walls and tall archway of the shrine's outer courtyard to the left, and clumps of shoulder-high grass and a few small pine trees right, marking the open fields surrounding the shrine. A full moon, haloed by clouds, drops into place to two sharp clacks of the ki. A STAGE ASSISTANT changes the sign on the pillar left indicating the scene and hurries off. Offstage shamisen begin playing the plaintive melody* Yachio, *"Eternity." Suddenly loud bata-bata tsuke beats alert us to the hurrying figures of MAMBEI, a farm youth, and his pretty sister, KOISO, slipping furtively out of the shrine grounds. He wears an ordinary country kimono of dark color, pulled up at the sides to show that he is wearing black traveling leggings, and he carries a plain straw hat. She has been a maid in the Ono household. She is dressed in a pale green kimono, the sash of which raises the hem for easier walking. Both wear straw sandals. He leads her forward by the hand. She cradles a small box wrapped in purple cloth to her breast. Frightened, they stop and peer into the windswept fields.]*

KOISO [*agitated*] : I'm sure he was a highwayman. He frightened me so, trying to slip his hand inside my bosom. [*She looks softly at* MAMBEI.] Dear Brother, I know you doubt Lord Harukaze's intentions, but he has given me the Ono family's precious poem card to keep until our child is born.

MAMBEI [*worried*] : It must be valuable. There was such commotion at the shrine just now. And they say the road is dangerous at night. Shall I carry it for you?

KOISO [*folding it to her breast*] : No. No. When we parted, my Lord Harukaze placed it in my hands as a memento of his affection. I shall carry it next to my heart.

[Music stops. Kaza Oto wind pattern swells ominously. A menacing figure steps out of the shadows by the shrine wall dressed in a brown padded kimono and wearing a gangster's black cloth over his head and face. It is SEIHEI, one of HAYAKUMO's men.]

SEIHEI [*harshly*] : Hey! You two! What luck we meet here! [*Poses, insolently, front.*] Eh, girl?

KOISO [*moving behind* MAMBEI *for protection*] : How terrible! That's the man!

[MAMBEI calms her and turns politely to SEIHEI. Seeing a samurai's two swords in the stranger's sash, he bows respectfully.]

MAMBEI: I am the farmer, Mambei, and this is my sister, Koiso. We are respectable people living in Ohara. Please help us, sir.

SEIHEI [*sneering*] : Help you? I'll help myself to the poem card the woman's carrying. I saw you sneaking a look at it in the shrine. It's the Ono Komachi treasure, isn't it?

[Kaza Oto wind pattern swells. Loud batan tsuke beats. He easily pushes MAMBEI aside. He holds out his hand imperiously and poses.]

Hand it over! Wretch!

KOISO [*covering the poem card with her sleeve*] : No, I have nothing like that.

SEIHEI: Give it to me!

KOISO: No thief will ever take it!

[SEIHEI tries to snatch it from her, but she slips out of his grasp. MAMBEI rises and takes her hand.]

MAMBEI: Quickly, Koiso. Run.

[Drum beats swell. They try to escape right, but at that moment KAZUMA, another of HAYAKUMO's men, swaggers on and blocks their path with outstretched arms. He is powerfully built and his coarse nature is evident in his reddish-brown makeup and a head of bushy black hair. Hoping to make himself look important, he wears clothes in shocking colors: brilliant orange and gold outer garment, bright green kimono, purple sash, and yellow socks.]

KAZUMA [*deep, harsh voice*] : Seihei! Well?

SEIHEI [*bows slightly to his superior*] : I was just about to take it.

KAZUMA [*malevolently looks at* MAMBEI *and* KOISO] : Hand it over quietly, or slash them through, Seihei! Slash them through!

tachimawari SEIHEI [*delighted*] : I will! I will!

[*The large drum plays slow, blooming* Midare, *"Agitation," indicating the arrival of an aristocrat. Loud tsuke beats accent the action.* KAZUMA *holds* MAMBEI, *as* SEIBEI *tries to wrest the poem from* KOISO. MAMBEI *breaks loose and hurries to help his sister. Irritated at the delay,* SEIHEI *pulls out his sword and forces the weaponless young man off right. For a time* KOISO *eludes* KAZUMA. *Finally she backs up to a small tree for protection. He forces her against a tree. She pushes him away. Suddenly a sickle flashes out from the tall grass around the tree and impales her in the stomach. A temple bell tolls in the distance. A shamisen plays* Shinobi Sanjū, *"Stealthy Melody": a single note plucked repeatedly, suspensefully, tapering off to silence.* KOISO *screams and struggles but she is held in a viselike grip. Her assailant, dressed in gray robe and hood, slowly emerges from hiding. The bell tolls.* Shinobi Sanjū *begins again. The assailant cruelly twists the sickle in* KOISO's *abdomen. Her scream gradually weakens. She dies and falls to the ground. The bell tolls. The man in gray removes his hood revealing himself as* HAYAKUMO. *The black and blue lines of makeup are stronger than before. He lifts the sickle above his head and poses in a triumphant mie to battari tsuke beats.* KAZUMA *is amazed to see the prince. He kneels respectfully.*]

KAZUMA: Ah, you, my Prince!

HAYAKUMO: Kazuma. Remove the poem card from her breast. Hmm. She's unusually pretty for a village girl.

[Kaza Oto *wind pattern plays softly in the background.* HAYAKUMO *passes sickle, robe, and hood to a* STAGE ASSISTANT. KAZUMA *removes the poem card case from* KOISO's *arms and also finds, to his surprise, a letter in her bosom. He passes the letter to* HAYAKUMO, *who reads it silently, but with evident satisfaction. The letter unfolds until it reaches the floor. Without a word,* HAYAKUMO *folds the letter and returns it to its envelope as* KAZUMA *holds up the poem card for the prince's inspection.* SEIHEI *trots on from the right, carrying a naked sword in one hand and* MAMBEI's *kimono in the other.*]

SEIHEI [*noticing* KOISO] : Ah, good, good! [*He kneels.*] My Prince, I chased that clod, Mambei, and caught him. With one stroke I cut the clothes off his back. To show him what a highwayman's made of, I snatched them up and sent him off naked!

HAYAKUMO [*strongly, facing* SEIHEI] : Ishihara Seihei, I place the poem card and this letter in your care!

[SEIHEI *kneels before* HAYAKUMO *and reverently receives the poem card in its case.* HAYAKUMO *points to the letter and smiles.*]

Using these, we will destroy the proud House of Ono and bring the world under our sway! The issue awaits us! We go to the Ono mansion now!

[SEIHEI *looks blankly at the prince.* HAYAKUMO *points to the letter, to*

MAMBEI's *kimono, to* SEIHEI, *and finally down the hanamichi.* SEIHEI *glances at the kimono he is holding. A look of understanding crosses his face. He nods delightedly and takes the letter.*]

Pass the poem card to Gemba.

SEIHEI: Yes, my Prince.

HAYAKUMO [*significantly*] : As for the letter . . . !

SEIHEI [*smiles broadly, delighted to play a part in* HAYAKUMO's *ruse*] : I will do it, my Lord!

[Kaza Oto *wind pattern swells.*]

HAYAKUMO [*calling toward the shrine*] : Gunnai! Gunnai!

[GUNNAI *leaps onto the stage from the archway stage left. He is a spy, dressed from head to foot in black, a black cloth covering his face as well. He carries a large object under his arm. He darts forward and kneels before the prince.*]

As you were told, take the object you carry to the Ono mansion.

GUNNAI [*bowing briskly*] : I will not fail.

HAYAKUMO [*to* KAZUMA] : It is fortunate you came, Kazuma. Let us visit your father now.

KAZUMA [*facing front*] : We will crush the House of Ono! Then, my father, Yatsurugi Gemba . . .

SEIHEI [*facing front*] : . . . will seize the House as feudal lord!

KAZUMA: The daughter Nishiki will be my wife!

SEIHEI: We owe everything to our Lord, the Prince!

KAZUMA: [*grandiloquently*] : We'll seize the House . . .

SEIHEI and GUNNAI: . . . through a little play!

share HAYAKUMO [*Smiling wickedly*] : Too small, too small! We'll seize the world in a grand masquerade![5] Ha, ha! Ha, ha, ha!

[*A sharp clack of the ki: the black drop falls, the moon disappears, and lights come up full on a scene of green hills and fields. The actors drop out of their roles. A* STAGE ASSISTANT *takes their sandals. They kneel in a row facing the audience.*]

kōjō HAYAKUMO [*deferentially, but with strong projection*] : Honored spectators, east and west. May you take your ease and attend our play with pleasure, we pray!

[*The four actors look out into the audience to the right, to the left, and up to the balcony, then bow very slowly, very low. Stick drum and flute play slow formal Kata Shagiri, "Half Shagiri," curtain music. The audience applauds and shouts approval as the curtain is pulled closed.*]

ACT II

yontateme ONO HARUMICHI MANSION ("WHISKER TWEEZERS" SCENE)

[*Two loud ki clacks. Offstage shamisen play a variation of "Eternity," lively Yachio Kuzushi, while small drum, stick drum, and flute play Haya*

5. The play on words, *hitoshibai* or plot (literally, "one play") and *ōshibai* or great plot (literally, "great play"), would have been especially appreciated by the audience because *shibai* was the usual word for a kabuki play or performance.

Mai, *"Quick Dance," from the nō theater. Ki clacks accelerate as the
curtain is quickly pushed open. The sign right reads "Ono Harumichi
Mansion Scene" and one left, "Whisker Tweezers Scene." The main room
of HARUMICHI's magnificent residence in Kyoto, raised off the ground,
faces an open garden. A small pine tree and low gate are right. Lowered
blinds cover the interior of the room. KAZUMA and HIDETARŌ, young
brother of HATA MIMBU, an Ono retainer, stand in the garden with their
swords drawn. HIDETARŌ is a delicate boy of twelve or thirteen. He wears
a pale blue kimono and darker divided skirt. Two sharp ki clacks signal
action to begin. They break the tableau and fight to alternating batan and
battari tsuke beats. They cross swords above and below. They pose in a
mie to battari tsuke beats. They strike simultaneously and pass, turn back,
and cross swords in a mie. KAZUMA forces HIDETARŌ to the ground and
is about to strike, when MAKIGINU, chief lady-in-waiting of the Ono
family, sweeps on from the left. She wears a conservative black kimono
and her hair is done up over her head. She kneels and forces the two men
apart with a commanding gesture. The three pose in a group mie to
battari tsuke beats. Through the following dialogue they hold the tableau:
KAZUMA, sword held over his head; HIDETARŌ, kneeling with sword
held back protectively; MAKIGINU, arms outstretched. Shamisen
continue* Yachio Kuzushi *in the background.*]

MAKIGINU [*disapprovingly, as if to two small boys*] : Here, here now, stop
this instant.

HIDETARŌ [*earnestly, in a child's voice*] : Lady Makiginu, please let me go.

KAZUMA [*harshly*] : Move out of the way! You'll be hurt!

MAKIGINU: Can your enmity be so deep you will not stop until I am
wounded? Tell me the reason, both of you.

KAZUMA: It was like this: in the middle of archery practice, Hidetarō burst
out laughing and said no matter how much I strove for excellence, "the
warped moral character of your father, Gemba, makes your striving
useless!"

HIDETARŌ: Everyone in the clan knows Gemba is wicked. Under his warping
influence no arrow of yours will fly straight. You insult my elder brother,
who is the most loyal Ono retainer. You call him a coward. You say he has
lost our House's most precious heirloom. And you would steal the Princess!
I won't allow it! Draw your sword and fight me! Fight me!

MAKIGINU: It shows little consideration for your lord to be dueling over a
personal matter. You shall not. You shall not!
[*They all pose. Music stops.*]

GEMBA [*from inside an anteroom left*] : You shall not stop them, Makiginu.
Kazuma, cut down the traitor's little brother. Cut him down.
[*Sliding doors open and* GEMBA, *elder adviser to the House of Ono, steps
out into the garden. He wears magnificent gold embroidered outer garments
over a lustrous tan kimono. His reddish-brown makeup indicates his evil
disposition. A short sword is thrust in his sash, he carries the long sword in
his left hand. He stops center.* MAKIGINU *hesitates, then kneels respectfully before him. At the same time,* HATA MIMBU *enters the garden*

unseen from the right. His light kimono and outer garments and white makeup indicate his virtuous character. He stands by the gate listening.]

MAKIGINU: My noble Gemba, are you urging them to fight?

[*Shamisen music resumes.*]

GEMBA: I am justified to say to my son "slay him." The elder brother, Mimbu, entrusted with protection of the House of Ono's precious rain-making poem, is negligent in searching for it, but the blockhead hasn't the stomach to disembowel himself! So, let Hidetarō die in his place!

[GEMBA *nods decisively to* KAZUMA, *but before anyone can move,* MIMBU *hurries in through the gate. A* STAGE ASSISTANT *removes his sandals. He holds a long sword ready to draw.*]

MIMBU [*firmly but politely*] : No. An inch of fault in one's self becomes a foot in another. We should set aside our mutual feelings of enmity. I devote myself loyally, night and day, to seeking out the criminal. What proof have you, to call Mimbu a cowardly samurai?

GEMBA [*snarling*] : The proof is our house's treasure is lost! It was entrusted to you and you allowed it to be stolen! The offense is yours, Mimbu! Loyalty commands you to disembowel yourself! Why shouldn't you be called a coward of a samurai?

kuriage

MIMBU [*ashamed*] : Well . . .

GEMBA: Slice your belly splendidly! Well . . . ?

MIMBU and GEMBA [*alternately, then in unison*] : Well, well, well, well! Well!

[*They face each other, strain forward, and are about to draw.*]

HARUMICHI [*inside the blinds*] : Wait, both of you. The court's problem will not be solved by Mimbu's committing self-immolation.

[*The blinds are rolled up to show* HARUMICHI *seated in the center of a magnificent reception room. Blossoming cherry trees and a misty landscape are painted on the rear wall. A striped silk curtain hangs to the floor before an archway in the center of the room.* HARUKAZE *sits to his father's right and a* SWORDBEARER *to the rear. Everyone on the main stage kneels and bows respectfully, except* GEMBA.]

GEMBA [*laughs rudely*] : Ha, ha! Are you getting senile, my Great Lord? The Emperor speaks but once: he has said he will inspect the poem card today. Do you expect him to countermand his own order?

HARUKAZE [*lips trembling*] : You may not kill yourself, Mimbu. It is for Harukaze to beg forgiveness of His Majesty! "Namu Amida Butsu! Namu Amida Butsu!"

[*He rises on his knees and is about to draw his short sword to disembowel himself.* MIMBU *gestures for him to stop.*]

HARUMICHI [*sternly*] : Be calm. Your deaths will mean nothing. Until the poem card is discovered, it is rash indeed to abandon the prospect of long life.

MIMBU and HARUKAZE [*contritely bowing*] : Yes, my Lord.

HARUKAZE: I shall follow your advice with all my heart. [*Looking at* MIMBU.] We will seek out the poem card immediately!

HARUMICHI: Can you do it?

MIMBU [*strongly*] : If the time comes that we fail, my young Lord and I stand
ready to die by the other's sword!

GEMBA [*vastly amused*] : Do you think sandals made of iron can be found,
though you search ten-thousand places in the Nine Mountains and the
Nine Seas? Fools! Ha, ha, ha, ha!

[*A call is heard from the rear of the hanamichi.*]

VOICE [*off*] : Announcing the envoy of Lord Toyohide of Bun'ya.

GEMBA [*frowning*] : What? An envoy from Toyohide? I don't understand.

HARUMICHI [*loftily*] : I await His Majesty's command to see the poem card.
Therefore, you shall greet this messenger from Lord Toyohide.

[*He nods slightly to* GEMBA *and* MIMBU. *They bow deeply.*]

GEMBA and MIMBU: Yes, my Lord.

[*Shamisen play quiet, slow* Yachio Kuzushi. *The blinds are lowered.*
KAZUMA *looks at* MIMBU, *laughs, and struts off left.* MAKIGINU *and*
HIDETARŌ *follow quietly. Music stops.* GEMBA *and* MIMBU *are alone.
They kneel by the gate, looking expectantly down the hanamichi.*]

VOICE [*off*] : Receive the envoy!

[*Shamisen play brilliant* Momo no Ki, *"Peach Tree," and small drums play
spirited* Daishō, *"Large and Small Drum." The curtain at the end of the
hanamichi flies open.* KUMEDERA DANJŌ *strides directly to the seven-
three position.* DANJŌ *is only a middle-ranking samurai, but he is ex-
travagantly dressed. His multilayered white silk kimonos, piped in pale
blue, are covered by stiff vest and split trousers richly embroidered in gold,
green, and black patterns. The voluminous costume and its vivid colors,
the reddish tinge to his otherwise white makeup, and two oversize swords
thrust in his sash convey an impression of boldness and strength.* DANJŌ
stands facing the audience, feet planted wide apart. Two RETAINERS
and two FOOTMEN *kneel behind him.*]

DANJŌ [*in a powerful, commanding voice*] : Enter and say, "Toyohide's
vassal, Kumedera Danjō, waits to present a request from his master."

RETAINER [*briskly*] : I shall, Sir.

[*He crosses on stage and stands before the gate. Music tapers off.*]
A request, my Lords!

MIMBU: Inform the envoy he may approach and state his business.

RETAINER [*facing* DANJŌ] : Enter, Sir.

DANJŌ: Follow me!

[*Entrance music resumes.* DANJŌ *is followed onto the stage by his small
retinue.* DANJŌ *stands unconcerned outside the gate, his hands tucked
casually inside the sleeves of his kimono. Shamisen continue* Momo no Ki
in the background as elaborate greetings are exchanged.]

MIMBU [*bowing*] : Ah, noble Danjō, it seems an eternity since we have had the
pleasure of last meeting. how distressing that you have been inconvenienced
by your journey as envoy today.

GEMBA [*cautiously*] : Indeed, it is noble Kumedera Danjō, as announced. I am

Yatsurugi Gemba, vassal to Minister Ono Harumichi, and of no importance whatsoever. Still, it is my fondest wish that we become intimates in the future.

DANJŌ [*easily*] : Well, well, so it's honorable Gemba, is it? By chance we haven't met before, but now we should be inseparable. I hope we'll become such friends, gold couldn't pry us apart!

GEMBA: These are grand greetings. [*Broadly gesturing.*] You may enter!

DANJŌ: Then I will!

[*Entrance music resumes. A* STAGE ASSISTANT *takes* DANJŌ's *sandals as he passes through the gate, and another places a low stool on the main stage left on which he sits. He rests a closed fan on his knee in studied nonchalance. His four attendants kneel behind him.* GEMBA *and* MIMBU *bow respectfully from a distance to the right. Two* STAGE ASSISTANTS *carry off the gate, as there is no further use for it. Shamisen continue* Momo no Ki *quietly in the background.*]

GEMBA [*grandly*] : And now, Danjō, I will listen to your message.

DANJŌ: Though uninvited, I am entrusted with this message from my Lord Toyohide: he wants to know about the strange illness that has struck Princess Nishiki so soon after his Imperial Lord Harumichi generously promised her in marriage to my Master. The purpose of my visit is to meet Lord Harumichi, learn from him in detail the nature of the sickness, return, and report the situation in full to my Lord.

[MIMBU, *who has been bowing respectfully, looks up.*]

MIMBU: We appreciate the purpose of your visit. We shall all rejoice when the princess is completely recovered from illness and the wedding celebrated.

GEMBA [*laughs roughly*] : Ha, ha! Why, Mimbu, you can turn this world upside down into the next and still the Princess won't recover! [*Looks at* DANJŌ *haughtily.*] You don't need to see Lord Harumichi. I can answer you soon enough: go back and tell your Master to forget the wedding which can't be, divorce her, and turn his thoughts to other things.

[DANJŌ *is angered. He stirs, then controls himself.* GEMBA *looks at him hopefully.*]

Ah, has it been wearisome for you, messenger? I know. Now you're going home. Please do, if you want. Go. Ha, ha! Go!

MIMBU [*shocked*] : Gemba, be quiet. You go too far when you say he may not meet our Lord and when you urge him to leave.

GEMBA [*swelling with pride*] : Though Lord Harumichi give his assent, though the Sun Goddess[6] show her approval, not even a chopstick may fall if Chief Retainer Gemba, of the House of Ono, shakes his head no!

MIMBU: Braggart! As long as Mimbu serves the House of Ono, we will see this wedding celebrated.

DANJŌ: Restrain yourself, Gemba. Surely you have a reason for suggesting divorce. What is it?

---

6. Amaterasu Ōmikami, Great Heavenly Bright Diety, chief among Shintō dieties and legendary ancestor of the Japanese emperors.

GEMBA [*leering*] : What would I hide? Your Princess cannot mingle in
human society!

DANJŌ: Hmm. No matter how strange or terrible her malady, divorce is out
of the question. I can't agree with your opinion. Forgive me for saying so,
but I shall see the Princess myself.

MIMBU [*very distressed*] : Of course, what you say is correct, yet she is
ashamed to meet people because of her illness.

GEMBA: Ridiculous! We will do as the messenger asks! [*Craftily, to* DANJŌ.]
It's best to pay cash: see her yourself and decide on the spot. [*Calls off.*]
Makiginu! Makiginu! Bring out the Princess!

WOMEN [*inside the blind*] : We shall.

NISHIKI [*faintly, from inside the blind*] : No, please, no. I do not wish to.
[*Shamisen play* Takara no Saku, *"Blossoming Treasure," and flute, drum,
and bells play* Midare *as the blind is raised.* PRINCESS NISHIKI *kneels in
the center of the room, dressed in a bright red "Scarlet Princess" kimono.
A thin cloth covers her head, half-hiding her lovely, delicate features.*
MAKIGINU *kneels to her right. Six women* ATTENDANTS, *dressed in
simple blue kimonos, kneel behind her in an arc. On the main stage*
DANJŌ, GEMBA, *and* MIMBU *bow.*]

DANJŌ: Ah, Princess Nishiki. I am Lord Bun'ya Toyohide's retainer, Kumedera
Danjō. I have come to the palace today, because the wedding has been
delayed so long our whole clan awaits anxiously. [*Jovially.*] I mean, more
than the whole clan, my Master is the one who waits anxiously, my Lady.
And I think the Princess, too, waits longingly for that day! Ha, ha!
[NISHIKI *raises her head to look at* DANJŌ. *She holds one hand at her
breast, the other at shoulder height, both modestly hidden inside their
sleeves.*]

NISHIKI [*faintly*] : Please listen, Danjō.
[*Shamisen resume* Takara no Saku *quietly in the background.*]
No woman was more fortunate than I, promised to the most attractive man
in the world, Bun'ya Toyohide, when this malignant disease crushed my
pride.

GEMBA: Since you're ill, become a nun! Wear black clothes and pray for a
better life in the future!

NISHIKI [*feebly protests*] : Gemba, how can you say that? When a woman is
unable to sleep with the man she adores, what future should she pray for?
No, I shall become no dreary nun.

DANJŌ: What you say is undoubtedly true, but still I've learned nothing of
your illness and I'm no nearer to an answer.

GEMBA [*delighted*] : That's right, that's right! See her disease with your own
eyes!

MAKIGINU [*protesting*] : But, my Lord . . .

GEMBA [*maliciously*] : Hah! I'll take off the robe!
[*The big drum rumbles* Doro-doro, *"Drum Roll," as* GEMBA *crosses into
the room and pushes* MAKIGINU *out of the way. He snatches off the robe
covering the Princess' head. A* STAGE ASSISTANT *holds a swatch of long*

hair over her head: it appears as if her hair is streaming upward in the air. They all react with amazement. The women ad-lib, "How terrible," "Poor Princess," "Look, again." NISHIKI covers her face and sobs.]

NISHIKI: Ahh! Quickly, I implore you, cover my shame.

[MIMBU *rushes into the room and takes the robe from* GEMBA.]

MIMBU: Be quiet, women! Pray as I recite the magic incantation Saint Narukami mercifully taught. Come! Come!

[*The women take out Buddhist rosaries which they fold in their hands.* MIMBU *holds the robe in the air over* NISHIKI's *head. Drum roll* Doro-doro *swells.*]

"Onabokia, onabokia, beirosha no makabodara, haraharitaya, sowaka, sowaka!"[7]

[NISHIKI's *hair subsides, and* MIMBU *covers her head with the robe.* Doro-doro *subsides. The Princess sobs pathetically.* GEMBA *and* MIMBU *return to their places.*]

GEMBA [*gloating*]: Well? What did you see? Was it strange? Was it frightening? The reason the Princess cannot mix in human society is this unheard-of affliction!

DANJŌ: [*places both hands on the hilt of his fan, thinking*]: This is remarkable. And does her hair not stand on end when the robe is placed over her head?

MIMBU: It does not. A charm, inscribed with the Incantation of Light and presented by Saint Narukami, was sewn into a thin robe giving it power, as you saw, to suppress the malady.[8] It is a blessing of the Gods and Buddhas.

DANJŌ: Hmm. I ask you all to arrange an audience with your Lord Harumichi. Will you convey my request?

[*He bows, as a matter of formality, to the higher ranking* GEMBA.]

MIMBU: It will be done. Please rest while your message is conveyed to our Lord.

GEMBA [*officiously*]: Makiginu! Accompany the Princess to the inner room!

NISHIKI [*pathetically*]: I am mortified to have my infirmity seen. How can I live? I wish to die.

MAKIGINU: Let us retire, my Princess . . .

WOMEN: . . . please.

[*Shamisen play* Takara no Saku, *and stick drum and flute play* Midare. MAKIGINU *comforts* NISHIKI *as the blind falls.* GEMBA *rises, looks haughtily at* DANJŌ, *and swaggers off left.* MIMBU *follows, crestfallen.* DANJŌ's *attendants bow and go off right, leaving him alone. Picking up his long sword, he crosses center, musing aloud about this strange affair. Shamisen continue* Takara no Saku *quietly in the background.*]

DANJŌ: A baffling illness. Sufficiency or insufficiency of blood determines many qualities of the hair, but a case of hair standing on end can't be

---

7. An incantation (*darani*) of the Shingon sect of esoteric Buddhism; used to cure illness.

8. The Kōmyō Shingon *darani*, literally, Light of the World, just recited, is written on the charm.

found even in the Rare Disease section of the Medical Encyclopedia! Hah! There's something strange about this.

[*He sits casually center, bored with waiting. Shamisen play* Nanakusa, *"Seven Flowers," and stick drum, small drums, and flute play* Shirabe, *"Entrance Tune." From the right* HIDETARŌ *brings on a tobacco tray. He places it before* DANJŌ *and bows. Shamisen continue quietly.*]

HIDETARŌ [*eyes modestly cast down, in a sweet voice*] : We have troubled you, honored envoy. I am Mimbu's younger brother Hidetarō. My brother believes you must be tired from your journey. While you are waiting to be announced in audience to our Lord Harumichi, please rest comfortably. I would be honored to attend your desires.

DANJŌ: My, how nicely you speak.

[*He looks closely and is delighted at* HIDETARŌ's *beauty. His eyes sparkle with anticipation.*]

So you are Mimbu's little brother? A good-looking boy like you will have a good future. Ha, ha! Tell me, do you practice archery and ride horses?

HIDETARŌ [*modestly, not looking up*] : I am studying archery of the Nasu school, but have not yet learned to ride.

DANJŌ [*feigning surprise*] : What? Not ride? A serious oversight in training.

[*Edging close, smiles broadly.*] Shall I instruct you?

HIDETARŌ [*flattered and flustered*] : Oh, sir, it would be an honor to submit to your guidance.

DANJŌ [*waving* HIDETARŌ *closer*] : Come closer! It will come easily with the right guidance, though there are bound to be one or two hard points along the way. Ha, ha! Most important are the hands and how skillfully they hold in their palms . . . the bridle!

[*Sliding up behind* HIDETARŌ, *he takes a hand and fondles it.*]

Here, here. I will teach you how to use your hands. Ahh, ahh! How soft your hand is.

[*He squeezes it and reaches around behind* HIDETARŌ *to grasp the other hand.*]

Now! Shall I teach you my secret art? Do you understand? Do you understand?

HIDETARŌ [*tremulously, he snuggles closer*] : Yes. Yes. Your secret art, sir.

DANJŌ: Press tightly against the flanks of your mount, thus . . .

[DANJŌ *squeezes* HIDETARŌ *between his thighs.*]

. . . firmly grasp the reins, thus . . .

[*He deliberately folds the boy in both arms and rocks him back and forth.*]

. . . and with your lips impart the secret art!

[*He leans his cheek against* HIDETARŌ's. HIDETARŌ *becomes frightened. He pulls free.*]

HIDETARŌ: You are perverted, sir!

[*He pushes* DANJŌ, *who falls, laughing good-naturedly, to the floor. Music resumes as* HIDETARŌ *tosses his head and runs off left. Music ends.*]

DANJŌ: He's a stiff-necked youngster! Ha, ha, ha, ha!

[*He looks directly at the audience and bows to them facetiously.*]

Shameful! Shameful, isn't it friends! Ha, ha! Waiting for an answer is a bore.

[*Shamisen play* Musume Nanakusa, *"Maid of Seven Flowers," in the background. A* STAGE ASSISTANT, *formally dressed in black kimono and rust-colored outer garments, hands* DANJŌ *a pair of tweezers, perhaps six inches long, with which he begins to pull whiskers from his chin, an act of masculine bravado.*]

Can't understand how her hair stands on end like that. The robe is slipped off and . . . *doro-doro-doro* . . . for the life of me I can't understand it.

[MAKIGINU *brings on a lacquered tea cup, places it beside* DANJŌ, *and bows politely.*]

MAKIGINU: Surely you are fatigued, good Danjō. Some time ago, the Princess herself set aside for you some Virgin Spring tea, and now she asks if you would like to taste it.[9] She makes it with her own hands and a single drop is delectable. It is my duty to offer you some.

[DANJŌ *slaps the tweezers down and turns to look her over appreciatively. Interpreting her words as a sexual invitation, he moves on his knees quickly to her side.*]

DANJŌ [*broadly*] : Well now that sounds like something to warm a man's heart. [*He seizes her hand and caresses it.*] Why, you know I'd be honored to take a sip of the Princess' royal tea, but at the moment I'd rather try a sip of yours, my dear.

[*He embraces her delightedly. She struggles to pull away.*]

MAKIGINU: I won't allow you to flirt, Sir. Here. Drink, I pray, from the Princess' cup.

share

DANJŌ [*salaciously*] : Ah, yes, but in a mere drop of her tea, my vital tea stalk can't stand on end![10] What I desire is a good swallow of your tea.

[*As he did with* HIDETARŌ, *he embraces her from behind. He tries to fondle her.*]

Tell me, is your tea brush still Virgin Spring? Hmm? Is it? Virgin Spring?

[*She breaks free and pushes him over.*]

MAKIGINU: How terrible you are! I'm a proper woman. I don't know what you're talking about. Hmph!

[*He laughs heartily. She makes a face at him, stamps, and flounces out. He sits up and looks at the audience.*]

DANJŌ: Ha, ha! That's two cups of tea I've been denied!

[*Cries from the audience,* "Don't give up," "Keep trying."]

Well then, I might as well drink this.

[DANJŌ *turns to the cup and drinks. As he does, a* STAGE ASSISTANT *substitutes a huge pair of tweezers for the smaller pair. It is fastened to*

9. *Hatsumukashi*, a select brand of tea (see Keene, *Chikamatsu*, p. 278) and hence something valuable here, means virginity. But also, in the slang of Kyoto's Shimabara licensed quarter, to have "tea" was to make love to a prostitute. We find in poems of the "Paradise Collection" (*Tōgenshū*, 1655), "The tea was delectable, incomparable," and "Though it was our first meeting, I had as much tea as I wanted."

10. When telling fortunes a piece of stem or stalk floating vertically in a cup of tea is a sign of good luck.

the end of a pole. The large drum beats Doro-doro: *the tweezers rise and hover in the air.* DANJŌ *rises on one knee, stamps, holds his long sword in the left hand, glares fixedly at the floating tweezers, and poses in a mie to battari tsuke beats.*]

What's this? The tweezers float in air?

[*Large drum, flute, and shamisen play ethereal-sounding* Kangen, *based on gagaku court music.* DANJŌ *presses the tweezers to the floor with his closed fan. Released, the tweezers again bounce and float in the air a few feet off the ground as* Doro-doro *swells.* DANJŌ *glares and poses in a mie to battari tsuke beats.*]

Released, they rise! A phenomenon!

[*The following movements and gestures are deliberately exaggerated for comic effect.* DANJŌ *has an idea. With a flourish, he takes the large silver pipe from the tobacco tray and slaps it on the floor. So that he can watch it carefully, he throws himself prone, rests his elbows on the floor, and with open palms mimes holding up his head. He crosses his eyes and poses in a powerful mie, glaring at the pipe a few inches away. It doesn't move. He kneels and takes a small dagger from the hilt of his long sword. When he places it on the floor, another dagger on the end of a long pole is immediately substituted for it: manipulated by a second* STAGE ASSIS-TANT, *dressed in formal kimono and outer garments, the substitute dagger rises and floats in the air.* Doro-doro *crescendoes.* DANJŌ *is amazed. Trying to understand what is happening, he steadies himself by pressing the pipe to the ground and looks first at the tweezers on his right and then the dagger on his left as they float gently in the air. Again, he crosses his eyes and poses in a powerful mie to battari tsuke beats. He nods in understanding and suddenly flips over onto his seat, leans on his arms with his back to the audience, and peers up inspecting the ceiling. In this position, he poses in a mie to battari tsuke beats. Shamisen play* Tentsutsu, "Hurried Entrance." *An uproar is heard off the hanamichi.* SEIHEI, *impersonating* MAMBEI, *forces his way past two protesting* SAMURAI.]

SEIHEI: Get out of my way, let me through!

FIRST SAMURAI: Wait, wait!

SECOND SAMURAI: Ruffian! You can't go in here!

DANJŌ [*heartily*] : Well, well. Isn't this the strangest house!

    [STAGE ASSISTANTS *clear away tweezers, dagger, and smoking tray. The actor playing* DANJŌ *drinks quietly from a hot cup of tea which a* STAGE ASSISTANT *unobtrusively brings out. In the meantime,* SEIHEI *is stopped at seven-three by the* SAMURAI. *He is wearing* MAMBEI's *clothes and carries, hooked onto a hoe which is slung over his shoulder, a small bundle and a teapot.*]

SEIHEI: I'm not a man to be stopped, no matter how many samurai try to stop me! Out of my way! [*He forces his way past the* SAMURAI *and swaggers onstage.*] I am Ohara Mambei, elder brother of Koiso who served this house. I have business with Lord Harukaze! Where is he? Why doesn't he come out?

[MIMBU *and* GEMBA *rush on from the left.* MIMBU *is scandalized by* SEIHEI's *behavior.* GEMBA *stands in the background, smiling and watching.*]

MIMBU: If you are Koiso's brother, you should behave as expected of a retainer of the House of Ono. You are impudent! Take him away!

FIRST SAMURAI: Come!

[SAMURAI *approach and are about to force* SEIHEI *off, when* HARU-KAZE's *voice is heard from inside the blind.*]

HARUKAZE [*quietly*] : Samurai, do not molest him.

[*The blind is rolled up to show* HARUKAZE *standing alone, with a worried expression on his face.*]

I wish to meet and converse with this man if he is Koiso's brother. You may leave, samurai.

[*The* SAMURAI *bows and goes off right.* SEIHEI *puts the hoe down with a flourish and stands center, arms defiantly folded across his chest.* HARUKAZE *sits, unsure how to proceed. Music ends.*]

Tell me, is Koiso well?

SEIHEI [*insolently*] : Hah! Harukaze here asks how she is! You damned murderer!

HARUKAZE: I? A murderer?

SEIHEI [*faking sadness*] : My dear sister Koiso . . . is dead!

HARUKAZE [*blanches*] : Koiso? How did it happen?

SEIHEI [*sneering*] : How did she happen to die? She was murdered . . . by you!

[*He stamps and poses.* HARUKAZE, MIMBU, *and* GEMBA *react with shock.* DANJŌ *sits quietly, hands folded over the hilt of his closed fan, so absorbed in thought he seems unaware of what is being said. Shamisen begin melancholy* Seki no Koman, *"Woman of the Barrier," in the background, to set the mood for* SEIHEI's *tale.* SEIHEI *pretends to cry. He controls himself and sits deliberately in the center of the stage, with the hoe beside him.*]

Listen and understand. You, "Lord" Harukaze, brought my sister into your house as a chambermaid for a salary of one and a half gold pieces a year.[11] She didn't go as your concubine. This Mambei isn't the kind that sells off his sister to some damned noble, hoping she'll be taken to bed so he can end his days loafing around like a cow in a mansion—like the one at Kotsushinchi that's as big as a racetrack—bought with buckets of cash he's milked from her.[12] Why did you make love to my innocent sister? Why did you gobble up her virtue on the sly? [*Shouting.*] Why? Why!

HARUKAZE [*flustered*] : Please, You are shouting. People will hear.

SEIHEI: Cats hear me. People hear me. I say what I have to say!

[SEIHEI *hits the ground with the palm of his hand and strikes a bravura pose.*]

11. About fifty dollars.
12. Undoubtedly referring to the teahouse "as big as a racetrack" that a noble's new concubine had purchased for her family in Kotsushinchi, Osaka, in 1739, three years prior to the play. It is an example of how contemporary events were worked into even the history portions of kabuki plays.

MIMBU [*trying to protect his master*] : Ruffian! You don't know what you're talking about. Take this fellow away, samurai!

GEMBA [*moving forward*] : Now here's a man. Mambei, you say what is hard to say. Speak frankly, don't be shy.

SEIHEI [*with exaggerated pathos*] : Ahh! You, Sir, are a good man. Pitiful little sister, it wasn't long before her belly puffed out.

[*He wipes away a tear and mimes a huge stomach. He takes out a folded letter from his kimono breast.*]

And then you sent a letter of dismissal from her post. Poor, dear sister, what could I do? I cared for you the best I could, but . . . was it your karma? [*He pretends to be so overcome he can't continue.*] Then, ah then, you suffered in labor terribly. You died writhing in agony. Ahh! When I think of it, when I think of it! Wah! Wah!

[*Music stops. He rises on his knees and pretends to cry. Since no tears come, he covertly pours tea on his hands and daubs his eyes. Almost smiling at his cleverness, he turns to the others, points to his dripping face, and wails loudly.*]

Wah! Wah! Wah!

[HARUKAZE *is too embarrassed to speak.* MIMBU *is innocently moved; he wipes away a tear.* GEMBA *feigns outrage.*]

GEMBA: What? Why that's just as if Lord Harukaze murdered her!

SEIHEI: Wah! Give me back my sister!

[*In a great show of grief, he weeps and at the same time holds out his hand as if expecting to have her returned.* HARUKAZE *blinks helplessly.*]

HARUKAZE: But . . . I . . .

MIMBU [*naively, amazed*] : Return your dead sister?

GEMBA [*ponderously*] : A most reasonable consideration.

[SEIHEI *drops his sad pose and turns belligerent again. He takes the bundle from the hoe and starts to unwrap it.*]

SEIHEI: Until my sister is returned, I'll hang on here and wait. I brought a soldier's rations and I'll use them!

[*To their astonishment, he opens a lunchbox of rice and other food. He picks up a pair of chopsticks and insolently begins eating.*]

MIMBU: In that case, I appeal to your reason.

[*He drops to one knee beside* SEIHEI *and takes out a packet of wrapped coins which he places on the floor.*]

On behalf of our young master, accept this small token of consideration. Use it to offer prayers which will lead your sister along Buddha's way in the afterlife. Please accept these two hundred ryō and leave.[13]

SEIHEI: What? Mambei is a man! Offer a hundred, two hundred, times this cheesy bit of cash, what do you take me for? [*He kicks the coins back to* MIMBU.] Return my sister!

[DANJŌ *casually puts down the pipe he has been smoking, pushes aside the tobacco tray, and turns to the others.*]

DANJŌ: Well, well, Mimbu, from what I can hear, you're in great trouble.

13. Between six and nine thousand dollars.

Shall I look into this for you?

MIMBU [*with obvious relief*] : We accept your advice gratefully. Please do so.

GEMBA [*snarling*] : And if you clumsily bite off more than you can chew, then what? Hah! We don't need your help!

DANJŌ [*chuckles*] : Why, I can do this more easily than my hand can touch my head.

[*Shamisen begin* Rokudan, *"Six Part Melody."* DANJŌ *picks up his long sword and crosses to* SEIHEI. *He kneels casually beside him.* SEIHEI *stops eating and glances apprehensively at* DANJŌ.]

Mambei. You're a rowdy fellow whose rudeness to those present is unforgivable, but, if as you say your sister's death is the cause of your distraction, out of consideration for this fact I will try to overlook your behavior. Now then, Mambei. Once your sister is returned, you will have no reason for complaint. Is that right? Good. Then your sister will be returned to you . . . now.

SEIHEI [*derisively*] : Hah! I'll take her! Give her back . . . here and now!

[SEIHEI *holds out his hand as if to receive* KOISO. *Music ends.*]

DANJŌ: Of course, someone has to get her. I know it's troublesome, but will you bring her back, Mambei?

SEIHEI [*flabbergasted*] : As long as Sister is returned . . .

DANJŌ [*smiling broadly*] : . . . you'll go? For your sister?

SEIHEI [*weakly*] : Heh, heh! I'll . . . go.

[*Shamisen resume* Rokudan. DANJŌ *holds out his hand nonchalantly. A* STAGE ASSISTANT *passes him a small writing table on the top of which are pen, ink, and writing paper. Unconcerned,* DANJŌ *picks up the pen and writes.*]

MIMBU: Danjō! How in heaven's name do you expect to bring back Koiso, who has departed from this world?

GEMBA: Ha, ha! I can hardly wait to hear your messenger's pearls of wisdom!

[DANJŌ *passes the completed letter to* SEIHEI *without deigning to look at him. Music fades to silence.*]

DANJŌ [*easily*] : Now your sister will return. Because she died in childbirth, she waits for you in hell's Lake of Blood.[14] Here, Mambei. Read this.

[*No one knows what the letter means.* SEIHEI *and* GEMBA *exchange worried glances.* HARUKAZE *looks at* MIMBU, *who shakes his head that he doesn't understand.*]

SEIHEI [*reading*] : "Following is an oral message: first, that the said person of Koiso, sister to Mambei of Ohara, is urgently required on earth; second, that in consideration of this fact she be allowed to return to the Land of the Living together with the bearer of this letter. Respectfully addressed to his Exalted Majesty Emma, ruler of Hades. Signed: Kumedera Danjō."

[*Looks up terrified. He cries out in despair.*] What in hell is this!

DANJŌ [*breezily, enjoying himself*] : What does it look like? If you go for your sister carrying this letter, you'll have her back in the Land of the

14. In popular Buddhism a woman who died in childbirth followed "the way of blood" after death that included dwelling in a Lake of Blood, one of the stages of hell.

Living in a jiffy. [*Confidentially.*] King Emma of Hades and I are as close as brothers. Just this past spring we had a chat by Amida Buddha Lake.[15] You know, Emma's aged a lot these last few years. So you set off like a good courier and bring back your sister. Quick. On your way.

SEIHEI [*falls back, terrified*] : Ehhh?

DANJŌ [*threatening quietly*] : A brother's love like yours is so rare in the world, my heart was touched. When you see Emma, ask him, "Are you well, these days?" And tell him Kumedera Danjō has never felt better! [*Rises on one knee and roars at* SEIHEI.] Well? Are you going? Will you take this message? Will you go to hell!

[SEIHEI *rises shakily to his feet. He and* GEMBA *exchange glances and pose. He licks his lips, trembling from head to foot. He grins sheepishly at* DANJŌ.]

SEIHEI: Heh, heh. It isn't that I don't want to go. I do, but even a little temple sightseeing in Kyoto or Osaka requires an auspicious day. If I'm going all the way to visit the dead in hades, I have to turn my sandals inside out. [*Comically, he points to his feet.*] I have to sew up a new rosary bag. [*He takes the cloth from around his head and mimes sewing it.*] I have to get white mourning clothes. [*He drapes the cloth over his arm.*] There's this and there's that, and I don't know what all that first has to be done. I . . . I . . . [*He breaks down and wails in terror.*] I'm going home!

[SEIHEI *rises and begins to edge away.*]

DANJŌ [*commandingly*] : Wait! Wait!!

[SEIHEI *bolts for safety.* DANJŌ *flicks a dirk, which strikes* SEIHEI *in the throat. He screams hoarsely and, clutching the dagger in his neck, falls dead.* GEMBA *rises, furious.*]

GEMBA: Danjō! Why did you kill Mambei? You have no right to act without permission here! Your conduct is beyond understanding! Would you destroy the House of Ono? [*He puts his hand on the hilt of his sword and leans forward glaring.*] Well, Danjō? Answer me! Answer me!

DANJŌ [*heartily*] : Ha, ha, ha, ha! "Who needs ask why the cat burglar sleeps in the day time?" [*Suddenly stern.*] That rogue isn't Mambei.

HARUKAZE and MIMBU: Ehh?

[DANJŌ *strikes a pose and leans forward. He speaks rapidly and forcefully.*]

DANJŌ: He thought no one would know Koiso's brother, but the farmers of Ohara are my master Toyohide's vassals. Early this month when Mambei was wounded he sought out my lord. "Yesterday Sister Koiso was attacked and killed in the Plain of Pines near Tree Island Shrine and a precious object entrusted to her by Lord Harukaze plundered. Investigate the incident," he begged. The matter was of grave importance to the House of Ono, so my lord gave responsibility for investigating the murder to me. The girl's corpse was thoroughly examined. The brother has been taken into

share

kuriage

15. A pond in the grounds of Wakō Temple in Osaka was popularly called Amida Buddha Lake because of a statue of Amida Buddha by its shore, ascribed to the reign of Emperor Kimmei (539–571).

temporary custody. I killed this creature because, from the beginning, it was obvious he had killed Koiso and intended to blackmail you. And there is more, much more.[16]

[DANJŌ *leaps to his feet and strides over to the body of* SEIHEI. *He takes from his breast the poem card wrapped in purple cloth. He kneels before* HARUKAZE *and folds back the cloth to show the card.*]

What do you see, my Lord? Is this not your family's precious poem card, restored to you?

[*All react.*]

GEMBA: What? The House of Ono's poem card . . . !

[*He moves swiftly to take the card from* DANJŌ, *who deftly holds it out of reach. They pose in a mie to battari tsuke beats:* DANJŌ *drops to one knee and holds up the card for everyone to see;* GEMBA *stands commandingly, heels together, sword in his left hand, his right hand grasping for the poem card.*]

DANJŌ [*roaring*] : A poem for which lives have been given! I will not pass it to you!

GEMBA [*enraged*] : To whom . . . then!

DANJŌ [*lightly*] : To you.

[*He places the poem card on* MIMBU's *open fan.* GEMBA *knows he is temporarily stymied; he moves back to the left and kneels.* DANJŌ *crosses center and again adopts a casual attitude as he kneels. A formally dressed* STAGE ASSISTANT *brings forward a cup of tea. Momentarily dropping out of character, the actor playing* DANJŌ *drinks a few sips to refresh himself. The actor resumes his role; the* STAGE ASSISTANT *removes the cup.*]

Well, you saw how magnificently I carried that off? Though, as usual, no one finds me polite. Now I'll stick my nose into one more affair. [*Forcefully.*] It's time to be presented to Lord Harumichi. Quickly. Let me see his Lordship.

HARUMICHI [*offstage*] : You shall.

[*Shamisen play brilliant* Takara no Saku *and stick drum, bells, and flute play* Midare *as the sliding doors at the back of the room open and* HARUMICHI *enters, followed by* NISHIKI, MAKIGINU, *and four* MAIDS. *As they enter, a* STAGE ASSISTANT *holds a black curtain in front of* SEIHEI *to cover his exit.* HARUMICHI *and the others kneel in the center of the room. Music ends.*]

I have heard from within what you have accomplished. What possibly could rival this joy?

DANJŌ [*energetically*] : The next happy event to follow will be when I settle once and for all the Princess' illness. Now then. Your illness, my Princess . . .

[*The large drum beats ominous* Doro-doro. DANJŌ *strides into the room. He lifts the robe from her head. Her hair streams upward into the air.* DANJŌ *and all the others gaze in fascination.* NISHIKI *trembles, in tears.*]

16. This section of the act in particular has led some Japanese commentators to describe it as an early detective story.

Promised restoration of her disgraced clan if she can bring rain, Lady Taema startles the lords with another request, "I would be most grateful to receive as my husband, Lord Toyohide, who sits before me." (*Taema:* Nakamura Shikan; *Prince Hayakumo:* Morita Kanya; *Mototsune:* Ichikawa Sadanji; *Toyohide:* Nakamura Senjaku) Page 106

The revolving stage turns, taking Act I, Scene 1, out of sight.

The high grass, pine trees, and tall archway of Tree Island Shrine, Act I, Scene 2, come into view. Page 107

Kazuma is amazed to see the man in gray is his master, Prince Hayakumo. The two men pose in a mie. (*Hayakumo:* Morita Kanya; *Kazuma:* Ichikawa Omezō) Page 109

At the signal of a ki clack the rear drop falls and the lights come up on a scene of green hills and a brilliant blue daytime sky. The actors drop out of their roles and kneel to address the audience (kōjō). Morita Kanya, as the troupe's senior actor, speaks to the audience from the center of the stage, "Honored spectators, east and west. May you take your ease and attend our play with pleasure." (*Hayakumo:* Morita Kanya; *Kazuma:* Ichikawa Omezō; *Gunnai:* Onoe Matsutarō) Page 110

The garden gate, having served its purpose of providing Danjō with an interesting entrance from the hanamichi, is taken away by two Stage Assistants dressed in black. One of Danjō's Attendants removes himself from the scene by facing upstage. The sign board reads "Ono Harumichi Mansion Scene." Page 114

Danjō is attracted by Hidetarō's youthful good looks. He clasps the boy's hands and embraces him, pretending to give the youngster lessons in horsemanship. "Press tightly against the flanks of your mount, thus, firmly grasp the reins, thus, and with your lips impart the secret art!" (*Danjō:* Onoe Shoroku; *Hidetarō:* Bandō Shuka) Page 117

Danjō slaps his silver pipe on the floor, throws himself prone, and poses in a mie, head "resting" on his hands. He glares. The pipe does not rise. (*Danjō*: Onoe Shoroku) Page 119

Iron dagger and tweezers float in the air, manipulated by two formally dressed Stage Assistants. Danjō crosses his hands over the pipe, closes his eyes, and considers the situation. Page 119

Suddenly he flips onto his seat, leans back, and gazes up at the ceiling, where Gunnai, the spy in Hayakumo's pay, is wielding a powerful magnet. Page 119

Mimbu crosses to give the poem card to Harumichi, who enters accompanied by female attendants. Danjō and Gemba bow respectfully. Stage Assistants hold a black curtain to cover Seihei's exit. (*Mimbu:* Onoe Kikuzō; *Danjō:* Onoe Shoroku; *Harumichi:* Sawamura Sōjūrō; *Harukaze:* Bandō Minosuke; *Gemba:* Nakamura Fukusuke) Page 124

The actor playing Danjō, momentarily dropping out of character drinks a cup of tea to refresh himself. He is attended by two formally dressed Stage Assistants, lesser ranking actors who are his disciples. (*Danjō:* Onoe Shoroku)

Page 124

When Danjō removes the robe, Princess Nishiki's hair streams upward into the air. (*Danjō:* Onoe Shoroku; *Princess Nishiki:* Bandō Tamasaburō; *Harumichi:* Sawamura Sōjurō) Page 124

Danjō forces Gunnai to the ground with the butt of his spear. The round object held by Gunnai is the magnet which caused Princess Nishiki's hair to rise in the air. "Now, fellow, someone put you up to this. His name! Quick! Tell me and I'll spare your life." (*Danjō:* Onoe Shoroku; *Gunnai:* Onoe Matsutarō) Page 125

Hmm! You wear, dear Princess, elegant pins and ornaments in your hair.

NISHIKI [*faintly*] : I do. They are silver pins fashioned in the latest court styles, made especially by my ladies for me.

DANJŌ [*starts*] : Ah! They are silver, are they? [*He looks closely at the ornaments.*] So! Now we will see whether the Princess suffers from a malady or not!

[*Doro-doro swells. DANJŌ pulls out the ornaments; the hair falls instantly. Drumming ceases. GEMBA is about to intervene, then thinks better of it. Keeping a watchful eye on GEMBA, DANJŌ returns to the garden and kneels. NISHIKI looks at DANJŌ gratefully.*]

NISHIKI: Ah. My appearance is no longer strange, my hair is restored to its proper place. How grateful, how happy I am.

DANJŌ [*strongly*] : Since the Princess is restored to health, the royal marriage can be consummated!

[*DANJŌ pivots on his knees to face HARUMICHI and bows.*]

GEMBA [*insolently*] : No. Her disease comes and it goes. There will be no rashly undertaken marriage here!

DANJŌ [*ironically*] : No need to feel anxious, Gemba. If I can find the cause of illness and doctor up the situation with these unskillful hands, why . . . I shall.

GEMBA [*sarcastically*] : Oh, I can hardly wait to see the treatment you prescribe. [*Suddenly furious.*] Show me! Show me!

DANJŌ [*glaring fiercely*] : Watch then! Yattoko, totcha, untoko na!

[*Kneeling, DANJŌ stamps his left foot forward to loud battari tsuke beats, yanks up on his trouser leg, and poses.*]

Yattoko, totcha, untoko na!

[*He does the same with his right leg and poses. Large drum and flute begin Mio Kagura. He stands, his trousers hitched up high. A formally dressed STAGE ASSISTANT helps him drop the right kimono sleeve. Ready for action, he seizes a long spear hanging on the wall and returns center stage. With a bravura flourish, he whips the spear over his head in his right hand, stamps forward with the left foot, crosses his eyes ferociously, and poses in a Genroku mie to battari tsuke beats and three beats of the large drum. He repeats the mie in the opposite direction. He draws himself up, turns, and thrusts the spear into the ceiling. With a cry of pain the spy, GUNNAI, tumbles down from the ceiling holding the magnet. DANJŌ forces him to the ground with the shaft of the spear. They pose in a mie to battari tsuke beats. Music stops.*]

DANJŌ [*rapidly*] : See the cause of the Princess' illness. I was mystified myself at first. Tweezers and dagger stood on end while the silver pipe did not. But then, when I saw the Princess' hair filled with specially wrought pins and combs in flower and butterfly designs, it came to me they must be made of iron that would leap into the air drawn by the power of a magnet secreted in the ceiling above! Someone spread the rumor that illness caused her hair to stand on end, so the vow between her and my master Toyohide would be broken. Hating this person's scheme to steal the

Princess for himself, I have pierced his magnet hocus-pocus with one spear thrust! Now, fellow, someone put you up to this. His name! Quick! Tell me and I'll spare your life.

[DANJŌ *raises the spear.* GUNNAI *looks to* GEMBA *for help.* GEMBA *glares back furiously.*]

GUNNAI [*petrified*] : A man will say anything to save his life. I was . . . hired . . . by . . .

[*The spy completely loses his nerve. He jumps up and runs, but* GEMBA *cuts him down from behind as he darts by. Loud batan tsuke beats.* GUNNAI *falls offstage, dying.* DANJŌ *seems not to have noticed.*]

DANJŌ: Things have turned out well: the poem card found, the House of Ono restored, the Princess' health returned. You, my Lord, have cause to rejoice.

[STAGE ASSISTANTS *have been helping* DANJŌ *put his sleeve back in place;* GEMBA *wipes the sword blade and returns it to its sheath. They exchange glances and kneel at the same time.* DANJŌ *bows politely to* HARUMICHI.]

No more felicitous occasion than this can be expected. Let us then begin felicitous preparations for a marriage.

HARUMICHI [*blandly, not committing himself*] : Indeed, a wedding requires preparation. The poem card has been returned and, now if rain does not fall, the bride shall enter her palanquin.

[DANJŌ *looks up, displeased by the implication.* HARUMICHI *decides to placate* TOYOHIDE.]

In honor of the occasion, I request my future son-in-law to accept this valuable sword as a gift from the House of Ono. Gemba, present the sword on my behalf.

[GEMBA *rises and faces* HARUMICHI, *receiving from him an expensively inlaid sword.* GEMBA *turns front, holding the sword by the tip of the scabbard, hilt in the air.*]

GEMBA [*glowering*] : As if unhindered, the wedding plans proceed. I exult for you.

DANJŌ: He receives the gift gratefully as your son-in-law. But more than this, my Master begs leave to present to his father-in-law a wedding gift.

HARUMICHI: And that wedding gift is . . . ?

DANJŌ [*powerfully*] : That wedding gift is . . . this, my Lord!

[DANJŌ *leaps up, pulls the sword from the scabbard* GEMBA *is holding and to batan tsuke beats, kills* GEMBA *with one stroke. As* GEMBA *falls, a* STAGE ASSISTANT *covers his head with a black cloth, and a second* STAGE ASSISTANT *floats a prop-head, on the end of a long pole, through the air until it rests on the stage.*]

As a wedding gift, my Lord Toyohide has rooted out the disease that attacked the House of Ono!

HARUMICHI: Truly, it is cause . . .

HARUKAZE and MIMBU: . . . for celebration!

[DANJŌ *sheathes the sword, kneels, and looks directly at the audience.*]

DANJŌ [*in a ringing voice*] : Let us offer our congratulations!

[*DANJŌ bows his face to the floor. Stick drum and flute play slow, stately Kata Shagiri. DANJŌ rises, bows to HARUMICHI, takes the gift sword from a STAGE ASSISTANT, and puts on his sandals with the help of a second STAGE ASSISTANT. Holding the sword at the scabbard end, the other hand tucked in his sleeve, he strides onto the hanamichi. At seven-three he stops and looks back. HARUMICHI rises and places an arm protectively around NISHIKI. HARUKAZE holds out the poem card on an opened fan. MIMBU bows respectfully. A single sharp ki clack: all pose in a strong mie to loud battari tsuke beats. Music becomes lively. The curtain is run closed. Three formally dressed STAGE ASSISTANTS come before the curtain and throw to the audience small souvenir towels on which is printed the name of the play. The audience applauds delightedly. DANJŌ smiles.*]

It's been a big part. I've done my best. Now, allow me to close the act!

hikkomi

[*He draws himself up, flicks the sword over his right shoulder, throws his left hand out before him, and, to furious uchiage tsuke beats which rise to a crescendo, taper off, then swell again, DANJŌ poses in a powerful mie. The curtain is pulled away from the offstage musicians' room, so they can watch DANJŌ. Stick drum, large drum, and flute play Miya Kagura, "Imperial Shrine Dance," and shamisen play Ama no Iwato, "Heavenly Rock Cave." A STAGE ASSISTANT helps. DANJŌ tucks the gift sword into his sash along with his other two swords. He tucks his hands inside his kimono sleeves and strides, assured and nonchalant, down the hanamichi and off as ki clacks accelerate. The curtain is fully closed, there is a single clack of the ki: large drum, stick drum, and flute play lively Shagiri, "Curtain Music," between acts.*]

gotateme

ACT III

SCENE 1   THE IMPERIAL PALACE GARDEN

[*Gradually accelerating ki clacks: the striped curtain is gently pushed open. The scene is a garden in the precincts of the Imperial Palace in Kyoto. Trees and shrubs are in the light green colors of spring. Mist softens the distant, airy view of hills behind. A stone footbridge, shaded by a willow, leads from up left across a small pond to a grass-covered mound center. The sign on the pillar right reads "Imperial Palace Garden." NISHIKI and TAEMA enter on the two hanamichi as the offstage CHORUS sings.*]

CHORUS [*to lyrical shamisen accompaniment*] :

Scattered clouds cover the moon, flowers in a mountain storm;
   An eveningtide of troubles though borne is painful.

[*NISHIKI wears a youthful pink kimono and carries the poem card in her right hand; TAEMA wears a sensuous lavender kimono of brocaded silk and carries a lacquered box. They stop at seven-three and face the audience,*] *unaware of each others' presence.* TOYOHIDE, *dressed in a powder blue kimono and wearing a lacquered wicker hat, enters the main stage. He removes the hat and poses. Now that he is away from the formal court situation, we see he is an exceptionally attractive man, handsome, suave, delicately refined. Music continues in the background.*]

TAEMA [*warm, passionate*] : I have been commanded to bring rain, but I cannot find my Master. And, ordered by Regent Mototsune, Lord Toyohide is now fasting in Tree Island Shrine, cut off from human contact for seven days and nights, praying to the gods. He should be here. How hungry he must be. [*Clutching the box to her breast tenderly.*] I so wish to be the one to appease his hunger.

NISHIKI [*gentle and youthful*] : I hurry to present Lord Toyohide with the poem card, recovered by the efforts of retainer Danjō, so it can cause the rain to fall, and I, as promised, shall be wed. [*She lowers her head modestly.*]

TOYOHIDE: Danjō successfully quieted the tumult in the Ono household, and yet did someone in the shadows pull the puppet Gemba's strings? Today, at the end of my prayers to Buddha, I heard a voice like a revelation saying "Destiny lies in the Imperial Garden, east in the direction of the Dragon and south to the Serpent." I am here, but what does it mean? [*Music becomes louder. He looks about wonderingly, then turns upstage. A* STAGE ASSISTANT *takes sandals and hat.* TAEMA *and* NISHIKI *come onstage. He turns front and the three see each other at the same time. Delighted and flustered, the women quickly kneel on either side of* TOYOHIDE *and bow prettily.*]

TAEMA and NISHIKI: Our Lord . . . Toyohide!

TOYOHIDE [*put out*] : Lady Taema? Princess Nishiki? Why are you here?

NISHIKI [*modestly*] : My Lord. I bring you the poem card.
    [TAEMA *tries to prevent her from reaching* TOYOHIDE. *He falls away. She passes the card to him. Opening it, he is relieved to see it is the lost heirloom.* TAEMA *pouts and turns away. He returns the card to* NISHIKI.]

TAEMA [*winningly*] : Knowing you would be ravished with hunger, I offer you my . . .
    [*She places the lacquered box of rice cakes at his feet, forcing* NISHIKI *to move away and poses beside him seductively, sleeves draped over his shoulders.* TOYOHIDE *disengages himself. She moves away and kneels.*]

TOYOHIDE: Nishiki. The poem card is for Regent Mototsune. Taema. My fast is not ended, so take the food and return home.

TAEMA: Cruel Lord Toyohide . . .

NISHIKI: . . . tell us, we pray . . .

TAEMA and NISHIKI: . . . what is in your heart?

TOYOHIDE [*torn between them*] : Ah, if I only could . . .
    [*To music, he turns to go away, but both of them rush to detail him.* TAEMA *tucks his right arm under hers. Alarmed,* NISHIKI *does the same with his left arm. He gently disengages himself and gestures for them both to go. They shake their heads "no."* TAEMA *pushes* NISHIKI *firmly out of the way and takes* TOYOHIDE's *hand, provocatively caressing it.*]

NISHIKI *kneels and looks imploringly at* TAEMA.]

NISHIKI: You are too forward. I am his true wife, joined by consent of his parents and mine.

TAEMA [*sharply*]: What are you saying? I am his first wife, joined flesh to flesh, his body and mine.

[*She smiles at him knowingly.* NISHIKI *is distraught. She clings to* TOYOHIDE. TAEMA *tries to pull him away. They tug him first one way, then the other. Losing patience, he pushes them both away and they flutter to the ground.*]

TOYOHIDE: I carry a grave responsibility. You must be reasonable and leave here at once.

[*Both bow and look appealing at him.*]

NISHIKI: For my Lord Toyohide, I will bring . . .

TAEMA: . . . rain without fail!

[TOYOHIDE *looks at first one then the other. His reply is ambiguous.*]

TOYOHIDE: Ah, yes, if only rain comes, peace will follow, and I shall rise in the world.

[*They move to him and kneel at his feet. He places his arms around them protectively. They pose. He gestures for them to go.* NISHIKI *takes the poem card from a* STAGE ASSISTANT *and goes off left;* TAEMA *glances provocatively at* TOYOHIDE *and moves slowly off right. Ominous* Kaza Oto *wind pattern, played on the large drum, rises and falls.*]

There was nothing strange about the garden before, yet the god of Tree Island Shrine appeared as Okina.[17] He spoke so vividly, surely he was a manifestation of my prayers. [*He notices the mound for the first time.*] Hmm. Is there significance to this tomb? And now this box of food, left by Taema. I will offer it and pray.

[*Booming large drum, bells, flute, and shamisen play* Kagura, *"Shrine Dance Music,"* as TOYOHIDE *picks up the box and places it reverently on the mound as an offering. He steps back, kneels, bows, and claps his hands two times in Shinto prayer.* HAYAKUMO *enters on the footbridge. He is fantastically dressed in a deep blue, silver, and gold nō-like costume of richly brocaded silk. The trousers are stiff and pleated. A gossamer outer cloak covers the heavy robe. A nō mask of Okina, wrinkled with age, covers his face. Carrying a staff in his right hand, he stands silently in the shadow of the willow tree.* TOYOHIDE *sees him and is struck dumb with amazement. Music stops.* TOYOHIDE *bows respectfully.*]

Oh, Deity, do you bestow your presence twice in answer to my humble petition? And what is significant in this particular part of the Imperial Garden, august Deity?

[HAYAKUMO *removes the mask in a grand gesture. His face is cruelly made up in heavy blue and black kumadori lines, suggesting more strongly than before his evil nature.*]

HAYAKUMO [*powerfully*]: It is I! Imperial Prince Hayakumo!

---

17. Literally, "old man": a symbol of longevity and the title of one of the oldest nō and kyogen plays.

TOYOHIDE [*turning away thinking*] : So, it is not the shrine deity in Okina's form, as I thought, but you Prince Hayakumo.

HAYAKUMO [*majestically*] : Indeed so, Toyohide!

[*Shamisen play stately* Biwa, *"Lute Melody," in the background.*]

The world's drought and the suffering of townsmen and farmers began from the day the infant Emperor was installed and Regent Mototsune decreed his ineffective policies. The punishment of Heaven visits us because Toyohide, too, betrays the trust of office! Though you are promised to Princess Nishiki, you are depraved and sleep with Lady Taema of the Clouds! Burdened with a woman's hatred, your heart is not fit for Buddha and the Gods. No matter how much you devotedly pray, the God of Tree Island Shrine will never bestow his favor!

TOYOHIDE [*shocked*] : Your Highness, what are you saying? You cannot be urging that His Majesty the Emperor abdicate?

HAYAKUMO: It is the Emperor's duty to take on himself the people's suffering. Hundreds of his subjects have been killed by this drought. Kanzō, enter!

KANZŌ [*off*] : Yes, my Prince!

[KANZŌ *trots on importantly from the left and drops to one knee before* HAYAKUMO.]

HAYAKUMO [*ominously*] : The number of stricken farmers in recent days is . . .

KANZŌ: Within the last two or three days a hundred and, all told, nearly a thousand farmers have died, Your Highness.

[KANZŌ *bows deeply.* TOYOHIDE *is unprepared for this fabrication.*]

TOYOHIDE: But, such numbers have not been reported!

HAYAKUMO [*cuttingly*] : Innocent Toyohide! Responsibility rests with the Divine Mikado! Who can forget the teaching of the Emperor Nintoku's[18] poem, "Seeing smoke rising from evening meals, I wondered if my people were happy." I retired from the palace to mingle with the people. Their hearts and mine are one. The number of dead reported by Kanzō comes from the lips of townsmen and farmers suffering agony themselves!

TOYOHIDE [*heatedly*] : Then, Your Highness, rather than urge our Mikado's abdication, step forward and lead the search for the seer Kiyoyuki whose prayers will surely bring rain.

HAYAKUMO: Ha, ha, ha, ha! The people's pain is the Emperor's sorrow, you say, but aren't you really protecting your own power? Rumors sweep the country that the drought continues as Heaven's punishment. Emperor Yōzei, though a child, has himself decided to abdicate!

TOYOHIDE: What? Can it be true?

[*A MESSENGER hurries down the hanamichi. He kneels at the seven-three position and bows.*]

MESSENGER [*formally*] : An imperial command, my Lords. The Regent of His Majesty summons you to attend him in the palace immediately on urgent affairs of state.

18. Reigned 313–399.

[MESSENGER *hurries off.* TOYOHIDE *bows to* HAYAKUMO *and turns to go.*]

HAYAKUMO [*triumphantly*] : As I expected! The Emperor's announcement of abdication! Toyohide. [TOYOHIDE *stops.*] You will place me on the Emperor's throne. You and Mototsune will recommend *me*!

TOYOHIDE [*proudly*] : No. We will delay replying to His Majesty and wait . . . for rain to fall!

[*He rushes onto the hanamichi to rapid bata-bata tsuke beats. At seven-three he stops, draws himself up resolutely, and poses in a mie to battari tsuke beats. Shamisen play* Azuma Jishi, *"Eastern Lion," as he moves quickly down the hanamichi and out of sight.* HAYAKUMO, *shaking with malevolence, watches him leave. Silence.*]

HAYAKUMO: The day I mount the Emperor's throne, torrents of rain will fall! Kanzō! Show me the compact sealed with their blood!

[KANZŌ *bows deeply. Rolling drum and crashing cymbals play* Midare. HAYAKUMO *moves ponderously center stage.* KANZŌ *cringingly takes the prince's mask, thin outer robe, and staff. He hands to* HAYAKUMO *a letter scroll and backs away.* HAYAKUMO *slowly unrolls and scans the scroll.*]

The lords who sign their names in blood, petitioning me to ascend the throne, are . . . hmm . . . hmm . . . Only Mototsune, Toyohide, and Ono Harumichi remain to oppose me. Although the House of Ono now seems at peace, their recent troubles have destroyed their prestige. When they offer their ancestor's sacred poem—to no avail—they will be laughed from court in shame!

KANZŌ: Their poem card cannot cause rain, my Prince?

[HAYAKUMO *holds the scroll in the air and strikes a grandiose pose.*]

HAYAKUMO: Never! Never! Whatever they try, I have my plans! No single drop of rain will fall!

KANZŌ [*deeply impressed*] : Then, Your Highness' great ambition will be achieved?

HAYAKUMO [*pondering, stalks slowly to the hanamichi*] : The only obstacles are Mototsune and Toyohide. While the drought continues, I must persuade the two of the wisdom of my rule. Come, we shall visit Regent Mototsune and his followers. Let us enjoy their futile discussions![19] [*He stops at the seven-three position.* KANZŌ *kneels behind him.*] Still, what the god announced to Toyohide troubles me. Ha, ha! No, the gods in Heaven favor me!

[*He poses, holding the scroll high over his head. Large drum, cymbals, and shamisen play stately* Midare. HAYAKUMO *flicks both sleeves over his arms and strides magnificently down the hanamichi and off, followed by* KANZŌ. *A moment of silence. The stage is empty. Large drum, stick*

19. "Let us visit Mototsune's 'Odawara Conference.' " In 1590 Toyotomi Hideyoshi beseiged Odawara Castle. Although the castle defenders discussed his terms of surrender for many months, they had not reached a decision when the castle fell to Hideyoshi. Hence, "Odawara Conference" is a disdainful term for any futile discussion.

drum, and cymbals crash, the flute joins Usudoro Abare, *"Disordered Rhythm," and shamisen play* Abare, *"Disorder." Sharp batan tsuke beats. The large rock on the top of the mount tips and rises in the air, lifted by an emaciated arm. With great effort* KIYOYUKI *emerges from the mound. He drops the boulder to the ground, collapsing over it. His formal court robe and trousers are pale blue. White hair falls to his shoulders, emphasizing his deep-etched, shriveled face. He blinks in the sun and shields his eyes. Shaking and half-demented, he searches feverishly until he sees the box. He seizes it, sits, and is about to eat. Music stops. Suspicious that the rice cakes may be poisoned, he looks carefully about. The large drum beats ominous* Mizu Oto *water pattern. He crawls weakly to the pond and throws in a rice cake. Water splashes as carp—manipulated by* STAGE ASSISTANTS—*strike and devour it. Drumming stops. He returns to the mound and starts devouring the rice cakes. Shamisen begins* Anton *quietly in the background.*]

KIYOYUKI [*between mouthfuls*] : Delicious. Ah, delicious. I've seen no food for a hundred days. How delicious! [*He looks about.*] It's been a long time since I've paid homage to the sun. How thankful I am!
[*He kneels and claps his hands fervently in gratitude.* TAKINO *enters silently on the footbridge and is amazed to see an old man worshiping the sun.*]
I've completely forgotten the taste of food, but thanks to the Goddess of Heaven, there's a feast before me. Ah, exquisite! Delectable!
[*He turns happily to the food again but* TAKINO *moves forward and interrupts him. Music stops.*]

TAKINO [*sternly*] : Do not move. The world is in turmoil and here I find a strange person who has slipped into the depths of the Imperial Garden. Who are you? Answer me. Your life depends on it!
[*She unties the cord fastening the dirk in her sash. She moves forward threateningly.*]
I am a retainer of Lady Taema and Endō Chikara's wife, Takino. I have seen you and you shall speak, whether you say you will or whether you say you will not! Well? Speak!
[*She poses with her hand on the dirk handle. He gestures for her to be calm. Shamisen begin quiet* Mochizuki.]

KIYOYUKI: Ahh, do not take that attitude. I am a person who has not seen the sun for a hundred days and, finding before me a feast of rice, offers gratitude to the bounty of the Sun Goddess. Truly, what should we be more grateful for than the brightness of the sun?
[*Clasping his hands together, he bows to the sun.*]

TAKINO: Ehh? What an incredible thing to say. Day after day blazing heat scorches the earth until not a drop of moisture remains. Do you mock the suffering of the Emperor and the people? [*She advances angrily.*]

KIYOYUKI: I do not joke. This is the truth.
[*Music stops. He draws himself up. His tone changes.*]
Takino, servant of Lady Taema! You do not recognize me, for my face has

changed in the hundred days I lived out of sight of the sun. I am Abe Kiyoyuki.

TAKINO [*falls back*] : What? You?

KIYOYUKI: I thought I had already died, but fate returned me to life to meet you here. I am fortunate. I am happy.

TAKINO: Is it really you? [*She looks closely. Recognizing him, she kneels respectfully.*] Master Kiyoyuki. It is you. But what brings you here, in this condition?

KIYOYUKI: The world's fate.

[*He looks about carefully. Shamisen begin delicate* Shinseki, *"New Barrier," in the background.*]

The drought searing the land is all the work of Saint Narukami. Filled with hatred for the Emperor, the Saint joined causes with Prince Hayakumo, withdrew to the depths of North Mountain, and there imprisoned the Dragon Gods and Goddesses of Rain so no drop of rain could fall in the Three Thousand Worlds of the Universe.[20] Because I knew, the Prince detained me out of fear I would inform His Majesty the Emperor. When he offered freedom if I would join their plan and I refused, I was buried alive. I should be dead, but Buddha and the gods of Shintō protected me. Blessed by the will of heaven, occult powers enabled me to lift the boulder from my tomb and emerge to pass this story on to you. If I die now, I will be content. I am grateful, grateful!

[*He clasps his hands together fervently, and bows toward the sun.*]

TAKINO [*eagerly*] : Then divine protection enabled you to lift the stone and escape death so you could offer incantations that will bring rain?

KIYOYUKI [*chuckling*] : No, Takino, I did not come out to offer prayers. When this Kiyoyuki fell into the bowels of hell, worldly desires of the Three Evil Ways—gluttony, bloodshed, and sexual passion—were forgotten. All except gluttony. The delicious smell of rice cakes roused me and I followed my nose to the surface.

TAKINO [*looking at the box*] : Why, the crest on the box is that of our house. These must be the rice cakes Lady Taema was bringing to the garden for Lord Toyohide.

KIYOYUKI [*touched*] : Can it be these came from Taema?

TAKINO: They did. And I, searching the garden for her, met you. How remarkable.

KIYOYUKI [*pondering*] : The tie to my disciple Taema is indeed unbreakable. [*Music ends.*]

TAKINO [*confidentially*] : But tell me, is there a way to placate Saint Narukami and free the gods and goddesses of rain?

KIYOYUKI: Yes, there is, there is.

[*He looks cautiously about and moves closer.*]

It will not be easy, for Narukami is Buddha's monk . . . yet there is a way.

20. In Buddhist cosmology a thousand worlds make one Small World, a thousand Small Worlds a Middle World, and a thousand Middle Worlds a Large World. Together they comprise the universe.

If Taema . . .

TAKINO [*stopping him*] : Shhh! "A man who emerges from a rock should know a rock has ears." Master, one moment. [*Crossing right and calling off.*] Monnosuke. Enter.

MONNOSUKE [*off*] : Yes, my Lady.

[*Large drum beats ominous* Mizu Oto *water pattern. She turns and kneels respectfully beside* KIYOYUKI. MONNOSUKE, *a young, low-ranking samurai, enters and kneels. Two* BEARERS *bring on a palanquin and squat beside it.*]

TAKINO [*looking meaningfully at* KIYOYUKI] : Go to my Lady's residence. Let master and pupil meet.

KIYOYUKI: Thank you, Takino. I must inform Taema before I die.

TAKINO [*forcefully*] : Monnosuke. Accompany this honored guest to the very door of the residence. Let no one see inside.

MONNOSUKE [*briskly*] : I will not leave his side until my Lady returns!

TAKINO: Be certain you do as I say.

MONNOSUKE [*bowing*] : I obey.

TAKINO [*gently*] : Master, please enter.

KIYOYUKI: Good Takino, I will go.

[*He moves to enter, but he is weak and he staggers. She catches him gently. They exchange looks. A sharp ki clack signals offstage* CHORUS.]

CHORUS [*sings* Kago Uta, *"Palanquin Song," to shamisen accompaniment and* Mizu Oto *drum pattern*] :

Come,

First we shall visit

The Princess . . .

[TAKINO *gestures for him to pass. He crosses slowly to the palanquin and turns back to look at her gratefully. She bows again. They pose. A sharp ki clack signals the end of the scene: a curtain, painted to represent the rock face of a mountain, drops in front of the scene. The large drum plays loud* Yama Oroshi *mountain storm pattern to hold the audience's attention as the scene is changed behind the curtain.*]

SCENE 2   A GROTTO ON NORTH MOUNTAIN ("SAINT NARUKAMI" SCENE)

[*Music changes to lively* Haya Tsutsumi, *"Fast Drum," played by the small drums and flute. The young monks* WHITE CLOUD *and* BLACK CLOUD *enter, one on each hanamichi. They are dressed in white kimonos covered in front by a black apron. Their heads are shaved and they carry black rosaries. They trot on comically, talking as they go, hands tucked up in their sleeves to ward off the mountain cold.*]

WHITE CLOUD: Have you heard? Have you heard?

BLACK CLOUD: I've heard. I've heard.

WHITE CLOUD: Have you heard?

BLACK CLOUD: I've heard.

[*They continue the exchange until they meet in front of the curtain center stage. Music ends.*]

WHITE CLOUD [*delighted to see his friend*] : What have you heard?

BLACK CLOUD [*foolishly*] : Everyone in Edo saying "Saint Narukami and the God Fudō" is a great play![21]

WHITE CLOUD: Donkey. Not that. I mean are people talking about our Master Narukami's secret rites?

BLACK CLOUD [*blankly*] : I haven't heard a thing.

WHITE CLOUD [*disgusted*] : You haven't? What he does is remarkable. Listen. [*Shamisen play delicate Haru wa Hanami*, "Spring Flower Viewing," *in the background.*]
The Emperor denied Saint Narukami's request that to him a temple be ordained, so, furious, he embarked upon austerities which have captured and bound the Dragon Gods of Rain in all the universe until not a drop of rain could fall. One hundred days have passed since the last single drop of rain has been seen. The land shrivels from dryness.

BLACK CLOUD: It's fine if you like your humidity low, but it must be hard for a farmer to stick his rice in the ground.

WHITE CLOUD: It's awe-inspiring to imagine Master's power.

BLACK CLOUD: It's the Emperor's own fault. He told a fib.

WHITE CLOUD [*scandalized*] : Shh! Being Master Narukami's disciple is a great honor. He is the needle, we are the thread. [*Mimes threading a needle.*]

BLACK CLOUD: Well, I'm worn to a frazzle—up the mountain every morning to help Master with his austerities, down the mountain to sleep. Three miles each way and it's cold up here.

WHITE CLOUD [*severely*] : If Master freezes, we freeze to death with him. That's what spiritual discipline means.

BLACK CLOUD: My legs have gone numb with the climbing, up and down, up and down.

WHITE CLOUD: I'm tired too, but I don't complain about it. You're a perfect dummy.

BLACK CLOUD [*snickering*] : If my tongue went numb I'd be a dumb dummy.

WHITE CLOUD: That would be a blessed relief.

BLACK CLOUD [*slyly*] : I've got medicine here that will take off the chill. You'll feel fit as a fiddle fast. How about a sip?

WHITE CLOUD: And is it good? I might try a drop.

BLACK CLOUD: It's the No-Death-No-Pain-Cures-a-Thousand-Complaints-Pharmaceutical-Preparation.

WHITE CLOUD: Well, where is it?

BLACK CLOUD: So precious I wouldn't dream of carrying it up my sleeve or in my sash. [*Gestures.*] I'll open the gates and bring it out.

21. The comic routine "Have you heard? Have you heard?" is found in many variations in scripts of *Narukami*. It seems to have been used first in the 1698 production and so was a well-established piece of business by 1742. Two, three, or four monks may appear.

WHITE CLOUD: Gates? You're going all the way down to the temple for it? There's no storehouse here.

BLACK CLOUD [*grinning*] : Yes there is. To groin a phrase, the medicine is up my crotch. Isn't that a perfect hiding place for something precious? Besides, crotch heat will hold the medicine at just the right temperature for drinking. [*He produces a small bottle of rice wine from between his legs.*] Here. [*Takes a wine cup from his sleeve.*] And here. [*Offers them.*] Here you are.

WHITE CLOUD: Dissolute, defiled, corrupted, filthy, worldly, dirty monk!

BLACK CLOUD: It's just a little wine.

WHITE CLOUD: Lord Buddha has enjoined murder, theft, lust, lies, and drunkenness. In the midst of our Master Narukami's strict meditation do you dare break the Buddha's commandment?

BLACK CLOUD: It keeps off the dampness.

WHITE CLOUD [*chuckling in spite of himself*] : So it does.

BLACK CLOUD [*raises bottle over his head*] : Since my elder objects, however, I'll smash this bottle to bits on the rock.

WHITE CLOUD: No, no! What a sacrilege it would be to waste Lord Buddha's bounty, for is not rice, multiplied a thousand times ten-thousand grains, nature's source of sake? It would be better if we must eliminate the sake to do so . . . by drinking it! Perhaps I'll have a sip.

[BLACK CLOUD *pours a cup.* WHITE CLOUD *downs it and sighs. Music stops.*]

Ahh. You know, when I toss off a cup like that, I feel as if I was being born in Buddha's promised paradise. I'll pour for you.

BLACK CLOUD [*drinks*] : Hmm, very good. But there's nothing to go with it.

WHITE CLOUD: Yes there is, yes there is. [*He brings out a dried octopus from between his legs.*] I knew we'd get famished. I brought an . . .

BLACK CLOUD: Octopus! A monk who'd eat flesh is depraved. Every servant of the Buddha takes a nip now and then, but eating meat in Master Narukami's place of meditation? I'll tell him.

WHITE CLOUD: You wouldn't.

BLACK CLOUD: Just see if I don't. [*Snatches octopus.*] Master! Master! White Cloud's eating octopus!

WHITE CLOUD [*snatches bottle*] : Black Cloud's drinking wine! Master Narukami!

BLACK CLOUD: White Cloud smells of fish!

[WHITE CLOUD *raps* BLACK CLOUD *sharply on the head with his knuckles to a loud ki clack. The rock curtain drops to the floor and is whisked away by* STAGE ASSISTANTS. *The sign reads "North Mountain Grotto Scene." It is the retreat of* NARUKAMI, *a Buddhist saint whose name means Thunderbolt. Towering gray and black rock cliffs hem in the scene. Rock steps ascend to a natural platform, right, which looks out onto a waterfall that plunges from above into a gorge below. A ritual straw rope, tied with sacred white papers, spans the waterfall. Left, a small, rustic pavilion roofed with thatch stands on a rock outcropping. The large drum booms out* Yama Oroshi *mountain storm pattern. The two monks kneel on either side of a small flight of steps leading up to the pavilion and piously take out rosaries.* STAGE ASSISTANTS *remove a blue and white striped curtain by the proscenium arch left. We see an* Ōzatsuma SINGER *and shamisen* PLAYER *seated on a dais.*]

ŌZATSUMA SINGER [*sings very slowly, in elaborate style, to deep shamisen music*] :

In the meantime, the great Saint Narukami,
   Blocks the flight of Dragon Gods and Goddesses,
   Confining the earth's rain.
Going deep into the mountains,
   He undergoes strict austerities,
   Before Buddha's altar.[22]

[*During the song* NARUKAMI *enters on the hanamichi. He is sunk in meditation. Wearing a thick silver-gray kimono, his hair has been uncut for three months and it reaches his shoulders. He holds a large Buddhist rosary before him. He stops at the seven-three position and turns toward the audience.*]

NARUKAMI [*rumbling voice*] : Hmm. Leaves are blown by the wind; in all things there is cause.

[*Ōzatsuma shamisen plays rapidly as* NARUKAMI *crosses ponderously to the platform. He kneels, facing the waterfall, and clasps his hands in prayer.*]

At this waterfall's rock-crushing stream, human impurity washed away,
I bend my spirit to achieve perfect meditation.

[*He faces the altar above which hangs a scroll painting of Fudō.*]

Praise to Buddha the all-powerful. Praise to the all-powerful Fudō.

[*He rings a prayer bell. The curtain covering the* Ōzatsuma *musicians is replaced. The large drum beats steady, suspenseful* Taki Oto *waterfall pattern. A bell is heard from the end of the hanamichi.*]

CHORUS [*sings offstage right to shamisen accompaniment*] :

Hail great Guardian God Fudō.
   Hail great Guardian God Fudō.

[*The sound of a struck prayer bell mingles with the repeated prayer to Fudō and insistent drum beating of* Taki Oto *waterfall pattern. The hanamichi curtain opens and* TAEMA *enters dressed in an elegant red kimono patterned with spring flowers. It is pulled off the right shoulder, showing an inner kimono. A black robe is folded over her arm. Though she strikes a prayer bell, her walk is languorous and extremely sensual.* TAEMA *pivots in a circle at seven-three looking about. She sees the waterfall, then* NARUKAMI. *She poses. The music ends. She takes a deliberately provocative pose and calls out in a pathetic voice.*]

TAEMA: Help me great Guardian God Fudō. Help me great Guardian God Fudō.

22. The syllable count of the song is unusually irregular (5–8–7–7–6–10–5–7–5) and is not maintained in the translation.

[*She waits to see what effect this will have.* NARUKAMI *turns front, still kneeling. His head is bowed, his eyes half closed. Still in meditation,* NARUKAMI *is scarcely aware of his surroundings. A* STAGE ASSISTANT *scurries onto the hanamichi with a tall black stool for* TAEMA *to sit on. She hands him the prayer bell and hammer. Spaced beats of the small drum are heard, first near and then far away, in the pattern called* Kodama, *"Mountain Echo," and shamisen gently play the same melody.*]

NARUKAMI [*rumbling voice*] : In the mountain is total silence, not a bird calls. Strange. Then why do I hear the sound of prayers to Buddha at this remote waterfall, deep in the mountains where a human footstep is rare? [*Calling in a detached manner.*] White Cloud. Black Cloud.

WHITE CLOUD and BLACK CLOUD [*waking and rubbing their eyes*] : Yes, Master?

NARUKAMI: Were you sleeping? Indolent monks.

WHITE CLOUD: How can you think that, Master? I wouldn't doze off. Not me. [*Points to* BLACK CLOUD.] Black Cloud was sleeping.

BLACK CLOUD [*pointing to* WHITE CLOUD] : You were, you were. What a thing, accusing me. Dear Master. I kept guard with eyes like saucers. I really did. White Cloud was the one sleeping.

WHITE CLOUD: I didn't doze off. You did.

BLACK CLOUD: You were sleeping, liar.

WHITE CLOUD: You were sleeping, dunce.

BLACK CLOUD: You!

WHITE CLOUD: You!

[*They rise on their knees, about to come to blows.*]

NARUKAMI [*undisturbed by their foolishness*] : Come. Is this the conduct of Buddha's servants?

[*They wilt, bowing their heads.*]

WHITE CLOUD and BLACK CLOUD: Yes, Master.

NARUKAMI: Good. Since you say you were not sleeping, surely you heard just now . . . ?

WHITE CLOUD and BLACK CLOUD: Heard . . . just now?

NARUKAMI: . . . in this distant grotto a woeful voice invoking Buddha's name? Did it only seem to be? Or was it truly . . . a ghostly spirit?

[*He pauses. Music stops. The monks tremble, frightened.*]

WHITE CLOUD and BLACK CLOUD: Ehhhhh?

NARUKAMI [*serenely*] : Both of you. Go to the foot of the waterfall and see what it is.

WHITE CLOUD and BLACK CLOUD: Ehhh?

NARUKAMI: Are you going?

WHITE CLOUD and BLACK CLOUD [*petrified*] : Yes . . . Master!

WHITE CLOUD [*whispering*] : Black Cloud. Our Master has spoken. You run down and see.

BLACK CLOUD: Oh, not me.

WHITE CLOUD: Yes, go.

BLACK CLOUD: Aren't you senior monk?

WHITE CLOUD: I am. What of it?

BLACK CLOUD: Don't you remember the feast at New Year's. Did I go and eat first? Or did you go and eat first?

WHITE CLOUD: It was New Year's. Obviously I went first. What of it?

BLACK CLOUD: Obviously you go and see first. That's what. You should go.

WHITE CLOUD: How can you talk about feasts and ghosts in the same breath? Since I'm your senior, you should do what I say.

BLACK CLOUD: Really? Every other time it's "I'm your senior, I'm your senior, I go first," isn't it? You go first this time.

WHITE CLOUD [exasperated]: Will you go?

BLACK CLOUD [waving him away]: After you.

WHITE CLOUD: Will you go I tell you!

BLACK CLOUD: You go, you!

WHITE CLOUD: Dunce! Should I thump your head in?

BLACK CLOUD: I'll thump yours back!

[They raise their fists to pummel each other. NARUKAMI, beginning to get angry, interrupts.]

NARUKAMI: Monks. What are you doing?

WHITE CLOUD [lamely]: Ahh . . . coming across a turnip, I thought I would mash it up and offer it most respectfully to you, Master.

NARUKAMI: Imbecile. What else should I expect from you. And what do you say?

BLACK CLOUD: Finding this Chinese sweet potato I thought I'd cut it up and bake it for Master's dinner.

[They raise their fists to their foreheads and bow.]

NARUKAMI: You are both fools.

WHITE CLOUD and BLACK CLOUD [bowing]: Yes, Master.

NARUKAMI: Enough quarreling. Go at once.

WHITE CLOUD and BLACK CLOUD [bowing lower]: Yes, Master.

[Shamisen play Haru wa Hanami. The monks rise and start to move right.]

WHITE CLOUD [turning back]: I was ready to go before. Really, I would have gone, but you had to make a fuss.

BLACK CLOUD: You didn't think I'd have let you go alone, did you? I would have gone with you. [Peers ahead.] Oh, isn't it creepy? You go ahead.

WHITE CLOUD [waving him to pass]: You go first.

BLACK CLOUD: No, you go first.

WHITE CLOUD: Go on, go on, I tell you.

BLACK CLOUD: I'll follow.

NARUKAMI [rumbling]: Will you two go!

WHITE CLOUD and BLACK CLOUD [wailing]: Yeeesss!

[They cautiously step forward, tiptoeing out of fright. They bend forward to peer ahead. They fall back, astonished by TAEMA's beauty.]

WHITE CLOUD: Fantastic! I've never seen anything so beautiful!

BLACK CLOUD: First class! Super grade A number one![23]

23. Black Cloud rates her jōjōkichi, the top ranking for a kabuki actor.

WHITE CLOUD: But . . . what do you suppose it can be?

BLACK CLOUD: Have you gone insane? It's a woman.

WHITE CLOUD: I know it's a woman, but what kind? I think she's not a human being.

BLACK CLOUD: I think you're right.

WHITE CLOUD: Then what is she?

BLACK CLOUD [*thinks*] : Do I know who she is!

WHITE CLOUD: Yes?

BLACK CLOUD [*almost swooning*] : She's an angel!

WHITE CLOUD: An angel? Why?

BLACK CLOUD: That beautiful creature is an angel. And do you see the robe over her arm? It's a robe of angel's feathers she's brought here to wash because our Master's spells have dried up all the water in the whole world.[24]

WHITE CLOUD: Weak head, weak eyes. She's a dragon princess.

BLACK CLOUD: Why do you say a dragon princess?

WHITE CLOUD: Because, you see, the incantations of our Master have dried the seas, the rivers, and the land until there is no place for a princess of the Dragon God of Rain to dwell, except this waterfall which happens to be the only water left on earth. She's come to join her family here. There is no doubt: she is a princess of the Dragon God of Rain!

BLACK CLOUD: That's bunk, monk. Whales don't have scales, but a dragon god princess does—and I don't see any. I don't see clams hanging from her sleeves. I don't see her getting seaweed plastered in her hair. [*Snickers.*] In front of the Master I said getting plastered! Look at her, she's exquisite! She's heavenly!

WHITE CLOUD: I tell you she is a princess of the Dragon God of Rain!

BLACK CLOUD: And I tell you she is an angel who has come from heaven!

WHITE CLOUD: She is a princess!

BLACK CLOUD: She is an angel!

WHITE CLOUD: Princess!

BLACK CLOUD: Angel!

WHITE CLOUD: Junior monk, you are contradicting your senior!

BLACK CLOUD: It's a free country, isn't it?

WHITE CLOUD: Ohhh! I'll thrash you within an inch of your life!

BLACK CLOUD [*mimicking*] : Ohhh! I'll put you in the hospital and you can foot the bill!

WHITE CLOUD and BLACK CLOUD: You! You!!

[*They raise their fists to fight. Music stops.*]

NARUKAMI: Silence. Since you will not obey, you shall sit and observe meditation.

WHITE CLOUD and BLACK CLOUD: We obey your command, Master Narukami.

NARUKAMI: Then do so. I shall see for myself.

---

24. Alluding to the feather cloak (*hagoromo*) of the celestial beauty who comes to earth and is forced to dance to have it returned, an incident dramatized in the nō play *Hagoromo*.

[*Sheepishly they sit beside the platform and take out their rosaries. No drums play* Itchō, *"Single Rhythm,"* NARUKAMI *rises and looks toward* TAEMA. *He rests his hand on a pillar of the pavilion and calls.*]
You there! You there! [*She does not respond.*] I don't understand. Standing before the craggy waterfall, having passed over a mountain trail difficult even for beasts of prey or birds, seems to be an aristocratic female form. How uncanny. [*Sternly.*] What are you?

TAEMA [*helplessly*] : I . . . Sir?

WHITE CLOUD and BLACK CLOUD [*simpering, mimicking her*] : I . . . Sir?

NARUKAMI: Silence.

WHITE CLOUD and BLACK CLOUD: Yes, Master.

NARUKAMI [*firmly*] : I am speaking to you.

TAEMA [*lowers her head pathetically*] : I am a woman living at the foot of the distant mountain, who has been parted from her dearest husband, Sir.

NARUKAMI: Parted from your husband?

TAEMA [*pretending to weep*] : Yes, your Reverence.

NARUKAMI: Parted and living, or parted in death?

TAEMA: Ah! This is the seventh day of the seventh week.

NARUKAMI [*somberly*] : The forty-ninth day of death?

TAEMA: Yes, your Reverence.

NARUKAMI [*raising the rosary to his forehead*] : "Namu Amida Butsu." Buddha Merciful All Hail, Buddha Merciful All Hail.[25]

[Kodama *drum pattern creates a lonely mood.* TAEMA *looks bashfully at* NARUKAMI, *then holds out the black robe for him to see.*]

waka TAEMA: "Though once a keepsake, you are now an enemy I must abandon; can I then perhaps begin to hope for forgetfulness."[26] And so I had thought to wash from this rough robe the dust of carnal life, yet the drought is everywhere, wells are dry, streams have stopped. I had heard of a waterfall in the venerable mountain where, in spite of drought, water miraculously never ceases flowing. [*Glances innocently at* NARUKAMI.] I only wish to cleanse away past carnal memories, so I can begin . . . life anew. [*She looks at the robe and pretends to weep.*] Enchanting husband. I miss you so. Can you guess what thought fills my heart? [*He does not understand what is happening, but he cannot take his eyes from her.*]

NARUKAMI: What a pitiful tale. It would appear you were close to him during your marriage?

TAEMA [*provocatively*] : He and I were very close. In heaven, like two proverbial birds, sharing one eye and one wing, inseparable. On earth, two trees with branches intertwined.[27] [*Smiles secretly.*] When I think back on it, so many interesting things occurred.

---

25. A Buddhist memorial service is held for the dead on the forty-ninth day after death.

26. A poem from the *Kokinshū*.

27. From the *Chōgonka*, a collection of poems by Hakurakuten (772–846), a Chinese writer greatly admired at the Heian court.

NARUKAMI [*piously*] : The road to salvation begins from carnal desire. Each
   word exchanged with this woman is ordained by Karma. Repent your
   unforgivable sins for his sake in the next life. I will hear your confession!
   [*He grasps the rosary in both hands and gazes intently at her. She meets
   his gaze, then modestly looks away.*]
TAEMA: If I speak, it would lighten the pain in my heart. [*She delicately
   touches her breast and looks at him.*] Should I speak?
NARUKAMI: Speak! Speak!
TAEMA [*rising briskly*] : Very well, I shall speak. And yet . . . it is so very far
   from here to where you are, the words I speak will not reach you in these
   echoing mountains. [*Pouting.*] I want to be near your side when I tell my
   story.
NARUKAMI [*catching his breath*] : True. Your voice mingles with the water's
   roar and is hard to hear. You shall approach. Come near! Come near!
   [*He makes a sweeping gesture for her to approach.*]
TAEMA: Then, I will . . . come close to your Reverence's side.
   [*The large drum beats steady* Taki Oto *waterfall pattern. She moves
   quickly toward* NARUKAMI, *as her* STAGE ASSISTANT *goes off with
   stool and hand properties.* WHITE CLOUD *and* BLACK CLOUD *run to
   stop her, clucking and waving their arms.*]
BLACK CLOUD: You mustn't, you mustn't.
WHITE CLOUD: By our Master's orders women are forbidden . . .
BLACK CLOUD: . . . within seven miles.[28]
WHITE CLOUD and BLACK CLOUD: Within seven miles you cannot go.
WHITE CLOUD: One and one make two.
BLACK CLOUD: And two can make three.
WHITE CLOUD: Women are abomination.
BLACK CLOUD: Sinful beyond words.
WHITE CLOUD: All hail the abacus. Click, click, add it up. One plus one
   makes three. [*He mimes counting with the beads of an abacus.*] It doesn't
   square.
BLACK CLOUD [*mimes ringing a prayer bell*] : Ding, ding.
WHITE CLOUD: Ding, ding, ding.
BLACK CLOUD: Out she goes.
   [*They block her way on either side, grinning foolishly.*]
TAEMA [*seeming to be bewildered*] : My, you say such strange things.
NARUKAMI [*considers*] : They are right to say them. No woman may
   approach my seat of meditation. Hmm. You shall sit with my monks close
   by on either side and speak. Speak!
TAEMA: Very well, your Reverence. I will tell my story here.
   [*She gestures magnanimously for them to sit. Covering their faces to hide
   their embarrassment, they kneel. Purposely delaying her story, she turns
   upstage while a* STAGE ASSISTANT, *dressed in formal kimono and outer
   garb, takes her sandals and the black robe. She turns coquettishly to the
   monks.*]

   28. A Buddhist holy place was to be kept undefiled for "seven miles in four
directions."

My two monks, will you listen, too?

NARUKAMI [*impatiently*] : If they do, will you speak?

WHITE CLOUD and BLACK CLOUD: We will, we will.

[*The monks put away their rosaries and look at her expectantly. She kneels between them and takes out a small black fan, partially covering her face with it. She poses alluringly. Shamisen play* Chigusa *love music and tinkling bells join in. She tells them her story hesitantly, with a great deal of seemingly innocent, but suggestive, pantomime, as if* NARUKAMI *were not there.*]

shikatabanashi TAEMA: I am embarrassed to say it, but I fell passionately in love with my lord not very long ago. It was in the middle of March last year. I had gone cherry-blossom viewing at Kiyomizu Temple, when a young lord, scarcely more than twenty, suddenly rose outside our canopy and peeked in at me, sitting inside our silken walls. [*Miming the action.*] How can I describe his nobility, his sweetness, in words? [*Behind the fan.*] Instantly, I knew this young lord was to be . . . my beloved.

WHITE CLOUD [*open-mouthed*] : Though you'd never seen him before?

TAEMA: Ah, his sweetness was such that, truly, from the nape of my neck . . .

[*Showing the nape of her neck, she leans toward him.*]

WHITE CLOUD: . . . a shudder?

TAEMA: A tremor went through my body.

BLACK CLOUD: You quivered?

TAEMA: I trembled. I turned hot. [*She fans herself.*] I turned cold. [*She hugs her breasts.*]

WHITE CLOUD: Ohh! I can't bear it!

[*The monks hug their chests, imagining the scene.*]

TAEMA: Then this young noble began to tease. First he seemed to be gazing at my face from afar, then he was not. [*Pretending to pout, she puts the fan away.*]

WHITE CLOUD: Was it delicious? Was it delicious?

BLACK CLOUD: Was it like eating sweet rice buns and honey?

TAEMA: My lord then took a fold of letter paper from his breast, dipped a writing brush in black ink, and quickly composed a poem which he ordered my serving maid to deliver.

[*Dipping her finger in ink, she mimes writing on the closed fan.*]

WHITE CLOUD and BLACK CLOUD [*eagerly*] : Did he write well? Did he write well?

TAEMA: Oh, he did. He did. The poem he wrote was very interesting.

WHITE CLOUD and BLACK CLOUD: Yes? The poem?

waka TAEMA [*"reading" from the fan*] : "Still yearning to see, one whom I have not really, seen nor have not seen . . ."

WHITE CLOUD: "Still yearning to see . . .

BLACK CLOUD: . . . one whom I have not really . . .

WHITE CLOUD and BLACK CLOUD: . . . seen nor have not seen?"

TAEMA: Ahh! How did the last half of his poem go?

[*As she had hoped,* NARUKAMI's *interest is aroused. He looks at her for the first time during the story. Music stops.*]

WHITE CLOUD [*stricken*] : Is this a thing you could forget?

BLACK CLOUD: If you'd written it on a plaque you could have stuffed it in your sash.

TAEMA [*pretending to think*] : "Still yearning to see, one whom I have not really, seen nor have not seen . . . "

NARUKAMI [*pleased with himself*] : "Can I live this way today, idly passing the time," is the last half of the poem, is it not?[29]

[*She claps her hand to her breast and looks at him as if he had said the most clever thing in the world.*]

TAEMA: Ohh! That is absolutely right!

[*The ambiguity of her response does not escape* NARUKAMI. *He gasps.*]

NARUKAMI [*thickly*] : And then? And then? What . . . what!

[*With a flourish, he pulls a small writing table before him, plants his elbows on it, rests his chin in his hands, and poses in mie, gazing fixedly at her. He holds the pose as she continues. Shamisen change to faster Nanakusa. The tempo of the story increases.*]

TAEMA [*back to the monks*] : Why, you can't imagine how interesting it then became.

WHITE CLOUD and BLACK CLOUD: Oh, we can, we can!

TAEMA [*brightly*] : Well then I called my maid. "Go ask his name," I said.

WHITE CLOUD and BLACK CLOUD [*eyes popping*] : Did he say, did he say?

TAEMA: Hateful man, he didn't say.

WHITE CLOUD and BLACK CLOUD [*clapping their hands to their cheeks in mock aggravation*] : Holy Buddha! Holy Buddha! [*They foolishly rub their rosaries.*] Hail the Glory of the Lotus Sutra!

TAEMA: Exactly: I recited the Fumon verse of the Lotus Sutra.[30] The charity of the Goddess of Mercy is a miraculous thing. That night, when others were asleep, I rose and found myself being guided, alone, to the middle of Saga Plain, where, I found, he lived.

WHITE CLOUD and BLACK CLOUD: Brave lady, brave lady!

TAEMA [*drawing back in fright*] : But then, I came to a broad river.

WHITE CLOUD: Naturally, naturally. The Big Dam River. The Cinnamon Tree River.

BLACK CLOUD [*snickering*] : A famous river.

TAEMA: Of course I wanted to cross, but there was no bridge, no ferry.

[*She mimes searching helplessly. Then she slaps her thigh in resolve.*]
Since there was no other way, I fixed my courage and crossed the river at night by the light of the stars. As a woman, I did a dauntless thing. Without thinking, I took my skirt . . .

[*She rises. Ostensibly turning away from the monks, but actually turning toward* NARUKAMI, *she delicately lifts the hem of her kimono to show a few inches of ankle. He starts and gazes in fascination. He pushes the table*

29. The poem is from the *Kokinshū* and is by Ariwara Narihira (833–880), one of the Six Great Poets of the Heian court. A man of Narukami's background could be expected to know it.

30. The twenty-fifth verse of the Lotus Sutra. It invokes Kannon Bosatsu, Goddess of Mercy.

away, grasping the rosary in both hands for support. She turns away as if embarrassed.]

WHITE CLOUD and BLACK CLOUD: You edged it up? You edged it up?

TAEMA: Not edge at all. I grasped it firmly and lifted it, entering the middle of the stream.

[*She is holding the kimono at thigh level. Lifting it with a jerk, as if by accident the front of the kimono opens in* NARUKAMI's *direction. He grasps the rosary harder.* TAEMA *and the monks now speak with obvious double meaning.*]

WHITE CLOUD and BLACK CLOUD: Brrr? Wasn't it cold?

TAEMA: Without a qualm, I splashed in. Splash, splash.

[*She raises the kimono and shows her leg each step she wades seductively through the river. The monks raise their kimonos and in turn each mimics her. They parade in a circle.*]

WHITE CLOUD: Splash, splash.

BLACK CLOUD: Splash, splash.

[*All three wade in unison, the monks simpering and giggling. The water gets deeper, their steps slow.*]

ALL: Splash, splash, splash. Splash. Splash.

WHITE CLOUD [*as if in ecstacy, waggling his hips*]: Oh! Deep! Deep!

BLACK CLOUD [*on tiptoe*]: I can't reach the bottom!

TAEMA [*adjusts her skirt and kneels*]: In time I reached the bank.

WHITE CLOUD [*sitting, grinning fatuously*]: Oh, damp, damp!

[*The monks wring out their kimono bottoms. She poses and speaks with deliberate intonation, so that* NARUKAMI *cannot misunderstand her meaning.*]

TAEMA: Though in the past I had disliked the slightest moistness caused by dew or love, now I pushed aside the short grass surrounding the small house in which my lord dwelled.

WHITE CLOUD and BLACK CLOUD [*weakly*]: Did you reach your destination?

TAEMA: When I quickly pushed open his rough gate and instantly entered, my lord said, "Ah! You have come!" [*She places her hand on* WHITE CLOUD's *thigh.*] He took my hand. [*She takes* BLACK CLOUD's *hand.*] And led me straight to bed. [*She looks down modestly.*]

WHITE CLOUD [*falling backward*]: Rapture! I melt!

BLACK CLOUD [*holding his hands over his lap*]: I don't know about you, but I'm as stiff as a log!

TAEMA [*demurely*]: We exchanged intimate stories. We burned incense and we drank sake. We hugged and tumbled, tumbled and hugged. Becoming unruly in our passion, we ended having a lover's quarrel. [*Miming both lovers.*] "Oh, stop it." "What if I don't?" "I'll pinch you." [*She pinches* WHITE CLOUD.] "I'll hit you." "Just try it once." "Well, I will," I said, and hit my lord on the head.

[*She slaps their bald heads. The hold their heads and wail.*]

WHITE CLOUD and BLACK CLOUD: Wah! Wah!

NARUKAMI [*entranced, he rises and poses with one foot on the top step*]:

And then. And then. Yes . . . what then?

TAEMA [*rising on her knees, miming*] : Very soon our quarrel grew heated. "I'll leave." "No, you will not leave." "I shall if I want," I said as I rose to go. He grasped my sleeve. "You are too heartless," he said. "Try to stop me if you want; I must leave." "No, stay." "Goodbye," I pulled my sleeve and broke away . . .

[*NARUKAMI is pulled, like the lover, toward TAEMA: he takes two steps forward, sways, and, to loud Yama Oroshi mountain storm pattern and batan tsuke beats, falls down the steps unconscious. He lies huddled on the ground. The monks rush to either side of him.*]

WHITE CLOUD: Master! Master!

BLACK CLOUD: Master has fainted!

WHITE CLOUD and BLACK CLOUD [*waving their arms helplessly*] : Master, Master!

TAEMA [*innocently*] : Dear Reverend.

[*The monks lift NARUKAMI to a sitting position. TAEMA hesitates, then rushes to the waterfall, as the large drum loudly beats Taki Oto waterfall pattern.*]

WHITE CLOUD [*on NARUKAMI's right*] : Ahh! His whole body . . .

BLACK CLOUD [*on his left*] . . . has grown cold.

[*TAEMA mimes dipping up water with her long kimono sleeve. She rises to bring it to NARUKAMI, but it spills. She puts her face into the water, rises, and hurries to NARUKAMI. She kneels beside him and, placing her lips against his, gives him the water. She massages his breast gently. The monks gasp. Feigning embarrassment, she backs away and kneels with her face to the ground. Music stops.*]

TAEMA [*softly*] : My Saint, my Saint.

NARUKAMI [*suddenly opens his eyes, his face unbelieving*] : Companion monks?

WHITE CLOUD: Praise to Buddha . . .

BLACK CLOUD: . . . Master has revived.

NARUKAMI: Something not of priestly nature has occurred. Engrossed without knowing it by the woman's tale, I fell unconscious from my seat of meditation. Yet, though my senses had fled, I think I felt a cool drop of water enter my mouth and revive me.

TAEMA [*modestly*] : Yes, it happened. From my mouth to yours, I transferred water from the stream.

NARUKAMI [*looks wonderingly at her*] : Ehh? Was the one who placed a drop of cool water on my lips . . . you?

TAEMA [*bowing*] : Yes, your Reverence.

NARUKAMI: And the one who pressed their flesh to mine to warm my breast . . . was you?

TAEMA [*bowing*] : Yes, your Reverence.

NARUKAMI [*considering*] : Hmm.

[*Suddenly he leaps to his feet and strikes her to the ground. Drum beats Yama Oroshi mountain storm pattern loudly.*]

Monks, watch her!

[NARUKAMI *swiftly returns to the pavilion. He turns and glares savagely at her. The monks drop to their knees facing* TAEMA.]

Ahh! Dangerous female!

[*Music changes to* Mizuki Sanjū, *"Moistness," played by shamisen.* NARUKAMI *speaks rapidly, rhythmically, with great force.*]

In ancient times there was a priest in India from Benaras called the Holy One-Horned Wizard.[31] Such was his wizardry he rode the clouds, he walked on water, until the day the Dragon Gods of Rain deluged the ground with endless downpour, when unthinkingly the Holy Hermit slipped and fell into a valley far below. Enraged, he cursed all the Dragon Gods living between the heavens and the seas, saying, "You caused the rain which caused the muddy earth to cast me down." With angry eyes the size of wagon wheels the Holy Wizard imprisoned all offending Gods of Rain. [*Slowly.*] He sealed them in a rock cave made magically inviolate by holy prayers hung upon a sacred rope. Drought seized the world, fields whirled with dust, everywhere the people suffered. Then the Emperor of that time conceived a plan by which the power of this Wizard would be destroyed. He called into his presence that lady of the court most perfect in countenance, Lady Sendara, and said to her, "Go to the grotto where the hermit dwells and with your sensual charms seduce this man so rain will fall." Vowing this, she sought him out, bewitched him with her sexual charms, and broke his secret spells. [*More and more rapidly.*] Black clouds filled the sky, rains deluged the land in torrents day and night, until, moistened, trees, grass, and the five grains came alive again. That silk-gowned woman drowned in lust a wizard of such power as he! Confess it, woman! Like her you are ordered by the Emperor to disrupt my meditation!

[*Music fades to silence.*]

And the one who has instructed you can be no other master of occult arts than Abe Kiyoyuki! Well? Answer in absolute truth, or on this spot you shall be ripped to pieces and flung away! Well! Well! Speak!

kuriage

[*He glares fixedly at her, plants his right foot on the top step, whirls the rosary over his head in his left hand, and poses in a fierce mie to battari tsuke beats.*]

TAEMA: Your suspicions overwhelm me. In truth it was my fondest dream to become your Reverence's disciple, but you allowed no one to approach. Then, distracted by your presence I told you of my intimate affairs. Now, since you doubt me, it is useless to go on living.

[*She weeps pathetically, then suddenly rises and gestures distractedly toward the waterfall.*]

I shall sink myself in the pool of the waterfall! May death vindicate my intentions! Yes!

[*Drum loudly beats* Taki Oto *waterfall pattern. Pressing her hands to her breast dramatically, she rushes toward the falls.*]

NARUKAMI: Stop her, monks!

31. The account is almost identical to that in book thirty-seven of the *Taiheiki* (ca. 1364–1374) and is undoubtedly from that source.

WHITE CLOUD and BLACK CLOUD: Yes, Master! Wait, please! Please, lady!
   [*They seize her by the arms at the brink of the fall and bring her back.*]
TAEMA [*helplessly*] : No, no. Let me go. Please let me die.
   [*She falls to her knees struggling, as they continue to hold her arms.* Taki Oto *fades away.* NARUKAMI *stands struck with admiration.*]
NARUKAMI: What impetuosity. In spite of once having sinned, your face radiates your true character. Admirable. [*Gravely.*] You must not die, for salvation does not lie in death.
TAEMA [*meekly*] : Yet, though I live . . .
NARUKAMI: Become a nun. Become a priestess.
TAEMA: Ehh?
   [*She breaks away from the monks. They kneel to her right.*]
NARUKAMI [*warming to the subject*] : Narukami will administer your tonsure. You will become a disciple of Buddha.
TAEMA [*wide-eyed*] : Do you mean that I may receive the tonsure at your hands, becoming a pupil of your very own?
NARUKAMI: You may.
TAEMA: Can this be true?
NARUKAMI: Does Narukami speak lightly or tell lies?
   [*He poses, proud and pleased with himself. She bows, making grateful, submissive little gestures as if overwhelmed by his masculine generosity.*]
TAEMA: Ohh! Master, I thank you from the depths of my heart.
WHITE CLOUD: Whew. I'm glad it's settled.
BLACK CLOUD [*grinning*] : So am I. Now when my habit tears I can get it sewn. We're in luck.
   [NARUKAMI *draws a straw mat forward and sits cross-legged.*]
NARUKAMI: Monks, go down the mountain. Bring razor and comb for the tonsure, and return.
WHITE CLOUD and BLACK CLOUD [*apprehensively*] : What, go?
NARUKAMI [*glaring at them*] : You won't go?
WHITE CLOUD: We're going, we're going. But . . . it's getting dark.
BLACK CLOUD: Couldn't we go tomorrow?
NARUKAMI: Do you revere your master's words? You have said you will go. You should disappear.
WHITE CLOUD and BLACK CLOUD [*sighing*] : Yes, Master.
   [*Drum beats quiet* Taki Oto *waterfall pattern. They rise and put on their sandals. Chattering and grumbling, they move toward the hanamichi.*]
WHITE CLOUD: Disappear. Disappear. I can disappear. [*Rhythmically.*] But when we vanish, the Master . . .
BLACK CLOUD: . . . and that woman . . .
WHITE CLOUD and BLACK CLOUD [*turning back to look*] : . . . will be alone together!
NARUKAMI [*glowering*] : What?
   [*The monks exchange knowing glances and grin foolishly. They puff out their cheeks, like a fat woman, and use girlish folk-dance gestures.*]
WHITE CLOUD: Goddess of Happiness! Goddess of Happiness!

BLACK CLOUD: Happy because she was . . .

WHITE CLOUD and BLACK CLOUD: . . . a priest's wife![32] Ha, ha, ha!

NARUKAMI: Rapscallions, both of you!

[*They run laughing to seven-three. Drumming stops.*]

WHITE CLOUD: Scold us as much as you want, Master is a snapping turtle . . .[33]

BLACK CLOUD: . . . poking up . . .

WHITE CLOUD: . . . against the Lady!

[*With closed fist, he gestures.*]

BLACK CLOUD: Oh, Master!

WHITE CLOUD and BLACK CLOUD [*salaciously*] : Poke, poke! Paddle, paddle!

[*Large drum and bell play religious* Zen no Tsutome, *"Zen Prayer," as the* CHORUS *sings the folk song* Zubonboe *to lively shamisen accompaniment. One monk waves his arms weakly and pokes stupidly about, exploring with his head, miming a presumably old and lethargic turtle, as the other laughs and waggles his hips.*]

CHORUS [*singing offstage*] :
Zubonbo ya! Poke, poke!
    Zubonbo ya! Paddle, paddle!
How scandalous having as a mate,
    An old turtle paddling in my pond.
    Zubonbo ya!

[*They laugh and point accusingly at* NARUKAMI. *They wave goodbye and dance off down the hanamichi as the audience applauds. Music stops.*]

NARUKAMI: Foolish fellows! Detestable pair!

[*She looks coyly up at him and bows very slowly.*]

TAEMA: And now, my teacher . . . ?

NARUKAMI: Already you call me teacher. If I am your teacher, you must become my pupil. Maintain a pure heart, and soon you will be ordained a nun.

TAEMA [*drawing back*] : When they return with the razor, will you cut off all my hair?

NARUKAMI: You'll have a clean-shaven pate before you know it!

[*She cries piteously. He looks bewildered.*]

Why do you cry?

TAEMA [*weakly, between sobs*] : When I think my black hair, each strand of which I smoothed a thousand times, is to be cut and thrown away . . .

NARUKAMI [*touched*] : You weep in sorrow?

TAEMA: I do.

[*Turning away, as if weeping, she thinks. Suddenly she rises on her knees and presses her fingers to her breast. She gasps and cries out in pain. She*

32. A pun on the word *daikoku*, which means both "God of Fortune" and "priest's wife."

33. The snapping turtle as a metaphor for the male sex organ is found in popular songs of the period.

does this several times, as the large drum beats ominous Yama Oroshi
mountain storm pattern.]

Ahh! Ahh! Ahhhh!

NARUKAMI: What is it? What is the matter?

TAEMA: The sorrow I feel has brought on a spasm . . . ahhhh!

[*She gasps pitifully and her body weaves from side to side. He stands
helplessly by her.*]

NARUKAMI: How dreadful. We don't have medicine. Ah! I could massage
your back.

TAEMA: I am too much trouble, dear Master. [*She has another spasm.*]

NARUKAMI [*righteously*] : In case of sickness all barriers are cast aside.
Here, now. Here, now.

[*With naive self-righteousness he stands behind her and very properly
rubs her shoulders. The drumming stops. Her cries subside. Silence.*]

TAEMA [*tiny, innocent voice*] : There is pain in my abdomen.

nureba
NARUKAMI: Ah, the source of pain must be in the pit of your solar plexus. I
have the power to cure spasms by the laying on of hands. Here, now.
Here, now.

[*As before, he approaches his task with utmost seriousness. He kneels,
placing his left hand on her shoulder, and deliberately inserts his right
hand into the breast of her kimono. He rubs a moment, then stops.*]

Does that feel good? Am I reaching the seat of your distress?

share
TAEMA [*innocently leans against him*] : Your kind hands touch my heart.

NARUKAMI [*rubbing*] : There, there. Is that better? Is it better?

[*His hand goes deeper inside her kimono. Suddenly he starts, and falls
back. He stands in amazement.*]

TAEMA [*meekly*] : What have you done?

NARUKAMI: My . . . my hand touched a wonderful thing.

TAEMA [*innocently*] : And what was that?

NARUKAMI: For the first time since I was born, my hand has been inside a
woman's kimono. There, on the middle of your chest, my hand touched
something soft, like two pillows hanging down with little handpulls on
the front.

TAEMA [*chiding*] : And you are called teacher? [*She hides her face as if
embarrassed.*] They are breasts . . . your Reverence.

NARUKAMI [*genuinely surprised*] : Breasts? Is that so? The breasts to which
I was indebted when, as a child, I gratefully drank my mother's milk?
What is a monk, that he forgets such a thing as breasts? I am dull, like a
wooden bridge.[34]

[*He strikes his head in wonder.*]

TAEMA: Such purity is laudable, Master.

NARUKAMI: And now, I shall discover the source of your illness.

[*No longer serious, he shows innocent delight in what he has discovered.
She rises on her knees to be more accessible. He stands behind her, with*

34. "To people he seems like a wooden bridge," in *Tsurezuregusa* (1330–1331) by
Kenkō Hōshi.

feet planted widely apart, his hand in her kimono. He rubs with broad gestures, his face shining with joy. Their bodies sway from side to side.]
Here now, here now. Ah, yes. Yes! Here are the breasts! How round and plump they are. [*His hand goes lower.*] Beneath them lies the stomach, cramped before it now lies soft to my touch. [*Hand goes lower.*] Next we reach the navel, Divine Seat of Life, Heaven's Center. [*Hand goes lower.*] Below Heaven's Center, the Sea of Seducing Vapors. [*Hand goes lower.*] Below the Sea of Seducing Vapors, Buddha's Pure Paradise! [*He holds her tightly.*] Is my touch pleasing?
[*They pose. Although he does not move, we see through his face his transformation into a creature of raging lust. Finally he looks down at her. Still feigning innocence, she returns his gaze.*]
TAEMA [*scarcely audible voice*] : Master . . . no more.
[*With a choked cry he rubs her deliriously.*]
NARUKAMI: Ahhh! I adore you! I worship you! My hope of reaching Buddha's Highest Paradise is gone. Only let me dwell in the bottom of the lowest level of heaven![35]
[*He embraces her in both arms. She escapes and they both fall back onto the ground.*]
TAEMA [*feigning surprise*] : Master. My Saint. What are you . . . ?
[*He faces her on all fours, pleading. His voice is slow, harsh, almost unrecognizable.*]
NARUKAMI: Would you say . . . I am mad?
TAEMA [*carefully*] : This is not your true nature.
NARUKAMI: Would you say . . . Buddha is offended?
TAEMA: You are a saintly monk who could not offend Buddha.
[*He rushes to her, seizes her arm, and shakes it violently. She pulls away. He towers over her.*]
NARUKAMI: I am damned! I am damned! Still living, but fallen into hell! Though damned, though sinking, what do I care! What do I care! Buddha himself was first a mortal. He had a wife as Prince Shitta, he had children. Say yes! Say yes to me!
[*He advances; she edges away trembling.*]
Refuse me and I shall transform myself on this very spot into a devil! I shall devour that beautiful throat and carry you into hell with me!
[*She buries her face in her kimono sleeve with a little cry. His face is tortured. His voice is terrible.*]
kuriage   Woman! Well! Well! What is . . . your . . . answer!!
TAEMA [*pretending fear but actually toying with him*] : My dear Saint . . .
NARUKAMI [*pressing*] : Do not refuse me!
TAEMA: Your Reverence . . .
NARUKAMI [*voice rising to a scream*] : Do not . . . refuse . . . me!
TAEMA [*prolonging his agony as long as she can before speaking*] : Yes, my Teacher.

35. The three levels of Buddhist paradise are each divided into three levels. Narukami had hoped to achieve the first level but now is content with the lowest, or ninth, level of salvation. Perhaps an erotic allusion as well.

NARUKAMI: Ahhh!

[*He collapses to the floor in relief. His lust evaporates and once more he is the naive and happy monk.*]

TAEMA [*chiding*]: Who ever walked the path of love with such a face as yours. It was frightening.

NARUKAMI: But . . . but will you?

TAEMA [*sweetly*]: If you want, I will.

NARUKAMI [*like an eager child*]: Death will be painless! To paradise![36] Come, come!

[*He rises gleefully and takes her hand, pointing to the pavilion. Pretending coyness, she pulls him back. He kneels beside her.*]

TAEMA: You're in such a hurry. Tell me, dear Teacher, are you determined to make me your wife?

NARUKAMI: There is a rule for marriage: plunge headlong into the pool.

TAEMA: Come now, do wait a bit. If you want to marry, I will, but a monk for a husband is hateful. [*She turns away pouting.*]

NARUKAMI [*jovially*]: They say a monk is good medicine for beriberi.

TAEMA: Will you quit the priesthood if I ask?

NARUKAMI: I'll do it this minute.

TAEMA: You'll become a man?

NARUKAMI: And fix my hair in the latest fashion.

TAEMA: [*wheedling*]: Will you, honestly?

NARUKAMI: I swear by the Founder of Buddhism!

[*He holds the rosary up to his forehead. She flounces.*]

TAEMA: Hmph. That oath stinks of Buddha. And your noble name too, "Saint" Narukami . . .

NARUKAMI [*placating her*]: Now, now, I can change the name.

TAEMA: Change it? To . . . ?

NARUKAMI [*slaps down the rosary, and poses proudly*]: The lecher, Ichikawa Danjūrō![37]

[*She smiles, he laughs heartily at himself. The audience applauds.*]

TAEMA [*modestly*]: We will be a loving couple.

[*He takes both of her hands and rises.*]

share   NARUKAMI: Come, come, let's begin our play!

[*The audience laughs at the pun.*]

TAEMA [*shaking him off*]: Again, you want to rush so. Before we become a couple, I want to drink our betrothal cup of wine.

NARUKAMI [*agreeably*]: We will, we will. We'll drink the cup. We have wine.

TAEMA [*surprised*]: Ehh?

NARUKAMI: And we have a sake cup.

[*A bell tolls in the distance. Shamisen play* Kin Aikata, *"Bell Melody," in the background.* NARUKAMI *crosses up to the rocks by the pavilion and*

36. *Rendai*, "lotus platform," where the statue of Buddha stands. Lotus also implies paradise, in this case sexual bliss.

37. Ichikawa Danjūrō Sukebei. A pun on the word *sukebei* (lecher), not a proper name but sounding very much like one because its two characters are used in many common names (*Suke*roku, Gon*suke*, Monno*suke*, Shin*bei*, Sem*bei*, Mam*bei*).

receives from a formally dressed STAGE ASSISTANT *a red lacquered "cup," almost twenty inches across, and a wooden cask of wine. Chuckling, he shows them to her.*]

The little monks thought they could hide these from me by the waterfall, but I saw them.

[*He sits, placing cask and cup between them.*]

TAEMA: Wonderful. Wishes come true. [*Picking up the cask.*] Here, you shall drink first.

NARUKAMI [*protesting*] : No, no. I've heard the proper way is that the wife drinks first, then passes the cup to the husband.

TAEMA: What a clever thing to say.

NARUKAMI: Here, here. [*He pours.*]

TAEMA: Not too much, not too much. I drink to our two existences, now and in the future.

[*Daintily she drinks the wine in three sips, as prescribed in the wedding ritual, then passes the cup to him. She takes the cask, but he will not let her pour.*]

NARUKAMI: No, no.

TAEMA [*hurt*] : Why not?

NARUKAMI [*embarrased, blurts it out*] : I haven't touched a drop in my life. I even hate cucumbers pickled in wine.

TAEMA: It may have been all very well to abstain before, but when you take a wife it is proper that you should drink.

NARUKAMI: But if it's something I can't stand?

TAEMA [*turning away, piqued*] : When I tell you to drink, will you not drink?

NARUKAMI [*bows contritely*] : I will do it. I will do it.

TAEMA [*still angry*] : Leave me alone.

NARUKAMI: Fill my cup, please, while I say I was wrong. I was wrong.

[*Music stops. They ad-lib much chatter back and forth as she presses the wine on him and he hesitantly accepts. She pours more and more sake in the cup until it is full to the brim. He lifts it to drink but the smell turns his stomach. She sniffs disdainfully at him. He strikes a pose. Large drum beats ominous* Doro-doro. *He gathers his courage and buries his face in the cup, drinking without pause until it is drained. The painting of Fudō hanging in the altar of the pavilion burns and disappears. He sits up, gasping. His head reels.*]

TAEMA: How do you feel?

NARUKAMI: For the first time since I was born, I have drunk sake. My stomach has turned upside down. [*He shivers and hugs himself.*] I'm cold.

[*She moves behind him and provocatively puts her arms around his shoulders.*]

TAEMA: Soon you will grow hot, I promise.

NARUKAMI [*politely*] : I return the cup to you.

TAEMA: I don't want to hear "return" during our nuptials.

NARUKAMI: Then let us say "take back?"

TAEMA: "Take back" is even worse.

NARUKAMI [*bowing with exaggerated politeness*] : Well then, please accept this cup as an humble gift.

TAEMA: You shall drink in celebration.

[*Although he protests, she begins to refill the cup.*]

NARUKAMI [*feebly*] : I can drink no more.

TAEMA [*angry*] : Will you not do what I tell you?

NARUKAMI [*sheepishly, holding the cup to his forehead and bowing*] : Ah, ah! Fill it, I beg you.

TAEMA: That's better.

NARUKAMI: Pour it full to the brim.

[*She leans forward on her knees to pour. Suddenly she pulls back in fright.*]

TAEMA: Ahhh!

NARUKAMI: What is it?

TAEMA [*hands to her breast*] : In the middle of the cup . . . is a snake!

NARUKAMI [*laughing*] : What silliness. There is nothing . . .

TAEMA: There is.

NARUKAMI: . . . here. Look. [*He looks and is startled.*] Ah, I see. It's not a snake. That is the sacred rope.[38] See.

[*He stamps forward with his left foot and brings the cup near her. He points into the cup, then at the rope across the waterfall. With a great show of fear, she looks first into the cup then up at the straw rope.*]

TAEMA: Indeed, it is a sacred rope.

NARUKAMI [*laughing heartily*] : Ha, ha, ha! You are a timid one!

TAEMA [*casually*] : What kind of rope is it?

NARUKAMI [*proudly*] : That is a miraculous rope.

TAEMA: Oh. And why?

NARUKAMI: A secret too precious to be spoken to anyone!

TAEMA [*submissively*] : Ah.

[*She backs away, as if accepting his refusal, but from time to time she glances surreptitiously at the rope. He lifts and drains the enormous cup. Her display of timidity has made him feel masterful, and he abandons caution. He poses. A distant temple bell tolls. Shamisen play* Kin Aikata *softly in the background.*]

NARUKAMI: I nurse a hatred for the Emperor and have imprisoned all the Dragon Gods of the world in this grotto. [*Bell tolls.*] Hung with secret prayers, the sacred rope binds them.

[*He puts the cup down and on one elbow, feeling the effects of the wine, confides in her.*]

Cut the rope and escaping, the Dragon Gods will bring down floods and torrents of rain. Ha, ha, ha!

[*He falls over, laughing loudly. The bell tolls. He faces her on all fours.*]

Absolutely, do not speak of this.

TAEMA: If the rope is cut . . . will rain fall? How remarkable. Should I . . .

38. *Shime*, a braided straw rope symbolizing and ensuring purity in Shintō.

[*She looks at the rope and almost rushes to it. The bell tolls. She catches herself and quickly picks up the wine cask.*]

. . . pour more wine? Come.

[*She overcomes his feeble protests and pours a full cup of wine. He gulps it down and sits in a blissful daze.*]

NARUKAMI: Ah! "North Mountain Cherry" is the name of a famous play![39]

TAEMA [*wheedling*] : You must drink three cups for marriage. But don't if you don't like me.

NARUKAMI: I didn't say I didn't like . . .

[*His voice fades off. He holds out the cup for her to fill, drains it, and falls over on his side. Music stops.*]

Around and around . . . and . . . around . . .

TAEMA: Master Narukami.

[*She helps him sit up. He rises unsteadily and takes her hand.*]

NARUKAMI: Come.

TAEMA: Yes.

CHORUS [*offstage, sings to shamisen accompaniment, indicating the passing of time*] :

waka
share
engo

No sooner used to,

Our evening's rain of pleasure, when the dawn of morning comes;

The sleeves of your sleeping robe, dampened in the morning mist.[40]

[*He leads her up the steps to the pavilion. She poses by the pillar, looking at the sacred rope. He draws her into his arms and they sink to the floor of the pavilion before the altar. He places a hand on her thigh. She leans against his chest. The blinds are lowered hiding them. A* STAGE ASSISTANT *clears away the cask and wine cup. Music ends.*]

TAEMA [*from inside the blind*] : Master. Wake up. Please, Master. Wake up . . . wake . . . up . . .

[*Her voice trails off. She knows he will not wake. A side blind is partially raised. The large drum beats* Taki Oto *waterfall pattern in a steady rhythm, gradually crescendoing through her scene.* TAEMA *slips out and rushes down to center stage. She kneels, facing the pavilion, and bows contritely.*]

Forgive me Narukami. I have been wicked. I did not want your fall, but it was our most gracious Emperor's command. [*She bows.*] As I promised . . . I will break the spell.

[*Shamisen and small drums play fast* Ishidan, *"Rock Steps."* TAEMA *quails when she sees how high the rocks are. But she tries to climb the steep rock steps to the waterfall, to scattered batan tsuke beats. Her long court robe hinders her and she trips again and again on the slippery rocks. Slowly she pulls herself up, using a creeping vine for support. At the top she poses to a roar of the large drum and battari tsuke beats. She kneels and unwraps a*

---

39. The last part of the play's full title, "Saint Narukami, the God Fudō, and North Mountain Cherry" (*Narukami Fudō Kitayamazakura*).

40. In waka form, except the third phrase is seven, rather than the usual five, syllables. "Rain," "dampened," and "mist" are engo related to lovemaking.

short dagger that she takes from her sash. She clasps her hands together in prayer. Music stops.]

Believing in the Three Jewels of Buddha[41] and pressing my head to the ground, I pray to the Twelve Deities of Heaven, the twenty-five Benevolent Gods, and to the Eight Dragon Gods: let rain fall. Believing in the Three Jewels of Buddha, I press my head to the ground.

[*Taki Oto drum beats swell. She rushes forward to cut the rope with her dagger, but icy spray drives her back. Again and again she tries. At last she forces her way up to the rope and cuts it through, to battari tsuke beats. Flute and stick drum burst into Hayabue, "Quick Flute," and the large drum plays Ama Oto rain pattern. She falls back in fright as Dragon Gods, one after the other, escape up the falls. The next instant lightning flashes and there is a roar of thunder. To bata-bata tsuke beats she flees onto the hanamichi. She stumbles and falls at seven-three. Silence. She turns back and looks fearfully at the pavilion. Music resumes. She rises, pivots completely, to show her beauty, and, to deliberate bata-bata tsuke beats, moves elegantly down the hanamichi and off. Lightning flashes. The large drum beats Kaminari Oto thunder pattern. Loud bata-bata tsuke beats. WHITE CLOUD and BLACK CLOUD lead a dozen white-clad monks onto the two hanamichi. They fold their arms in their sleeves and try to protect their faces from the pouring rain. They call out as they run.*]

MONKS: Master! Saint Narukami!

[*The blinds of the pavilion are raised. In the dim light of the storm we can only make out that NARUKAMI is on his hands and knees, and that his head is down. WHITE CLOUD and BLACK CLOUD hurry up to the steps to greet him. The others remain stage right.*]

WHITE CLOUD [*relieved*] : Ah, Master, here you are. Here you are. Agh! He smells!

BLACK CLOUD [*covering his nose*] : He's been drinking wine!

MONKS: Ahh! Master!

[*They all notice the hanging ends of the rope. They gape and tremble.*]

WHITE CLOUD: Our Narukami's secret spell has been broken!

BLACK CLOUD: The sacred rope is cut, the Dragon Gods . . .

MONKS: . . . escaped and gone!

WHITE CLOUD: And so the rains . . .

MONKS: . . . come pouring down!

[*Large drum beats furious Ama Oto rain pattern. The monks tremble and hug themselves.*]

BLACK CLOUD: Lightning and thunder . . .

MONKS: . . . flash and roar!

[*Lightning flashes, Kaminari Oto thunder pattern swells. The monks fall to their knees, terrified.*]

Buddha save us! Buddha save us!

[*The sound rouses NARUKAMI. He moves, but his face cannot be seen.*]

NARUKAMI [*fearsome, demonic voice*] : What! It rains!

41. Buddha, the sutras, and the priesthood.

Lady Taema and Princess Nishiki, both in love with Toyohide, enter simultaneously on two hanamichi to begin Act III, Scene 1, set in the Imperial Palace
Garden. (Kamigata Jōruri musicians, in the background, accompany dance
sequences in this production.) (*Taema:* Nakamura Shikan; *Nishiki:* Bandō
Tamasaburō; *Toyohide:* Nakamura Senjaku) Page 127

Hayakumo wears the nō mask of Okina, the deity of longevity. (*Hayakumo:* Morita Kanya) Page 129

Hayakumo's disguise is removed, showing facial makeup which is more villainous than in previous scenes. He reads from the scroll the names of his supporters. "The lords who sign their names in blood, petitioning me to ascend the throne, are . . . hmm . . . hmm . . . Only Mototsune, Toyohide, and Ono Harumichi remain to oppose me." (*Hayakumo*: Morita Kanya) Page 131

Narukami innocently massages Taema's breast to relieve her pain. "I have the power to cure spasms by the laying on of hands. Here, now. Here, now. Does that feel good? Am I reaching the seat of your distress?" (*Narukami:* Onoe Shoroku; *Taema:* Nakamura Shikan) Page 150

"What silliness. There is nothing here. Look. It's not a snake. That is the sacred rope. See." (*Taema:* Nakamura Shikan; *Narukami:* Onoe Shoroku) Page 154

Narukami begins his transformation into the Thunder God. His wig and makeup are changed. He drops his kimono top showing a white inner kimono woven with a lightning design. (*Narukami:* Onoe Shoroku)

Basting threads holding the sleeves of the white inner kimono are pulled out. The kimono top falls to reveal a third kimono embroidered with great orange, red, and yellow flame patterns. Page 157

To signify his abandonment of Buddhism, Narukami rips a sutra in two. He poses in a ferocious mie, holding the ends of the sutra as Stage Assistants lift the costume around him in order to increase his size. (*Narukami:* Onoe Shoroku) Page 158

The imperial envoy, General Sakuramachi, speaks to Taema, "In his benefi-
cence, the Emperor proclaims, 'the marriage to Lord Toyohide, as previously
pledged, shall be speedily arranged.' Do you humbly accept his will?" (*Retainer:*
Nakamura Fukusuke; *Taema:* Nakamura Shikan; *Toyohide:* Nakamura Senjaku;
Sakuramachi: Ichikawa Omezō) Page 160

The Guardian God Fudō, holding sword and rope with which to subdue wrongdoers. A flaming penumbra rises behind him. At his right kneels the Rushana Buddha reincarnated as a child, as dark and fearsome as Fudō himself. (*Rushana:* Onoe Rokuya; *Fudō:* Onoe Shoroku) Page 163

The final tableau of *Saint Narukami and the God Fudō*. Autumn maple leaves frame a distant perspective of mountain peaks rising above the clouds. The God Fudō is flanked by the Kannon Bodhisattva and the Rushana Buddha. Though defeated, Prince Hayakumo mounts a small platform center where he poses formally with drawn sword overhead. On his right, Takino, Taema, and Toyohide move into final poses, and on his left, Sakuramachi and Retainer pose strongly. Geki Bushi Singers sit on a dais to the side. (*Rushana:* Onoe Rokuya; *Fudō:* Onoe Shoroku; *Kannon:* Bandō Shuka; *Takino:* Onoe Taganojō; *Taema:* Nakamura Shikan; *Toyohide:* Nakamura Senjaku; *Hayakumo:* Morita Kanya; *Sakuramachi:* Ichikawa Omezō; *Retainer:* Nakamura Fukusuke) Page 164

MONKS [*clasping their rosaries*] : The rains pour!

[*Tremendous burst of* Ama Oto *rain pattern on the large drum.*]

NARUKAMI: What! It thunders!

MONKS: The thunder roars!

[*Roar of* Kaminari Oto *thunder pattern. Lightning flashes.*]

NARUKAMI: Why does the rain pour? [Ama Oto *rain pattern.*] Why does the thunder roar? [Kaminari *thunder pattern and lightning.*]

watarizerifu   WHITE CLOUD [*rising*] : Because, dear Master, you were ruined by a woman just now.

BLACK CLOUD: We asked her name and where she fled.

THIRD MONK: She is Lady Taema of the Clouds . . .

FOURTH MONK: . . . most beautiful lady of the Court . . .

WHITE CLOUD: . . . by the Emperor's command, come to seduce . . .

MONKS: . . . our Master!

NARUKAMI [*terrible voice*] : Ehhh? The woman came to destroy my power? Aghhh!

[*He lifts his head slowly during the speech. He is transformed; bold black and deep blue lines around his mouth and eyes have turned his face into a mask of ferocious evil. His head is topped with a great bush of black hair. With a cry he rips his rosary in two. He cocks his head, plants his right foot on the top step, flings his arms wide, and poses in a furious mie, to battari tsuke beats. The monks fall to the ground. Shamisen again play Mizuki Sanjū in the background. As NARUKAMI speaks, two monks and a STAGE ASSISTANT help him slip off his kimono top, revealing a white kimono with a jagged silver pattern representing lightning.*]

For each inch of good a foot of evil blocks our way! [*He throws down the rosary.*] The secret spells are shattered! I have transgressed Buddha's laws and incur Buddha's wrath! So be it then: I shall become a living Thunder God and pursue you, woman, to the ends of the earth! Hah, hah! How easy it will be!

[*He rises majestically, towering over* WHITE CLOUD *and* BLACK CLOUD. *He hurls a sutra to the right, another to the left. They are acc dion-folded and they flutter open into long streamers. Again the monks . . NARU-KAMI poses in a ferocious mie. The small curtain stage left . . s to show the Ōzatsuma SINGER and shamisen PLAYER.*] [42]

ŌZATSUMA SINGER [*accompanied by the shamisen*] :

Spirit of Thunder and Lightning, Narukami,

    Concentrating mind and spirit, to search out,

   To approach and overtake her.

[WHITE CLOUD *and* BLACK CLOUD *seize his arms and pull him first one way then the other. With a powerful gesture he throws them off; they fall, pulling out basting threads in his sleeves and a STAGE ASSISTANT pulls down his silver and white kimono top to reveal beneath it a third kimono, silver with a brilliant pattern of orange and yellow leaping flames repre-*]

---

42. A form of narrative singing used in kabuki during the Genroku period and derived from Geki Bushi.

senting the power of lightning. The two terrified monks leap down from the pavilion to the ground below. NARUKAMI rips a sutra in half and throws both halves to the monks. Each holds an end as NARUKAMI poses in a mie to battari tsuke beats.]

NARUKAMI [*fiercely*] : East to Outer Beach in Ōshu!

[*He tosses the other ends of the sutras to the monks and crosses to the pillar right.*]

ŌZATSUMA SINGER: West to Demon Island in Chinzei!

[*He wraps his left leg and both arms around the pillar, crosses his eyes, and poses in a hashiramaki, or "wrapped-around-a-pillar," mie, to battari tsuke beats. A STAGE ASSISTANT spreads out the fallen kimono top behind him, to make the figure seem larger and more powerful.*]

NARUKAMI: South to the Falls of Nachi in Kumano!

[*He crosses to the pillar left.*]

ŌZATSUMA SINGER: North as far as the Wild Sea of Echigo![43]

[*He poses in an identical hashiramaki mie, with arms and legs wrapped around the pillar.*]

NARUKAMI: To places no human ventures!

[*Small drums and flute again play rapid Daishō. He takes the Diamond Scepter from the altar and, holding it over his head, leaps onto the main stage.[44] Brandishing it, he passes through the monks formed in two lines to batan and battari tsuke beats. The monks form a human platform center stage. NARUKAMI is lifted onto it. Raising both hands over his head and holding the scepter in his teeth, he poses in a mie, sleeves held out for effect by a STAGE ASSISTANT, to battari tsuke beats.*]

ŌZATSUMA SINGER [*slowly*] : Go a thousand miles!

NARUKAMI [*almost a scream*] : Leap ten times a thousand miles!

tate

[*Large drum plays* Yama Oroshi *mountain storm pattern as stick drum and and flute resume music at a deliberate tempo. Batan and battari tsuke beats alternate, as the monks begin a stylized fight with NARUKAMI, attempting to restrain him. One at a time, the monks try to seize his arms, but he easily shrugs them off. He passes between them, brushing them to either side. They form a single line and try to push him back. He counters, forces them back two steps, then with a bravura gesture sends them falling like a string of dominoes. NARUKAMI mounts the rock steps and seizes the cut rope. He stands with his feet together, holding the rope over his head in his right hand, in a Fudō mie, to battari tsuke beats. He hurls the rope at the monks. One catches it and is bowled over. He hurls the other half of the rope and another monk rolls over catching it. A monk climbs the steps to halt NARUKAMI. He is flipped in a somersault off the platform onto the main stage. NARUKAMI rushes down and poses with his foot on the body. The monks rush forward protesting. A dummy is*

43. The outer limits of Japan are described in these words in the *Soga Monogatari* (mid-fourteenth century). The same passage is used at the climax of another aragoto play, *Yanone* (The Arrowhead).

44. A short metal rod with bulging ends that is used as a weapon to quell evil, especially in Shingon Buddhism.

substituted for the prostrate body. NARUKAMI *raises the dummy over his head. The monks fall back terrified. He hurls the dummy at them and it bounces from hand to hand, down the line of white figures and out of sight off left. To furious bata-bata tsuke beats,* NARUKAMI *rushes onto the hanamichi.*]

MONKS: Master! Master!

ŌZATSUMA SINGER: [*elaborately ornamented vocal pattern to shamisen accompaniment*] :

Indeed, the pursuing Narukami . . .

[*At seven-three* NARUKAMI *turns back and glares at the monks. They fall to the ground shielding their faces. A sharp ki clack.* NARUKAMI *faces the audience.*]

Follows in her footsteps!

[*Uchiage tsuke beats gradually rise to a crescendo, fade away, then swell again, as* NARUKAMI *raises his arms high over his head, crosses his eyes, and poses in a mie to battari tsuke beats and loud beats of the large drum.*

hikkomi

He begins a powerful stylized exit. Glaring fiercely he pulls back one step, draws himself up, and leaps forward onto the left leg. Music changes

tobi roppō

to lively Tobi Sari, "*Leaping Exit,*" *played by the large drum, stick drum, and flute.* NARUKAMI *holds the pose a long moment, then again pulls back, draws himself up, and leaps forward onto the right leg. Arms powerfully thrusting forward he leaps, at first slowly and with great deliberation, then gradually faster and faster, down the hanamichi and out of sight to the sound of thundering drums and bata-bata tsuke beats. The audience applauds. The curtain is run closed. A ki clack signals drums and flute to play* Kata Shagiri *between acts.*]

rokutateme

ACT IV

SCENE 1   BUN'YA TOYOHIDE'S MANSION

[*Two ki clacks: the curtain is run open. The large drum beats* Ama Oto *rain pattern and ki clacks accelerate, then fade to silence. Behind the main striped curtain a blue sky curtain masks the set. A single ki clack: action begins. Four* FARM WOMEN *cross the stage gossiping. They wear blue and brown cotton kimonos and are bare-footed. They hold straw hats over their heads.* Ama Oto *rain pattern continues softly in the background.*]

FIRST WOMAN: My, my, how it rains. The blessed rain is like the first dream of the New Year come true.

SECOND WOMAN: If it goes on this way, there'll be floods soon.

THIRD WOMAN: Is it really Lady Taema who did it?

FOURTH WOMAN: She seduced Saint Narukami and, though he pursued her, she was protected by Kumadera Danjō.

FIRST WOMAN: She's the most alluring woman on earth, they say. What man could resist her?

159   Saint Narukami and the God Fudō

SECOND WOMAN [*laughing*]: Look at us any way you like, we're just
    pumpkins and squash!
THIRD WOMAN: Well, let's take our pumpkin heads over to our Lady Taema's
    residence and thank her.
FOURTH WOMAN [*giggling*]: They say she's gone to Lord Toyohide's
    chambers.
FIRST WOMAN: Then at long last the two . . . have wet each other clean
    through, you can be sure of that!
SECOND WOMAN [*with a sly wink*]: And standing here in the rain, I'm getting
    wet . . .
ALL: . . . clean through!
    [*They laugh bawdily and cross off right. A sharp ki clack signals the
    curtain to fall. It is whisked away by* STAGE ASSISTANTS. *A beautifully
    appointed room in* TOYOHIDE's *residence is flooded with light. Silver and
    golden cloud designs decorate the walls. Sliding doors at the rear are
    painted to represent a garden scene, featuring the large drum and curtains
    marking a stage for court bugaku dance performances. Large drum, flute,
    and shamisen play elegant* Kangen *court music.* TOYOHIDE, *an elderly*
    RETAINER, *and* TAEMA *are kneeling on the right side of the room,
    greeting an imperial envoy,* GENERAL SAKURAMACHI, *who is regally
    seated on a tall stool center.* TAKINO *and* MAIDS *flank the aristocrats at
    the back of the room.*]
TOYOHIDE [*bowing formally*]: Welcome, General Sakuramachi, bearer of the
    Emperor's will. Forgive the thousand-fold inconvenience we cause you.
SAKURAMACHI [*loftily*]: Upon this occasion, the Dragon Gods' virtuous
    strength has been released through the endeavors of Lady Taema of the
    Clouds and rain has fallen. From the Imperial person to his lowest subject,
    our ecstasy knows no bounds. In his beneficence, the Emperor proclaims,
    "The marriage to Lord Toyohide, as previously pledged, shall be speedily
    arranged." Do you humbly accept his will?
    [TOYOHIDE *and* TAEMA *bow in assent.*]
TOYOHIDE [*strongly*]: The land is tranquil. In gratitude we hear the voice of
    our Majesty resounding on this auspicious occasion. Joyfully we accept
    his will.
TAKINO: It is a case of "rain settling the earth."[45]
MAID: Lady Taema brilliantly deposed her rival, Princess Nishiki.
TAKINO: We congratulate you . . .
WOMEN: . . . Lady Taema.
TAEMA [*modestly*]: It was not through my strength. The Heavens, the
    Benevolent Gods, and the Dragon Gods guided me.
    [*Music stops.*]
RETAINER: Let us pray your marriage will last a thousand years. Drink from
    the nuptial cup three times three! [*Calling off.*] Bring on the wedding cup!
MAID [*offstage*]: We shall, Sir.

45. Ambiguous, but in addition to its literal meaning the line suggests Taema has
"settled" the political turmoil in the land. And rain suggests Taema's use of sex to
dispose of Narukami.

HAYAKUMO [*offstage, at the end of the hanamichi*] : The wine cup . . . shall wait!

[*All look expectantly down the hanamichi. Stick drum, small drum, and flute play exciting Hayamai, "Fast Dance." Prince HAYAKUMO moves grandly onto the hanamichi. He wears a flowing silver and white court robe and Chinese red trousers that trail away behind him. He wears a gold hat and carries the plain wood symbol of high office. His face, deeply lined in black and dark blue, bespeaks uncompromising evil. Bata-bata accelerates then tapers off as he reaches seven-three.*]

TOYOHIDE: Prince Hayakumo, what does this mean?

HAYAKUMO: You shall hear! Listen!

[*He sits on a tall stool a STAGE ASSISTANT brings onto the hanamichi. Shamisen play Shizen Bushi, "Song of Nature," and small drums play Daishō in the background.*]

Your Prince is the one whose virtue brought this rain. For thirty-seven days I have undergone austerities at Tree Island Shrine, until the shrine's god answered my prayers with rain. To claim Taema responsible is rank impertinence! She is my consort! Through your negligence, this virtuous prince has not ascended to the throne!

TOYOHIDE: You are committing fearful treason, Prince Hayakumo! Do you not know Abe Kiyoyuki has proclaimed you the cause of the world's drought?

HAYAKUMO [*glaring fiercely at* TOYOHIDE] : Do you dare . . . !

TOYOHIDE [*rises on his knees, and edges in aggressively*] : Stop! My retainer Kumadera Danjō has slain Narukami.[46] Kanzō, Hachirō, and the other conspirators have been bound, showing your treason to be . . . a bubble on the water!

HAYAKUMO [*rising*] : Yahhh! Intolerable! So! I will take the palace and the imperial throne myself! I shall become Japan's Demon King! I shall raze the temples and shrines! Taema! Come!

[*He crosses on stage. He throws his hat to the ground and reaches for* TAEMA.]

TOYOHIDE [*rising*] : No! Guards, guards!

[TOYOHIDE *stands protectively in front of* TAEMA. *Blinds slowly fall to cover the tableau in the room. Large drum booms out Mitsu Daiko, "Triple Beat," fighting pattern. Five GUARDS run on from either side of the stage and encircle* HAYAKUMO *with their spears. With the help of a* STAGE ASSISTANT *he drops the top of his kimono to reveal a brilliant orange kimono beneath it. Another* STAGE ASSISTANT *pulls basting threads in the sleeves, dropping them to reveal a third kimono boldly patterned in black and gold. The Prince's hair streams down either side of his face. Uchiage tsuke beats crescendo then fade away. He holds the blade of his long sword up, turns front, and to battari tsuke beats, poses in a mie, eyes crossed and mouth evilly twisted. Large drum, stick drum, flute, and*]

_____

46. The scene in the 1742 production in which Danjō kills Narukami and Narukami's ghost torments Taema has not been performed since the original production and is not translated here.

shamisen play rhythmic Ōdaikoiri, "Large Drum." Batan and battari tsuke beats alternate, as HAYAKUMO with easy dignity repulses the futile attacks of the GUARDS. He seizes the spears of one man on each side and throws them in opposite directions. Two other GUARDS cross spears in front of the prince; he slices their spears in two. The GUARDS on his left attack one after another, but they are deftly avoided by HAYAKUMO. A sweeping cut with his sword flips the last GUARD into the air in a full somersault. HAYAKUMO places his foot on his back, glares wickedly, and the GUARDS tumble backward, feet in the air. They rise and rush past him stage right. Music stops. He turns on them ferociously. Holding the sword threateningly over his head, he forces them step-by-step down the hana-michi and off, to accelerating bata-bata tsuke beats and booming Mitsu Daiko. He poses in a grandiose mie, sword held over his head, to battari tsuke beats.]

TOYOHIDE [*inside*] : Hayakumo! Wait!

HAYAKUMO [*sneering*] : You? Hah!

[*TOYOHIDE rushes on to rapid bata-bata tsuke beats. He has dropped the top of his court robe, showing a pale lavender kimono beneath it. He faces HAYAKUMO and they pose in a mie to battari tsuke beats. The small drums and flute play rapid, energetic Tsukkake, "Speedily," as they fight in elegant, stylized movements. They slash simultaneously, pass by, turn, and cross swords again. They pose in a mie to battari tsuke beats. Music changes to slower Daishō Iri, "Large and Small Drum," played by shamisen and small drums, as the fight continues. They circle, strike high then low, and cross behind each other. They pose in a mie to battari tsuke beats. A cloud descends as the large drum and tsuke accelerate alternating double beats, doron and batan. The two try to attack, but an unseen power paralyzes them. They stagger and fall unconscious as the cloud reaches earth hiding them from sight. Silence. The lights dim, except stage left where a platform comes into view on which are seated two Geki Bushi SINGERS and two shamisen PLAYERS.[47] The SINGERS bow and raise their texts respectfully.]*

GEKI BUSHI SINGERS [*singing in rich, soaring, and elaborately embellished style*] :

A drop of water in a bottle.
Pieces of incense burning, in the brazier,
   Shed a light, no person can avoid,
   Reaching evil deeds, beyond human morality.[48]
Wonder of Wonders!
The living body of All Wise Fudō Myōō,
   Is manifested here!
We are grateful!

47. An early form of narrative singing (jōruri) in Edo favored by Danjūrō I.

48. Fudō is one of five aspects of the Great Light Buddha (Dainichi Nyorai), who sheds an all-powerful light over the world.

SCENE 2 PRINCE HAYAKUMO'S SUBMISSION ("FUDŌ" SCENE)

[*A sharp clack of the ki: large drum rolls and stick drum, flute, and cymbals play Sōgaku. A second ki clack: the set changes. TOYOHIDE's residence begins to lower, bringing into view a rocky mountain top with a range of mountains in the background. Light streams down from the sky, striking patches of mist which hang in the distant valleys. Seated in the center, on the highest peak, is Buddha in his fearsome aspect as the guardian FUDŌ. Flames rise up behind him in a penumbra. His body is earthen-colored, his hair is in small curls, he holds a golden rod in his right hand—with which he chastises evil—and a rope for binding sinners in his left, as in statues of the diety. To his left stand the gentle figure of the Kannon Bodhisattva as a child holding a golden lotus. To his right is the Rushana Buddha, also reincarnated as a child, almost as dark and as frightening as FUDŌ himself. A third single ki clack signals the scene to begin. Shamisen, large drum, bells, and flute play dignified Ongaku, "God Music," in the background.*]

FUDŌ [*a voice like doom*] : Hayakumo! All men behold me! I am the God Fudō, Guardian of the Great Light Buddha, suppressor of devils and demons, made manifest before you here as the living Fudō! Behold my evil-destroying presence, bearing a miracle from the Gods of Heaven and the Benevolent Deities!

GEKI BUSHI SINGERS [*rapidly, emotionally*] :
Wondrous revelation!
   A miracle!
[*A thunderous roll of Doro-doro on the large drum. The cloud covering HAYAKUMO and TOYOHIDE is whisked away by STAGE ASSISTANTS. HAYAKUMO rises and faces front, his face malevolent.*]

HAYAKUMO [*voice rising to a scream*] : Agghhhhh! Will you destroy my ambition's dream!
[*HAYAKUMO whirls on FUDŌ, raising his sword to attack. The large drum and tsuke alternate double beats, doron and batan, at an accelerating tempo. HAYAKUMO tries to strike, but FUDŌ's power makes him stagger back. Again and again the prince tries, each time with less strength, until he falls to his knees exhausted.*]

TOYOHIDE [*rising on his knees*] : We are grateful. You have exorcised and cast down the Prince's evil designs. We are grateful!
[*He presses his hands together and bows toward FUDŌ. Shamisen, large drum, flute, and bells resume Ongaku. TAEMA, followed by TAKINO, enters on the main hanamichi; SAKURAMACHI and RETAINER enter on the left hanamichi. They stop at seven-three and face the audience. Music fades.*]

TOYOHIDE [*declaiming*] : When the brightness of this Land of the Sun was cast into shade . . .

TAEMA: . . . by divine providence of the Gods of Heaven and the Benevolent Deities, Guardian Fudō appeared . . .

163 Saint Narukami and the God Fudō

SAKURAMACHI: . . . the dark clouds scattered . . .

RETAINER: . . . evil dispelled . . .

TAKINO: . . . a wondrous miracle of strength . . .

TOYOHIDE: . . . shining before . . .

ALL: . . . our astonished eyes!

FUDŌ: Witness this proof of Buddha's mercy!

[Ongaku *music resumes. The two groups pass onto the stage, keeping their backs to the audience so as to remove themselves from the scene. HAYA-KUMO faces first SAKURAMACHI and then TOYOHIDE in a ceremony offering thanks for full houses during the run of the play: he takes up his sword and cuts the air three times, writing the character "large" (大), then two times, writing the character "entry" (入), or "full house." Loud* batan tsuke *beats punctuate each stroke. STAGE ASSISTANTS place a small platform left of center. Music stops. A sharp* ki clack *signals the cast to move into a final tableau, as* uchiage tsuke *beats gradually rise to a furious crescendo. HAYAKUMO mounts the platform and poses with sword held horizontally over his head as a STAGE ASSISTANT lifts up the kimono top behind him; RETAINER leans in toward the prince; SAKURAMACHI looks triumphantly front; TOYOHIDE holds his sword in readiness; TAEMA stands glancing over her shoulder at TOYOHIDE; TAKINO kneels respectfully; the GODS are immobile. A sharp* ki clack: *lights come on full. The group freezes into position in an* emen, *or "pic-ture,"* mie *to loud* battari tsuke *beats. Loud applause accompanies the curtain as it is slowly pulled closed to accelerating* ki clacks. *Two soft* ki clacks: *the large drum plays lively* Uchidashi. *The play is concluded.*]

Chronicle of the Battle of Ichinotani

Ichinotani Futaba Gunki

by Namiki Sōsuke, Namiki Shōzō I, Namiki Geiji,
and Asada Itchō.

A five-act history (jidai) play written for the Toyotake Puppet Theater in Osaka, *Chronicle of the Battle of Ichinotani* opened in December 1751 and ran for twelve months. The chief author is Namiki Sōsuke (also called Senryū), who had collaborated with Takeda Izumo and Miyoshi Shōraku a few years earlier in writing the "Three Great Masterpieces" of jōruri for the rival Takemoto Puppet Theater. When this theater suffered a disastrous decline in popularity in 1750 and Sōsuke decided to move to the Toyotake Puppet Theater, he brought with him a mature knowledge of jōruri drama and theater. He had completed the third act of *Chronicle of the Battle of Ichinotani* when he died in September 1751. Other writers attached to the theater completed the remaining two acts and the full play opened two months after his death.

Several related plots are woven together in the full play. Since the premier production, however, only the "Atsumori's Camp" and "Suma Bay" scenes from the second act and "Kumagai's Battle Camp" scenes from the third act have been staged. They concern the story of Kumagai's sacrifice of his son. All are translated here. The place of these scenes in the original play is shown below. The five acts (*dan*) of the play are divided into: opening scene (*kuchi*), continuing or middle scene (*tsugi* or *naka*), and final scene (*kiri*) which may consist of an opening and a conclusion (*tsume*). A travel scene (*michiyuki*) occurs between the third and fourth acts.

Act I (*shodan*) { Opening scene (daijo)
Middle scene (naka)
Final scene (kiri) { Opening (kuchi)
Conclusion (tsume)

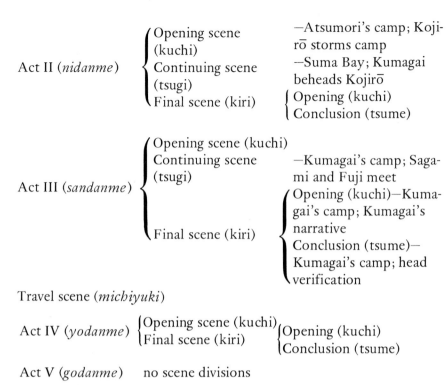

Act II (*nidanme*)	Opening scene (kuchi)	—Atsumori's camp; Kojirō storms camp
	Continuing scene (tsugi)	—Suma Bay; Kumagai beheads Kojirō
	Final scene (kiri)	Opening (kuchi) / Conclusion (tsume)

Act III (*sandanme*)	Opening scene (kuchi)	
	Continuing scene (tsugi)	—Kumagai's camp; Sagami and Fuji meet
	Final scene (kiri)	Opening (kuchi)—Kumagai's camp; Kumagai's narrative / Conclusion (tsume)—Kumagai's camp; head verification

Travel scene (*michiyuki*)

| Act IV (*yodanme*) | Opening scene (kuchi) | Opening (kuchi) |
| | Final scene (kiri) | Conclusion (tsume) |

Act V (*godanme*)   no scene divisions

The tragedy of Kumagai's killing his own son out of loyalty to his lord, Yoshitsune, is heightened by the circumstances in which the playwright has skillfully placed his hero. To carry the substitution (migawari) to a successful conclusion Kumagai must deceive both Lady Fuji and his wife: he must conceal the truth from his wife, whom he wishes to console but cannot, and he must accept Lady Fuji's hatred in spite of the fact that he has not slain her son. Even more interesting is the unique way in which the child sacrifice scene is repeated: in Act II Kumagai beheads his son, then in the following act he relives the terrible moment in a beautifully written narrative which leads up to the head verification. This is dramatic writing which is brilliant and deeply moving. To some contemporary interpreters, the play is seen as a denunciation, not a glorification, of giri in feudal Japan and a criticism of the inhumanly cruel demands made of parents and children by this ethical system.

Few changes in the jōruri text are made for kabuki performance. Several sections of passed-along dialogue are kabuki additions, as is Kumagai's effective final exit down the hanamichi (which is not a usual part of the jōruri stage). Offstage geza music is added to the usual Takemoto music for kabuki productions, especially for opening and closing the curtain and for battles. Most of the puppet tricks (*karakuri*) are retained, such as the scene of horses and riders swimming out to sea, growing smaller with each passage across the stage (accomplished by changing puppet size in jōruri and by having children act the roles of the warriors in kabuki).

The text presents no problem, for the kabuki version is very similar to the original jōruri text. Kabuki texts can be found in Atsumi Seitarō, ed., *Nihon Gikyoku Zenshū* (vol. 28, 1928), and Toita Yasuji, ed., *Kabuki Meisakusen* (vol. 2, 1955). An annotated jōruri text of the "Kumagai Battle Camp" scenes in Yūda Yoshio, ed., *Bunraku Jōrurishū* (Collection of Jōruri Puppet Plays; Tokyo: Iwanami Shoten, 1965) was also consulted. Stage directions are primarily from performances at the Kabuki-za, Tokyo, February 1967, and the National Theater of Japan, February 1968. Professor Mildred Tahara kindly allowed me to compare this translation with her recent translation of the "Kumagai Battle Camp" scenes.

Chronicle of the Battle of Ichinotani

ACT I

SCENE 1   ATSUMORI'S CAMP

[*The striped kabuki curtain is slowly run open to clanging of battle alarm cymbals playing Tōyose, "Approach," and alternating beats of the large drum and clacks of the ki. The scene is the battle camp of the Heike forces at Suma Bay. It is night and all that can be seen is a towering palisade of sharpened logs marking outer fortifications. A heavy gate, some ten feet high and also made of sharpened logs, opens into the camp. No one is in sight. A single sharp ki clack signals the Takemoto NARRATOR and accompanying shamisen PLAYER to begin. They are offstage left, on a second level where they follow the action of the play unseen behind a bamboo blind. The Takemoto shamisen sound is thick and heavy and easily distinguishable from the lighter, brighter sound of the usual Nagauta shamisen of kabuki, in the geza offstage right.*]

NARRATOR [*singing in a rich, strong voice to shamisen accompaniment*] :
Unbridled drinking leads to debauchery. Unrestrained indulgence in pleasure leads to its own bitter grief. Sorrowful indeed is the end of opulence. After twenty brief years of prosperity, the Taira clan has abandoned the capital to attacks of the Minamoto, establishing an encampment at Suma Bay. With the wide ocean at the front, steep Hiyodorigoe Mountain at the rear, deep First Valley at the side, walled with high palisades made of sharp palings running to the water's edge, the camp appears impregnable. The Taira troops, over which fly banners of red, are led by young Lord Atsumori, acting in place of his father, Minister of State Tsunemori. It is the beginning of the third month. The night is dark, even the moon is hidden, as Kojirō Naoie, the only son of the Minamoto chief, Kumagai . . .
[*Drums and cymbals sound Tō̄yose battle alarm. Shamisen play Jindate, "Before the Camp." KOJIRŌ rushes onto the hanamichi to loud bata-tata*

tsuke beats. He stops at the seven-three position and looks around him. The delicate white of his refined features is set off by the light blue of his kimono which can be seen beneath gold- and indigo-colored armor. His hair is tied back with a broad gold band. He flourishes a spear and poses in a mie to battari tsuke beats.]

. . . a lone warrior hurrying under the light of the stars into the enemy's battle camp . . .

[KOJIRŌ *moves silently up to the main gate.*]

. . . draws a single breath and glances in all directions.

KOJIRŌ [*in a firm but delicate voice*] : Ah! Fortunately I am the first to make my way here. Before the others arrive, I must cut my way in. I shall!

NARRATOR [*singing*] : Although he rushes in every direction, there is no crevice in the palisades. As he wonders what to do, faintly from inside, the sound of court music . . .

[*Softly, from the geza offstage, drift the sounds of* Sōgaku, *a gagaku court melody, played by large drum, flute, bells, and small drum.* KOJIRŌ *listens fixedly as the* NARRATOR, *accompanied by the Takemoto shamisen, continues.*]

Now, when even the mountain wind ceases and the sea waves become calm, melancholy sounds of music stir us deeply. Unconsciously, Kojirō strains heart and ears to hear . . .

KOJIRŌ [*sadly, looking front, as court music continues*] : The tale my parents told me, that aristocrats of the capital are refined and sensitive, is, I now see, true. In the midst of this world's strife not the sound of clashing weapons but tasteful playing of strings and flute and the singing of poetry mark time's passing. Surely, I am heartless, country-born, a clod. I treat these exalted people as our enemies and raise the sword of bloodshed against them—how wretched it is!

[*He lets his spear drop to the ground. His head falls and he poses.*]

NARRATOR [*singing to shamisen accompaniment*] : Saying "how wretched it is," young Kojirō's heart is touched, and unconsciously the tears fall. Suddenly, the sound of running from behind! The warrior Hirayama rushes forward lance in hand!

[*Loud bata-bata tsuke beats break* KOJIRŌ's *reverie. Cymbals, large drum, and gong play* Tōyose. HIRAYAMA, *a Genji warrior, rushes onto the hanamichi. He is dressed in dark armor and breeches and carries a sword and long lance. Long hair falls about his shoulders, framing a ruddy, heavy face. He stops at seven-three and peers into the dark.* Sōgaku *court music resumes in the background.*]

HIRAYAMA [*harshly*] : Who are you, friend or enemy?

KOJIRŌ: Is it you, Sueshige?

HIRAYAMA: So the friend is you, Kojirō? [*He walks onto the main stage.*] It would never have entered my head that you would be here before me. Admirable, admirable! If it were any other person I would fight to lead the charge, but I was not the first to arrive and since this is your first battle, I grant you the honor of being first into the enemy camp. Don't hesitate! Slice your way in! Cut them down!

KOJIRŌ: No, Hirayama. Listen to the court music. Truly, the elegant ways of the palace are far removed from ours.

HIRAYAMA: You don't understand at all, young Kojirō. Listen: in ancient times Shōkatsu Kōmei, his forces surrounded and beseiged by Shiba Chūtatsu, having exhausted every stratagem, mounted the camp tower where he calmly burned incense and played the koto. Seeing this and suspecting a trap, Chūtatsu foolishly led his troops away.[1] Ha! This music is the same thing! Don't let it put you off. Quickly, attack the camp and earn your fame. Or, if you are afraid, Kojirō, I will lead the attack!

KOJIRŌ [*humiliated*] : How can you say . . .

HIRAYAMA [*crudely laughing*] : Are you a coward?

kuriage

KOJIRŌ: Well . . .

HIRAYAMA: Well . . . ?

BOTH [*alternately, accelerating until they are speaking simultaneously*] : Well, well, well, well, well!

HIRAYAMA [*leaning in, sneering*] : Will you attack? Well? Well!!

[*Court music stops.* HIRAYAMA *gestures for* KOJIRŌ *to go. Distraught,* KOJIRŌ *looks first at the gate then at* HIRAYAMA.]

NARRATOR [*singing to shamisen accompaniment*] : Cleverly urged on, Kojirō Naoie cries out in a hot-blooded voice . . .

KOJIRŌ [*passionately*] : I challenge the Heike enemy in their camp!

[*To battari tsuke beats,* KOJIRŌ *faces the gate. He twirls the spear, and faces resolutely front. He speaks in time to rhythmic music of the Take-moto shamisen.*]

nori

I am Kumagai Kojirō Naoie, only son of Kumagai Jirō Naozane, clan leader of all samurai of Musashi Province! Come face me—I am the vanguard of the Genji! Come out and fight! Come out and fight!

[KOJIRŌ *poses with his spear held overhead.*]

NARRATOR [*singing to shamisen accompaniment*] : His cries are answered by an uproar within the camp. Pushing open the gate, the enemy pour out.

[*Drums and alarm cymbals sound* Tōyose. *The gate swings ponderously open and ten* SOLDIERS, *dressed in dark blue and white uniforms, and carrying swords and spears, surround* KOJIRŌ.]

SOLDIERS: You won't escape!

tate

[*Drums, cymbals, and alternating batan and battari tsuke beats accompany the brief battle between* KOJIRŌ *and the* SOLDIERS. KOJIRŌ *vigorously forces them against the gate and, to bata-bata tsuke beats, chases them into the camp where the fighting continues.* HIRAYAMA *looks through the open gate, is about to follow, then hesitates.*]

NARRATOR [*singing to shamisen accompaniments*] : While Hirayama is wondering what to do, Kumagai Jirō Naozane, pierced to the heart with worry that his child leads the vanguard, rushes on, feet flying in the air.

[*During the narration,* KUMAGAI *moves swiftly onto the hanamichi to bata-bata tsuke beats and* Tōyose. *He is dressed in gold and orange armor*

1. An incident described in the Chinese historical novel *The Romance of Three Kingdoms* (*San Kuo*) and the basis of a well-known Peking opera, *The Ruse of the Empty City.*

covered with a cape of purple, the color of the Minamoto, and wears a
general's battle helmet topped with deer's antlers. He stops at seven-three.]

KUMAGAI: Ah, Hirayama, where is Kojirō?

HIRAYAMA: He was just here asking what he should do. Do not plunge into
the middle of the Heike camp single-handed, I said. Wait until the main
force has come, I urged. But he's young. He slashed headlong through
the gate!

KUMAGAI [*thunderstruck*] : Dear God, he did?

NARRATOR [*sings to fast shamisen accompaniment*] : A furious lion whose
cub is lost . . .

tate
[*KUMAGAI rushes onstage to bata-bata tsuke beats; drum and cymbals
play Tōyose. Six SOLDIERS run out of the gate and attack him. KUMA-
GAI snarls with fury and slashes past them into the camp. They turn and
follow him in with loud cries.*]

. . . he forces past the enemy into their camp. Hirayama smiles to himself
as he sees this.

HIRAYAMA: Ha, ha, ha! Just as I planned, just as I planned! Father and son
are rats in my trap, surely destroyed by now! [*In time to rhythmic music
of the Takemoto shamisen.*] Damn Kumagai, I've watched him rise in Genji
nori
favor, but now my time has come. Without lifting a finger, the enemy does
my work better than the Wind God. In their struggle for life and death the
strength of father and son is such the enemy will be hard pressed. Let them
fight hard. Let them die! [*Music stops and HIRAYAMA speaks rapidly.*]
Then I will enter and defeat the Heike, rising to whatever heights of fame
I could wish! Ha, ha! Ha, ha! Clever, clever!

NARRATOR [*sings to shamisen accompaniment*] : He is in boisterous spirits
when the cries of many men are heard from inside the gate. He stands as if
to defend himself against opponents, but Kumagai Jirō Naozane dashes
through the gate clutching his son to his side.

[*To loud bata-bata tsuke beats, KUMAGAI enters supporting a figure
dressed like KOJIRŌ, but actually ATSUMORI.*]

KUMAGAI [*rapidly*] : Good Hirayama, my son Kojirō has been wounded. I
must take him to camp for care. Remain and earn glory.

NARRATOR [*singing to shamisen accompaniment*] : So saying over his
shoulder, he rushes away as if flying.

[*During the narration, KUMAGAI moves quickly past HIRAYAMA,
holding the helmet over his "son's" face, onto the hanamichi. He glances
back over his shoulder at HIRAYAMA and poses in a mie at seven-three to
battari tsuke and drum beats. Then he moves deliberately off the hanamichi
to accelerating bata-bata tsuke beats, drum, cymbals, and Takemoto
shamisen.*]

SOLDIERS [*rushing out of the gate*] : Yaaaaaah!

tate
[*Batan and battari tsuke beats; drums and cymbals play Tōyose to accompany the fight. The SOLDIERS face HIRAYAMA with drawn swords. He
slashes through them, one by one, with his spear. They re-form and
attack. He forces one to the ground and poses, foot on his back, in a mie.*]

174   Chronicle of the Battle of Ichinotani

Lively nō drums and flute, and offstage shamisen play Hayabue, *"Quick Flute." Two, then four,* SOLDIERS *attack with their swords;* HIRAYAMA *forces them back into the gate, following them. The stage is empty. Silence. As drums and flute furiously play* Hayabue, *a young warrior dressed as* ATSUMORI—*actually* KOJIRŌ—*rides out of the camp mounted on a white steed. His face is white, his armor and accouterments are burnished gold and red. He drives* HIRAYAMA *before him onto the hanamichi where he poses, sword held high over head, in a mie to battari tsuke beats. A sharp ki clack. Drums and flute resume* Tōyose *and* Hayabue *at a furious pace and loud bata-bata tsuke beats accompany* "ATSUMORI" *as he forces* HIRAYAMA *down the hanamichi and out of sight. A sharp ki clack. A light blue "wave" curtain falls across the stage ending the scene.*]

nidanme tsugi   SCENE 2   SUMA BAY

[Nami Oto *wave pattern and* Tōyose *continue between scenes.* STAGE ASSISTANTS *place straw, rocks, and clumps of rushes and grass in front of the curtain to indicate the sea edge.* Nami Oto *swells and ends. Silence. The stage is empty. Takemoto shamisen begins a plaintive melody.*]

NARRATOR [*sings plaintively*] : Yearning for the sight of Prince Atsumori, distraught upon the beach at Suma Bay . . .

[Nami Oto *wave pattern is played on the large drum and* Kodama, *"Mountain Echo," on the small drums. The curtain at the rear of the hanamichi opens and* PRINCESS TAMAORI *enters. Her pale face is set off by a scarlet kimono and long red trousers. Her hair hangs long down her back. She carries a spear in one hand and moving lifelessly, trails a purple cloak behind her. Her kimono is off the right shoulder, indicating her distraught state. Between phrases of narration she calls out plaintively, "Lord Atsumori," "My Prince, are you here?"*]

. . . Princess Tamaori, with tear-soaked sleeves, a sharp dagger near her breast, wanders here and there in the spring breeze, beneath the hazy moon.

[*She poses at seven-three, then moves onto the main stage calling pathetically.*]

She searches about her. Suddenly, the vague form of a man appears silhouetted against the early eastern clouds. It is the warrior Hirayama, fleeing on a mountain trail that leads to Suma Bay. As he sees Princess Tamaori . . .

[HIRAYAMA *rushes on from the left to fast bata-bata tsuke beats, holding a drawn sword. Music stops. Seeing the Princess, he sheathes his sword.*]

HIRAYAMA [*gloating*] : Can it be Princess Tamaori? This is a lucky meeting!

[*To loud batan tsuke beats, he seizes her by the sleeve. Takemoto shamisen plays softly in the background.*]

From the first, when I fell in love with you at the capital, you dazzled my eyes. I could not forget you sleeping or awake, until, unable to contain myself, I spoke to your father Tokitada, who promised you would come to me in marriage. Now, praise the Gods, I have you and will make you my wife. Come.

NARRATOR [*singing to shamisen accompaniment*] : Though he takes her hand, she shakes him off.

[HIRAYAMA *seizes her hand and pulls. To sharp batan tsuke beats, she frees herself and backs away. Takemoto shamisen music continues in the background.*]

TAMAORI [*innocently*] : Do not speak so. Whether my father gave permission or not, I am pledged to Atsumori unto our second lifetimes. We are searching for each other now. Should he die, we die together. Do not interfere.

NARRATOR [*singing to shamisen accompaniment*] : Turning to go, she is stopped.

[*He crudely steps on the hem of her kimono.*]

HIRAYAMA: Ha! Search for Atsumori as much as you want, look for him at the bottom of the ocean, you won't find where he's gone!

[*With a laugh he turns front releasing her kimono. She faces him.*]

TAMAORI [*frightened*] : Oh, and why?

HIRAYAMA [*smiling*] : Because Atsumori has just been killed by me.

TAMAORI: Ahh! Atsumori killed, you say?

HIRAYAMA [*unconcerned*] : He is.

TAMAORI: Ahhhh!

[*She falls back, presses her hand to her breast, and poses. She mimes the words of the narration.*]

NARRATOR [*singing quietly to shamisen accompaniment*] : Delicate, the Princess sinks beneath her grief. Unaware of others' eyes, she raises her voice in tearful cries and falls prostrate upon the ground.

[*Head down, she weeps. Suddenly she takes out the small dagger and rises.*]

TAMAORI: Prepare yourself, enemy of my husband!

NARRATOR [*rapidly to shamisen accompaniment*] : Saying "enemy of my husband," and slashing out, her wrist is seized.

[*She tries to cut HIRAYAMA, striking left and right to batan tsuke beats, but he easily avoids her weak movements, then seizes her wrist with his left hand puts his right on the hilt of his sword threateningly. Takemoto shamisen music continues in the background.*]

HIRAYAMA [*harshly*] : You! Do you try to oppose me? I should show no mercy! [*Laughs.*] My, the softness of your hand is just what I expected! You misunderstand me, after all. Change your affections completely, yield, and I will cherish you as my wife. Well, Princess? Will you have me? Will you?

[*He presses her hand to his cheek, then, moving behind her, tries to press his cheek against hers.*]

NARRATOR [*singing to plaintive shamisen accompaniment*] : Honeyed words, "will you, will you," draw tears of anger.

TAMAORI [*breaks away and kneels*] : Ahh! To speak of yielding myself to a detestable samurai, who in normal times would not even dare approach, is revolting. You are loathsome to me!

NARRATOR [*singing to fast shamisen accompaniment*] : Again she slashes; he seizes and holds her fast.

[*She rises and slashes to batan tsuke beats. He easily seizes her wrist and holds her helpless.*]

HIRAYAMA [*matter-of-factly*] : So. Will you become my wife?

kuriage   TAMAORI: Well . . . ?

HIRAYAMA: Do you hate me?

TAMAORI: Well . . . ?

BOTH [*alternately faster until they speak simultaneously*] : Well, well, well, well!

HIRAYAMA: Say you hate me and I'll kill you. Well? Well?!

[*Coldly he throws her to the ground, unsheaths his sword, and poses, back to the audience, heels together, and sword upraised, in a soku mie to battari tsuke beats. Takemoto shamisen plays plaintively in the background.*]

TAMAORI [*weeping*] : Kill me, if you are such a beast. Oh, is there no one who will slay this person for me?

NARRATOR [*singing to plaintive shamisen accompaniment*] : She is piteous in her agony; strong-willed Hirayama's anger wells up.

HIRAYAMA [*faces her, furiously*] : Agh, hateful bitch! On top of rejecting me, you spew out insults! It would be intolerable to let you live, watching you bloom for another man. You'll see what my vengeance is for being cruelly tormented!

[Nami Oto *wave pattern ominously swells. In desperation she rises and slashes to batan tsuke beats.*]

NARRATOR [*singing to shamisen accompaniment*] : As the raised sword is plunged through her breast . . .

[*With a single stroke he drives the sword into her body. She gasps and staggers.*]

. . . a single gasp of agony! From the rear battle cries!

[*Shouts mingle with alarm sounds of the large drum and cymbals playing Tōyose. Panic-stricken, he throws the Princess into rushes at the side of the stage and runs onto the hanamichi to loud bata-bata tsuke beats. He holds the naked blade in front of him and poses in a strong mie to battari tsuke beats.*]

Without a backward glance he runs away.

[*To accelerating drum and tsuke beats* HIRAYAMA *rushes off. A* STAGE ASSISTANT, *dressed in black, unobtrusively removes* TAMAORI's *dropped spear and dagger.* Nami Oto *wave pattern swells. A sharp ki clack. The wave curtain falls and is whisked away by* STAGE ASSISTANTS *revealing Suma Bay framed by towering cliffs on either side. Small pine trees, rocks, and clumps of grass edge the water. The deep blue ocean extends as far as the eye can see. The stage is empty. Nō drums and flute from the geza off right play* Issei, *"One Voice," as the* CHORUS *sings, in austere nō style, a passage from the nō play "Atsumori."*]

CHORUS [*off right, accompanied by nō drums and flute*] : "In the meantime, massed Heiki warriors, from the Emperor down, rushed to the waters' edge in time to board ships, the Emperor's among them, before they stood out to sea."

NARRATOR [*sings to Nami Oto wave pattern and shamisen accompaniment*] : The enemy have slipped away by road, and Prince Atsumori hurries to inform his father Tsunemori, aboard the Emperor's ship.

shuraba

[*During the narration, "ATSUMORI" moves elegantly onto the hanamichi astride his horse. To Takemoto shamisen, nō drums playing* Kakeiri, *"Hurried Entry," and* Nami Oto *wave pattern ATSUMORI circles the stage looking for his father. The horse, played by two actors, delights the audience by prancing and pawing the earth. A flotilla of ships appears on the horizon. ATSUMORI spurs his horse into the water, and the horse, neck outstretched as if swimming, carries its rider through the "ocean" toward the Emperor's ship and out of sight. ATSUMORI, now played by a child actor on a toy horse, reenters swimming toward the boats, giving the impression of being far out to sea.*]

NARRATOR [*singing as the music continues*] : And as he does, from the rear, Kumagai Jirō Naozane . . .

KUMAGAI [*offstage at the rear of the hanamichi*] : Wait! Wait!!

[*Furious bata-bata tsuke beats. KUMAGAI rides a black horse onto the hanamichi as nō drums play* Tsukkake, *"Speedily," and cymbals and large drum play* Tōyose.]

NARRATOR: . . . shouting loudly and whipping his horse, enters pursuing!

KUMAGAI [*at seven-three*] : Do I see before my eyes an exalted general of the Taira? Do you show your heels to an opponent? Come back! I challenge you! Meet Kumagai Jirō Naozane, leader of the samurai of Musashi! Come back! Come, come! [*Roaring.*] Fight me! Fight!!

NARRATOR [*singing to shamisen, drums, and cymbals*] : Raising his fan and opening it, he calls, "wait for me, wait."

[*KUMAGAI beckons to ATSUMORI with his fan, painted gold with a rising sun emblem in the center. Tsuke, drums playing* Daishō, *"Large and Small Drum," cymbals, and Takemoto shamisen crescendo. KUMAGAI whips his horse across the stage and into the ocean in pursuit of ATSU-MORI. He passes ATSUMORI and disappears from view.*]

NARRATOR [*slowly singing to shamisen accompaniment*] : Is not hearing an opponent's challenge reason to pause? Atsumori reins in his horse . . .

[*ATSUMORI stops his horse and faces front.*]

. . . Kumagai presses forward, together they raise their swords high . . .

tate

[*KUMAGAI, now also played by a boy actor on a toy horse, appears to be far out to sea, approaching ATSUMORI. They draw miniature swords and face each other. Batan and battari tsuke beats punctuate the battle.*]

. . . morning sun glints like lightning on their blades, attack and turn, attack and turn, clang, clang . . .

[*Striking at each other, they charge, turn, and charge again.*]

. . . the sleeves of their armor flutter, flutter, in the wind of Suma Bay . . .

[*Without flinching they trade blows face to face.*]

. . . flocks of sea plovers, flocks of sea plovers, burst skyward, ebbing, surging, ebbing again . . .

[*They cross swords and, reflecting the narration, first one then the other seems to prevail.*]

. . . diamond for diamond, dross for dross, decision is impossible!

KUMAGAI [*facing front, in a child's high voice*]: Now, let us grapple!

ATSUMORI [*facing front, in a child's high voice*]: Yes! Let us!

NARRATOR [*singing to shamisen accompaniment*]: Though astride their horses, they grasp each other and wrestle. Feet slide from their stirrups, and they fall between both steeds.

[*Loud* Nami Oto *wave pattern. They throw their swords into the sea, rein their horses side by side, reach over and grasp each others' forearms. A sharp ki clack. They pose in a mie to battari tsuke beats as a blue wave curtain drops to cover them. Stick drum and flute play lively* Hayabue. *As the music continues,* ATSUMORI's *horse, riderless, prances across the stage and down the hanamichi to bata-bata tsuke beats. A sharp ki clack. The blue wave curtain falls and is whisked away. The scene is the same. As stick drum, flute, and large drum play* Ōdaikoiri, "*Large Drum,*" *and* uchiage *tsuke pattern swells, fades, then again crescendoes,* ATSUMORI *and* KUMAGAI *rise on a lift center stage, hidden by a red cloth held in front of them by two* STAGE ASSISTANTS. *The cloth is taken away and we see* KUMAGAI *holding* ATSUMORI *to the ground. They pose in a mie to battari tsuke beats. A ki clack: action begins.*]

NARRATOR [*singing to shamisen accompaniment*]: In an instant, Kumagai seizes Atsumori and pins him to the ground. [*Music ends.*]

KUMAGAI: Your destiny has reached its end. Speak out your name, so its fame will increase my glory. [*Meaningfully, as he looks intently into* ATSUMORI's *eyes.*] Have you a final request in this life? Ask and I will not fail to fulfill it.

NARRATOR [*singing slowly, with great emotion, to shamisen accompaniment*]: He speaks with great courtesy . . .

[KUMAGAI *releases* ATSUMORI, *sheathes his sword, and sits on a stump stage right. A* STAGE ASSISTANT *removes* ATSUMORI's *helmet.* ATSUMORI *sits cross-legged center.*]

ATSUMORI [*gravely*]: You are a generous spirited and noble warrior, though an enemy. I will count it the greatest honor of my life to be killed in war by one such as you. When I left for the field of battle I abandoned thoughts of family and of self.

NARRATOR [*sings slowly to shamisen accompaniment*]: He has no request for this life, for he knows no existence in it.

[*Takemoto shamisen continues softly in the background.*]

ATSUMORI: Yet, it is difficult to forget the kindness of my father and mother. They will grieve deeply when they hear I have died in battle. After I am slain, at least do not fail to deliver this body to my father, to assuage their grief. Know that I am . . . Minister Tsunemori's youngest son . . . Atsumori!

NARRATOR [*sings slowly to shamisen accompaniment*]: Pronouncing the name is an agony. Kumagai is not wood or stone, tears stream from his seeing eyes.

[KUMAGAI, *until now impassive, drops his head forward, then with an effort straightens. He nods resolutely, tucks the fan into his belt, crosses to* ATSUMORI, *and kneels beside him.*]
What does he think raising him up . . .
[KUMAGAI *bows humbly, as to one of higher rank, and gestures for* ATSUMORI *to rise.*]
. . . brushing the dust, brushing it from his armor?
[*With his fan,* KUMAGAI *pats the dust from* ATSUMORI'*s armor. He brushes clean* ATSUMORI'*s helmet and sword and passes them to him.* KUMAGAI *moves a respectful distance away, kneels, and bows deeply to* ATSUMORI. *Music stops.*]
KUMAGAI: Your noble bearing speaks witness that you are the son of Minister Tsunemori. To save one person cannot lose our victory. No one is here: make your escape. Quickly, quickly!
[KUMAGAI *looks intently at* ATSUMORI, *points down the hanamichi with his closed fan, slaps his chest with the fan, and bows deeply.*]
NARRATOR [*sings slowly to shamisen accompaniment*] : "Quickly, quickly," he says. Gracefully, Prince Atsumori . . . [*Music stops.*]
ATSUMORI [*gently*] : You may help me to escape, but the Heike cannot escape destiny. Rather than be dishonored by a common soldier cutting me down at some future time, quickly, kill me yourself.
NARRATOR [*sings very slowly to shamisen accompaniment*] : Facing west, he clasps his hands . . .

[*Nō drums plays melancholy* Kodama, *"Mountain Echo" pattern, distant thunder rolls are heard, and Takemoto shamisen plays quietly in the background. With great dignity,* KUMAGAI *rises and stands to the side.* ATSUMORI *sits cross-legged center and slowly removes his armor, gloves, and swords. He places his helmet on top of the armor and a short dagger directly in front of him. Silence. He folds his hands in prayer.*]
. . . closes his eyes, and waits.
[ATSUMORI *closes his eyes and bows his head expectantly.* KUMAGAI *stands, as if petrified. A loud chord from the Takemoto shamisen,* KUMAGAI *starts.*]
KUMAGAI [*in a choked voice*] : Prepare . . . yourself.
NARRATOR [*continuing*] : Compassionately, Kumagai repeats Buddha's name in his heart, as he moves behind and lifts Buddha's sword that will sever earthly ties!
[*A* STAGE ASSISTANT *takes* KUMAGAI'*s fan.* KUMAGAI *moves behind and just to one side of* ATSUMORI. *He draws his long sword and raises it above his head. He draws a sharp breath, then slowly lowers the sword.*]
In appearance like a precious jewel . . .
[*Gently* KUMAGAI *places his hand on* ATSUMORI'*s cheek and turns his head.*]
. . . overwhelmed by pity and remorse his heart breaks, he hesitates . . .
[*The sword trembles in* KUMAGAI'*s hand. He turns away trying to gain control. Without a word,* ATSUMORI *closes his eyes and bows his head*

again. Suddenly KUMAGAI *raises the sword as if to strike. He trembles. His face is anguished.*]

. . . the hand that holds high the great sword weakens, his mind dissolves in tears, it is not possible to strike. Thus agonized time slips away from Kumagai . . .

[KUMAGAI *cannot strike. He falls to his knees. Suddenly drums and cymbals sound Tōyose battle alarm. To loud battari tsuke beats* KUMAGAI *looks down the hanamichi and poses in a strong protective mie.*]

. . . when from the opposing hill Hirayama!

[HIRAYAMA *rushes onto the hanamichi followed by two* SOLDIERS. *At seven-three he mounts a small platform which is placed on the hanamichi by two* STAGE ASSISTANTS. *It is decorated with a pine tree and indicates a hilltop some distance away.*]

HIRAYAMA [*calling out*]: Kumagai! You! Kumagai!! Traitor! You capture a Heike general and are about to let him go? Kill them, men, kill them both! [*He poses.*]

NARRATOR [*chants without shamisen*]: He hurls out abuse! Kumagai starts with surprise! What should he do? He stands in silence.

[KUMAGAI *starts, then slowly looks down at* ATSUMORI, *eyes wide with shock. He lowers his eyes and stands immobile, deep in thought.*]

ATSUMORI [*quietly*]: Ah. Will you fail, Kumagai? Do not let this chance pass and earn a coward's disgraceful name. Quickly, cut off my head and prove yourself.

[ATSUMORI *looks up at* KUMAGAI. HIRAYAMA *sits ostentatiously on a camp stool placed beside the platform by a* STAGE ASSISTANT.]

NARRATOR [*singing to shamisen accompaniment*]: It destroys his heart, looking with unseeing eyes into the noble face turned up to him!

KUMAGAI [*deeply aware of the irony of his words*]: My only son, called Kojirō, whom you match exactly in age and appearance, was wounded in this morning's battle leading the attack, so I was forced to lead him to our battle camp. [*Glancing covertly at* HIRAYAMA.] Deeply concerned, out of a father's love for his son, I could not help but reflect that taking your life here will cause your mother and . . . your father . . . Tsunemori . . . grief.

[*His voice breaks. He slaps one hand on top of the other to control their trembling. He turns away from his son and begins to sob silently.*]

NARRATOR [*sings to shamisen accompaniment*]: Brave warrior though he is . . . tears flow uncontrolled.

ATSUMORI [*faces* KUMAGAI]: Dull-witted Naozane. You would abandon companions as villains and welcome enemies as friends. Take my head quickly and pray for my soul in death. If not, I can kill myself.

[*Quickly* ATSUMORI *takes up the dagger that has been in front of him and is about to unsheath it.* KUMAGAI *rushes forward and seizes* ATSU-MORI's *hand to stop him.*]

KUMAGAI: Do not do it!

ATSUMORI: Will you disgrace yourself, coward?

KUMAGAI: But, I . . . !

kuriage

ATSUMORI [*gently*] : Then cut off my head. Well?

KUMAGAI: Well . . . ?

BOTH [*alternately, increasing in speed until they are speaking simultaneously*] : Well, well, well, well, well!

ATSUMORI [*agonized voice*] : Do it quickly! Decapitate me!

[ATSUMORI *rises on one knee, pulls loose his hair, bites hard on it to control himself, and again sits cross-legged with his hands rigidly clasped in prayer.*]

KUMAGAI [*calm, resolved*] : If father and son both pray for each other's salvation, in future lives surely they will dwell together on the same lotus blossom. "Namu Amida Butsu. Namu Amida Butsu." Buddha Merciful All Hail.

NARRATOR [*sings in a highly emotional voice to shamisen accompaniment*] : His head . . . falls to the ground!

[KUMAGAI *raises the sword high over his head and with a single stroke decapitates his son. Loud shamisen and batan tsuke beats. ATSUMORI falls backward. A* STAGE ASSISTANT *covers his head with a black cloth, at the same time placing a property head beside the body.*]

Though shameful in people's eyes . . .

[KUMAGAI *wipes the sword in the crook of his arm, sheathes it, and slowly sinks to his knees. Afraid to look at the head of his son, he gropes blindly for it.*]

. . . cradling the precious head in his arm . . .

[*Finding the head, he cradles it gently.*]

. . . he raises his voice in an anguished cry!

[*Takemoto shamisen accompanies* KUMAGAI's *action. He rises on one knee, slowly brings the head before him, looks down at his son's face, then falls back with an anguished scream. Batan tsuke beats. He rises and faces* HIRAYAMA. *Takemoto shamisen continues rhythmically in the background.*]

nori

KUMAGAI: No other than Kumagai Jirō Naozane has severed the head of Imperial Prince Atsumori, unmatched among the Heike clan! (*Thrusts the head forward.*] Witness it!

HIRAYAMA [*rises and gazes intently at the head*] : I, samurai Hirayama, witness the act!

KUMAGAI [*voice rising in a hoarse scream*] : Victory!

HIRAYAMA: Victory!

SOLDIERS: Victory!!

[*Sound of drums and cymbals playing* Tōyose *from the rear of the hanamichi.* HIRAYAMA *strides down the hanamichi and off, followed by the* SOLDIERS. KUMAGAI *watches him depart. In the silence he gradually relaxes.* Nami Oto *wave pattern begins softly, creating an atmosphere of suspense.*]

NARRATOR [*sings to shamisen accompaniment*] : Is it unquenchable longing for her husband that rouses Princess Tamaori, lying faint on the sand?

Prince Atsumori, played by a child actor on a toy horse, appears to be at a distance in the ocean. Kumagai, pursuing on the black horse, is still in the foreground and is played by an adult actor. "Wait for me, wait. Is not hearing an opponent's challenge reason to pause?" (*Atsumori:* Bandō Yachimaru; *Kumagai:* Matsumoto Koshirō)

Far out at sea, Kumagai and Atsumori are played by child actors. "Kumagai presses forward, together they raise their swords high. Morning sun glints like lightning on their blades, attack and turn, attack and turn." (*Kumagai:* Kataoka Hideji; *Atsumori:* Bandō Yachimaru) Page 178

Kumagai has captured Atsumori (actually Kumagai's son Kojirō). In deference to the fact that his opponent is supposedly the son of the Emperor, Kumagai kneels respectfully before him. "To save one person cannot lose our victory. No one is here: make your escape. Quickly, quickly!" (*Kumagai:* Matsumoto Koshirō; *Atsumori:* Nakamura Kichiemon) Page 180

Kumagai draws his sword and prepares to kill Atsumori. "Facing west, he clasps his hands, closes his eyes, and waits." (*Kumagai:* Matsumoto Koshirō; *Atsumori:* Nakamura Kichiemon) Page 180

"His head falls to the ground!" Kumagai, unable to look at the head of his son, gropes blindly for it. A Stage Assistant in black kneels behind him. (*Kumagai:* Matsumoto Koshirō) Page 182

Kumagai thrusts the head forward for Hirayama on the hanamichi to see. "No other than Kumagai Jirō Naozane has severed the head of Imperial Prince Atsumori, unmatched among the Heike clan! Witness it!" (*Kumagai:* Matsumoto Koshirō) Page 182

The act ends as Kumagai is left alone on stage, cradling the precious head of his son. He grasps the bridle of his horse for support, plants his feet wide apart, and strikes an agonized mie pose. Note the crossed left eye. (*Kumagai:* Matsumoto Koshirō) Page 185

The formal striped curtain is pushed open on the scene of Kumagai's Battle Camp. Farmers read the signboard containing the implied order that Kumagai must kill his son. " 'Cut off a branch of flowers, cut off a finger,' it seems to say." Page 186

"Ahh! Isn't it Lady Fuji?" "Your voice . . . is it Sagami?" Sagami recognizes Lady Fuji standing outside the gate. (*Fuji:* Nakamura Kichinosuke; *Sagami:* Nakamura Mannojō) Page 188

"My son's enemy! Kumagai!" Hearing that Kumagai killed her son Atsumori, Lady Fuji unsheaths her dagger and strikes. He avoids her blows and forces her back. (*Sagami:* Nakamura Mannojō; *Kumagai:* Ichikawa Somegorō; *Fuji:* Nakamura Kichinosuke) Page 193

TAMAORI *pulls herself painfully from the beach grasses toward* KUMA-GAI.]

TAMAORI [*weakly*] : Ah, wait, please. What cruel person has killed Prince Atsumori? At least let me see his face one final time as a remembrance.

NARRATOR [*sings to shamisen accompaniment*] : Speaking in a faint voice, deeply wounded, she approaches Kumagai, who is embracing the head.

KUMAGAI [*cautiously*] : Who asks for Prince Atsumori?

NARRATOR [*sings to shamisen accompaniment*] : "Ah, to meet him," is her dying breath.

TAMAORI [*clutching her wound*] : I am Prince Atsumori's betrothed, Princess Tamaori.

KUMAGAI [*turns, surprised*] : Is it Atsumori's bride, Princess Tamaori?

TAMAORI: He is dead? Then, his head . . . [*She gropes blindly for* KUMA-GAI.] My eyes! I . . . can't see!

KUMAGAI [*softly*] : Cannot see?
[*He kneels beside her and passes his hand before her eyes. When she makes no response he sighs, relieved that she cannot give them away.*]
How pitiful. Here is the head . . . of Prince Atsumori.

NARRATOR [*sings to shamisen accompaniment*] : As it passes from hand to hand, she catches her breath and cradles it on her lap, near death with pain.
[KUMAGAI *gently places the head in her lap. Imagining the head to be* ATSUMORI's *she embraces it weeping. Suddenly drums and cymbals sound* Tōyose *alarm.* KUMAGAI *hurries toward the hanamichi to bata-bata tsuke beats and looks into the distance. Music ends.*]

TAMAORI [*faintly*] : Dearest Atsumori, it is pitiful that your life should come to this. [*She caresses the head.*] I longingly sought you everywhere since you departed for battle, when the Genji warrior Hirayama Mushadokoro seized and forced his love on me. I tried to slay him by surprise but, being a woman, as you see I was wounded. Dearest Atsumori, we two . . . share the same sad end . . . together . . .

NARRATOR [*sings plaintively to shamisen accompaniment*] : "At least I want to die seeing your face as we part," she thinks, but . . .
[TAMAORI *places the head upright on the ground before her. She loses track of it. As she gropes frantically, she gasps with pain and falls back, clutching her breast.*]
. . . her heart fills with the pain of her dreadful wound.

TAMAORI: I cannot even see . . . how inconsolable!

NARRATOR [*continuing*] : Lovingly she strokes the head, cherishing a memory of his final words in life to her, "afterward" . . . spoken in the evening as the flute played.
[*Shaking with pain, she cradles the head and caresses it.*]

TAMAORI [*growing weaker*] : Though our love was unfulfilled in this life, in future lives assuredly it will last eternally . . .

NARRATOR [*continuing*] : "I am bound to you in love, my husband," she says . . .
[*She holds the head in trembling hands before her face.*]

. . . pressing to her face, folding to her breast . . .

[*She presses the head to her cheek, then to her breast.*]

. . . mind driven to distraction, uncontrolled voice rising . . .

[*Weeping distractedly she falls forward, to batan tsuke beats.*]

. . . in the cries of Suma Bay's sea plovers. Sleeves dipped in an ocean's tide of tears . . .

[*She rises to her knees, holding the head before her face.*]

. . . ebbing now as life's breath ebbs, seeing that the time of death has come . . .

[*Desperately she strains forward, gazing with sightless eyes for a final glimpse of ATSUMORI.*]

. . . her . . . life . . . expires.

[*She dies holding the head tightly to her breast, slowly collapsing to the ground.*]

Shocked and grieving, Kumagai stands deep in thought.

KUMAGAI: How sad it is that two noble young people, like budding flowers who knew nothing of life but springtime days at court, should come to this: their bodies now lie on lonely Suma Bay, too remote for any visitor to honor their graves.

NARRATOR [*sings to shamisen accompaniment*] : He weeps bitter tears of grief.

[*He begins to cry, then immediately checks himself and looks cautiously down the hanamichi for signs of soldiers. Nō drums play melancholy Kodama, "Mountain Echo" pattern and rolling thunder is heard in the distance. KUMAGAI kneels beside TAMAORI and to batan tsuke beats tries to take the head. She holds it tightly in death and he is forced to gently bend back each finger to release it.*]

KUMAGAI [*softly*] : Let worldly attachments be dissolved that you may enter Buddha's Pure Land. "Namu Amida Butsu. Namu Amida Butsu."

NARRATOR [*sings quietly in an extremely slow and free tempo to shamisen, Kodama drum pattern, and distant rolls of thunder*] : There is no escape for it, there is none . . .

[*Reverently, KUMAGAI places the head on the tree stump right.*]

. . . taking Atsumori's cape, he covers her body.

[*He places her body on a raft of small logs, half-hidden in the rushes stage left. He spreads over her the bright red cape which had covered ATSU-MORI's armor.*]

Atsumori . . .

[*KUMAGAI cuts a piece of cloth from his own purple cape, kneels beside the stump, spreads the cloth on the ground, places the head on it, and, after a long last look at his son, ties up the ends of the cloth. He carefully puts the wrapped head back on the stump.*]

. . . imperial corpse placed and covered.

[*KUMAGAI removes the purple cape from his armor and, with the help of a STAGE ASSISTANT, holds it in front of ATSUMORI hiding their move-*

ment to the raft. *The cape is spread over* ATSUMORI, *and the two bodies lie side by side under red and purple cloth. Instrumental music continues as* KUMAGAI, *profoundly depressed and moving as in a dream, finds his spear. Placing the hilt against the logs, he gently pushes the raft out to sea. Watching it move away, he hurls the spear in its wake. He strains to see them as long as possible. As they go out of sight, he drops his head and sobs silently.* KUMAGAI's *black horse enters and stands stage right. Narration resumes.*]

Taking in the reins and securing them . . .

[KUMAGAI *crosses to the horse and picks up the trailing reins.*]

. . . and tightly cinching the saddle . . .

[*He dusts off* ATSUMORI's *armor and places it on the saddle, where a* STAGE ASSISTANT *helps secure it. To instrumental music,* KUMAGAI *continues his melancholy pantomime. He picks up* ATSUMORI's *dagger and long sword. He looks at one, then the other, and sighs deeply as he thinks of his son. He passes them to a* STAGE ASSISTANT, *who fastens them to the saddle.* KUMAGAI *lifts the helmet, gazes at it a moment, and places it on the pommel.*]

. . . cradling the head in his bow arm . . .

[*He takes up the head and holds it under his left arm.*]

. . . he grasps the bridle in the other. Hearing the melancholy clop of hoof against rock, brings to mind the sadness of that parting in the Dandoku Mountains . . .

[KUMAGAI *leads the horse center and brings its muzzle close to his head.*]

KUMAGAI: . . . when Prince Shitta's young groom said farewell to his master . . .

NARRATOR [*continuing*] : . . . eons ago.[2]

[*The horse rears and paws.* KUMAGAI *turns his back to the audience to calm the horse.*]

Amid falling tears . . .

[*With one arm around the horse's neck* KUMAGAI *sobs convulsively, though no sound is heard. He releases the bridle and turns front gazing at his son's head. His knees buckle and he sinks to the floor where he weeps unabashedly. The horse nuzzles him from behind. Drum and cymbals sound* Tōyose. *Rising to his feet he controls his tears. He grasps the bridle firmly with one hand, cradles the precious head in the other, plants his feet wide apart, and poses in a strong mie to loud battari tsuke beats. He holds the pose as the curtain is run closed to loud* Kakeri, *"Rushing," played by offstage shamisen, small drums, and flute,* Nami Oto *wave pattern, and accelerating ki clacks. Music fades away. A sharp ki clack. Drums and flute play lively* Shagiri *between acts.*]

2. Alluding to the sorrow of his young groom when Buddha, then Prince Shitta (Siddhartha in Sanskrit), left to seek enlightenment.

ACT II

KUMAGAI'S CAMP

sandanme tsugi

[*Music changes to* Toki no Taiko, *"Time Drum," of the large drum. Ki clacks accelerate as the curtain is slowly drawn open. The scene is* KUMA-GAI's *battle camp in First Valley, facing Suma Bay. The main room, raised and with an open veranda fronting it, faces the audience. The rear and sides of the residence are closed off by sharp palings draped with white curtains that bear the Kumagai family crest. A cherry tree in full bloom grows to the right. Beside it is an official notice board that reads, "Here stands a rare double-flowering cherry tree from the south. If a branch is cut by any person, his punishment, following the ancient case of the Maple Tree, shall be to cut off one finger for one branch cut. The second month of the third year of Juei."* [3] *Music ends. A single sharp ki clack signals narration to begin.*]

makura

NARRATOR [*singing to shamisen accompaniment*] : Even the heavens turn. Some day will the moon shine over Suma Bay through cleared skies? The Heike drift on waves off Yashima Island in the bay, while among the prospering Genji host, unsurpassed Kumagai has established his camp in First Valley by Suma Bay, encompassing within its impenetrable palisade of felled trees, a youthful tree in full bloom, known as Kumagai's cherry tree. Passersby, of whom some can read and some cannot, crowd about staring at the notice board which forbids the cutting of a single flower.
[*During the narration, four* FARMERS *enter and crowd around the notice board. They wear pantaloons, leggings, short cloaks of dark blue and brown cotton, and straw sandals. They carry hoes and rakes over their shoulders.*]

FIRST FARMER: That's a fine cherry tree, isn't it? Look at the blossoms.

SECOND FARMER: Not the tree, look at the notice. The Priest Benkei wrote it they say. But I can't read one character.

THIRD FARMER: The tree is protected by General Yoshitsune. [*Puzzled.*] "Cut off a branch of flowers, cut off a finger," it seems to say.

FOURTH FARMER [*frightened*] : That scares me. Instead of a flower, cut off a finger? Sounds like they want our heads.

FIRST FARMER [*wide-eyed*] : Just standing here I feel like I'm stepping on a tiger's tail!

SECOND FARMER: Quick as a wink . . .

THIRD FARMER: . . . before we break a branch . . .

ALL: . . . we had better leave!
[*They hurry off right to loud drum beats. The stage is empty.*]

NARRATOR [*sings to shamisen accompaniment*] : Having traveled a long distance, Kumagai's wife, Sagami, approaches . . .
[*The curtain at the rear of the hanamichi opens and* SAGAMI *enters, wearing a gold brocaded kimono tied with black and gold sash and covered*

3. 1184.

with a plain black traveling robe. At seven-three she stops and looks toward the camp. Her accompanying RETAINER and BEARER kneel behind her.]

. . . immersed in thoughts of son and of husband, seeks out the palings of the battle camp, and recognizes on the white curtains their family crest.

SAGAMI: We are here at last. [*To the* RETAINER.] You may go ahead.

[*The* RETAINER *bows and leads the way. They stop at the gate.*]

RETAINER: Attention inside!

NARRATOR [*sings to shamisen accompaniment*] : Hearing the noisy call, Tsutsumi Gunji comes out.

[*The large blue and silver sliding doors to the inner room open and GUNJI, a family retainer, enters. He is soberly dressed in olive and gold kimono and stiff outer garments and wears a samurai's two swords.*]

GUNJI: Who approaches our master's gate? [*He is amazed to see* SAGAMI.] My Lady, what are you doing at the battle camp?

SAGAMI: Ah, Gunji. You are looking well.

GUNJI [*bowing*] : Thank you, Madam. But first you must come in. Please enter.

SAGAMI: If I may.

[*Occasional chords of the Takemoto shamisen accompany their deliberately paced actions.* GUNJI *opens the gate and kneels. The* RETAINER *takes* SAGAMI's *straw hat and walking stick.* SAGAMI *enters followed by the* BEARER, *who places the small boxes he is carrying next to the veranda and helps* SAGAMI *remove her black traveling robe and replace it with another robe of gold brocaded silk that matches her kimono. The* BEARER *takes her sandals and goes out the gate. Both attendants bow.*]

SAGAMI: You may rest now.

RETAINER and BEARER: Yes, my Lady.

[*They close the gate and go off right.* SAGAMI *climbs the short steps to the main room and sits in the place of honor left.* GUNJI *kneels to the right. Bright sounding geza shamisen, offstage right, play* Musubi Aikata, *"Bound Together," quietly in the background.*]

SAGAMI: Tell me, are my husband and son well?

GUNJI: Both are well, my Lady.

SAGAMI: Please tell my husband I am here, Gunji.

GUNJI [*bowing*] : Master has gone to the temple today, and Kojirō has not recently been seen with our lord. Are you not tired from your long journey, my Lady? Please retire and rest.

[*Music stops.* SAGAMI *nods assent and is about to rise.*]

NARRATOR [*sings to shamisen accompaniment*] : As they are exchanging numerous greetings, Prince Atsumori's mother, the court lady Fuji . . .

[*Alarm drums and cymbals sound. Lady* FUJI *runs onto the hanamichi. She is dressed in black and pulls a straw hat low over her face. She carries a small dagger in her hand ready for use. She stops at seven-three and looks anxiously behind her.*]

. . . fleeing from the jaws of the tiger, hurries under falling blossoms toward the battle camp.

[*To loud drums and cymbals playing* Tōyose *and bata-bata tsuke beats she runs under the cherry tree and leans against the gate. She poses as cherry petals fall.*]

FUJI [*calling urgently through the gate*] : Pursuers are close behind. Please conceal me!

GUNJI [*startled, answers stiffly*] : This is a camp at war. You'll find no refuge here.

SAGAMI [*compassionately*] : Wait, Gunji. A woman understands a woman's plight. [*She rises and goes to the gate. Opening it, she has one quick look at* FUJI *before she conceals her face.*] Ahh! Isn't it Lady Fuji?

FUJI [*cautiously looking out*] : Your voice . . . is it Sagami?
[*They joyously recognize each other.* SAGAMI *kneels politely before* FUJI, *formerly her mistress at the imperial court.*]

SAGAMI: Imagine meeting again unexpectedly . . .

FUJI: . . . after so long. You are well I hope . . .

SAGAMI: . . . and you? My!

FUJI: My!

TOGETHER: My, my!

SAGAMI: Please enter, my Lady.

FUJI: Forgive me. If I may.
[SAGAMI *places her hands delicately before her and bows low. She gestures politely for* FUJI *to enter.*]

NARRATOR [*sings to shamisen accompaniment*] : She is welcomed with an open heart.
[SAGAMI *passes* FUJI's *straw hat and sandals to a* STAGE ASSISTANT, *who whisks them away.* FUJI *loosens her robe, goes up the steps, and sits in the place of honor left.* SAGAMI *kneels opposite her.* GUNJI, *after closing the gate, kneels behind his mistress and bows low.*]

GUNJI: Clap if I can be of service, my Ladies.

NARRATOR [*sings to shamisen accompaniment*] : Gunji then rises and leaves.
[GUNJI *bows, rises, and exits through the sliding doors center. The two women look fondly at each other.* SAGAMI *glances to each side to see that they are alone, then bows.*]
Sagami, at last, bows . . .
[*Offstage shamisen play dignified* Goshiki, *"Five Colors," in the background.*]

SAGAMI [*warmly*] : Truly, an age has passed like a dream since the time you resided in the palace, an intimate of the Emperor, and I, infatuated with the warrior Satake Jirō, then on duty at the palace too, was forced to flee with him to the east. You could not know it, but it pleased me to hear how, after you had conceived by his Majesty, you were betrothed to Lord Tsunemori, Chief Minister of the Heike clan, and shared in the time of Heike power and prosperity. Then, when this war between Heike and Genji brought the scattering of the Heike clan, I was worried for your safety. How relieved I am to see your Ladyship's smiling face.

FUJI [*smiling*] : Dearest Sagami, it is good to see you well. My, my. I heard you were carrying a child when you went away and I do not even know if you gave birth to a girl or a boy. How is the child?

[*Offstage* Goshiki *stops.*]

NARRATOR [*sings to shamisen accompaniment*] : Let two women meet even briefly and, happy in their tears, piled-up words tumble forth. Eyes glistening, Lady Fuji . . .

FUJI: Man cannot escape adversity. The son I gave birth to and raised to become a handsome youth, dear Atsumori, has been slain in battle, while my husband, standing to sea off Yashima Island, has left me alone to face I cannot imagine what future! Can you understand my despair?

NARRATOR [*continuing*] : As she laments plaintively . . .

[*The two women dab eyes with kimono sleeves.*]

SAGAMI [*bowing sympathetically*] : No wonder you are distraught. I will consult with my husband. Out of consideration for the kindness you have shown us in the past, please entrust your welfare to us. While my husband was a member of the imperial Northern Guard he was called Satake Jirō, now his name is Kumagai Jirō Naozane. He is well known, the commander of all samurai forces in Musashi Province.

NARRATOR [*singing to shamisen accompaniment*] : Hearing this, Lady Fuji . . . !

FUJI: The warrior you married as Satake Jirō is now Kumagai Jirō?

SAGAMI [*modestly*] : He is.

FUJI: This Kumagai Jirō is . . . your husband?

[FUJI *rises on her knees wide-eyed, then slowly sinks back.*]

NARRATOR [*continuing*] : . . . calms her shocked heart.

FUJI [*deceptively quiet*] : Do you remember, dear Sagami, when your adultery was discovered at the palace and the Emperor decreed your imprisonment? It was I who interceded and made possible an escape with Satake Jirō through the great gate at night?

SAGAMI [*warmly*] : How could I forget your kindness?

FUJI: If you have not forgotten then you will return that favor by helping me slay an enemy.

SAGAMI: Kill someone? Who?

FUJI [*looks at* SAGAMI *piercingly*] : Your husband. Kumagai.

[SAGAMI *recoils.*]

SAGAMI: Ehh? You harbor such enmity?

FUJI: I do! [*She weeps.*] The man who killed Prince Atsumori is . . . your husband Kumagai!

[FUJI *falls forward weeping.*]

SAGAMI: Can this be true?

FUJI: Have you not heard?

SAGAMI: I have just arrived after the long journey from the east. Now to hear your story . . . It is unbelievable! [*Trying to mollify* FUJI.] Allow me to ask my husband the truth of this when he returns.

NARRATOR [*sings to shamisen accompaniment*] : Struggling to speak through their tears . . .

SENTRY [*off, at the rear of the hanamichi*] : Announcing Lord Kajiwara!

FUJI: Why should he come here?

SAGAMI [*worried*] : He must not see you. Quickly . . .

> [*They rise.* SAGAMI *urges* FUJI *toward the small room left.* FUJI *stops at the door.*]

FUJI: When Kumagai returns . . .

SAGAMI: . . . I will ascertain the truth . . .

FUJI: . . . and if he is my son's slayer . . .

SAGAMI: . . . though my husband, he is your enemy.

FUJI [*intensely*] : Slay him without fail.

SAGAMI [*weak and close to tears*] : You may . . . trust me.

FUJI: Then, dear Sagami . . . !

SAGAMI: Lady Fuji . . . !

> [FUJI *goes into the small room left.* SAGAMI *closes the sliding doors and stands alone perturbed. She exits through the doors center.*]

NARRATOR [*sings to shamisen accompaniment*] : Entering immediately, Heiji Kagetaka seats himself in the place of honor.

> [*Drums play* Toki no Taiko, *indicating the entrance of an evil person.* KAJIWARA *strides onto the hanamichi. He wears dark-colored battle dress: armor, leggings, straw sandals, and a samurai's two swords. His face is dark and cruel. Without ceremony he enters the room and sits left.* GUNJI *comes through the doors center, kneels right, and bows politely.*]

GUNJI: What can I do, my Lord?

KAJIWARA [*rudely*] : Call your Master.

GUNJI: Master Naozane resolved to offer prayers at the temple today. Be so kind as to entrust any message to me.

KAJIWARA: What? Kumagai's left camp? Agh! [*Shouting off.*] Heh! Soldier! Bring in the old stonecutter!

SOLDIERS [*off, at the rear of the hanamichi*] : Yes, my Lord!

NARRATOR [*sings to shamisen accompaniment*] : Saying "yes," they drag before Heiji the innocent looking stonecutter Byakugo Midaroku.

> [Toki no Taiko *resumes. Two* SOLDIERS *bring* MIDAROKU, *bound with ropes, down the hanamichi and force him to the ground by the veranda. He is an old man. A cloth hides his white hair. He wears work clothes: grey and white striped leggings, pantaloons, and cotton kimono. Music ends.*]

KAJIWARA: Well, old man, who ordered you to make a monument for Atsumori? Since all the Heike have been driven into the western seas, a two-faced Genji samurai must be your benefactor. Confess it! I'll torture you with boiling lead, slice you down the back, rub salt in your wounds if you lie! Well, you old fool?

MIDAROKU [*lightly ironic*] : Your accusation is absurd. I told you, Atsumori's spirit requested the grave marker. He placed the order and vanished. I don't care if he had no interest in buying a monument to the Five Roads to Virtue, but it's the principle of the thing, and he didn't pay me a penny, principal or interest. At least I'd have borrowed his soul fire as a night light to work by if I'd known what he was up to. Should I send a bill to the

share

devil? I can't shake money from a shade in hades, so, believe my story or not, the best one you'll get this side of Nirvana is: I did a favor to Atsumori's ghost. "Namu Amida Butsu, Namu Amida Butsu."

NARRATOR [*sings to shamisen accompaniment*] : His words are as slippery as eels.

GUNJI: You can see that talking to him is like pounding nails into rice paste. Please rest inside a while, Sir.

KAJIWARA [*though furious, bides his time*] : It's obvious who ordered you to carve the marker. When Kumagai returns, the three of us will have this out face to face! Take this fellow in! Gunji, lead the way!

NARRATOR [*sings to shamisen accompaniment*] : The old stonecutter is forcibly led away. Kajiwara is ushered into the inner room.

[*To Toki no Taiko music, the* SOLDIERS *roughly take* MIDAROKU *off left.* GUNJI *ceremoniously escorts* KAJIWARA *into the inner room. The stage is empty. The first section of the act is concluded; the final section, or climax, begins. The Takemoto* NARRATOR *and his accompanying shamisen* PLAYER *appear on a small revolving platform to the left of the stage. They wear formal black kimono and stiff sky-blue outer garments. They bow deeply to the audience. The* NARRATOR *lifts the play text to his forehead in a gesture of respect. They bow again. For the remainder of the play they remain in sight.*]

NARRATOR [*sings, slowly and with melodramatic facial expression, to the music of his shamisen accompanist*] : The sun is declining in the west when Sagami slides open the center doors to wait for her husband's late return.

[SAGAMI *enters and crosses slowly to the center of the room, where she kneels looking into the distance patiently.*]

SENTRY [*off, at the rear of the hanamichi*] : The Master has returned!

NARRATOR [*continuing*] : Does Kumagai Jirō Naozane, slayer of Atsumori in the flower of youth, understand life's impermanence?

[KUMAGAI *appears on the hanamichi. He wears a formal kimono of white silk, covered by rich trousers and vest made of gold brocade. A temple bell tolls. Deep in thought, head sunk on his chest, he slowly approaches the camp.* SAGAMI, *seeing him, claps twice.* GUNJI *appears and, at* SAGAMI's *command, opens and kneels respectfully beside the gate.* SAGAMI, *too, kneels and bows very low.*]

Though a fierce warrior, he is capable of compassion, and returning home his heart is full.

[*He pauses at seven-three and gazes at the Buddhist rosary grasped tightly in his hand. Slowly he crosses to the gate. He looks back at the notice board, then enters.* GUNJI *takes his sandals and closes the gate. The gate will not be used again, so it is taken away by two* STAGE ASSISTANTS.]

He looks at his wife, Sagami . . .

[*Angered that* SAGAMI *is there, he faces front, slaps his thigh, and strides up the steps into the room, where he immediately sits.*]

. . . with stern displeasure, and goes to sit without speaking.

[SAGAMI *and* GUNJI *kneel right, facing* KUMAGAI. *To distract his master,* GUNJI *speaks immediately.*]

GUNJI [*bowing*] : Lord Kajiwara arrived a short time ago, wishing to discuss with you an investigation he is making of the stonecutter Midaroku, whom he has brought with him. He is waiting in the inner room, Master.

NARRATOR [*sings to shamisen accompaniment*] : He spins out the details.

KUMAGAI: What is he investigating, I wonder? In any case, see that he is offered sake.

[*Still trying to protect his mistress,* GUNJI *hesitates.* SAGAMI *covertly gestures for him to stay.*]

Serve him wine, I say. What are you waiting for? Go!

NARRATOR [*sings to shamisen accompaniment*] : Severely scolded, he has no choice . . .

[*When* GUNJI *rises to leave,* SAGAMI *pulls on his sleeve to hold him. Frightened, he politely frees himself and goes out the center doors.*]

. . . Sagami pleads with her eyes and, though Gunji leaves, his heart remains behind. Watching him go, Kumagai speaks . . .

KUMAGAI [*harshly, to cover his grief*] : You! Wife! What do you mean coming here? When I left home you were strictly warned not to disturb us, but you have paid no attention. You also know women are forbidden to enter a battle camp! Insolent, brazen woman!

NARRATOR [*sings to shamisen accompaniment*] : Before his angry display, Sagami hesitantly . . .

SAGAMI [*bowing politely*] : Your rebuke is justified, dear Husband, but I worried about Kojirō going into his first battle until I could not sleep. So, wondering if I would only walk a mile, would I learn how he is, or if I walked five miles, would I have word from him, I found I had traveled seven miles down the road, then ten, and before I knew it one hundred miles . . . until I was in the capital. [*Hoping to disarm him, she laughs decorously.*] Ha, ha, ha, ha, ha! [*She covers her face with her partly open fan. Still unmoved, he looks stonily ahead.*] Arriving in the capital and hearing stories on every hand about the battle raging at First Valley, what parent would not be drawn to where her child was? Forgive me, I beg you. [*She bows, then looks up happily.*] Is Kojirō well?

NARRATOR [*rapidly chants without shamisen accompaniment*] : The question draws a harsh reply from Kumagai!

KUMAGAI [*strongly*] : Agh! When a warrior enters the battlefield he abandons life! It shows cowardly clinging to affections, to ask if Kojirō is well. [*Pause, he steals a glance.*] And, if he were slain, what would you do? Well?

SAGAMI [*slowly, with dignity*] : You misunderstand. Should Kojirō die, even in his first battle, my heart would be at ease as long as the opponent who met and slayed him was a worthy general.

NARRATOR [*sings softly to shamisen accompaniment*] : Her brave words match the thought in his heart. His face softens as he speaks . . .

KUMAGAI: Listen, then: by wresting from Hirayama Mushadokoro the honor of advancing to the head of our troops, Kojirō distinguished himself. Single-

handed he slashed his way into the Heike camp. Though he was slightly
wounded in the struggle, he has brought eternal glory to our family.

SAGAMI [*startled*] : What? It was not a fatal wound?

KUMAGAI: Ah. I see regret is written on your face. [*He poses strongly. His
right hand rests on his closed fan. He glares at her.*] Answer me! If his
wound were fatal, would you grieve?

SAGAMI [*with difficulty she dissimulates*] : It is not that. I was moved to ask
out of joy that his efforts were at least meritorious to the extent that he
was slightly wounded. [*She pauses and looks closely at* KUMAGAI.] Were
you with Kojirō then?

KUMAGAI [*gesturing with the closed fan*] : I was. From the time of his first
danger we were together in the battle. I took him, protesting, under my
arm and carried him back to camp. Later, to my incomparable glory, I
took the head of their rear-guard commander, Prince Atsumori!

[KUMAGAI *poses.* SAGAMI *falls back with a gasp.*]

NARRATOR [*rapidly to shamisen accompaniment*] : At his words Sagami pales
with shock, while behind, the Emperor's intimate listens . . .

FUJI [*rushing from the room left*] : My son's enemy! Kumagai!

NARRATOR [*continuing*] : Unsheathing her dagger, she cries "Kumagai!"
He uses her scabbard . . .

[FUJI *slashes at* KUMAGAI *several times to loud batan tsuke beats. He
fends off the blows with the empty scabbard.*]

KUMAGAI: Who calls me an enemy?

NARRATOR [*continuing*] : . . . pressing her to the floor.

[*Forcing her to the floor, he does not see her face.*]

SAGAMI: Do not be hasty. She is our Lady Fuji.

KUMAGAI: What? Lady Fuji? [*He lifts her up enough to recognize her. He is
aghast.*] Truly it is Lady Fuji!

NARRATOR [*continuing*] : Meeting so unexpectedly, he leaps back and bows
in respect.

[*He takes the dagger from her hand and starts to bow to her.* FUJI *seizes
his long sword and is about to draw. To show his sincerity he quickly
removes the short sword from his sash and pushes it toward her, making
himself unarmed. In time to rhythmic shamisen chords he gradually forces
her back with placating gestures. He looks* FUJI *directly in the eye, then
prostrates himself before her. For the moment she is unable to kill him, but
her desire for revenge is undiminished.*]

FUJI: How inhuman, Kumagai, to take the head of a mere child in combat.
[*She weeps loudly. Recovering, she nods to* SAGAMI.] You have sworn to
kill your husband.

SAGAMI: But I . . .

FUJI: Did you lie before?

SAGAMI: But . . .

FUJI: Will you help me?

kuriage   SAGAMI: Well . . .

FUJI: Well?

BOTH [*alternately, then faster until they are speaking in unison*] : Well, well, well, well!

FUJI [*hand on hilt of KUMAGAI's long sword*] : Well? Sagami! Will you?

SAGAMI [*weakly, after an anguished pause*] : I . . . will!

NARRATOR [*continuing*] : "I will," she replies, though her breast feels paralyzed!

SAGAMI [*bowing, the words scarcely audible*] : My Lord Naozane. Knowing all the while Prince Atsumori is the noble seed of an Emperor, you felt obliged to slay him. There must be some reason. If there is . . .

SAGAMI and FUJI: . . . I pray . . .

NARRATOR [*continuing*] : They speak as if suffocating . . .

[FUJI *seems ready to draw* KUMAGAI's *long sword, but* SAGAMI *gestures for her to stop. The two women look at each other.* FUJI *slowly sinks to the floor.*]

. . . tears fall unrestrained.

[*They weep bitterly and loudly.*]

KUMAGAI [*looking coldly ahead*] : What nonsense. In this war all Heike warriors are enemies. Why should we forgive Atsumori, a Heike prince, or anyone else, when we're fighting for our very lives?

[*Outraged, she is about to draw. He falls back on one hand and calms her with a gesture.*]

Listen to me, Lady Fuji, what happens on the battlefield is beyond human power. Resign yourself to it. I will relate to you the tale of that day, and how Prince Atsumori died in battle.

NARRATOR [*sings melodramatically, with great emotion, to shamisen accompaniment*] : He settles himself and begins to narrate the tale!

[FUJI *threatens to draw. He gestures for her to be calm. She sits reluctantly. He moves forward and poses on his knees, grasping the closed fan in his right hand.*]

monogatari

KUMAGAI [*strongly*] : Now then, it had come to pass that during the long night of the sixth, at the time clouds in the east were beginning to brighten, among the throng of Heike warriors who assaulted our vanguard of two—Hirayama and Kumagai—one man stood out . . .

NARRATOR [*continuing*] : . . . "unsurpassed in scarlet-laced armor, forcing even Hirayama to cease fighting and flee to safety on the beach!"

[KUMAGAI *places the fan on the floor, gestures strongly, lifts the closed fan, strikes his chest with it, and points into the distance, miming the action described in the narration.*]

nori

KUMAGAI: What a fearless young samurai! "Come back," I shouted, "don't waste yourself on a fleeing enemy when I, Kumagai, am here!" [*Calling off.*] "Come back! Come back!"

NARRATOR [*continuing*] : Holding the fan, he motioned him to return . . .

[KUMAGAI *points off with the fan, flicks it open, and still on his knees poses in a mie to battari tsuke beats, the fan held against his chest.*]

. . . until he turned his horse's head, and blows twice, three times, struck on the wave-struck shore.

[KUMAGAI *closes the fan and, to* batan tsuke *beats, strikes his thigh, as if whipping a horse.*]

nori

KUMAGAI: "Let us grapple," I said; "Yes," he replied.

NARRATOR [*continuing*] : Casting long swords away, they crash to the earth between their horses!

[*He moves the fan back and forth as if the two were grappling over it, opens it, and suddenly presses it down to the floor.*]

FUJI [*trembling*] : Ah! Then did you hold down the young warrior?

KUMAGAI: Looking closely at his face, I saw he was some sixteen years old, the same age as my son, a court child with blackened teeth and eyebrows delicately plucked, surely still living with his parents. Thinking of their deep agony and of my own affection for a son, I lifted him to his feet.

NARRATOR [*continuing, slowly*] : Brushing off the dust . . .

[KUMAGAI *mimes brushing the dust from his sword.*]

KUMAGAI: "Quickly! Flee"!

FUJI: Did you urge him to go? Then you did not intend to slay him?

KUMAGAI: Though I urged him, "quickly, flee," "no," he replied, "once thrown to the ground by the enemy, I am dishonored. Take my head quickly . . . Kumagai!"

FUJI: What? Did he say, "take my head"? What a noble phrase!

[*She collapses, weeping loudly.*]

KUMAGAI [*straining for control*] : My Lady, please! When I heard this, all the more tears welled in my breast.

[*Forcing back tears, he presses the closed fan against his chest.*]

Ahh, what if my son Kojirō had been thrown to the ground by the enemy and was about to lose his life in this same way. The way of the samurai is not so base! Though I seized my long sword . . .

NARRATOR [*sings in loud, melodramatic tones to shamisen accompaniment*] : "I hesitated! I could not draw!"

[KUMAGAI *seizes his long sword. Rising on his knees, he stamps one foot on the top step of the stairs and poses in an anguished* mie *to loud* battari tsuke *beats. In time to shamisen chords, several times he tries to draw. The* NARRATOR *strains forward and slaps the stand for emphasis; his face contorts as he cries out* KUMAGAI'*s agony.*]

"Then I heard! From the mountaintop behind me, routed Hirayama cried out!!"

KUMAGAI [*chants powerfully, in time to the rhythm of the* Takemoto

nori

shamisen] : "Kumagai! You are a traitor! He is at your mercy, yet you dream of helping Atsumori," he called out to me! Ahhhh!!

[*With a prolonged cry,* KUMAGAI *falls forward. He steadies himself by leaning on the upright closed fan. Quietly, but emotionally, he continues.*]

"There is nothing I can do. Have you any final words? If so, speak and I will . . ."

[*He breaks off and puts his hands to his eyes.*]

NARRATOR [*continuing*] : Eyes brimming with teardrops . . .

KUMAGAI: "Father is safely at sea, but mother's welfare weighs upon my heart. In this unsettled world, yesterday's clear skies have clouded. My single request, Kumagai, is that you help my mother in the difficult life to come." There was nothing else to do but . . . strike off the child's head! [*Screaming.*] Thus I fulfilled the custom of the battlefield!

[*The two women rise on their knees in horror, then sink back weeping loudly. KUMAGAI's face twists in agony, he rises on one knee, holds the open fan before his chest, and poses. He throws the closed fan to the floor in a gesture of revulsion. His chest heaves with sobs and he prostrates himself on the floor. The three weep together.*]

NARRATOR [*sings quickly to rapid shamisen accompaniment*] : In the midst of his narrative, Lady Fuji . . .

FUJI: Had he truly loved his mother, could he not have hidden in the capital as his father urged . . .

NARRATOR [*continuing*] : ". . . instead of setting out for First Valley? Ah, how I bitterly regret that, when you bravely dressed in armor . . ."

[*Rising on her knees,* FUJI *mimes bidding* ATSUMORI *farewell.*]

FUJI: . . . I urged you, joyfully, to go!

NARRATOR [*continuing*] : "Though I was resolved, my heart bursts with anguish!"

[SAGAMI *and* FUJI *look comfortingly at each other, then fall forward, weeping loudly and wiping their eyes. In her grief* FUJI *turns away.* KUMAGAI *sits impassively. Spoken narration continues without shamisen accompaniment.*]

Thinking, "how natural her grief," Sagami deliberately raises her lamenting voice.

SAGAMI [*eloquently*] : No, my dear Lady. Among all the host that fled by ship to Yashima Harbor, only one, Prince Atsumori, remained behind to earn through death greater fame than a hundred-thousand mounted warriors. Would you be happy if he quaked in hiding, the object of people's jibes and laughter? How disgraceful that would be.

NARRATOR [*sings to shamisen accompaniment*] : As she is admonished, Kumagai . . .

KUMAGAI [*turns to SAGAMI, soberly*] : Excellent, Wife. It will not do for a lady of the court to remain here. Go with Lady Fuji at once, anywhere she wishes. [*He faces* FUJI *gravely.*] Resign yourself, my Lady. I must prepare for Lord Yoshitsune's inspection of Prince Atsumori's head. Gunji, are you there? Gunji? Gunji!

[*The two women bow very low.* KUMAGAI *replaces the short sword in his sash and takes the long sword in his hand. He rises and looks intently at* FUJI.]

NARRATOR [*continues*] : Calling, he goes out of the room.

[KUMAGAI *gestures to* FUJI *to be restrained, then strides out through the doors center which automatically open and close for him. Silence. A time bell tolls in the distance. The final section of the climax begins.* SAGAMI *rises and helps* FUJI *put on her outer robe. Plaintive, poetic narration continues.*]

sandanme kiri
(tsume)

As the sunset bell tolls time's uncertain passing, the lights of the battle camp light up more and more . . .[4]

[*The bell tolls again. Two boy* SERVANTS *bring on small glowing lanterns.*]

. . . the grief of stricken Lady Fuji.

[SAGAMI *sheathes the small dagger and hands it respectfully to* FUJI. *She kneels and bows. The bell tolls.*]

FUJI [*sadly, to quiet Takemoto shamisen accompaniment*] : When I think of him, pity overwhelms me. He carried an object next to his flesh, from which, until his death, he was never parted: this flute called Green Leaves. [*She takes out a small flute wrapped in cloth.*] It proves how strong is the bond between mother and son that this flute, which Atsumori gave the stonecutter as payment to raise a marker over his grave, should mysteriously come into my hands.

[*She gazes wonderingly at the flute.*]

NARRATOR [*slowly sings to shamisen accompaniment*] : "If the soul still remains on earth, why do you not appear before me?"[5]

FUJI: You do not hear my voice, my son. Ahh! What memories are contained in this flute!

[*She folds back the cloth and gazes longingly at the polished bamboo tube.*]

NARRATOR [*continuing*] : Pressing it inconsolably to her breast, she laments.

[FUJI *presses the flute to first one cheek then the other. She cradles it tenderly in long kimono sleeves and holds it tightly to her breast. She sinks to the floor, weeping loudly.*]

SAGAMI [*drying her tears*] : The flute should be a consoling memento, its notes, even more than a chanted Darani prayer, leading his soul through all obstacles to repose. Dearest mistress, let its sound be Prince Atsumori's voice.

[SAGAMI *looks inquiringly at* FUJI.]

NARRATOR [*continuing*] : In accordance with her urgings, Lady Fuji . . .

[SAGAMI *looks off and claps twice. A boy* SERVANT *enters, listens to* SAGAMI's *whispered order, bows, and retires.*]

Although tears flow into the holes of the flute and fingers tremble, the notes rise clear.

[*Except for chords of the Takemoto shamisen, the following actions are performed in silence. Two boy* SERVANTS *enter from the inside room. One carries a black lacquered pitcher of water and matching basin, the other an incense tray. They put them down and bow. The first* SERVANT *pours water over* FUJI's *hands, then moves back respectfully. The second* SERVANT *passes a small white towel to* SAGAMI, *who in turn passes it to* FUJI, *who carefully dries her hands. The towel is passed back the same way. The first* SERVANT *now pours water on* SAGAMI's *hands, and the*]

4. "More and more" (*itodo*) is a kakekotoba. In translation the line may be read "light up more and more" or "more and more the grief."

5. The soul remains on earth forty-nine days after death in Buddhist belief.

towel is handed to her by the second SERVANT. *When the towel is returned, the first* SERVANT *picks up the pitcher and basin, bows very low, and swiftly carries them off. The second* SERVANT *slides the incense tray before* SAGAMI *and bows. She, in turn, very respectfully places it in front of* FUJI *and bows low to* FUJI *with her back to the audience. The second* SERVANT *quickly exits, and the doors center close.* FUJI *takes the flute from inside her kimono, unwraps it, and holds it before her reverently. Putting the flute in her lap, she places a pinch of incense on burning coals in the small bowl on the tray. She places her hands together and bows her head. Curls of smoke rise in the air.* FUJI *gestures to* SAGAMI. SAGAMI *bows, moves to* FUJI, *kneels, and, rising again, takes the incense tray and places it beside the sliding doors left.* SAGAMI *places a pinch of incense on the coals and clasps her hands in a silent prayer. Now that her hands are purified and incense offered to* ATSUMORI's *soul,* FUJI *raises the flute to her lips.*]

Bound by ties of love between mother and son . . .

[*Gentle notes of* Tsukebue, *"Flute Accompaniment," rise and fall. The shadow of a man appears on the translucent paper doors. Narration quickens.*]

She catches one fleeting glimpse of a form, vague as shadows of a heat wave, cast on the sliding paper doors. "Surely it is Atsumori!"

FUJI: My child! My beloved!

NARRATOR [*continuing*] : Rushing forward, she is stopped and calmed by Sagami.

[FUJI *rises in great agitation.* SAGAMI *gently but firmly stops her.*]

SAGAMI: Dear Lady, please listen. The spirit of the dead may appear in the smoke of incense.[6] When Fujiwara Sanekata died in exile, his soul's longing for the capital was so great he returned in the form of a sparrow. While this form you see may be such a spirit, it is said the ties of parent and child last but one lifetime. If you approach, his spirit will surely vanish.

FUJI: No, no! Isn't it said souls of the dead wander on earth for forty-nine days before incarnation? At least a single word . . . !

NARRATOR [*continuing*] : Shaking loose, breaking loose . . . !

[FUJI *shakes off* SAGAMI's *politely restraining hand. Three times* SAGAMI *tries to prevent* FUJI *from reaching the doors, but in the end* FUJI *forces* SAGAMI *to the floor and rushes to the doors.*]

When the sliding doors rattle open there is no figure to be seen, only a suit of scarlet-laced armor standing in its place.

[FUJI, *with the help of* STAGE ASSISTANTS, *slides the doors open to show, not a person, but a suit of stacked armor in an otherwise empty room. Both women fall back in surprise.*]

FUJI [*tremulously*] : Was the shadow only this?

SAGAMI [*on her knees, gently*] : Did you imagine this form, in the longing of your heart?

6. According to Chinese legend, the spirit of the Empress Li appeared in the smoke of incense offered in her memory.

FUJI: Oh, Sagami!

SAGAMI: Dearest Lady!

NARRATOR [*continuing*] : Bound in yearning, unheedingly . . .

[FUJI *turns to look again at the armor.* SAGAMI *watches her, then turns away and mimes her grief.*]

kakekotoba

. . . they cry out[7] their weeping lament.

[FUJI *sinks to the floor. Both women wipe their eyes as they cry rhythmically in unison.*]

Time slips by. Then Kumagai Jirō Naozane enters carrying the head case. Sagami pulls her husband's sleeve.

[*The sliding doors center open and* KUMAGAI, *a deeply melancholy expression on his face, slowly enters. He carries under his left arm a round case, made of plain wood, used to contain a head taken in battle or execution.* KUMAGAI *wears formal court dress: a deep green kimono is covered by a stiff upper garment and long, trailing trousers of the same color with a wide gold band across the center.* SAGAMI *politely holds his sleeve so he cannot move.*]

SAGAMI [*modestly*] : Dear Naozane, the life of mother and child together ends here. Allow them to take final leave of each other at least.

NARRATOR [*sings dramatically to shamisen accompaniment*] : Lady Fuji, still in tears . . .

FUJI [*weeping*] : Kumagai, have you not a child, too? Understand what is in a parent's heart. Even wild beasts grieve for their children. Have pity, allowing me one last glimpse.

NARRATOR [*continuing*] : Though wretchedly imploring him . . . !

[*She sinks to her knees and pulls on his other sleeve. The women flank him.*]

KUMAGAI [*severely*] : No! Until the head has been identified, permission cannot be given to view it!

NARRATOR [*continuing*] : As he pulls free and moves between them, about to go . . .

[*He pulls first one sleeve free, then the other, and deliberately descends the steps. Suddenly the clear, refined voice of* YOSHITSUNE *is heard offstage.* KUMAGAI *stops and looks back.*]

YOSHITSUNE [*off*] : Kumagai! Kumagai, do not depart with Atsumori's head! Present it to Yoshitsune! I shall verify it immediately!

NARRATOR [*continuing*] : With the call of "I shall verify it immediately," the door flies open to reveal . . . General of the Army Yoshitsune!

[*Nō drums play Itchō, "Single Rhythm," creating a military mood. The center doors slide open to reveal* YOSHITSUNE, *the Shōgun's younger brother. He wears armor threaded with gold, black leggings, and red shoes. His handsome face is powdered a delicate white. A gold and white silk cape partially covers his heavy armor.*]

As one, Jirō Naozane, his wife as well, and also Lady Fuji fall prostrate.

---

7. In translation "cry out" may mean either "scream" or "exhaust."

199 Chronicle of the Battle of Ichinotani

Yoshitsune takes his seat . . .

[YOSHITSUNE *strides to the place of honor left. He sits on a camp stool and rests his feet on a bearskin rug, both just placed there by his* SAMURAI. *He holds a large war fan firmly in his right hand.* KUMAGAI *quickly mounts the steps and kneels center stage, while* SAGAMI *and* FUJI *kneel unobtrusively in the corner of the room right. They bow flat to the floor. Four* SAMURAI *squat on their heels behind* YOSHITSUNE *keeping guard. The music stops.*]

YOSHITSUNE [*elegantly, yet with great inner strength*] : Kumagai, to delay in presenting the head for verification and to request leave, in the midst of battle, cast doubt on your intentions. I have heard your conversation from beginning to end, concealed in the inner room. I command you: this instant produce Atsumori's head!

NARRATOR [*sings slowly, dramatically, to shamisen accompaniment*] : Hearing his words, Kumagai . . .

[KUMAGAI *rises on one knee. He looks at* YOSHITSUNE, *then at the notice board right.*]

. . . strongly answers, "yes" . . .

[KUMAGAI *nods his head, resolved. Looking at* YOSHITSUNE *he says, "yes," and bows very low.*]

. . . moves quickly to the young cherry tree, where there is planted . . .

[*He strides to the veranda by the cherry tree and, reaching out, pulls the notice board from the ground. Soft batan tsuke beats accompany the action.*]

. . . a notice board, which he pulls from the ground . . .

[*Very deliberately he brushes dirt from the end of the stick with paper taken from the breast of his kimono.*]

. . . and places, unafraid, before Lord Yoshitsune.

[KUMAGAI *places the notice board on the floor before* YOSHITSUNE, *kneels, and bows.*]

KUMAGAI [*strongly, composed*] : A short time ago at Horikawa Palace, my Lord Yoshitsune made known his will to one of his vassals by means of a poem fastened to a mountain cherry. In the same way here, Priest Benkei has written on this notice board your command to take Atsumori's head. In obedience to my Lord's decree, as written here, the head has been taken! Undertake, then, its verification!

kubijikken   NARRATOR [*ponderously singing to shamisen accompaniment*] : When he lifts open the lid . . . !

[KUMAGAI *begins to lift the head case lid.* SAGAMI *recognizes* KOJIRŌ.]

SAGAMI: Ahh! That head is . . . !

NARRATOR [*sings rapidly to shamisen accompaniment*] : Struck by the truth, the wife rushes forward; Lady Fuji strains to see!

[*With lightning speed,* KUMAGAI *claps the lid back over the head.* SAGAMI *rushes forward, but he brushes her down the steps with the notice board.* FUJI, *straining to see, is prevented from approaching by* KUMAGAI, *who presses her back, using the notice board as a pole.*]

KUMAGAI [*harshly*] : Stop! You may see the head after our Lord has verified it! You will be silent now! Silence!!

[*The last word is drawn out in an agonized cry. They pose in a tableau. The audience applauds.*]

NARRATOR [*continuing, emotionally*] : Kumagai's admonition . . .

[*Both women try to move forward. KUMAGAI shakes his head fiercely and pushes FUJI back with the board.*]

. . . calls them to shame . . .

[*He glares commandingly at SAGAMI; she slowly falls back.*]

. . . wanting to approach but unable to . . .

[*KUMAGAI raises the notice board over his head. FUJI, suddenly released, plunges headlong down the steps.*]

. . . racked by unendurable anxiety!

[*To loud battari tsuke beats they pose in a mie: KUMAGAI flicks a long trouser leg forward, plants his foot loudly on the top step, presses the notice board, upside down, against his shoulder and glares at the women; SAGAMI and FUJI, kneeling on either side of the stage, face KUMAGAI, hold up a hand to protect themselves, then fall forward, sobbing bitterly. The audience applauds the mie. YOSHITSUNE makes no sign that he is aware of what is happening.*]

Circumspectly, Kumagai Jirō Naozane proceeds.

KUMAGAI [*gripping the board emotionally*] : Prince Atsumori is the Emperor's offspring, residing in the Emperor's Southern Palace. [*Glances significantly at the notice board.*] "Rare double-flowering cherry tree from the south: if any person strikes off the flower of one branch, he must strike off the flower of the other."[8] Inferring what your intentions might be, I have struck off his head to correspond with the flower of your command!

[*His words are a strangled scream. His body trembles violently.*] Has my Lord's will been fulfilled? Or has Kumagai misunderstood? Pronounce judgment!

NARRATOR: He cries out!

[*The NARRATOR's voice quivers with emotion, his face contorts, his eyes start, he rises on his knees and with shaking hands grips the ends of his vest to keep control of himself. KUMAGAI throws down the notice board, and with a single gesture takes the lid from the case and thrusts the head of KOJIRŌ before YOSHITSUNE. The NARRATOR's voice becomes hushed.*]

8. Kumagai's interpretation of the order contains several involved puns. The word for bud, *futaba*, is written with the character meaning "youth," but audiences would be reminded of the more common way of writing futaba, with characters meaning "two" and "leaf," referring to the double leaf that accompanies a budding flower, thus suggesting Atsumori and Kojirō, who are budding or flowering youths of the same age. Being the Emperor's son, Atsumori is "rare" or precious; it is "rare" or fortunate that Kojirō, so like Atsumori, would be available for substitution; and a double-flowering cherry tree itself is a rarity. The order (*isshi o kiraba, isshi o kiru beshi*), previously read "if you cut one branch, you must cut one branch [or finger]," here is read "if you cut one child, you must cut one child," for "one branch" and "one child" are written with characters having the same pronunciation (*isshi*).

Yoshitsune smiles and initiates the inspection.

[YOSHITSUNE *opens his fan in a languid movement, holds it before his face, turns toward the head, then slowly lowers the fan.* KUMAGAI *looks intently into* YOSHITSUNE's *eyes trying to read his lord's expression.* YOSHITSUNE *nods slightly as he recognizes* KOJIRŌ. *He continues to gaze at the pale face of the dead boy as he speaks delicately, yet deeply moved.*]

YOSHITSUNE: Ahh. You have read Yoshitsune's heart to spare the flower. The head is well taken. [*He pauses.*] Now, let those present who are related pay final honor to this head which unmistakably . . . is Atsumori. [YOSHITSUNE *lowers and closes the fan.*]

NARRATOR [*sings slowly, emotionally, to shamisen accompaniment*] : After hearing these words . . .

[KUMAGAI *bows and moves, on his knees, to the veranda.*]

KUMAGAI [*scarcely audible*] : Here, Wife. [*He places the head before her on the veranda.*] Show Prince Atsumori's head to Lady Fuji.

[*He looks warningly at her. She slowly raises her eyes to meet his. A look of understanding passes between them. He retires upstage.*]

SAGAMI [*bowing*] : Yes.

kudoki NARRATOR [*sings plaintively, melodically, to shamisen accompaniment*] : Saying no more than "yes," the wife . . .

[SAGAMI *rises, anguished, unable to look at the head of her son. She grips the lapels of her heavy outer robe and sinks to her knees weeping.*]

. . . lifts the pitiful head in her hands . . .

[*Struggling against her emotions, she rises and crosses to the head. At last, she turns and looks, but cannot bring herself yet to touch it. She takes folded paper from her breast, bites down hard on it to gain control of herself, turns away, and stands in a grief-stricken pose, head rhythmically bobbing up and down like a puppet to express her conflicting emotions. The audience applauds.*]

. . . with brimming eyes she gazes upon the changed face of her dead son . . .

[*She lifts the head from the floor and cradles it in the crook of her arm. In time to the music she walks forward carefully, one step at a time.*]

. . . her breast, choked with bitter grief, her body quaking . . .

[*She staggers, catches herself, then sinks to the floor. Holding the head out at arm's length, at last she gazes at it, lovingly, as she rocks from side to side. Her head bobs in grief and she weeps bitterly.*]

. . . ahhh! . . . the head in her trembling hands . . .

[*Taking the paper from between her teeth, she cradles the head in the crook of her arm and wipes* KOJIRŌ's *face. She puts the paper away. Holding the head directly before her in both hands, she rises on her knees and looks longingly into* KOJIRŌ's *face. Her hands and body tremble, the head moves rhythmically up and down.*]

. . . seems to be nodding . . .

[SAGAMI *and* NARRATOR *cry in unison.*]

SAGAMI: . . . as he did, when turning back at the gate, he smiled upon me!

When I recall his features . . .

[*She clutches the head to her breast and presses her cheek against KOJI-RŌ's.*]

NARRATOR [*continuing, emotionally*] : . . . how tragic . . .

SAGAMI: . . . how pathetic!

NARRATOR: Her voice stops in her throat!

[*Her body is wracked with sobbing so violent no sound can escape. Then gradually her despairing cries alternate with those of the NARRATOR until they are loudly weeping in unison to shamisen accompaniment.*]

SAGAMI [*tearfully*] : Dear Lady Fuji. Look. Lamented Prince Atsumori's . . . head!

[*Putting a piece of clean paper beneath it, SAGAMI places the head on the floor facing FUJI. FUJI, still kneeling with her back to the audience, slowly looks over her shoulder. Seeing the head of KOJIRŌ, she turns to SAGAMI in wonder.*]

FUJI: What? That head is . . . ?

SAGAMI [*crying out*] : Yes, it is!

[*To Takemoto shamisen accompaniment, SAGAMI quickly covers the head with the trailing end of her robe, as if to protect it, and cries anew. She looks meaningfully at FUJI and partially uncovers the head.*]

Look carefully upon this head. May it dispell your rancor. You should, indeed, pay homage . . . pay homage to it!

[*Covering the head again, she cries softly in time to the rhythm of the Takemoto shamisen.*]

Ahh, this head . . . at the time I was secretly pregnant by Kumagai at the palace, and forced to flee to the east to give birth . . . this head . . . you, too, gave birth to a child who became . . . Prince Atsumori! Together we carried a child in our wombs when parted from our homes.

NARRATOR [*continuing pathetically*] : That, after sixteen years of separation, a maid in waiting could be of service to her lady . . .

[*SAGAMI looks down at the head under the robe. She waves her hands in the air distractedly.*]

. . . surely is an act of Karma!

[*SAGAMI falls forward over the head. She and the NARRATOR cry in unison.*]

SAGAMI [*frantically*] : At least, in death were his . . .

NARRATOR [*continuing*] : . . . "last moments brave?" she asks in tormented fear.

[*She lifts the robe to peer at her son's face, then drops the robe with an agonized expression on her face. Tearfully she hugs the head in the robe to her breast.*]

The husband does not even blink before his lord, though tears stream from his eyes . . .

[*KUMAGAI grips his fan tightly, his lips tremble, but he does not speak. SAGAMI carries the head to the veranda and gently replaces it on the base of its carrying case.*]

Were he to speak a word of consolation, he would choke on tears, he would spit blood!

[SAGAMI *falls to the floor, leans back first on one hand, then on the other. Suddenly she rises and runs to embrace KOJIRŌ's head once more, but KUMAGAI firmly gestures for her to go back. She collapses on the floor weeping.*]

Lady Fuji, in tremulous voice . . .

FUJI: Ah, dear Sagami, it had not crossed my mind until now that Kumagai had compassionately sacrificed your son for mine. With what words can I thank you? As to how he could play his flute and show his shadow on the doors—now I understand.

[*She faces* YOSHITSUNE *and bows deeply, indicating she knows he arranged these events. Suddenly battle alarms—a conch shell and drums and cymbals playing* Tōyose—*sound offstage.*]

NARRATOR [*rapidly*]: Carried by the wind, the conch shell's battle cry clamorously pierces the ear! Roused by its sound, Yoshitsune . . .

YOSHITSUNE [*briskly*]: Kumagai. The conch shell sounds assembly. Prepare yourself. Prepare for battle!

NARRATOR [*sings rapidly to shamisen accompaniment and swelling battle alarm*]: Obedient to his words, Kumagai hurries from the room.

[KUMAGAI *bows, picks up his long sword, and goes into the center room. One of the SAMURAI puts the cover on the head, and moves the case to one side.*]

Kajiwara Heiji, who has been listening all the while, bounds from the garden gate!

[KAJIWARA *lopes on from the garden left, sneering and shaking his fan at* YOSHITSUNE. *Music stops.*]

KAJIWARA: I heard you, I heard you! [*Laughs harshly.*] I expected something like this, so on the excuse of investigating the stonecutter, I've done some spying! [*He runs to the hanamichi.*] The Kamakura Shōgunate will be pleased to hear that Yoshitsune and Kumagai want to save Atsumori! Ha, ha! Just wait!

NARRATOR [*continuing, at a furious tempo*]: He shouts over his shoulder as he rushes off, when, from behind, a stonemason's steel chisel pierces his back as cleanly as a dagger's blow!

[KAJIWARA *runs down the hanamichi to rapid and loud bata-bata tsuke beats. As he goes out of sight, sharp batan tsuke beats and a cry of pain are heard.*]

With a single cry, breath and life expire! As the General is thinking, "Who has done this," the old stonecutter enters.

[MIDAROKU, *holding a stone chisel in his hand, runs on from the left, looking anxiously down the hanamichi. Seeing* YOSHITSUNE, *he assumes a pose of innocent old age.*]

MIDAROKU: Well, well. A piece of worthless trash blocking your way has been removed and a recent conversation has set my mind at ease. I will take my leave.

NARRATOR [*continuing*] : . . . he says, turning to go.

[*To Takemoto shamisen accompaniment* MIDAROKU *crosses toward the hanamichi.*]

YOSHITSUNE [*elegantly*] : Wait, old man.

MIDAROKU [*kneels cautiously*] : What is it you wish, my Lord?

YOSHITSUNE: Identify yourself.

MIDAROKU: I have nothing to conceal. I am an old stonecutter: Byakugo Midaroku from Mikage Village.

YOSHITSUNE: Then stand. You may go.

[*Relieved,* MIDAROKU *bows and crosses onto the hanamichi with small, slow steps of an elderly person. As he reaches seven-three* YOSHITSUNE *suddenly glares at him.*]

Munekiyo, wait! Yaheibyoe Munekiyo! Wait!

NARRATOR: Surprised at Yoshitsune's words, he gasps but shows an innocent face.

[MIDAROKU *stops and guilelessly calls down the hanamichi.*]

MIDAROKU: Hey, Yahei! Our Commander is calling you! Hey there, Yahei!

[*He kneels and bows contritely to* YOSHITSUNE.] No person called Yahei is here, your Lordship.

YOSHITSUNE: The saying is true: "when man is touched by extreme hatred, sorrow, or joy, these three are not forgotten through a lifetime." I recall with joy how, long ago, when my mother Tokiwa nursed me at her breast, your kindness saved her, my brothers, and myself from freezing in the snows of Fushimi outside the capital. Although I was only three years old, I remember your face and can clearly picture, whether you conceal it or not, the mole between your eyes. You disappeared soon after Councilor Shigemori died. It is good to see you well, Grandfather.

[YOSHITSUNE *slaps the closed fan into his left fist, then grasps it firmly, as he looks intently at* MIDAROKU.]

NARRATOR [*sings to shamisen accompaniment*] : Hearing this, Midaroku briskly returns . . .

[MIDAROKU *rises. He slaps his thigh resolutely and, dropping his innocent look, stamps on stage. A* STAGE ASSISTANT *removes his sandals. He tucks the chisel away in his kimono and removes the cloth covering his forehead.*]

. . . staring at Yoshitsune's face as if to bore a hole through it!

[*He boldly mounts the steps and thrusts his face close to* YOSHITSUNE's.]

tatekotoba

MIDAROKU [*fearlessly*] : Your insight is monstrous! They say Lao Tzu was born wise,[9] that by the age of three Chuang Tzu could read a man's face! But you, Yoshitsune!

[*He faces front and sits. A* STAGE ASSISTANT *helps him drop his kimono top, showing a samurai's white underkimono beneath it, and take off his cap, revealing a thatch of snow white hair. No longer acting the devious commoner, we see him as he really is: a proud samurai.*]

9. Said to have been born an old man with white hair.

Had I not overlooked you that time, long ago, there would have been no general to breach the cliffs at Tekkai and at Hiyodorigoe and to reduce the Heike fastness at Suma Bay. Had I not saved Yoritomo's life, the Heike would be ascendant now. Aghh! The greatest error of my life was helping you! Because of you, Lord Shigemori knew the Heike faced a perilous future. He advised me, at the time of his death, to renounce the warrior's life, go into hiding, and offer masses in memory of all the Taira who might fall. I took under my care the only remaining Princess of the Taira family[10] and retired to Mikage Village with three thousand gold ryō[11] which was intended for memorial services at the Heike ancestral temple at Iozan. Throughout Banshū Province, at Nachi and Mount Kōya—at Heike mausoleums everywhere—I erected gravestones for those already departed, each memorial, each one, sprung from the bitter tears of its unknown donor . . . Yaheibyoe Munekiyo!!

[*He points to himself and screams his name as if it were a curse.*]

Although I had not seen Atsumori since he was an infant and could not possibly remember his face, without knowing why, I somehow felt the man who came to order Atsumori's marker was a noble of the vanquished Heike, so I accepted his commission happily, never dreaming he was ordering a stone memorial on this shore for salvation of the soul of Kojirō, whose fate had changed his! Agh! The will of heaven is beyond man's understanding, but for the two infants whom I saved from death— Yoritomo and Yoshitsune—to become leaders who would utterly annihilate the greatest Taira nobility . . . !

NARRATOR [*emotionally sings to shamisen accompaniment*] : ". . . is fate too cruel to bear!"

[MIDAROKU *clasps his hands supplicating heaven. His body shakes with emotion. He grinds his teeth.*]

MIDAROKU: I am the traitor among the Heike who betrayed their trust! How the spirits of dead Taira lords and warriors will vent their hatred on me! Ahhh! Munekiyo! Wretched man!!

[*Like one demented, he tears his hair. He strikes his chest and arms.*]

NARRATOR [*at the same high pitch of emotion*] : First raging, then contrite, his tears . . . challenge a waterfall! Ahhhhh!

[MIDAROKU *tumbles down the steps and collapses, weeping bitterly in unison with the* NARRATOR. *The music quiets. Pause.*]

Wise since birth, General Yoshitsune says . . .

YOSHITSUNE [*sensing* KUMAGAI's *presence offstage*]: Ah, it is you, Kumagai. Bring the box of armor from the small room.

NARRATOR [*sings quietly to shamisen accompaniment*] : Kumagai Jirō Naozane enters from within. Bearers place an armor box before their Lord. [KUMAGAI *enters slowly from the inner room. He wears battle dress: dark armor, gloves, leggings, and helmet. He kneels to the right of* YOSHI-

10. Shigemori's daughter, Princess Koyuki.

11. Between \$90,000 and \$135,000.

TSUNE. *Two* BEARERS *bring out a large wicker box and place it on the main stage in front of* YOSHITSUNE.]

YOSHITSUNE [*carefully*] : Old man, deliver this box of armor to the princess. Do it . . . Midaroku!

MIDAROKU [*surprised*] : Midaroku, did you say? Ah, I see. A Genji general can't ask Munekiyo, friend of the Heike, for a favor! Ha, ha! Isn't this an interesting situation?

[*He chuckles and assumes his previous guise of innocent old age.*]

I could do what you request, but armor for a girl? It seems inappropriate. I'll just peek inside . . .

[MIDAROKU *trots casually to the box and unties the lid.*]

NARRATOR [*sings to shamisen accompaniment*] : When he lifts the lid and looks inside . . . !

[*Opening the lid, he sees* ATSUMORI. FUJI *rushes forward.*]

FUJI: Ahh! Is it . . . ?

[MIDAROKU *claps the lid on the box. She tries to open it. He holds the lid tightly with one hand and pushes her back with the other.*]

MIDAROKU [*quietly, but prolonging each word*] : There is . . . nothing . . . inside.

[*She hesitates, then tries to open the lid again. He pushes her back gently and shakes his head. He looks at her meaningfully.*]

Even a traitor would be satisfied. Give thanks to Kumagai, for . . .

[*He picks up the notice board and looks at it with tears in his eyes.*]

. . . strike off the flower of one branch, strike off the flower of the other. Ahh! How grateful we are!

[*He bows to* KUMAGAI *and* YOSHITSUNE, *weeping quietly in gratitude.*]

NARRATOR [*sings to shamisen accompaniment*] : Hearing this, Sagami turns to her husband . . .

SAGAMI [*dabbing her eyes*] : Though I am resigned knowing my child's death was an act of loyalty, still, how could Kojirō and Atsumori, opponents in the battle, be exchanged?

KUMAGAI [*gruffly*] : I have told you: I carried Atsumori from the field pretending he was wounded. Obviously, it was Kojirō that Hirayama challenged and Kojirō's head I took!

NARRATOR [*continuing*] : She weeps at his harsh words.

SAGAMI: You are inhuman, Kumagai! He is not your child alone. After I have come one hundred, two hundred miles hoping anxiously to see his face, how can you scold me, saying nothing of what you have done except "obviously it was Kojirō's head I took?"

NARRATOR [*continuing*] : She has reason to weep bitter tears and raise her voice. The General understands her feelings.

[KUMAGAI *sits impassively.* SAGAMI, *bent over, weeps loudly.*]

YOSHITSUNE [*clearly*] : Kumagai. The time has come to depart for battle in the west. Prepare yourself.

KUMAGAI [*quietly, bowing*] : My Lord, please grant the leave I have requested.

YOSHITSUNE: I understand. From time immemorial, the samurai has fought for fame in life in order to pass on glory to his heir. Should one's son die before him, the will to battle dies, too. I grant your request, Kumagai. Enter monkhood in good spirits and offer services for the repose of my parents' souls, I pray.

NARRATOR [*sings quietly to shamisen accompaniment*] : This compassionate command is heard gratefully, as he loosens his sash, slipping off his armor . . .

[KUMAGAI *bows to* YOSHITSUNE, *then takes off his battle dress. Beneath the helmet his head is shaven and beneath his armor he wears a monk's black cloak and plain grey kimono. A* STAGE ASSISTANT *stacks armor, helmet, gloves, and breeches beside* KUMAGAI.]

Seing this, Sagami says . . .

SAGAMI [*amazed*] : But . . . Kumagai . . . !

KUMAGAI [*calmly, holding a Buddhist rosary in his hands*] : I am doing nothing strange. In the midst of strife the General has generously granted my deep desire to renounce the world. From this moment, let me take the monk's name Renshō and turn my steps toward Amida Buddha's Western Paradise, where Kojirō, embarked before me upon the Nine Stages of Bliss, and I shall one day sit together on the same lotus. Buddha Merciful All Hail. "Namu Amida Butsu, Namu Amida Butsu, Namu Amida Butsu."

NARRATOR [*very slowly sings to shamisen accompaniment*] : Commendable . . . and . . . heart-breaking!

dangiri

[KUMAGAI *lifts the rosary to his forehead and prays.* NARRATOR *continues briskly.*]

Thinking "a long stay brings misfortune," Midaroku plans to tie up the

share

affair and quickly leave.

[MIDAROKU *kneels in front of the armor box and tries to tie it onto his back, slipping his arms into large loops of rope fastened to either side of the box.*]

MIDAROKU: Yo, ho! Yo, ho! Yo, ho!

[*To Takemoto shamisen chords, he tries to rise several times, each time falling back because the load is so heavy. Panting, he tucks one leg under him, plants the notice board firmly in the ground, and, to accelerating shamisen music, manages at last to rise to his feet. He staggers left, then right, and finally stands straight. He poses in a mie, notice board against his shoulder, to loud battari tsuke beats. He speaks rhythmically, in exact time to chords of the Takemoto shamisen.*]

nori

Lord Yoshitsune! What if Prince Atsumori gathers once again remnants of the Heike clan and returns evil for good?

YOSHITSUNE [*continuing the rhythmic style of speech*] : It would be no more than heaven's just retribution, for when Yoshitsune and his brother Yoritomo were saved they rewarded with evil the kindness done to them.

KUMAGAI [*strong, normal speech*] : Truly, when that time comes, the vanity of this world abandoned, unfettered to any man, Kumagai will stand apart from the bloody carnage and help equally the tortured souls of both Genji and Heike dead . . .

Kumagai concludes the narrative account (monogatari) of Atsumori's death. He strikes a pose with the open fan held to his chest. "There was nothing else to do but strike off the child's head! Thus I fulfilled the custom of the battle-field!" (*Sagami:* Nakamura Jakuemon; *Kumagai:* Ichikawa Danjūrō) Page 196

Lady Fuji plays Atsumori's flute in the hope that his spirit will appear before her. "Bound by ties of love between mother and son, she catches one fleeting glimpse of a form, vague as shadows of a heat wave, cast on the sliding paper doors. 'Surely it is Atsumori!'" (*Fuji:* Nakamura Kichinosuke)

"Then Kumagai Jirō Naozane enters carrying the head case. Sagami pulls her husband's sleeve." (*Sagami:* Nakamura Ganjirō; *Kumagai:* Onoe Shoroku; *Fuji:* Nakamura Shikan) Page 199

Kumagai prevents Sagami and Fuji from seeing the head in the case. He poses
in a mie. "Stop! You may see the head after our Lord has verified it! You will
be silent now! Silence!!" (*Sagami:* Onoe Baiko; *Kumagai:* Matsumoto Koshirō;
Yoshitsune: Ichikawa Somegorō) Page 201

Yoshitsune views the head and asserts that it is Atsumori's. "You have read Yoshitsune's heart to spare the flower. The head is well taken." (*Kumagai:* Onoe Shoroku; *Yoshitsune:* Onoe Baiko) Page 202

Sagami shows Lady Fuji the head of Kojirō. "Look carefully upon this head. May it dispell your rancor. You should, indeed, pay homage, pay homage to it!" (*Sagami:* Nakamura Mannojō) Page 203

"When he lifts the lid and looks inside . . ." Midaroku sees Atsumori alive and well in the box.

Lady Fuji rushes forward to see if Atsumori is in the box. Midaroku pushes her gently back. "There is nothing inside. Even a traitor would be satisfied. Give thanks to Kumagai." (*Yoshitsune:* Nakamura Kichiemon; *Midaroku:* Ichikawa Chūsha; *Fuji:* Nakamura Kichinosuke) Page 207

Kumagai abandons his life as a warrior and prepares to leave as a wandering monk. (*Sagami:* Onoe Baiko; *Kumagai:* Matsumoto Koshirō; *Yoshitsune:* Ichikawa Somegorō; *Midaroku:* Onoe Shoroku; *Fuji:* Sawamura Sōjūrō) Page 209

Kumagi exits to Ōzatsuma shamisen music. The curtain covers the main stage isolating Kumagai on the hanamichi. (*Kumagai:* Ichikawa Somegorō; *Ōzatsuma Musician:* Kashiwa Isanosuke) Page 210

NARRATOR: . . . offering prayers for their salvation.

[KUMAGAI *raises the rosary to his forehead and eyes.* MIDAROKU *looks at* KUMAGAI *and laughs wryly.*]

nori MIDAROKU [*speaking in strict rhythm of the Takemoto shamisen*]: When that time comes, Midaroku will abandon this world and return as Mune-kiyo!

KUMAGAI [*speaking normally*]: Thoughts of a monk's black robes fill my heart. I shall become a disciple of Priest Hōnen, submitting to his teaching in Black Valley. [*Faces* YOSHITSUNE.] May your good fortune increase, my Lord.

NARRATOR [*sings to shamisen accompaniment*]: Saying this, wife joins husband . . .

[KUMAGAI *sits on the steps. A* RETAINER *passes to* SAGAMI *straw sandals which she ties to* KUMAGAI's *feet.*]

. . . the stonecutter, together with Lady Fuji, stand beneath the eaves of the encampment.

[FUJI *kneels by* MIDAROKU *and looks questioningly at the box.*

MIDAROKU *indicates with a reassuring nod that* ATSUMORI *is safe in his care. From opposite sides of the stage the two women and two men exchange parting glances.*]

SAGAMI and FUJI [*slowly in unison*]: If destiny allows . . .

NARRATOR: . . . say the women . . .

KUMAGAI and MIDAROKU: . . . we shall meet again . . .

NARRATOR: . . . say the men.

YOSHITSUNE [*interrupting in a clear, commanding voice*]: Live your lives in good health!

NARRATOR [*sings to shamisen accompaniment*]: Hearing their Lord's will, with tears of gratitude, tears of sad remembrance . . .

[KUMAGAI *looks at* YOSHITSUNE *with an expression of gratitude. He bursts into tears and bows down to the ground. After a moment he rises, and* SAGAMI *puts over his shoulder a monk's alms bag and gives him a plain straw hat and walking staff, passed to her by the* RETAINER. *He takes a few steps to the right, holding hat and staff limply at his sides.*]

. . . reminded, the General takes into his own hands Kojrō's head.

[*Receiving the head from a* SAMURAI, YOSHITSUNE *rises and extends it, face forward, toward* KUMAGAI.]

YOSHITSUNE [*with a catch in his clear voice*]: This shall be consecrated at Suma Temple, that the unblemished name of . . . Atsumori, inscribed in gold, shall live for generations to come.

[*They pose for a moment in silence, then express their unbearable anguish in linked dialogue of alternating phrases of seven and five syllables.*]

watarizerifu MIDAROKU: Though we pity the flower, mentioned on the sign . . .
shichigochō FUJI: . . . of Musashibō Benkei, we must pity more . . .

SAGAMI: . . . the forsaken samurai . . .

RETAINER: . . . pride of warrior thrown aside . . .

KUMAGAI: . . . a traveler whose place of rest will never be known . . .

YOSHITSUNE: . . . in this transient and mutable . . .

ALL [*in unison*] : . . . world of man!

NARRATOR: Tears cloud their voices!

[KUMAGAI *bows to* YOSHITSUNE, *then to* MIDAROKU. *As he turns to go,* SAGAMI *reaches out to stop him. He brushes past her and walks onto the hanamichi.*]

YOSHITSUNE: Kumagai!

[YOSHITSUNE *holds out* KOJIRŌ's *head. Slowly* KUMAGAI *turns back. Though he has renounced the world, he cannot help wishing for a final view of his son.*]

KUMAGAI [*anguished*] : Now that I am entering Buddha's blessed land . . . all cares have vanished!

[*He turns away from* KOJIRŌ *to gain control over himself, trying to forget the ties of earthly affections, but he cannot. Again he turns to look at his son.*]

Ahh! Sixteen years have passed, like a single day! Ahh! It is a dream, a dream!

[*Numbly he lifts his hand to wipe away a single tear. He turns his back on* KOJIRŌ.]

NARRATOR [*quietly sings to slow shamisen accompaniment*] : A single teardrop of dew, splashing to the ground; from a holly leaf sprinkled, by winter's first snow; melted in the sun's clear light . . . how like Kumagai![12]

[*A single sharp ki clack signals the final tableau:* KUMAGAI *collapses to his knees at seven-three and buries his head in the straw hat;* FUJI *starts to cross to* KUMAGAI, *but* MIDAROKU *forces her back with the notice board;* SAGAMI *looks at* KUMAGAI, *then falls forward weeping;* YOSHITSUNE *holds the head firmly in both hands. All pose in a strong group, or hippari, mie as the stick drum is struck loudly three times in the*

hikkomi

Dangiri pattern. The curtain is slowly closed to loud, accelerating ki clacks. KUMAGAI *remains huddled over on the hanamichi. The edge of the curtain is pulled back to allow the geza musicians to see* KUMAGAI. *An Ōzatsuma shamisen* PLAYER *enters from the wings and stands immediately behind* KUMAGAI, *one foot placed for balance on a small stool brought out by a* STAGE ASSISTANT. *Very faint and distant sounds of drums and cymbals playing* Tōyose *are heard from the rear of the hanamichi, then silence.* KUMAGAI *rises, thinking of the active and honored life he is renouncing. The Ōzatsuma shamisen begins to play soft, widely spaced, tenative chords of* Urei Sanjū, *"Sorrowful Melody." Drawn once again by the memory of the son he killed,* KUMAGAI *slowly pivots to look back. His shoulders are slumped, the hat and staff hang loosely in his hands. Music stops. He stands motionless, silently recalling the past. Then very quietly the Ōzatsuma shamisen plays* Okuri Sanjū, *"Departing Melody." He blinks back tears and forces himself to turn his back forever on his former life. He looks down the hanamichi, thinking of the unknown future. For a*

12. Alluding to the light of Buddha's salvation.

*moment he is overwhelmed by anguish and melancholy. His lips tremble
and his hands shake. He controls himself, slowly raises the hat over his
head, half glances back over his shoulder again, then drops his head
forlornly and poses. Hesitantly, as if worldly ties held him back, he begins
to leave, each deliberate footstep accented by* Tōyose *drum and cymbals,
and* Ōzatsuma *shamisen music. He pauses, looks up once more, then, with
an expression of agonized resolve, he pulls the hat sharply down in a
gesture of humility and runs faster and faster down the hanamichi and off
to accelerating music and loud bata-bata tsuke beats. In complete silence
the hanamichi curtain closes behind him, the corner of the main curtain is
pulled closed, and the* Ōzatsuma *musician goes off right. A sharp clack of
the ki signals drums and flute to play* Shagiri. *The performance is concluded.*]

Love Letter
from the Licensed Quarter

Kuruwa Bunshō

The dance play (buyō geki) *Love Letter from the Licensed Quarter* is a descendent of the Yūgiri-Izaemon prostitute-buying (keiseigai) plays of the Genroku period. It has had an involved history and can be variously dated. The earliest play dramatizing Izaemon's love for the courtesan Yūgiri was written for kabuki in 1678. Chikamatsu Monzaemon wrote *Seventh Anniversary of Yūgiri's Death* for Sakata Tōjūrō in 1684. None of the texts of these, nor of the score of other, Genroku plays about the lovers has come down to us, but it seems likely that Chikamatsu borrowed heavily from them when he composed, in 1712, the three-act jōruri play *Yūgiri and the Straits of Naruto. Love Letter from the Licensed Quarter* is based on the first act of this play. Many kabuki dance plays in later years took Chikamatsu's puppet text as a point of departure. Some of these used Takemoto music, others Tomimoto, Kiyomoto, or Tokiwazu music. The dance play version titled *Love Letter from the Licensed Quarter* was first performed in 1780. It is the only kabuki play about Yūgiri and Izaemon now regularly staged.

Izaemon is a model for wagoto leading man roles and Yūgiri for courtesan roles. The comic-erotic mood of the play is typical of prostitute-buying plays. Izaemon is heir to a wealthy merchant family. Because he has been disowned, he and Yūgiri allow a samurai family to adopt their seven-year-old son. Further developments of this story are taken up in the second and third acts of the jōruri, but they are not staged in kabuki. Overlaid on the prostitute-buying situation is the later style of dance play. Three types of music accompany the dance and mine sections of the version translated here. Takemoto puppet and Tokiwazu dance ensembles sit onstage in view of the audience; the standard kabuki Nagauta ensemble sits in it usual place offstage right. When the sung text is in alternating phrases of seven and five syllables (shichigochō), it is translated into English lines of the same syllable count. All the Tokiwazu and Nagauta songs are written this way. In keeping with the narrative function of Takemoto music, the majority of the Takemoto sections are in prose. In fact, the final dance-mime section of the play—the love scene between Izaemon and Yūgiri—is entirely sung prose. Chikamatsu's jōruri text provides about half of the lines; the other half were written for kabuki performances. Nagauta lyrics and most Tokiwazu lyrices are kabuki additions. The opening rice-pounding scene, only indicated in the puppet play, is expanded into a longer, more ribald scene, and the sections of connected dialogue (watarizerifu) are a kabuki specialty not found in the jōruri.

The translation is based on texts in Atsumi Seitarō, ed., *Nihon Gikyoku Zenshū* (vol. 27, 1928), and Toita Yasuji, ed., *Kabuki Meisakusen* (vol. 3, 1956). An annotated text of Chikamatsu's jōruri on which *Love Letter from the Licensed Quarter* is based is in Shigetomo Ki, ed., *Chikamatsu Jōrurishū* (Chikamatsu's Puppet Plays, vol. 1; Tokyo: Iwanami Shoten, 1958). Most stage directions are from the performance by Nakamura Ganjirō II and Nakamura Senjaku III, playing Izaemon and Yūgiri respectively, at the Misona Theater, Nagoya, October 1967.

Love Letter
from the Licensed Quarter

SCENE 1   OUTSIDE THE YOSHIDA BROTHEL

[*Stick drum and flute play lively* Tōri Kagura, *"Shrine Dance Procession,"
and shamisen play* Shikoru, *"Harden," behind the striped kabuki curtain.
Two ki clacks. Ki clacks accelerate as the curtain is run open. The main
entrance of Yoshida House,*[1] *in New Town licensed quarter, Osaka,
opening onto the street. Lattice strips cover the front of the house. A
festive display of a Shintō sacred straw rope hanging under the eaves and
great tubs of cut bamboo, plum, and pine branches flanking the entry in
the center of the stage indicate that it is the New Year season. Music tapers
off. Silence. The stage is empty. A single ki clack: music resumes. Shouts
are heard from inside the house. A group of male* SERVANTS *bursts
through the curtain in the entry. They wear short happi coats over plain
cotton kimonos. They carry a large tree stump as a mortar and a long-
handled maul for pounding the traditional New Year's rice-cake dough.
One* SERVANT *puts a huge ball of rice dough in the hollow of the stump.
As the others clap their hands and sing, the* SERVANT *with the maul
strikes rhythmically, moving around the stump in a circle.*]

SERVANTS [*sing* Kome Tsuki, *"Rice Pounding," to the accompaniment of
shamisen and small drums*]:
Pounding rice five men are right, pound together in rhythm;
　When a great lord is passing, even he must stop to watch.
[*They repeat the song several times, until the* SERVANT *who is pounding
drops the maul to the ground and plops down cross-legged.*]

FIRST SERVANT [*wiping his forehead*]: Whew! I could use a drink.
[*The others laugh and hoot.*]

SECOND SERVANT [*playfully slapping his shoulder*]: He'd rather pound the
mochi[2] with debutante whores or old women . . .

　1. Yoshida House is an *ageya* or house of assignation. In 1678, the time of the play, a
customer did not visit the house where a courtesan lived. Instead he met her at an
ageya where they were entertained and where they spent the night.
　2. *Mochi*, a small rice cake, is a traditional New Year's delicacy. The dough is prepared
by pounding steamed rice in a pestle, so "to pound mochi" meant in popular parlance
sexual intercourse.

THIRD SERVANT: . . . but he can't today. The Awa millionaire's bought them all.

FOURTH SERVANT: So our pounding goes into rice cake!

[*They laugh good-naturedly.*]

watarizerifu

FIFTH SERVANT: Each year it's the custom to make felicitous rice cakes . . .

SIXTH SERVANT: . . . to celebrate the New Year . . .

SEVENTH SERVANT: . . . the first business of the year . . .

EIGHTH SERVANT: . . . is drinking, treated by the master of Yoshida House.

NINTH SERVANT: If there's trouble abroad, why the only trouble . . .

TENTH SERVANT: . . . is drinking our fill!

FIRST SERVANT: Remember last year, when the great courtesan Oyama took a shine . . .

SECOND SERVANT: . . . to the best . . .

THIRD SERVANT: . . . singer and dancer at the feast?

FOURTH SERVANT [*puffing up*]: I'll do my best this year . . .

FIFTH SERVANT: . . . in the hope she'll fall for me!

[*They all laugh, and some jokingly push the* FOURTH SERVANT.]

SIXTH SERVANT: Forget it. Let's stuff ourselves . . .

SEVENTH SERVANT: . . . and hope the Awa patron treats us . . .

EIGHTH SERVANT: . . . to his Awa-cakes . . .[3]

NINTH SERVANT: . . . and maybe some of his girls!

TENTH SERVANT: Oh, how great . . .

ALL: . . . that would be!

[*Shamisen resume* Shikoru *and stick drum and flute* Tōri Kagura. HIRA-OKA, *a wealthy samurai from Awa*,[4] *appears on the hanamichi. He is dressed in sober but expensive dark kimono and cloak. He is escorted by four adult* MAIDS, *two teahouse* GIRLS, *and two* CHILD MAIDS, *whose brilliant colored kimonos catch the eye.* HIRAOKA *stops at seven-three and faces the audience. Music stops.*]

HIRAOKA: "Even travelers can't help being late sleepers, when the year end comes,"[5] someone has written. I have come from faroff Awa, at New Year, to see the whores of Osaka and drink love's liquor from the pink blossoms of wintertime. I proclaim it publicly: I want to meet the famous courtesan Yūgiri. Sweet girls, skilled in love's affairs, intercede for me. Five days straight I have waited at Yoshida House for her. Please arrange it, please.

watarizerifu

FIRST MAID [*sweetly flattering*]: A lord so enamored that he lets his heart stray to the port of Osaka, far from home, is surely a millionaire who knows the ways of love . . .

SECOND MAID: . . . for among all the courtesans of New Town Quarter, the famous one you visit unceasingly is Evening Mist of Fan House.

THIRD MAID: We deeply understand your passion, and wish your quest to meet her meets success, yet . . .

---

3. Since Awa can mean either an area of the island of Shikoku or millet, the line can mean either "millet cakes" or "(the man from) Awa's cakes."

4. On Shikoku Island facing Osaka across the Inland Sea.

5. Travelers who had long distances to cover on foot were notoriously early risers in Japan. But even they slack off and share in the festivities which mark the end of the year.

FOURTH COURTESAN [*sadly*] : . . . since mid-autumn she has been ill . . .

FIRST SERVANT [*confidentially*] : . . . master and mistress both worry about forcing things too much . . .

SECOND SERVANT: . . . but she has pride and with luck her heart might melt . . .

ALL: . . . tonight.

HIRAOKA [*fervently*] : And so please intercede, please.

FIRST MAID [*bowing*] : In any case, great millionaire . . .

ALL: . . . do come this way.

> [*Shamisen and stick drum play* Migi no Uta, *"Song of the Right," as the procession crosses onstage. A black-robed* STAGE ASSISTANT *places a folding stool center.* HIRAOKA *sits and fans himself importantly. The others flutter around him. Music stops.*]

FIRST SERVANT [*bowing obsequiously*] : Welcome, welcome . . .

SERVANTS [*in unison*] : . . . great millionaire from Awa.

HIRAOKA [*jovially*] : Well, well. I see you are all lined up before me. Tell me, is the mochi pounding over?

watarizerifu   FIRST SERVANT [*ingratiatingly*] : We finished it off a moment ago. A generous patron came to Yoshida House this New Year . . .

SECOND SERVANT: . . . passing out tips to us every day, so we really put our hearts in it.

THIRD SERVANT: Why, you made us feel so good . . .

FOURTH SERVANT: . . . we beat the rice in rhythm . . .

FIFTH SERVANT: . . . as a welcome . . .

ALL [*bowing*] : . . . Master.

HIRAOKA [*frowning*] : I wish I had seen it. But I have come daily to see Yūgiri.

> [*A* FIFTH MAID *hurries from the entrance and bows to* HIRAOKA.]

FIFTH MAID: Ah, have you just returned, sir? Wonderful news. It must have been the auspicious mochi pounding. When our master personally went to Yūgiri and implored her, as you might expect of a high-ranking courtesan, she consented, for the honor of Yoshida House, to appear today!

HIRAOKA: You say Yūgiri will come out?

watarizerifu   FIRST SERVANT [*rubbing his hands gleefully*] : If Yūgiri is coming out, let's go quickly in . . .

SECOND SERVANT: . . . to the banquet hall and feast and drink . . .

THIRD SERVANT: . . . as we usually do . . .

ALL: . . . at our great lord's pleasure!

HIRAOKA: Here, here, now. You don't have to say it. As if I didn't know!

> [*Laughing, he throws a handful of coins onto the ground. The* SERVANTS *eagerly scramble for them.*]

ALL: Thank you! Thank you, sir!

watarizerifu   FIRST SERVANT [*slyly*] : They say a millionaire has sticky fingers![6]

---

6. *Nurete de awa,* part of a proverb meaning to handle "millet with wet fingers" (that is, to get rich without effort) leads into *awa no odaijinsama,* "Awa's millionaire." *Awa* is a kakekotoba. *Nurete* also suggests his fingers are wet with love.

SECOND SERVANT: When you're alone with Yūgiri . . .

THIRD SERVANT: . . . side by side in Yoshida's private cottage . . .

FOURTH SERVANT: . . . you'll be today's mochi-pounding pestle . . .

FIFTH SERVANT: . . . she a mortar dripping with love . . .

SIXTH SERVANT: . . . never ceasing through eternity!

SEVENTH SERVANT: Congratulations . . .

ALL: . . . on getting in her bed!

> [*There is nothing salacious in their attitudes. They laugh good-naturedly.*
> HIRAOKA *waggles his fan at them.*]

HIRAOKA: Flatterers! Flatterers!

FIRST SERVANT [*expansively*] : Then, great millionaire, enter the banquet hall . . .

HIRAOKA: . . . come with me, all of you . . .

ALL: . . . with pleasure, sir!

> [*Shamisen play fast* Sugagaki *brothel music.* HIRAOKA *rises and leads the way through the curtain into Yoshida House. The others follow ad-libbing "This will be a great feast," "I'll drink all day," "We'll never have a feast like this one."* SERVANTS *carry off the mortar and pestle. Music fades. The stage is empty. Two ki clacks: paper doors slide open stage left revealing a raised platform on which are seated three Takemoto* SINGERS *and three shamisen* PLAYERS. *After a short shamisen introductory section, the* LEAD SINGER *sings a capella.*]

LEAD SINGER:

Winter's woven hat of straw covered with grime;
Letter-paper kimono frayed at sleeves and knees.

share

SINGERS [*in unison, to shamisen accompaniment*] :

A heath fern blown by the wind, enduring during;
Hiding concealed though he is, in past times it was not so.[7]

A windblown flower, chin tucked into his collar . . .

> [*Shamisen continues to play as the lights come up on the hanamichi and* IZAEMON *enters. He wears a "paper kimono," supposedly made of Yūgiri's love letters, that shows his poverty. The characters of her "letters" are embroidered in silver thread on the purple and black silk patches that make up the kimono. A sedge hat hides his face. A short sword is tucked in a plain black sash. He wears straw sandals. Hunched over against the bitter winter cold, he has tucked his arms inside his kimono sleeves. He walks slowly, wearily. At seven-three he stops and looks toward Yoshida House. He turns back and faces the audience. Takemoto singing resumes to shamisen accompaniment.*]

SINGERS: Teeth clamped tight still chattering in the evening cold.

> [*He shivers and hugs himself. He steps back, stumbles, and recovers his balance. He blows gently on his hands to warm them. His head shakes as if crying.*]

---

7. This complicated passage contains many puns. Part of the line goes *kaza fukishinogu* (to bear the blowing wind) *shinobugusa* (fern), *shinobu to suredo* (though he hides).

Protruding sword hilt and guard are worn smooth with age;
  End of the scabbard cut short by the approaching year's end.[8]
[IZAEMON *brushes dust from his kimono sleeve, then pulls out the thin red inner kimono of his right sleeve and places it protectively over the sword hilt. He holds the scabbard tip gently in his left hand, sighing. He looks toward the house and slaps his thigh determinedly. He tucks his hands once more into his sleeves and walks onstage, arrogant and pathetic, a fancy, funny, and thoroughly miserable young man.*]

LEAD SINGER [*chanting rapidly, without shamisen accompaniment*] : Like a hunted fugitive he peeps furtively into the brothel.
  [*He parts the split curtain in the entry and calls inside. His voice is delicate and wan.*]

IZAEMON: Are you there, Kizaemon? [*Pouting.*] Kiza. Kiza.

LEAD SINGER [*singing to shamisen accompaniment*] : Haughtily, fan held before his nose . . . young men pour from the house!
  [*IZAEMON poses facing front with his left hand tucked arrogantly in his breast. He flicks his fan half open and holds it before his face. Offstage stick drum and shamisen play* Odoriji, *"Dance Music." A dozen* SERVANTS *rush out brandishing brooms. Music softens.*]

ALL [*ad-libbing*] : Yes, Master Kizaemon is in. He's here. Who wants him?

FIRST SERVANT [*contemptuously, looking* IZAEMON *up and down*] : Ehh? What kind of windblown ghost are you?

SECOND SERVANT: Damned scarecrow, what do you mean impudently calling . . .

THIRD SERVANT: . . . "Kiza, Kiza," to a gentlemen?

FOURTH SERVANT: You talk as bold as a spender spewing out a thousand gold pieces!

FIFTH SERVANT: Idiot. What shack did they throw you out of?

SIXTH SERVANT: Don't stand before Master Kizaemon's gate . . .

SEVENTH SERVANT: . . . with your face covered, blabbing like you owned the world!

EIGHTH SERVANT: Impudent beggar . . .

NINTH SERVANT: . . . know your place . . .

TENTH SERVANT: . . . or you'll see what it means to joke with us!
  [*They turn their backs on him.* IZAEMON *lowers the fan and poses.*]

IZAEMON [*blithely*] : Who cares about a thousand gold pieces? His name is Kizaemon. I'll call him Kiza if I like. Now, I want to meet him.
  [*He flicks open the fan and poses, pouting. The* SERVANTS *are incensed. They push their sleeves up, tie towels around their heads, and raise their brooms to beat him. Stick drum and shamisen play* Odoriji.]

ALL: Meet him? What nerve! Meet this!

LEAD SINGER [*chanting rapidly*] : Brooms whirl! Kizaemon rushes out!
  [KIZAEMON, *the owner of Yoshida House, flicks open the entry curtain*

---

8. Traditionally all debts had to be paid at the end of the year. A person down on his luck might have to settle for wearing a short sword that has been cut down from a broken long one.

and enters, frowning. He is middle-aged and wears a formal black cloak and tan divided trousers over a townsman's gray kimono. He restrains his employees with a gesture.]

KIZAEMON [*dignified*] : Come, come. There should be no disturbance on the day for auspicious New Year's rice-pounding. Think of what would happen if you injured someone with your brooms.

[*Though* IZAEMON *looks thoroughly disreputable,* KIZAEMON *bows politely.*]

I am Kizaemon. But who are you? Why do you want to meet me?

[IZAEMON *does not move or speak.* KIZAEMON *edges in and tries to peer under the hat.*]

LEAD SINGER [*sings to shamisen accompaniment*] : Peering under the sedge hat . . .

IZAEMON [*delicately, pouting*] : It's me, Kiza.

[IZAEMON *lifts the hat slightly to show his face.* KIZAEMON *falls back astonished.*]

KIZAEMON: Ehh? Master Izaemon?

IZAEMON [*feigning the reason he has come*] : I've wanted to meet you. So I've come.

[IZAEMON *tucks his hands in his sleeves, tosses his head, and poses.*]

KIZAEMON: Welcome, young Master, welcome!

[*He bows very low and wipes away a tear. He turns to the* SERVANTS *severely.*]

See what you've done. Who did you think this was? It is our honored Master Izaemon. Put up your brooms. Drop your sleeves. Apologize and hope the Master will be good enough to forgive you. [*Bows to* IZAEMON.] Please, please forgive us.

[*The* SERVANTS *look sheepishly at one another, adjust their clothes, and kneel abjectly before* IZAEMON.]

watarizerifu
FIRST SERVANT: We were rude without thinking.

SECOND SERVANT: We were inexcusably careless . . .

THIRD SERVANT: . . . not to know a valued customer.

FOURTH SERVANT: Please, excuse the dreadful thing . . .

ALL: . . . we have done.

IZAEMON: Then you will not beat me?

ALL [*bowing*] : Oh, no.

IZAEMON: And you won't scold me any more?

ALL [*bowing*] : Oh no, Master.

IZAEMON [*still piqued*] : You've made a mistake, have you?

FIRST SERVANT: We blundered, we blundered. In years we haven't made . . .

ALL [*prostrating themselves*] : . . . such a blunder!

IZAEMON [*pleased with himself*] : Hmph. I should say you haven't.

KIZAEMON: Be quick now. Fix a room for our young master.

[*Bowing and ad-libbing apologies, the* SERVANTS *tumble over each other in their hurry to escape inside.*]

They're a troublesome bunch of boys. Ha, ha, ha! But, my how strange to see you like this. [*He shakes his head sadly and blinks back tears.*]

When I heard you had been disowned, two, three times I searched as far as Nara and Fushimi. How good to see you again! Come, we will go to your favorite small room. We have two years of tales to exchange. Please come this way.

[*Deeply moved,* KIZAEMON *takes the trailing sleeve of* IZAEMON's *kimono to guide him.*]

LEAD SINGER [*sings to shamisen accompaniment*] : As he tugs upon the sleeve . . .

IZAEMON [*pathetically trying to maintain his dignity*] : Here. Here. Kiza. My kimono is paper, your touch is rough . . . rough.

LEAD SINGER [*slowly, singing to shamisen accompaniment*] :

Pull on it and it will tear, hold it and a crease remains;
  Wandering through December.

[IZAEMON *brushes loose his sleeve, pats it gently, and poses holding it protectively to his chest.*]

In olden times the servants rushed forth to greet him;
  Now they come out to meet him with poles raised high.

[KIZAEMON *backs off politely.* IZAEMON *gestures warningly to* KIZAE-MON *with his fan, then tucks it back into his sash. He slips both arms nonchalantly inside the breast of his kimono and poses, sulking.*]

Removing his straw sandals and deep woven hat;
  Grandly he swaggers into the small banquet room.

[*He stamps and kicks off his right sandal. Instantly a black-robed* STAGE ASSISTANT *takes it away.* KIZAEMON *removes his wooden clogs and places them before his honored guest.* IZAEMON *steps into them and stands proudly in his newfound height. He unties the cord under his chin and removes the hat. His face has delicate features and is powdered white. Courtesans, forced to entertain the coarsest men, find the handsome gentleness of a man like* IZAEMON *extremely attractive. The audience applauds and shouts, "We've waited for this."* IZAEMON, *striving to maintain his dignity, flicks open his fan and turns to go.* KIZAEMON *respectfully holds his hat and gestures that it would be wiser not to enter.* IZAEMON, *determined to meet* YŪGIRI, *pulls his hat free and stamps loudly on the floor with his clog. He pouts.* KIZAEMON *bows low to his customer.* IZAEMON *smiles and passes the hat to a* STAGE ASSISTANT. *Overcome with shame at his pathetic state,* IZAEMON *holds the fan before his face. Then he flicks the other arm inside his sleeve, lifts his nose in the air, and swaggers into Yoshida House as if he owned it. Stick drum and shamisen play* Odoriji. KIZAEMON *admires* IZAEMON's *sensuous gait. He does a comic imitation: he picks up* IZAEMON's *sandals, hikes up his trousers, and walks mincingly inside.*]

SCENE 2   A GUEST ROOM IN THE YOSHIDA BROTHEL

[*A single ki clack signals the change of scene: lights partially dim, the front of Yoshida House is flown and the pots of pine and bamboo disappear right and left. A second ki clack signals lights to come up full. A guest room in the brothel. Snow scenes are painted on large sliding doors at the rear to the right. Left are sliding doors covered with translucent paper. New Year offerings and hanging decorations brighten the room. The Takemoto SINGERS and shamisen PLAYERS remain in view. Offstage Odoriji music swells. Two young MAIDS enter and place lighted lamps at the rear of the stage. A STAGE ASSISTANT in formal dress places a charcoal brazier under a frame which is covered by a gaily colored quilt to make a heater. This is put center stage. KIZAEMON enters from the right carrying small lacquered trays of sweets and of cakes. He puts them beside the heater. The MAIDS kneel by the door and bow. IZAEMON breezes in, his mood completely changed. He is at ease and smiles happily. After two years of penniless wandering he relishes being pampered again. KIZAEMON places a cushion by the heater and gestures for IZAEMON to accept it. He takes it as if it were his right. The MAIDS slip away, closing the door behind them. KIZAEMON kneels a respectful distance away and bows very low to welcome IZAEMON. He speaks with marked deference, merchant to important customer.]*

KIZAEMON: I can't say how good it is to see you well. Ah, it's so cold outside again today, please warm yourself.

IZAEMON [*grandly*] : I shall. Ahh. It's warm. It's warm.

[*He tries to pretend nothing is wrong, but he is chilled to the bone from the January cold and he cannot help shivering. Sliding his legs under the quilt, he rubs his hands pathetically.*]

KIZAEMON: The chill in the air is terrible. Young Master, you must be cold. Ah, my cloak!

[*The STAGE ASSISTANT places a tray holding a black cloak beside KIZAEMON. He crosses to IZAEMON and gently places the cloak over his trembling shoulders.*]

LEAD SINGER [*singing sadly to shamisen accompaniment*] : He lightly drapes the cloak . . .

IZAEMON [*noticing the cloak, half melancholy, half proud*] : A generous gift is presented to frozen Izaemon. Out of understanding for your feeling, he accepts it.

[*As if he were dressed in the height of fashion, he precisely arranges the folds of the cloak and ties the breast cord in a perfectly shaped knot. He inspects the look of the cloak and is satisfied.*]

LEAD SINGER [*occasional shamisen chords punctuate chanted phrases*] : Kizaemon carefully, gazes at the form, newly dressed in borrowed cloak. [*Offstage shamisen and stick drum play Odoriji quietly in the background. KIZAEMON blinks back tears of sympathy.*]

KIZAEMON: It is clear why people say man's fate is unknowable. Who would have thought Izaemon, honored young master of Fuji House, would ever wear Kizaemon's cloak, though it be made of Chinese silk or antique gold brocade.[9] When I think how pained you must feel, hot tears boil forth.

---

9. Paraphrased from the *Wakan Sansai Zue*, a 105-volume encyclopedia, whose first volumes were published the year before the play was written.

[*His voice breaks. He places open palms to his eyes.* IZAEMON *saunters airily left.*]

IZAEMON: Ah, Kiza, no. I'm not the least bit in fashion, but I don't care. Do I complain, do I complain? No. No one really knows this Izaemon. Though I've come to look like this, I don't feel vexed. And do you know why? [*He preens.*] There's a saying, "no one thinks it strange to see a horse or cow bearing heavy loads of logs, but people cheer to see a cat or a mouse do it." I suppose I shouldn't say it, but I stand undaunted though I've nothing but a paper kimono to my name. On and on, I carry on, carrying a crushing debt of half-a-million dollars.[10] For I am Fujiya Izaemon, Japan's greatest man!

[*He smirks and poses with both hands tucked inside his kimono breast.*]
My fortune is my person, my person is my gold, and so . . . ohhh, I'm cold. I'm cold.

[*The audience laughs as he drops his pose and scurries to the heater to warm his hands.*]

KIZAEMON [*gravely*] : How fortunate for you, you are your fortune. And how auspicious for us that you bring your body of gold to Yoshida House in time to celebrate the New Year. Before long your disinheritance will be revoked and then you will return as before. That will be a happy day. [*Calls off right.*] Ume, where are the New Year's offerings? Bring an offering for eternal youth, quickly, in the spirit of the New Year.

UME [*off*] : I'm coming.

LEAD SINGER [*singing to shamisen accompaniment*] :
Saying "I shall," his wife Ume places on the shelf;
    An offering of new leaves, pomegranates, dried chestnuts,
    Tangerines, and oranges, variously arranged.

[KIZAEMON's *wife* UME, *carries on a small wooden tray heaped with fruits and nuts. She places it as an offering in the alcove up left, then kneels beside her husband. She wears a matron's dark blue and gray kimono. Two* MAIDS *place a lacquered wine pitcher and cups beside* IZAEMON, *bow, and exit right, closing the sliding door after them.*]

IZAEMON [*coyly*] : Yes, Ume, it's me you see.

UME [*bowing repeatedly*] : Ah, welcome, Master Izaemon! Welcome! Since you've gone we've worried about you endlessly. And now to see you . . . [*She breaks off, nearly in tears.*] Ah, it is good to see you!

IZAEMON: You have not changed at all, Ume. [*Savoring his misery.*] Congratulations.

UME [*bowing*] : Thank you.

IZAEMON: And now, having congratulated you, it is time to ask some questions.

---

10. Eleven thousand gold ryō; worth between $330,000 and $500,000. Even allowing for the fact that Izaemon is deliberately exaggerating the figure to gain sympathy, great sums were required to cut a fine figure in the licensed quarter. It was because Izaemon had squandered much of the family fortune that he had been disinherited two years before. The play does not make clear what type of business Fuji House is in, but it is a merchant family.

[*He thinks of* YŪGIRI *and rises on his knees, yearning for her. Then he catches himself and looks ahead proudly.*]

sutezerifu

Why is it since I've been here you haven't uttered one word about Yūgiri? Are the rumors I have heard true—that pining for me, she has fallen ill?

share

[*Emotionally.*] Does Evening Mist, unsubstantial, fade and die?[11] Well, Kizaemon, tell me. What has happened? Are you silent because you think I'll snivel? Why should I cry? I . . . will not . . . cry. I want to hear her story, so I can laugh.

[*His eyes fill with tears at the thought of* YŪGIRI. *His lips tremble. To control himself, he grasps the charcoal tongs and poses. The tongs slip and he falls over. He laughs sheepishly and adjusts his kimono.*]

LEAD SINGER [*sings to shamisen accompaniment*] :

The voice which says "I will not, I will not cry"
  Is clouded over by tears of anxious concern.

[*Delicately he pulls out the red inner kimono sleeve and daubs his eyes.*]

KIZAEMON [*quickly, bowing low*] : Surely we were impolite not to speak of Yūgiri before. Your feeling is natural. [*To* UME.] Ume, tell Master Izaemon the news.

[*He gestures for her to move forward. She sits quietly with hands folded in her lap.*]

UME: In every way it would be better for you to talk with the young master.

KIZAEMON [*annoyed*] : A woman's better at something like this.

UME [*stubbornly*] : It's men's work and you should do it.

KIZAEMON: Is there no difference between a man and a woman? A woman is responsible in the house. You should tell him.

UME: No, you should tell him.

KIZAEMON [*firmly*] : You shall be the one to speak!

UME: If it's hard to do, it's always my work. Ho, ho, ho!

[*The men smile. She moves closer to* IZAEMON.]

In the middle of autumn, Yūgiri fell sick with worry, but happily, Master Izaemon, her spirits have revived. She stayed secluded in her room and I worried that she would only get worse, but fortunately a wealthy samurai from Awa has requested her.

IZAEMON [*shocked*] : What?

UME: For days he has insisted she must come out for New Year. At last she has consented. She meets him in the inner room today.

[IZAEMON *rushes desperately to her. Like a little boy pleading for a favor from his mother, he falls to his knees, placing both hands on her waist.*]

IZAEMON: Really, is it true? Are you fibbing to me?

UME: If you want to know whether it's true or not, look through the doors yourself.

LEAD SINGER [*sings rapidly to strong shamisen accompaniment*] : Izaemon's face is stricken!

---

11. A play on the name Yūgiri, Evening Mist, which combined with *kieru* (fade away) can mean "evening mist vanishes" or "Yūgiri dies."

Izaemon stops at the seven-three position on the hanamichi. "Winter's woven hat of straw covered with grime; letter-paper kimono frayed at sleeves and knees." A Stage Assistant holds a lighted candle, as if to light the actor's face. (*Izaemon:* Nakamura Ganjirō) Page 220

In front of Yoshida brothel Izaemon meets its owner. "I am Kizaemon. But who are you? Why do you want to meet me?" (*Kizaemon:* Bandō Mitsugorō; *Izaemon:* Nakamura Ganjirō) Page 222

Waiting for Yūgiri's arrival, Izaemon feigns indifference, lacing his fingers over his knees. (*Izaemon:* Nakamura Ganjirō) Page 230

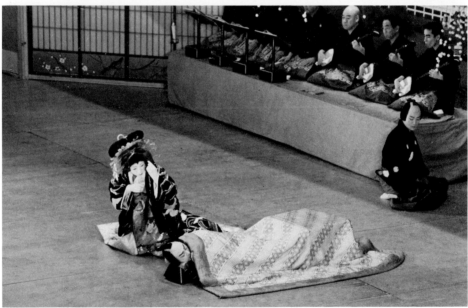

Yūgiri enters from the inner room. She pivots gracefully to face upstage, then slowly turns to gaze over her shoulder at Izaemon, who pretends to be sleeping. (*Izaemon:* Kawarazaki Gonjūrō; *Yūgiri:* Ichikawa Monnosuke)

Yūgiri kneels beside Izaemon as a Stage Assistant watches. "Do open your eyes. I am ill." Singers (Kiyomoto in the illustration) continue, "Although death long ago would have come surely; until today the thread of life is unbroken, held firm by compassionate Gods and the Buddha." (*Yūgiri:* Nakamura Utaemon; *Izaemon:* Kataoka Nizaemon) Page 231

"This Izaemon labors night and day to earn a living for he carries a debt of eleven thousand ryō. He has to sleep whenever he can, so he thanks you not to disturb him. Miss Street Slut." (*Yūgiri:* Nakamura Senjaku; *Izaemon:* Nakamura Ganjirō) Page 232

"Stop it! Don't come close to me! I may have been disinherited, but no
courtesan who's been kicked and tumbled in the next room gets near Fujiya
Izaemon!" (*Yūgiri:* Nakamura Senjaku; *Izaemon:* Nakamura Ganjirō) Page 232

"There's no harm done if a customer kicks you. Because if there's no lust in him you can't make a living. Agh!" Izaemon turns away from Yūgiri. (*Yūgiri:* Nakamura Utaemon; *Izaemon:* Kataoka Nizaemon) Page 233

"From the day our flirtation, thin as watery blue, became deep-dyed with loving one another, have such ties of love been known even in Cathay?" She kneels beside him. They hold the robe between them and pose. (*Yūgiri:* Ichikawa Monnosuke; *Izaemon:* Kawarazaki Gonjūrō) Page 234

A Clerk from the House of Fuji announces that Izaemon's family will ransom Yūgiri. The lovers pose as the curtain is closed. (*Izaemon:* Kataoka Nizaemon; *Yūgiri:* Nakamura Utaemon; *Clerk:* Kataoka Gatō) Page 237

[*In time to rhythmic chords of Takemoto shamisen music,* IZAEMON *rises and turns toward the sliding paper doors left. He scarcely knows what he is doing. The cloak falls unnoticed to the floor. Like a drunken man, he reels and staggers to the doors. His hands tremble so violently he can hardly grasp them, then he flings them open revealing an empty room with another set of sliding doors at the rear. Music gradually accelerates. Dancing in time to the music, he throws these doors open and stands transfixed at the sight of the shadows of* YŪGIRI *and* HIRAOKA *cast on the thin paper of yet another set of inner sliding doors. They are drinking and gesticulating animatedly. Their heads blend together. He falls back helplessly. Silently he appeals to* UME.]

LEAD SINGER: For a moment there are no words he can utter!

[UME *approaches with the cloak. He turns wildly, as if to burst through the doors into the adjoining room. Then his resolution ebbs and he turns to* UME. *She drapes the cloak over his shoulders, kneels, and restrains him by placing both hands on his sash. They pose. The cloak slips to the floor and a* STAGE ASSISTANT *whisks it out of sight. Takemoto shamisen play quietly in the background.*]

IZAEMON [*wretchedly*]: Oh! She seems in miraculously good spirits all right. In my good-natured way, I couldn't conceive of such a thing happening. It's true, from the time the world began, who has ever heard of a sincere whore or a bespectacled blind man?[12] You think I came here today wanting to see Yūgiri's face. How mortifying. I didn't at all. [*Nose in the air.*] There's not a smidgen of love left in my heart for that . . . harlot, but as you know the wretch bore me a son. He's just seven this year.
[*Sinks to his knees with a self-pitying sigh.*]
One of your old crones said he'd been put out for adoption, but I don't believe he's been adopted. I suppose you've had him strangled . . . and his body thrown away. Ohhhh!
[*He rises and stamps in pique.* UME *and* KIZAEMON *exchange shocked looks.* IZAEMON *is oblivious to everything except his own problems.*]
There's no mistake about it: I thought I was a rake buying a whore, but what I raked up was trash.[13]

UME [*protesting*]: But why do you say that?

IZAEMON [*petulant*]: Can you ask why? I've spent a fortune and all I've got from her are love letters—eleven thousand ryō of waste paper! [*He gestures with his fan.*] Why, if I piled them up, I'll bet I could build Mt. Fuji in papier-mâché! Oh, look. [*He sinks slowly to his knees.*] I've soaked my precious paper kimono crying out useless tears. How absurd.
[*He realizes he has been daubing his eyes with the trailing sleeve of his kimono. Gently he wipes the dampened right sleeve. This finished, he flips both arms inside his kimono, stands erect, and strikes a martyred pose.*]

12. "No one has seen a sincere prostitute nor a picture of a *karyōbinga* rooster" (a mythical bird mentioned in Buddhist sutras) in Chikamatsu's text is usually changed to this easier form. Few in the Japanese audience would understand the original.
13. A pun on *keiseigai* (buying a prostitute) and *kamikuzukai* (trash man).

share

And now, before the seams of my kimono sleeves disintegrate, I think I shall go.

[*With his nose in the air and a self-pitying look on his face, he sashays toward the door, hoping of course to be stopped. UME kneels before him, blocking his way.*]

UME: Master Izaemon, let the fact that the guest in the inner room is no ordinary person be food for thought.[14]

IZAEMON [*brightly*] : Hah! He could be a fancy dish or pot luck for all I care. I've had my fill, thank you!

UME: You mustn't fly off the handle so, young Master.

IZAEMON: If I do, I'll hit her with it. Hmph! "Evening Mist." I haven't missed her evenings!

LEAD SINGER [*singing*] : Hiding her smile . . .

[*UME can't help smiling. Proud of his witticisms, IZAEMON nods grandly to them and starts to go. She detains him by holding his sleeve.*]

IZAEMON: No, I'm thinking of going away. You shouldn't try to prevent me.

[*He pulls gently on his sleeve; she continues to hold it.*]

I'm going to go.

[*He pulls again but she does not release her hold. He claps his hands delightedly.*]

I know what I'll do. I'll walk around the room.

[*UME covers a smile and releases his sleeve. He adjust his kimono and fixes his hair, as if getting ready for a public promenade. Takemoto shamisen play occasional chords as accompaniment. He flicks his arms inside the kimono sleeves and casually circles the room. He passes the doors to the inner room, then stops, drawn back irresistibly toward them. He is enraged to see the shadows on the paper doors. He clenches his fists. He is about to throw the doors open, but then realizes he is powerless to interfere. Furious at his impotence, he stamps toward the door.*]

Ahh! I'm going!

[*UME restrains him. He pretends to struggle.*]

UME: Do not go. I'll warm some sake.

IZAEMON: No, no. I'm leaving. [*Hesitates.*] Or should I stay? Or should I go? [*Blithely.*] I'll just take a nap.

[*In an instant he is curled up under the quilt of the heater, head resting on his arm and for all the world asleep.*]

KIZAEMON [*in a whisper*] : You didn't have to say so much about Yūgiri.

UME: Eh? "Tell him, tell him," you said. I told him, that's all.

KIZAEMON: You didn't have to jabber on and on. Well, get him a pillow. Quickly, now.

UME: Yes, yes.

[*A STAGE ASSISTANT passes her a headrest which she gently places*]

share

share

14. The guest is Hiraoka's wife, who is caring for the child of Izaemon and Yūgiri. She has come disguised as her husband. This is not important in the versions of the play performed now, for none of the preceding nor following acts are done. This line and following ones contain a number of puns on food and dishes.

under IZAEMON's *head.* IZAEMON *pretends to be asleep.* KIZAEMON *and* UME *tiptoe to the door. Fondly, they look back at* IZAEMON.]

KIZAEMON: It's so like the young master, he hasn't changed a bit. In the past, I honored him like the God of Fortune and now he's destitute. Yet he doesn't grudge us our good life. Ah, he's the son of a great family for certain. In the end, he'll apologize or the family will relent. He'll be taken back, I'm sure. Stay here ten thousand days, young Master.

LEAD SINGER [*singing to shamisen accompaniment*]: There is fondness in their hearts as they leave the room. Looking after them, Izaemon . . .
[*They slip silently through the doors up right and close them.*]

IZAEMON [*sighs and sits up*]: That kind couple still cares for me, even as I am. I can never forget it. Comparing them with Yūgiri . . . agh!
[*His heart is torn by the thought of* YŪGIRI *with another man. Yet there is nothing he can do. Fuming, he flounces over to the wine tray and plops down on his knees. A half-dozen graduated wine cups stand in a pile. He carelessly tosses the small ones over his shoulder. When he reaches the last, large, saucerlike cup, he fills it and lifts it to his lips. He stops, gazing forlornly ahead.*]
How changed is my appearance. What hasn't changed is the gaiety of the quarter.
[*He doesn't really like sake, but he tosses the drink down and then chokes. Offstage Nagauta singing begins from the geza.*]

SOLO SINGER [*lyric singing to shamisen accompaniment expressing* YŪGIRI's *feelings*]:
Looking back through time;
    Even one's bitter grief is remembered fondly.
[*Noticing a drop of wine on his precious kimono sleeve, he wipes it away.*]
More painful still than meeting an endearing man;
    At Osaka's barrier gate are the world's lessons.[15]
[*He puts away the wine cup, slaps his thigh determinedly, and begins to mime playing a shamisen.*]

IZAEMON [*wistfully*]: Play away, play away. Hearing that song reminds me of autumn a year ago, when we viewed the moon, enraptured, from our private room. We were so happy.
[*He realizes he should be angry. He folds his arms across his chest.*]
Of all people, to think that you would deceive me . . .
[*He clenches his teeth and makes a fist, looking about for someone on whom to vent his anger. Then, realizing how foolish he looks, his shoulders slump.*]

SOLO SINGER [*continuing offstage*]:
The flow of their affections blocked unexpectedly;
    Turns into stagnant marshland, a brackish pool.
[*Seeing no way out, he drops down by the wine tray, pours and drinks*

15. The Osaka barrier was one of the great barriers which had to be passsed in traveling between Kyoto and Edo, and in poetry its mention suggests melancholy parting.

recklessly. He seizes the headrest and rushes to the sliding doors as if to hurl it into the inner room. He feels the seams of his paper kimono straining. Quickly he drops the headrest to the floor. Again his mood changes: like a pampered prince, he delicately arranges the kimono's folds and poses.]

IZAEMON [*lightly, ruefully*] : It's true, every person in the world feels love and sorrow. But an outcast like me isn't even considered. When I rage or pout in the corner, no one pays any attention. Very well then, I'm going home. Hmph. Sincere harlot. I'm going home.

[*To occasional chords of offstage Sugagaki shamisen music, he arranges his dress, and walks elegantly to seven-three on the hanamichi. He tries to pose grandly, arms tucked inside his kimono sleeves, but the effect is marred by a hangdog look in his eyes. He faces the audience, speaking with deep melancholy.*]

I have been shown kindness by some. Forgive me, for leaving without saying goodbye . . . Kizaemon.

SOLO SINGER [*continues offstage*] :
The heart's innermost feelings go misunderstood;
    Until the moonlight makes clear our affection.

[*He turns back for what he intends to be a final look, but he cannot take his eyes from the doors separating him from YŪGIRI. Without realizing what he is doing, he runs back pell-mell, clambering over the heater in his haste. He stops, knowing he can't do anything, and sits inelegantly on the heater. A single ki clack: doors upstage right open showing a Tokiwazu ensemble of four SINGERS and four shamisen PLAYERS seated on a dais. They wear formal black kimonos and outer garments of deep green.*]

TOKIWAZU SINGERS [*in a high, lyric style to shamisen accompaniment*] :
How pitiful she, this Yūgiri;
    Times of long ago flow past, fond remembrance.

[*A CHILD MAID, dressed in brilliant red kimono with trailing sleeves, demurely brings on YŪGIRI's tobacco tray. She places it beside IZAEMON and exits. He pretends indifference until the MAID is gone, then he almost falls from the heater in his excitement. He straightens his kimono and slicks down his hair with moistened palms. He cannot decide how to receive YŪGIRI. First he plans to treat her formally: he kneels at the far edge of the room, placing his hands deliberately on his knees and looking coldly ahead.*]

Within the inner chamber her heart leaps with joy;
    Ties of their affection still happily undestroyed.

[*A second CHILD MAID, dressed like the first, places a small tray of sweets beside the tobacco tray and exits. It is torture for IZAEMON to keep from peeking to see if YŪGIRI is coming. Finally he cranes his neck to look. She isn't there. He gets an idea: he claps his hands and tiptoes to the door, tripping and almost falling on the way. He tries to peek in. Then he hides at the side of the door, ready to shout "Surprise!" when she enters. Again he changes his mind. He sits cross-legged, fingers laced over his knees.*]

Breast from breast and heart from heart a mountain divides;
  And just as much divided by the sliding doors.
[IZAEMON *gives up his pose on the heater and jumps to his feet. Now frantic over her impending arrival, he tries out various attitudes—aloof, stern, friendly, casual—but in the end abandons them all to slide under the quilt. With one motion he scoops in the headrest and feigns sleep. Tempo of Tokiwazu music quickens. The sliding doors center open and* YŪGIRI *enters, followed by the two* CHILD MAIDS. *Her blushing pink kimono is almost completely hidden by a long outer robe of black silk embroidered with cranes and pine branches symbolic of the New Year. A thick wad of folded paper held before her downcast eyes hides her face. She enters slowly, moving sensuously.*]

kudoki
Yearning to glimpse his dear face from morning till night,
  She joyfully approaches, rushing to his side.
[*She drops the paper from her eyes and looks up. Her white face is delicately formed and extremely beautiful. Fans shout the actor's name. She pivots gracefully to face upstage, then slowly turns her head to gaze over her shoulder at* IZAEMON. YŪGIRI *embodies all the attractive features of the Genroku courtesan; she is physically alluring, accomplished, sophisticated, and, in spite of her profession, can lose her heart to an attractive man. She is deeply in love with* IZAEMON.]
I bring my body next to yours, within the same robe;
  Let it cover both of us, quickly let us sleep;
  Enfolding holding him fast Yūgiri weeps.[16]
[YŪGIRI *dismisses the* MAIDS *with a gesture. They exit up center. Looking at* IZAEMON, *she has to stifle tears. Quickly she crosses beside him and drops to her knees. With a deliberate gesture, she sweeps the trailing robe protectively over him.*]
YŪGIRI [*speaking with exquisite sadness, each word greatly prolonged*] :
  Izaemon. Izaemon. Do open your eyes. I . . . am ill.
TOKIWAZU SINGERS [*continuing*] :
  Although death long ago would have come surely;
    Until today the thread of life is unbroken,
    Held firm by compassionate Gods and the Buddha.[17]
[*She falls back as if in sudden pain. She immediately pretends nothing has happened, posing sadly, gazing at his closed eyes.*]
  "Have you no feeling of yearning for me?
    Don't you wish to see my face?" she asks tenderly.
    Hoping to rouse him she lifts and cradles his head.
[*She places her hand gently on his shoulder and rocks him back and forth. She leans closer, half-cradling his head in her arms. He does not react. Hurt, she pokes his shoulder.*]
TAKEMOTO SINGER [*to shamisen accompaniment*] : She sharply pushes
  him . . .

16. The Tokiwazu lyrics are particularly rich with puns, internal rhymes, and engo.
  17. In popular belief Shintō gods or the Buddha could hold a person back from death with an unseen rope (*hikaezuna*).

[IZAEMON *sits up and pushes her away. He adopts a lordly attitude, not even looking in her direction.*]

share

IZAEMON [*rudely*] : Here, here. What are you doing, Miss Whatever-they-call-you. Miss Evening Mist—or is it Miss Evening Meal?[18] —I'm not like you, indolently carousing around at the year's end. This Izaemon labors night and day to earn a living for he carries a debt of eleven thousand ryō. He has to sleep whenever he can, so he thanks you not to disturb him. [*Coldly, over his shoulder.*] Miss Street Slut.

[*He slaps the floor for emphasis, pulls in the headrest, and snuggles down under the quilt.*]

TAKEMOTO SINGER [*singing to shamisen accompaniment*] : Rolling over on his side, he pretends to snore . . .

YŪGIRI: Izaemon! You have no reason to speak that way. Why are you angry? Tell me or you will not sleep. I shall not allow it.

[*She shakes his shoulders, first gently, then more firmly when he does not move. Suddenly he sits up, shaking her off.*]

kuzetsu

IZAEMON [*coldly furious*] : Stop it! Don't come close to me! I may have been disinherited, but no courtesan who's been kicked and tumbled in the next room gets near Fujiya Izaemon! See here, Miss Streetwalker, come back in spring when the weather suits your trade. Now get out. Get out! [*He flicks open his fan and waves her away as if she were some kind of loathsome beggar. He stamps away left to be rid of her.*]

TAKEMOTO SINGERS [*in unison*] : Though he says, "get out, get out . . . "

[*She gasps and covers her mouth to hide her anguish. Suddenly afraid he has gone too far, IZAEMON peeps at her from behind his open fan.*]

YŪGIRI [*faintly*] : What? You call Yūgiri a streetwalker?

IZAEMON: Can you say you don't know why? When you let a samurai kick his way into your affections, that's what you are, a streetwalker, I say!

share

TAKEMOTO SINGERS [*singing in unison to shamisen accompaniment*] :[19] "Felicitous morn," some write[20] this New Year.

[*He points to his foot and mimes kicking her. He thrusts his leg forward again, this time with erotic suggestiveness.*]

IZAEMON: Furthermore, he probably did it wearing clogs! Hah!

[*IZAEMON stamps and derisively scuffs his foot in her direction.*]

TAKEMOTO SINGERS [*continuing in unison*] :

Highly stilted passages honor the year end;

"Felicitous morn," some write this New Year.

[*Takemoto shamisen and small offstage drums play strong, rhythmic accompaniment as IZAEMON, in a fit of pique, drops to his knees by the food trays and pelts YŪGIRI with soft rice cakes. He is about to throw*

18. This is a direct translation of a rather cruel pun on the name Yūgiri-*dono* (Miss Evening Mist) and the made-up word *yūmeshi-dono* (Miss Evening Meal).

19. Chikamatsu here paraphrases the lyrics of a New Year's song of low-class street entertainers (*manzai*) to whom Izaemon has just compared Yūgiri, calling her a *manzai geisei*, "street prostitute."

20. Chikamatsu intends *sorai* (is) to suggest samurai, as in translation "some write" could be heard in performance as "felicitous morn, samurai, this New Year."

the cake stand as well, until he notices it is similar in shape to the small nō shoulder drum. Instantly forgetting his anger, he dances and mimes playing the drum. YŪGIRI *slowly lowers her head, weeping.*]

IZAEMON [*cruelly*] : In any case, it's all part of a day's work, isn't it. There's no harm done if a customer kicks you. Because if there's no lust in him you can't make a living! Agh!

[IZAEMON *drops the stand. He coldly turns from* YŪGIRI *and poses with his arms tucked in the breast of his kimono.*]

TAKEMOTO SINGERS [*continuing in unison*] :
Youths lustfully greet their revered streetwalkers;

kakekotoba   Highly stilted passages[21] honor the year end;
    "Felicitous morn," some write this New Year.

[IZAEMON *flicks open his fan and turns on* YŪGIRI *spitefully.*]

IZAEMON: If a samurai can kick Yūgiri, so can a merchant. If a merchant can kick you, so can Izaemon. Kick, kick, kick!

[*He has worked himself into such a rage he can scarcely speak. He stamps repeatedly on the floor, then plops down by the trays.*]

Ah, Kiza! Who cares if it's mochi or stale rice for a street slut!

[*He knocks the tray to the floor. Suddenly facing her, he pulls back his kimono sleeve and raises his fist.*]

TAKEMOTO SINGER [*sings rapidly to shamisen accompaniment*] :
His long pent-up grievances burst out in tearful words;
    Pulling tobacco tray close he lights the long pipe.

[*He tries to smoke, but is so furious he can't get the tobacco into the small bowl and can't hold the pipe still enough over the coals to get a light. This enrages him even more. He knocks the tobacco out and half turning to her, raises the pipe as if to strike her. She recoils. With an expression of helpless disgust, he whirls front and slams the pipe onto the floor. He sighs.*]

He adopts an attitude of cool unconcern.

[*He turns his back on her and sits with fingers laced casually around his knees. He poses sadly. A* STAGE ASSISTANT *takes off trays and cakes.*]

TOKIWAZU SINGERS [*sing slowly to lyric shamisen accompaniment*] :

kudoki   Though they may say the bitter grief Yūgiri feels;
    Teardrops brimming in her eyes to be so reviled;
    Is natural in a quarrel between two lovers.

[*To stifle her tears* YŪGIRI *clenches the wad of tissue between her teeth. Rising on her knees, she poses, gazing at* IZAEMON. *She puts most of the paper back in the front of her kimono. The rest she rolls into a ball, which she almost throws angrily at his back. It hurts her that he seems so unconcerned, and she tucks the paper away in her sleeve pathetically.*]

21. Chikamatsu's kakekotoba in this line is *ashida* (high clog) which also suggests *ashita* (morning). Courtesans worn tall clogs, often fourteen inches high, when they paraded through the quarter. "Stilted passages" becomes the kakekotoba in translation. The line can be taken to mean "streetwalkers' highly stilted passages" (parade on clogs) or "stilted (poetic) passages honor the New Year."

233 Love Letter from the Licensed Quarter

From the day our flirtation, thin as watery blue,

engo

Became deep-dyed[22] with loving one another;

[IZAEMON *tucks both hands in the breast of his kimono. He rises grandly and turns to go. Quickly she blocks his way. Gently placing her hands against his chest, she forces him back one, two, three steps. Pretending unconcern, he drops to one knee. She kneels beside him and arranges his hair with a pin that she takes from her elaborate hairdo. Although this is a sign of deep affection, he shakes her off, sulking.*]

Have such ties of love been known, even in Cathay?

[*He rises to leave again, but she drapes her arms over his shoulders to restrain him. With an elegant movement he pivots, holding the lapel of her robe so it falls from one of her shoulders and onto his in one motion. She kneels. They pose holding the robe between them. Then he breaks away, wearing the robe himself. With a disdainful shrug, he poses.*]

Flaunting our great affair, I lived joyously;

[*He shivers and huddles under the robe, then, like a sulking boy, pulls the robe over his head. A hand snakes out from the robe hunting for a pipe. She hurries to his side, picks up a pipe, wipes it with her sleeve, and offers it to him.*]

Though people spoke slanderously of my obligations.

[*Peeping out from the robe and seeing her grief-stricken face, he is almost moved, but his hand gets tangled in the bulky sleeve as he reaches for the pipe and he ends up angry once more. Together, they lean over the coals of the tobacco tray to light their pipes. She purposely brings her pipe near his, only to have him knock it out of the way so he can go first. He raises the pipe as if to strike her. When she recoils, he slaps the pipe down loudly on the floor and poses with his back to her.*]

TAKEMOTO SINGER [*sings to slow shamisen accompaniment*]:

Though seen sharing the same bed, sleeping back to back;

They stretch the fragile ties of love unthinkingly.

[*They rise and stand back-to-back. She blinks back tears; he sighs with self-pity. Thinking of their unhappy situation, he slowly drops to his knees. She kneels beside him and when she reaches out to touch his shoulder, he coldly brushes the hand away.*]

Their lovers' quarrel ended, morning bells sounding;

kakekotoba

Hatefully it seems to them, the birds sing at dawn.

[*He rises and crosses elegantly to the heater where he sits in a swaggering pose, hands tucked into the back of his sash. She kneels at his feet. She takes one of the sleeves of the black robe and wraps it around her arm, tying them together. She looks up imploringly. They pose.*]

Love cannot be as you wish, it goes its own way;

Yet the only happiness in this broad world;

True love to true love.

---

22. There is a double engo in these lines (*mizuasagi omoisometa*): water engo (*mizu* means water and *someta* dyed in liquid); and color engo (*mizuasagi* means watery blue and *someta*, dyed, implies color).

[*She leans against his thigh seductively. Still not mollified,* IZAEMON *pushes her away and throws off the robe, which a* STAGE ASSISTANT *quickly takes off. She pulls his sleeve to show him a letter scroll that she takes up from a small tray stage left. He snatches it from her, extends it like a telescope, and peers at the audience. He lifts it as if to strike her. She gently retrieves the scroll, then throws it across stage with a flourish. It unrolls some ten or twelve feet, stopping in front of* IZAEMON. *They hold opposite ends of the love letter. They recall the past, posing sadly. Then he remembers he is angry with her: he yanks on the letter, ripping it in half. She sinks to the floor, her half of the crumpled letter clutched to her breast. Again they pose.*]

TAKEMOTO SINGER [*chants in regular rhythm to strong shamisen accompaniment*] : "Can you still think of Yūgiri as a prostitute?"

[*Reading the letter and recalling the past, she is near tears. He lets it slip idly from his fingers, circles the stage nonchalantly, and slides under the quilt to go to sleep.*]

"Am I not really your wife? I had just turned fifteen the year end we met. Now our child is seven."

[*With the love letter dangling a few inches from his face,* IZAEMON *can't resist the impulse to see what* YŪGIRI *has written. He comes across a complimentary passage. Flattered, he beams and nods approvingly. He catches himself and rolls over as if asleep.*]

"When writing your family, isn't it true that I sign 'Izaemon's wife' without any blame?"

[*She rises on her knees and points to the letter. He shrugs and thrusts his hands deeper into the quilt.*]

"If you feel bitterly toward me, I too have reason to feel bitterness toward you."

[*Passing the letter to a* STAGE ASSISTANT, *she reaches under the quilt from the opposite side of the heater, searching for his hands. With a childish smirk, he lifts the heater, quilt and all, and crosses past the startled* YŪGIRI *to sit stage left.*]

"A full year and more has passed without a word of news."

[*She kneels beside him, lovingly putting her arms around his shoulders. He shrugs free and escapes, with the heater, to the other side of the stage.*]

"Worrying about you constantly, I became ill."

[*Very agitated,* YŪGIRI *rises, not knowing what to do. She feels a sharp pain and, uttering a tiny cry, collapses to the floor.*]

Can it be you have not noticed her wasted form, her life but barely extended by ointments and potions, massages and acupuncture?

[*He rushes to her and begins to massage her back. This has no effect, so he crosses to the door, calling for help in mime. In the end he stands helplessly watching her.*]

"I had thought to greet you with, 'I have waited for our meeting so long,' but instead I am met with abuse."

[*He pours a cup of wine for her, but her accusing face shames him so he*

turns away and passes the wine over his shoulder. She places her hands on his sash and looks up into his eyes. He is deeply moved. They pose.]
"If you think I no longer love you, why don't you just kick me, why don't you just beat me?"
[*He proudly circles the stage and drops under the quilt again. She poses, holding a lavender and red silk scarf which a STAGE ASSISTANT has passed to her. She holds it up for him to see: on it are the intertwined crests of the actors playing* YŪGIRI *and* IZAEMON, *showing the linking of their lives.*]
"Yūgiri is dying. My only prayer: that I may see your smiling face."
[*She crosses behind him and gently forces him to his knees. She poses with the cloth clenched between her teeth to stop the pain. Then she falls to the floor, quietly weeping.*]
Raising her tearful voice, "How can you remain so heartless, hating me this way," she gropes across the floor. Thinking neither of past nor of future, their hearts are turbulent.
[*They grope toward each other. Center, their hands touch. He places his hands on her thighs. She looks up coquettishly. They embrace, reconciled. They hear someone approaching. He scurries to the door. She rises on her knees and places her palms together in prayer. He kneels beside her and gently separates her hands with his own clasped palms, indicating it is for him to pray, not her. They sit silently, heads bowed. Then both begin to weep quietly. Suddenly loud bata-bata tsuke beats are heard. Stick drum and shamisen play lively* Odoriji. IZAEMON *moves protectively behind* YŪGIRI. KIZAEMON, UME, *and the* MAIDS *file on from inside and kneel. They are beaming and chattering animatedly. Music changes to rhythmic, rapid* Hayawatari, *"Rapid Crossing." The curtain at the end of the* hanamichi *flies open and a procession of eighteen clerks and servants from the House of Fuji march on. They wear conservative brown and blue kimonos. Each carries a heavy, locked strongbox, filled with gold pieces. They chant in unison as they walk, "Essa! Essa! Essa!" Music fades away.*]
UME [*bowing*] : Wonderful news, young Master! Your family has relented. They wish you back and all the people of your house are here to welcome you.
IZAEMON [*with a delighted expression*] : Really? They aren't angry any more?
KIZAEMON: Nothing could be greater cause for rejoicing! Enter! Enter!
[*He waves the procession onstage.* Hayawatari *resumes. The men stack the boxes in an impressive pyramid in the center of the stage. Each box contains a thousand ryō, together enough to retire* IZAEMON's *debts and release* YŪGIRI *from her contract.*] [23]
MEN [*bowing*] : We rejoice for you, young Master!

23. The amount—eighteen thousand ryō, or between $540,000 and $800,000—presumably in the chests, is not to be taken literally. The point is that a certain number of chests must be brought in to make an appropriately big pyramid on stage.

IZAEMON [*almost dancing for joy*] : How marvelous! What great good
fortune! Come everyone! Clap with me!
[*All join him in the ritual ten hand claps—three, three, three, one—that
celebrate an auspicious event.*]
ALL [*bowing to* IZAEMON] : We offer our congratulations!
[IZAEMON *preens delightedly.* YŪGIRI *and* UME *exchange knowing
glances and smile.* IZAEMON *struts back to get* YŪGIRI's *black robe from
a* STAGE ASSISTANT. *She rises and they exchange positions. He drapes
the robe over her shoulders.*]
TOKIWAZU SINGERS [*sing slowly, lyrically to shamisen accompaniment*] :
Izaemon's eyes twinkle in carefree happiness;
   The name of Yūgiri shall bloom, like a spring flower;
   Before admiring eyes, through all the ages.
[YŪGIRI *drops to her knees and faces front.* IZAEMON *sits possessively
on the money boxes, grins, and flicks open his fan. He glances happily at*
YŪGIRI. *A single ki clack. The cast poses in a group, or* hippari, mie *as*
Odoriji *swells and the curtain is run quickly closed to a crescendo of ki
clacks. Two ki clacks signal large drum to play* Uchidashi, *which concludes
the performance.*]

The Scarlet Princess of Edo

Sakura Hime Azuma Bunshō

by Tsuruya Namboku IV, Sakurada Jisuke II, and Tsuuchi Genshichi

The Scarlet Princess of Edo was performed as the February-March production at the Kawarazaki Theater in Edo in 1817. The chief author, Tsuruya Namboku IV, was sixty-two years old and at the height of his writing powers. (His best known play, *The Ghost of Yotsuya*, was written when he was seventy.) Namboku often identified the historical "first part" (*ichibanme*) of an all-day play and the contemporary "second part" (*nibanme*) in his texts. *A Supporter's Bridge of Return* (1813) is divided as follows:

Ichibanme
    Mitateme (Act I): Scene One; Scene Two; Scene Three
    Yontateme (Act II): Scene One; Scene Two; Scene Three
    Gotateme (Act III): Scene One
    Rokutateme (Act IV): Scene One; Scene Two; Scene Three
                        (*ōzume*, finale)
Nibanme
    Jomaku (Opening Act): Scene One; Scene Two
    Ōgiri (Conclusion): Dance act

In other plays Namboku made no formal distinction between history and domestic parts and numbered acts consecutively from beginning to end. *The Scarlet Princess of Edo* is of this type, written in seven acts: Prologue (*hottan*), Act I (*jomaku*), Act II (*nimakume*), Act III (*sanmakume*), Act IV (*yonmakume*), Act V (*gomakume*), and Act VI (*rokumakume*, or *ōzume*, finale). Nonetheless, the play follows the usual history-domestic structure: the history part contains the Prologue, Act I, and Act II; Act IV is similar to a michiyuki lovers' journey scene and can be considered a dance act substitute; Acts V and VI, centering on Gonsuke, are sewa or contemporary; with the last scene (*ōzume*) returning the play to the historical worlds of the first part. *The Scarlet Princess of Edo* was the main play (hon kyōgen) on the bill, followed by a dance scene, "The Five Seasons." *The Scarlet Princess of Edo* was so popular that its fifth and sixth acts were restaged for the April program at the Kawarazaki Theater. These acts, starring the scoundrel Tsurigane Gonsuke, have been revived a number of times since. Most of the original play was revived in 1967 at the National Theater of Japan (although Gunjibei's "Village School" scene and several shorter scenes were cut to reduce the play's running time).

Namboku wove together three major worlds (sekai) in the play. Seigen's love for Princess Sakura was a popular theme, having first been staged in jōruri as early as 1674. In kabuki, Danjūrō I played the role of Seigen in 1694 at the Murayama Heiemon Theater in Kyoto. Namboku already had used the Seigen-Sakura World in two plays before *The Scarlet Princess of Edo.* The second world he took up was, if anything, even more famous. Concerned with the struggle for succession within the Yoshida clan, it was usually called the Sumida River World because the murder of the clan lord took place along the banks of that river. Since 1688, the first year of the Genroku era, it had been dramatized regularly in kabuki. Into these two historical worlds Namboku wove the gangster (kizewamono) world of Tsurigane Gonsuke. The practice of weaving several worlds together into a single plot laid in a single period reached its highest point of development during the time Namboku was writing and is sometimes called *naimaze* ("intertwine").

Ostensibly, *The Scarlet Princess of Edo* takes place during the Kamakura era (Umewaka's father was a retainer of the Shōgun Yoritomo), but in fact the entire play is permeated with the spirit and attitudes of Namboku's own time. The contemporary or sewa nature of the play can be seen in the figure of Gonsuke, who like many others during the droughts and riots of the Kasei period turned to petty crime as a living. For those on the losing side, a quarrel for succession (*oiesōdō*) within a feudal house was the ultimate catastrophy, for it meant that hundreds of samurai, perhaps thousands of retainers and hangers-on, were abruptly dismissed with no means of livelihood. The desperate lives of Seigen and Sakura when they are made outcasts, Zangetsu and Nagaura reduced to murder and thievery in the most miserable surroundings, and Sakura being sold into prostitution were typical events of the time (it is said Namboku was familiar with the reported case of a daughter of an imperial family who had turned to prostitution in the Shinagawa district of Edo in the early 1800s). The more respectable unemployed samurai turned to teaching calligraphy, as does Gunjibei.

As was customary, Namboku was assisted by other playwrights. Early editors have suggested that the spectacular "Kiyomizu Temple" and "Cherry Valley" scenes are the work of Sakurada Jisuke, but this opinion is not supported in the most recent edition of the play. "Gunjibei's Village School" scene is modeled structurally on jōruri plays. The substitution of the head of one's child and brother (migawari) in order to protect one's lord is a situation taken straight from jōruri, but its manner of dramatization is not like jōruri at all. The young people are slain with a minimum of hesitation and neither before nor after their deaths do the surviving relatives indulge in the elaborate, tearful laments typical of jōruri. It is notable that the scene is not accompanied by jōruri narration.

Considering the extreme length and complexity of the plot, the large cast of characters, and the varying moods of its different scenes, the play is remarkably cohesive on the whole. A major exception is the Gunjibei scene which, because its cast of characters is wholly new and its plot is peripheral, tends to stand apart from the rest of the play. The scenes of Sakura returning from the brothel half-whore and half-princess, Zangetsu and Nagaura being expelled from the temple in their underwear, Seigen appearing as a ghost and boring Sakura with it all, and Gonsuke cheerfully black-mailing Ojū and Sentarō are superb examples of the skill with which Namboku drew comedy from incongruity of situation and character. Of special interest are long sections of dialogue cast in seven-five (shichigocho) form which sound exceptionally beautiful when spoken aloud, and which Namboku uses with good effect throughout the play (Sakura and Gonsuke in Act I, Sakura and Seigen in Act IV, and Gonsuke, Ojū, and Sentarō in Act VI). Danjūrō VII, who was then only twenty-eight, had three roles written for him: Seigen, Gonsuke, and Hanbei. Namboku deliberately wrote quick-changes (hayagawari) into the play to entertain the audience as Danjūrō changed from role to role (in Acts I, V, and VI especially).

The play concludes as do many of Namboku's full-length plays: Sakura is restored to her position according to the dialogue, although visually we see the curtain close on a group pose in which Sakura's retainers Hanbei and Shichirō are surrounded by constables trying to capture Sakura. We know all will turn out well, but in order to end the play on a peak of intensity the curtain is closed before the action's final resolution occurs. This theatrically effective convention was widely used and is used in kabuki today. The "concluding dance scene" (nibanme shosagoto), which Hanbei announces in the last line of the play, was the well-known "Five Seasons Dance," celebrating the varying moods and colors of the five festival seasons. It was intended as a vehicle for Iwai Hanshirō to appear in a brilliant finale. It was an independent dance piece (ōgiri) and not considered part of Namboku's main play (hon kyōgen), which ends at this point.

The text of the complete play in Takeshiba Sōtarō, ed., *Tsuruya Namboku Zenshū* (Complete Plays of Tsuruya Namboku, vol. 6; Tokyo: San'ichi Shobo, 1971), is translated, except for minor elisons made for the sake of clarity. Also consulted was the text in Tsubouchi Shōyō and Atsumi Seitarō, eds., *Dai Namboku Zenshū* (Complete Works of the Great Namboku, vol. 8; Tokyo: Shunyōdō, 1925), and the text of the 1967 National Theater of Japan production, as adapted and directed by Gunji Masakatsu. Stage directions are taken primarily from the 1967 production.

The Scarlet Princess of Edo

hottan

PROLOGUE   ENOSHIMA CLIFF SCENE

[*Warning clacks of the ki, heard from behind the striped kabuki curtain, signal that the play is about to begin. The large drum offstage plays rising and falling* Nami Oto *wave pattern and shamisen play* Zen no Tsutome, *"Zen Prayer." Sharp sounds of bells and hand drums, playing* Maigo Gane, *"Lost Child," are heard from the rear of the theater. Shouts and cries mingle with the music. Blue lights come up on two hanamichi, one left and one right, that run through the audience. Curtains at the end of the hanamichi are flicked open and a group of shaven-headed* PRIESTS *enters on each. The* PRIESTS *wear white kimonos covered with black outer garments. One group is led by a temple* SAMURAI, *the other by a temple* OFFICIAL. LANTERN BEARERS *precede and follow them. They strike drums and bells and call out as they peer into the darkness.*]

SAMURAI's GROUP: Reverend Priest!

OFFICIAL's GROUP: Little Monk!

SAMURAI's GROUP: Reverend Seigen!

OFFICIAL's GROUP: Shiragiku!

[*The two processions meet before the curtain.*]

SAMURAI: What? Do you mean the boy is missing as well as Reverend Seigen?

OFFICIAL: We're searching for the boy everywhere. But honorable Seigen? Is he gone too?

SAMURAI: Then it must be. The two have gone off together.

OFFICIAL [*sadly shaking his head*] : Such a tender child.

SAMURAI [*urgently*] : It's far past midnight.

OFFICIAL: Let us continue the search. Hurry everyone.

ALL: Reverend Seigen! Shiragiku! Reverend Priest! Little Monk!

[*Rising and falling wave pattern,* Nami Oto, *blends with the bells, hand drums, and cries of the searching men. The two groups pass each other and go off in opposite directions. Two sharp ki clacks: the stage blacks out. Soft but gradually accelerating ki clacks accompany the opening of the curtain.*

A stark, jagged rock is silhouetted against the blue nighttime sky. A sign-post identifies the scene as Enoshima, a rocky peninsula near Kamakura, notorious for lovers' suicides. The rising and falling sounds of Nami Oto *wave pattern create a lonely, forbidding atmosphere.*]

uta jōruri CHORUS [*singing offstage*]:
    Fragile grasses of passion seeded unknowing;
      Unattended grow rampant in alluring hues;
      Which fade as the wind's gusts blow blade from blade apart,[1]
    [*A single ki clack signals rapid bata-bata tsuke beats and loud* Nami Oto. SHIRAGIKU *hurries down the main hanamichi. He is a delicately attractive boy of twelve or thirteen, dressed in a pink silk kimono that has feminine style flowing sleeves and tucked up skirts. Face, hands, and feet are powdered white and his hair is in a youthful ponytail.* SHIRAGIKU *falls at seven-three, trembling in fear and exhaustion.* SEIGEN, *a tall and impressive monk in a simple silver-gray kimono, kneels by him and embraces him tenderly. A temple bell tolls. They pose. As the* CHORUS *continues,* SEIGEN *rises, places an arm protectively around the boy's shoulder, and looks carefully about. Again they pose.*]

uta jōruri CHORUS [*singing offstage*]:
    "Though the flower falls and dies it takes root again";
    Attainment of Buddha's law is but illusion;
      Yesterday a passing dream, its deep passion nothingness;
      The carnal way of the world is sensuous abandon;
      Nothing restraining our steps on the path of lust.

engo   Harbored thoughts held at bay, they flee from men's eyes;
      To watery Enoshima's dark destination;
      This pure white chrysanthemum dressed in Buddha's black;
      Tightly held by ties of love is Shiragiku;
      Whose trembling fallen visage remains before us.
    [SEIGEN *gently helps* SHIRAGIKU *to his feet. The boy looks back longingly;* SEIGEN *shakes his head, points instead to the rock, takes the boy's hand, and leads him slowly onto the stage. The temple bell tolls.* SHIRAGIKU *starts with fright, then sinks to his knees.* SEIGEN *and* SHIRAGIKU *look into each others eyes. Each places a hand on the sign-post for support. Close to tears, they pose.*]

SEIGEN [*emotionally*]: My dearest Shiragiku. To go on living, knowing we are the playthings of Karma and that fellow priests are making light of our love, is impossible. I should die alone but cannot, inflicting, in my weakness, misery on a budding flower. Do not hate me, please.

SHIRAGIKU [*gently reproving*]: Dearest Master Seigen, how could I hate you, who lavished affection on me, a mere page, and filled my heart with happiness? I am the one who should die, for I aroused your Reverence's

---

    1. *Uta jōruri,* or "song jōruri," is a type of dance music—Takemoto, Tokiwazu, Kiyomoto, or one of the less often employed forms such as Kato Bushi or Geki Bushi. Namboku does not indicate here which he wishes but he often called for Kiyomoto.

desire willingly. May I be reborn a maiden so we can live together in future lives as man and wife.

[SHIRAGIKU *looks appealingly at the priest.* SEIGEN *takes* SHIRAGIKU's *hands tenderly in his.*]

SEIGEN: How pitiful your words are. I, who once served the Lord of Ōshū, Date Chikahira, was then known as Shimizu Kiyoharu. My younger brother, Shinobu Sōta, became an evil person as he grew older, until I had to leave my master's service, severing forever a brother's ties.[2] Three years passed and I became a monk at Hasedera Temple in Kamakura. Indeed, it is the Karma of past lives that when we met I seethed with desire, faltering in my duties to Lord Buddha. From dawn throughout the day I yearned for you, waiting for each night when I could in secret ecstatically receive your love. How I regret that my illicit passion should have led you to this pathetic fate!

[SEIGEN *places an arm protectively around* SHIRAGIKU's *shoulders.*]

SHIRAGIKU [*childishly earnest*]: I am prepared. Do not pretend regrets, beloved Master Seigen. We have exchanged eternal vows, our hearts' desires inscribed here . . .

[SHIRAGIKU *takes from his breast a small lacquered incense case wrapped in purple silk.* SEIGEN *reacts seeing it.*]

SEIGEN: Next to my heart I, too, carry this . . .

[*Takes out the lid to* SHIRAGIKU's *case, also wrapped in purple silk.*] Disciples of the Buddha cannot write a pledge of love with the blood of cut fingers nor fix upon their bodies a sign as others do. Instead, our names inscribed upon an incense case, to bind our love forever . . .

[*In the darkness they cannot read the inscriptions. Just then the moon appears from behind the clouds.* Nami Oto *wave pattern crescendos.* SEIGEN *leads* SHIRAGIKU *by the hand partway up the rock steps. They pose, bodies bent backward, each with an arm placed gently around the other's waist. Holding his lacquered case up to catch the moonlight,* SHIRAGIKU *reads.*]

SHIRAGIKU: "Kiyo" for "Sei" and "haru" for "gen," your true name, Kiyoharu inscribed on this case.

SEIGEN: On its lid, the brush has traced the name "Shiragiku"—White Chrysanthemum—in strokes unchanging through the years. Sharing the same precious object symbolizes our shared love.

[*They look at each other feelingly.* SEIGEN *resolutely slaps the lacquered lid, quickly folds the cloth over, and puts it away inside his kimono. Taking* SHIRAGIKU's *hand, he leads him slowly, tenderly, to the top of the towering rock.*]

uta jōruri   CHORUS: Not only woman can be in this mortal world;
               Closest companion to man, his dearest lover.

2. It serves no dramatic purpose for Namboku to make Seigen and Gonsuke (disguised as Shinobu Sōta) brothers. This is a joking reference to the fact that because Danjūrō VII was playing both roles the characters could be expected to have a brotherly resemblance.

Brother to Spring's plum blossom is Autumn's flower;
   The blooms of Arihara, White Chrysanthemum.
Youthful locks cast a shadow of ancient beauty;
   Across our memories and in ages to come;
   This place shall be called the Rock of the Temple Page.

[SHIRAGIKU *draws back from the cliff edge instinctively. He falls weakly to his knees and clings to* SEIGEN.]

SHIRAGIKU: Our resting place is the ocean's swirling waters. Reverend Seigen!

SEIGEN: Dearest Shiragiku!

[SEIGEN *kneels beside the boy. They embrace.* SHIRAGIKU *presses the priest's hands to his cheeks. They wipe away their tears, compose themselves, turn toward the dark sea, and clasp their hands in prayer.*]

SHIRAGIKU: "Namu Amida Butsu." Buddha Merciful All Hail.

[Nami Oto *wave pattern crescendos.* SHIRAGIKU *clutches the incense case in his left hand, rises suddenly, and without a word leaps from the rock into the sea below. Loud batan tsuke beats. A splash of water flying up from the sea behind the rocks drenches* SEIGEN.]

SEIGEN: You have jumped, my child. How could you? I join you, dear rash Shiragiku!

[Nami Oto *swells. He rushes to the cliff edge, then falls back shuddering.*]
I would die for you without a thought, but . . . the cliff is so high, I'm terrified.

[*Shaking, he hugs his shoulders. He teeters at the cliff edge, torn between love for* SHIRAGIKU *and fear of death. Then he sinks to the ground, powerless to fulfill his vow. Drum pattern changes to ominous* Usu Doro, *"Suspenseful Drum Roll," presaging the appearance of a spirit. A pale green ball of fire—the "soul fire" of the dead* SHIRAGIKU—*rises from the water and hovers in the air unseen by* SEIGEN *over his head. In tears,* SEIGEN *clasps his hands and prays.*]

SEIGEN: "Namu Amida Butsu. Namu Amida Butsu." Buddha Merciful All Hail.

[SEIGEN *falls forward as the curtain is slowly pulled closed to quiet ki clacks.* STAGE MANAGER *enters from the right. He wears a formal black kimono covered by light blue wide-shouldered vest and split trousers. He kneels before the curtain center stage, places his closed fan before him, and speaks to the audience in ringing, formal tones.*]

kōjō   STAGE MANAGER: Ladies and gentlemen! Today's play, of which the Prologue set before Enoshima's Rock of the Temple Page has just concluded, spans a period of seventeen years. You will see in the New Kiyomizu Temple scene set in Kamakura how the story of Seigen and his love for Shiragiku after an interval of seventeen years intertwines with the legend of Princess Sakura. [*Bows.*] Ladies and gentlemen, this I respectfully announce!

ACT I

SCENE 1   NEW KIYOMIZU TEMPLE

[*A single ki clack signals* Gyōretsu Sanjū, *"Processional," music to begin. The* STAGE MANAGER *swiftly exits. Gradually accelerating ki clacks accompany the opening of the curtain. Drums, shamisen, and bell play* Shaden, *"Temple,"* Daibyōshi, *"Big Rhythm," and* Teragane, *"Temple Bell," in unison. It is the hills of Kamakura in spring: cherry blossoms, as far as the eye can see, show pale pink against distant green foilage. At first nothing is visible center stage, then the facade of the main hall of New Kiyomizu Temple rises into view. The massive structure is bright red and its panels are carved and painted in blue and gold.* SHICHIRŌ, *a samurai of the Yoshida clan, and* MATSUWAKA, *Yoshida's son and heir, pose center.* SHICHIRŌ *wears conservative olive-colored kimono and outer garments. The pale blue kimono of* MATSUWAKA *has the soft trailing sleeves of a court child's dress and is covered with light lavender cloak and trousers figured with silver thread.* GENGO, *stage left, and* GUNSUKE, *stage right, kneel in a pose. Both wear two swords and the garments of lesser samurai.* SAMURAI *retainers kneel in two rows upstage. Two strong beats of the large drum and bell conclude the music when the temple is fully in view.*]

SHICHIRŌ [*strongly, posed front*] : How dare you say I lie, Gengo Sadakage? Deny it or you will not leave our master's presence alive!

GENGO: Shichirō, you improperly petitioned for rule of the Yoshida clan to pass on to our young master, falsely stating Minister Koresada had died of illness, when in fact our lord was set upon and killed last February while returning from duties at Kamakura Palace. Even the Miyakodori scroll was stolen. Our Reverend Majesty the Emperor alone bestows the rank of Minister of State, which honored our late lord. And clan succession is decided by the Kamakura Shōgun. Since this power has been delegated to Honorable Seigen, Chief Abbot of Kiyomizu Temple, our clan's petition should be directed to the Shōgun through him. Why do you not directly state the facts of our lord's death? Deception risks discovery and punishment, and extinction of the House of Yoshida!

SHICHIRŌ [*caustically*] : It is obvious our petition for succession will not be favorably received if we rashly report Lord Koresada's death to the authorities when we do not even know his murderer's identity. How can you suggest our heartfelt efforts to bring peace and longevity to the House of Yoshida, which has endured through the generations, are unworthy? In itself this is treachery to the clan!

GENGO [*rising*] : Ehh? My loyalty is unquestioned! I won't stand for your scurrilous remarks, Shichirō!

SHICHIRŌ: You won't permit them? Gengo, since when does the dull blade of disloyalty draw blood?

249   The Scarlet Princess of Edo

GENGO: I will show you!

SHICHIRŌ [*facing him*] : Do you think you can?

[*They pose, hands on sword hilts, ready to draw.*]

GUNSUKE [*fearlessly*] : My lords, this is not an appropriate time for precipitous action. Do not draw, I beg of you.

MATSUWAKA [*quietly*] : I observe you each have reason to your dispute. Were there time, a conclusion could be reached. However, I ask you both to place above all else in your hearts our effort to petition Priest Seigen today regarding the succession. Do this for the welfare of our clan.

SHICHIRŌ and GENGO [*subsiding, but still angry*] : Yes, my Lord.

GUNSUKE [*strong but respectfully*] : We must first of all consider how the well intentioned dispute between such important clan members as Master Shichirō and Gengo will affect young Lord Matsuwaka. It is disrespectful for a young retainer to speak so, but I earnestly beg you set your differences aside.

[*He bows low.*]

SHICHIRŌ: Hm. You are a courageous young fellow. [*Glancing at* GENGO.] Since it is the wish of Lord Matsuwaka . . .

GENGO: . . . shall we defer this matter? [*Glares at* SHICHIRŌ.] Together, without rancor . . .

SHICHIRŌ and GENGO: . . . shall we confer?

[*They nod in agreement and pose.*]

GUNSUKE [*bowing low*] : For the peace of our house, reflect calmly, my Lords.

MATSUWAKA: Momentarily my heart was pained, now I am relieved. Let us proceed to the temple precincts and approach Priest Seigen.

SHICHIRŌ [*to the attending samurai*] : Quickly, everyone.

GENGO: Accompany your master.

SAMURAI: We shall.

[MATSUWAKA *rises and turns to go. Drums, bells, and shamisen play* Shaden *and* Daibyoshi. *The others rise and follow* MATSUWAKA *as he crosses stage left. The jingling of a bridle is heard behind the hanamichi curtain.*]

SHICHIRŌ: The sound of a bridle?

MATSUWAKA: Who can it be?

AKUGORŌ [*offstage*] : Matsuwaka! I bear a command! Do not move!

[*Bells and drums play loudly as* AKUGORŌ *rides a coal black horse onto the hanamichi. He wears a dark kimono, split riding skirt and cloak, and riding boots. He carries a whip. His face is dead white with dark black lips and eyebrows, the makeup of a refined villain. He poses at seven-three.*]

watarizerifu   MATSUWAKA: Iruma Akugorō . . .

SHICHIRŌ: . . . appears on his horse . . .

GENGO: . . . in fiery spirit!

MATSUWAKA: What is the command . . .

ALL: . . . he bears?

[*They glance at each other apprehensively.* AKUGORŌ *rides onto the main stage and dismounts. The horse is led away. He sits left in the place of honor.*]

AKUGORŌ: Now hear me. I bring a private message from Chief Magistrate Yorikazu, who concerns himself because of his close relation with the House of Yoshida. He has heard the rumor that, contrary to your report, Minister Koresada was murdered and the precious Miyakodori scroll purloined; that following this, the young prince Umewaka, seeking vengeance, was slain on the banks of the Sumida River; and that, furthermore, Prince Matsuwaka and his sister, Princess Sakura, plan to meet secretly with the Priest Seigen in Kamakura to influence his decision on a clan successor.[3] Produce the Miyakodori scroll to prove these rumors false, Matsuwaka, if you can. If you cannot, the world will know you are traitor first to his Imperial Majesty and second to the government of the Kamakura Shōgun. The private wish of Magistrate Yorikazu is that these rumors be investigated . . . by me!

[*Everyone reacts in amazement.*]

MATSUWAKA [*openly*]: Not only father's death and brother's, but the loss of the scroll, is already . . .

SHICHIRŌ [*strongly, breaking in*]: Wait. A groundless rumor does not trouble me, though it is told everywhere, even reaching the attention of his Majesty our Shōgun. The truth is our lord and the prince passed away while paying casual visit to the eastern provinces. Let them inquire.

AKUGORŌ [*glowering*]: Well then, if the rumor is incorrect, you have the Miyakodori scroll. Shall I examine it now?

[MATSUWAKA *starts, then poses.*]

SHICHIRŌ: The fact is, the Miyakodori is in possession of the temple abbot. Inspect it after purification ceremonies have been performed, if you wish.

AKUGORŌ: What? Today, you . . . ?

SHICHIRŌ [*bows slightly*]: Until tomorrow morning, we beg your leave.

GENGO [*poses carefully*]: Once Lord Akugorō was betrothed to Princess Sakura, and though the engagement was broken off some good feelings remain, I am sure, so until tomorrow morning . . .

AKUGORŌ [*grandly*]: . . . requests Gengo, model of loyalty. Though word of Princess Sakura's infirmity ended my betrothal, you are Prince Matsuwaka's vassal. I cannot refuse your plea.

MATSUWAKA: Then my Lord Akugorō . . .

AKUGORŌ: . . . until tomorrow, when the scroll . . .

SHICHIRŌ: . . . shall determine our young lord's fate!

[*They all pose.*]

3. The Sumida River World concerns the two young heirs of the Yoshida clan, Umewaka and Matsuwaka, whose names mean Young Plum and Young Pine. Namboku adds a sister to the plot, Princess Sakura or Princess Cherry, to round out the three trees so often mentioned in Japanese poetry: plum, pine, and cherry. He also intends the characters to be a takeoff (*modoki*) of the famous triplets—Umeōmaru, Matsuōmaru, and Sakuramaru—in the puppet play *The House of Sugawara* (1746).

Now, my Prince, let us present ourselves within the precincts of the temple.

[*To* Shaden *shamisen music,* MATSUWAKA *and his retinue rise and mount the temple steps, disappearing from sight along the temple balcony.* GENGO *addresses* AKUGORŌ *as he would his master.*]

GENGO [*angry*] : What nerve, Master Akugorō. Shichirō knows they don't have the scroll, but he pretends they do!

AKUGORŌ [*uneasy*] : He must have some plan in agreeing to inspection of the scroll, yet how could he when it was we who had the old man killed and scroll stolen?

GENO [*looks carefully about*] : From Shinobu Sōta . . .

[*He takes a letter from his breast and hands it to* AKUGORŌ.]

AKUGORŌ [*reading*] : "In accordance with your request, I have cut down the Minister, and have taken into possession the Miyakodori scroll, to be conveyed to Lord Iruma Akugorō upon receipt of 2,000 gold ryō.[4] Signed, Shinobu Sōta." A reward of 2,000 ryō?

GENGO: Impudent, greedy wretch, how dare he? Still, if he doesn't get the money, the scroll is . . .

VOICES [*off*] : Make way! Make way!

AKUGORŌ [*quickly putting the letter inside his kimono*] : To the hut by the waterfall where we will speak of this in detail. Quickly, quickly!

GENGO [*bowing*] : Master, lead the way.

[*A roll of the large drum, bells, and flute begin stately* Sōgaku, *"Court Music."* AKUGORO *and* GENGO *look at each other, nod in determination, and slip off left. Two magnificently costumed processions enter simultaneously. Princess* SAKURA *and her party enter from inside the main temple. She wears a red embroidered "scarlet princess" kimono with flowing sleeves. It is covered with a cloak of the same design. Her face is white and a glittering tiara sets off an ornate hairdo. She walks with eyes modestly downcast, flanked by* NAGAURA *and* IOZAKI, *chief ladies-in-waiting. They are dressed in heavy brocaded robes and kimonos of sober hue. She is served by a* PAGE, *dressed in a young boy's delicate kimono and outer garments. Five court* LADIES, *in brightly colored kimonos, and five* MAIDS, *in kimonos of pale pink, follow her and kneel on the balcony.* SAKURA *stands center, above the steps. The second procession enters on the* hanamichi, *led by* SEIGEN, *now chief abbot of the New Kiyomizu Temple. He is dressed in a robe of purple silk, over which is a pure gold cloak fastened with a cord of red braid. An umbrella of state is held over his head and two temple* SAMURAI *clear the way.* SEIGEN *is followed by* ZANGETSU, *second in command of the temple, clothed in gold silk,* CHIKŌ, *a temple official, six* PRIESTS *wearing white robes, two more* SAMURAI, *and two* FOOTMEN.]

CHORUS [*sings offstage,* Hana Furite, *"Falling Petals," as* Sōgaku *continues*] :
Wondrously the flowers are falling;
  Smell the fragrance of incense in four directions;

---

4. Between $60,000 and $90,000.

How appealing is the music of the moment;
    The appealing sound of music.
[SEIGEN *sees* SAKURA *and stops at seven-three, impressed with her beauty. He poses sanctimoniously, clasping a pale blue rosary in both hands. She sees him.*]

SAKURA [*formally*] : Ah, exalted Reverend Seigen, pray detain yourself a moment.

SEIGEN [*dignified*] : A vision of the "Five Precepts" in elegant adornment, a princess of imperial lineage, like the treetops in bloom, halts us for some reason. [*Carefully looks her way.*] But first, her Ladyship is . . . ?
[*The temple bell tolls. All pose.*]

ZANGETSU [*unctuously*] : Dwelling, in a word, at Cherry Blossom Valley hermitage . . .

CHIKŌ: . . . daily importuning ordination as a nun . . .

PRIESTS: . . . Yoshida's daughter . . .

SEIGEN: . . . Princess Sakura? Ah! We go!
[*A roll of the big drum, bells, and flute, and Sōgaku processional music resumes. With great dignity SEIGEN and his retinue cross onto the stage. At the same time SAKURA and her retinue move down from the balcony. STAGE ASSISTANTS place wooden benches covered with red cloths downstage. SEIGEN and SAKURA meet center, pass, and sit with their retinues stage left and stage right, respectively. In SAKURA the habit of easy command mingles with modesty. She covers her face with her trailing sleeve.*]

SAKURA: This unworthy one who has sinned has yearned to meet you, most honored Seigen, to accept your intercession. Blessed Buddha's guidance leads me upon your path today, and hence, do . . .

NAGAURA [*bowing respectfully*] : . . . grant the request of Princess Sakura.
[*Shamisen plays* Hana Furite *in the background. Single beats of the large drum and bell loudly punctuate the rhythmically spoken phrases of the women.*]

IOZAKI [*speaking strongly*] : It was Princess Sakura's heartfelt intention;
    to petition your Worship for intercession; on behalf of her brother,
    to become the new clan lord. Instead she heard Priest Seigen's praises
    loudly sung; and seeking to leave this world of mortal sorrow; begs great
    Seigen accept her as his disciple; guiding her sinner's footsteps along
    Buddha's Way.

FIRST LADY [*gently chiding*] : Not waiting for permission, Princess Sakura;
    insisted upon living in the hermitage; in Cherry Blossom Valley midst
    towering mountains. Determined to abandon this inconstant world; not
    even spring's bursting flowers can arrest her gaze.

SECOND LADY: Endeavoring in some way to lift her spirits; we entreated our
    princess, for a single day; to stroll the shell-strewn sands of Seven Mile
    Beach; bathed by the refreshing air of the spring season . . .

THIRD LADY: . . . being a short way to walk to the ocean's shore; thinking it
    would divert her, at least a little; to tread the new blades of grass growing
    on the path; gazing on the distant view, softened in the haze . . .

watarizerifu
shichigochō

FOURTH LADY: ... though the princess acquiesced to our entreaties; unmoved by the sea breezes ruffling her skirt hems; not for even as long as a puff of wind blows; did she lift her eyes upon nature's great wonder ...

FIFTH LADY: ... for her heart was most hasty of all in the party; fixedly dwelling upon an early return ...

NAGAURA: ... indeed this determined but transient flower; blown upon the mountain gale of Buddha's precepts; is no other person than ...

ALL: ... Princess Sakura! [*They bow.*]

ZANGETSU [*piously*]: You speak lightly of ordination. Hardship strews the path to Buddhahood, and merely looking at the princess' frailty rouses me to pity. Why, with such beauty, are you resolved to be a nun?

watarizerifu

CHIKŌ [*unctuously*]: In ancient times Buddha bestowed as his commandments "Five Admonitions" of behavior, the first of which is "Kill not." Thou shalt not kill man with alluring glances.

FIRST PRIEST: "Steal not," is his second admonition. Steal not from man, nor should woman steal a patron's illicit love.

SECOND PRIEST: "Lie not," is his third. To attract a repugnant patron ...

THIRD PRIEST: ... dissemble not, nor falsely seek to please him.

FOURTH PRIEST: Speak not of entering the nunhood before austerities have been endured.

FIFTH PRIEST [*giggles*]: What tragic waste should a young maid drink sake and transgress Buddha's law.

ZANGETSU: Abandon this foolish plan ...

ALL: ... we earnestly pray!

[*The temple bell tolls. Piously the* PRIESTS *lift their rosaries and bow.*]

SAKURA [*protesting politely*]: That cannot be. Exalted Reverend Seigen, ordain this one who desires to leave the carnal world.

SEIGEN [*ponderously, not looking her way*]: It is as the monks have said. Irrespective of good works, the hope of entering upon Buddha's holy way is separated from its achievement by an abyss. My lady is a budding flower. Should the seeker of Buddha's law commit a single transgression, hellfire is his destiny. Beware, Buddha's judgment is severe. [*Temple bell tolls.*] Forego tonsure, marry your betrothed, and assure your clan's posterity. This is the better course.

SAKURA: Though your advice falls on grateful ears, affliction by some unmentionable, carnal sin ... [*She cannot continue.*]

NAGAURA [*gestures with her left hand*]: Since birth our princess has been unable to open the five fingers of her left hand.

watarizerifu

SEIGEN [*starts, then recovers quickly*]: What? In birth, the princess' left hand ...

SAKURA [*turning her head in embarassment*]: ... was clenched, a defect perhaps caused by destiny or Karma of a past life?

[*Shyly she extends her closed left hand from the kimono sleeve.*] For this reason ...

NAGAURA: ... the suit of Princess Sakura's betrothed ...

ALL WOMEN: ... has been withdrawn.

[*They bow toward* SEIGEN. SAKURA *covers her face in shame.*]

SAKURA: Ashamed to show myself in public, unable to join the society of humankind, let me reduce my sins' severity by rejecting mortal cares and pledging myself to Buddha's Way. And, so I may offer masses for the souls of my father and Umewaka, grant this humble request, I pray.

[*She glances shyly at him. He notices her look, reacts, and faces front.*]

SEIGEN: Indeed. That one of such tender years desires nunhood arouses in me great sympathy. [*He considers. The music stops.*] Merciful Buddha does not hear supplication in vain. Through his charity, man's Karma can be broken in an instant. [*Looks piercingly at* SAKURA.] How old did you say you were?

NAGAURA [*bowing*]: She is, your Excellency, seventeen years old.

SEIGEN: Come. Join our voices in the Nembutsu Sutra, appealing to Merciful Buddha!

[IOZAKI *leads* SAKURA *down center. With utmost dignity* SEIGEN *rises and faces* SAKURA. *The* PRIESTS *stand in two rows behind him.* SEIGEN *closes his eyes, and slowly rubs his rosary in both hands. The* PRIESTS *do the same.*]

SEIGEN [*sonorously chanting*]: Buddha . . . Merciful!

[*Buddhist prayer bell rings out clearly.*]

PRIESTS: All . . . Hail!

SEIGEN: "Namu Amida Butsu!"

[*The prayer is slowly chanted again and again.* SAKURA's *left arm trembles. The large drum beats* Usu Doro *as* SAKURA's *whole body shakes uncontrollably and her eyes start with fear. Suddenly the fingers of her left hand fly open. An* ACTING ASSISTANT, *behind* SAKURA, *drops onto the floor a small black lacquered box.*]

watarizerifu PAGE [*moving forward, picks up the box*]: From within your hand . . .

SAKURA [*amazed at her open hand*]: Look, look, somehow my hand . . .

ALL WOMEN: . . . indeed, your hand has opened . . .

PRIESTS: . . . by the sutra just recited.

SAKURA [*receiving the box from the* PAGE]: From my hand this . . .

IOZAKI [*receiving the box from* SAKURA]: . . . delicate incense case has fallen, lacquered black and, inscribed in gold, on its back written . . . the name "Kiyoharu."

[SEIGEN, *without a word holds out his hand for the incense case.* SAKURA *returns to the bench and sits.* SEIGEN *receives the box.*]

SEIGEN [*facing front to conceal his emotions*]: It is . . . surely it is! They say the morning dew, fallen upon the mulberry and dispersed by the sun, falls again the following day. Time passes but we do not know when the souls of the dead return. "Does not the yearning spirit, though interred to earth, hold to the Wheel of Karma, and return to life again?" These are the ancients' teachings. "Namu Amida Butsu, Namu Amida Butsu!"

[*Oblivious to the others, the box slips from his fingers and he clasps his rosary passionately as he offers fervent thanks to Buddha. Shamisen begin quiet* Sode Kuguru *in the background.*]

SAKURA [*immersed in her own thoughts, she does not notice* SEIGEN] :
Even in my dreams, I would not have imagined . . .

IOZAKI: . . . in her hand an incense case. Reverend Seigen . . .

ALL WOMEN: . . . how can it be? [*They bow.*]

[SEIGEN *and the* PRIESTS *return to their places.*]

NAGAURA [*simpering*] : My goodness, your Excellency, I'd like some sutras read too if they can turn me into a young girl.

IOZAKI: And now, Princess Sakura, showing no reserve . . .

FIRST LADY: . . . from among the world's men . . .

SECOND LADY: . . . choose with easy heart . . .

THIRD LADY: . . . the finest lord of the land . . .

NAGAURA: . . . is insignificant before our Lady.

[*The* PAGE *wraps the incense case in the purple cloth and gives it to* SAKURA.]

SAKURA [*firmly*] : No. Though deeply grateful for this auspicious event, my heart is set upon a nun's ordination.

ZANGETSU [*making a show of amazement*] : How unreasonable you are, Princess Sakura, your defect rectified, with no grounds for unhappiness, to seek nunhood . . .

CHIKŌ: . . . tonsure and black garb . . .

PRIESTS: . . . is an act we cannot . . .

[*Music stops.* SEIGEN *poses.*]

SEIGEN: Fellow monks, you are mistaken. There is only one path to sever ties of lust, to destroy sins of past incarnations, to enter Buddha's Western Paradise.

SAKURA [*looking directly at him for the first time*] : Is my petition to be granted?

IOZAKI [*amazed*] : Princess Sakura . . .

ALL WOMEN: . . . may become a nun?

SEIGEN [*strongly*] : Buddha's ways are strange. "Namu Amida Butsu." Buddha Merciful All Hail.

[*Large drum, shamisen, and bell play* Shaden *as* MATSUWAKA *and* GUNSUKE *rush onto the main stage from the balcony of the main hall. They kneel beside* SAKURA. *Music stops.*]

MATSUWAKA [*quietly respectful*] : Is it true, dear Sister, though your infirmity is gone . . .

GUNSUKE [*bowing deferentiallly*] : . . . you resolve, unshaken, to be ordained?

SAKURA: Yes, Matsuwaka, my wish is granted.

SEIGEN: After saying mass for the souls of the departed, I shall come to your retreat, Princess, and perform in the Valley of the Blossoming Cherry . . . your . . . induction. [*Softly, front.*] The investiture shall be . . . Seigen's!

SAKURA: I wish only to be led to Buddha's arms. My Teacher!

[*Innocently but provocatively she opens her arms toward him. He rises, overcome with emotion, speaking to himself.*]

SEIGEN: Princess, you, too, seventeen this year? How swiftly the years have passed, until today, overwhelmed by memories of Enoshima's departed love, aroused by this lacquered case . . .

[*He stops, unable to continue. She looks at him solicitously.*]

SAKURA: Master?

SEIGEN [*eyes shining, faces her*] : We experience here the very limits of
Karma's recurring cycle of birth and death!
[*Solemn Sōgaku processional music by large and small drums, flute,
bells, and pan-pipe.* SEIGEN *flicks the rosary over his left, then right
shoulder as a sign of benediction. The large drum rolls, and* SEIGEN *leads
his retinue off left in stately procession.*]

CHORUS [*repeats* Hana Furite *with* Sōgaku *as they exit*] :
Wondrously the flowers are falling;
    Smell the fragrance of incense in four directions;
How appealing is the music of the moment;
    The appealing sound of music.

SAKURA [*to her maids*] : I return to the hermitage.

NAGAURA: Do not leave the world . . .

ALL WOMEN: . . . so hastily.

MATSUWAKA: After today, will my sister be no more?

GUNSUKE: A flowering cherry should not end in a pit. Think, my Lady, of
the House of Yoshida.

SAKURA [*sweetly*] : No thought exists in my mind but ordination. [*To the
maids.*] You are to come, everyone.
[*She turns to go.* MATSUWAKA *rushes forward, kneels, and politely holds
her trailing sleeve.*]

MATSUWAKA: Wait, Sister. Please.

SAKURA: I bear no love for this transient world.
[*Drums, shamisen, and bells begin* Shaden. SAKURA *gently pulls her
sleeve from* MATSUWAKA's *fingers. Holding the cloth-wrapped incense
case in her extended left hand, she serenely crosses down the hanamichi
followed by her retinue.* NAGAURA *follows, hesitates, then runs off
down left after* SEIGEN's *procession. Music ends.*]

MATSUWAKA: My sister will not listen.

GUNSUKE [*respectfully*] : Firmness of purpose is admirable. Yet the scroll of
our clan must be discovered by tomorrow, or . . .

MATSUWAKA: . . . the House of Yoshida will be no more.

GUNSUKE: We arrived too late to move your worthy sister. Quickly let us
find Shichirō, young Master. Surely he will have a plan.
[*Lively* Shaden *music resumes.* GUNSUKE *gestures for his master to
proceed.* MATSUWAKA *nods in agreement. They both move quickly up
the steps and along the balcony left until they are out of sight.* ZANGETSU
is pulled on stage by NAGAURA. *Music continues softly in the background.*]

NAGAURA: I've got to say it.

ZANGETSU [*protesting*] : We're in the middle of services for the dead,
Nagaura. What the devil is it?

NAGAURA [*scolding*] : You called me an old witch, a pastepot hag.

ZANGETSU: Ah, that. [*Piously.*] "Our innermost thoughts reflect on the
face," Buddha has said. I have to hide our intimacy from others.

share

257 The Scarlet Princess of Edo

NAGAURA: Did you insult me in public on purpose?

ZANGETSU: Of course, Woman.

NAGAURA [*pouting*] : I couldn't know that. I was going to take the compact of love we swore before the gods and tear it to pieces. [*She brings out a letter.*]

ZANGETSU: Don't be foolish. Here, I'll keep it.

[*He snatches the letter from her and tucks it in his kimono breast.*]

NAGAURA [*coquettishly slaps his arm*] : I'm older than you, Zangetsu, by just a few years, but when we're together . . . oh, Zangetsu!

ZANGETSU: Seigen is a sanctimonious fraud. You watch, Nagaura, when he slips, I'll be there to shove him out of Kiyomizu with nothing but a tattered umbrella to his name. Would you like to be wife of the abbot of Kiyomizu Temple?

NAGAURA [*simpering*] : Wife? I feel like the goddess of love!

ZANGETSU: Hm, speaking of the goddess of love, that Princess Sakura is a luscious thing, isn't she? If she knew more about life she wouldn't be so eager to become a nun.

NAGAURA: What do you care? Unless you and she . . .

ZANGETSU: What? [*Patting her shoulder.*] Could I forget my wife?

NAGAURA: Is it the truth?

ZANGETSU: You know it is.

NAGAURA: I'm so happy! [*She squeezes him in an embrace.*]

MAID [*calling from offstage*] : Lady Nagaura.

ZANGETSU: What? Who's that?

NAGAURA [*petulant*] : With each inch of good goes a foot of evil.

ZANGETSU: Quit fussing. We can't be seen together.

[*Drums, bells, and shamisen resume* Shaden. NAGAURA *tries to stop* ZANGETSU, *but he slips out of her grip and trots off left. Seeing him leave, she turns to go. To loud batan tsuke beats she bumps into AKU-* GORŌ, *striding on with* GENGO *from stage right.* AKUGORŌ *wears a deep wicker hat which hides his identity. Music stops.*]

NAGAURA [*surprised*] : Ah, Matsui Gengo.

GENGO [*bows obsequiously*] : Lady Nagaura.

AKUGORŌ: Hmm. This is Princess Sakura's favorite maid?

GENGO [*bowing*] : Yes, Master, it is.

AKUGORŌ [*removes the hat and smiles coldly at* NAGAURA] : You are fortunate to meet Iruma Akugorō, Princess Sakura's former betrothed. Now that her deformity is cured, she may renew her bond to me. Old woman, pass to her this love letter stating my intention.

[*He takes a letter from the breast of his kimono and offers it to her. Indignantly refusing it, she turns away.* GONSUKE—*actually* SHINOBU SŌTA *in disguise—silently appears stage left. He wears a commoner's plain blue kimono, tucked up in the back for easy walking so that his bare legs show. His face is covered with a growth of whiskers. He listens a moment, then slips off, unnoticed.*]

NAGAURA: Ha! I will not. From the beginning you knew her hand was crippled. When her love was flawless you shamed her. Get someone else to take your letter. Ha, ha, ha!

[*Laughs scornfully, covering her mouth with a closed fan.*]

AKUGORŌ: Long-tongued crone! Do not take the letter then, but no one insults Iruma Akugorō.

[*He takes a step toward* NAGAURA, *who backs away frightened.* GENGO *restrains* AKUGORŌ, *pulling on his sleeve.*]

GENGO: My, my, Lady Nagaura, what are you saying?

NAGAURA: Hmph. What do I care?

[*Nose in the air, she runs off to bata-bata tsuke beats.* AKUGORŌ *puts his hand on his sword. Again* GENGO *restrains him.*]

AKUGORŌ: Take your hands off. Spiteful female, I will . . .

GENGO: But think, my Lord, if you kill Princess Sakura's servant, she will be frightened, and . . .

AKUGORŌ [*pulls away*]: I see you are right. Yet who will deliver . . .

[GONSUKE *enters in time to hear the last line. Insolently, he leans against the steps left, arms crossed inside the breast of his kimono.*]

GONSUKE [*nonchalantly*]: Want me to take it?

AKUGORŌ: Eh? It is . . .

GENGO: . . . the one who wrote the letter . . .

AKUGORO: . . . Shinobu . . .

GONSUKE: Quiet! Don't use my name, I've told you. I heard you just now. It won't take me long to deliver a letter. I'll do it. Just be sure to pass over 2,000 ryō.

[*Though the samurai are his social superiors,* GONSUKE *treats them with barely concealed contempt.*]

AKUGORŌ [*pompously*]: On the event of Princess Sakura's reply . . .

GENGO: . . . we undertake to guarantee gold will promptly . . .

GONSUKE [*insolently*]: Crap. Who wants your guarantee? I did a job in February. I want cash. Pay up or you won't find it funny.

AKUGORŌ: I understand your feeling, but there have been special circumstances. Soon, now, a mountain of coins will . . .

GONSUKE: In the meantime, one more job? [*Shrugs disdainfully.*] The letter, then . . .

GENGO [*officiously*]: Deliver it safely, returning with favorable reply to Lord Akugorō . . .

[*By chance, a* MAID *enters from the steps left, unseen.* GENGO *kneels, receives the letter from* AKUGORŌ, *and ceremoniously hands it to* GONSUKE. GONSUKE *puts it away in his kimono and turns to go.* AKUGORŌ, *flustered, turns first to* GENGO, *then to* GONSUKE.]

AKUGORŌ: Stop! Where is . . . ?

GONSUKE [*smiling knowingly*]: . . . the precious Miyakodori? Right here.

[*He pulls from his kimono breast the scroll, secured like a talisman around his neck with a cord. Grinning, he slides it from its cloth wrapping for them to see.*]

This is my insurance that you'll come across with 2,000 ryō.

MAID: What? The Yoshida house treasure? Here?

[*She rushes at* GONSUKE, *but he easily pushes her aside. She holds him by the kimono sleeve. They pose to batan tsuke beats.*]

GONSUKE: Bitch! Let go!

MAID: I have seen the precious scroll of state! Our princess . . .

GONSUKE [*coldly*] : . . . will never know!

[*He tucks the scroll away and drags the girl to the edge of the temple moat. As drum beats* Mizu Oto *water pattern, he flicks a small towel around her neck and strangles her. Double batan tsuke beats. He kicks her body into the moat.* Taki Oto *waterfall drum pattern crescendos. A splash of water flies up and wets* GONSUKE. *Indifferently he brushes the water from his kimono.* AKUGORŌ *and* GENGO *stand amazed.*]

GONSUKE [*ironically sings a refined nō song*] : "The sunset bell tolls . . ."

AKUGORŌ and GENGO: But you have committed murder . . .

GONSUKE [*sauntering past them*] : "Scattering the cherry blossoms . . ."

AKUGORŌ and GENGO: . . . in the temple.

GONSUKE [*looking back contemptuously*] : What's that, you two? "Beside the mountain temple."

[*Standing at seven-three he looks down the hanamichi. Bringing his fists out of the breast of his kimono, he strikes an arrogant pose. Loud battari tsuke beats. Drums, shamisen, and bells resume stately* Shaden. GONSUKE *strides off down the hanamichi, scratching his whiskers. Music fades.*]

AKUGORŌ: That Sōta is audacious.

GENGO: On the day you present to the clan their precious Miyakodori, saying, "I have found it for you," you will rule the House of Yoshida. That day Princess Sakura will become your splendid bride.

AKUGORŌ: When that time comes, Gengo, you shall rise to whatever rank you ask. But should she refuse me, when I become Lord of Yoshida, we will . . .

GENGO [*eagerly*] : . . . abduct the princess?

AKUGORŌ [*triumphantly*] : Just so!

[*They pose.* Shaden *music resumes.* GENGO *bows obsequiously and gestures for* AKUGORŌ *to proceed.* AKUGORŌ *strides off stage right followed by* GENGO. *The stage is empty for a moment. To accelerating bata-bata tsuke beats* MATSUWAKA *rushes down the steps followed by* GUNSUKE. MATSUWAKA *has removed his cloak, to more easily draw his sword. Both hands are on the hilt.* GUNSUKE *stops his master, clinging to his kimono sleeve. Music ends.*]

GUNSUKE: Young Master, stop.

MATSUWAKA [*impetuously*] : Words cannot erase the stain of shame which darkens the House of Yoshida. I am heir. I am responsible. Tell my dear sister our honor is redeemed with blood.

[*He tries to release his sleeve.* GUNSUKE *quickly blocks his way by kneeling before him.*]

GUNSUKE: Without the scroll your family cannot rule. You must not take your life while it is still not found. [*He bows contritely.*]

MATSUWAKA: Yet . . . ?

GUNSUKE: Master, Shichirō reports . . . [*He whispers in* MATSUWAKA's *ear.*] As for the scroll . . .

MATSUWAKA [*surprised*]: . . . while I am in hiding, you and Shichirō will search it out . . . ?

GUNSUKE [*bowing*]: . . . and restore the rule of the House of Yoshida. Now you must go to Musashi Province and stay with Yamada Gunjibei, a former retainer.

MATSUWAKA [*hesitates, then agrees*]: I shall do as you suggest.

[*Master and retainer hold each others' gaze for a moment.* MATSUWAKA *nods, then turns to leave. Music resumes and ominous* Usu Doro *drum pattern begins.* GENGO *strides on from the right, blocking the way with outstretched arms. Music stops.*]

GENGO: Stop, Prince Matsuwaka. Lord Akugorō acts on orders of the Kamakura Shōgun. [*Harshly.*] You're not slipping out of here without an explanation.

MATSUWAKA [*shocked*]: But you are a Yoshida retainer, Gengo.

GUNSUKE [*moves to protect his master*]: How dare you block the prince's path and speak insultingly?

GENGO [*snarling*]: Eh? Brash young fool!

[GENGO *seizes* MATSUWAKA's *arm to loud batan tsuke beats.* GUNSUKE *quickly breaks* GENGO's *grip and forces him back.*]

GUNSUKE: You outrage our young master! Traitor!

[*Drums and flute play lively* Daibyōshi *and intermittent tsuke beats accompany their stylized fight.* MATSUWAKA *flees up the steps to rapid bata-bata tsuke beats. At the end of the veranda, unable to go further, he seizes the umbrella traditionally fastened to the temple wall. While* GUNSUKE *holds* GENGO *by the collar,* MATSUWAKA *opens the umbrella, and using it to break his fall, leaps onto the main stage. He escapes onto the hanamichi to rapid bata-bata tsuke beats. He poses in a mie at seven-three to loud battari tsuke beats. Shamisen play* Hayame, "Lively Melody." MATSUWAKA *hurries down the hanamichi out of sight to gradually accelerating bata-bata tsuke beats.*]

GENGO [*furious*]: Wretch, you've let him get away!

GUNSUKE: Traitor, don't you know your time has come?

[Kaza Oto *wind pattern rises and falls. They draw and fight.* GUNSUKE *stuns* GENGO *by striking him on the head with the back of his blade.* GENGO *falls to the floor.*]

GUNSUKE: I am coming, Prince.

[*Loud bata-bata tsuke beats as* GUNSUKE *runs onto the hanamichi. At seven-three, he poses in a strong mie to battari tsuke beats. Shamisen playing* Hayazen, "Fast Zen," *drum and bells playing* Haya Sōban, "Fast Gong," *and tsuke accompany* GUNSUKE's *hasty exit. A sharp ki clack: the stage revolves. Large drum and bell play* Haya Sōban *as the Kiyomizu Temple drops from sight on the elevator and, simultaneously, the next scene revolves into view.*]

SCENE 2   CHERRY VALLEY HERMITAGE

[*A rustic building with thatched roof, set in the hills behind Kiyomizu Temple is seen. Cherry trees bloom on either side. Spring flowers grow in clumps here and there. Twig fences partially hide the house. There is a low, free-standing gate right. Forest birds call. A bell tolls. A sharp ki clack signals the scene to begin. Lights come up showing* NAGAURA, LADIES, *and* MAIDS *kneeling on the veranda. Holding their rosaries, they pray in unison.*]

ALL: "Thereupon did the Buddha of Infinite Mercy rise from his seat and bare his right shoulder respectfully."

NAGAURA [*sighs wearily*]: When I read the words of blessed Kannon's prayer they sound as dreary as a Chinese Taoist talking in his sleep. Not at all like the lovely illustrated prayer scrolls I'm used to looking at.

watarizerifu   FIRST LADY [*giggles*]: It's just as Lady Nagaura says. I read the words but I haven't the least idea . . .

SECOND LADY: . . . what they mean? We could ask the monks here, they should know.

THIRD LADY [*laughs decorously*]: Ha, ha! Other than His Excellency Seigen, there's not a priest at Kiyomizu Temple . . .

FOURTH LADY: . . . true, not one who looks as if he could read a prayer . . .

FIFTH LADY: . . . though they know the latest music from kabuki and songs of love. You can be sure . . .

FIRST LADY: . . . they all, everyone of them . . .

ALL: . . . stink of worldly evil. Ha, ha, ha!

[*They decorously hide their faces behind their sleeves.*]

NAGAURA: Here, here. Do not speak evil of the monks. As in the kabuki song "The Maid of Dōjō Temple," we should be chanting sutras to help Princess Sakura along Buddha's road to enlightenment. At least you know Kannon's prayer. Recite it instead of gossiping about the monks.

SECOND LADY: But, you spoke first: a Chinese Taoist talking in his sleep . . .

NAGAURA: I? When?

ALL [*bowing low to cover their smiles*]: Just now.

NAGAURA: You're making it up.

ALL: Lady Nagaura, what a barefaced lie!

[*They giggle and cover their faces. Shamisen play* Zen no Tsutome. ZANGETSU *and* PRIESTS *enter from the left. They stand facing the women. Music ends.*]

ZANGETSU [*officiously*]: Reverend Seigen requests our presence . . .

PRIESTS: . . . hence we are here.

[*As the women move right, the* PRIESTS *take places on the veranda left.*]

NAGAURA [*touching* ZANGETSU's *sleeve playfully*]: My, my, it's Reverend Zangetsu . . .

WOMEN [*tittering*]: . . . come for tonsure?

watarizerifu   ZANGETSU [*irritated*]: No, no. Tonsure follows ordination, which Reverend Seigen will perform after the Bell of Rest has tolled.

Seigen comforts Shiragiku before the boy leaps to his death. (*Seigen:* Morita Kanyai; *Shiragiku:* Bandō Tamasaburō) Page 247

"Wait, Sister. Please." Matsuwaka politely pulls Sakura's sleeve to prevent her from leaving. (*Sakura:* Nakamura Jakuemon; *Matsuwaka:* Ichikawa Monno-suke; *Shichirō:* Kawarazaki Gonjūrō)

Sakura, holding the cloth-wrapped incense case in her left hand, exits down the hanamichi. She holds the hand of her chief Lady-in-Waiting, Iozaki, for support. (*Iozaki:* Bandō Shūchō; *Sakura:* Nakamura Jakuemon) Page 257

Iruma Akugorō removes the wicker hat to reveal his identity. (*Akugorō:*
Bandō Minosuke; *Gengo:* Iwai Hanshirō) Page 258

Gonsuke strangles the Maid who has discovered he has stolen the Yoshida
family scroll. (*Gonsuke:* Bandō Mitsugorō; *Maid:* Bandō Moriya) Page 260

Having killed the Maid in the precincts of a Buddhist temple, Gonsuke strikes a contemptuous mie pose on the hanamichi, hands thrust through his kimono and baring his chest. (*Gonsuke:* Bandō Mitsugorō) Page 260

"I come, my Ladies, with a message for Princess Sakura. Here. Take a look, Princess." Gonsuke slaps Akugorō's love letter down before Sakura. (*Gonsuke:* Bandō Mitsugorō; *Sakura:* Nakamura Jakuemon) Page 264

Gonsuke entertains the ladies with a ghost story. "He bares his arm and grabs that ghost by the collar." The Page and Maids see the tattoo on his arm. (*Gonsuke:* Bandō Mitsugorō) Page 266

Sakura exposes on her arm a tattoo identical to Gonsuke's. He reacts with amazement. (*Gonsuke:* Bandō Mitsugorō; *Sakura:* Nakamura Jakuemon)

They compare tattoos, then pose in a mie. Page 267

Gonsuke and Sakura begin their love scene. In an erotic gesture he trusts his leg across her lap. "You'll do what?" Page 268

He embraces her. She lowers her head in shame. "I'll be yours eternally." Page 269

Casually he unfastens the sash of her kimono. She turns, letting it unwind.

He thrusts his hand into the bosom of her kimono.

He pulls her to him. They kiss. Page 269

"Princess Sakura has defiled the temple!" The blind of the Cherry Valley Hermitage is raised. Zangetsu, in yellow robes, holds the incense case. Akugorō, Gengo, and Shichirō stand outside, momentarily shocked speechless. Page 270

Gengo and Zangetsu strip Seigen of his gold cloak and purple kimono. (*Gengo:* Iwai Hanshirō; *Seigen:* Morita Kanya; *Zangetsu:* Ichikawa Yaozō) Page 273

Seigen is thrown down the stairs. He rises on one knee, clasping Sakura's incense case in his hands. (*Sakura:* Nakamura Jakuemon; *Seigen:* Morita Kanya) Page 273

Zangetsu rushes to retrieve his love letter from Nagaura. Shichirō snatches it away. "A written oath of love between you and Nagaura! Your crime requires banishment." (*Seigen:* Morita Kanya; *Akugorō:* Bandō Minosuke; *Zangetsu:* Ichikawa Yaozō; *Shichirō:* Kawarazaki Gonjūrō) Page 274

CHIKŌ: We bring perfume for purification, to wash away the world's filth.

FIRST PRIEST: Monks in unison shall chant the sutra . . .

SECOND PRIEST: . . . loudly invoking Buddha's blessing . . .

THIRD PRIEST: . . . that in an instant your mortal body . . .

FOURTH PRIEST: . . . shall be renewed in purity.

ZANGETSU: Therefore, please tell Princess Sakura . . .

ALL: . . . the reason we are here.

SOLO SINGER [*offstage sings* Ito ni Yoseji, *"Melody For Strings," to shamisen and bell accompaniment*]:

> The flower even, out of love is shrouded by thought of a single cloud;
>> Fallen in love in the past, beyond time the lovers are joined;
>> In deep darkness of the chamber.

waka SAKURA [*reciting from behind the blind*]: "Only from today when looking will the mirror's face be wet with tears; do not tell other people of your remembered image."

[*The blind is raised, revealing Princess* SAKURA *seated before a mirror having her waist-length hair combed by* IOZAKI. *She is dressed in chaste white kimono. A* PAGE *waits upon her.* WOMEN *and* PRIESTS *bow. Shamisen continue* Yoseji *melody in the background.*]

NAKAURA: Princess Sakura . . .

ALL: . . . we have disturbed you.

SAKURA [*speaking to herself*]: At last honored Seigen assents to my often repeated wish to exchange this miserable self for the black robes of a nun.

IOZAKI: To think that now the hair I daily dressed is to be cut forever. I want to cry.

[*She and others wipe away tears.*]

Forgive these fumbling fingers, Princess.

SAKURA [*serenely*]: There is no need to express apologies. Nagaura. A nun requires no earthly possessions. To you I leave my scarlet kimono. The rest of my belongings are for all of you.

NAGAURA [*delighted*]: Thank you, my Princess.

SAKURA: My heart is light. Bring everything.

[*Music becomes louder. She nods to the* MAIDS. *Several rise and go into the inner room, returning with clothes, candles, incense, combs, and cosmetic boxes.* NAGAURA *distributes them to the women.*]

ZANGETSU [*shakes his head in disapproval*]: You are too kindhearted, Princess. After your head is shaved it will be too late to let the hair grow in again. And if even you aren't tempted, a beautiful nun tempts others. [*Rubs his head and smiles knowingly.*] It's not for an unimportant priest to advise a princess, but becoming a nun isn't natural.

watarizerifu SAKURA: Nothing shakes my resolve. Each moment that brings me closer to my ordination . . .

ZANGETSU: . . . increases my feeling . . .

ALL [*bowing*]: . . . of compassion.

SAKURA [*gazing at the incense case*]: I cherish the symbol of my deliverance. Everyone take . . .

IOZAKI: . . . your rosaries . . .

ALL: . . . and pray.

[*Music stops. They bow to SAKURA. A MAID moves the mirror to one side and places before SAKURA a black lacquered stand holding incense and live coals. SAKURA lifts a pale blue rosary before her face. She drops pinches of incense on the coals: coils of smoke rise in the air. ZANGETSU and the PRIESTS retire to the inner room. The WOMEN open missives bound in brocade.*]

ALL: "Busetsu, Ze Fumonbon, Jishichū Hachiman Shisen Shushō." The teaching of Buddha, the Lotus Sutra, mercy for the agonies of the multitudes. Hail the Supreme Law of the Lotus Sutra.

[*They chant the Lotus Sutra to tinkling prayer bell and shamisen playing Zen Aikata, "Zen Melody." During the prayer GONSUKE strides jauntily onto the hanamichi, talking as he goes.*]

GONSUKE: It's taking long enough to get there. Ah, there it is. Beg your pardon, ladies, beg your pardon.

[*He crosses onto the main stage and, not waiting to be acknowledged, blithely interrupts their chanting. All look up, shocked at such insolent behavior to women of the court.*]

PAGE: What? Who is this person?

GONSUKE [*grinning*] : Me? Oh, just an humble messenger.

[*Before anyone can prevent him, he enters the room and sits casually in their midst. The WOMEN pull away in fright. He continues as if nothing were wrong.*]

What have we here? Prayers for Lady Sakura? Let's hold on a minute now ladies.

IOZAKI [*sputtering*] : How dare an uncouth creature like yourself approach her ladyship? Will you not . . .

WOMEN [*bowing elegantly*] : . . . depart from here?

GONSUKE [*shrugs easily and moves a few inches away*] : Of course, of course.

NAGAURA: What is the meaning of this insolent appearance?

GONSUKE: As you wish. I come, my Ladies, with a message for Princess Sakura. [*On his knees, he leans toward SAKURA and, taking the letter from his breast, slaps it on the floor in front of her.*] Here. Take a look, Princess. Eh?

NAGAURA: Do you think you can approach her without going through us? Low, impudent fellow. Leave this room at once!

GONSUKE [*unperturbed*] : Fine. I'll step outside and leave it to you ladies.

[*He sits on the edge of the veranda to get into his sandals, then moves stage right, where he squats on his haunches to wait. SAKURA opens her eyes, folds her sutra book, and for the first time is aware of the letter.*]

SAKURA [*reading the envelope*] : "To Princess Sakura . . . from Lord Akugorō."

[*WOMEN are scandalized.*]

NAGAURA: On the errand I was solicited for?

GONSUKE [*lightly mocking*] : In that humble capacity, I have come.

SAKURA [*returning to her rosary, she speaks with aloof distaste*] : At the very moment I am to enter the Way of Immaculate Submission, a worldly missive offends my eye. Remove it from my presence.

GONSUKE [*enjoying her discomfort*] : Such a letter is loathsome, Princess?

SAKURA [*elegant*] : I wish this message of carnal desire cast away from me. [*Music stops.* NAGAURA *picks up the letter, crosses toward* GONSUKE, *and contemptuously flings it in his face.*]

GONSUKE [*unruffled*] : Don't you want to read it?

NAGAURA [*losing her temper*] : Persistent, detestable wretch! Will you not leave?

SAKURA: Once severed from earthly desires, it is an act steeped equally in sin to be moved by your lord's pleas or to refuse them.

GONSUKE [*secretly pleased, he strikes a pose*] : Then, Princess, you've no reply at all?

IOZAKI [*bowing respectfully*] : I hesitate to speak, my Lady, but carefully consider what you do. [*Shamisen resume* Zen Aikata *in the background.*]

watarizerifu
shichigochō
Rather than casting off this common world; which by all appearances you find repugnant; for an unseen afterlife which we cannot know; enjoy life as mortal man, taking pleasure as it comes. Princess, is not this letter from Lord Akugorō; a fortunate occurrence, indeed some sort of sign?

FIRST LADY: Surely it is as she says, Princess Sakura . . .

SECOND LADY: . . . living is more interesting as husband and wife . . .

THIRD LADY: . . . so follow the world's way, in which marriage is . . .

FOURTH LADY: . . . determined for womankind by man and god.

NAGAURA: Forego tonsure and nunhood, we pray my Lady . . .

ALL [*bowing*] : . . . contemplate, nay, consummate, a happy marriage!

SAKURA [*delicately*] : No matter, I shall not. [*The music stops.* SAKURA *continues her silent prayers, dropping from time to time another pinch of incense on the coals.* GONSUKE *glances her way, scratching his whiskers as he decides what to do next.*]

GONSUKE: Ah, Princess, you're a tough-minded one. But it's a fact men and women feel emotions. Why, Ladies, did you know there's a ghost running loose here in Kamakura? [WOMEN *ad-lib cries of alarm.*]

NAGAURA: What in the world . . .

ALL: . . . do you mean? [GONSUKE *smiles and leans forward. He tells his story with animated gestures.*]

shikatabanashi
GONSUKE: Since you ask, I'll tell you the whole thing. There was a girl near here that all the men were crazy about, a dead ringer for the actor Hanshirō.[5] One dull fellow from the countryside was so far gone he wouldn't leave her side. She didn't glance his way, but he tagged her night and day, stumbling along in a daze, just sick with love. Then one day he

5. Iwai Hanshirō V (1776–1847), so highly acclaimed he was accorded the unusual honor of being troupe manager though an onnagata, was playing the role of Sakura.

up and died. Now they say his ghost comes back to haunt the girl in broad daylight. She started having convulsions. No one knew what to do. Her parents had the priests say prayers of course, but nothing seemed to work, when just then a young buck passing by from Edo heard the story. "A ghost?" he said. "What the hell do you think of that. Why, I haven't seen a ghost in a long time. I think I'll wait around and have a talk with him." And with that he's off to the girl's place. He lights up a pipe and sits waiting. Suddenly—doro, doro, doro—a blue light pops out, and there comes this skinny-looking ghost with a pale face moaning, "Poor me! Poor me!" Well, this young guy jumps up with a good-natured shout.
[*Relishing the role,* GONSUKE *makes a fierce face and pushes back his kimono sleeve, exposing a tattoo mark on his left arm.*]
He bares his arm and grabs that ghost by the collar. "Hah! Damned moron spook! Ghosts are supposed to come out at night!" With that he knocked him down shouting, "What do you mean showing up in the daytime?" And the ghost answered in a pitiful voice . . .
FIRST LADY [*breathlessly eager*] : Yes, yes, what . . .
ALL: . . . did the ghost say?
GONSUKE [*acting it to the hilt*] : Why, "I'm afraid of the dark," he said!
[WOMEN *laugh decorously. Her prayers disturbed, the princess glances up. She sees* GONSUKE's *tattoo.*]
SAKURA [*tiny, incredulous voice*] : A . . . tattoo . . . ?
GONSUKE [*dropping his kimono sleeve*] : Beg your pardon, Princess.
SAKURA [*rising on her knees, she looks intently at* GONSUKE] : Then you . . . ?
[*The rosary slips from her fingers. She cannot speak.*]
IOZAKI [*noticing nothing*] : It is time for final preparations, Princess.
[*She nods a command to the women. They bow, rise, and cross to assist* SAKURA. *The princess stops them with a faint gesture.*]
SAKURA: Stay. [*Improvising.*] My ears, which should admit no evil, have been defiled by an untruthful tale. Ten times I shall recite the Lotus Sutra, to cleanse away the stain before Priest Seigen arrives. Retire and leave me, all.
FIRST LADY [*reproving*] : But, Princess, we should . . .
NAGAURA [*cutting them off*] : Not a word. Do as your mistress tells you.
WOMEN [*bowing*] : We obey.
[*Shamisen and tinkling bells play* Yoseji. *The* WOMEN *rise and go inside, taking with them all the objects except the incense stand, which is placed beside* SAKURA. *Last to leave is* NAGAURA, *who glances curiously at the princess before closing the sliding doors.* SAKURA *and* GONSUKE *are alone.* GONSUKE *stands and stretches nonchalantly. He slaps the letter against his thigh, then tucks it away. Music stops.*]
GONSUKE: I get sleepy sitting. I'll tell Lord Akugorō there's no reply. Taking his letter, I'll go.
[GONSUKE *turns to go. Her voice trembles, breathless.*]
SAKURA: No. You shall not go.

GONSUKE [*stops*] : Oh? Is there something else?

SAKURA: There is . . . something else, You may come here.

GONSUKE [*alert, moves to the veranda and poses*] : And now that I'm here?

SAKURA: Do not be reserved. Come closer.

GONSUKE [*surprised in spite of himself*] : What? That's too much, Princess.

SAKURA: It is a small thing.

[*She rises on her knees and looks up into his eyes. He returns her look coolly, then decides he has nothing to lose. Briskly he brushes off his kimono and drops it down to cover his legs. He walks into the room and kneels to her right some distance away. He bows properly, but without humility.*]

GONSUKE: By your leave, here I am, Princess.

SAKURA [*shyly chiding*] : You need not be so coldly formal. You may inform me now . . .

GONSUKE: Eh? What should I . . . ?

SAKURA: . . . of your true identity. You need not conceal it.

GONSUKE [*startled*] : What?

[SAKURA *places her left hand on her kimono sleeve and poses.*]

SAKURA: Behold. Observe well.

[*An* ACTING ASSISTANT *helps her remove her chaste white kimono, revealing beneath it a pink kimono patterned with bursting cherry blossoms. Coyly she slides next to him and with her left hand raises the right kimono sleeve—exposing a red and blue tattoo mark identical to GON-*SUKE's. *He can scarcely believe his eyes.*]

GONSUKE: You saw my tattoo . . .

SAKURA: . . . on your arm . . .

GONSUKE: . . . that night? Then you were the one . . . ?

[*In a vulgar gesture, he yanks his kimono open and sits cross-legged beside her. He pulls up his kimono sleeve. They compare tattoos. She averts her head in shame; he laughs harshly. They pose in a mie to battari tsuke beats. Shamisen and koto offstage begin the romantic melody Rokudan, "Six Part Melody." The following section, written in alternating phrases of seven and five syllables, is spoken in a highly musical, rhythmic manner.*]

watarizerifu
shichigochō

SAKURA [*shyly, unable to meet his gaze*] : What happened afterward was that gradually; with each day and night that passed, there increasingly; welled within me tender and loving memories. How can I ever forget the spring of last year; the cold of February lingering in the air; when by my nighttime pillow, creeping stealthily; appeared a burglar's dark form dimly before me; black hood covering his head, his face in darkness. Before I knew it, frightened, my trembling hand seized . . .

GONSUKE [*roughly bragging*] : . . . without a thought I yanked her straight back into bed! Like it or not I pulled her tightly up to me; to mark the sudden death of spring's virginity; chalk it up to my good luck that I'm still alive; for not thinking my night's work had taken much time; calls of morning birds startled us awake at dawn; I rose to slip away, silent as I'd come . . .

SAKURA [*tears fall, her mouth trembles, remembering*] : . . . clinging to a
stranger's sleeve, urging him to stay; one brief glimpse upon that arm, a
mark of manhood; pink blossoms of a cherry and a temple bell; shown pale
in the morning light of the crescent moon; with face still unknown to me,
we parted and then . . .
[*Back to back, they raise their sleeves. Each looks at the other's tattoo
and poses.*]

GONSUKE [*laughs*] : . . . then surprised as hell I heard someone shouting
"thief"; you know damned well I wanted to clear out of there! Still I
thought to myself then, "this one's a beauty; a cute bud of a girl six- or
seventeen; that I wouldn't mind meeting again somewhere . . ."

SAKURA: . . . yes, how I wished to meet you, yet I blush with shame; at what
I did to assure my love would be known; fixing upon my right arm for
future meeting . . .

GONSUKE [*marveling*] : . . . red temple bell and cherries, exactly like mine!
I didn't know you liked it all that much, Princess!

SAKURA [*passion overcoming her modesty*] : You came here today to me
bearing love's message . . .

GONSUKE [*amazed*] : . . . true enough I was bringing you a love letter.

SAKURA: We see in this chance meeting . . .

GONSUKE: . . . in Kamakura . . .

SAKURA: . . . our destiny unraveling . . .
[*She looks at him provocatively. He stands, flicks open his kimono to bare
his legs, and sits with a flourish.*]

GONSUKE: . . . mighty damn well! Ha, ha!
[*Music stops. They pose in a mie to battari tsuke claps. Music resumes.*]

SAKURA [*covering her face bashfully*] : One more thing I must speak of that
happened that night; there grew within my body a child of our love.
Fearful of court gossiping, and with just a maid; I fled into the country
where our child was born.

GONSUKE: What? You puffed up? For god's sake after one time? [*Dis-
interested.*] And the brat?

SAKURA: Rather than abandon our infant, he was placed for care with a
servant of Lady Nagaura. [*She moves closer.*] Though you were unknown
to me, we met by Buddha's grace. Karma links our lives together.
[*She places her hand hesitantly, but coquettishly on his thigh. He hugely
enjoys the situation.*]

GONSUKE: And, Princess, this business of turning into a nun . . . ?

SAKURA: Since meeting you again . . .

GONSUKE: You'll go on being a Princess?

SAKURA: . . . since meeting you . . .

GONSUKE [*coolly smiling*] : Yes?

SAKURA: I shall . . .
[*He roughly embraces her and thrusts his bare leg, in an erotic gesture,
across her lap.*]

GONSUKE: You'll do what?

SAKURA [*faintly*]: I'll be . . . yours . . . eternally.

[*She buries her head in shame. Matter-of-factly he puts his hand inside the breast of her kimono.*]

GONSUKE: Ha, ha, ha! Be the footman's princess! It's been a long time . . . Princess.

SOLO SINGER [*offstage sings* Tada Uta, *"Plain Song," to shamisen accompaniment*]:

The flower even, out of love is shrouded by thought of a single cloud.

nureba

[*Casually* GONSUKE *begins to unfasten* SAKURA's *kimono sash. She turns and, frightened, falls to the floor. They pose.*]

GONSUKE [*cynically*]: Well? Are you my wife or not? With a wife you do as you like.

SAKURA: Then . . . do as you like, however . . .

GONSUKE: However . . . this is what I'll do.

[*Music continues. He pulls on the sash. She acquiesces by turning, letting the sash unwind. They pose, the long sash stretched between them. He pulls the sash and she falls against him, panting with emotion. He thrusts his hand into the bosom of her kimono. They kiss, her kimono sleeve delicately covering their faces. He rises and abruptly crosses right to the pillar where he poses indifferently. He undoes the knot of his stiff sash. Holding it, she falls back on the floor and looks up at him. In a bravura gesture he sweeps back the loosely hanging kimono to expose his body naked except for a loincloth. He sits provocatively beside her. She looks at him passionately as the blind falls to cover them from view.*]

SOLO SINGER [*continues* Tada Uta, *"Plain Song"*]:

Fallen in love in the past; without time the lovers are joined;
  In deep darkness of the chamber.

ZANGETSU [*reenters*]: Damned old hag! I only meet her for the money. That oath of love turns my stomach. Ugh!

[*Ruefully he looks at the letter. He is about to put it away when he notices the blind is down. He tiptoes over to peek in at the princess. He hears someone approaching and in his haste to leave drops the letter. He slips off left as* AKUGORŌ *and* GENGO *stride onto the hanamichi. They stop at seven-three.*]

AKUGORŌ: While we wait for that scoundrel Sōta to return, Princess Sakura may already have taken her vows.

GENGO: Until he returns with a reply, Master, it's best to bear the fellow in silence.

AKUGORŌ: No, I will see for myself.

[*Ominous* Kaza Oto *wind pattern. They cross stealthily onto the main stage. A distant temple bell tolls. They slip through the gate. Loud bata-bata tsuke beats:* SHICHIRŌ *rushes on from stage left.*]

SHICHIRŌ: Lord Akugorō, I beg to report: the Miyakodori scroll has just been stolen and young master Matsuwaka has been kidnaped! It happened so suddenly I feel it must be the work of *tengu* forest spirits. I earnestly ask that you consider our clan's new situation.

AKUGORŌ: You lie, Shichirō. There are no forest demons here.

SHICHIRŌ [*bluffing*] : What I say is true. Have you the scroll to prove me wrong?

AKUGORŌ [*stymied*] : What? No, I have not but . . .

SHICHIRŌ: Well, then?

[*They pose, glaring at one another.*]

SAKURA [*behind the blinds*] : Without fail we shall be lovers in future lives, too.

AKUGORŌ: The princess' voice . . .

GENGO: . . . behind the blind?

AKUGORŌ [*thundering*] : Gengo, investigate!

[*Drums and flute play fast* Daibyōshi. GENGO *tries to pass.* SHICHIRŌ *prevents him, pressing him to the floor. They pose in a mie to battari tsuke beats. During the pose* ZANGETSU's *voice is heard from within the blind. The music stops.*]

ZANGETSU: Princess Sakura has defiled the temple!

[*The blind is raised.* ZANGETSU *is seen standing over the disheveled princess. He holds the incense case.* LADIES *file on and kneel stage left.* SHICHIRŌ *moves left, notices the dropped letter, and picks it up. There is only time to read the address before he tucks it away.*]

SHICHIRŌ: What? Princess Sakura . . . ?

ZANGETSU [*sanctimoniously*] : . . . has indulged in carnal lust.

AKUGORŌ: This is outrageous!

NAGAURA [*entering from within*] : What? Can it be our Princess erred?

IOZAKI [*entering, sees* SAKURA's *appearance*] : Ah! Indeed, such a scandalous . . .

WOMEN: . . . appearance.

SAKURA [*covering her face with her sleeve*] : From the world's eyes I hide my face in mortification.

AKUGORŌ [*livid*] : What? *You* are mortified? Zangetsu, what scoundrel has dared . . . ?

ZANGETSU: As I came in he slipped away quick as a wink. But he left behind a piece of evidence.

AKUGORŌ: Evidence?

ZANGETSU [*patting the incense case*] : Inside this cloth . . .

SHICHIRŌ: Inside?

ZANGETSU: . . . evidence of immorality.

AKUGORŌ and GENGO [*facing front*] : Without delay, show us evidence.

[ZANGETSU *passes the incense case in its purple cloth to* AKUGORŌ. *Just as he is about to fold back the cloth,* SEIGEN's *commanding voice is heard within.*]

SEIGEN: Cease your altercation!

[*The temple bell tolls. Shamisen play* Kin Aikata, *"Bell Melody."* SEIGEN *makes a grand entrance from up center. He sits in the seat of honor stage left.* SAKURA, *in embarrassment, moves away right.* PRIESTS *enter and kneel on the main stage right. Music continues softly in the background.*]

SHICHIRŌ: Honored Seigen . . .

NAGAURA: . . . how have you . . .

WOMEN: . . . arrived unseen?

SEIGEN [*covering his surprise and chagrin*] : The time had come for Princess
Sakura to don robes and take the tonsure, so I came through the garden,
alone and in haste. But I arrived too late: she already has transgressed. It is
Buddha's will that by my action her as-yet-unconsecrated flesh has
yielded to temptation. She merits no strong rebuke, therefore.

AKUGORŌ [*sputtering with rage*] : That is not so. She may not be confirmed,
but she—Princess of the House of Yoshida—is an adulteress!

GENGO: Furthermore, her lust has defiled Buddha's temple. Her sin can't be
dismissed. My Lord, within the cloth . . .

[*Music stops. The temple bell tolls. AKUGORŌ sits on a tall stool brought
forward by a STAGE ASSISTANT. AKUGORŌ deliberately begins to
peel back the cloth. SHICHIRŌ stops him.*]

SHICHIRŌ: Yet no partner has been seen so there cannot be a crime. To speak
of evidence and investigation, my Lord Akugorō, is unsuitable to one of
noble family. First, what indiscretion . . . ?

FIRST PRIEST: Indeed, noble Seigen will be prone to overlook this insult if
adequately appeased.

AKUGORŌ: A priest thinks like a priest. But a samurai . . .

GENGO: Quickly, the evidence . . .

[*AKUGORŌ opens the cloth.*]

AKUGORŌ: An incense case. The front is covered with a grass design, on the
back is inscribed the name "Kiyoharu." [*Temple bell tolls.*] Or, read the
characters the Chinese way . . . "Seigen." I understand.

[*He rises and crosses into the room. He seizes SEIGEN's left arm as if he
were a prisoner.*]

The Princess' partner is . . . Seigen! High Priest Seigen is conspirator in
fornication!

SHICHIRŌ: Are you mad? The virtuous priest of Kiyomizu . . .

IOZAKI and NAGAURA: . . . is partner to the princess?

ZANGETSU: My, my, do you truly hold . . .

AKUGORŌ: . . . an incense case with his name, Seigen, written on the back.

ZANGETSU [*pretending sympathy*] : Ah. I see, I see. Our foolish priest gave
it to her as a pledge. [*Shakes his head.*] My, oh, my!

SAKURA [*rises on her knees*] : It cannot be. The incense case was in my
possession . . .

WOMEN: . . . before your indiscretion?

AKUGORŌ [*deliberately*] : Lying beside the princess did you not, Seigen, did
you not drop inadvertently proof incontrovertible of your lechery?
[*Thrusts the case before SEIGEN's eyes.*] Well, did you not, foul priest?

SAKURA [*faintly*] : My Lord, what you insist upon is impossible.

SEIGEN [*loftily*] : In truth, to love man or woman is to embrace putrescent
flesh. Even in regard to the Great Way of Compassion which led to
enlightenment in ancient times, there are instances in which some have

strayed from the proper way, but as for myself I have had no carnal knowledge of Princess Sakura. It is a fact, known by those present, that the incense case you call your evidence previously fell from the princess' hand.

watarizerifu

NAGAURA: Yes, yes, all of us . . .

WOMEN: . . . can testify . . .

MONKS: . . . all of us . . .

ALL: . . . that this is true.

SHICHIRŌ: Everyone here knows that incense case. The Priest Seigen would never . . .

AKUGORŌ: No! You are servants to the princess. The monks are his disciples. The testimony of underlings is worthless.

watarizerifu

ZANGETSU [*hiding a smile*] : You mean, no matter what excuse is given . . .

AKUGORŌ: . . . nothing can change the fact that on the case's back the name Seigen is written!

SEIGEN: And so, I am stigmatized a corrupt priest . . .

AKUGORŌ, GENGO, and ZANGETSU: . . . by this evidence inescapable!

SAKURA: No matter what you say, Reverend Seigen is innocent.

AKUGORŌ: Then if not Seigen, did some other man . . .

GENGO: . . . seduce you? Well? Name him!

AKUGORŌ [*leans in threateningly toward* SEIGEN] : Have you, Priest, an explanation? Have you?

SEIGEN [*unable to answer*] : I . . .

GENGO [*to* SAKURA] : Who is your seducer?

kuriage

SAKURA [*unable to speak*] : Well . . .

GENGO: Well?

AKUGORŌ: Well?

SEIGEN: Well . . .

[*First alternately, then in unison, they speak at increasing speed.*]

ALL: Well, well, well! Well!

AKUGORŌ: You have no word, no syllable of answer? Answer me! Answer . . . me!

[*They stand over the victims, glaring down accusingly, and pose.* SAKURA *and* SEIGEN *sit mute, heads bowed.*]

ZANGETSU [*sits beside* SEIGEN, *rubbing his hands obsequiously*] : Well, well, well. This is most distressing, most distressing indeed. The proof shows, Master Seigen, no one else but you are the culprit.

[SAKURA *and* SEIGEN *react.* ZANGETSU *calms them with a deprecatory gesture.*]

Now, now. Charity to mankind. Is that not right? Priestly duty lies in helping our fellow man. We must then, Master Seigen, Princess Sakura, hide from the eyes of man this monstrous crime. Since this case of yours . . .

AKUGORŌ [*loftily*] : . . . assuredly proves . . .

ZANGETSU [*still smiling, places case beside* SEIGEN] : . . . salacious lustfulness! Concern for human charity demands . . . we send this priest on a tour of the provinces.[6]

FIRST PRIEST [*beseeching him*] : Is there nothing you can say, dear Reverend Seigen . . .

PRIESTS: . . . to defend your innocence?

SEIGEN: The scriptures tell of the monk from Cathay, fallen into hell, saying "Buddha prays for all mankind, though mankind prays not for Buddha." In spite of following the glorious Way of the scriptures and having committed no sin against Buddha, man suffers the agonies of hell. Out of sympathy and for the sake of others, I truly . . .

ZANGETSU: . . . have sinned and are fallen into hell, partner in lust, Reverend Seigen!

ALL: Ahh!

SHICHIRŌ [*desperately*] : In such circumstances it is unjust.

SEIGEN: I could vindicate myself, but what of Princess Sakura? Let me now act for another. [*Holding the case tenderly.*] Wherever it may lead.

ZANGETSU: No doubt about it, Reverend Seigen is the culprit.

AKUGORŌ [*roughly seizes* SEIGEN's *arm*] : Whoremaster! Despoiler of virgins! Rip the polluted robes from the stinking bell-ringer!

GENGO: Yes, Master!

ZANGETSU: You deceived us, Master! Now pay for your wickedness!
[*Bell tolls three times. Ad-libbing, they move to either side of* SEIGEN *and remove his gold cloak and purple outer kimono. A* STAGE ASSISTANT *helps them. When* SEIGEN *is stripped to his simple white under-kimono, he is thrown sprawling down the short flight of stairs onto the main stage to batan tsuke beats. His accusers pose above him.*]

AKUGORŌ, GENGO, ZANGETSU: Sinful, wicked priest!

CHIKŌ [*shocked*] : You go too far!
[PRIESTS *begin to rise.* GENGO *steps forward with his hand threateningly on the hilt of his sword.*]

AKUGORŌ: Move closer and you all . . .

AKUGORŌ, GENGO, ZANGETSU: . . . are guilty equally!
[PRIESTS *fall back, cowed.* AKUGORŌ *poses grandly.*]

AKUGORŌ: Throw the priest among the outcasts as warning to adulterers.

NAGAURA: And Princess Sakura?

AKUGORŌ [*savoring this most of all*] : She has willfully seduced Buddha's priest and polluted Buddha's temple. Until remanded otherwise, she is detained . . . in my custody.

WOMEN: Princess Sakura must . . . ?

SAKURA [*frightened*] : . . . go with your Lordship?

AKUGORŌ: Return my affection and I might consider . . .

SHICHIRŌ: . . . restoring the House of Yoshida?

6. A play on words the audience certainly must have enjoyed. The ostensibly Buddhist phrase *tera o hiraku* (open a temple) also was kabuki slang for playing in the provinces.

AKUGORŌ: Never! Its demise is irrevocable.

[*He poses, glaring at* SHICHIRŌ. ZANGETSU *rubs his hands ingratiatingly and bows many times.*]

ZANGETSU: Heh, heh. I'm sure your Lordship will agree the next temple abbot should be me. Heh, heh!

SHICHIRŌ [*remembering the letter, takes it out*] : That shall not be, depraved Zangetsu.

ZANGETSU [*pretending amazement*] : Oh? Why is that?

SHICHIRŌ [*quickly scanning the letter*] : A written oath of love . . .

ZANGETSU: Ahhh!

[*He rushes to retrieve the letter.* SHICHIRŌ *pushes him to the ground.*]

SHICHIRŌ: . . . between you and Nagaura!

NAGAURA: Ahh!

SHICHIRŌ: Your crime requires banishment.

ZANGETSU: Damn! This is a fine mess!

[*The temple bell tolls. The large drum beats* Kaza Oto *wind pattern. Cherry petals flutter to the ground, around and over* SEIGEN, *indicating the evanescence of worldly things.*]

AKUGORŌ: Sakura! Seigen! Rise!

[*The bell tolls. Cherry blossoms scatter and fall to the ground.*]

waka SEIGEN [*poignantly*] : "Before the blossoms fall from the cherry's branches unexpectedly; in the fullness of our life does not sadness engulf us?" I, a disciple of Buddha, am accused of sinning against another.

[*He stifles tears.* SAKURA *rises on her knees.*]

SAKURA: Forgive, I pray, a wretched princess, who has caused false calumnies to be raised against you, esteemed Reverend Seigen. I quail before your righteous disfavor. Forgive me, please.

[*She clasps her hands in an appeal for forgiveness. The temple bell tolls in the distance.* SEIGEN *looks keenly at her, trying to control his mounting agitation.*]

AKUGORŌ: Sakura!

GENGO: Seigen, stand!

SEIGEN: How clear it is: after seventeen years, the unrequited spirit of Shiragiku . . .

[*She scarcely hears his words, but the tone of his voice and his gaze disturb her.*]

SAKURA: Ehh?

[*Both look away.*]

SEIGEN: . . . was destined to return. Oh, blessed be the Wheel of Karma!

[*He rises on one knee, clasps the incense case passionately, and poses. He is quietly triumphant that, though he has lost his position, soon he will be reunited with the reincarnation of* SHIRAGIKU. *The temple bell tolls. A sharp* ki *clack.*]

AKUGORŌ: Stand, I say!!

[*The temple bell tolls, the large drum beats soft* Kaza Oto *wind pattern, and shamisen begin* Hana ni Utsurou, *"Drifting Flower." The group moves into tableau:* SEIGEN *stands clutching rosary and incense case;* AKUGORŌ

holds SAKURA's *hand possessively, as* SAKURA *looks appealingly at*
SEIGEN; ZANGETSU *tries to rise but is pushed to the floor by* SHICHIRŌ;
NAGAURA *casts a furtive glance at* ZANGETSU; *and* GENGO, *hand on
sword hilt, faces down the protesting* PRIESTS. *Soft ki clacks swell then
fade, as the curtain is slowly walked closed on the tableau. A single loud ki
clack signals drums and flute to play lively* Shagiri, *"Curtain Music,"
between acts.*]

nimakume   ACT II

INASE RIVER SCENE

[Kaza Oto *wind pattern and accelerating ki clacks accompany the opening
of the striped curtain. It is the following day. The scene is a debris-
littered bank of the Inase River, near Kamakura, a short distance from
Kiyomizu Temple. A band of outcasts lives here.* BANHACHI, *the group's
leader, sits in front of a hut of reeds. High grass and stunted trees surround
it. A small fire burns stage right.* KITAROKU *is washing large radishes in
the river. Others are sprawled on the ground, drinking sake from rice bowls.
They wear an assortment of rags and patched kimonos. They are unshaven
and filthy.*]

ZUBUROKU [*a youngster*] : You've been drinking since morning, Boss. Is
   something up?

BANHACHI: I don't drink for nothing. You bet there is. Here, Kid, have some.

ZUBUROKU: Yeh, Boss, great.

OKESHICHI: Hey, Kitaroku, what're you up to?

KITAROKU [*rises from his washing*] : Me? There ain't no pickles to go with
   the sake, so I yanked some radishes out of the field. I'm trying 'em raw
   with salt. [*Chews.*] Awful! [*He spits.*]

KOYASUKE [*laughing*] : You're crazy. That stuff'll kill your stomach. My old
   man bawled me out when I did that as a kid.

KITAROKU: I didn't ask you to eat.

KOYASUKE: Who then?

   [*They move in ready to fight.*]

BANHACHI: Stay away from each other or you'll be at it again. Listen,
   Kitaroku, quit thieving like a pack rat. I'll get it if the fields are picked
   clean.

   [*Temple bell tolls in the distance.*]

ZUBUROKU: Is the bell for some festival at the temple?

BANHACHI [*disgusted*] : Read the signs.

ZUBUROKU [*seeing them for the first time*] : Oh. They're new.

BANHACHI: Everyone else knows. [*Shakes his head.*] Hell of a thing, a
   Kiyomizu priest bedding down with a Yoshida family princess.

ZUBUROKU [*innocently*] : Sex ain't right.

OKESHICHI: You don't have to worry about it.

ZUBUROKU: Aw, shut up.

OKESHICHI [*eagerly*]: What's in it for us?

BANHACHI [*shrugs*]: Who knows? She'd be dead now, if she weren't almost married to a noble. And it's only because Seigen is the "People's Buddha" they haven't beheaded him. They're lucky. Instead of losing their lives, they'll be whipped in public . . . then banished to live with us.

[*All react with surprise.*]

ZUBUROKU: They're coming here?

BANHACHI: We'll see what's in it for us. [*Laughs.*] One's an imperial princess, the other's a priest from a great temple! It's something to celebrate, ain't it, them living with us! Ha, ha!

[*They roar with laughter. Bells, flute, and drums begin Sōgaku. SAKURA's retinue of court MAIDS enters on the hanamichi escorted by three SAMURAI in rich court dress and followed by PORTERS carrying large lacquered boxes containing SAKURA's belongings. The procession stops momentarily at seven-three, then moves grandly on stage. BANHACHI looks knowingly at his men. They hide smiles and adopt an ingratiating attitude, falling back as if in awe of the SAMURAI and kneeling with their faces to the ground. The MAIDS kneel and the SAMURAI sit on camp stools placed for them stage left. The music ends.*]

SAMURAI [*officiously*]: Are you creatures responsible for this place?

BANHACHI: My men and I guard the road and fields, Sir.

SAMURAI [*to chief* MAID]: These are the ones.

FIRST MAID [*elegantly*]: Our visit is burdensome for you. But we are servants to the House of Yoshida concerned for the life and safety of our Princess Sakura, who as punishment for her disgrace is to be publicly exposed by the Inase River. We beg you to befriend the princess and show her mercy.

SECOND MAID [*bowing*]: We wish to make easier the entrance into your society of our dear princess, who, of imperial lineage, until today has not even seen an outcast.

THIRD MAID: Though forbidden to do so, we offer with all our hearts this small gift.

[*A PORTER passes paper parcels of gold coins forward.*]

FOURTH MAID: We pray you will all be compassionate toward Princess Sakura.

BANHACHI [*bowing low*]: Ah, thank you, Ladies. Say "thank you" to the ladies.

ALL [*bowing vigorously*]: Thank you, my Ladies!

FIRST MAID: By all means say nothing of our visit to anyone.

BANHACHI [*smiling*]: To no one, my Ladies, to no one.

[*Zen no Tsutome music begins. CHIKŌ and the PRIESTS enter in procession on the hanamichi. At seven-three CHIKŌ sees the MAIDS and stops. BANHACHI quickly scoops up the money.*]

CHIKŌ: Have you come, my Ladies, on Princess Sakura's behalf?

FIRST MAID: And you to intercede for Reverend Seigen? How sad it is . . .

SECOND MAID: . . . that because of indiscretions . . .

ALL: . . . they must suffer punishment.

CHIKŌ: Please do not say that.

[CHIKŌ *nods to the others and the procession proceeds. They kneel stage left facing* BANHACHI. *The* MAIDS *move right. Music ends.*]

The more one speaks of it the worse the fault becomes. We are borne down by the truth that beloved master Seigen, a living Buddha in this sinful world, has been destroyed by a woman. Yet we, his pupils, are of one mind. We cannot abandon him and so we have brought gifts of supplication, honored outcasts. [*Nods to* PRIESTS.] Offer your greetings with the gifts.

FIRST PRIEST [*pushing forward wrapped package of gold coins*]: Hey there, you outcasts. Come here.

[BANHACHI *scowls and turns away.*]

SECOND PRIEST: Here, here, that's no way to speak. What you should say is exactly opposite. [*To* OUTCASTS.] From this day on, Master Seigen will be living amongst you. Heh, heh, heh, heh. We are just worthless monks, acolytes from Kiyomizu Temple. Among them I am no one important, but I ask that when our manacled master appears today, graciously accept him into your midst. Be hospitable to him in all ways, we beg. [*He bows low.*]

FIRST PRIEST: Heh, heh, heh, heh! Did I ever put my foot in it! These gifts are given with a pure heart. Because our master is a fallen priest he may eat some fish and so, with this small gift perhaps you can . . .

BANHACHI [*taking the money*]: Ha, ha, ha. Sounds like he's an easygoing priest. Thank you, thank you.

CHIKŌ: No, no, it is for us to thank you. As for the money, it is a small amount. Use it as you wish. Enjoy yourselves drinking wine together. Seigen has fallen from Chief Priest of the great temple of Kiyomizu to being a beggar. Allow him what freedom is possible while he is among you, we pray.

BANHACHI: Thank you, thank you. [*Weighing the two packages of money in his hands.*] Ho, ho. A hundred ryō of gold at least. Well, well.

ZUBUROKU: A hundred ryō? Let me see it.

OTHERS: Let me! Let me!

BANHACHI: Shut up. Don't shout. [*To* MAIDS *and* PRIESTS.] For beggars, it's like lightning striking!

[Toki no Taiko, *"Time Drum," music begins.* GENGO *with two* SAMURAI *enter on the hanamichi, escorting* PORTERS *who are carrying two palanquins. At seven-three* GENGO *stops and is amazed to see the* MAIDS *and* PRIESTS. *Furious, he strides center stage and faces them. Music ends.*]

GENGO: It will cost your lives to help the depraved priest and his mistress, just as it will cost me mine if I allow you to show them mercy! You shall not intercede!

watarizerifu FIRST MAID: It is not as you think, noble Gengo.

SECOND MAID: We do not come to interfere . . .

THIRD MAID: . . . but only bid . . .

FOURTH MAID [*bowing*]: . . . our mistress farewell.

CHIKŌ: We cannot part from our teacher, who to us is like Buddha himself.

GENGO: Hm. Since she is the child of my master, relenting should not result in my execution. You have permission, but for a short time.

ALL: You will allow us?

GENGO: Don't be long.

ALL [bowing] : We thank you.

GENGO [gruffly] : Outcasts.

BANHACHI [bowing low] : Yes, sir?

GENGO: Are you prepared to guard this site?

BANHACHI [expansively] : Yes, my Lord, like you told us.

GENGO: And take charge of the prisoners?

BANHACHI: Like you said, my Lord.

[BANHACHI signals his men. They roll two straw mats onto the ground, seize poles, push up their sleeves, and stand guard.]

GENGO: Samurai, bring forth the convicted prisoners.

FIRST SAMURAI: Priest Seigen . . .

SECOND SAMURAI: . . . Princess Sakura . . .

BOTH: . . . come forth!

[The temple bell tolls. Shamisen play Saigyo, "Monk." PORTERS raise the palanquin blinds, and SEIGEN and SAKURA, dressed as previously, step out. OUTCASTS seize their arms and force them to their knees on the rough straw mats. Music ends.]

GENGO [gloating] : Now, listen! Nefarious monk, you have defiled the temple of your samurai lords. For this you deserve to have your head cut off, but out of mercy one hundred lashes in public, expulsion from the priesthood, and exile to a life among outcasts shall be your punishment.[7] For this be grateful. And you, Princess Sakura, have lewdly consorted with this priest and are responsible for the loss of the Miyakodori scroll. You shall be punished with the priest and exiled as an outcast. Offer thanks that you have been saved from death by your imperial birth. Take them, outcasts!

SEIGEN [clasping his rosary] : In truth, the image of the moon shining pure and eternal over the boundless ocean of enlightenment is destroyed by wind-driven waves of the Five Corruptions and Six Desires.[8] I am accused of wetting my sleeves with the dew of lust. Though unjustly charged, I do not think of myself now but only of my temple's welfare. Serve it well.

CHIKŌ [bowing] : Representing the priests of Kiyomizu, we have come . . .

PRIESTS [bowing] : . . . to greet you.

FIRST MAID: Dear Mistress . . .

MAIDS: . . . we grieve for you.

[They bow. SAKURA does not look at them, but speaks resolutely.]

7. In reducing Seigen and Sakura to hinin, literally, "non-human," the government is punishing them with the most severe penalty short of death. Excluded from all legitimate groups in society (warrior, farmer, artisan, merchant), the hinin has no rights, can own no property, cannot appeal to the law for protection against any wrong suffered. He quite literally is assumed not to exist in society any longer. Such a fate for the highborn would be more galling than death or banishment.

8. Buddhist salvation and purity may be symbolized by the moon's rays.

SAKURA: I rejoice in your solicitude, yet having sinned I greet you in shame. Therefore, in the future your kindness cannot be accepted.

watarizerifu

SECOND MAID: How resolute you are. We are in your debt and wish to follow you . . .

THIRD MAID: . . . across the fields . . .

FOURTH MAID: . . . deep into the mountains . . .

MAIDS: . . . allow us, my Lady.

[*They rise to join* SAKURA.]

SAMURAI: Women, stand back!

CHIKŌ [*brings out small packet*]: Dear Master, I completely forgot. We, at Kiyomizu, have blessed this special medicine with ten-thousand prayers. Take it to use in perilous times to come, we beg you.

[*He pushes it toward* SEIGEN, *who picks it up wonderingly and puts it into the breast of his kimono.*]

SEIGEN: Homeless am I in the Three Worlds, of what use is medicine? My heart is crippled. I am grateful to you. Dear disciples. Do nothing more for me or you will be punished. Return to the temple.

PRIESTS: But, Master . . .

GENGO: Rise and leave. [PRIESTS *hesitate.*] Go!

CHIKŌ: If it is fated . . .

SEIGEN: . . . we shall meet again.

[Saigyo *melody resumes. The* PRIESTS *rise and exit left reluctantly.* TOWNSPEOPLE *enter from both sides of the stage, gawking at the sight of two criminals of high status put on public display. They laugh and poke at them. The* OUTCASTS *hold them back with poles. Music changes to lively* Hayame. NAGAURA *is pulled onto the* hanamichi *by* JŪSAKU, *a middle-aged peasant woman dressed in somber blue kimono and brown breeches. She carries* SAKURA's *baby, tightly wrapped.*]

JŪSAKU [*shrilly, angrily*]: I'm telling you to hurry up!

NAGAURA [*trying without success to break free*]: Don't go so fast.

JŪSAKU: Move!

NAGAURA: Please be more quiet.

JŪSAKU [*stopping at seven-three*]: Just like your name, you've got a big mouth, woman.[9] You badgered me to take the child, but you've paid me nothing.

NAGAURA: What can I do? I've no milk in my breasts. Ah, we're at the place my princess is to be exposed.

JŪSAKU: Then hurry.

[*Music continues as they cross onto the stage.* NAGAURA *is shocked to see* SAKURA's *appearance, but pretends that nothing has changed. Music ends.*]

NAGAURA [*bowing*]: Indeed, I consider myself fortunate to meet you here, noble Princess.

JŪSAKU [*disgusted*]: Stop the highfalutin court manners. Do you think

9. Nagaura means "long bay," suggesting a large mouth.

you're in heaven? If you'd a bit of feeling for the kid you'd have lived up to your agreement. But you didn't, so take him back.

[*Thrusts the child at* NAGAURA.]

NAGAURA: It's true I promised you money, but there is none as the child is illegitimate.

JŪSAKU [*looks shrewdly at* NAGAURA] : Hm, so that's it. I was sure you'd snitched the adoption money yourself. Well, Princess, she hasn't paid me. Are you going to? Let's have it now. Or I'll yank the kimono off your back and pawn it!

NAGAURA: Here. Stop that. Dearest Princess, since from today you're an outcast, I'm not your attendant and I can't raise the child. Now, it's best for you to take it. [*Chattering callously.*] Hugging an infant to your breast is a big part of your new trade. One infant carried on the back gains a man's sympathy and earns a silver coin. Our sort does it all the time.

share "With beggars and potatoes, young sprouts bring in money," they say.

[*The child cries.* NAGAURA *thrusts it at* SAKURA.]

Ah, ah, here it is. My, see how your breasts are still sticking out. It shows you are a true mother!

SAKURA [*recoils*] : I cannot, before the eyes of everyone. My lady Nagaura, it is for you . . .

NAGAURA [*impatiently*] : How can I take care of him? Without any money what can I do? He's yours, so squeeze him tight.

[*She forces the wailing child on the princess.* SAKURA *hesitantly opens the breast of her kimono to suckle it.*]

JŪSAKU: All right, you've got your kid back. Let's have the money you owe me.

FIRST MAID [*rising*] : As for the money, let us . . .

GENGO: Here, here. Get back. Stop her.

SAMURAI [*forces her down*] : Sit down!

NAGAURA: No matter what you say, there is no money. Will taking the kimono satisfy you?

JŪSAKU: Yes, yes.

[*They try to strip* SAKURA. GENGO *stops them.*]

GENGO: How can you help this farm woman and insult your mistress in this manner?

NAGAURA [*blandly*] : She's taking what's owed her.

GENGO: Old sow! A woman's a woman, but you're mad. [*To the* OUT-CASTS.] Move them back.

NAGAURA and JŪSAKU: Impertinent! She owes me!

SAMURAI [*pushing them into the crowd*] : Get back. Quickly!

NAGAURA and JŪSAKU: It's our right.

SAMURAI: Back, back, I say.

GENGO: Show mercy and those asking for mercy will be everywhere. Yet in what country is a woman suckling an infant turned out to beg? Ahh! Where has that infant of hers come from? Were it my own master, I'd not show mercy! Seigen, crawl before me like a dog and like a beast receive one hundred lashes of the cane in public view. Kneel!

semeba

[SEIGEN *bends forward. With obvious satisfaction,* GENGO *strikes* SEIGEN *on the back, each time to* batan tsuke *beats. The movements are rhythmic; the cane does not touch.* SEIGEN *collapses to the floor.*] Princess Sakura, though affianced to my Lord Akugorō you have sinned against him. Many are those who love lechery. Now I, Matsui Gengo Sadakage, will beat you in public until you ache to the marrow of your bones!

[OUTCASTS *pull* SEIGEN *upright.* GENGO *moves between the two prisoners. He alternately strikes* SEIGEN *and* SAKURA *to* batan tsuke *beats. They writhe in pain.* MAIDS *try to intervene;* SAMURAI *and* OUTCASTS *hold them back. To loud* bata-bata tsuke *beats,* SHICHIRŌ *rushes down the hanamichi and onto the stage. He forces* GENGO *back. They pose.* SHICHIRŌ *speaks as rapidly as he can, trying to rattle* GENGO.]

SHICHIRŌ: Gengo Sadakage, what does this mean! Striking your mistress!

GENGO: You know I am ordered to perform this duty. When it is my duty, Matsui Gengo strikes mercilessly even though I strike my mistress. Nothing will prevent me!

SHICHIRŌ: Ha, we know what you're doing. But you will never take over the Yoshida family which so loves the princess.

GENGO [*startled, but hiding his reaction*]: Ehh?

SHICHIRŌ: This is the act of a traitor. Gengo, you were in Kamakura, why act as if you know nothing of the turmoil in our clan?

GENGO: I'm concerned with just this internal matter: the princess' immorality.

SHICHIRŌ: Then one attached so closely should have known.

GENGO: Well . . .

SHICHIRŌ: Set aside the duty to beat your mistress you have just now been exercising so zealously.

GENGO: But, when the order has come from on high . . . ?

SHICHIRŌ: Didn't our clan superiors order us to be alert during this time of troubled succession?

GENGO: Yes, but . . .

SHICHIRŌ: And do you think beating your mistress is an act of loyalty?

kuriage

GENGO: Well . . .

SHICHIRŌ: Well . . . ?

[*They begin alternately, then speed up until they are speaking simultaneously.*]

GENGO and SHICHIRŌ: Well, well, well, well! Well!

[*They stand face to face, about to draw.* SHICHIRŌ *presses his bluff as far as he can.*]

SHICHIRŌ: You treat our lady inexcusably. You should kill yourself in shame. Apologize, or from this moment consider me your enemy, Gengo Sadakage!

GENGO [*blustering*]: You rant like a masterless samurai inviting death. I wish I could finish you now. But wash your neck clean; soon enough your head will roll. I shall report this to our superiors.

SHICHIRŌ: Do, and we'll see on whose neck the blade falls.

281 The Scarlet Princess of Edo

GENGO [*turning pale*] : Madman! [*To the* OUTCASTS.] The princess is not to leave this spot.

OUTCASTS: Yes, Sir.

GENGO: Unforgivable insult. Come!

[*Large drum plays* Toki no Taiko. GENGO *turns and goes off left, followed by* SAMURAI *and* OUTCASTS. *Music ends.*]

FIRST MAID: Ah, Master Shichirō, thank heaven you have come!

SHICHIRŌ [*now that* GENGO *is gone, he can express his true feelings*] : How can you women speak of thanks? My arguments may have parried Gengo's violence for a moment, but they can't restore our princess. [*To* SAKURA.] My Lady, although you must become a wandering outcast, recover the Miyakodori scroll so your house will flourish again . . .

SAKURA: Like the swirling shoals of the Izuka River, man's heart is change-able. I am ashamed I did not suspect Gengo's unfaithfulness to my brother's cause. I deserve punishment.

watarizerifu   FIRST MAID: Hearing your words our hearts are moved . . .

SECOND MAID: . . . they deeply pain us . . .

ALL: . . . my Lady.

SHICHIRŌ: Enough. Stop this chatter and return to the mansion.

MAIDS: Leave her alone? How pitiable.

SHICHIRŌ: Go back. You can't help our princess. Return to the curtained and scented beds of the palace. Princess, whatever the hardship of the future—wandering in the open, loitering at the margin of human society, spending nights wrapped in a rough straw mat—the enemy of your father and brother . . .

MAIDS: But . . .

SHICHIRŌ [*implacably*] : . . . must not be forgotten.

[*Shamisen play quiet* Saigyo. SHICHIRŌ *forces the protesting* MAIDS *off.* SHICHIRŌ *and* SAKURA *exchange a final look, then he turns and quickly follows the women.* SAKURA *and* SEIGEN *are left alone. A temple bell tolls in the distance.* SEIGEN *looks with ill-concealed rancor at* SAKURA *nursing the baby.*]

SEIGEN: Princess Sakura. Through what hatred did you connive to make me a criminal and turn me into a miserable beggar? The more I think of it, the more vile you are.

SAKURA [*meekly*] : Hearing your bitterness, what can I say? In brief, while living in Kitashirakawa a thief stole my heart. Though we spent but one night together, in my body lodged the seed of his love.

SEIGEN [*pained*] : So that is what happened. While I thought you came to Kiyomizu Temple seeking guidance as you fled the turmoil of the world into nunhood, in fact I was branded a criminal . . .

SAKURA: . . . unfairly by acts for which I deeply apologize. Through the power of your mercy the hand which for seventeen years had been closed by the King of Hades opened. Unknown to me the man who in different form had fathered my child that night in the capital, first appeared as

Akugorō's messenger then vanished, while the fallen incense box inscribed with the name Kiyoharu became proof of your guilt. Forgive me please.

SEIGEN: Ahh! In truth, the disaster of deceit. It is the punishment of Karma. Using my earthly name, Tonoinosuke Kiyoharu, I had loved several youths and then the young page Shiragiku, who abandoned his life in a pact of love that I through cowardice and want of compassion failed to fulfill. Now, the world turns and scorns us. For me, the spirit of dead Shiragiku . . . [*He looks passionately at* SAKURA].

How quickly, the Wheel of Karma . . . seventeen years . . .

SAKURA [*holding her baby tightly*] : What do you mean?

SEIGEN [*meaningfully*] : "Comfort mankind," is Buddha's command.

SAKURA [*frightened*] : Ehhh?

[SEIGEN *is about to approach her when* BANHACHI *suddenly appears. They eye him suspiciously and pull apart. He adopts a rough, jocular attitude as he drops to his haunches between them.*]

BANHACHI: Ha, ha! I suppose you're talking about the past, but nothing can bring that back. People say you and her didn't have the nerve to carry off a lovers' suicide. Look here, Seigen, you've been beaten and set out in public as a sinner. Face it, you're finished as a priest. But you could earn a piece of change here and there on the side. Can't you speak? [SEIGEN *shudders involuntarily.* BANHACHI *shrugs and turns to* SAKURA.]

Hey there, Princess. What about you? You're one of us but I can see you ain't cut out for the life of singing street beggar.[10] Ha, ha! You brought his honor down for a hell of a tumble. So why don't you go marry him and live together man and wife? That's the thing to do.

SAKURA: I have endured more in a single day than could be imagined, but to talk of marriage is beyond bearing.

[*She pulls away.* SEIGEN *is furious at* BANHACHI *for frightening* SAKURA *and disturbing his plans.*]

SEIGEN: Loathsome. Detestable. Such words defile Buddha's disciple. I will not listen. "Namu Amida Butsu, Namu Amida Butsu." [*He prays.*]

BANHACHI [*suddenly sympathetic*] : Ah, Master Seigen, you've got the wrong idea. It's all right if she's got two husbands. Let her take three husbands or five. Even for a princess it don't matter. These days that's the style. [*He slaps his thigh and laughs.*] I tell you, a shaved head don't suit you no more. Grow some hair and you're in business. It don't have to be down to your shoulders, you know. Ha, ha! [*He gets wine and offers a cup to* SAKURA.] Princess, serve your fallen husband a drink to start off your new lives as outcasts, like us. You know, Princess, I could get you two out of here. Slip enough cash my way, why I'd set you up as townsmen, or farmers, or whatever you want.

SAKURA [*anxiously*] : Do you say, even though we are under punishment . . .

10. *Onna taiyū*, wandering female jōruri singers, were reputed to be drawn mainly from among outcasts.

BANHACHI [*expansively*] : . . . I can get you out of this racket and back to
normal lives.

SAKURA: And we could lead normal lives away from this outcast group?

BANHACHI: That's what I said.

SAKURA [*bowing*] : Then I ask: please arrange it.

BANHACHI: And then you're a real beauty. I ain't had an upbringing, but
any man would take you out of here. I don't lie. Leave it to me. I'll dig
you up a patron quick enough. Now that I know, I'll dash off and get you
a husband, a lover. Wait right here. [*Contemptuously to* SEIGEN.]
Well, Reverend, ain't you the cold one. Just to spite you, I'll bring back a
fine husband if there's money in it. You'll be sorry when that time comes,
eh? A priest's a stubborn fool. Hey, Princess, soon you'll have all the
husbands you could want. Wait here. I'll be back soon.
[*Shamisen and hollow gourd play* Mokugyo, *"Gourd," as* BANHACHI
runs off down the hanamichi. SEIGEN *slowly opens his eyes. Seeing he is
alone with* SAKURA, *he slides close to her.*]

SAKURA [*humiliated and numb, she turns to* SEIGEN *for help*] : Reverend
Seigen, this existence is unbearable another moment. Save me from a
beggar's life.

SEIGEN [*feigning reserve*] : I wish I could, Princess, but how can a priest
dedicated to Buddha offer help to a woman? Were I but a samurai, as I was
before becoming a priest . . .

SAKURA: "Like the flow of a river, who can know where our wretched life
will end?" What will become of me in this fleeting world?

SEIGEN: Indeed, how exceptionally painful it must be for one who has been
delicately raised, protected even from the force of the winds. Here,
Princess Sakura, take this sacred medicine as protection for the struggles
ahead.
[*Pretending to be overwhelmed with sympathy for her, he presses the
medicine into her hands.*]

SAKURA [*bows prettily*] : Your offer of assistance is gratifying when it
would be but natural for you to feel resentment toward me. What thanks
can I . . .
[SEIGEN's *passion for the princess is becoming almost uncontrollable.
He pulls her close.*]

SEIGEN: Do not speak. A priest offers succor. Now I am guiltless, but seventeen years ago a White Chrysanthemum fell . . . Shiragiku.

SAKURA: Again, Shiragiku?

SEIGEN: The falling of a flowering chrysanthemum was Seigen's sin. The
world is shown my punishment, but nowhere in the world can forgiveness
for such a sin be found. But from this day the vows pledged by this fallen
priest in a former life to Shiragiku shall be yours . . . [*He seizes her hand.*]
. . . Princess Sakura!

SAKURA [*not understanding*] : I am unworthy of this sudden generosity.
How grateful I am. [*She bows.*]

SEIGEN: You make a depraved priest indescribably happy. Our lives are joined, and though I am a fallen monk, Princess, let us formally celebrate our marriage vows.

SAKURA [*amazed*] : What? You and I . . .

SEIGEN [*pleading*] : As a sign our hearts are united, when I give you my strength, though my body be buried in the earth, my spirit will find its way to you. A pillow shared one night binds us together in the afterlife. Dear Princess, do not fear.

SAKURA [*pulls away cautiously, hoping not to antagonize him*] : I am filled with joy knowing you wish to guard and protect this unworthy person, but as you know I have a child and so, to another man, I . . .
[*A dark figure appears behind the hut, half-hidden by the rushes.* SEIGEN *clings to* SAKURA.]

SEIGEN: You cannot refuse. You cannot. Do you doubt my love?

SAKURA: No. I do not, but . . .

SEIGEN: You do. In your presence then I renounce celibacy.
[*He rises to his knees, and in a frantic gesture tears in two his rosary. To batan tsuke beats he flings the pieces to the ground.*]

SAKURA: Your rosary . . .

SEIGEN: . . . as proof of my devotion, dispelling any doubts.
[*He passionately embraces her. The dark figure steps from the bushes, pushes them apart, takes the baby, and to batan tsuke beats, strikes a dynamic pose.*]

SAKURA [*holding his sleeve*] : My infant. How can you?

AKUGORŌ [*cruelly*] : Have you already forgotten your betrothed? I am Akugorō!
[*With a flourish, he takes off the black cloth covering his face.*]

SEIGEN [*relieved, thinking he means no harm*] : Ah, it is you, my Lord.

AKUGORŌ [*scornfully*] : Depraved sutra mumbler! Silence!
[*He poses. One shamisen plays* Sugomi, *"Horror," in the background.*]
I heard you promising yourself, abominable priest, to Princess Sakura. This puling infant you gave birth to, Princess, this bastard by an unknown man, will be hostage until you answer my proposal.
[*As if he would choke the baby.*]

SAKURA [*clinging to his arm*] : Can you be so heartless?

AKUGORŌ: Your reply then is . . . ?

SAKURA: My reply is . . .
[*Music stops.* SEIGEN *is frantic.*]

SEIGEN: No, no! Do not reply! I will protect you, Princess!

AKUGORŌ [*coldly furious*] : You dare stand in the way of my love? Black-robed, incense-smelling hypocrite!
[SEIGEN *tries to recover the child, but* AKUGORŌ *easily pushes him to the ground to batan tsuke beats. He puts his foot on the priest's back. The three pose.*]

SEIGEN: I am the cause . . .

SAKURA [*interceding*] : Reverend Seigen did not . . .

AKUGORŌ: I will decide Seigen's fate. The child will suffer, Princess. Accept my love, or . . .

[*The child cries as* AKUGORŌ *begins to twist its throat.*]

SAKURA: Please, my baby . . .

[*She clutches at the child. He shakes her off, then seizes her hand.*]

AKUGORŌ: Agh, this is tiresome. Come, Princess.

SEIGEN: You shall not . . .

AKUGORŌ: Troublesome priest!

tachimawari

[AKUGORŌ *kicks* SEIGEN *from under his foot to batan tsuke beats. Shamisen play fast* Hayame, *the large drum beats* Mizu Oto *water pattern, and batan and battari tsuke beats punctuate a brief struggle in pantomime.* SEIGEN *strikes at* AKUGORŌ *with his cane stick three times. Avoiding the blows,* AKUGORŌ *takes the stick from* SEIGEN *and jabs it into his stomach.* SEIGEN *sinks to the ground by the hut, gasping for breath.* AKUGORŌ *seizes* SAKURA *by the hand and draws her, struggling, into the outstretched arms of* SHICHIRŌ, *who rushes on from stage right. Music ends.*]

SHICHIRŌ: Iruma Akugorō!

AKUGORŌ: Shichirō! Out of my way!

SHICHIRŌ: Why you are dragging Princess Sakura, with her child . . . ?

AKUGORŌ: What of it?

SHICHIRŌ: The child, Lord Akugorō!

AKUGORŌ: Agh! This is tiresome!

[*Music resumes.* AKUGORŌ *rids himself of* SAKURA, *pushes* SHICHIRŌ *to one side, and to rapid bata-bata tsuke beats, rushes off right with the child.*]

SHICHIRŌ: Good god, what is he doing!

[SHICHIRŌ *pursues him.* SAKURA *tries to follow, but* SEIGEN, *on his knees, clings to her. Music ends.*]

SEIGEN: I won't let you, I won't let you leave Seigen for an unknown man's child.

SAKURA [*distraught and struggling*] : Your desires are not those of a disciple of the Lord Buddha. When I come back with my child I will reply. Until then, wait . . .

[SEIGEN *holds her fiercely.*]

SEIGEN: I understand that it is your child, but for you I have fallen into hell. Don't you see what you mean to me? My Dearest!

SAKURA: This is too much. The more you speak the more unreasonable you become. I must find my child. Let me go for just a moment.

SEIGEN: I will never let you go. You are trying to deceive me. [*Holds her tightly.*] After I have been disgraced, slandered in public, do you think I will let anything stand between us? Until you have shared my pillow, you will not leave my side by so much as an inch!

[*Music changes to* Sugomi *and* Mizu Oto. *As they struggle,* GENGO *runs between them, pushes* SEIGEN *to the ground, and seizes* SAKURA's *hand.*]

GENGO: Come, Princess. Lord Akugorō wants you at his mansion.

SEIGEN [*blocking their way*] : You shall not take her. You shall not! I will follow you . . .

[GENGO *forces* SEIGEN *to the edge of the river bank.* SEIGEN *loses his balance and, clutching wildly, grasps* SAKURA's *trailing kimono sleeve.* SAKURA *takes the opportunity to flee left, and her sleeve, held by* SEIGEN, *is ripped off. With a scream,* SEIGEN *falls into the river and disappears.* Mizu Oto *and tsuke beats crescendo.*]

GENGO [*gloating*] : Come, Princess!

[*Music continues.* SAKURA *fends off* GENGO. *A sharp ki clack signals the stage to revolve. To loud battari tsuke beats they pose in a strong mie, he stage right, she stage left by the hut, expressing unresolved opposition. As the stage turns and they disappear from sight, another part of the river bank comes dimly into view. Clouds obscure the full moon.* AKUGORŌ, *holding the child aloft, and* SHICHIRŌ, *arms wide, blocking his way, stand posed on the river bank. A sharp ki clack signals action to begin. Music changes to* Hayame Aikata *and* Mizu Oto. AKUGORŌ *and* SHICHIRŌ *leap down onto the main stage and pose in a strong mie to battari tsuke beats. They hold their poses as they speak.*]

AKUGORŌ: You won't have her bastard!

SHICHIRŌ: Even though it is Princess Sakura's child of shame I will have it!

[AKUGORŌ *tries to pass* SHICHIRŌ, *who in turn grasps the baby. They struggle for possession of the child, then to free their hands for fighting, place it up stage.* SHICHIRŌ *grasps* AKUGORŌ's *kimono lapels and accidentally discovers a letter tucked inside.*]

SHICHIRŌ [*holding* AKUGORŌ *at bay with one hand, reads*] : "To Matsui Gengo Sadakage, from Shinobu Sōta."

AKUGORŌ [*furious*] : Here!

SHICHIRŌ: I don't understand how this letter can be from Shinobu Sōta. The most wanted burglar and second-story man in the country writing a secret letter to Gengo Sadakage? Until this is explained . . .

AKUGORŌ: . . . you will be silent! Child! Pass the letter here!

SHICHIRŌ: Not until I've read it!

[*Music swells.* AKUGORŌ *snatches back the letter. The outcasts* OKE-SHICHI *and* ZUBUROKU *sneak up behind* SHICHIRŌ *and pinion his arms.*]

OKESHICHI: Good move, eh, Boss?

AKUGORŌ [*viciously*] : Dump him in the river!

ZUBUROKU: Got you!

OKESHICHI: Right, Boss!

tachimawari [*Music changes to* Zen no Tsutome. AKUGORŌ *looks at the letter, tucks it into his kimono and hurries off right.* SHICHIRŌ *breaks away. The* OUTCASTS *attack. He draws his sword and with two swift strokes kills them. They fall to the ground and roll offstage, "dead."* SHICHIRŌ *wipes the blade clean, then rushes after* AKGUORŌ. *The stage is empty. Music stops. Silence. Then a temple bell tolls.* Mizu Oto *water pattern swells; shamisen play forboding* Hayasanjū, *"Rapid Melody." To batan*

287 The Scarlet Princess of Edo

tsuke beats, a groping hand rises up from behind the river bank. SEIGEN, *disheveled and exhausted, pulls himself out of the river. Using a weeping willow tree for support, he poses in a mie to battari tsuke beats,* SAKURA's *rent kimono sleeve held fast between his teeth.*]

SEIGEN [*calls weakly*] : Princess. Princess Sakura. Flee, but you will not escape me. I am dissolute and disgraced because of you, sweet Princess. Where are you? Princess Sakura?

[*He stumbles toward the hanamichi. The baby cries.* SEIGEN *starts. Seeing the child on the ground, he crosses back.*]

What? Princess Sakura's child? Who could have abandoned it? It will soon be food for wild beasts if it is left here. [*Picks it up.*] You remind me, your father is my enemy. Yet you may lead me to Princess Sakura.

[*He carries the infant gently onto the hanamichi. He stumbles and falls at seven-three. A sharp ki clack. The bell tolls and the curtain is silently closed behind him. The baby cries.* SEIGEN *rises, looks at the child, notices* SAKURA's *sleeve and recalls her. He stifles a bitter sob.*]

Ahhh! Princess . . . Sakura!

[*Shamisen play soft* Kyōran, *"Demented Melody." Mizu Oto water pattern is heard in the background.* SEIGEN *looks into the distance, straining to see* SAKURA. *The baby wails. Moved by the baby's helpless cries, he jiggles the bright red kimono sleeve like a puppet to quiet the child, at the same time he looks anxiously about him for sign of the princess. Torn between caring for the child and rushing after* SAKURA, *he moves as quickly as he can. Drums and flute play spirited* Shagiri *between acts.*]

sanmakume

ACT III

SCENE 1   OSHIAGE VILLAGE STORE

[*The curtain is run open to* Daimoku Taiko, *"Prayer Drum" pattern, and accelerating ki clacks. The scene is a street on the edge of Oshiage Village near Edo. A small gate leads into trees and grass of a garden off right. On a large rock is painted "Buddha of Knowledge." In the center of the stage is an unpretentious country store selling locally gathered herbs, cakes, and sake. Sitting on camp stools before the store are three young men in plain kimono wearing two swords. They are low-ranking samurai:* KANGORŌ, KANZŌ, *and* GORŌJI. *Gambling, they shout for sake.* OSHIGE, *the wife of* GUNSUKE, *looks up from the charcoal over which she is roasting snails. A servant,* DOTESUKE, *bustles in carrying a dish of rice. Quickly he puts it down to refill their bottle from a wine barrel in the store. Local* VEN-DORS *of herbs and vegetables pass by hawking their wares. The samurai pay no attention, drunkenly calling for their wine.*]

KANGORŌ: Hurry up!

KANZŌ [*shaking his fist*] : Bring my drink!

GORŌJI: And get those snails roasted!

OSHIGE: I'll have them to you soon, Sir.

DOTESUKE [*fawning*] : Here we are, Sir. [*Pours wine.*] You're going fishing from the river dike, I suppose?

GORŌJI: Hmph, should we go fishing? Fresh river fish hit the spot.

KANGORO: I'd rather fish for Edo geisha.

GORŌJI: Not if we can't have wine.

[*They laugh and drink.* OSHIGE *brings the snails. She is dressed as a village woman, and is wearing a servant's apron.*]

OSHIGE: I'm sorry it took so long, but they're well done.

KANGORO: Good job. Here, Auntie, have a drink, eh? [*Offers cup to her.*]

OSHIGE [*waving it away*] : Thank you, Sir, but I can't drink.

KANGORO: Why's that? Because it's my cup, you won't drink?

OSHIGE [*bowing humbly*] : Oh, no, Sir. It's just that sake and I don't . . .

DOTESUKE [*foolishly*] : My, my, drink from their cup and thank them for it. Then have a sip from my cup, too! Hee, hee!

KANZŌ [*very drunk*] : Right. It's damned ill-bred to refuse a drink from a samurai. [*He turns away and drinks.*]

GORŌJI: Kangoro is softhearted. He might let you off, but I won't be trifled with. You can take a small cup if you want, Woman, but you'll drink!

[*He throws snails on the ground and thrusts a small cup at her.*]

OSHIGE: You are rude, Sirs, after I say I cannot, to insist.

KANZŌ: When we're drinking, you drink. It's an old story, Lady.

KANGORO [*picking up a large cup*] : We'll compromise then. Use this one.

OSHIGE [*losing patience*] : How annoying you are.

[*She is reprieved by the arrival, stage right, of* HANBEI, *to Daimoku Taiko music. He wears a dark kimono and the two swords of a samurai. A large wicker hat completely hides his face. He sits on a camp stool, brought forward by a* STAGE ASSISTANT.]

OSHIGE [*bowing*] : Welcome, Sir. Shall I bring a cup of tea?

[*She starts to cross to him.* KANGORO *pulls her back.*]

KANZŌ: Hey! He gets no tea until you drink!

OSHIGE: But he's a customer.

ALL: So are we.

OSHIGE [*smoothly*] : First the tea. [*Crosses to* HANBEI.] It is certainly a beautiful day. Tea, Sir?

HANBEI: If it is no trouble, please.

[Daimoku Taiko *resumes. She bustles off into the store.* SŌDOKU, *the village herb doctor, enters from the right. Music ends.*]

KANGORO: Welcome, Doctor, welcome.

SŌDOKU [*crosses and stands beside the samurai*] : Ah, Master Kangoro. You're having a picnic in the country, I see. Enjoy yourself.

KANZŌ: How can we? You've stopped seeing your patients. You've abandoned us.

SŌDOKU [*protesting*] : That's not so. I've just been too busy.

KANZŌ: What kind of doctor is too busy to see a sick man?

GOROJI [*sarcastically*] : They don't call you Doctor Poisoner for nothing.[11] The world must be full of fools that don't care if they live or die, to have you as their doctor.

SODOKU [*laughing it off*] : Goroji, you like to slander me. Talk about people throwing away their lives. I've heard a pretty story: in Kamakura they're searching for the adulteress Princess Sakura, who has escaped from her intended, Lord Iruma.

GOROJI: And that's not all. They say they're searching for young Prince Matsuwaka, who's on the run from some crime or other. Say, Kanzo! We'd be in for a big promotion if we captured those two. What do you think?

KANZO: There's no point in capturing them. The way a samurai rises in this world is by taking a few heads.

[HANBEI *listens intently.*]

But that's a remote possibility. Tell me about the girl, Sodoku. What did you find out? Hm?

SODOKU: Ah, the daughter of the masterless samurai? My boy, she stammers so you wouldn't believe it.

KANZO: I already know that. I told you it's not important.

SODOKU: Well, although she stammers, she's, ah, talented in writing calligraphy.

GOROJI [*scornfully*] : Who doesn't know that? Isn't her father a calligraphy teacher?

SODOKU: I've heard something about him. It seems he's recently engaged her to a samurai.

GOROJI: Damn. Then the rumor is true. Have you heard, Kanzo?

KANZO: What does it matter? He's penniless. If I insist, he can't refuse. Did you talk to him?

SODOKU: Until I was blue in the face. When he was sick the other day, I went to see him. [*Confidentially.*] I don't know if it's true or not, but they say he's taken a young fellow into the house.

KANGORO: Eh, a young man in the house?

KANZO [*face set*] : He is handsome?

SODOKU [*relishing the telling*] : Of course, I don't actually know if there is a young man or not, but the rumor is they're having an affair.

[HANBEI *starts.*]

SAMURAI [*together*] : They're what?

SODOKU: And something even more urgent: he's supposed to be her betrothed's younger brother!

KANZO: This youngster is making love to the girl, is he?

GOROJI: Then we should demand an answer immediately. Let's go, let's go.

DOTESUKE [*agreeably*] : I'll lead the way. And come back with some gossip.

SODOKU [*nervously*] : Don't repeat what I told you.

KANZO: Yes, I will, every word. Come along. Be our witness.

GOROJI: That's right.

11. Sodoku, literally, "source of poison."

SŌDOKU [*holding back*] : No, no. I don't like this. Take someone else.

KANZŌ: Come along.

[*They pull him protesting across the stage.*]

SŌDOKU: This is a bad joke, friends.

KANZŌ [*laughing*] : Come, I'll pay for your tea.

DOTESUKE [*bowing*] : Thank you, Sir, thank you.

GORŌJI: Let's go, let's go.

SŌDOKU: Listen to me. Take someone . . .

GORŌJI: You are coming with us. Sneak of a sawbones!

[*They pull him off right,* DOTESUKE *following, to* Daimoku Taiko *music.* OSHIGE *brings on an earthenware teapot. A* SERVANT GIRL *pours a cup of tea.*]

OSHIGE: I'm sorry. I've kept you waiting. Please drink a little.

HANBEI [*removes hat*] : Thank you. By the way, there is something I would like to ask. Do you know if a masterless samurai by the name of Yamada Gunjibei recently moved to these parts?

OSHIGE [*startled*] : Eh? How fortunate you should ask—I serve Master Gunjibei myself. He lives at Koume in Kawaramachi, where he teaches calligraphy.

HANBEI: Hmm. Did you say the respected Gunjibei teaches calligraphy . . . ?

OSHIGE: Yes, he does.

HANBEI: The pieces fit together.

[*He poses in thought.*]

OSHIGE: Eh?

HANBEI: Nothing. How does one go there?

OSHIGE [*cheerfully*] : Let me take you.

HANBEI: Your shop is open.

OSHIGE: The girl will take care of it. [*Cutting off his protest.*] Allow me to show the way. This way, please.

[*Shamisen play* Zaigō, *"Country District." A sharp clack of the ki signals the stage to revolve.* HANBEI *and* OSHIGE *pass through the gate and are carried out of sight.*]

SCENE 2   GUNJIBEI'S VILLAGE SCHOOL

[*As the stage revolves, an old village house with patched paper in the sliding doors comes into view. To the left is a small temple with white offertory paper hanging from the eaves. A sign outside the house reads, "Calligraphy Instruction: Yamada Gunjibei." On the inside wall hang small wooden boards on which names of pupils are written. In the center of the room white-haired* GUNJIBEI *sits behind a small desk, instructing* HANJŪRŌ, *younger brother of* HANBEI, *in recitation of the Confucian classics.* HANJŪRŌ *is dressed in the delicate, long-sleeved kimono of a noble youth.* KOHINA, *the teacher's young daughter, is teaching writing to* OFUMI, *a village pupil. Both girls wear bright, long-sleeved kimonos. A clack of the ki, and action begins.*]

OFUMI [*reciting as she writes*] : " 'Will you take me flower viewing, to see the cherry trees blooming on the banks of the Sumida River?'[12] I entreated again and again.''

GUNJIBEI [*reading formally*] : "Succeed through righteous conduct, may your name live in posterity, honor your parents—this is the sum of virtue."

HANJŪRŌ: "Be obligated first to your parents, second to your superiors, and last to yourself."

OFUMI [*turning the page and copying*] : "I am grateful to have received your recent letter."

GUNJIBEI: For some time now, you have done nothing but study, Hanjūrō . . . [*He coughs.* HANJŪRŌ *and* KOHINA *move quickly to his side.*]
No, don't bother about me. This old illness is nothing.

HANJŪRŌ: We are worried, Master, it comes back so strongly.

KOHINA [*stuttering*] : H-H-Hanjūrō is right. Here, l-l-let me.[13] [*She rubs his back.*]

GUNJIBEI: Ah, Daughter. I wish I knew why the cough recurs; perhaps because I am growing old, perhaps it's the spring weather. Ah. It's annoying to be ill.
[GUNJIBEI *rests.* HANJŪRŌ *ladles a cup of hot water and brings it to his master.* OFUMI *continues her lesson. Shamisen play* Tentsutsu, *"Hurried Entrance," as* DENROKU, *a village official, enters on the hanamichi, carrying a cloth-wrapped package.* GUNSUKE, *wearing a townsman's heavy cotton kimono tucked up at the waist and a plain cotton cloak, comes on after him. Paper umbrellas tied to a pole are slung over his shoulder in the manner of a peddler. They stop at seven-three.*]

GUNSUKE: What are you carrying there, Denroku?

DENROKU: Wanted pictures of two fugitives came from the government today. I'm showing them around the village.

GUNSUKE: Fugitives, eh? [*He poses. Solicitiously.*] It's a nuisance being an official. Where are you going now?

DENROKU: Straight to your place.

GUNSUKE [*casually, to cover his surprise*] : To my place? That is a bother, isn't it?
[*They cross to the entry gate.*]
Please go in. I'm home, Master.
[*They go in and sit before* GUNJIBEI. *Music stops.*]

HANJŪRŌ: You're back soon, Gunsuke.

KOHINA [*stammering*] : W-will you have some t-tea?

GUNSUKE: That's kind of you.

GUNJIBEI: It looks as if you've come home with as many umbrellas as you went out to sell. I take it you didn't reach the market?
[GUNSUKE *notices* DENROKU *looking suspiciously at the closed doors. He decides to tell a tale to distract* DENROKU's *attention.*]

shikatabanashi   GUNSUKE: That's right. I was on my way there, Master, with the batch of umbrellas I'd just made, when, crossing Big River Bridge, I happened to

---

12. An obvious reference to the Sumida River World and Princess Sakura (Cherry).
13. It is characteristic of Namboku to depart from the usual and make Kohina, a gentle and sympathetic character, a stutterer.

share

glance to the north and there were thunder clouds piling up like mountain peaks. A moment later the rain came pouring down. My umbrellas were to sell, not to use, so I turned tail and ran straight back. It's funny, isn't it—to run from the rain carrying a bundle of umbrellas over your shoulder? I guess there's plenty of funny business in the world. Ha, ha, ha!

[*He glances meaningfully at* GUNJIBEI.]

GUNJIBEI [*smiling*]: Indeed. Who should bother buying an umbrella if even the umbrella seller is driven home soaking wet by the rain? Ha, ha! [*Cautiously.*] Now, Denroku, what brings you to my humble house?

DENROKU: I have come with a government notice.

GUNJIBEI: What kind of notice?

DENROKU: Warning of two fugitives. Please look at their pictures.

[*He opens the cloth-wrapped package and takes out two sketches.* GUNJIBEI *puts on spectacles to inspect them.*]

GUNJIBEI: These are the fugitives? [*He reads.*] "Princess Sakura." "Prince Matsuwaka."

[DENROKU *cranes his neck, trying to peer into the room left.* GUNJIBEI *gives no indication that he has observed him.*]

GUNSUKE [*considering*]: Is that so? These pictures are of Princess Sakura and Prince Matsuwaka, wanted by the authorities?

GUNJIBEI: But is it not so that they are fugitives due to the slander which Iruma and his men have brought to the Emperor's ears?

HANJŪRŌ: If so, then my brother Hanbei and this matter . . .

[*He looks at the two older men and pauses.*]

GUNSUKE [*flaring*]: And so you've come to see if the two criminals are here in this house?

DENROKU [*hastily*]: Not at all. You teach boys and girls here. What if the fugitive youngsters suddenly were to show up and try to become your pupils. That's why I came.

GUNJIBEI: I am relieved. And the pictures?

DENROKU: I will leave them here. Guard them carefully.

GUNJIBEI [*coldly polite*]: I am sorry for the trouble I have caused you.

[*Shamisen resumes* Tentsutsu. *Acutely uncomfortable,* DENROKU *bows and hurries off right. The three men sit morosely, as shamisen continue in the background.*]

GUNSUKE: They will press the search vigilantly, Master.

GUNJIBEI [*sadly*]: My error was slight, yet I was dismissed from rank, forced to live with my daughter as a vagabond. My only happiness has been thinking of the time when the flower would blossom, but each day I grow older and, though my daughter is fairly attractive, her stammering remains as it was at birth. [*Sighs.*] Your brother Hanbei has betrothed her, such is his virtue . . .

[GUNJIBEI *breaks off, unable to continue. Music stops.* HANJŪRŌ *bows respectfully.*]

HANJŪRŌ: This dismissed samurai's only excuse for living here, half-student, half-refugee, dependent on your kindness is that family connection.

GUNSUKE [*near tears*]: The efforts of a worthless retainer have not prevented misfortune from overwhelming my masters. The thin ribs of the umbrella break under the strain.

GUNJIBEI: Old ribs crack . . .

GUNSUKE: . . . yet we hardly eke out a living.

[*A bell tolls eight times. GUNJIBEI rouses himself and smiles for KO-HINA.*]

GUNJIBEI: Is it two o'clock so soon? Spring days pass by so quickly. Daughter, the children may go home.

[*Shamisen resume* Zaigō. *GUNJIBEI rises and enters the small room left. KOHINA turns and calls to the children, embarrassed at having to speak.*]

KOHINA: I-it is t-t-two o'clock, ch-children.

[*Three or four BOYS and GIRLS run excitedly out of the inner room. They arrange writing cases and scrolls for carrying.*]

FIRST BOY: Two o'clock, two o'clock! I'm going straight to Kawarasaki Theater to see kabuki. Who's coming with me? I'll buy rice cakes when we go through Kobiki. I'll buy but afterward you pay me back. Or I'll tell your fathers!

SECOND BOY: All you do is eat. You shouldn't speak that way. Pay your respects.

FIRST GIRL [*bowing*]: We'll come tomorrow, Miss Kohina.

FIRST BOY: I could eat an actor's crest, I'm so hungry.

OFUMI [*innocently*]: Whose crest would you eat?

FIRST BOY: Danjūrō's. It's three rice boxes![14]

OFUMI: But . . . but . . .

share FIRST BOY: It's the end of everything when a girl says "butt." How's yours, Ofumi? Ha, ha!

OFUMI [*hurt and angry*]: You've a filthy mouth.

FIRST BOY: I'll make yours just as dirty.

[*He paints OFUMI's lips black with his writing brush, as others hold her down. All the children bow and run off. OFUMI follows, crying. GUN-SUKE notices paint on one of the umbrellas and picks it up.*]

GUNSUKE: They've spattered paint on the umbrella. Children. Such foolishness.

[*He washes the paint off with a ladle of water and places the opened umbrella in the entry to dry. KOHINA picks up SAKURA's picture and shows it to HANJŪRŌ.*]

KOHINA: It p-pains to think of the p-princess s-suffering so.

HANJŪRŌ: My brother, too, suffers. He left me here because he must wander looking for her.

[*The two look sadly at the picture. GUNSUKE moves to the temple left.*]

GUNSUKE [*to himself*]: You are right. The princess is being hounded from one end of the country to the other because she happens to be engaged to

14. A joke alluding to Danjūrō's family crest, which was prominently displayed on the kimono he wore in every role, including Hanbei in this scene.

Lord Akugorō. While inside this country temple dedicated to the spirit of the plum . . .[15]

GUNJIBEI [*from inside*]: Gunsuke. I need you a moment, Gunsuke.

GUNSUKE: Yes, Master, I am coming.

[*Shamisen play* Goshiki, *"Five Colors". With a quick glance at the temple, he enters the main room and goes through the doors to GUNJIBEI's room.*]

KOHINA [*slowly, with great effort*]: I-it is heartb-breaking, not t-to speak, a c-cripple like the p-princess, whose m-misery, I-I would g-gladly lighten, exchanging my w-worthless l-life, for h-hers. To your b-brother Hanbei, I w-write . . .

[*Resolutely she rises, gets the open umbrella, and writes a poem on it. HANJŪRO takes the umbrella and reads.*]

waka

HANJŪRO: "Flower of youth broken, trailing sleeve torn asunder, of what matter now are the unjust assaults of the wind and the falling rain?" Your meaning is not certain, unless . . . you intend to sacrifice . . .

[KOHINA *covers her face and bows low.*]

KOHINA: Yes.

[HANJŪRO *looks at her with deep admiration and sympathy.*]

HANJŪRO: Kohina. You are indeed gentle and tenderhearted.

[*She weeps silently. Soon his lips tremble, and tears flow down his cheeks.*]

CHORUS [*sings* Tada Uta, *"Plain Song," offstage*]:
The pine tree in the midst of
    Wisteria blossoms.

[*During the song,* OSHIGE *guides* HANBEI *onto the hanamichi. They stop at seven-three.*]

OSHIGE [*pointing*]: The house is there, Sir.

HANBEI: Please lead the way.

OSHIGE: Yes, Sir.

[*Shamisen play* Tada Aikata, *"Plain Melody," in the background. They cross to the main stage. She opens the gate and ushers him in.*]

OSHIGE: Come in, don't be formal.

HANBEI: If I may. Thank you.

[HANBEI *removes his hat and moves left to the place of honor in the main room. Music stops.*]

HANJŪRO [*amazed*]: Brother Hanbei, why are you . . . ?

[*Recovering, he bows in greeting.*]

HANBEI [*cold and formal*]: I apologize for not writing. [*Bows formally to* KOHINA.] Kohina, I trust your father is well.

KOHINA [*flustered and embarrassed*]: Y-y-yes . . . [*She bows to cover her confusion.*]

15. A reference to *The House of Sugawara.* After death, Lord Sugawara's spirit lived on as a plum tree and a temple was dedicated to it.

HANBEI [to OSHIGE] : I offer apologies for the trouble that looking after my younger brother must have caused you. I acted inexcusably.

OSHIGE [waving off the apology] : Goodness, we've done nothing. As you saw, I run a store, and my husband has a side job, when we're not helping the master here. Its been no trouble to take the boy.

HANJŪRŌ [eager to have news from his brother] : Hanbei, have you heard about them searching for Princess Sakura?

HANBEI [coldly] : I have heard the story. And others as well.

[The brothers' eyes meet. HANBEI's anger is apparent; HANJŪRŌ is hurt, not knowing what is wrong. They pose.]

Now, is your master at home? Is he?

HANJŪRŌ [trying to please his brother] : Yes, Brother. He is inside. I will . . .

GUNJIBEI [from inside] : No. I will come.

[Shamisen play Tada Aikata as GUNJIBEI enters from center stage. He has changed to formal samurai costume and carries a samurai's two swords. HANBEI moves right, so GUNJIBEI can sit in the place of honor, left.]

Ah, Inanoya Hanbei. I am glad you look well. [He bows.]

HANBEI [bows formally] : It is a source of joy to find you unchanged. I cannot sufficiently express my gratitude for the care you have given my younger brother during the time I have been searching for banished Princess Sakura. It was too much to have expected.

GUNJIBEI [protesting] : Don't say such formal things. You're too polite for the man who asked, in spite of her infirmity, to marry my daughter.

[Turning to OSHIGE angrily.] Where's his tea? What are you thinking of?

OSHIGE [bowing repeatedly] : How rude of me. Immediately.

GUNSUKE [already filling a cup] : Yes, Master. Tea for Master Hanbei.

HANBEI: It is not necessary.

[As GUNSUKE serves the tea, HANBEI sees him for the first time.]

Now you are in service here?

GUNSUKE [bowing politely] : Gunsuke, sir. With my wife I now serve former samurai Gunjibei.

HANBEI: This woman is your wife?

[Indicating OSHIGE, who bows low.]

GUNSUKE: My better half, Sir. Ha, ha! As you can see, our master lives in a poor way and we do what we can to help. She peddles wine and snacks by the roadside, a penny a swallow. I have my handiwork. I make umbrellas.

[Takes umbrella and hands it proudly to HANBEI.]

HANBEI: You do this for a living? [He sees the poem and reads.] "Flower of youth broken, trailing sleeve torn asunder, of what matter now are the unjust assaults of the wind and the falling rain?"

GUNJIBEI [looking carefully] : Hm. Isn't it Kohina's writing?

HANJŪRŌ [hesitantly, but wanting to tell the truth] : Yes, Kohina, a few minutes ago . . .

GUNJIBEI [surprised] : . . . scribbled on the umbrella?

HANJŪRŌ: As I was looking on.

HANBEI [his face tightens] : Kohina's poem, shown to my brother? A clever piece of work.

[*He closes the umbrella and poses strongly, as the others watch, unsure of his meaning.*]

GUNSUKE [*lightly scolding*] : And the result is—one umbrella wasted!

GUNJIBEI [*severely*] : You should be ashamed of yourself, when you know how hard we work to earn a living. [*Seeing KOHINA's downcast face, his anger turns to concern.*] Now, Daughter, don't be embarrassed. Come, come, address your affianced properly.

KOHINA [*stammering, as her father leads her by the hand*] : I-I-I . . .

GUNJIBEI [*deprecatingly*] : Do you see, Hanbei? Ha, ha! She is like a little child.

[*He stands looking down at her. Tears of love and sadness come to his eyes. She kneels beside HANBEI, bowing her face to the floor, ashamed and confused.*]

HANBEI [*deliberately formal*] : In that you are mistaken. Though young in years, perhaps, she writes in a superb hand. To an unlettered man such as myself, the precise import of her poem is unclear, yet, one thing is certain. It is a love poem.

GUNJIBEI [*kneeling*] : Oh?

HANBEI : From the poem's intent it is clear your daughter is a talented writer. The lines relate to each other most skillfully.

GUNJIBEI [*bowing*] : Is that so? A father is grateful to hear words of praise for his daughter. I thank you.

HANBEI [*still coldly formal*] : Your words are gracious.

[*The bell tolls seven times.*]

Is it four already? It will soon be evening.

HANJŪRŌ : Are you leaving already then, Brother?

HANBEI : Do you ask when I leave because you want me to go? However, before dusk sets in . . .

[*The others gasp. HANJŪRŌ bows to cover his humiliation.*]

GUNJIBEI [*protesting*] : It's been so long. Let us drink together.

HANBEI : That is not necessary.

GUNSUKE [*eagerly*] : Have a long talk. Besides it looks like rain. Why don't you spend the night, Master Hanbei?

OSHIGE : The very thing, though we have nothing to offer except some soup. Husband, get . . .

GUNSUKE [*quickly*] : I know. Get wine.

GUNJIBEI : Excellent, excellent. For my daughter's sake let us drink to your engagement.

[*GUNSUKE stops in the entry to watch.*]

HANBEI : You show the solicitude of the old. In that case, I will stay a while longer.

GUNJIBEI [*warmly*] : Daughter. Hanjūrō. Show him to the small sitting room.

HANJŪRŌ [*warmly*] : I shall. This way, Brother.

HANBEI [*formally*] : With your permission, Father-in-law.

GUNJIBEI : Son-in-law.

OSHIGE : Husband!

GUNSUKE : I know! The wine!

[*Shamisen play* Tada Aikata. GUNJIBEI *and* HANBEI *bow to each other.* HANBEI *rises and is escorted through the sliding doors upstage by* HANJŪRŌ *and* KOHINA. OSHIGE *follows closing the doors after them.* GUNSUKE *goes out through the gate to buy wine.* GUNJIBEI *sits alone, deep in thought.*]

GUNJIBEI: For months Hanbei has not visited nor has he sent word. Suddenly he appears today. I wonder.

[*To* Daimoku Taiko *music* KANZŌ, KANGORŌ, GORŌJI, SŌDOKU, *and* DOTESUKE *come into view on the hanamichi, talking animatedly.*]

DOTESUKE: Ah, there it is.

KANGORŌ: Over there?

KANZŌ: This is going to be fun.

KANGORŌ [*laughing*] : I'll play the drums.

KANZŌ: Hello, hello! Anybody home?

[*Without waiting to be invited, they open the door and stand in the entry.* GUNJIBEI *overlooks their rudeness and greets them politely.*]

GUNJIBEI: Ah, are neighbors visiting my poor house? Please, please, sit up here.

KANGORŌ [*sitting casually in the entryway*] : Never mind. This is fine.

GORŌJI: Any place is the same to me, but as long as we have to sit somewhere, let's go where the mat is cleaner.

[*He moves into the room and sits.*]

KANZŌ [*following*] : Do you have to be rude? [*Smiling.*] Gunjibei, my friends and I have seen you many times, but we've never spoken. I am Ushijima Kanzō. [*Bows.*]

KANGORŌ [*bows*] : Ishihama Kangorō.

GORŌJI [*bows*] : And Imado Gorōji here . . .

ALL: . . . make your acquaintance.

GUNJIBEI: My, my, what fine introductions. Yes, I've seen you about, but I'm an old man and didn't ask who you were. What can I do for you?

KANZŌ: Old Gunjibei, answer the question the doctor asked you the other day.

GUNJIBEI: Do you mean about my daughter?

KANZŌ: Yes. You've put off an answer. Tell me now: yes or no?

KANGORŌ [*harshly*] : We're his friends and we've come to see . . .

GORŌJI: . . . he's satisfied. So, Gunjibei . . .

KANZŌ: . . . we'll have the girl now!

GUNJIBEI [*politely, composed*] : Well, well. Everything else aside, asking for her hand does me great honor, as she is the daughter of a fallen samurai. I thank you from the bottom of my heart. [*He bows formally.*] But, it happens she is engaged.

KANZŌ: Who's the man?

GUNJIBEI: His name is Inanoya Hanbei, like myself a former samurai.

KANZŌ [*scathingly*] : Old man! I may not be a great lord, but I'm a samurai intimate with the government in Kamakura. Don't get angry, but how can a teacher of scribbling make a living with a worthless dismissed samurai living in his house as son-in-law? Better me, than him.

KANGORŌ [*picking the umbrella up disdainfully*] : Look. He lives by covering the ribs of old umbrellas. What's this? A poem?

[GUNJIBEI *tries to retrieve the umbrella, but* KANZŌ *snatches it and reads.*]

KANZŌ: I see, I see. Just what this means I don't know. [*Menacingly.*] But we know a former samurai is trying to help the fugitive princess. It had better not be your daughter's man, or you're in trouble. And now this poem written on an umbrella . . . strange, isn't it, Friends?

KANGORŌ: Think about it, old man.

GUNJIBEI [*protesting*] : You are ill-mannered and you speak nonsense. If a former samurai becomes the son of a former samurai, that should trouble no one. I will thank you to leave without another word. As far as my daughter is concerned, I forbid her to see you.

KANZŌ [*pale with anger*] : You refuse?

GUNJIBEI [*setting his jaw*] : I do.

KANZŌ: You have humiliated a samurai. Whatever you say, I'll have Kohina. Break in and get her!

[*They start to enter.* GUNJIBEI *rises and blocks their way.*]

GUNJIBEI: Do you dare break into my house?

KANZŌ: I won't be trifled with. Do you understand!

[*The two friends pin* GUNJIBEI's *arms, as* KANZŌ *rushes inside. He returns, pulling* KOHINA *by the hand.*]

GUNJIBEI: Such flagrant rudeness, to force my daughter . . .

[*They start to leave.* GUNJIBEI *blocks their way but is pushed aside.* HANBEI *rushes in. He throws* KANZŌ *to the floor and puts his arm protectively around* KOHINA. *They pose.*]

HANBEI: If you move I'll cut you to pieces.

KANZŌ, KANGORŌ, GORŌJI [*comically*] : Ahh! This is the son-in-law?

HANBEI [*eyes blazing*] : Though I'm not a samurai now, I still know how to fight. Do you come here wearing a samurai's swords to dishonor a samurai's daughter? Well? What has she done to deserve this? I'm her husband. Make me your opponent. Well? Do I fight the three of you?

KANZŌ: Ha, ha, if you are Kohina's husband, my friends and I made a mistake.

GORŌJI [*quickly*] : Yes, yes. We were drunk. Bad wine caused bad judgment.

DOTESUKE [*sputtering*] : What? I'm to blame? You're heartless.

KANZŌ: We didn't know you were the affianced . . .

HANBEI: . . . of Kohina. Well I am.

[*The three look at each other and nod in agreement. Afraid to use their swords on* HANBEI, *they mask their cowardice behind insults and innuendo.*]

KANZŌ: Isn't it a sight? A splendid husband, like Buddha, so loving to his bride . . .

KANGORŌ: . . . he cannot see the worm in the apple. A young worm . . .

GORŌJI: . . . with long locks . . .

HANBEI: . . . which has . . .

share KANZŌ [*insolently*] : . . . wormed its way into a soft heart that writes suspicious words on an old worm-eaten umbrella! Ha, ha, ha!

[*With a flourish he holds up the umbrella and points to the poem.*]

GORŌJI: Think about it. You'll see the connection between a deposed samurai, Yamada Gunjibei . . .

DOTESUKE [*eyes wide with horror*] : . . . and the House of Yoshida? Can it be?

GORŌJI: Truly, the princess and the prince . . .

HANBEI: What do you say!

share KANZŌ [*foolishly*] : Prints of kabuki will be good . . .

ALL: . . . for New Year's gifts.

[Daimoku Taiko *music resumes.* DOTESUKE *rushes off frightened. The three samurai put on their sandals and swagger noisily outside. At seven-three they hold a whispered conference.* KANZŌ *and* KANGORŌ *exit down the hanamichi talking loudly,* GORŌJI *slips back through the gate and hides in the bushes by the house. Music ends.*]

GUNJIBEI [*kneeling, bows contritely*] : I apologize for their unspeakable actions.

HANBEI [*sitting left in the place of honor*] : Drunken loiterers cause disturbances. It cannot be helped. However, there is something I wish to say as your son-in-law. Could someone overhear?

GUNJIBEI [*surprised*] : Besides ourselves, there is no one. Ah, yes. Gunsuke's wife. [*Turns and claps twice.*] Oshige. Come here a minute.

[*Shamisen play* Goshiki. HANJŪRO *and* OSHIGE *enter from the center sliding doors and sit to the right of* GUNJIBEI. *Music softens.*]

HANJŪRO [*bowing*] : Is there anything I can do?

OSHIGE: Did you call, Master?

GUNJIBEI: As you know, everyday I pray for long life before the image of Fudō. I have a guest today. Please pray for me, Oshige.

OSHIGE: What if, while I am gone . . . ?

GUNJIBEI [*somberly*] : Our needs can be satisfied by my daughter.

OSHIGE: Yes, Master.

[*She bows, rises, and crosses to the door. Aware that something is wrong, she turns and looks meaningfully at* KOHINA. *Slowly* KOHINA *meets* OSHIGE's *gaze.*]

Take care, Kohina. Of your father. Of your guest. Of . . . Hanjūro. Remember, take care.

[*With the slightest of nods,* KOHINA *indicates assent. They pose.*]

GUNJIBEI: Haven't you left yet?

OSHIGE [*bowing quickly*] : I am going, Master.

[*Shamisen continue* Goshiki. OSHIGE *looks behind her once more, then swiftly goes out the gate and off right. Music stops.*]

GUNJIBEI [*with great dignity*] : There are no listening ears. Anything now . . .

HANBEI: . . . may be said. Come here, Hanjūrō.

HANJŪRŌ [*bowing*] : Yes, Brother.

> [HANJŪRŌ *crosses and sits next to his brother.* HANBEI *looks coldly ahead.*]

HANBEI: The fact is, you have made love secretly to Kohina, my betrothed.

HANJŪRŌ [*overwhelmed, scarcely able to speak*] : How can you think . . . ?

KOHINA [*tries desperately to speak*] : W-w-what? I-I-I . . . ?

HANBEI [*cutting their protests short*] : Naturally, Brother, you do not admit it. But you, Gunjibei, know it is true.

GUNJIBEI [*prepared for unpleasant news, he is nonetheless shocked*] : Father and daughter, we share this house from morning to night. She speaks of nothing but her happiness that you care for her and are to be her husband. Your brother, too, shows only joy that you will marry. You cannot believe these two have . . . been immoral.

HANBEI: I have proof.

GUNJIBEI [*starting*] : What?

HANBEI: The poem written on the umbrella. Look.

GUNJIBEI: What? The poem, my daughter wrote . . . ?

KOHINA: . . . o-on the u-umbrella, is . . . ?

HANJŪRŌ [*bowing strongly*] : . . . no proof, my Brother.

HANBEI [*reading*] : "Flower of youth broken, trailing sleeve torn asunder, of what matter now are the unjust assaults of the wind and the falling rain?"

KOHINA [*near tears*] : In p-p-place of the p-princess . . .

HANBEI: No. It is a love poem.

KOHINA [*looking at him with fright*] : Eh?

HANBEI [*gravely*] : Read the poem carefully. It tells of Kohina's secret love. Without doubt "flower of youth broken" means she has given herself to a man. And, having transgressed, she flaunts her disdain of being discovered and "unjustly assailed." You see this, do you not, Gunjibei?

KOHINA: B-but w-w-why d-do y-you t-t-think . . . ?

GUNJIBEI: Dear Kohina, be calm. I know it would be impossible for you to be wicked with Hanjūrō.

HANBEI [*relentlessly*] : No, Father-in-law, you are wrong. It is true Kohina and I did not exchange betrothal cups of wine, but nonetheless she is my wife. Precisely because she lived with her father, I allowed my younger brother near her. Yet they have shamed us both. Gunjibei, this is hard for an old man to hear, but I must speak: if they go unpunished, you and I are not samurai and we should rip open in shame our old, wrinkled bellies. Inanoya Hanbei cannot hold up his head as a samurai. Can you?

GUNJIBEI: Let me question my daughter. If I find no grounds for suspicion, your honor and mine will be restored. And if you question your brother . . .

HANBEI [*nods firmly*] : I shall. Hanjūrō, you have heard: you have humiliated your elder brother, made a mockery of his life as a samurai. The truth! Speak!

HANJŪRŌ: Brother Hanbei, your words come from a hardened heart. It is true I might at some time commit some wrong. But can you believe I would act improperly toward Kohina . . . your betrothed, my brother's wife? Kohina, you are wrongly accused. Upset and in haste it is doubly hard for you to speak, I know.

[*Takes a scroll, opens it, and places it in front of her. He opens a writing box and places it beside the scroll.*]

But you can write, "I have done nothing." Here.

KOHINA [*taking the brush*] : I-I-I . . .

[*She writes on the back of the scroll.*]

HANBEI [*scornfully*] : Spew out whatever lies you like. I've known your transgressions a long time.

[*He deliberately jars her arm with his closed fan. The writing is smeared and she tries to correct it.*]

Kohina, you can cry and you can sob, but do you think you can make a fool of your husband by scribbling on the back of a scroll falsehoods from the back of your mind?

[*He jars her arm. Again the writing is smeared and she tries to correct it.*]

I discover you are an imbecile. You smear my honor as you smear this scroll.

[KOHINA *cries out in frustration. She rips the scroll to pieces, then, frightened by her rashness, sobs.*]

HANJŪRŌ [*to* KOHINA] : What can I say to dispute my elder brother's words? I am filled with pity for you, Kohina. You are blameless, yet because we two have been close friends, are the same age and have similar tastes, people imagine we have been indecent. It is a terrible joke but natural.

HANBEI [*ruthlessly cutting in*] : And because your licentiousness is common gossip, your brother's honor is defiled. Since you won't admit your sin, as a warrior should, must your brother cut open his belly?

HANJŪRŌ: Brother, you would . . . ?

HANBEI [*rising on one knee and looking into* HANJŪRŌ's *eyes*] : If you think killing myself would be regrettable, confess your sin.

HANJŪRŌ [*stuggling to reply*] : This is cruel. Absolutely nothing has . . .

HANBEI: You deny it?

HANJŪRŌ: On my oath to Buddha.

HANBEI: Hide it, and I end my life.

HANJŪRŌ: Brother, you are rash.

HANBEI: Then will you admit your guilt?

HANJŪRŌ: My guilt . . . ?

HANBEI: If not, I kill myself.

HANJŪRŌ: Brother!

HANBEI [*agonized*] : Do you force your elder brother to throw away his life? Will you not absolutely confess your guilt?

[HANJŪRŌ *bursts into tears.* GUNSUKE *returns from the store with a bottle of wine; as he looks in the gate he immediately senses the situation. He puts the bottle down and moves outside the gate where he listens unseen.*]

HANJŪRŌ: Tears cannot help. If, when I explain I am blameless, you say you will commit suicide, then, though I am not at fault . . .

HANBEI [*forcefully*] : Do you admit your impropriety with Kohina?

HANJŪRŌ [*eyes downcast*] : Though I have not sinned . . .

KOHINA [*trying one final time to speak*] : W-wait, then I-I t-t-too . . . !

HANBEI [*caustically*] : My bad name is already known.

KOHINA: A-and so y-you . . . ? It's u-u-unfair . . .

HANJŪRŌ [*quietly*] : The world's evil is heard a thousand miles. Since you heard that I have sinned, then I must be . . . guilty.

[*He drops his head and cries.*]

KOHINA [*frantically*] : It's a l-lie, Hanjūrō!

HANBEI: There. His confession is before you, Father.

GUNJIBEI [*grief-stricken, he looks at* KOHINA] : Though the wedding cups were never exchanged, a samurai's word is his oath. And now that their guilt is proven . . . ?

[*He looks at* HANBEI *and poses.*]

migawari   HANBEI [*with no outward sign of emotion*] : I shall execute my brother.

GUNJIBEI [*falls back in alarm*] : Ahh!

[*They all pose. In a single movement* HANBEI *draws his sword and stands.* HANJŪRŌ *looks at his brother, then quietly clasps his hands together in prayer, closes his eyes, and leans forward slightly, offering his neck to* HANBEI's *blade.*]

HANBEI [*almost inaudibly*] : As I expected.

HANJŪRŌ [*surprised*] : What?

[*A sudden look of understanding passes between the brothers.* HANJŪRŌ *composes himself and with one blow* HANBEI *strikes off his head. A* STAGE ASSISTANT *places a prop head beside the body and a black cloth over the actor's head to cover it from view.* KOHINA *gasps and tries to rise, but* GUNJIBEI *holds her in place.* HANBEI *kneels and takes up his brother's head. Agonized, he strives to keep his voice level.*]

HANBEI: He was my blood brother, Gunjibei, yet you note the consequence of transgression.

GUNJIBEI [*controlling his voice with difficulty*] : How reasonable. Splendid warrior.

HANBEI: And, now, you . . .

GUNJIBEI: . . . partner in his lechery . . .

KOHINA [*terrified*] : I-I . . .

[*Slowly* GUNJIBEI *reaches out and takes her hand. He pulls her beside him. They pose.*]

GUNJIBEI: Daughter of a samurai . . . fortunate to have lived to be sixteen, you have done nothing wrong I know.

KOHINA: Your d-doubts are g-gone?

GUNJIBEI [*holding her close to him*] : You are innocent. Nevertheless, I am a samurai.

migawari   KOHINA [*startled, she pulls away, then, as she looks at* HANJŪRŌ, *she accepts the situation*] : Yes, Father.

303   The Scarlet Princess of Edo

[GUNJIBEI *rises. She clings to his knees. They pose. Gently, he removes her hands. She sits back and composes herself.* GUNJIBEI *draws his long sword, and cuts off* KOHINA's *head with a stroke. A STAGE ASSISTANT covers her head with a black cloth and places a prop head beside her body.* GUNSUKE, *who has entered the room as witness to the execution, kneels beside* GUNJIBEI. *He wipes the blood from the sword with a small cloth, and* GUNJIBEI *returns it to its scabbard.*]

GUNSUKE [*looking at* GUNJIBEI *with admiration*]: In your breast . . .

GUNJIBEI: My Son, I present to you the head of your intended bride . . .

[*He presents* KOHINA's *head to* HANBEI, *who takes it. He cradles a head under each arm. They pose.*]

HANBEI [*voice choking*]: You, too, are a samurai.

GUNJIBEI [*carefully*]: And you show loyalty to your lord.

HANBEI [*realizing* GUNJIBEI *understands his mission*]: Ahh!

GUNJIBEI [*tears drop from his eyes*]: Let them be wedding gifts.

[GUNJIBEI *takes the portrait of* SAKURA, *and looks at it.* HANBEI *reverently places the two heads in the center of the stage.*]

HANBEI: If they are useful . . .

GUNJIBEI: . . . to the princess, forever in the future . . .

HANBEI: . . . Kohina and I shall be . . .

GUNJIBEI: . . . husband and wife. I am grateful.

GUNSUKE [*kneeling*]: For our lady, Kohina will substitute . . . but, your brother died for nothing, like a dog.

HANBEI: No, my brother, too . . .

[HANBEI *crosses quickly to the small temple left, and swings open the door.* MATSUWAKA *steps out. All pose.*]

MATSUWAKA: Ah! "How pitiful, that these two . . . "[16]

HANBEI: No, my Prince! Quickly!

[*The prince returns to the temple, and* HANBEI *closes the door.*]

GUNJIBEI: Inside? He?

HANBEI: Now you know. The twig may be cut, but the branch remains.

[HANBEI *picks up the head of his brother.*] For the sake of the prince . . .

GUNJIBEI [*picks up the head of* KOHINA]: . . . for the sake of the princess . . .

GUNSUKE [*picks up the umbrella*]: . . . knowingly she wrote her heart's riddle here.

HANBEI: Unfortunate Kohina . . .

[*They pose.* GOROJI *emerges from hiding by the gate.*]

GOROJI: Two pieces of evidence!

[GOROJI *slips in, takes the picture, and seizes the umbrella.* GUNSUKE *forces him to the ground.*]

GUNJIBEI: From an ant's hole . . .

GUNSUKE: . . . the dike will crumble!

HANBEI: Let us take care. Farewell!

[*A single sharp clack of the ki.* GOROJI *moves right with picture and umbrella.* GUNSUKE *blocks his way. The four pose in a powerful group mie to battari tsuke beats. As they hold the mie, the curtain is closed*

16. Paraphrased from *The House of Sugawara.*

ACT IV MIMEGURI SHRINE SCENE

MIMEGURI SHRINE SCENE

[*Two ki clacks: the large drum beats irregular-tempoed, rising and falling*
Ama Oto, *representing the sound of falling rain. Slowly the curtain is
walked open to shamisen playing* Kofukuji no Tsutome, *"Kofuku Temple
Prayer," and quiet clacking of the ki. The scene is the entrance to Mimeguri Shrine near Asakusa in Edo, looking dark and dismal in the evening
rain. A massive Shintō arch of gray stone spans a flight of stone steps
leading to the top of the Sumida River embankment. Dim lights of houses
can be seen across the river. Stumpy pines and clumps of grass grow here
and there.* KANZŌ *and* KANGORŌ *are crouched around a small fire
right, trying to keep warm.* GENGO *stands aloofly apart. Music stops. A
single loud ki clack: action beings.* KANGORŌ *squints into the dark sky.*]

KANGORŌ: Isn't this rain ever going to stop?

KANZŌ [*shivers*] : I'm soaked to the skin. Ah, Master Gengo, you have
   nothing to keep off the rain. It's sad for you.

GENGO: Standing in the spring rain has no agony to compare with a samurai
   dispossessed. How galling to have been dismissed by my Lord Akugorō,
   because the dog Sōta would not turn over the scroll I hired him to seize.
   That wretch blackmails us for a golden fortune, while clan rule escapes
   our grasp. Agh! [*Turns to others.*] I rely on your help.

KANZŌ: Leave it to us, Master Gengo. We're watching the suspicious writing
   master who moved into the village. He's the father of Kohina we were
   telling you about. No mistake, this out-of-work warrior is a Yoshida family
   retainer.

KANGORŌ: They must have Prince Matsuwaka hidden. They may even know
   where Princess Sakura is.

GENGO: Good! Remember, wherever the prince is you will see his man
   Gunsuke. So the prince and princess must be there. Hm, that fellow
   Gorōji you left behind, why isn't he back yet?

KANZŌ: I don't know. He was left to watch Kohina, but . . .
   [*They turn back to the fire. Shamisen play* Zen no Tsutome. *To rapid
   bata-bata tsuke beats* GORŌJI *runs on carrying the umbrella and picture.
   He crosses directly to the fire. Music ends.*]

GORŌJI [*bowing to* GENGO] : Master Gengo, I am here.

GENGO: So, you're back. [*Strongly.*] At the house of Gunjibei you saw the
   lackey Gunsuke, did you not?

GORŌJI: Just as you say. I watched Kohina like a hawk, but it wasn't the way
   we thought. Old Gunjibei sliced off his daughter's head!

KANZŌ and KANGORŌ: He did what? Why? Why?

GORŌJI: I'll tell you why: with the princess wanted, the princess' champion
   Inanoya Hanbei urged the old man to restore his samurai honor, so he

305 The Scarlet Princess of Edo

cut off poor Kohina's head! They plan to palm off the girl's head as Princess Sakura's. I know it. I've brought the poem she wrote on the umbrella and Sakura's picture as proof. [*Shows them.*] See.

KANZŌ: The picture's soaked. Here, I'll dry it out.

[*He plasters it on the pillar of the arch near the fire. GENGO reads the poem and nods with understanding.*]

KANGORŌ: And what about the youngster?

GOROJI: That Hanbei cut off his own brother's head! I tell you it's a plot.

[*They all pose. GENGO faces front, triumphantly.*]

GENGO: The matter is beyond doubt: the fugitive Matsuwaka is concealed in that house. Gunsuke is there. Come, let us . . .

KANZŌ [*listening*] : Wait. That sound . . . it's Gunsuke . . .

GENGO: . . . coming here? Then, all together . . .

ALL: . . . we understand!

[*GUNSUKE rushes onto the hanamichi to loud, rapid bata-bata tsuke beats. His right kimono sleeve is pulled down for action and he carries a naked sword. He seizes GOROJI, then sees GENGO.*]

GUNSUKE: Ah! Matsui Gengo Sadakage!

GENGO: Deceitful hireling, Gunsuke!

GUNSUKE [*freeing GOROJI, and posing*] : Gengo. At long last . . .

GUNSUKE and GENGO: . . . we meet.

GUNSUKE: Traitor to our house, Gengo Sadakage, where is the Miyakodori scroll? I know you have it! Hand it to me, now!

[*GUNSUKE holds out his hand. GENGO turns away contemptuously.*]

GENGO: Silence, menial! I know nothing of the scroll's disappearance. But the clever poem on the umbrella and Kohina's sacrifice we know. So confess it all: where are you hiding the prince?

KANZŌ: Talk fast, or when Matsui Gengo raises a finger, I'll cut you down.

GUNSUKE: You know this much about the princess and Matsuwaka?

GENGO: Enough to have you killed. Wretch, what is your plan?

KANZŌ [*grinning*] : Your worthless life is over. Prepare to say . . .

ALL: . . . your prayers!

GUNSUKE: Insolent braggarts. Don't trifle with me. Come, the four of you, face Gunsuke, your opponent! "Like the beating of wings, like the sad cries of the gulls and water fowl from the Sumida River bank at Mimeguri Shrine . . ."

tate

[*They begin to fight as a pleasure boat, filled with singing geisha, passes up the river behind them. Shamisen, drums, nō flute, and small bell play spirited* Gion Bayashi, *"Gion Rhythm." Batan and battari tsuke beats punctuate the action. GUNSUKE strikes with his sword right and left, moving past KANZŌ and GOROJI. He poses in a mie, holding the four at bay. GUNSUKE attacks; GENGO slashes deep into GUNSUKE's abdomen. A STAGE ASSISTANT pulls down GUNSUKE's kimono, revealing a blood-stained undergarment, and loosens his hair, which falls wildly to his shoulders. Thinking the wounded young man will be easy to kill, the four attack at the same time. GUNSUKE uses the open umbrella as a shield. It*] is slashed to ribbons. GUNSUKE *fights his way up the steps to the top of the bank. As they attack up the steps, he kills them one by one, pushing their bodies off the bank into the river. As each falls,* Mizu Oto *water pattern crescendos.* GUNSUKE *collapses, dying of his wounds. A temple bell tolls. Music changes to lonely, tentative* Shinobi Sanjū, *"Stealthy Melody."*]

Ahh! How intolerable! At the very moment I should be a winged arrow for my master, I writhe regretting my wounds! Life is at an end for Gunsuke . . .

seppuku   [*He plunges the sword into his stomach.*]

"Namu Amida Butsu! Namu Amida Butsu!"

[*Trembling in agony, he rises, pulls out the sword, and leaps into the river. Loud* Mizu Oto *water pattern. A group of gulls rise, startled, and fly along the embankment. A temple bell tolls. Music stops. Frogs in the river croak loudly.* Ama Oto *rain pattern is heard quietly in the background. Dim blue lights come up on both* hanamichi. SEIGEN, *carrying the infant, enters on the right* hanamichi; SAKURA *enters on the left* hanamichi.]

meriyasu   SOLO SINGER [*offstage sings* Doku Gin, *"Solo Air," to shamisen accompaniment*]:

Reminded of seagulls at Mimeguri Shrine;
  Their forms steeped in misery, rain-drenched in sorrow;
    "Where is my lover?" the plovers cry.

[*They stop at seven-three, exhausted.* SEIGEN *shields the child from the rain with a farmer's torn straw hat.* SAKURA's *bright kimono sleeve can be seen still wrapped around the baby.* SAKURA *wears a short rain cape of straw over a peach-colored kimono. Her hair is no longer elegantly arranged, but hangs down her back. She stands weakly, trying to keep off the rain with a tattered paper umbrella. A temple bell tolls. They look center, though they cannot see each other in the darkness. Crows caw from the trees. Frogs croak. Shamisen play melancholy* Doku Gin *in the background. They speak plaintively, in rhythmic phrases of seven and five syllables. Their thoughts, independent at first, gradually fuse.*]

waka   SAKURA: "Does the flock of birds, rising high into the air, now before my eyes; foretell safety for my child, or what else we do not know?"

warizerifu
shichigochō   SEIGEN: Dedicated though I was to Buddha's service; still there is living no man made of stone and wood. For the sake of another this Seigen was swayed; the one word "love" obsessing my heart and body. How dreadful this all becomes, how despicable.

SAKURA: Thinking back upon that night at Buddha's temple; in order to save the thief who was my lover; the esteemed priest was brought to degradation; a crime for which punishment now heavily falls; by the Sumida River on a rain lashed form; altered in appearance now . . . Princess Sakura.

SEIGEN: When I think of how my soul sinks in misery; deeper each day for her love, then I long to meet; that she may see the anguish caring for the child; causes me unknown to her, for if I could now . . .

SAKURA: . . . what person where extends to him the hand of succor; raising my child to manhood, my babe just one glimpse . . .

307   The Scarlet Princess of Edo

SEIGEN: . . . in one meeting to reproach with mounting bitterness . . .

SAKURA: . . . of my beloved infant, my darling child . . .

SEIGEN: . . . the parent of this child, Princess Sakura . . .

SAKURA: . . . to meet again . . .

SEIGEN: . . . to see you!

SAKURA: Oh, Merciful Buddha . . .

SEIGEN: . . . let the princess . . .

SAKURA: . . . let the child . . .

SEIGEN: . . . please let us . . .

BOTH [*together, drawn out*]: . . . meet . . . one . . . more . . . time!

> [*A temple bell tolls in the distance. Hearing it, they are reminded of how greatly their fortunes have changed. They pose, anguished. They remain unaware of each other.*]

SOLO SINGER [*offstage sings* Doku Gin *to quiet shamisen accompaniment*]:
Their forms steeped in misery, rain-drenched in sorrow;

"Where is my lover?" the plovers cry.

> [Ama Oto *rain pattern grows louder. They shield their faces with hat and umbrella and move hesitantly into the rainy darkness. Blindly approaching each other, they almost meet, but a flurry of rain sends them fleeing in opposite directions. She mounts the steps center; he stumbles into the fire right. The child cries.* SAKURA *freezes in a pose, then looks back over her shoulder in the direction of the cry.* SEIGEN *cuddles the baby.*]

SEIGEN: There, there. You're hungry and soaked through from the rain. No wonder you cry. [*Looking down.*] What's this? Ashes of a fire? If only I can resurrect its blaze!

> [*Shamisen play* Doku Gin Aikata, *"Solo Air Melody."* SEIGEN *crouches. He rakes twigs into the ashes and fans them with the hat.* SAKURA *closes the umbrella and, standing halfway up the steps, peers into the darkness.*]

SAKURA: Whose fretting child the traveler carries, I cannot discern. In darkness neither black nor white are known, but if my child lives, surely he will be blessed if I give this one my breast. And . . . if he is dead, merit will speed his way to Buddhahood. The baby shall be held by me.

> [*She takes a step toward the child, then stops.*] I am society's transgressor. Will not revealing myself be cause for later regret? Still, to forsake a crying infant . . .

> [*She looks with pity toward the unseen child, but is not strong enough to act. She turns away.*]

SEIGEN: Wind and rain put out the fire no matter what I do. Ah, if it would only stop. What's this?

> [*Searching for twigs his hand falls on* KOHINA's *umbrella. Eagerly he opens it and places it over the fire. He blows on the ashes and fans them. Smoke rises. He coughs and falls back. Flames spring up.*]

Praise Buddha! Now, little one, your clothes will dry.

> [*He cuddles the baby in one arm and spreads the red kimono sleeve on the edge of the umbrella to dry.* SAKURA *turns as the fire lights. The characters of the poem are clearly silhouetted against the flames.*]

"You dare stand in the way of my love? Black-robed, incense-smelling hypo-
crite!" Akugorō poses with his foot on Seigen's back, holding Sakura's baby.
(*Akugorō:* Bandō Minosuke; *Seigen:* Morita Kanya; *Sakura:* Nakamura
Jakuemon) Page 285

Akugorō jabs Seigen in the stomach and tries to drag Sakura away with him. (*Akugorō:* Bandō Minosuke; *Sakura:* Nakamura Jakuemon; *Seigen:* Morita Kanya) Page 286

Gengo forces Seigen to the edge of the river bank. Seigen loses his balance and, clutching wildly, grasps and tears off Sakura's kimono sleeve. (*Sakura:* Nakamura Jakuemon; *Gengo:* Iwai Hanshirō; *Seigen:* Morita Kanya) Page 287

Searching for her infant, Sakura approaches the Mimeguri Shrine on the main hanamichi. (*Sakura:* Nakamura Jakuemon) Page 307

Simultaneously Seigen enters on the second hanamichi. He carries her baby and is looking for Sakura. In the darkness and the rain they do not see each other. (*Seigen:* Morita Kanya)

Seigen examines the medicine Sakura has thrown to him at the fire. A Stage Assistant follows a prompt book to Sakura's left. (*Seigen:* Morita Kanya; *Sakura:* Nakamura Jakuemon) Page 309

SAKURA: "Flower of youth broken, trailing sleeve torn asunder, of what matter now are the unjust assaults of the wind and the falling rain?" In truth, how like myself.

[SAKURA *sees* SEIGEN *for the first time, crouching low over the fire, his face hidden. She sees the kimono sleeve.*]

A torn kimono sleeve? A priest in tattered garments? Indeed, what memories they recall!

[SEIGEN *notices* SAKURA's *portrait on the arch. His lips move as he reads to himself the caption, "Princess Sakura." Music fades away.*]

SEIGEN [*voice choking with emotion*] : More than any other, dearest Princess Sakura . . . !

[*The baby wails.*]

SAKURA: My heart is touched by the wandering priest. [*Loudly.*] Medicine as alms.

[*She throws the packet of medicine beside the fire.* SEIGEN *picks it up, wondering at the familiar voice.*]

SEIGEN: That voice . . . ?

SAKURA: That child . . . ?

[SEIGEN *looks down at the packet. He recognizes it as the one he gave* SAKURA. *He looks up, amazed. For the first time* SAKURA *sees* SEIGEN's *face and, thinking she recognizes him, starts to rush down the steps. Just then he leaps to his feet, accidentally kicking aside the umbrella. A flurry of rain falls to* Ama Oto *rain pattern and the insistent sound of a repeatedly struck bell. Instantly the fire is quenched and they are plunged into darkness. They freeze in a pose. Melancholy and lonely sounding* Sorabue, *"Empty Flute" and* Tsutsu Izutsu, *played by a single shamisen, begin in the background. Desperately,* SEIGEN *climbs the steps groping for* SAKURA; *at the same time she descends the steps toward the fire. They pass in the dark.* SEIGEN, *at the top of the embankment, realizes he has missed his chance to find her. He slumps with weariness and disappointment.* SAKURA *reaches the fire and finds no one there. Wondering if it was* SEIGEN *and her son, she stands pensively looking into the dead ashes. The rain falls harder still. They raise their umbrellas. The temple bell tolls twice. They pose, subdued and melancholy, as the curtain is pulled closed to muted clacking of the ki. A single loud ki clack signals flute and drums to play spirited* Shagiri *between acts.*]

gomakume

ACT V

IWABUCHI HERMITAGE SCENE

[*Two clacks of the ki: shamisen play* Anton *and drums and bell* Zen no Tsutome. *Ki clacks rise to a crescendo as the curtain is run open. It is several weeks later, late afternoon and evening. The scene is a dilapidated hermitage near the village of Iwabuchi, outside of Edo. The main room of the hermitage, drab and water-streaked, faces the audience. On the right is a small temple to Saint Jizō, protector of children, separated from the main room by a gate. Left, a weeping willow looms over a graveyard plot. ZANGETSU, who has been reduced to running the hermitage, stands outside in a dirty gray kimono. He is breaking up a large barrel-shaped coffin with a hammer. In the room NAGAURA, now his common-law wife, sits before a mirror fixing her hair. SEIGEN, unseen as yet, sleeps behind a low screen. CHŌHACHI, a local farmer, and KUROHACHI, a rag-and-bottle man, sit on the veranda of the room, their feet on the ground outside. KANROKU, a slave-trader, sits apart from them, casually smoking his pipe. A single clack of the ki signals the action to begin.*]

KUROHACHI [*craftily*] : Hey, Zangetsu, is the old priest really better?

ZANGETSU: A little better this morning.

CHŌHACHI: And so you're breaking up his coffin.

    [*They laugh.*]

NAGAURA [*testily*] : It's a used coffin. Where do you think we get firewood?

CHŌHACHI: You use coffins for firewood?

NAGAURA [*facing him, abruptly*] : Nothing's wasted here. Firewood from coffins, and we sell the small pieces. We turned an old carrying case into a lantern. Our teabags come from corpses' clothes.

KUROHACHI: That's disgusting. It's filthy. [*Bobs his head, laughing.*] Still, it's not far from what I do, going from mortuary to mortuary every day buying up old clothes.

KANROKU [*knocking the ashes from his pipe casually*] : By the way, remember what I asked you to do? Did you get any?

ZANGETSU [*shaking his head*] : Not yet. It's hot enough, but the devils aren't out this year. There just aren't any snakes about. I hear you have a wild man from the mountains in a freak show.

KANROKU: That's right, I've got him in the sideshow up in Ryōgoku, and in a day or two I'm adding a woman snake-handler.

CHŌHACHI [*eagerly*] : If I see any snakes I'll catch 'em for you. I've got some dried lizards. They'd be great for your wild man's dinner.

ZANGETSU [*rises, stretching his sore back*] : What about it, Kanroku? Buy lizards for your wild man.

KANROKU [*laughs*] : He eats them every day. Here. Let's see.

    [CHŌHACHI *hands a small bag to* KANROKU, *who looks inside.*]

    What're these?

CHŌHACHI: Blue lizards.

KANROKU [*handing the bag back in disgust*] : You're something. Who'd eat a blue lizard? Try it once and you'd be a dead man.

CHŌHACHI: They're poison?

KANROKU: Deadly poison.

ZANGETSU: I never heard blue lizards were poison.

CHŌHACHI: Damn! I walked my legs off catching 'em!

    [*They turn away.* ZANGETSU *puts his tools away.*]

KUROHACHI: Hey, Zangetsu, what do you have to sell?

ZANGETSU: Ha! Nothing! It's a lousy time. No one's died, and that parasite is still sponging off us. [*Gestures to where* SEIGEN *is sleeping.*] Unless the old woman wants to sell her robe or . . . what about your hair pins, Woman?

[*Proudly* NAGAURA *gets out her hair ornaments and the robe* SAKURA *gave her.*]

NAGAURA: I have clothes and more hair ornaments than you would believe. Here. They are mine and they are not for sale.

KUROHACHI [*slyly*] : What can you do with a bright kimono and gold pins, Auntie?

NAGAURA: What a man you are! Can't you guess? I'll wear them and sashay down the street!

[*She waggles her hips. They all laugh.*]

CHOHACHI: Imagine, an old woman in a girl's kimono! Folks'll be fit to be tied.

KANROKU [*slaps his thigh*] : I have it. I'll put you next to the snake woman. An old hen dressed to the teeth will bring them in faster than the devil's daughter. Ha, ha! Oh, you'll be a great attraction!

KUROHACHI: Not to me!

CHOHACHI: I want my money back!

[*The men laugh.* NAGAURA *turns away in a huff.*]

NAGAURA: Spiteful old men.

KUROHACHI: Well, I have to be going. Coming, Chohachi?

[*He picks up his bundle.* CHOHACHI *bows to* ZANGETSU, *who sits smoking. They go off right, laughing and chatting.* NAGAURA *rises and goes inside.* KANROKU *looks about to be sure the others are gone. He slides near* ZANGETSU.]

KANROKU [*confidentially*] : Say, Zangetsu, I've got some real news. I came across a terrific beauty wandering along the road from Terashima Field this morning. She pretended to be lost, but the way she sauntered along— it's a put-on. I pulled her off the street into my place. Now I can't get her out. The neighborhood's crawling with toughs waiting for a prize like this. I can sell her for one sweet price if someone doesn't sniff her out first. But I need a quiet place to hide her, Zangetsu . . .

ZANGETSU: Ho, ho! What's the problem? Bring her over as fast as you can.

KANROKU: Good. Hmm. I can't just take her down the street. She's so great everyone would notice. If there was only something I could disguise her in . . .

ZANGETSU: Well, well, that's not so difficult. Dress the woman in anything you want. Bring her along. [*He eyes* KANROKU.] Ho, ho. I have it. Take the old lady's robe. I'll give her some excuse . . .

NAGAURA [*off*] : You will, will you? Dress some street slut you've never seen in my precious wedding kimono? [*Opens the sliding doors and glares at him.*] You're mighty free with my things. How dare you? You're a fool. [*Closes the door.*]

ZANGETSU [*shrugging*] : That's the way it is, then. Bring her some way.

KANROKU: I have to have something to disguise her in.

ZANGETSU: Ah, ah! Right before our eyes. Here. Use this.

[ZANGETSU *gets* SEIGEN's *black robe that is draped over the screen.*]

KANROKU: A monk's robe. Anything. Who cares? Even a battered princess can't walk the streets naked! Now, we have to cover her face too.

[ZANGETSU *gets* SEIGEN's *battered hat from the wall.*]

ZANGETSU: Take the straw hat. It will go with the robe.

KANROKU: I'll dress her and be back in an instant. [*Winks.*] You'll see what she's like.

ZANGETSU [*rubs his hands gleefully*] : Hurry, Kanroku, hurry!

KANROKU: I'm on my way.

[*Shamisen play* Anton *and drums and bell* Zen no Tsutome. KANROKU *rises and trots onto the hanamichi carrying the robe and hat. At seven-three he passes* OJŪ, *a woman of about thirty, dressed in a conservative purple and blue striped kimono. In spite of her ordinary dress she is obviously of the samurai class. She is the wife of* SHICHIRŌ, *unknown to either* ZANGETSU *or* NAGAURA. *For the sake of the Yoshida family, she is searching for* SAKURA's *child. She crosses to the gate. Music ends.*]

OJŪ [*politely bowing*] : Excuse me, Sir, is this Iwabuchi Hermitage?

ZANGETSU [*perfunctorily*] : Yes, yes. What is it?

OJŪ: Forgive me, please. I live near Asakusa. My only child died, and my grief is inconsolable.

[ZANGETSU *looks up to see an attractive woman. His attitude immediately changes. Eagerly he opens the door for her.*]

ZANGETSU: Ah, is that so, my good woman?

OJŪ: Shortly after his death I heard of your temple, where merciful Saint Jizō intercedes for children who . . . [*She pretends to cry.*] We are promised only a short life on earth, but at least the living can help the dead attain salvation by praying to Buddha. I beg you, perform services in his memory.

[*She opens a small bundle and takes out coins wrapped in white paper. She places them in his hand and bows respectfully.* ZANGETSU *hefts the coins, tucks them away, and chuckles good-naturedly.*]

ZANGETSU: My, my, how politely you ask. As master of the hermitage, I promise to pray my heart out for the little dear's soul. Very sad, very sad, indeed. And the child . . . ?

OJŪ: An only child, still a baby when smallpox carried him away.

ZANGETSU: My, my! "Namu Amida Butsu. Namu Amida Butsu."

OJŪ: Before I go, may I pray to Saint Jizō myself?

ZANGETSU [*effusively*] : Of course you may, of course. Buddha will be honored having you by his side. Heh, heh!

OJŪ: Then excuse me. I won't be a minute.

[*Shamisen play* Anton *and drums and bell play* Zen no Tsutome *as* OJŪ *bows politely and enters the ramshackle temple.* ZANGETSU *looks after her.*]

ZANGETSU [*to himself*] : A young woman coming to pray like that. Admirable. Damn good figure, too. What a waste. A ripe young thing like that . . .

NAGAURA [*entering*] : Eh? What ripe young thing are you talking about?

ZANGETSU [*unconcerned, closes the gate*] : A good-looking woman just went in to pray.

NAGAURA [*outraged*] : What? Good-looking, you say? Why you lecherous incense-sniffer!

[*To loud batan tsuke beats, she grabs his ear and pulls him to the floor. They face each other, on their knees.*]

ZANGETSU: Don't call me an incense-sniffer. Hag!

[*He pushes her; she sprawls on the floor.*]

NAGAURA: Hag? You dare call me that?

[*Her rhythmic, regal speech contrasts with her disreputable appearance.*]

shichigochō

Now in my declining years am I condemned; to this ten-foot square hovel of a hermitage; I the Princess Sakura's favorite lady; a woman of Yoshida, of noble station; lured by a dissolute priest to my destruction? I'm a hag,

share

am I? As far as I'm concerned you look like Bajū the horse-faced actor.[17] Mule! Ass!

ZANGETSU [*sarcastically*] : One female turns up and you scream with envy. Caterwauling bitch.

NAGAURA: Bitch? You . . . you babbling Buddha-head!

ZANGETSU: Foul-mouthed baboon!

NAGAURA: Baboon? Baboon!!

[*They scuffle to* Namameki Okashimi, *"Comic Lewdness," a playful melody, and to batan tsuke beats. Spluttering with rage,* NAGAURA *pummels him. He trips her. She tries to rip the kimono from his back. Intimidated, he crawls away, but she shoves him into the screen with a crash.* SEIGEN *and the baby are seen lying side by side under a quilt. The child wails.* SEIGEN *wakes. He is shockingly wasted from illness; his hair is uncombed, his face is gaunt, his ribs show black through the front of a dirty gray kimono. He holds* SAKURA's *kimono in trembling hands.* ZANGETSU *and* NAGAURA *bow in a show of solicitude.*]

ZANGETSU: Most honored Reverend Seigen . . .

NAGAURA: . . . are you feeling better?

[*He does not seem to hear. Shamisen play quiet* Mokugyo, *as* SEIGEN *speaks in a rasping voice.*]

shichigochō

SEIGEN: The kimono pattern is as I remembered it; her scent lingering faintly on the trailing sleeve; am I dreaming a vision or can this Seigen; with his beloved once more, with his dear lover; within this mortal world . . . ?

[*Soundless, racking coughs cut off his reverie. He crumples forward, clinging to the robe.* ZANGETSU *helps him to a sitting position.*]

ZANGETSU: Ah, dear Master, do not speak of what is unreal.

SEIGEN [*dazed*] : Zangetsu? Lady Nagaura? Can it be you? And this robe, how did it . . . ?

[OJŪ *comes stealthily out of the temple and listens by the gate.*]

17. One more instance of a character being likened to the actor playing the role, here Ōtani Bajū playing Zangetsu. The lines also contain a rather elaborate play on words: *bajū* means "horse-ten," Zangetsu calls Nagaura *baba*, or "old hag," and she retorts that he is a *baba uma*, literally "race-track (baba) horse (uma)."

NAGAURA [*bows politely*] : A gift from Princess Sakura from the time I served her at the mansion.

shichigochō

SEIGEN: Just a few moments ago while I was sleeping; I saw in a dreaming state, you Princess Sakura; toward whom my deep bitterness welled as if to cry out; when the crying of the infant aroused consciousness; my eyes slowly opening to look on this robe. Indeed this truly happened. You do, Princess Sakura, remember me, do you not? Can it be you do not know my tribulation; since the night we were parted at the river bank; from that wretched beginning, this Seigen; took in your child and raised him as he would his own; in spite of the calumny heaped upon a priest; who wandered homeless in the hope that someday the child; would somehow lure you to him, Princess Sakura; and so in this way at last meet with you once more! [*As if listening.*] Ah, why can I not hear you, Princess Sakura! How impossible it was for me to have known; when we two exchanged our vows of unchanging love; that would last from previous lives into the future; and we made the heartfelt pledge to die together; in youthful indiscretion; that by cowardice I would be led to error; so the more precious in this, all now that remains . . .

[*He takes out the incense case from his breast. Speaking normally.*]

So precious I keep it close to my heart. Ah, to meet and give it to you.

shichigochō

When I remember that night at Mimeguri Shrine; passing by one another in the rainy dark; the medicine you threw down by the flickering fire; when you heard the crying sound of an unseen child; was the very medicine Seigen earlier; had given to you, Princess, by the Inase River. When I think that it was you whom I was seeking; from whom I was helplessly parted in the dark; and now here to see without even knowing it; Princess Sakura's dearly cherished crimson robe; doubly I feel my heart being crushed to extinction. Ah, such precious elegance!

[SEIGEN *gazes at the kimono in one hand and the incense case in the other. He poses. Music stops.* ZANGETSU *thinks the case contains money* SEIGEN *has received to care for the baby. He bows solicitously.*]

ZANGETSU [*craftily*] : Then, dear Master Seigen, are you caring for Princess Sakura's child?

[SEIGEN *realizes he has gone too far. He quickly hides the case in the breast of his kimono.*]

SEIGEN: No, no, no. A priest vows to help all men. Why I spoke her name, I do not know. Perhaps she appeared in an unchaste dream. "Namu Amida Butsu. Namu Amida Butsu."

[*He prays to hide his confusion. The child wails.* ZANGETSU *is annoyed.*]

NAGAURA: Reverend Seigen, a man cannot rear an infant, and I can't help with my withered breasts.

ZANGETSU: This crumbling house is no place to raise a child, dear Master.

SEIGEN: What can I do?

[OJŪ *throws open the door and enters.*]

OJŪ [*resolutely*] : There is a way.

SEIGEN: Ehh?

OJŪ [*bows*] : I could not help hearing of your trouble, Reverend Seigen, raising the child. My only child has died. In place of it I will care for this motherless one.

SEIGEN [*hesitantly*] : Your words seem trustworthy. He has no breast to suck and cries constantly so that surely he will become ill.

ZANGETSU [*callously*] : We can't even get a wet nurse. Remember what happened to that woman?

NAGAURA: What a person she was. She just gobbled up the coins I gave her and off she went. What do you say, Zangetsu, should we ask her to take the child?

OJŪ [*improvising*] : Ah, if you agree, the child will live in my home in Sanya. My husband serves several restaurants there—his name is Sentarō of Ariake. I am his wife, Ojū. [*She bows.*]

SEIGEN: Since you sound reliable, and it would be good for the child . . .

[ZANGETSU, *delighted, leaps up to get the child.*]

ZANGETSU: Generous woman, we are ever in your debt.

SEIGEN [*relieved*] : For the child's sake I ask it.

[OJŪ *receives the baby. She notices* SAKURA's *kimono sleeve.*]

OJŪ: Is this a torn kimono sleeve?

SEIGEN: It is all the clothes he has. Such merciful charity you show him.

[SEIGEN *weeps as* OJŪ *deftly wraps the child in a cloth she takes from her bundle. She return the kimono sleeve to* SEIGEN *and, cuddling the child, moves quickly to open the gate.*]

OJŪ: Do not worry about the child, please. Before you know it he'll be back, his smiling face . . .

ZANGETSU [*protesting*] : There's no need, absolutely none . . .

NAGAURA: . . . Madam, take him and go.

SEIGEN: Care for him, Madam . . .

[*Shamisen play* Anton *and drums and bell* Zen no Tsutome. NAGAURA *waves* OJŪ *away and closes the door behind her.* ZANGETSU *sighs with relief. Overjoyed to have* SAKURA's *baby,* OJŪ *hurries onto the hanamichi and out of sight. Music ends.*]

SEIGEN: There are still some in the world who can show pity. But pitiless is the owner of this robe . . . Ah, my chest! I am dizzy!

[*He clutches his chest in a spasm of pain.*]

ZANGETSU: Come, dear Master, lie down. Here, here. You mustn't catch cold.

[ZANGETSU *pretends to fuss over* SEIGEN, *helping him lie down. He replaces the screen. He poses. A temple bell tolls. Stealthily* NAGAURA *beckons to him.*]

NAGAURA: Psst. Psst. What was it he took out just now? Did you see it, Zangetsu?

[*The bell tolls.*]

ZANGETSU [*matter-of-factly*] : I saw it. I saw it. It's a purse for sure. The sooner it's finished the better. [*He sees the discarded bag of dried lizards.*] Ah! That's it. Into the hot water . . .

NAGAURA: . . . blue lizards?

> [*The bell tolls. Ominous* Kaza Oto *drum pattern.* ZANGETSU *tiptoes to the fire, lifts the lid of the teapot, and stirs into the water a small amount of blue powder from the bag.* NAGAURA *holds her breath.*]

ZANGETSU: Now . . .

NAGAURA: For Reverend Seigen . . . ?

ZANGETSU: . . . a drink of poison. [*Bitterly.*] What of it? If we don't poison the bag of bones today, he'll be dead tomorrow anyway. I say good riddance. Ha! Damned sponging hypocrite, he should thank us for ending his misery.

NAGAURA [*simpering*] : Poison is simple, simple is best. It's boiling, Zangetsu.

> [Kaza Oto *softens.* ZANGETSU *kneels by the fire and with a wooden dipper fills a teacup with the liquid, warding off the poisonous vapors with his sleeve.* NAGAURA *cringes.* ZANGETSU *crosses to* SEIGEN *and carefully places the cup by his head. He lifts the screen and leans it against the back wall. He and* NAGAURA *kneel at a respectful distance from the priest. Music stops.*]

ZANGETSU [*solicitously*] : Are you awake, dear Master? We have brought some medicine.

> [*Slowly* SEIGEN *sits up.* ZANGETSU *pushes the cup toward him.*]

SEIGEN: Medicine, for me?

ZANGETSU [*heartily*] : Oh, yes, dear Master. The wife and I grieve that we can't usually offer medicine, but the color of your face today roused us to pity. We got this from the doctor in the village. It's best piping hot. Heh, heh! Here, Master Seigen.

> [SEIGEN *peers into the offered cup, feeling instinctively that something is wrong. He poses.*]

SEIGEN: Mankind's birth and death are decreed by Karma. Unlike an ordinary person, a priest commits grievous sin if he tries to halt his death. What others would thank you for is repugnant to me. Please throw out the potion. I do not wish to alter fate.

> [*He pushes the cup away.*]

NAGAURA [*gently, mollifying him*] : Indeed, it is so, but please drink one sip . . .

ZANGETSU [*offers the cup again*] : . . . of this special brew.

SEIGEN [*drawing back*] : I said there is no need. I do not want . . .

ZANGETSU: . . . our medicine? [*Politely holds the cup to* SEIGEN's *lips.*] One sip, good Master . . .

SEIGEN: No.

ZANGETSU: . . . will do you good. Come . . .

SEIGEN: No, no.

ZANGETSU: . . . drink.

> [SEIGEN *pulls away frightened.* ZANGETSU *drops the pretense of solicitude. He throws* SEIGEN *to the floor, to batan tsuke beats, and thrusts the cup to his lips. Harshly.*]

You will drink it, Seigen!

> [*Shamisen play* Sugomi. Kaza Oto *wind pattern continues softly.* ZANGE-TSU *holds* SEIGEN. *They pose.*]

So you sniffed out our plan and to keep from drinking made a pretty speech about Karma? Then you know I'm a desperate man. Yes, Seigen, the cup is . . . poison.

SEIGEN: I was right to be suspicious. You are a pair of wicked . . .

ZANGETSU: Bah! You'll stop grumbling when you're dead! Here, help me, Nagaura.

NAGAURA: Drink . . .

ZANGETSU: . . . damn you!

SEIGEN: No! I won't drink poison!

ZANGETSU: You will drink, you will!

[*Music grows louder. Tsuke beats accent SEIGEN's struggle. NAGAURA takes the cup from ZANGETSU and tries to force the poison down SEIGEN's throat, as ZANGETSU holds him. SEIGEN clenches his teeth, then stuffs SAKURA's kimono sleeve into his mouth. ZANGETSU rips the sleeve away and sits on SEIGEN's chest. SEIGEN strikes the cup: the poison splashes across his face. He screams and turns away. ZANGETSU wraps a cloth around SEIGEN's neck and twists, as NAGAURA beats him with a piece of kindling. A STAGE ASSISTANT quickly alters SEIGEN's makeup. When SEIGEN manages to turn front, we see that a large purple blotch disfigures the left side of his face.*]

NAGAURA: One side of his face . . . it's horrible!

ZANGETSU [*not letting go, peers over SEIGEN's shoulder*] : For heaven's sake, be quiet. The poison scarred his face is all. He's not strangled yet, so . . . [*Music and tsuke swell. ZANGETSU yanks hard on the end of the cloth, twisting it tightly around SEIGEN's neck. SEIGEN claws the air in agony. He falls to the floor, rolling under the bed quilt. Savagely ZANGETSU and NAGAURA beat him with sticks, stopping only when they are exhausted. ZANGETSU pulls the quilt away. SEIGEN lies motionless; blood—applied by a STAGE ASSISTANT—flows from his mouth. Music stops. ZANGETSU and NAGAURA pose.*]

NAGAURA [*fearfully*] : Is he dead? Is he, Zangetsu?

ZANGETSU [*whispering*] : Wait. I'll see if his breath's stopped.

[*He holds his hand over SEIGEN's mouth.*]

NAGAURA: Well? Is he? Is he?

ZANGETSU [*matter-of-factly*] : Hm. He is. He is. Gone for good.

NAGAURA: Quick, the money, Zangetsu! Get the money!

[*ZANGETSU bites through the cord fastening the case around the priest's neck. He grins and hefts the package. His face falls.*]

ZANGETSU: What's this?

NAGAURA [*trembling in anticipation*] : Is there money? Is there?

ZANGETSU [*unwrapping the cloth*] : It's wrapped like a stack of gold pieces, but . . . it's too light. [*Opens case.*] Damn. An incense case! [*He tosses it in the corner.*] We've broken our backs for nothing.

NAGAURA: That can't be helped. But, Zangetsu, what are we going to do if people start saying we murdered him?

ZANGETSU: Hm. What should we do? It's all over if the neighbors see him. Still, he was a sick man. It's enough to say he died.

NAGAURA: Yes.

ZANGETSU: I'll cover him up with the bedding. [*He folds the bedding over* SEIGEN.] There, that does it. If anyone asks what happened, just say, "Reverend Seigen passed away from mortal illness."

NAGAURA: I will, I will. [*Looks at* SEIGEN.] How long is he going to stay that way?

ZANGETSU [*considering*]: How long *can* he stay that way? You go out and bring back the gravedigger, Gonsuke.

NAGAURA: But . . . Gonsuke? Is it safe?

ZANGETSU: He's a good-for-nothing, but if we do it ourselves he'll be suspicious. Go fetch him. Hurry.

NAGAURA [*bustles over to the gate*]: I'm going, I'm going, Zangetsu dear. [*Pertly turns back.*] Shall I take a little stroll?
[*They laugh. She turns and trots off right as shamisen play* Anton *and drums and bell lively* Zen no Tsutome. *Music softens.*]

ZANGETSU: Well, well. The crime is finished in a wink. Still, he was a priest. I should say a prayer for him.
[*He hides* SEIGEN *with the screen and, kneeling before the Buddhist alter upstage, piously rubs his rosary beads and mumbles a prayer.* GON-SUKE *saunters on from the right, carrying a hoe and a shovel over his shoulder.*[18] *He wears an old, patched kimono casually tucked up in the back. Music ends.*]

GONSUKE [*bored*]: "Come quick," she said, so Gonsuke's here. Did someone bring in a stiff?
[*Quickly* ZANGETSU *rises. Joking and gossiping at high speed, he edges* GONSUKE *away from* SEIGEN.]

ZANGETSU: Ah, Gonsuke. Hello, hello. It's no poor soul brought in. It was, bless us all, poor Reverend Seigen, come to us for aid and comfort such a short time ago. Alas, he's gone, passed away in illness this very day.

GONSUKE: The old priest died? Too bad.

ZANGETSU: In an instant he was gone.
[*They stop left by the willow tree.*]

GONSUKE: Do you want to put him here?

ZANGETSU: Right here, right here, good Gonsuke. Nothing could be better. I'll help you. Just a minute. I'll help you.
[*Shamisen play* Mokugyo *in the background. Batan tsuke beats mark each shovel of dirt* GONSUKE *throws out of the grave.* ZANGETSU *ties back his sleeves and is soon helping. As they shovel, a trap opens in the stage and a grave appears. Lights come up on the hanamichi.* KANROKU *leads* SAKURA *on by the hand. She wears* SEIGEN's *hat and black robe. A purple hood covers her face. At seven-three she forces him to stop.*]

SAKURA [*elegantly*]: Good Sir, you lead me, pray, to what abode?

KANROKU: Girl, I told you. Cut out the fancy talk. Now, do you see that nice place over there? It's quiet and there's a woman in the house. That's where I'm taking you.

---

18. As one of the many unemployed rōnin of the period, Gonsuke had to scrape together a living any way he could. It is not strange that he moves from place to place in and around Edo and from job to job during the play.

SAKURA: You pay me undeserved honor, Sir.

KANROKU: Ah, ah! The big words never stop. Come on.

[*They cross onstage. Music ends. KANROKU calls through the gate.*]
Are you there, Zangetsu? I have the girl.

ZANGETSU: Ah, Kanroku, come in, come in!

[ZANGETSU *drops his kimono in back to look more dignified, and crosses to meet them. He tries to see what she is like, but cannot. GON-SUKE continues digging.*]

KANROKU: Isn't she something? I put her in one of my wife's old hoods, so no one could see her cute face on the way.

ZANGETSU [*chuckling*]: Ho, ho, you're a sexy little riddle! Can you fix it up, Kanroku?

KANROKU: Can I? I'm a specialist when it comes to bargaining with Kozu-kappara[19] madams. Here's what we'll do: I'll leave the girl with you and go alone to make the deal. You're her father or brother, I'll say. Then the two of us take the girl to the whorehouse . . .

ZANGETSU: And I say I'm her brother?

KANROKU: You ask for cash. Be sure to ask for cash.

ZANGETSU [*admiringly*]: That's a smart trick. We'll have the money in our hands tonight, then?

KANROKU: Would I come with a female I couldn't sell? Do your part, that's all. [*To* SAKURA.] Don't go away. I won't be long. [*To* ZANGETSU.] I'll have it settled and be back before you know it. Remember, I'm leaving the little jewel in your care.

[ZANGETSU *sees him through the gate, bowing and rubbing his hands in anticipation of the money.*]

ZANGETSU: Yes, yes, hurry, hurry. I'll watch her like a hawk.

[*Shamisen plays* Mokugyo. KANROKU *crosses onto the hanamichi. At seven-three he stops and turns back.*]

KANROKU: Stay right there, girl. You hear?

SAKURA [*elegantly*]: Return without delay, for I shall be alone in this place while you are at an unknown destination.

KANROKU: I'll be back, I'll be back. Listen to her. Ever hear anything like that?

ZANGETSU: "Return without delay." Ho, ho! Amazing!

KANROKU: I'm off.

[SAKURA *bows politely.* KANROKU *runs off. Music stops.* ZANGETSU *turns to* SAKURA, *oozing friendliness.*]

ZANGETSU: There, there, dear girl, don't be afraid. You're safe from harm with me. We're no big noisy temple, just a little country chapel dedicated to Jizō, protector of children. I, my dear, am the chaplain. Set your heart at ease.

SAKURA [*bows regally*]: Your intention, my good priest, is a source of gratification. You should not, Sir, abandon me.

[*Hearing* SAKURA's *voice*, GONSUKE *stops work, amazed.*]

19. A brothel district of the most sordid kind, unlicensed and illegal, at the edge of the city.

ZANGETSU: Hoo! That's a damned patronizing speech. Don't you worry about being abandoned, Dearie. [*Tries to see her face.*] Here now, there's no need to be afraid. It's turned a trifle hottish. Let's take off that stifling hood? Heh, heh!

SAKURA: If it is certain . . .

ZANGETSU: No harm will come of it.

> [*He removes her hat and hood and is dumbfounded to see* SAKURA. GONSUKE *puts down his shovel and slips behind the tree to watch unseen.*]

> You? Princess Sakura?

SAKURA [*looking carefully at him*] : And are you not the priest . . . ?

ZANGETSU [*piously*] : . . . of Kiyomizu, Zangetsu. How good it is to see you, my Lady. Welcome, welcome. Please come inside, my Lady.

> [*He leads her into the room, holding her hand as long as he dares. He helps her remove the black robe. She wears only a thin, pale pink kimono beneath it. Wearily, she sinks down, stage left in the place of honor. Kneeling right, he lets his gaze linger on her figure. He speaks smugly.*]

> All worldly things, they say, must change, but my, my, to think of Princess Sakura, dressed like this, here in my rude hovel . . . Hmmm.

> [*He is reminded of* SEIGEN. *Half to himself.*]

> It must be destiny. I'd get nowhere if he were here. Killing him off was heaven-sent.

SAKURA [*partly overhearing*] : Kill, my good priest? Your words are frightening.

ZANGETSU: No at all. I was saying I should . . . ah . . . kill the pesky mosquitoes buzzing about, though heaven-sent, should they bother my Lady. Heh, heh!

> [*Pretending to swat mosquitoes, he slides closer to* SAKURA.]

> It's a chilly spring but already mosquitoes are biting. Ha, ha! With the wind turned chill you'll catch your death of cold in such a thin kimono, Princess. Let me help you keep warm, my Lady.

> [*He scurries upstage to get* SAKURA's *old "scarlet princess" robe.* NAGAURA *returns. Seeing* ZANGETSU *with* SAKURA, *she conceals herself outside the gate.*]

SAKURA [*at a loss*] : The kimono I used to wear?

ZANGETSU: You remember? It is the very robe you gave to Nagaura in parting, at Kiyomizu Temple.

SAKURA: Then . . . my dear maid . . . ?

ZANGETSU: . . . lives here in the hermitage. My Princess, come put on your old robe. You just follow me and don't worry about a thing.

> [*Shamisen play* Mokugyo. ZANGETSU *rises and takes her by the hand. He covers his actions with a constant stream of reassuring chatter.* SAKURA *looks about expectantly for* NAGAURA *and allows herself to be led into the small room left. Music softens.*]

GONSUKE [*scowling darkly*] : It's the princess, no mistake. What the hell is she doing here?

NAGAURA: What is depraved Zangetsu up to? How dare he bring Princess Sakura into my house and dress her in my clothes? Ah, it's clear what's on his mind! He's going to set her up as his wife on the sly! How infuriating! [ZANGETSU *returns with* SAKURA *now wearing the "scarlet princess" kimono.* NAGAURA *and* GONSUKE *step back out of sight. Music stops.*]

ZANGETSU: There we are. That's a good girl. You've shed your drab clothes and shine like the Cherry Blossom Princess of old in the kimono you once gave to your maid Nagaura. [*Pointing to the box of hair ornaments.*] Everything is here you might need. Just settle right in.

SAKURA: Has dear Nagaura really come to live under this roof?

ZANGETSU: That's right. Don't you worry about a thing. We'll be by your side to ward off the slightest trouble. In exchange for that, Princess, won't you agree to the request I made a Kamakura? [*She sits. He leans over her from behind.*]

SAKURA: Kamakura? What do you mean?

ZANGETSU: You should know what I mean. Heh, heh. It's a lewd thing to say, but you made me passionate back at Cherry Valley, Princess. Before anything could come of it though, the trouble over Seigen erupted at the hermitage. But there's no one here to stop us. So, let me tell you, Princess . . . [*He tries to put his hand in her kimono. She shakes him off.*]

SAKURA: You are impudent. I do not permit your wickedness.

ZANGETSU [*dropping his cajoling tone*]: Do not permit? Listen, girl, things are different now. You're no better than a tramp. Whether you like it or not, I'm having you.

SAKURA: You are a miscreant. Do not touch me. [*Shamisen play strong melody* Amba. *Batan tsuke beats punctuate their short struggle.* ZANGETSU *roughly embraces* SAKURA. *She tries to pull free but cannot. He straddles her, fumblingly trying to undo her sash.* GONSUKE *and* NAGAURA *burst into the room.* GONSUKE *sends* ZANGETSU *sprawling.* NAGAURA *holds him by the collar. Music stops. They pose in a mie to battari tsuke beats.*]

GONSUKE: Discovered! Whoremonger!

NAGAURA: Discovered! Adulterer!

ZANGETSU: Ah, ah! The gravedigger! The old woman!

NAGAURA [*pounding him*]: Yes, it's me. [*To* SAKURA.] Your lady-in-waiting.

SAKURA [*relieved*]: Dear companion, it pleases me to see you here.

NAGAURA: Agh! With my own eyes I saw you take the robe from him and put it on—the one you gave me. He's my man, Princess. You were stealing him away! [*She turns her back on* SAKURA *and slaps the floor in anger.*]

GONSUKE: Damned sutra mumbler! [*Laughs harshly.*] I, gravedigger Gonsuke, have found a wife stealer! [*Strikes a brash pose.*]

ZANGETSU: What do you mean, you tramp? Your wife? Married to the princess? Ha, ha, ha! You're mad! [*Tries to rise.* GONSUKE *shoves him to the floor.*]

GONSUKE: I'm not mad and it's not a lie. Princess Sakura is mine.

SAKURA [*recognizing* GONSUKE] : Is it you, from whom I was parted after briefly meeting at Kiyomizu . . . ?

GONSUKE: You bet. You swore undying love to Tsurigane Gonsuke. [*To* ZANGETSU.] This is my wife the Princess, the Princess my wife. [*Looking fiercely at* SAKURA.] I'm your husband, eh, Princess?

SAKURA [*modestly*] : Indeed, this gentleman is my precious master, toward whom I shall allow no improper behavior. A wife serves her husband even into the life hereafter. We are pledged eternally. My words are the truth. [NAGAURA *and* ZANGETSU *exchange astonished glances.*]

GONSUKE: Do you hear? We're man and wife. What the hell do you mean getting fresh with my wife? Well? To get an answer do I have to cut off your fat head? [GONSUKE *pulls a butcher knife from his sash.* ZANGETSU *falls back, but is undaunted.*]

ZANGETSU: It won't be easy to take. Look here, Gonsuke, how can I believe you're married? Where's the license? Where's your proof?

GONSUKE: Proof more certain than a license . . . is this! [*With a proud flourish* GONSUKE *flicks up the kimono sleeve to reveal his tattoo.*]

ZANGETSU [*protesting*] : A tattoo? What proof is that?

GONSUKE: It's my symbol—symbol of Tsurigane Gonsuke, digger of corpses' graves. [*He bares* SAKURA's *forearm, revealing her tattoo. She hides her face.*]

NAGAURA: It's too fantastic to believe . . .

ZANGETSU: . . . the princess' arm, tattooed like yours?

GONSUKE [*proudly*] : Man and wife united with the words "our destiny" written on our flesh. We two bear a beauty mark of mutual love.

ZANGETSU [*at a loss*] : Well, then . . . ?

kuriage   GONSUKE [*threateningly*] : Yes, then?

ZANGETSU: Then . . .

GONSUKE: Then?

GONSUKE and ZANGETSU [*alternately at increasing speed*] : Then, then, then, then!

yusuriba   GONSUKE: Then, lecher, I'll have your damned head! [GONSUKE *slides his right arm free of the kimono sleeve and sits resolutely on the floor. He slaps the knife before him, crosses his legs, and, holding one big toe in an uncouth gesture, poses in a mie to battari tsuke beats.* ZANGETSU *crawls meekly to* NAGAURA *for protection.*]

ZANGETSU: I wish it was a dream. I wish it was a dream.

NAGAURA: See what your wenching has come to? A carnal heart brings calamity. Gonsuke, let me intercede for him. I saw it all, but had no part in his wicked scheme. Won't you be conciliated?

GONSUKE [*contemptuously*] : The only way a woman is going to save that fathead is to come up with a fat ransom and do it quick.

NAGAURA: Is that what you suggest? A ransom? As you know, we have no estate at our disposal. [*Simpering.*] And as newlyweds we've no money. Would you be content with a ransom of one hundred gold ryō?

GONSUKE [*trying to hide his delight*] : What? A hundred ryō?

NAGAURA [*continues smoothly*] : Paying as deposit one-tenth of one ryō now.

GONSUKE: Miserable bitch! Am I a fool? What the hell will a tenth of a gold ryō buy? Pay up or I'll take his head!

[GONSUKE *picks up the knife and rises as if to attack.* ZANGETSU *cowers behind* NAGAURA.]

ZANGETSU: Offer him more, please, Wife, please!

NAGAURA: Very well. You are incorrigible, but even now not wholly hateful. [*Bows to* GONSUKE.] How much will satisfy you, Gonsuke?

GONSUKE [*sitting cross-legged*] : What can you squeeze from a corpse-washing reprobate priest? Here's what I'll do. Give me the broken-down temple, the house, what's in it, and your clothes down to your bare skins. The whole lot's not worth a damn but I'll settle for it.

ZANGETSU: Yah! On top of the house and all the furniture . . .

NAGAURA: . . . you want me naked, too?

ZANGETSU [*wailing*] : You'll ruin us!

GONSUKE [*laughs*] : Should I take your head?

ZANGETSU [*wilting*] : Ah, ah! What can I do?

GONSUKE [*harshly*] : Hand it over!

ZANGETSU: You'll have it. You'll have it. [*Pleads with* NAGAURA.] Dearest Wife, take off your clothes for my sake.

NAGAURA [*acts the pouting young maid*] : I won't do it. Shame on you, embarrassing me.

ZANGETSU: Don't babble when my head's at stake. You said you'd fix it. Give him your clothes.

[ZANGETSU *takes off her long sash and is peeling off her kimono when* GONSUKE *seizes* ZANGETSU's *clothes from behind, and with a single deft motion whirls* ZANGETSU *around and whisks off his kimono.* ZANGETSU *and* NAGAURA *tumble down the steps. They clutch their undergarments and look down at their bare legs, astonished that they have been so suddenly dispossessed.*]

GONSUKE [*poses*] : Riffraff! Trash! House, temple, clothes . . . everything here is mine. Get out, both of you!

[ZANGETSU *and* NAGAURA *parody the typical scene of pathetic, star-crossed lovers forced to flee because of their transgressions.*]

NAGAURA [*tiny, pleading voice*] : Ah! Lord Zangetsu . . .

ZANGETSU [*nobility itself*] : Ah! Lady Nagaura . . .

BOTH: Alas! Our condition is indeed pitious.

[*They delicately wipe away tears with their sleeves.* ZANGETSU *looks into the sky. He shivers and pulls his under kimono tightly around him.*]

ZANGETSU: Too cruel to be borne, the heavens darken and rain seems about to fall. Good Gonsuke, lend us one umbrella, as is customary in these sad cases.[20]

GONSUKE: That's easy. Have this elegant one.

[*From a rack on the wall, he takes a common paper umbrella and disdainfully throws it at* ZANGETSU's *feet. Quiet* Ama Oto *rain pattern begins. With a sigh* ZANGETSU *picks up the umbrella, symbol of their wandering to come, and helps* NAGAURA *rise. They face front and pose, pitifully. They speak in an exaggeratedly poetic manner.*]

shichigochō

ZANGETSU: "Great melancholy rain drops splatter from the sky . . .

NAGAURA: . . . the devil himself would weep . . .

BOTH: . . . to behold our woe."

michiyuki

[*Rain pattern continues. As the* CHORUS *sings romantic* Omoi Kasanaru, "To Remember Again," *they enact in delicate mime a lovers' "travel dance." He tucks her hand under his arm, nods to her bravely, and leads her through the gate. Like a young maiden, she walks daintily, glancing about. Outside the gate they stop. He opens the umbrella and holds it protectively overhead. She hides her face in embarrassment. He strikes a manly pose, then wistfully notices that the umbrella is hanging in shreds. They move in gentle dance steps onto the hanamichi.*]

CHORUS [*sings* Omoi Kasanaru[21] *to shamisen accompaniment*]:
My heart is troubled endlessly worried;
Especially in the evening sadness comes . . .

[*At seven-three they silently weep and cling together under the umbrella. The audience laughs and applauds. Suddenly* ZANGETSU *drops his melancholy pose. Closing the umbrella with a flourish, he turns to the musicians in the room offstage right.*]

ZANGETSU [*ebullient*]: Cut it! Cut! Musicians, play something with life in it!

[*Drums and bells strike up the rollicking rhythm* Kangara, "*Bright Beat,*" *and shamisen join in with* Suika Busuika, "*Chic and Vulgar.*" ZANGETSU *tosses the umbrella to* NAGAURA *and they begin a comic folk dance. They circle one another energetically. She snuggles up to him; he gives her a playful push that sends her sprawling. He dances off laughing. She flourishes the umbrella and dances after him to accelerating bata-bata tsuke beats.* GONSUKE *watches them go out of sight as the music fades away.*]

GONSUKE: Damn fools!

[*He sits carelessly stage left, in the place of honor.* SAKURA, *who has been cowering upstage, sits in the subservient position to his right.*]

SAKURA: My abiding wish has been to meet you, dear Husband. From the beginning I have served you, though you are of common parentage and of lowly breeding. Our deep vow has been ill-fated. Our poor child . . .

GONSUKE: What'd you do with the brat, Princess?

20. A priest expelled from a temple was allowed to take with him nothing except one paper umbrella with which to ward off the elements.
21. Taken from the kabuki dance play *Sagi Musume* (1762).

Zangetsu kneels by the fire and with a wooden dipper fills a teacup with poison, warding off vapors with his sleeve. Nagaura watches. (*Nagaura:* Sawamura Gennosuke; *Zangetsu:* Ichikawa Yaozō) Page 316

"You'll stop grumbling when you're dead! Here, help me, Nagaura. Drink, damn you!" Zangetsu throws Seigen to the floor and tries to force him to drink the poison. (*Nagaura:* Sawamura Gennosuke; *Zangetsu:* Ichikawa Yaozō; *Seigen:* Morita Kanya) Page 317

Zangetsu strangles Seigen with a towel. Poison splashed on Seigen's face disfigures it with a large purple blotch. (*Nagaura:* Sawamura Gennosuke; *Zangetsu:* Ichikawa Yaozō; *Seigen:* Morita Kanya) Page 317

Zangetsu removes the hood and sees that the woman brought to him by
Kanroku is Sakura. "You? Princess Sakura?" (*Sakura:* Nakamura Jakuemon;
Zangetsu: Ichikawa Yaozō)

"I was saying I should kill the pesky mosquitoes buzzing about, though heaven-
sent, should they bother my Lady." Zangetsu pretends to swat a mosquito
with his fan. Page 320

Nagaura and Zangetsu see Sakura's tattoo. "It's too fantastic to believe . . . the princess' arm, tattooed like yours?" (*Nagaura:* Sawamura Gennosuke; *Zangetsu:* Ichikawa Yaozō; *Gonsuke:* Bandō Mitsugorō; *Sakura:* Nakamura Jakuemon) Page 322

Stripped of their clothes and all they own, Zangetsu and Nagaura are driven from Iwabuchi Hermitage. (*Zangetsu:* Ichikawa Yaozō; *Nagaura:* Sawamura Gennosuke; *Sakura:* Nakamura Jakuemon) Page 324

"Do not deny our ties of love ordained by Karma. I adore you! I adore you!"
Panting with desire, Seigen clutches at Sakura. (*Sakura:* Nakamura Jakuemon;
Seigen: Morita Kanya) Page 328

"Will you love me? Or shall I kill you, Princess?" Seigen picks up Gonsuke's knife to attack Sakura. (*Sakura:* Nakamura Jakuemon; *Seigen:* Morita Kanya) Page 328

To ward him off, she throws sutras from the altar. They pose in a mie. Page 329

She trips, he clings to the pillar threatening her. They pose in a mie.

Seigen emerges from the open grave, the knife embedded in his throat. Page 329

Gonsuke and Sakura on the hanamichi at the conclusion of Act V. He flicks
a straw mat over their shoulders and they pose. (*Gonsuke:* Bandō Mitsugorō;
Sakura: Nakamura Jakuemon) Page 330

Seigen's ghost rises among the gravestones beside the hermitage. He clutches
at and is partially hidden by trailing willow branches. (*Seigen:* Morita Kanya)
Page 330

[*Because* SAKURA *has been raised at court, she does not understand vulgar language. She continues unperturbed.*]

SAKURA: . . . contemplating his sweet memory, I wonder where he may be?

GONSUKE: The hell with him any way! We're young. We'll have more fun without him.

SAKURA [*shyly but eagerly leans against him*]: Though you left without a word, my heart has not wavered in devotion. You shall not leave this abandoned one again.

GONSUKE [*a hard laugh*]: Relax, Princess. Would I throw away a good thing? [*He casually puts his hand in her breast.*] In the old days, you had to be a noble's son, with a pretty mug, decked out in purple silk and wearing a warrior's two swords, to be lover to a princess. It's a twisted world now, isn't it, when a princess loves a gravedigger? Ha, ha, ha! Eh, Princess. I won't throw you out. And you won't leave me, eh?
[*He puts his hand more deeply into her bosom. She submits ecstatically, then rises and embraces him from behind, letting trailing kimono sleeves fall over his shoulders. She poses provocatively.*]

SAKURA: I shall never forsake you. I am alone in the world. You shall be this one's protector.
[GONSUKE *leans back, hands clasped casually around one bare knee.*]

GONSUKE: Don't worry, I'll take care of you. But you'll live as I do. I'm a beggar; I haven't a cent. You'll wear a cotton kimono, with a cheap sash wound around your gut, not like that. [*Nods at her expensive clothes.*] You'll get along without maids, servants, lacquered hair, and combs. You'll quit blacking your teeth, till they go white like the teeth of the rest of us dogs. You'll sleep with a dozen others in the room and get up at dawn. If you can't say "yes" to life in a pigsty, forget about living with me!

SAKURA [*sincerely, for she understands none of it*]: Having no experience of the heavenly things you describe, pray instruct me in what I should do.
[*She bows prettily.* GONSUKE *likes what he hears, but still considers her a liability.*]

GONSUKE: You won't do unless you're cheapened up. But I haven't time to teach you. I've got work to do. [*He thinks.*] Hmmm. I wonder? Could we farm you out some place for lessons in vulgarity?

SAKURA [*innocently*]: Would such instruction differ from composing song and poetry?

GONSUKE: Damned right it would. [*He poses.*] Now, who would take in someone like you? [*He slaps his thigh and chuckles.*] Of course. You can go to Kozukappara. Checking you into a whorehouse there should do the trick. I'll have a talk with that pimp Kanroku. [*Turns to* SAKURA.] Listen, Princess, I'm going out to fix you up with a job. While I'm gone, don't go away. Wait here, eh?

SAKURA [*obedient, yet unconsciously as to one of lower class*]: I shall do and go where you suggest. Yet, as I will be alone at night in this lonely hut and feeling trepidation, I ask that you return in haste.

GONSUKE [*annoyed at her tone*] : Hell, what are you afraid of? I may bring
  someone with me, so fix yourself and be ready to go. [*Rises.*] It's getting
  dark. I'll light a lamp. [*At the lamp he strikes a flint.*] Damn! No oil.
  Maybe there's some in the altar lamps. [*Going up toward the altar, he
  sees* SEIGEN.] My God. Isn't he a gruesome sight.
SAKURA [*frightened*] : What is it?
GONSUKE [*crosses behind and embraces her*] : Nothing. Nothing to be afraid
  of. Just . . . don't go near the altar, Princess. [*Rises cheerfully.*] You
  won't need a light. I'll be back soon. Remember, you wait here.
  [*She nods dutifully. He steps down onto the main stage. A roar of
  thunder. Lightning. He stops and looks up at the sky.*]
  It's going to pour, I'd better be off.
  [*He looks at her, then poses front with a satisfied look. Shamisen play
  Anton as the thunder roars. He trots through the gate onto the hanamichi,
  tucking up his kimono in back as he goes. At the sight of* GONSUKE's
  bare legs, SAKURA *is unconsciously aroused. She rises on her knees and
  looks longingly after him. Without a backward glance he strides down the
  hanamichi and out of sight. Music stops. Thunder subsides.*]
SAKURA: Come back quickly. Yes, come quickly. It is frightening to be alone.

kudoki

  [*Her glance falls on the mirror and she recognizes it as her own.*] Before
  this mirror each morn and eve, at the palace in times past, the familiar
  sight of a few stray locks, in an oiled and lustrous coiffure . . .
  [*She sets up the mirror. Stifling tears, she arranges her hair as the* CHORUS
  sings.]
CHORUS [*sings* Kuroi Kami, *"Black Hair"*] :
  Remembering when;

kakekotoba

    Lustrous black hair was bound, to be alluring;
  Loosened in nighttime sleep, scattered as soft down;
    Importuning him to share, this pillow till dawn.
  [SAKURA *arranges ornaments in her hair and puts on the three-tiered
  tiara. She looks at her image in the mirror and poses, near tears. Suddenly
  she sees the incense case reflected in the mirror.*]
SAKURA: What? Can it be . . . ? [*Quickly picks it up.*] It is the incense case
  fallen from my fingers at Kiyomizu Temple a short time ago! [*Looking
  closely.*] Inscribed with the same pattern on lid and box, and on the back
  is written . . . "Shiragiku." What does it mean?
  [*She sees her torn kimono sleeve. She holds both tightly, breathless with
  excitement.*]
  And the sleeve, rent from my kimono on the banks of the Inase River?
  How can both case and sleeve be at this hermitage? Ahh! That dark night
  then, in the rain at Mimeguri Shrine, the priestly form I saw was surely . . .
  Reverend Seigen, who now is here!
  [*Thunder and lightning.*]
  I would wish the thunder were less frightening.
  [*She peers eagerly into the gathering darkness for* SEIGEN. *A roll of
  thunder forces her right, then left. At the veranda, she looks out into the*

graveyard. A blinding flash. Lightning strikes a limb from the willow tree. Smoke rises from the charred trunk. SAKURA falls unconscious. Silence. Ominous Kaza Oto wind pattern begins. The screen trembles. A palsied hand appears over the top of the screen, then a second. SEIGEN staggers to his feet. Not quite dead, he has been shocked into consciousness by the lightning bolt. His face is grotesquely disfigured. A Buddhist prayer bell is repeatedly struck. SEIGEN stumbles to the stone water basin and drinks from the wooden dipper. He clings to a pillar of the veranda, his face contorted with pain. He can barely speak.]

SEIGEN: Beaten . . . left for dead . . . did I fall unconscious?

[*SAKURA recovers. In the dim light she cannot recognize him.*]

SAKURA: That voice? Are you . . . ?

SEIGEN: A young woman here? Is it . . . ?

SAKURA: Again that voice. Are you . . . ?

SEIGEN: Ahh! Is it truly . . . ?

SAKURA: Reverends Seigen?

SEIGEN: Princess Sakura!

[*He rushes to embrace her but collapses after a few steps. She is terrified. He clutches his throat with one hand and manages to snare the hem of her kimono with the other. The Buddhist bell sounds repeatedly. With maniacal intensity he forces words from his agonized throat.*]

Cruel Princess Sakura. You have forgotten Seigen, who was disgraced by you! Since that night we parted in the rain by the Inase River, I have carried your child everywhere in the hope of finding you! I have been banished, tortured, made an outcast for your love! Princess, I adore you! I adore you!

SAKURA: That is true. I was the one who spoke the falsehood and caused your disgrace. You asked for my answer. But because of my weak nature I have had a child by a secret lover. I fully accept the blame for your fall which resulted when he appeared by chance at Kiyomizu.

SEIGEN: It is the child you gave birth to whom I have cradled in my arms! It was your child . . .

SAKURA: Truly, my child was with you?

SEIGEN: It was my hand which raised him. His cursed father . . . who is he?

SAKURA: Of unspeakably low birth, yet it is fate that I love his child.

[*With the grip of a dying man SEIGEN draws her beside him.*]

SEIGEN: Listen to what could not be spoken before . . . to the tale of our hundred lives together! Listen . . . dearest Shira . . . Shiragiku!

SAKURA [*remembering*]: Shiragiku?

SEIGEN: That distant night on Enoshima's cliffs . . . Seigen remained among the living . . . while my beloved, seeking the way of love . . . leaped to death in the sea. The young page Shiragiku . . . was you Princess Sakura . . . in . . . a . . . former . . . life!

SAKURA: I? Shiragiku's incarnation? Oh, it cannot be!

SEIGEN: At birth . . . did your hand not . . . clutch his incense case? Shiragiku's?

[*Feverishly he presses her hand against his cheek. She is stunned by the truth of what he says. He embraces her from behind and they sink to the floor.*]

Through previous lives . . . into endless time . . . Seigen's love for Shiragiku! Princess, you are Shiragiku!

[*He forces her to put an arm around him. He places a trembling hand on her breast. With mounting excitement, he rubs her breasts until she nearly faints in revulsion.*]

Do not deny our ties of love . . . ordained by Karma. I adore you! I adore you!

[*Panting with desire, he presses against her.*]

SAKURA [*pleading*] : Pitiful Reverend Seigen, though you love me through generations, it is an illicit passion. I already have a husband. [*Bows politely.*] Set aside, good Seigen, your desires.

SEIGEN [*gathering his strength*] : Seigen will never abandon your love. Never. Our passion shall be consumated. Agonized life flickers to an end . . . already damned eternally for sinning . . . your refusal means nothing.

[*He clutches his chest and grimaces in pain. The prayer bell is struck insistently. SAKURA shudders and turns away. He seizes the knife left on the floor by GONSUKE.*]

If you were slain, heartless woman . . . and I . . . bliss would be ours together, sharing the same lotus leaf. Accept me now . . . or will you die . . . for . . . our . . . love?

[*SAKURA turns. She sees the knife and gasps but, as if hypnotized, she seems unable to flee. He edges toward her.*]

If our ties in this life are weak . . . marriage in the next will make them strong! Die for me!

SAKURA: I . . . I . . . !

SEIGEN: Or will you . . . love me now?

SAKURA: I . . . !

kuriage

SEIGEN [*drawing out the word*] : Well . . . ?

SAKURA [*drawing out the word*] : Well . . . !

BOTH [*alternately, then simultaneously*] : Well, well, well . . . well!

SEIGEN [*harshly*] : Will you love me? Or shall I kill you, Princess?

koroshiba
tachimawari

[*He is beside her. Gasping in agony, he brings the knife up to her throat. The hypnotic tie between them snaps. She breaks away; gently he attempts to murder her. Instrumental music alternates with song; Kaza Oto wind pattern of the large drum rises and falls; action sequences, punctuated by batan and battari tsuke beats, culminate in mie poses. The mood and tempo of fighting, though gradually rising to a climax, is deliberate throughout. Because the combat is expressed in formal patterns, the scene is at once terrifying and beautiful. SEIGEN slashes at her right and left, but his efforts are ineffectual. Moving quickly out of his reach, she avoids rather than opposes him. As a result, there is little physical contact. He manages to seize her arm but she slips free. He falls to the floor, off-balance. She runs to the altar where accordion-pleated sutras are stacked high. She*] *throws them one after another; he tries to fend them off with the knife, but they gradually entangle his arms. They pose in a mie to battari tsuke beats: she is near the altar; he stands right center in a sea of paper. The final sutra is stretched in an arc between them.*]

CHORUS [*sings slow Jizōkyō, "Saint Jizo's Prayer"*] :
I touch my brow to your feet revered Saint Jizō;
Blessed Saint, Blessed Jizō.

[*The fight continues at a slower pace. He clings to the hem of her kimono, rises, and holds the knife to her breast. She breaks away and restrains him from behind. He slashes over his head. They fall apart. Tripping, she falls to the floor by the pillar left. They pose in a mie to battari tsuke beats: he clings to the pillar leaning toward her, knife raised; she kneels facing him, bent backward to avoid the blade. Twice he rushes at her and stumbles; the knife wedges between the floor mats. He steps on the train of her kimono. She pulls free and he tumbles down the steps. They pose in a mie to battari tsuke beats: he lies on his back brandishing the knife; she kneels on the steps above him, hands clasped pleadingly. The CHORUS ends. Shamisen play faster Kasai, "Edo Melody." They rise. She avoids several dangerously close lunges. In desperation, she wrests the knife from him. He crawls along the ground toward her, lifting his hands in supplication.*]

SEIGEN: Kill me . . . please!

SAKURA: No. Please, Reverend Seigen. Stop.

SEIGEN: Then kill yourself!

[*He tries to embrace her. She does not want to use the knife against SEIGEN, so she throws it over his head and it falls into the grave. She sighs with relief and does not fend off his embrace. Feverishly he clutches at her breast. She shudders and pushes him away. He plunges head first into the grave. Silence. Drum and tsuke swell. SEIGEN rises in the grave. He has fallen onto the upturned blade and it is embedded in his throat. Blood from the wound streams onto his chest.*]

SAKURA [*kindly*] : Are you all right? Reverend Seigen?

SEIGEN: You . . . have . . . killed . . . me. Shameless . . . woman . . .

[*She turns and sees him. She clasps her hands and prays almost inaudibly.*]

SAKURA: Reverend Seigen, absolve this one of your death, I pray.

[*He shakes his head, unable to speak. On the verge of death, he nevertheless staggers from the grave in one final attempt to embrace SAKURA. She avoids him. He collides with the veranda pillar, and the knife is driven deep into his throat. Batan tsuke beats. The prayer bell is struck repeatedly. SEIGEN clings to drooping willow branches for support. Convulsions wrack his body and he dies, falling among the gravestones. Lights come up on the hanamichi. Kaza Oto wind pattern. Shamisen play loud and lively Hayame. GONSUKE runs on to fast bata-bata tsuke beats. He comes up behind SAKURA, lying huddled center. Music stops.*]

GONSUKE [*casually*] : I'm back.

[*SAKURA lets out a terrified scream. He leaps back, startled.*]

For God's sake, don't surprise me like that! What's the matter?

[*She throws herself at his feet, sobbing.*]

SAKURA: The recent thunderbolts frightened me.

GONSUKE [*scoffing*] : Hah! You highborn ones are babies. Who's going to buy you if you're a coward? Listen, it's all set. They need a woman at the Four-Six House in Kozukappara.

SAKURA [*still in shock, she bows politely*] : It is my wish that you decide. Your judgment will be acceptable.

GONSUKE: Your wish is it? I'm your husband, you'll do as I say. You're going to a whorehouse and you're going to work. Understand? [*Blithely.*] Learn the lingo and pick up a common touch. You are one hell of a sight in that outfit. But then, flashy goods sell! Ha, ha! Come on, Princess, we'll check you in.

[Kaza Oto *wind pattern.* GONSUKE *is in high spirits. Flicking a straw mat from a hook in the entry, he throws it over their shoulders. He leads her through the gate and onto the hanamichi.* SAKURA *trembles violently. The flute plays eerie* Netoribue, *"Ghostly Flute," and the large drum* Doro-doro, *"Drum Roll," indicating the appearance of a spirit.* SEIGEN's *ghost stands among the gravestones, half hidden by willow branches. He beckons to* SAKURA *with both limp arms. A pale green ball of fire—the spirit or "soul fire" of* SEIGEN—*bobs in the air over the priest's head. At seven-three* SAKURA *stands rooted, then she is pulled back as if on strings. Tsuke and drum crescendo. She collapses.* GONSUKE *kneels beside her, unaware of either the apparition or the soul fire.*]

GONSUKE: What is it?

[SAKURA *looks from* SEIGEN *to* GONSUKE. *The left side of* GON-SUKE's *face is disfigured with the same blue blotch as* SEIGEN's. *She gasps.*]

SAKURA [*weakly*] : Your face . . . like Seigen!

GONSUKE [*harshly*] : It's me!

SAKURA [*gazing back and forth between them*] : Truly, you are . . .

GONSUKE [*proudly*] : . . . I am Gonsuke, girl!

[*He flicks the straw mat around the two of them. The soul fire moves from* SEIGEN *across the stage. It floats in the air over their heads, rising and falling at the end of a long pole, manipulated by a black-robed* STAGE ASSISTANT. SAKURA *sees the soul fire. She knows that* SEIGEN's *vengeful spirit is now tied to her and that in death* SEIGEN *has willed his disfigurement on his rival* GONSUKE. *She ruefully accepts the fact that hereafter she will have no control over her life.*]

SAKURA [*sardonically*] : Since I'm to be poisoned . . .

GONSUKE: What?

SAKURA: . . . I assure you, I'll drink the cup down.

GONSUKE [*not understanding*] : No need, Girl, I'll take care of you!

[*A single ki clack. They pose. Accelerating ki clacks accompany the closing of the curtain behind them. Shamisen play* Yari Sabi, *"Rusted Spear," stick drum and flute* Tanuki Bayashi, *"Badger Rhythm," and large drum* Doro-doro. *The soul fire bobs overhead.* GONSUKE *struts proudly.* SAKURA *moves with new strength down the hanamichi. They go out of sight. Drums and flute play lively* Shagiri *between acts.*]

rokumakume   ACT VI

SCENE 1   A STREET IN YAMANOSHUKU VILLAGE

[*Two sharp clacks of the ki: the act begins. The curtain is run open to the sounds of a time bell and a wailing child. The scene is a side street in a mountain village: a police box is right, fire buckets are piled up left by an open well, and a black curtain behind the scene indicates that it is night.* KINBEI, RIHEI, MOKUBEI, *and* YUMEIZAEMON *enter carrying lanterns. They are village officials on their nightly rounds.* SANTA, *the night watchman, enters crying, "watch for fire," and banging his metal pole on the ground. The baby wails loudly. Everyone stops, amazed to hear a child in the street.* SANTA *follows the sound to an old basket, half hidden in a rubbish pile by the fence. He brings the basket to* KINBEI.]

KINBEI [*flustered, refuses the basket*] : Why is it such things happen when I'm responsible?

RIHEI: That's true. Put Kinbei on night watch and there's bound to be trouble.

YUMEIZAEMON: It may be an abandoned child, but it gets cold all the same. We can't leave it here. Should we put it in the police box?

MOKUBEI: What if a stray dog comes along and makes a meal of it? Where would we be then?

KINBEI [*looking for a way out*] : First we should know when the child was abandoned.

SANTA [*thinks*] : It wasn't there when I made rounds at two, and it's just three now.

KINBEI [*sighs*] : Then it was during my watch.

RIHEI: Should we get someone to take it in?

MOKUBEI [*searches for money in the basket, finding none*] : You have to pay foster parents and there's nothing here.

KINBEI: This is going to cost the village money.

YUMEIZAEMON: By the way, I don't see Gonsuke. He's on duty, too.

SANTA: He said he'd be here soon.

YUMEIZAEMON: He's the biggest cheat I know. His face is horrible. So's his disposition.

RIHEI [*nodding*] : He's a dreadful person with a disgusting face.

MOKUBEI: He makes me ill.

KINBEI [*frowning*] : We won't settle this business if he hears you've slandered him behind his back. Would you say this to Gonsuke's face?

ALL: No, no. Not me.

KINBEI: You aren't men at all. Look at you, all you can do is talk.

[*The child cries. They look into the basket. The time bell tolls.* GONSUKE *hurries on from the right. He carries a lantern. His face is still disfigured, but he is now dressed, like the other men, in conservative townsman's dark kimono and cloak. GONSUKE has used his possession of the Iwabuchi temple and house to establish himself as a reputable householder in the village. As a landowner he is also a ward official. He wears his new respectability lightly.*]

GONSUKE [*heartily*] : Councilmen of the ward, you've been waiting. Lots of business kept me. [*Sees the basket.*] What's this? An abandoned brat?

KINBEI: It's an abandoned boy, about two years old. We're discussing what to do with it.

RIHEI: It's got to have milk.

GONSUKE [*shrewdly*] : That's right, you need a woman to nurse the kid. What kind of heartless person would raise the thing for two years, then throw it out? [*Makes a show of deep concern.*] You know, Kinbei, it'll cost the ward hard cash to get someone to take the kid off your hands.

KINBEI [*officiously*] : The ward will have to pay two gold ryō, even three. We know that very well. Don't we councilmen?

[*Others nod in agreement.*]

GONSUKE [*briskly*] : Well then, I know how to settle this in a flash. I haven't got a son and if three ryō go with the kid, I'll take him in. The cash will pay off some of the cost of raising him, and I'll gain a son. Well, do I take the brat?

KINBEI: This is sudden. Hm. It would relieve the ward of responsibility, and surely the village elders will approve. [*He decides.*] The boy is yours. Do you agree, councilmen?

RIHEI: The sooner it's settled the better.

YUMEIZAEMON: We can collect three ryō quick enough.

GONSUKE [*slyly*] : But you'll have to feed him yourself at least until tomorrow.

KINBEI [*protesting*] : I know three ryō isn't much, Gonsuke. Still you should take him now.

GONSUKE: I don't have to pick a brat out of the street to have a son, you know. I can marry. I can have my own. [*Looks at them coolly.*] Three ryō is on the cheap side, don't you think? Add another half.

[*All react with surprise.*]

KINBEI: Three and a half ryō?

GONSUKE: That's right.

KINBEI [*temporizing*] : We will think about it, Gonsuke.

[GONSUKE *flicks his arm in his kimono sleeve and poses, looking hard at* KINBEI.]

GONSUKE: The abandoned brat will come with three and one half gold pieces, or not at all!

KINBEI [*resigned*] : Very well, three and a half then.

GONSUKE: Fine. Now that we're agreed, seal the bargain.

[*They clap in unison ten times, indicating agreement. Everyone is relieved to have an awkward situation resolved. They bow and congratulate each other.* KINBEI *takes the basket from* SANTA.]

KINBEI: Now then, Gonsuke, this is what I'll do: I'll take the boy now, my
wife will nurse him, and later in the morning we'll bring the child and the
money to your place.

[*They all bow to* GONSUKE *and ad-lib goodbyes. Shamisen play* Mokugyo
as they go off with the baby. Alone, GONSUKE *poses, highly satisfied.
The time bell tolls.*]

GONSUKE: Three ryō won't go far. My real treasure is the House of Yoshida
scroll that hangs like Buddha's talisman around my neck.

[*He pushes the scroll out the front of his kimono and gazes at it. In
silence a palanquin appears on the hanamichi.* GONSUKE *quickly puts the
scroll back inside his kimono. A young* SAMURAI *leads the palanquin
onto the main stage, pays the bearers, and waves them away. He approaches*
GONSUKE.]

SAMURAI [*politely*] : Excuse me, good Sir.

GONSUKE [*warily*] : What do you want?

SAMURAI: Does a householder named Gonsuke live in the neighborhood?

GONSUKE: I'm the landowner Gonsuke. Who wants to know?

SAMURAI: That person is you? Come.

[*He leads the way to the palanquin. The curtain is flicked open and*
AKUGORŌ *steps out. He and* GONSUKE *measure each other with their
glance and pose.*]

AKUGORŌ [*regally*] : I shall be some while. You may retire.

SAMURAI: As my Lord wishes.

[SAMURAI *bows and goes off right.* GONSUKE *feigns casual deference,
but he watches* AKUGORŌ *carefully every moment.*]

GONSUKE: So, you've come to call on Gonsuke? You, who at Kiyomizu . . .

AKUGORŌ [*pompously*] : . . . entrusted to your hand a letter to no avail. In
secret I have come tonight for one purpose and that alone: to complete the
undertaking of which we spoke before. I am here to take possession of the
Yoshida scroll.

GONSUKE: Ah, is that so? You've come for the Yoshida scroll? Which . . . I
have.

AKUGORŌ: Exactly so.

GONSUKE [*indifferent*] : It's here and I've no use for it. [*Takes it out.*] I'll be
glad to be rid of it. It weighs me down. But, I was promised by Matsui
Gengo . . .

AKUGORŌ [*grandly*] : I know what was pledged. Is that the scroll?

GONSUKE: It is.

[AKUGORŌ *extends his hand in a grandiose gesture. Casually* GONSUKE
passes the scroll to AKUGORŌ, *who quickly opens it and scans it.*]

AKUGORŌ: Beyond doubt it is the Yoshida scroll! I acknowledge its receipt.
You have done well. Much will come your way.

[AKUGORŌ *turns to go.* GONSUKE *strikes a brash pose.*]

GONSUKE: Lord Akugorō! When you begged me to steal the Miyakodori you
said I'd be rewarded. But you forget what I asked for: two thousand ryō.
I'll take the money now, if you don't mind.

AKUGORŌ [*frostily*] : Indeed? We shall undertake to convey your just reward in due time. And now, without further discussion, we shall retire for the evening.

GONSUKE: Oh, no! Keep your promise. I risked my life. I killed two men for the scroll. You can say it's a lot of money, but isn't ruling the House of Yoshida worth two thousand ryō? If you think so, pay me now. If not . . . give back the scroll.

AKUGORŌ [*with thinly disguised hatred*] : What? Is your petty tradesman's heart quaking that you may lose some gold coins, Gonsuke? Do you question my honor? Iruma Akugorō is not so contemptible. [*Darkly.*] In proper time you will receive your due.

GONSUKE: You say later. I say now is the time. The place is here. [*Poses.*] The money, great Lord Akugorō!

AKUGORŌ: Unreasonable treasonable rogue, I do not carry . . .

GONSUKE [*cutting him off*] : If you haven't got cash, go get it! Hand it over . . . or else the scroll!

[*GONSUKE reaches for the scroll. Suddenly AKUGORŌ draws and slashes. GONSUKE leaps aside and defends himself. They cross swords and pose in a mie to loud battari tsuke beats.*]

AKUGORŌ [*snarling with fury*] : Wretch! Madman!

GONSUKE [*laughs harshly*] : You're the mad one, not me!

AKUGORŌ: Insolent! You are my enemy, Gonsuke!

tate

[*Batan and battari beats alternate. Shamisen play Ishidan, "Stone Steps." AKUGORŌ strikes ponderously. GONSUKE parries several times, then agilely slips under AKUGORŌ's blade and strikes the sword from his hand. He slashes his opponent from chest to thigh. AKUGORŌ clings to GONSUKE. GONSUKE places the scroll between his teeth to free his hands and with a powerful, two-handed upward thrust into the body, kills AKUGORŌ. GONSUKE poses in a mie, sword held out at arm's length. He puts the sword away and notices the well.*]

GONSUKE [*laughs*] : A corpse and a well! Ha, ha!

[*He turns to kick the corpse into the well. Nearby a rooster crows loudly. GONSUKE starts, then poses.*]

Even dawn startles . . . the murderer.

[*The time bell tolls four in the morning. A rooster crows. Shamisen play Yotsutake Bushi, "Four Bamboos." As the stage revolves, GONSUKE kicks AKUGORŌ into the well and the scene of GONSUKE's lodgings comes into view. Action continues without a break.*]

SCENE 2   GONSUKE'S HOUSE IN YAMANOSHUKU

[*As the revolving stage stops, the faint sounds of Yatai Bayashi, "Street Stall Melody," the lively music for the Three Shrines Festival, can be heard from offstage shamisen and drums. The scene is the main room of GONSUKE's house in Yamanoshuku, modestly furnished but obviously the home of a substantial person. A curtain center leads to rooms inside.*]

*Paper sliding doors indicate a small room left. Entry to the street is by a
wooden sliding door right. TSUNAEMON, a moneylender, enters from the
right, remonstrating with OJŪ and her husband SENTARŌ, who is
really the Yoshida retainer, SHICHIRŌ incognito. TSUNAEMON is sleek,
well-fed, and dressed in unobtrusive but expensive dark wool kimono and
cloak. SENTARŌ wears a commoner's cheap cotton kimono of black
and white checks. The moneylender is sputtering and fuming. Music fades.*]

TSUNAEMON: No, no, Sentarō. I don't care if it still is dark. Take me straight
to his house!

OJŪ [*trying to placate him*] : Please forgive him, Sir.

SENTARŌ: Let him complain to the landlord. Who cares? He can yell to the
village head if he wants to.

OJŪ: Shh! People can hear. We should keep this to ourselves.

SENTARŌ: What difference does it make? I don't care who hears.

[TSUNAEMON *beats on the door.*]

TSUNAEMON [*turning to him*] : You talk outrageously. I'll see you pay for
this, Sentarō. You were lent ten gold pieces for three days. Why didn't you
send your wife when the three days were up? Since you didn't, your
landlord's going to hear about it.

SENTARŌ: Don't bother. I'll see him, to report you.

TSUNAEMON [*sputtering*] : Unprincipled wretch!

[TSUNAEMON *pounds on the door.*]

OJŪ [*trying to distract him*] : I don't blame you for being angry with such a
man. Why, he will do anything to earn a bit of cash. Listen: he's gone as
far as selling the child we took in to raise.[22] He drives me to distraction.
It's natural for you to be angry, but, please, won't you . . .

TSUNAEMON: . . . pardon your husband? Certainly not. [*Stops and looks
closely at her.*] Did he really, as you say, sell a baby?

OJŪ [*feigning tears*] : Oh, he did, Sir!

TSUNAEMON: You're a disgusting fellow.

SENTARŌ [*not intimidated*] : Why disgusting? Because I pawn a baby? It's an
old country custom.

TSUNAEMON [*he pounds and still no one comes*] : He isn't home. Why did
you bring me when he's not here? [*Pounds again.*] Landlord! Open up!

SENTARŌ [*caustically*] : He puts a lock on the outside of the door to
impress people. He's inside. [*Shouts.*] Open up in there!

TSUNAEMON: Wake up, landlord! Wake up! This is a mortuary!

[*Shamisen play* Yatai Bayashi. GONSUKE *swaggers on from the right.
Without a word, he seizes* TSUNAEMON *and throws him to the ground.
Batan tsuke beats.*]

GONSUKE: Who the hell are you? I come home to find a nervy bastard
caterwauling in front of the door.

[*He takes a key from his kimono and opens the door.*]

22. It is unclear why Shichirō, a staunch retainer of the Yoshida clan, would sell
his mistress' child. But the action is in keeping with his assumed role of a swaggering
and impulsive Edo gambler.

Sentarō. Is this fellow from your place?

SENTARŌ: Yes, Landlord Gonsuke.

[*They enter.* GONSUKE *sits stage left in the place of honor. He crosses his legs and nonchalantly settles down for a smoke as if the others weren't there.* TSUNAEMON *dusts himself off and kneels right. Fuming, he tries to regain his dignity.* OJŪ *and* SENTARŌ *close the door, then sit unobtrusively behind* TSUNAEMON. *Music stops.*]

TSUNAEMON: See here. Are you the landlord, the master here?

[GONSUKE *doesn't reply.* TSUNAEMON *looks uncomfortable.*]

I am Tsunaemon, moneylender of the Ōgyō firm. What gives you the right to seize me by the neck as if I were a . . . a day-old kitten? Landlord, you're an illiterate, unreasonable know-it-all.

GONSUKE [*lightly sarcastic*] : Like you say, I'm not educated. You said something else, too. You said my house is a mortuary. But that can't be. I'm here and I'm alive. Explain it, since you're the smart one.

[TSUNAEMON *realizes he cannot win this argument. He becomes conciliatory.*]

TSUNAEMON: Landlord, I was wrong to have said it. But it's your responsibility to control a tenant's actions. [*Officiously.*] I would like you to guarantee in writing the debts of your tenant Sentarō.

GONSUKE [*shouting*] : Do what?

SENTARŌ: Please, Master, let me tell the whole story. This is the honest truth. As you know, the Three Shrines Festival is coming up and no one wants to be a piker then, so I borrowed ten ryō from this fellow for the celebration. I had to have the money but he wouldn't give it before I signed a contract pledging my wife if it wasn't repaid in three days. Well, the three days are up now and he says he wants Ojū, or he'll take it up with you, Master.

GONSUKE: He's trying to get his collateral, is he? Ha! Forget it, fellow.

TSUNAEMON [*exploding*] : Forget it? I won't! A landlord's responsible for his people's debts. You can't leave it like this. No Sir, I'm not satisfied. Either guarantee his debt or I'm going to the village council!

nanori

GONSUKE [*grandiloquently*] : Shut your mouth, blowhard! I'm no fat cat that spills out his guts because a shyster like you makes a noise. Virtue I never knew, but I've plenty of training in vices. [*Strikes a bravado pose.*] I'm Tsurigane Gonsuke. With a bit of cash I bought a landowner's rights.[23] Of my boarders, no one wins the prize for filial piety. I haven't been here long, but when they're in trouble they run to me, 'til, hell, my front yard looks like a prison gate! I welcome to my property the pick of the crop of thugs and thieves, and the man who'll put a rope around his parent's neck gets his room rent free!

---

23. The power of money had become increasingly important by the Kasei era. In spite of Shōgunate regulations merchants could buy social position that infringed on the prerogatives of the samurai class. Even a rogue like Gonsuke is able, with a small amount of money, to buy land and with it respectability and a place on the ward council.

OJŪ [*hopefully*] : Do you hear that, Husband?

SENTARŌ [*bows to* GONSUKE] : You, Sir, are an understanding master.

TSUNAEMON: Heavens. He's a lunatic. [*Changing his tactics.*] Sir, you paid good money for your property. You can understand how it is with me. He agreed to pledge his wife as security and . . .

GONSUKE [*grinning wickedly*] : You don't get her. It's damned well usury asking a wife as collateral on a three-day loan. [*Leans in confidentially.*] Would you like me to tell that to the council? I will, if you don't get the hell out of here. Clear out, before I bash in your head!

[GONSUKE *threatens* TSUNAEMON *with the tobacco tray.* TSUNAEMON *crawls to the edge of the room and picks up his sandals.*]

TSUNAEMON [*ruefully*] : You're an excitable man, Landlord. Ahem. Isn't he, Sentarō?

SENTARŌ [*curtly*] : On your way if you're finished.

TSUNAEMON: I'm going. [*Crosses to the door.*] I'm going, but this is too absurd for words.

GONSUKE [*ominously*] : Then leave without any. Go, silent as death.

TSUNAEMON [*cowed and mortified*] : I'm going, I'm going, silent . . . as . . . death.

[*Shamisen, drums and bells play* Take ni Naritaya, *"I Want to Become a Bamboo,"* and Shoden Bayashi, *"Sacred Melody."* TSUNAEMON, *holding his sandals in his hand, tiptoes through the door and off right, thoroughly defeated.* SENTARŌ *faces* GONSUKE *humbly. Music stops.*]

SENTARŌ: With just a few words you settled it. Wife, offer thanks.

OJŪ [*bowing*] : Your firmness showed him to be a man of mean spirit, Master.

[*Shamisen play* Yatai Bayashi. KINBEI, *his wife carrying the baby, and the other councilmen enter from the right. They come directly to the door and open it. Music softens. They ad-lib greetings.*]

GONSUKE [*casually but politely*] : Kinbei, come in, come in.

[*They remain standing in the entry, anxious to be finished.*]

KINBEI: Thank you, but we meet with the elders soon. We've collected from the ward. Please receive three and a half ryō and the child.

[KINBEI *pushes a stack of paper-wrapped coins toward* GONSUKE. GONSUKE *hooks them with his pipe, hefts their weight, and smiles as he slips them inside his kimono.* KINBEI's *wife passes him the baby. It cries, and* GONSUKE *dumps it unceremoniously in* OJŪ's *lap. He resumes smoking.*]

Our agreement is concluded. We are grateful, Gonsuke. It's still early, we'll leave so you can rest.

GONSUKE [*lightly*] : I'll watch over the kid. And thanks for the money.

[*Music resumes. The visitors bow and hurry off, obviously relieved.* OJŪ *uncovers the baby's face. The baby cries. She and* SENTARŌ *recognize the child as* SAKURA's. *Music fades.*]

OJŪ [*involuntarily*] : Ahh!

GONSUKE: He isn't your kid, but he's hungry; since you're here, why don't you give him your breast?

[GONSUKE *sits smoking.* OJŪ *and* SENTARŌ *exchange glances. They rise and quietly slip to the door with the child.*]

SENTARŌ: We will let you rest, Master.

[*They ease the door open and are about to leave. Without warning* GONSUKE *leaps up and blocks their way. He looks at them haughtily and poses.*]

GONSUKE: Sentarō, stay where you are! You, Woman, give the brat his lunch!

OJŪ: Then you know the child is . . . ?

SENTARŌ: Quiet! Do not tell . . .

GONSUKE [*he slams the door closed*] : Nothing goes on here Gonsuke doesn't know!

yusuriba

shichigochō

[*Shamisen play* Kawaigarareta, *"Once Loved." The two sit dejectedly.* GONSUKE *swaggers back and sits. He poses with his legs crossed, holding a pipe in his right hand. He speaks grandiloquently, relishing the power he holds over them.*]

The kid means nothing to me still I took him in; for even three gold pieces are better than none. I knew who had the child, who abandoned him; lodger in my tenement, Sentarō; if a rope around your neck is a frightening thought; hand over to your landlord twenty ryō of gold; pick up the little bastard and clear the hell out!

[OJŪ *and* SENTARŌ *are amazed.*]

SENTARŌ: You mean you took the waif in knowing all the while; your purpose was extorting from me twenty ryō?

OJŪ: Twenty ryō of gold you say? He must pay it now?

GONSUKE: You have that much haven't you?

SENTARŌ: I have twenty ryō?

GONSUKE [*posing grandly*] : In your wife Ojū you have!

OJŪ *and* SENTARŌ [*pose*] : Ehhh?

GONSUKE: If I keep the damned brat here someone's got to nurse him; I've a tenant luckily whose wife is giving milk; as security she stays to suckle the kid; until Sentarō returns to pay up twenty ryō! [*Grins at* SENTARŌ.] Does the cunning of your landlord impress you, Sentarō?

SENTARŌ [*impressed in spite of himself*] : To use an abandoned child to earn twenty ryō . . .

GONSUKE [*front*] : . . . is one hell of a good plan, don't you think it is?

OJŪ: Then it's settled: I'll remain in lieu of ransom . . .

GONSUKE [*his turn to be surprised*] : You'll hock yourself for him?

OJŪ: If not my husband . . .

SENTARŌ: If I'm arrested . . .

[*Both think of* SENTARŌ's *duty to find the Yoshida scroll.*]

GONSUKE: You'll leave her with me?

OJŪ [*obliquely giving permission*] : Indeed, Sentarō, you must . . .

SENTARŌ [*acknowledging*] : . . . from this instant surely I . . .

GONSUKE [*roars with laughter*] : . . . must check your wife with Gonsuke! Ha, ha, ha!

[*They pose.*]

CHORUS [*sings* Take ni Naritaya, *and drums and bell play* Shoden Bayashi]:
Let me become a bamboo, straight-growing and tall . . .
[*During the song* SENTARŌ, *boiling with resentment, yanks up the hem of his kimono and rushes through the door. He slams it closed and runs onto the hanamichi. In his haste he almost knocks down* KANROKU, *leading a palanquin carried by two* BEARERS. SENTARŌ *rushes past them and out of sight.* KANROKU *knocks at* GONSUKE's *door.*]

KANROKU: Gonsuke, are you there?

GONSUKE: It must be Kanroku. Come in.

KANROKU [*pops his head in*]: Ah, you're here. Good, good. [*To* BEARERS.]
Wait there.
[BEARERS *bow and squat beside the palanquin.* KANROKU *enters and crosses to* GONSUKE, *who remains sitting. The baby cries.* KANROKU *looks at* OJŪ *in amazement.*]
What's this, Gonsuke? Have you taken a wife with a child?

GONSUKE: Don't talk like a fool. Hard cash went with the abandoned kid, so I took him in. She's a tenant's wife.

KANROKU: You are a strange one. You've got a wife but you send her out as a prostitute. Then you pick up a kid without mother or father and bring in a woman to feed it.

GONSUKE; Easy come easy go. When it's time, I'll cull 'em out.

KANROKU: You're the hardest man I ever met, Gonsuke. But, listen, there's something we have to talk about. I brought your wife back. She's no good at Kozukappara any more.

GONSUKE [*uninterested, lights a pipe*]: Hmmm.

KANROKU: Listen to this.
[*He settles down to tell his story. Shamisen play* Take ni Naritaya *in the background.*]
I set her up in a place of her own, because one look at her and you knew she was a nice piece of goods. From the beginning she was the talk of the quarter. Customers fought to try out the new "Scarlet Princess of Kozukappara." Then the word got around that she talked and acted like the daughter of a court noble. It made men blush. Scared them speechless. The wife worked hard to get rid of her stuck-up ways. With the man's tattoo on her arm, we called her the "Cherry Bell Princess." Soon customers lined up to get in. We passed out numbers like a butcher shop.

GONSUKE: Hell, if she's got customers, why bring her back?

KANROKU [*confidentially*]: Someone, I don't know who, began whispering about town, "a ghost comes out when the whore lays down." I had to move her. We went to another part of the quarter. Gonsuke, guess what happened? The ghost followed right along. Everywhere I took her, the ghost was there, too.

GONSUKE: You mean a ghost is tailing the princess?

KANROKU [*nods vigorously*]: That's right.

GONSUKE [*gloomily*]: If your story's true, it may be the ghost that ruined my face.

KANROKU: Oh? I knew your face wasn't always like that. I thought you had an accident.

GONSUKE [*laughs off his premonition*] : You've told a weird story, Kanroku. Anyway, I don't care how good-looking she is, who wants her with a ghost tagging along? Not me.

[*He turns away to smoke.* KANROKU *is not put off so easily.*]

KANROKU: I've brought her home. There's no other place for her. [*Calls off.*] Send her in. Then go off and have a drink.

FIRST BEARER: Yes, Sir. We'll be across the street.

[*The men lift the side flap of the palanquin and trot off right. Shamisen play* Inshu, *"Master of the House."* SAKURA *rises indolently from the palanquin. She is markedly changed. She wears a thin, erotically draped kimono, its garish pattern of the type affected by cheap prostitutes. A cloak falls provocatively off one shoulder. Her hair is deranged. She saunters carelessly into the room.* OJŪ *is thunderstruck to see her husband's mistress, but she hides her reaction.*]

GONSUKE: So. You've been around and now you're back. Did the pimps get their money's worth, Princess?

[*He laughs.* SAKURA *poses indolently. Her speech unconsciously alternates between the vulgar idiom of a harlot and her old, elegant court speech. The effect is humorously incongruous.*]

SAKURA: You don't have to worry, I made out all right. What's good enough for a trick ought to be good enough for . . . you, oh, most cherished husband. So what if I moved around?

[*She sees* OJŪ *and the baby.* OJŪ *is unknown to her, and she does not recognize the baby. She crosses spitefully to* GONSUKE *and hooks the tobacco box away from him. She strikes it repeatedly with her pipe to get his attention.*]

Hey, where'd you pick up the broad? You presume upon my good nature should you imagine I would tolerate . . . this old bag shacked up here. In this Land of the Rising Sun, sufficient space does not exist to encompass two of us . . . let alone a puking brat. If she wishes, let her suckle, let her rear the child . . . out of my god-damned sight. I find the infant offends my sensibilities. So, Gonsuke, Let's knock it off!

[*She hikes one knee up under her chin in an undignified pose and smokes.* GONSUKE, *vastly amused, does not bother to glance her way.*]

GONSUKE: Hey, Kanroku, she learned a few things since she went with you. Still, some of the princess shows through. Ha, ha!

KANROKU: Birth tells. Rub a tarnished gold piece and it shines.

SAKURA: What do you guys know? From break of dawn through the night . . . ah, drop it, who cares.

GONSUKE [*good-naturedly*] : I see, I see. She's chopped down the middle: half princess, half bitch.

[*The men laugh.*]

SAKURA: Where'd you snatch the snot-nosed kid? If you desire to bring a son to manhood, did I not give birth? For God's sake, Gonsuke, at least you could raise your own bastard.

[*Stretching out, she leans indolently on one elbow.*]

GONSUKE: Don't be stupid. He brings in money.

KANROKU [*rubbing his hands together*] : How true, my Friend, say what you like, money comes first. Gonsuke, your wife is back, but the seal that's fixed to her contract is mine. At Kozukappara they thought she'd work out, so you were paid twenty ryō in cash. Now they call me a liar and want their money back. I don't have it, you do. Return the twenty ryō, Gonsuke.

GONSUKE [*lightly*] : You're a born fool. Since you've come this far with the wife, leave her, Kanroku. But hell, I haven't any money, not a coin.

KANROKU [*mournfully*] : Then there's nothing else to do but take the princess back. I suppose they'll turn her into a streetwalker, a "pearl of the night." I suppose they'll beat me. It's in their hands.

[*He rises abruptly and takes her hand.*]

Well, Princess, back to the whorehouse you go.

SAKURA: Do you propose to return me to that place once again? [*Pulls her hand loose.*] Cut it out. Indeed, rudely to seize my hand reveals your lack of breeding. [*She slaps her pipe on the floor and poses.*] Damned disgusting pimp!

KANROKU: Talk all you want, the money's got to be settled.

GONSUKE [*briskly*] : All right, Kanroku, I'll settle.

KANROKU: But, you're broke you said.

GONSUKE: You'll be satisfied. Just listen.

[*He beckons KANROKU over and whispers in his ear. KANROKU brightens.*]

KANROKU: In her place?

GONSUKE [*grinning*] : Is it a good idea?

KANROKU: It's a great one!

GONSUKE [*casually to OJŪ*] : Hey, Missus. You go with this fellow to Kozukappara and stand in at the whorehouse for a while.

OJŪ [*dumbfounded*] : What? Work in Kozukappara, in place of . . . your wife?

GONSUKE [*heartily*] : It won't be long. Sentarō can pick you up later, when he pays me twenty ryō. You do it for a while, Missus, all right?

OJŪ [*pretending aloofness*] : Though your strange wife's affairs are no concern of mine, I will go as her substitute out of consideration for my husband's honor.

[*She bows, secretly pleased that she can help the princess.*]

GONSUKE [*impressed*] : Lady, you're a regular son of Edo.[24]

OJŪ: Spare your flattery. I will go, but my husband . . .

GONSUKE [*expansively*] : . . . will have everything explained.

OJŪ: I leave the child in your care.

---

24. Impulsiveness and generosity are typical of the Edokko, or native-born Edoite.

[OJŪ *places the child on the floor.* KANROKU *ushers her into the palanquin. In silence she looks back at* SAKURA *and poses. The* BEARERS *carry her swiftly onto the hanamichi, followed by* KANROKU.]

CHORUS [*sings* Giri to Nasake, *"Duty and Compassion" to slow shamisen accompaniment*] :
Duty and human compassion,
    Struggle within one heart.
[SENTARŌ *rushes onto the hanamichi, halting the palanquin at seven-three.* OJŪ *looks warningly at him.*]

SENTARŌ [*elliptically, trying to find out what has happened*] : Ojū, faithful to Yoshida . . .

OJŪ: . . . Sentarō, my husband . . .

SENTARŌ: . . . do you take the place . . . ?

OJŪ: . . . of our master's princess.
[SENTARŌ *understands, though the words mean nothing to* KANROKU, *who is amazed that* OJŪ's *husband does not object.*]

KANROKU: You agree?
[SENTARŌ *nods with resolution. He hands* OJŪ *a letter of divorce, which he has just had prepared, that releases him to continue looking for the Miyakodori scroll.*]

SENTARŌ: Here. It is a letter of divorce.

OJŪ [*bows gratefully*] : I am pleased.

SENTARŌ: This severs our relations.[25]

OJŪ [*reading*] : "To Lady Ojū, from Awazu no Shichirō." I understand.

KANROKU: Bearers, on your way!
[*The* BEARERS *carry the palanquin off, followed by* KANROKU.]

CHORUS [*repeats* Giri to Nasake] :
Duty and human compassion,
    Struggle within one heart.
[SENTARŌ *moves stealthily up to the door, listens a moment, then moves into the bushes at the rear of the house.*]

GONSUKE: Well, wife, it's been a hell of a long time. Why don't I get out the bedding, eh?
[*He goes into the small room left and brings out folded bedding which he drops beside* SAKURA.]

SAKURA: God, not again! How blessed to contemplate one night alone, in which my pillow is not a hated enemy.
[GONSUKE *puts the baby at the foot of the bedding under a blanket.*]

GONSUKE: Don't let the kid bother you. He'll have to sleep down there.

SAKURA: That's lousy. [*Kicks the covers off the baby with her foot.*]
Scrawny runt. The child is detestable.

GONSUKE [*stretching out*] : Quit complaining. I'm sick of it. Hey, Wife, is it like he said? Does a ghost pop out when you lie down?

25. He legally releases her from their marriage so she will not share in any punishment he might incur in continuing to protect Matsuwaka and search for the Miyakodori.

SAKURA [*lies down, bored*] : Do not speak of ghosts, I pray.

GONSUKE: Praying won't keep them away! Ha, ha! I know what will though. [*He gets a short sword from the closet upstage and shows it to* SAKURA.] It doesn't look like much but it's a prize blade. If your ghost comes out, don't be bashful. Run him through.

SAKURA [*leaning indolently on one elbow*] : Is the blade, I pray, considered valuable?

[*He tucks the sword under the pillow and sits cross-legged beside her.*]

GONSUKE: It is. It's rusty now but in its time it's carved up lots of men. [*The baby cries. He carelessly shoves it with his foot.*] Hey. Shut up, you.

[*Shamisen play* Giri to Nasake *as* SANTA *enters from the right. He knocks on the door, then peeks in, holding the lantern before him. He sees* GONSUKE *and bows. Music softens.*]

SANTA: Excuse me Sir, the council is meeting. They're asking for you. I was sent . . .

GONSUKE: Tell them I wasn't home.

SANTA: They are meeting about the money. [GONSUKE *looks up.*] And they're drinking.

GONSUKE [*rises*] : There's always something when you're a landowner. You wait, Wife, right here.

SAKURA: Don't worry. I'll be asleep. Alone.

[*Music becomes louder.* GONSUKE *gets a cloak from the closet and puts it on. Holding the lantern before him,* SANTA *leads* GONSUKE *off right.* SAKURA *rises and watches them go. The music stops. The time bell tolls.*]

SAKURA: He went off without lighting a lamp. Where does he keep one? Ah, it's a bore.

[*The time bell tolls. Soft, ominous* Kaza Oto *wind pattern begins. Shamisen play* Mimeyori, *"Beautiful Eyes." She yawns and stretches. She searches for a lamp. From the small room left we hear the sound of steel and flint. A glow brightens the paper doors.* SAKURA *re-enters with a lighted lamp which she places on the floor beside the bedding.*]

Oh, to sleep one night alone. Long ago only the zither sounded in the early evening. For a gloomy place like this though, we should hear bright theater music, not the zither.

[*She sits and pushes the child to one side with her foot.*]

Hey, Kid, I need a nap. Move over.

[*She stretches out luxuriously. After a moment the baby wails. Wearily, she rolls over and pats the baby.*]

Hey, don't cry on me, Kid. Now, now, now. Don't cry.

[*The child is quiet. Shamisen and drum are silent. She looks at the baby. The irony of the situation strikes her. She poses, on the verge of tears.*]

Ahh, to think . . . that I too in this same way once cradled my child; bud of the House of Yoshida and now abandoned; alike in form and childish sound, wretched and alone; my own beloved baby . . .

[*She forces thoughts of the past from her mind.*]

A squalling kid reminds me of brawling short-timers. God, what paradise to rest a night before going back to work!

[*She sighs and picks up a pipe. She tries to light it over the coals of the tobacco tray, but the coals are dead. She leans toward the lamp for a light. Doro-doro crescendos, indicating the appearance of a ghost. The lamp slides out of reach. Thinking it was her imagination, she leans in again to light her pipe. Again the lamp slides away. Wearily she rises to inspect the room. She finds nothing. Suddenly she shivers and pulls her kimono tightly around her. The stage darkens.*] [26]

The night breeze is chill.

[*She slides under the covers and pulls them around her neck. Doro-doro becomes louder. She sits up. The ghost of SEIGEN appears, dressed in a dirty gray kimono. His emaciated figure seems about to disintegrate. His arms hang limp, his head bends grotesquely to one side. He seems to float in a pool of pale green light. Doro-doro subsides. Annoyed, SAKURA knocks the ashes from her pipe into the tobacco tray.*]

So, it's you again is it, old Seigen's ghost? What do you want now? You follow me as if it were your right, but it's time you listened to reason.

[*She poses. Shamisen and flute play eerie Netoribue.*]

I moved and I moved but you followed me every place, until my best patrons left. Why? Did you want to ruin my business? Destroy my livelihood? Your ghastly appearance once terrified me. But now I know these nightly visits are just the working out of Karma. You don't frighten me. I'm used to you, Mister Apparition, and your incessant visits grow tiresome. Get out. It's dawn. It's time for you to disappear. So, go on, go home, scat! How depressing having a priest as a customer.

[*She gestures roughly for him to go. He doesn't move. She sighs.*]

Listen to me, Reverend Seigen. I may have been Shiragiku in a former life, but the misery you bear isn't my fault. Quit hanging around, quit nagging me. Because you're wretched, you hold me cheap. And I'm tired of it. Your rotting corpse belongs in the grave, not here. I loath it. Get out of my sight!

[*She slaps the pipe on the floor and contemptuously turns her back on him. Doro-doro grows louder. SEIGEN raises his arms. She senses his response and turns.*]

What? What is it you want?

[*SEIGEN points to the child, then to SAKURA. She reacts. He repeats the gesture.*]

This is the infant . . . born of my womb? And your jealous spirit lives on in my husband? Can it be true? My . . . own . . . child?

[*Music swells. SAKURA rushes tenderly to the child, but SEIGEN raises his hand and she is forced back. She tries again; again he gestures her*]

26. Kabuki was performed in the daytime. To let in the light, wooden shutters running the length of the theater under the eves were opened. Here Namboku's stage direction reads: "Close the shutters and darken the stage."

344   The Scarlet Princess of Edo

away. SAKURA *falls to her knees, weeping. She clasps her hands in supplication.*]

Knowing my grief, will you keep me from my child? Relent, Reverend Seigen, I beseech you.

[SEIGEN *does not move. Desperately, she draws* GONSUKE's *sword. Drum and tsuke alternate double beats as she attacks. With a limp gesture he easily repels her. She sinks to the floor. Music swells.* SEIGEN *glides through a panel in the wall and is gone. The green light fades and is replaced by the warm glow of the lamp. Silence.* SAKURA *rushes to embrace her baby.*]

To think I did not know you.

[*The child cries. She opens her kimono and places the child to her breast.*] You yearn for a mother's milk, proof we are bound by ties of blood. Past sins erased memory of my beloved child's face. I am your mother. You are my child. Pitiful one, fated to be born to misery.

[*Weeping, she clings to the crying child. Yatai Bayashi festival music is heard in the distance.* GONSUKE *enters from the right, dragging his cloak. He has been drinking and his walk is unsteady.*]

GONSUKE: Hey, Wife, here I am. I'm back. I'm home. Hey, Princess. You sleeping?

SAKURA: It took you long enough.

GONSUKE [*plops down on the bedding*] : Of course, of course. We were drinking. We tossed it down like nobles. [*Sees the child.*] You're nursing the brat? Forget it. Little bastard. Don't know where he came from. Leave him be, leave him be.

SAKURA: He'll be asleep soon. The least you could do is meet your own child.

GONSUKE [*fuzzily*] : Meat? It was good tonight. Goat meat. Ha, ha! Kid meat. I can't drink any more. Do everything in secret. Did you pull in a lot of customers tonight? [*She moves as if to fix the bedding.*] If you put that bedding away I'll kill you.

SAKURA [*bitterly*] : We're not in a brothel now. This is your house.

GONSUKE: That's stupid. I already went past my house.

SAKURA: It is your house, I tell you.

GONSUKE: Yeh? It really is? Then throw that pukey kid out of my house! Get rid of him.

[*As he starts to pick up the child to throw him out, a letter falls from his breast.* SAKURA *quickly picks it up and reads the address.*]

SAKURA: "To Matsui Gengo, from Shinobu Sōta."

[*Uncertain of what he has heard, he puts the child back and turns.* SAKURA *hides the letter.*]

GONSUKE: Hm? You walked the streets in Matsui, too? Ha! You'd better turn a trick one way or another, Wife. Come here.

[*He pulls her roughly by the hand and crosses upstage to get a jug of wine and a cup. He forces her down on the bedding.*]

Here. Have a drink. Come on, have a drink.

SAKURA: I will. I will drink with you, my Lord.

[*He holds the cup out to her, but she turns away coquettishly. Unseen, she holds the letter toward the lamp and furtively reads it. He turns away, surly at her rebuff.*]

GONSUKE: You've no damn right playing high and mighty aristocrat with me, Princess. I wasn't born a flunky or a gravedigger. I'm a samurai, a real samurai, do you hear?

[*He downs the cup and pours another. SAKURA looks up from the letter, shocked.*]

SAKURA: As a samurai, your name was . . . ?

GONSUKE [*half-hearing*]: Name? Something never spoken.

SAKURA: Shinobu . . . Sōta . . . ?

[*She poses, holding the letter behind her back. He struggles to comprehend, but his mind is befuddled by the wine.*]

GONSUKE [*mumbling*]: Hmm? You know a lot, Wife?

SAKURA [*ominously*]: Yes, I do.

GONSUKE: If you do, you should know enough to drink when your lord and master commands.

SAKURA: No, no, dear Husband. The man must drink first. Allow me, dearest Master.

[*Playing the wheedling courtesan, she pours for him. He drinks unsteadily.*]

GONSUKE: I drank like a lord before. I'll drink like one again. [*Drinks.*] I don't give a damn if you boast you're a princess. What do I care. Overnight I'll be a great noble. And the reason? This.

[*He takes out the wrapped scroll. SAKURA starts, but cannot identify it.*]
It looks like an amulet and it is. It's the guardian of my rise in the world, the Miyakodori scroll. Who holds the rolled scroll? Danjūrō! Ha, ha, ha!

SAKURA [*encouraging him*]: Imagine, in your possession. Yet, how could you have . . . ?

GONSUKE [*boasting, holds up the sword*]: How? I took this sword. I killed the owner of the scroll with it and then cut down a kid of twelve or thirteen who happened onto Edo's Sumida River bank. I had to run. For awhile I was Gengo's flunky, then came this grubby life. But I hung tight to my treasure all the time, talisman that will make Tsurigane Gonsuke Lord of Wineland, Prince of Sake Castle. Ha, ha! Then we'll drink like lords every day!

[*He does not notice SAKURA's horrified reaction. She controls herself with great effort, then leans against him provocatively.*]

SAKURA: Are you being truthful? Is it not a boastful tale designed to impress this one?

GONSUKE [*preening*]: It's true. I did it. Slick as a monkey sliding down a tree. Ha, ha, ha! Because you're the daughter of a court noble, being wife to a samurai lord is . . .

[*Sliding a hand into her breast, he suddenly stops, realizing he has said too much. He pulls away.*]
Not so. What I said just now is a lie. I made it up. It's all lies. All of it, lies . . . lies. Lies.

share

share

Sakura hooks the tobacco box. Gonsuke is unconcerned. "Hey, where'd you pick up the broad? You presume upon my good nature should you imagine I would tolerate . . . this old bag shacked up here." Sakura's speech alternates between court speech and vulgar idiom. (*Ojū:* Sawamura Sōjūrō; *Sakura:* Nakamura Jakuemon; *Gonsuke:* Bandō Mitsugorō) Page 340

Sentarō (actually Shichirō) watches the palanquin carrying his wife, Ojū, to a life of prostitution. (*Kanroku:* Bandō Yagorō; *Sentaro:* Kawarazaki Gonjūrō) Page 342

"Hey. Shut up, you." Gonsuke shoves the baby with his foot to quiet it. (*Gonsuke:* Bandō Mitsugorō; *Sakura:* Nakamura Jakuemon) Page 343

Left alone, Sakura reaches to light her pipe over the flame of the lamp.
Mysteriously it moves out of her reach. (*Sakura:* Nakamura Jakuemon)
Page 344
Gonsuke is too drunk to notice Sakura reading the letter that brands him as
her father's killer. (*Gonsuke:* Bandō Mitsugorō; *Sakura:* Nakamura Jakuemon)
Page 346

Sakura cuts the throat of her child, because its father is the murderer of her father. Gonsuke lies in a drunken stupor. (*Gonsuke:* Bandō Mitsugorō; *Sakura:* Nakamura Jakuemon) Page 347

Sakura plunges the sword into the stomach of the sleeping Gonsuke. He wakes and places his foot on her waist to hold her off. They pose in a mie. (*Sakura:* Nakamura Jakuemon; *Gonsuke:* Bandō Mitsugorō) Page 347

Sakura plunges the sword into Gonsuke's side as he struggles with her. He gasps, his fingers claw the air. (*Gonsuke:* Bandō Mitsugorō; *Sakura:* Nakamura Jakuemon) Page 348

SAKURA [*sweetly*] : Drink one more cup of wine, dear Husband. Please drink.

GONSUKE [*waving her away*] : I can't, I can't. I'm not bottomless Yuranosuke, out of a kabuki play.[27] I'm Gonsuke! Ha, ha, ha, ha! That's good, that's good!

[*Laughing at his own joke, he accepts more wine from* SAKURA.]

SAKURA: Here, don't go to sleep. Drink another cup. Drink up. Drink.

[*She forces several cups on him. Gasping, he waves her away. He falls on his back in a stupor. Her urgings trail off. She shakes him; he does not move. Silence. Cautiously, she removes the scroll from inside his kimono and bites through the cord which holds it. Soft batan tsuke beats. She unrolls the scroll in the light of the lamp. She recognizes it and weeps with gratitude.*]

The House of Yoshida is restored. Blessed favor that my brother's murderer and my father's is found.

[*She brings the scroll to her forehead, then puts it safely away. Without a sound she unsheathes the sword.*]

How pitiful that you are his son. This blade ended Father's life. Now you are enemies, my husband and . . . my . . . son. Please forgive me.

[*Her eyes fill with tears. She raises the sword. The baby cries in his sleep. Doro-doro swells. She covers his face with a quilt, then plunges the sword into his throat. The crying ceases abruptly.*]

"Namu Amida Butsu. Namu Amida Butsu."

koroshiba

[Kaza Oto *wind pattern rises and falls. A single shamisen plays* Sugomi. SAKURA *now moves with deadly assurance. She throws* GONSUKE's *cloak over the lamp and in the semi-darkness poses in a fierce mie, holding the bloody blade high over her head. Battari tsuke beats. A temple bell tolls in the distance. She drops to her knees and frees her right arm of the restricting kimono sleeve. She poses. The bell tolls. Stealthily she crosses to* GONSUKE *and drops to her knees beside him. The bell tolls. Using both hands, she plunges the sword into his stomach. Batan tsuke beats; music swells.* GONSUKE *screams, struggling to sit up. He slides off the kimono top to reveal a bloody wound below his ribs. They pose. The bell tolls.*]

GONSUKE [*in terrible agony*] : Princess! You do this . . . to your husband?

tachimawari

[*They rise and fight in slow, stylized movements accompanied by tsuke, shamisen, and drum. Each sequence ends in a mie, emphasized by battari tsuke beats. She attacks; he stumbles to the floor. He places his right foot against her waist, holding her off. She raises the sword. They pose.* GONSUKE's *hair, loosened by a* STAGE ASSISTANT, *falls to his shoulders. He struggles to take the sword from her, but lacks the strength. He falls against a pillar. They pose.* SANTA, *making his rounds, hears the commotion and peeks through the door. He runs off to sound the alarm.* GONSUKE *seizes* SAKURA's *kimono and manages to pull her to the floor. They pose. Music swells. They rush past each other simultaneously, and as*

---

27. Oishi Yuranosuke, one of the heroes of *Chūshingura: The Treasury of Loyal Retainers*. As a ruse he pretends to be a drunkard.

share

347   The Scarlet Princess of Edo

they turn back the sword plunges into GONSUKE. GONSUKE *gasps and clutches his side. His fingers stiffen. He dies. Silence. The sword slips from* SAKURA*'s trembling hand.*]

SAKURA: For though he was evil and for salvation of father and of son, I now consecrate to Buddha . . .

[*She cuts a lock of her hair as an offering to help them attain Buddhahood. Suddenly alarm signals of clacking bamboo are heard off right. Shamisen play rapid* Hayame. SAKURA *wipes the blade and sheathes it. A dozen villagers crowd on from the right. They carry sticks and clubs, some carry lanterns. Though eager to see a woman murderer, they are afraid to enter the house. They mill about outside. Clutching the sword and the scroll,* SAKURA *cautiously slides the door open. She sees the crowd of villagers and freezes.* SENTARŌ, *mingling with the crowd, sees the scroll and sword and guesses what has happened. He slips unobtrusively away to bring the news to* HANBEI.]

VILLAGERS: Murderer! Murderess!

[*They threaten her with sticks and clubs. She slams the door to* batan tsuke *beats. All pose. A sharp* ki *clack: the curtain is run closed to soft, continuous* ki *clacks. Drums, flute, and bell play fast* Yatai Bayashi *between scenes.*]

ōzume

FINALE   THREE SHRINES FESTIVAL SCENE

[*Two* ki *clacks: the curtain is run open. Shamisen, drums, and flute play brilliant* Itcho, *"Single Rhythm." Tsuke beats rise to a furious climax as* HANBEI *comes into view on a trap rising in the center of the stage. Behind him a black curtain covers the set.* HANBEI *is dressed as* SAKURA, *his face covered.*[28] *A large wicker hamper is strapped to his shoulders. To* battari tsuke *beats he poses. Music changes to* Yatai Bayashi. HANBEI *runs onto the hanamichi to rapid* bata-bata tsuke *beats, stopping when he sees a festival parade approaching. A dozen young* MEN, *dressed in light green kimonos and wearing large boatlike hats, dance toward him playing* binzasara *sound-makers.* HANBEI *tries to escape down the second hanamichi, but his way is blocked by a second group of celebrants, young* GIRLS *dressed in boys' pale blue and pink kimonos and trousers. They strike jangling metal staves on the ground in time to their dance movements.* HANBEI *moves center. The two groups pass in front of him. They notice him. Suddenly the men step out of their green kimonos, revealing short black costumes underneath. They are* CONSTABLES *in disguise, searching for* SAKURA. *They surround* HANBEI. *Music stops.*]

CONSTABLES: Do not move!

28. An example of a quick-change (hayagawari). Throughout the play Danjūro has been making quick-changes as he has alternated playing Seigen and Gonsuke in quick succession. Here he appears as Princess Sakura only a few moments after being seen as the murdered Gonsuke. In a few more moments he will drop his disguise as Sakura and become Hanbei. Within perhaps twenty minutes Danjūro is seen playing four roles.

tate

[*With their metal rods of office, they hold* HANBEI *fast. All pose in a group mie to battari tsuke beats. A sharp ki clack: the black curtain falls and is whisked away by* STAGE ASSISTANTS, *revealing the colorful scene of the Asakusa Kannon Shrine in Edo. The main gate is an imposing structure, painted Chinese red and gold. An enormous paper lantern hangs in the archway. Cherry trees fill the background with a sea of pink blossoms. Music resumes.* HANBEI *throws off the* CONSTABLES. *They face him from both sides of the stage.*]

watarizerifu
shichigochō

FIRST CONSTABLE [*following tempo of music*]: Brazen woman, murderer . . .

SECOND CONSTABLE: . . . we will apprehend you . . .

THIRD CONSTABLE: . . . during the festivities . . .

FOURTH CONSTABLE: . . . of Asakusa Kannon . . .

FIFTH CONSTABLE: . . . Three Shrine Festival!

    [*They press in on* HANBEI. *Suddenly he throws off his disguise. They fall back astonished. They rush forward again and surround him.*]

FIRST CONSTABLE: Miscreant surrender . . .

ALL: . . . the princess to us!

    [SHICHIRŌ *rushes on. The two fight with the* CONSTABLES *and press them back. All pose in a group mie to loud battari tsuke beats.*]

SHICHIRŌ: Inanoya Hanbei, has the stolen Miyakodori scroll been restored?

HANBEI: Through Princess Sakura's long travail it is in our possession. And the crime of our Lord's death and young Umewaka's righteously avenged.

SHICHIRŌ: And the princess . . . ?

HANBEI: Concealed in this hamper for protection. Let us together . . .

SHICHIRŌ: . . . go to the mansion. The House of Yoshida will be restored!

FIRST CONSTABLE: But Princess Sakura is a murderess!

ALL: You shall not move!

HANBEI: We shall!

    [*They all pose in a group mie to battari tsuke beats. Drums, flute, and bell burst into fast* Kinjishi, *"Lion Song," as the cast breaks from the pose and kneels to face the audience.*]

HANBEI: Ladies and gentlemen! Following this we pray you will enjoy our program's concluding dance scene!

    [*Small drums play* Uchikomi, *"Frenzied Beating." The cast rises and poses in a group mie to loud battari tsuke beats. The curtain is slowly run closed to accelerating ki clacks. Drums and flute play* Shagiri.]

Appendix A Sound Effects: Ki patterns

One of the most distinctive sounds in a kabuki performance is the sharp and pentrating clack of wood clappers, ki or hyoshigi, being struck together in the air. The particular brilliance and almost musical quality of the ki sound stems from the fact that extremely hard, fine-grained wood is used (oak is best, cherry is second-best) and the ki's curved ends reduce the point of contact between the two pieces of wood to the barest minimum thereby assuring a sharp and clear sound. (Similar clappers are heard at jōruri puppet performances and at sumo wrestling, but the sound is less distinctive.) The main purpose of the ki is to provide cues during a performance. Its reverberating sound can always be clearly heard over dialogue or music or even the clamor of the audience.

Generally speaking, three types of ki patterns are heard which relate to three different functions within a performance: single clacks provide the immediate cue for something to happen; double clacks prepare cast and crew for an impending action; continuous clacks accompany an on-going action through to its conclusion. Anyone working in the theater, as well as the audience, could follow the course of the play—the period of preparation preceding, the opening and closing of the act curtains, the start of dialogue and action, the introduction of an onstage musicial ensemble, the turning of the revolving stage, the positioning of the main actor on the hanamichi—just by listening to the signals coming from the ki. If the primary function of the ki is technical, to run the performance, to stage-manage it, it also is true that for most lovers of kabuki its sound creates a mood and an atmosphere in which the action on stage takes on greater effectiveness (this is particularly true of the continuous patterns).

The main ki patterns heard in kabuki and their function in performance are given below. In order to indicate the general nature of the sound heard each ki clack is shown by a circle, its size suggesting loudness and the distance between circles suggesting time between sounds. These should be considered approximations only; the volume and the tempo of the patterns will be varied to suit each scene.

tomegi ("stopping ki"): a double clack that ends drum and flute music
 (*chakutō*) about fifteen minutes before the start of the play ○ ○

nicho ("two clacks"): a loud double clack, ten to fifteen minutes before the
 start of the play, that signals jūichicho to begin ○ ○

jūichicho ("eleven clacks"): a series of soft, widely spaced, gradually
 accelerating clacks that continues until the curtain is ready to open and
 warning cast and crew of the time remaining before the curtain; also called
 mawarigi, "walking-around ki," because the person beating the ki moves
 about through the backstage area

∘ ∘ ∘ ∘

∘ ∘ ∘ ∘ ∘ ∘ ∘

ki o naosu ("changing ki"): very loud double clacks that mark the end of
 jūichicho, warn the cast to be in place, and signal the curtain to open ○ ○

kizami ("continuous pattern"): beginning loudly, accelerating, and tapering
 off, it accompanies the pushing open of the curtain

○ ○ ○ ○ ○○○○○○○○○○○○○○○∘∘∘

tomegi a double clack (as above): the first beat ends kizami and the second
 signals for the action of the plan to begin ○ ○

ki o ireru ("insert ki"): within a scene either a single clack to signal a curtain
 to fall, the stage to revolve, the moon to drop into place, or some other
 scenic change ○

 or a double clack to introduce a group of onstage musicians (*debayashi* or
 degatari), the first clack signaling their appearance and the second cueing
 them to begin singing and playing ○ ○

tsunagi ("linking"): soft double clacks spaced about ten seconds apart while
 scenery is being changed between scenes

∘ ∘   ∘ ∘   ∘ ∘   ∘ ∘

kigashira ("head ki"): a very loud single clack after the last line of dialogue
 in bravura style play, coming between the uchiage and the battari patterns
 beat out by the tsuke during the play's final group mie pose ○

hon maku ("true curtain," also *maku*, "curtain," or *dara maku*, "beat
 curtain"): one of two major curtain-closing ki patterns, loud spaced clacks
 that gradually accelerate and then soften, for history plays as a rule

○ ○ ○ ○ ○ ○○○ ○○○○○ ○○○○○∘∘∘

hyōshi maku ("rhythmic curtain"): the second major curtain-closing
 pattern; soft, regularly spaced clacks gradually crescendo and then fade
 away

∘∘∘∘∘∘○○○○○ ○ ○ ○ ○ ○ ○ ○ ○ ○○○○○∘∘∘∘∘

Shagiri dome ("stopping *Shagiri*"): double clacks signaling the end of the
  day's performance; heard after the curtain is closed and Shagiri music is
  finished ◯ ◯

The purpose of the kizami and the hon maku patterns is the same: first to
draw the audience's attention toward the stage and the curtain through very
loud, widely spaced clacks, and then gradually to release the audience's
attention as the clacks softly fade away. Actually the two patterns are almost
identical: one opens the curtain and one closes it. In contrast to these very
strong and arresting patterns, hyōshi maku softly insinuates itself into the
listener's consciousness, crescendoes slightly for effect, then tapers off into
silence. Created in the late eighteenth century, it is used most often for the
conclusion of domestic acts. Namboku favored it over hon maku in most of his
plays (the text of *The Scarlet Princess of Edo* calls for hyōshi maku to close
all acts except one). The curtain may also be drawn in silence, usually to
allow the main actor to move onto the hanamichi prior to an exit without the
ki attracting the audience's attention away from him and to the stage (for
example, *Saint Narukami and the God Fudō*, Act II and Act III, Scene 1).

A pattern of drum beats also may be played simultaneously with a continuous ki pattern. At first the sounds alternate, but as they speed up they
become simultaneous. Several drum patterns can be used. One often heard is
a pattern of single large drum (ōdaiko) beats with single ki clacks. The fusion
of two different sound patterns is called *kakeai*, "alternation." Kakeai
accompanies the opening of the first act curtain of *Saint Narukami and the
God Fudō* and *Chronicle of the Battle of Ichinotani*.

Appendix B   Sound Effects: Tsuke patterns

The beating of two hard wood clappers, somewhat shorter than the ki but otherwise similar in shape, on a flat board placed on the stage floor is called tsuke (or *tsukeuchi*, "beating the tsuke"). The sound of the tsuke is flatter and duller than that of the ki. Its function is to reinforce movements and dialogue of the actors through punctuating beats of sound. Tsuke probably was not used in kabuki until around 1700; since then it has become an inseparable element of performance. It may have been inspired by fast drum beats (*ranjo*) that accompany the entrance of *bugaku* court dancers. Apparently the first time tsuke made its appearance in kabuki it accompanied the entrance of Shintō gods and demons. Now any important acting moment may be accompanied by tsuke patterns. Whereas ki serves a technical function in the staging of kabuki, tsuke's function is dramatic: it helps the actor express the emotions and meaning of the play.

Almost all combinations of tsuke sequences can be broken down into four main patterns: *hirote*, "single hand" (or *hirote utsu*, "single-hand beat"), is a single, sharp beat; batan is a double beat (left, right); battari is a triple beat (left, left, right); and bata-bata is a continuous beating pattern (alternating left and right). The last three are onomatopoeic words indicating the sound of the tsuke pattern.

A single loud hirote beat (●) can emphasize the falling of a pot to the floor, one person slapping another, striking with a fan, hitting the floor with the flat of the hand while speaking, and similar small actions. Batan (● ● or ● ●) emphasizes larger actions: a sword stroke, a person falling to the ground, or a hero strongly planting his foot preparatory to performing a mie. Tumbling to the ground is accompanied by several consecutive batan patterns that taper off (●●   ●●   ●●   ●●   ••). The main function of battari (● •●) is to accentuate upward and downward head movements of the mie pose. Batan can be used for this also, and the choice lies with the actor. Therefore, the same mie might be accompanied by either—

	(head up)	(head down)
battari:	●	•●
or batan:	●	●

Rapid entrances and exits (most often along the hanamichi) are accompanied by bata-bata beating. In a history play this starts slowly and loudly, then accelerates to give an impression of great strength:

(●　　●　　　●　　　●　　●　　　●　●●●●●●●●●);

in a domestic play bata-bata maintains a steady pace and volume, producing an unobtrusive effect:

(● ● ● ● ● ● ● ● ● ● ● ● ● ● ● ● ● ●).

Bata-bata usually does not taper off into silence (as the continuous ki patterns do) but ends abruptly as soon as the actor reaches his destination.

These four patterns are joined in fighting scenes (tachimawari) to provide a virtually continuous sequence of varying sounds. The person beating the tsuke watches the action and moment by moment may vary the sequence if he wishes, but in general the function of these patterns can be described as: bata-bata for exits and entrances; alternating batan and battari to match major tate (units of fighting choreography) movements; battari or batan for mie; and hirote during a continuous or repetitious sequence of movements.

I have left till the end the most exciting tsuke pattern of all: uchiage, literally "beating-rising," which leads into the final mie of a play (or sometimes an act of a play) that is held as the curtain is closed. The longest single pattern of tsuke, it can last upward of twenty to thirty seconds. It starts slowly and very loudly, accelerates to a furious pace, suddenly softens, then quickly swells to maximum volume as the beats spread apart and stop. As emotion is built to a climax by uchiage, the full cast moves into their final tableau position. As they hold this position a single sharp ki clack (kigashira) sounds. Heads circle and lock into position in the final mie to battari tsuke beats. This sequence can be shown as follows:

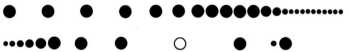

As an example of how the different patterns are put together, a section of the fight between Sukeroku and Ikyū from *Sukeroku: Flower of Edo* follows. Just over a minute long, it describes the sequence of movements and their accompanying tsuke patterns as performed in May 1967 at the Kabukiza, Tokyo. (The chart is marked in two-second intervals; b = batan; B = battari; H = hirote; BB = bata-bata; S = Sukeroku; I = Ikyū.)

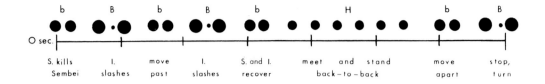

O sec.

b　　　　B　　　　b　　　　B　　　　b　　　　　　　　H　　　　　　b　　　　B

S. kills　　I.　　　move　　I.　　　S. and I.　　meet　and　stand　　move　　stop,
Sembei　　slashes　　past　　slashes　　recover　　　back-to-back　　apart　　turn

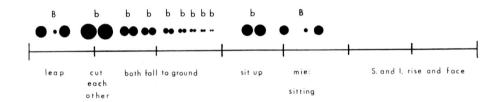

H　　　　　　　　　　　　　　B　　　　　　　B　　　　B

S. moves close to I.　　　　　mie: S. kneeling,　　　　S.　　　move
　　　　　　　　　　　　　　　I. standing　　　　　stands　　apart

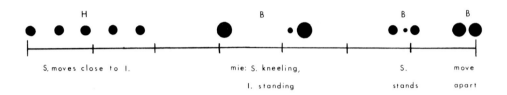

B　　b　　b　b　b　b b b b　　b　　B

leap　　cut　　both fall to ground　　sit up　　mie:　　　S. and I. rise and face
　　　each　　　　　　　　　　　　　　　　sitting
　　　other

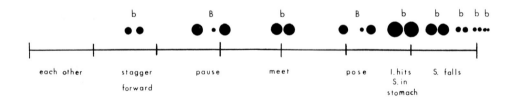

b　　　　B　　　　b　　　B　　b　　b　b b b

each other　　stagger　　pause　　meet　　pose　I. hits　S. falls
　　　　　　forward　　　　　　　　　　　　　S. in
　　　　　　　　　　　　　　　　　　　　　stomach

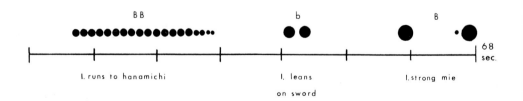

BB　　　　　　　　　　b　　　　　　B
　　　　　　　　　　　　　　　　　　　　　　　　　68
　　　　　　　　　　　　　　　　　　　　　　　　　sec.

I. runs to hanamichi　　　　I. leans　　　　I. strong mie
　　　　　　　　　　　　on sword

Appendix C Geza Music Cues

It is not necessary to write down in a cue book the sequence of ki or tsuke patterns that accompany a performance. The number available is small and patterns occur in a relatively fixed relationship to the staging techniques or acting which they accompany. The ki or tsuke sequence required for a given play is simply learned during rehearsal (if it is not already known) and played by ear in performance. The cuing of geza music is more complicated. Performances today can call upon a repertory of some four-hundred selections in Edo-style plays (and an almost equal number, though different selections, in Kyoto-Osaka-style plays). Onstage musical ensembles—Tokiwazu, Takemoto, Kiyomoto, and others—provide most musical accompaniment for dance plays so that in them we find the smallest number of geza selections (only 8 in *Love Letter from the Licensed Quarter*); similarly, in puppet adaptations most music is played by Takemoto musicians (in the two-and-a-half-hour performance of *Chronicle of the Battle of Ichinotani* only 19 geza selections are required). However, geza music plays almost constantly throughout *Sukeroku: Flower of Edo*, and in all-day plays the number of geza songs, melodies, and percussion rhythms integrated into the action of the play is very large (*Saint Narukami and the God Fudō* calls for 60 and *The Scarlet Princess of Edo* 69). Because selections are repeated, the number of occurrences of geza music can run into the hundreds in a long play (185 times in *The Scarlet Princess of Edo*). This complexity of music use requires offstage musicians in the geza to follow a cue book (*tsukechō*) in which the sequence of musical selections is written out. Geza songs (*uta*), shamisen instrumental melodies (*aikata, sanjū*, and other terms), and flute and percussion patterns (*narimono*) are included. Tsuke, "accompaniment" (*chō* means "book," hence "accompaniment book"), here indicates musical accompaniment and is not related to the word for the wooden clappers.

The example following is page eight of a twelve-page tsukechō used by Kineya Rokurirō, the head geza musician of the Kikugorō Kabuki Troupe, when performing *The Chronicle of the Battle of Ichinotani*. At the top of the page (in translation on the left) the cue for each geza selection is given. The usual kinds of cues are action (curtain opening, for example), a phrase of dialogue with the speaker indicated (Kajiwara: "Gunji, lead the way!"), or, in a puppet adaptation as here, a line of the chanted jōruri text ("Heiji Kagetaka . . ."). Cues to end music, given at the bottom of the page, are of the same sort. Cues do not always give the exact moment to begin or end; rather they are reminders to the musicians of what is coming next. In the example, the vague direction *sugu*, "soon," is the cue for Musubi Aikata. The musicians know the function of that melody in the play is to establish a mood for the few speeches which Sagami and Gunji have together; when the dialogue begins they will begin.

The title of the song, melody, or drum pattern is given in the center of the page. Repeats of the same music are indicated by *onajiku*, "same." Song lyrics usually are written in as well for they tend to be brief, seldom more than a line or two. Although the selection of music for a classic play is fairly well fixed now, changes can occur from production to production because different musicians are playing, actors insist upon special music of their own choice, or a scene needs to be cut or extended, speeded up or slowed down.

A page from a geza music cue book (*tsukechō*) for *Chronicle of the Battle of Ichinotani*, "Kumagai's Camp Scene," giving six music cues. The cues, which read vertically in Japanese, need to be read across the page in English translation.

Starting cue	Music name	Ending cue
Open curtain		
①	Toki no Taiko music	
		Curtain is open
Soon		
②	Musubi Aikata music	
		All [begin] exit
Lady Fuji: "Forgive me."		
③	Goshiki Aikata music	
		Lady Fuji: "Do as you wish . . ."
Lady Fuji: "Forgive me."		
④	Same music	
		Until jōruri
Jōruri text: "Heiji Kagetaka . . ."		
⑤	Toki no Taiko music	
		All have entered
Kajiwara: "Gunji, lead the way!"		
⑥	Same music	
		Kajiwara and others have exited

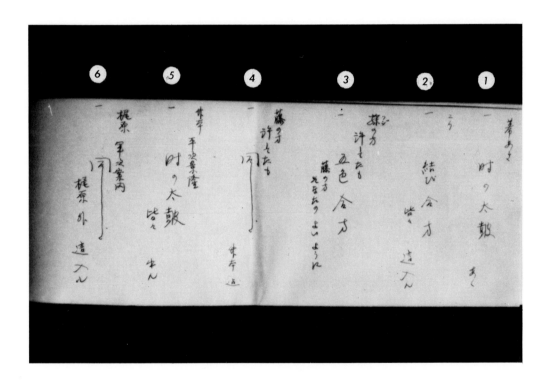

Glossary

aka hime: "scarlet princess," role type, so-called because of the scarlet kimono worn by a princess or daughter of nobility.

akutai: a speech of deliberate insult.

Amida Butsu: Amida Buddha, through whose mercy paradise can be entered.

aragoto: literally, "rough style," a bravura acting style, specialty of the Ichikawa Danjūrō acting line.

arahitogami: literally, "violent man-god," a powerful human whose spirit, after death, remains on earth and is worshiped as a kind of deity.

bata-bata: onomatopoeic word for continuous beating of tsuke; emphasizes rapid entrance or exit of a character.

batan: onomatopoeic word for two-beat tsuke pattern.

battari: onomatopoeic word for three-beat tsuke pattern, the second beat being a soft, often almost inaudible, grace-note preceding the third; accompanies mie.

bon: late summer festival honoring spirits of the dead and occasion for plays about characters who died tragically.

budōgoto: scenes of warriors fighting.

buyō: generic term for dance; *see also* shosagoto.

buyō geki: literally, "dance play," a play with strong dramatic content performed in dance style.

daijo: "great opening," the opening scene of the first act of a puppet drama.

dan: an act of a puppet play.

dangiri: final portion of kiri section of an act in a puppet drama; builds to strong musical climax.

de (deha): entrance scene of major character on the hanamichi.

dendenmono: *see* maruhonmono.

dōkeyaku: comic role.

Edo: Tokyo; also Edo (or Tokugawa) period, 1600–1867.

eiri kyōgenbon: "illustrated play script," portions of dialogue and a summary of the action of a play with monochrome illustrations, published and sold to advertise a play.

engo: "related words," synonyms or words related in meaning; an important verbal device used in both poetry and prose.

ennen: a dance of longevity, originally religious but secularized in early kabuki.

furi: pantomimic movement executed to musical, usually song, accompaniment in jōruri and in buyō.

futatsume (also futateme): "second piece" on a kabuki program. A brief piece unrelated to the main play.

gagaku: music that accompanies bugaku court dances or can be played in concert; supported at the imperial court from the seventh century.

Genroku: era name, 1688–1704; when used to describe the period of early flowering of urban culture includes the period 1688–ca. 1730.

geza: offstage right location for musicians and singers who provide standard musical accompaniment during performance; hence also music from that location.

gidayū kyōgen: a play adapted from puppet drama and using the gidayū style jōruri music created by the singer Takemoto Gidayū. *See also* maruhonmono.

giri: duty or obligation.

godanme: "fifth act" of a puppet play.

gomakume: "fifth act" of a kabuki play.

goroawase: comic rhyming.

goryō: a vengeful deity or spirit of a deceased person.

goryōe: a festival including music and dancing to propitiate a vengeful spirit or deity.

gotateme: "fifth piece" of a kabuki program and third act of the main play.

goten: a setting or scene in the imperial palace.

hanamichi: ramp through audience connecting stage to rear of auditorium used for major entrances and exits. Literally, "flower way," probably first used to bring flower gifts to the stage.

han buyō: a play performed in part through dance; literally, "half-dance."

handō: a comic villain.

Heian: era name, 794–1185; period of imperial court rule during which Kyoto was the nation's capitol.

hikkomi: exit down the hanamichi; literally, "withdrawal."

hon kyōgen: "main play," always consisting of multiple acts and beginning after the futatsume.

Hōreki: era name, 1751–1764, during which many puppet plays were adapted to kabuki.

hottan: an introductory scene that may open the main play; literally, "prologue."

hyōshigi: *see* ki.

ichibanme: "first part," or history section, of a main play.

ichiyazuke: literally, "overnight pickles"; a play dramatizing the latest news of the day.

iken: a scene in which a character strongly expresses his opinion to another; an admonition scene.

inga: *see* karma.

ippon chōshi: type of elocution in which the voice continues at a rapid rate with little variation; literally, "single rhythm."

Itchū Bushi: an early style of narrative singing used to accompany dance or important entrances or exits; now replaced by later music styles.

jidaimono: history play of any type; also specifically those history plays set in the Heike period (1156–1185). *See also* ōchomono and oiemono.

jidai-sewamono: mixed history and domestic play.

jitsuaku: literally, role of a "true villain."

jitsugoto: role of a mature and sincere hero; one type of tachiyaku role.

jitsu wa: "in reality," a scene in which a disguised character reveals who, in reality, he or she is; a connecting link between history and domestic plots in the same play.

jobiraki: the "opening" or first piece written especially for that month's program, brief and independent of the main play.

jo-ha-kyū: aesthetic concept of "introduction-development-climax," governing structure of gagaku music and of nō drama and performance.

jomaku: literally, "introductory act"; the first act of a main play.

jōruri: a general term for narrative music and, hence, for puppet plays performed to this style of music.

jūhachiban: literally, "the eighteen," meaning the eighteen favorite plays of the Ichikawa family, selected by Danjūrō VII in the middle-nineteenth century.

kabukimono: early term for a kabuki actor. Literally, "far-out thing."

kabuki odori: "kabuki dance," which originally distinguished kabuki from other popular performing arts.

kakeai: *see* warizerifu.

kakekotoba: "pivot word"; in prose or poetry a word which has one meaning when read with the phrase preceding it and another with the phrase following.

kaomise: the first production of the new season, usually in the eleventh lunar month, which introduced the actors engaged at a particular theater for that season; literally "face showing."

karakuri: special theatrical effects in puppet performances.

karma: also inga; Buddhist belief that a person's actions during one lifetime will determine his destiny in future reincarnations.

Kasei: contraction of Bunka era (1804–1817) and Bunsei era (1818–1830); cultural period noted for its decadence.

kashagata: role of mature or elderly woman.

katakiyaku: role of a villain.

Katō Bushi: type of early dance music performed by amateurs in kabuki.

keiseigai: literally, "buying a prostitute"; a play based on hero's visit to a brothel, especially in Kyoto and Osaka.

ki (or hyōshigi): two hard wood clappers, about a foot long and two inches square, struck together near the slightly curving tips to produce a clear, almost musical, penetrating sound. Used to cue curtain, entrances, scenery changes, music, or dialogue.

kiri: the final, and most important, section of an act of a jōruri play.

kiri kyōgen: short domestic play following a history play and ending the day's program, either in kabuki or jōruri.

kiwamono: a play about a recent event; literally, "seasonal goods."

Kiyomoto: a type of kabuki dance music created in 1814, noted for its lyrical quality.

kizami: continuous pattern of ki clacks that accompanies opening or closing of the main curtain.

kizewamono: type of play about gangsters and other commoners in the lowest social level; a sub-category of sewamono.

koeban: claque; literally, "voice group."

kōjō: announcement to the audience by an actor or the stage manager.

kojōruri: "old jōruri," puppet plays prior to 1686.

kōken: a stage assistant, either a member of the backstage crew who moves scenery or an actor who assists another actor on stage.

koroshiba: a murder scene.

kubijikken: verification of the identity of a head to assure that the intended death of a person has in fact occurred; a standard scene type, especially in jōruri plays.

kuchi: opening section of a jōruri act.

kuchiake: *see* mitateme.

kuchidate: process of improvising a play during performance; literally, "creating orally."

kudoki: scene of lamentation; also portion of a musical composition played and sung during a lamentation scene.

kugeaku: one sub-category of villain role; a villain who is a prince or high-ranking member of the imperial court.

kumadori: makeup style utilizing bold designs of bright red, blue, gray, or black, especially in aragoto acting.

kuriage: a writing and vocal technique of pressing an opponent for a reply in increasingly insistent manner, thereby "raising up" the emotional tension of the scene.

kuzetsu: "lovers' quarrel," a standard section of a brothel-visiting scene.

kyōgen: in kabuki the generic term for a play or drama of any type. Also the independent comic plays staged between nō plays in a nō-kyōgen performance.

makura: literally, "pillow"; sung narrative that introduces a jōruri act.

maruhonmono: a kabuki play based on a jōruri text (literally, "fully-written text"). Also dendenmono (for the sound of the Takemoto shamisen) or gidayū kyōgen (play using Takemoto Gidayū music).

Meiji: era name, 1868–1912; the initial period in which Japan was opened to the West.

meriyasu: a type of solo geza song used to accompany tender scenes in which a female character mimes, without dialogue, her state of mind.

miarawashi: to "disclose before another's eyes" one's true identity through a complete costume change in view of the audience.

michiyuki: a "journey" scene, performed as dance.

mie: acting technique of assuming a powerful pose; includes preparatory movements, circling of the head on the neck, and final pose with fixed glare, often including crossed eyes; usually accompanied by battari pattern of tsuke.

migawari: substitution of one person, usually a child and relative, in order to effect the escape of another. A standard scene type, especially in jōruri.

minarai: a "see-and-learn" playwriting apprentice.

mitate: writing technique of placing contemporary characters and events in past eras, most commonly Kamakura (1185–1333) or Ashikaga (1336–1568).

mitateme: literally, "third piece" on a program and the first act of the main play. Also called jomaku in Edo and kuchiake in Kyoto and Osaka.

modoki: deliberate imitation of a prior play, act, or scene to allow the audience to draw comparisons.

monogatari: literally, "storytelling"; a scene in jōruri where a male character recounts a tragic event in great detail.

Nagauta: the basic type of kabuki music, used as background from the geza or onstage in dance plays; only type of kabuki music which incorporates drums and flute with shamisen.

nagori: "farewell" performance, given to honor a departing actor or a character in a play.

naimaze: writing technique of "interweaving" several plots from different worlds into a single story.

naka: *see* tsugi.

nani-nani zukushi: a running pun.

nanori: "name-saying," a speech in which a major character grandiloquently announces to an opponent or rival his great qualities.

nembutsu: invocation of Amida Buddha; nembutsu odori was one of the dances Okuni performed in secularized form.

nibanme: "second part" of a play, the domestic section.

nidanme: second act of a jōruri play.

nimakume: second act of a kabuki play.

ninjō: spontaneous human feelings of sympathy toward others.

nirami: crossing one eye over the other to accentuate strongest type of mie.

nori: brief lines of dialogue spoken in rhythmic cadences that "ride" Takemoto shamisen music in puppet-derived plays.

nureba: a specifically erotic love scene; literally, "wet scene."

nuregoto: acting style suitable for a love scene or the specific business involved in a love scene.

ōchōmono: "imperial court play," one type of history play, concerning the court of the Emperor in Kyoto during the Heian era (794–1185); also ōdaimono.

ōdaiko: large drum on which different ceremonial and atmospheric patterns are beat.

ōdaimono: "court history play." *See* ōchōmono.

oiemono: "feudal house play," a type of history play about samurai clans of the Edo period but placed in an earlier historical period.

oiesōdō: struggle for succession in a feudal house; the basic situation dramatized in oiemono plays.

ōgiri: "finale," a dance piece that ends the day's program.

Okuni kabuki: the original style of kabuki performance, created and performed by the young woman Okuni.

onnagata: male performer of female roles.

onna kabuki: kabuki performed by troupes of women, ca. 1603–1629.

ōodori: "grand dance," group dance by whole company ending a day's program.

ōotoshi: a concluding section of tearful lamentation in jōruri, one of several types of climax possible; literally, "great conclusion."

otokodate: role of a chivalrous commoner, brave and devil-may-care.

otokogata: actor of male roles, a term used mostly in very early kabuki.

Ōzatsuma: a type of early kabuki shamisen music and singing.

ōzume: final scene or act of the jidai or history section of a play.

rakugo: comic storytelling.

rokumakume: "sixth act" of a kabuki play.

rokutateme: "sixth piece" of a kabuki program and fourth act of a main play.

rōnin: member of the samurai class who has no master to serve and hence is unemployed and without social position.

roppō: a dynamic, often tempestuous, exit on the hanamichi by a major character (very occasionally entrance as well); literally, "six directions" movement.

ryō: gold coin of fluctuating value, generally worth thirty to forty-five dollars.

Sanbasō: name of dance play celebrating good luck and longevity, adapted from the nō play *Okina*, performed as ritual piece to open the day's program.

sandan (sandanme): "third act" of a puppet play.

sange: Buddhist ceremony of expiation.

sanmakume: "third act" of a kabuki play.

saruwaka: comic role, probably derived from kyōgen comedies.

satsujinmono: a murder play.

sekai: "world," a group of historically known figures and situation around which a play is created.

seppuku: suicide by disembowelment; literally, "stomach-cutting." (Harakiri is vulgar form of the term.)

sewa: domestic or contemporary.

sewamono: a domestic or contemporary play concerning the lives of commoners.

shamisen: three-stringed plucked lute that is basic kabuki musical instrument.

share: pun.

shichigochō: verse or prose written in alternating phrases of seven and five syllables; literally, "seven-five pattern."

shichisan: "seven-three," a position on the hanamichi, seven-tenths of the distance from one end and three-tenths from the other end, where an actor stops and poses.

Shimabara kyōgen: a play set in the Shimabara brothel district of Kyoto; a type of keiseigai play.

shinjū: a double suicide by lovers.

shiritori monku: a type of humorous rhyme in which the end word of a phrase is repeated, with a different meaning, as the first word of the following phrase; literally, "end-taking phrase."

shodan: "first act" of a puppet play.

Shōgun: supreme military ruler, of the samurai class.

shosagoto: a dance piece.

shukō: plot.

shuraba: battle scene between warriors, usually as part of an army in combat.

sutezerifu: ad-libbed dialogue.

tachimawari: fighting scene.

tachiyaku: general term for male leading roles.

Takemoto: narrative style singing and shamisen music created by Takemoto
  Gidayū for jōruri puppet plays, used in kabuki adaptations of these plays.

tanka: *see* waka.

tanzen roppō: one type of roppō, a swaggering walk.

tate: formalized fighting movements, used especially in group fighting.

tateoyama: leading roles played by the onnagata actor.

Tenmei: era name, 1781–1788.

teoigoto: "wounded scene," showing suffering of wounded and dying hero.

tobi roppō: one type of roppō in which aragoto hero leaps and bounds down
  hanamichi; literally, "leaping roppō."

tōdori: backstage manager of a theater among whose duties was speaking the
  kōjō.

Tokiwazu: a type of kabuki dance music created in 1747; combines narrative
  and lyric qualities.

Tomimoto: a type of kabuki dance music created in 1748; now largely superseded by Kiyomoto.

tōshi kyōgen: a "straight-through play," that is, a single play lasting all day.

tsugi: "next," the section of a jōruri act which follows the opening section; or
  naka, "middle" section.

tsuke: two hard wood clappers beat on a board placed on the stage floor;
  patterns emphasize and underscore actors' movements.

tsume: when kiri section of a jōruri act is divided into two, this is second and
  concluding portion; literally, "end."

tsurane: long speech by a major aragoto character delivered in rhythmic,
  melodic manner.

uchiage: literally, "rising-beating"; long tsuke pattern that accompanies the
  most important mie in a play.

ukiyoe: wood-block genre prints, often of actors or scenes from kabuki.

wagoto: "soft style" acting favored in Kyoto and Osaka, largely created by
  Sakata Tōjurō.

waka (or tanka): a poem of 31 syllables, in phrases of 5-7-5-7-7 syllables.

wakashūgata: an actor of adolescent male roles.

wakashū kabuki: performances of kabuki by troupes of young boys, and the
  period 1629–1652 during which these were the only kabuki performances
  allowed; literally, "young boys' kabuki."

waki kyōgen: "house play" identified with a particular theater and regularly performed in the early morning hours as a convention; short and usually dance.

warizerifu: writing technique; long, independent speeches by two main characters are divided into alternating sections, often in shichigochō; literally, "divided dialogue"; sometimes called kakeai, "exchange."

watarizerifu: writing technique in which a single speech is parceled out to a number of characters, the last line being delivered in unison; literally, "passed-along dialogue."

yakuharai: melodic and rhythmic style of elocution, usually applied to a major speech in shichigochō.

yarō kabuki: "adult male kabuki," performed by troupes of adult males, and the period of these performances, from 1652 until Genroku.

yatsushi: "in disguise"; standard situation in oiemono in which disguised hero enters licensed quarter to visit a courtesan.

yodanme: "fourth act" of a puppet play.

yonmakume: "fourth act" of a kabuki play.

yontateme: "fourth piece" of a kabuki program and second act of the main play.

yoten: chorus of low-ranking opponents who engage hero in choreographed tate fighting scene.

yūjo kabuki: "prostitutes' kabuki," performed by troupes of prostitutes, and the period of these performances, ca. 1603–1629; also onna kabuki.

yusuriba: an extortion or blackmail scene.

zagashira (zatō): literally, "theater head"; the leading actor of a troupe who also functioned as its manager.

zatō: see zagashira.

Selective Bibliography

Arnott, Peter D. *The Theatres of Japan.* New York: St. Martin's Press, 1969. A nontechnical appreciation of kabuki in current performance.

Atsumi Seitarō, ed. *Nihon Gikyoku Zenshū* (Complete Japanese Drama). 50 vols. Tokyo: Shunyōdō, 1928–1932. Four hundred complete and abridged kabuki plays; not annotated.

Bowers, Faubion. *Japanese Theatre.* New York: Hermitage House, 1952. A general account, mostly about kabuki. Three plays are translated in an appendix: *The Monstrous Spider, Gappo and His Daughter Tsuji,* and *Sukeroku.*

Brandon, James R., with Tamako Niwa. *Kabuki Plays: Kanjinchō and The Zen Substitute.* New York: Samuel French, 1966. Translations with stage directions of two dance plays.

—— ed. *Traditional Asian Plays.* New York: Hill and Wang, 1972. Production scripts of *The Subscription List* (*Kanjinchō*) and *The Zen Substitute* as well as the nō *Ikkaku Sennin* dramatizing the Saint Narukami theme.

Dunn, Charles James, and Bunzō Torigoe, trans. and ed. *The Actors' Analects: Yakusha Rongo.* New York: Columbia University Press, 1969. Accounts by Genroku actors of their art and their lives.

Engeki Hyakka Daijiten (Encyclopedia of Theater). 6 vols. Tokyo: Heibonsha, 1960–1962. A major source of information.

Ernst, Earle. *The Kabuki Theatre.* Revised ed. Honolulu: University Press of Hawaii, 1974. A complete descriptive study.

—— ed. *Three Japanese Plays.* New York: Oxford University Press, 1959. Contains the kabuki play *Benten the Thief* as well as the jōruri *The House of Sugawara* often performed as kabuki.

Gunji Masakatsu. *Buyo: The Classical Dance,* trans. Don Kenny. New York: Walker/Weatherhill, 1971. An illustrated introduction to kabuki dance.

—— *Kabuki.* Tokyo: Kodansha, 1968. Brief authoritative text, lavishly illustrated.

—— *Kabuki Jūhachibanshū* (Collection of Eighteen Famous Plays). Tokyo: Iwanami Shoten, 1965. An excellent annotated edition.

—— *Kabuki no Hassō* (Formation of Kabuki). Tokyo: Kobundo, 1959. Emphasizes the religious background of early kabuki.

—— *Kabuki: Yōshiki to Dentō* (Kabuki: Forms and Traditions). Tokyo: Gakugei Shorin, 1969. Valuable for its examination of writing and performance conventions.

Halford, Aubrey S. and Giovanna M. *The Kabuki Handbook.* Tokyo: Tuttle, 1952. Contains more than a hundred play synopses.

Hamamura Yonezo, et al. *Kabuki.* Tokyo: Kenkyusha, 1956. A collection of essays.

Ihara Toshirō. *Kabuki Nempyō* (Chronology of Kabuki). 8 vols. Tokyo: Iwanami Shoten, 1956–1963. A useful chronological listing of performances, play titles, actors, and commentary, from 1559 to 1907.

Izuka Tomoichirō. *Kabuki Saiken* (Survey of Kabuki Drama). Tokyo: Daiichi Shobō, 1926. Over 6,000 plays discussed according to subject matter.

Kawatake Mokuami. *The Love of Izayoi and Seishin,* trans. Frank T. Motofuji. Tokyo: Tuttle, 1966. The second, fourth, sixth, and seventh acts of an all-day play—now performed as a separate "true" domestic play.

Kawatake Shigetoshi. *Kabuki: Japanese Drama.* Tokyo: Foreign Affairs Association of Japan, 1958. A random description by a major scholar.

—— *Kabuki Jiten* (Dictionary of Kabuki). Tokyo: Jitsugyō no Nihonsha, 1957. Small and good.

—— ed. *Kabuki Meisakushū* (Famous Kabuki Plays). 2 vols. Tokyo: Kodansha, 1936. Contains seventeen annotated texts, mostly of Edo plays.

—— *Kabuki Sakusha no Kenkyū* (Study of Kabuki Playwrights). Tokyo: Tōkyōdō, 1940. Playwrights and their works presented chronologically.

—— *Nihon Gikyokushi* (History of Japanese Drama). Tokyo: Nan'undō, 1964. A third devoted to introducing major kabuki playwrights and their plays.

—— *Nihon Engeki Zenshi* (Complete History of Japanese Theater). Tokyo: Iwanami Shoten, 1959. Contains a detailed history of kabuki.

Kawatake Toshio. *A History of Japanese Theater, II: Bunraku and Kabuki.* Tokyo: Kokusai Bunka Shinkokai, 1971. Stresses characteristics common to both kabuki and jōruri plays.

Keene, Donald. *Chūshingura: The Treasury of Loyal Retainers.* New York: Columbia University Press, 1971. A classic play of kabuki and jōruri.

—— trans. *Major Plays of Chikamatsu.* New York: Columbia University Press, 1961. Eleven jōruri plays, some of which are also staged as kabuki.

Kincaid, Zoe. *Kabuki: The Popular Stage of Japan.* New York: Macmillan, 1925. The first important book published in English on kabuki.

Malm, William P. *Nagauta: The Heart of Kabuki Music.* Tokyo: Tuttle, 1964. The standard work on kabuki music.

Ogasawara Kyōko. *Kabuki no Tanjō* (Birth of Kabuki). Tokyo: Meiji Shoin, 1972. A reinterpretation of early kabuki based on firsthand sources, largely popular songs.

Scott, Adolphe Clarence. *The Kabuki Theatre of Japan.* London: George Allen and Unwin, 1955. A descriptive account with emphasis on acting and plays.

—— trans. *Kanjincho: A Japanese Kabuki Play.* Tokyo: Hokuseido, 1953. A dance play.

Segawa Jōkō. *Genyadana: A Japanese Kabuki Play*, trans. A.C. Scott. Tokyo: Hokuseido, 1953. A "true" domestic play.

Shuzui Kenji. *Kabuki Geki Gikyoku Kōzō no Kenyū* (Study of the Structure of Kabuki Drama). Tokyo: Hokuryūkan, 1947. Applies dramatic theories to specific plays.

Suwa Haruo. *Genroku Kabuki no Kenkyū* (Study of Genroku Kabuki). Tokyo: Kasama Shoin, 1967. A new examination of early kabuki.

Tachimawari no Kata to Yōgo (Forms and Terminology of Fighting Movements). 3 vols., Bandō Yaenosuke, ed., in *Kyōzai* (Educational Materials), series 2. Tokyo: Kokuritsu Gekijō, n.d. Stick drawings and terminology for fighting movements.

Takano Tasuyaku and Kuroki Kanzō, eds. *Genroku Kabuki Kessakushū* (Masterpieces of Genroku Kabuki). 2 vols. Tokyo: Waseda Daigaku Shuppanbu, 1939. Forty-four illustrated play digests from Kyoto-Osaka and Edo; not annotated.

Takaoka Nobuyuki. *Kabuki no Kyakuhon* (Kabuki Playscripts.) Tokyo: Hobundō, 1943. Major plays analyzed in detail.

Takeshiba Sōtarō, et al., eds. *Tsuruya Namboku Zenshū* (Complete Plays of Tsuruya Namboku). 12 vols. Tokyo: San'ichi Shobō, 1971– . A well-edited but unannotated edition.

Toita Yasuji, ed. *Kabuki Meisakusen* (Collection of Kabuki Classics). 15 vols. Tokyo: Sōgensha, 1952–1957. A large and accessible collection, unannotated.

—— *Kabuki: The Popular Theatre*, trans. Don Kenny. New York: Walker/Weatherhill, 1970. An illustrated introduction.

Tsubouchi Shōyō and Atsumi Seitarō, eds. *Dai Namboku Zenshū* (Complete Works of the Great Namboku). 17 vols. Tokyo: Shunyōdō, 1925–1927. Superseded by the Takeshiba edition, but still valuable.

—— and Yamamoto Jirō. *History and Characteristics of Kabuki: The Japanese Classical Drama.* Yokohama: Yamagata, 1960. Essays interesting for their nineteenth-century viewpoint.

Urayama Masao and Matsuzaki Hitoshi, eds. *Kabuki Kyakuhonshū* (Collection of Kabuki Plays). 2 vols. Tokyo: Iwanami Shoten, 1960. An excellent annotated edition of six plays with an introduction.

Yamamoto Jirō, et al., eds. *Kabuki Jiten* (Dictionary of Kabuki). Tokyo: Jitsugyō no Nihonsha, 1972. A one-volume encyclopedia.

Index